THE RUSSIAN REVOLUTION

LENIN

THE
RUSSIAN REVOLUTION
1917–1921

BY

WILLIAM HENRY CHAMBERLIN

VOLUME ONE

WITH A SELECTED BIBLIOGRAPHY OF
RECENT WORKS ON 1917
BY DIANE KOENKER

PRINCETON UNIVERSITY PRESS
PRINCETON, NEW JERSEY

Published by Princeton University Press, 41 William Street, Princeton, New Jersey 08540
In the United Kingdom: Princeton University Press, Oxford

Copyright © 1935 by The Macmillan Company
Selected bibliography © 1987 by Princeton University Press

Library of Congress Cataloging in Publication Data will be found
on the last printed page of this book

Reissued with a new introduction, February, 1952

First Princeton Paperback printing, 1987
LCC 87-3719
ISBN 0-691-05492-4
ISBN 0-691-00814-0 (pbk.)

This edition is reprinted by arrangement with Macmillan Publishing Company,
a division of Macmillan, Inc.

Clothbound editions of Princeton University Press books are printed on acid-free paper,
and binding materials are chosen for strength and durability. Paperbacks, while
satisfactory for personal collections, are not usually suitable for library rebinding.

Printed in the United States of America by Princeton University Press,
Princeton, New Jersey

9   8   7   6   5   4   3

INTRODUCTION TO NEW EDITION

SEVENTEEN years have passed since this history was first published. The world significance of its subject has grown in retrospect. The Soviet Union plays a much larger and more formidable role in American foreign policy calculations than it played in 1935.

At that time communism was in power only in Russia. Plausible reasons could be alleged for believing that it could not or would not conquer in countries with differing historical backgrounds and national cultures. Now communist political and economic methods have prevailed over a vast Eurasian land mass, from China to Czechoslovakia. Approximately one-third of the population of the globe lives under some form of communist rule. It would seem that both the basic ideas of Marx and Lenin and the practical means by which the Russian communists obtained and held power deserve the understanding that can only be the result of careful study and analysis.

The text of the history is unchanged in the new edition. It was written as a chronological factual record, based on examination of communist and anti-communist sources, of what occurred during the eventful years of revolution and civil war. It seemed inadvisable to alter this record in any way because of shifts in international political conditions and in the climate of public opinion.

One might have expected a history published seventeen years ago to become outdated in some details through the discovery and publication of new material. It has not happened in this case, I think, because of the special and unusual conditions which govern research by Russian or foreign historical scholars in Russia.

Many books, pamphlets and newspapers which I was able to obtain and consult during the period from 1922 to 1934 when I worked on the history in Moscow would not be available to a research student at the present time. A prolonged political purge which led to the execution of many of the most eminent figures in the first years of the Soviet regime has played havoc with Soviet Russian historiography.

v

Side by side with the trial and execution of such leading "old Bolsheviks" as Rykov, Bukharin, Zinoviev, Kamenev, Pyatakov, Krestinsky, there was a systematic attempt to blacken their past reputations and to deny or discredit their activities during the Revolution. Many books and pamphlets by Trotsky and lesser communist heretics like Shlyapnikov could be picked up in secondhand bookstores during the relatively mild atmosphere of the twenties.

Now censorship has made a clean sweep of all such material. It is uncertain when, if ever, a reasonably objective appraisal of events and personalities will be possible, on the basis of what is now accessible to research students in the Soviet Union.

Some of the material on which this history is based has been eroded by time, as well as by censorship. Soviet newspapers of the revolutionary years, badly printed on inferior paper, were disintegrating and becoming illegible during the time of my own research in Moscow.

Cultural contacts between the Soviet Union and foreign countries have never been close or intimate. In the strained political atmosphere of recent years these contacts have almost ceased to exist. To the best of my knowledge no independent historical scholar has been able to conduct research in the Soviet Union for many years.

Despite the political restrictions which prevent a normal interchange of scholars and students between the United States and the Soviet Union, there has been a notable growth of interest in Russian studies in this country since the war. I hope the republication of this detailed account of the greatest social revolution of the modern age will be of service to students who are interested in the origin, background and early vicissitudes of the Soviet state which rose on the ruins of the former Russian Empire.

WILLIAM HENRY CHAMBERLIN

Cambridge, Massachusetts
January 6, 1952

INTRODUCTION

THE present history is the fruit of twelve years of study and research, mostly carried on in the Soviet Union. From the time when I arrived in Moscow in 1922 I conceived the idea of composing a narrative of the Bolshevik Revolution and of the period of civil war which followed it. With the constant and devoted co-operation of my wife, who read through endless files of newspapers and historical magazines relating to the period under discussion, I commenced to burrow into the vast stock of source material contained in histories, memoirs, newspapers, historical magazines, and archive materials.

The time which I could devote to research was necessarily limited while I was carrying on regular journalistic work in Russia as correspondent for *The Christian Science Monitor*. Through the kindness and generosity of the John Simon Guggenheim Memorial Foundation, which awarded me a Fellowship for a period of eighteen months, I was enabled to suspend journalistic work and to devote myself during the years 1933 and 1934 to the actual writing of the history, based on the mass of source material which I had collected during earlier years.

I chose as the starting-point of my history the downfall of the Tsarist regime in March, 1917, and as the concluding point the introduction of the New Economic Policy in March, 1921, which represented the beginning of an entirely new phase in Russian social and economic development. The four years which passed between these two events present a gigantic historical panorama, always moving and dramatic, heroic, or tragic, or both, according to one's point of view: the panorama represented by the establishment of a new social order, based on extreme revolutionary theories, in a huge country with a vast population that had always stood somewhere between Europe and Asia in the character of its political and economic institutions.

The fascination of describing such an epoch of human history

is obvious. Equally obvious are the historian's difficulties, especially in dealing with events after the beginning of the civil war, when Russia was largely cut off from the outside world. No one could be more conscious of the imperfections of my history than I am. Not a few details in the complicated course of revolution and civil war are still obscure and debatable and await the patient efforts of the specialized research scholar of future generations. I always found myself confronted with a rigorous problem of selection and compression in writing a history of manageable length. A full record of all the aspects of Russian political, economic and social life, of the many and varied campaigns of the civil war would require the services of a staff of trained historians, with an encyclopedic amount of space at their disposal.

At the same time there seemed to be adequate reasons for endeavoring to convey to foreign readers an account of the main events of Russian revolutionary history. No work covering the period which I have selected and based on an extensive study of Russian original material is in existence. The fact that I was able to talk personally with many of the actors in the events which I described, both on the Red and on the White side of the political, economic and military front, gives, I hope, somewhat more living quality to the narrative. Moreover, having arrived in Russia for the first time after the conclusion of the period which I describe, I feel that I am in a better position to achieve an attitude of objective detachment than a Russian, whose sympathies are almost inevitably strongly enlisted on one side or the other in the fierce struggle that shook up his country's existence to the depths and most probably strongly affected his own personal fate.

Just because my work is something of a pioneer in its field I have been at special pains to place the establishment of the facts in the foreground and to offer only as much personal interpretation as seemed quite indispensable. In the opening chapters of the work I have endeavored to convey some idea of the background against which the Revolution took place; in the closing chapter I have attempted to answer some of the questions which the course of the narrative would almost inevitably excite. Appendices devoted to translations of decrees, governmental declarations, notes and other documents present in full a certain amount of material which is referred to or cited partially in the narrative, and create an illustrative background for the history as a whole. All dates are given according to the Western calendar.

In conclusion I should like to express my appreciative gratitude for the willing aid and coöperation in my studies which I received from the staff of the Library of the Communist Academy in Moscow and of the Russian Foreign Archive in Prague. The conclusions which I formed on the basis of research in these two institutions are, of course, entirely independent, and I alone am responsible for these.

WILLIAM HENRY CHAMBERLIN

New York, N. Y.
December 19, 1934.

SELECTED BIBLIOGRAPHY
OF RECENT WORKS ON 1917

by Diane Koenker

MANY monographs, memoirs, and collections of documents have been published since the original edition of Chamberlin's work, although none has completely replaced his synthesis. Nor can this updated bibliography be as comprehensive as the original one published in Volume II of this history. The works listed below represent a small selection of studies on the 1917 revolution that deserve mention, both because of their contribution to the historical understanding of 1917 and for their value as further bibliographic guides. For reference to many other important studies and collections, in Russian, English, and other languages, the reader is encouraged to consult the bibliographies in the works cited here.

ANWEILER, OSKAR. *The Soviets: The Russian Workers, Peasants, and Soldiers Councils, 1905–1921*. New York, Pantheon, 1974. Translation of a study by a leading German scholar.

AVRICH, PAUL. *The Russian Anarchists*. Princeton, Princeton University Press, 1967. Offers insight into an important but often overlooked element of the revolutionary movement.

BROWDER, PAUL, AND ALEXANDER KERENSKY (editors). *The Russian Provisional Government, 1917*. Stanford, Stanford University Press, 1961. 3 vols. Documents selected by the Prime Minister of the Provisional Government.

CHERNOV, VICTOR. *The Great Russian Revolution*. New Haven, Yale University Press, 1936. History by the leader of the Socialist Revolutionary Party.

COHEN, STEPHEN F. *Bukharin and the Bolshevik Revolution*. New York, Knopf, 1973. Important study of a major Bolshevik leader and theorist.

DANIELS, ROBERT V. *Red October*. New York, Scribner's, 1967. Reinterpretation of the October revolution which stresses its unplanned character; challenges Trotsky's version.

DEUTSCHER, ISAAC. *The Prophet Armed: Trotsky, 1879–1921*. New York, Vintage, 1954. First volume of the classic three-volume biography of Trotsky.

FERRO, MARC. *Bolshevik Revolution: A Social History of the Russian Revolution*. London, Routledge & Kegan Paul, 1980. Norman Stone, trans. Social history from a proponent of the *Annales* school in France.

———. *Russian Revolution of February 1917*. Englewood Cliffs, N.J., Prentice-Hall, 1972. J. L. Richards, trans.

FISCHER, LOUIS. *Life of Lenin*. New York, Harper & Row, 1964. Standard biography.

GETZLER, ISRAEL. *Kronstadt, 1917–1921: The Fate of a Soviet Democracy*. Cambridge, Cambridge University Press, 1983. Detailed study of the radical naval fortress that aided the Bolshevik seizure of power.

GILL, GRAEME J. *Peasants and Government in the Russian Revolution*. New York, Barnes and Noble, 1979. A study of government agrarian policy rather than of peasants themselves.

HASEGAWA, TSUYOSHI. *The February Revolution: Petrograd 1917*. Seattle, University of Washington Press, 1981. Detailed synthesis of the fall of the monarchy and first days of the new regime.

HAUPT, GEORGES, AND JEAN-JACQUES MARIE. *Makers of the Russian Revolution*. Ithaca, Cornell University Press, 1969. Translated autobiographies of several dozen Bolshevik leaders.

KATKOV, GEORGE. *Russia 1917: The February Revolution*. London, Collins, 1967. Emphasis is on conspiracy theories of the revolution.

KEEP, JOHN L. H. *The Russian Revolution: A Study in Mass Mobilization*. New York, Norton, 1976. Important and massive study of the urban and agrarian revolutions.

——— (editor). *The Debate on Soviet Power: Minutes of the All-Russian Central Executive Committee of Soviets: Second Convocation October 1917–January 1918*. Oxford, Oxford University Press, 1979.

KOENKER, DIANE. *Moscow Workers and the 1917 Revolution*. Princeton, Princeton University Press, 1981. Social history of the revolution in Russia's second city.

MANDEL, M. DAVID. *The Petrograd Workers and the Fall of the Old Regime*. London, Macmillan, 1983.

———. *The Petrograd Workers and the Soviet Seizure of Power*. London, Macmillan, 1984. Workers' revolution from a sociological and political perspective.

MAWDSLEY, EVAN. *The Russian Revolution and the Baltic Fleet: War and Politics, February 1917–April 1918*. New York, Barnes and Noble, 1978.

MEDVEDEV, ROY A. *The October Revolution*. New York, Columbia University Press, 1979. George Saunders, trans. Interpretation by a major Soviet dissident Marxist historian.

MELGUNOV, S. P. *Bolshevik Seizure of Power*. Santa Barbara, ABC-Clio Press, 1972. History by a participant who opposed the October revolution.

MILIUKOV, PAUL N. *The Russian Revolution*. Vol. 1: *The Revolution Divided, Spring 1917*. Gulf Breeze, Fla., Academic International Press, 1977. Tatyana and Richard Stites, trans. Historical treatment by one of the leading figures in the Kadet party and Provisional Government; further volumes in preparation.

PETHYBRIDGE, ROGER. *The Spread of the Russian Revolution*. London, 1972. Essays on aspects of the revolution usually ignored: press, transport, propaganda.

———— (editor). *Witnesses to the Russian Revolution*. New York, Citadel, 1967. Fragments of firsthand accounts, organized as a chronological narrative of the revolution.

PIPES, RICHARD. *The Formation of the Soviet Union: Communism and Nationalism, 1917–1923*. New York, Atheneum, 1968. Detailed political study of the revolution and civil war in Russia's borderlands.

RABINOWITCH, ALEXANDER. *Prelude to Revolution: The Petrograd Bolsheviks and the July 1917 Uprising*. Bloomington, Indiana University Press, 1968.

————. *The Bolsheviks Come to Power: The Revolution of 1917 in Petrograd*. New York, Norton, 1976. Meticulously researched studies of the Bolshevik party at all levels of activity in 1917.

RADKEY, OLIVER H. *The Agrarian Foes of Bolshevism*. New York, Columbia University Press, 1958. Classic study of the Socialist Revolutionary Party.

RALEIGH, DONALD J. *Revolution on the Volga: 1917 in Saratov*. Ithaca, Cornell University Press, 1986. The first non-Soviet account of the revolution in the Russian provinces.

ROSENBERG, WILLIAM G. *Liberals in the Russian Revolution: The Constitutional Democratic Party, 1917–1921*. Princeton, Princeton University Press, 1974. Important political history and major study of the Kadet party in revolution and civil war.

SAUL, NORMAN E. *Sailors in Revolt: The Russian Baltic Fleet in 1917*. Lawrence, Kans., Regents Press of Kansas, 1978.

SMITH, S. A. *Red Petrograd: Revolution in the Factories*. Cambridge, Cambridge University Press, 1983. Social history focusing on the theme of workers' control.

SUKHANOV, N. N. *The Russian Revolution 1917*. Princeton, Princeton Uni-

versity Press, 1984. Joel Carmichael, ed. Brilliant observations by a non-Bolshevik socialist participant in 1917.

SUNY, RONALD GRIGOR. *The Baku Commune, 1917–1918: Class and Nationality in the Russian Revolution*. Princeton, Princeton University Press, 1972. Pioneering study of the revolution away from central Russia.

TSERETELLI, I. G. "Reminiscences of the February Revolution." *Russian Review* 14 (1955): 93–108, 184–200; 15 (1956): 37–48. Memoirs of the Menshevik leader.

VOLINE. *The Unknown Revolution*. New York, Free Life Editions, 1974. Important anarchist perspective.

VON MOHRENSCHILDT, DMITRI (editor). *The Russian Revolution: Contemporary Accounts*. New York, Oxford University Press, 1971.

WADE, REX A. *Red Guards and Workers' Militias in the Russian Revolution*. Stanford, Stanford University Press, 1984. Well researched, focused on Petrograd but looks at other locations as well.

————. *The Russian Search for Peace*. Stanford, Stanford University Press, 1969. Socialist and Provisional Government's attempts to end the war.

WILDMAN, ALLAN K. *The End of the Russian Imperial Army*. Vol. I: *The Old Army and the Soldiers' Revolt (March–April 1917)*. Princeton, Princeton University Press, 1980. Major social history of the army; a second volume extending to October is forthcoming in 1987.

CONTENTS

ILLUSTRATIONS

1

THE RUSSIAN REVOLUTION

VOLUME ONE

CHAPTER I

SOCIAL FORCES IN RUSSIAN HISTORY

THE course and character of the Russian Bolshevik Revolution and of the Soviet state which emerged from it were profoundly affected by ten centuries of Russian organized social life, with their accumulation of public and private institutions, customs and habits of thought. The influence of the past on the mighty social upheaval of 1917 was of a twofold character. It had created a Gordian Knot of class and social antagonisms which could only be cut by the sharp sword of revolution. And at the same time the heavy hand of the Russian past left unmistakable imprints on the psychology and character and ultimate outcome of the Revolution itself.

The arena on which the drama of Russian history has been played is the vast Eurasian plain, which nature itself seemed to have destined for political unity. One can travel two thousand miles from the Arctic Ocean to the Black Sea or the Caucasus Mountains and twice that distance from Russia's western frontier to Lake Baikal without encountering natural boundaries in the shape of high mountain ranges. Rich in some mineral resources and in forests, with a number of large navigable rivers, the Eurasian plain is subject to two natural disadvantages which unmistakably retarded Russia in its material and cultural development. The severe winters and the short planting seasons lower the productivity of agriculture, while the landlocked character of the territory around Moscow, the centre from which the building up of the Russian state proceeded, seriously obstructed trade and other intercourse with the outside world and contributed to the building up of a psychology of primitive isolation.

A very important factor in Russian development was the essentially Eurasian character of the Russian state. From the dim, half legendary days of the tenth and eleventh centuries, when the princes of Kiev went out to battle against the Pechengi, Polovtsi and other nomads, down to the systematic conquest of Central Asia in the nineteenth century Russia has been in constant contact and intermittent conflict with the Asiatic peoples of the steppe, Tartars,

1

Turcomans, Turks, Kirghiz and others. This struggle with the nomadic and semi-nomadic tribes of the steppe is generally recognized as one of the major forces in Russian historical development. In the eloquent words of the historian Kluchevsky:

"We remained in the rearguard of Europe; we guarded the rear of European civilization."[1]

There can be no reasonable doubt that this very process of struggle with the East helped to impart certain Asiatic traits to Russian character and Russian state administration and justified Plekhanov's characterization of the Russian social order as "too Europeanized in comparison with Asia and inadequately Europeanized by comparison with Europe."[2]

European influences gradually made themselves felt in Russia, and as early as the sixteenth century the Muscovite state was a power to be reckoned with in Eastern Europe. But there was always something foreign and artificial about the progress of European culture and technique in Russia. To a large extent Western innovations were introduced and sometimes imposed from above; they scarcely touched the masses of the people. It remained debatable whether Russia was the most Eastern of European powers or the most Western of Asiatic powers. Appropriately enough for a Eurasian state, Russia's religion and its conceptions of law and government, together with its forms of medieval religious art, came from Constantinople, capital of an Empire that also served as a bridge between Europe and Asia.

It is noteworthy that medieval visitors to Russia from such West European countries as England and Germany carried away the impression that they had been visiting an Eastern despotism. So the Englishman Fletcher writes: "Their method of government is very similar to the Turkish, which they apparently try to imitate. Their government is purely tyrannical; all its activities are directed to the advantage and profit of the Tsar alone, and, moreover, in the most clear and barbarous fashion." And the German Baron Gerberstein makes the unflattering observation that "it is uncertain whether the roughness of the people demands a tyrant-ruler or whether this people became so rough and cruel as a result of the tyranny of the ruler."

The beginnings of Russian organized life are associated with the cities of Kiev, on the Dnieper, in Southwestern Russia and with Novgorod, on the Volkhov, in the Northwest. Both cities lay on convenient river trade routes; and the princes of Kiev built up an

extensive state, carried on war and trade alternately with the Byzantine Empire and accepted Christianity from that source toward the end of the tenth century.

The Kiev state began to decline in the twelfth century, partly as a result of the continual pressure of the steppe tribes, partly because the princes were continually engaged in feuds among themselves and there was a perceptible drift of population in a northeastern direction, toward the Upper Volga and its tributaries. The ruin of Kiev was completed during the Tartar Conquest, which took place in the first half of the thirteenth century; and the task of serving as the nucleus of a new Russian state, which finally became strong enough to cast off the Tartar rule, fell to the princes of Moscow.

By pursuing a policy of caution and conciliation in relation to the Tartars the Moscow "grand princes," as the rulers of the territory were called, extended their possessions at the expense of their more adventurous and weaker neighbors; and in 1380 the Grand Prince Dmitry Donskoy won the first major victory over the Tartars at the Battle of Kulikovo. This victory was not altogether decisive; the Tartars returned from time to time, pillaging the country and levying tribute; and Russia's dependence upon the Asiatic conquerors was finally shaken off only during the reign of Ivan III (1462–1505), who completed the unification of the northern part of Russia under his rule and married Sofia, the niece of the last Emperor of Constantinople.

The grandson of Ivan III, Ivan IV, known as The Terrible (1533–1584), first assumed the title of Tsar and carried hostilities into the land of the Tartars, capturing Kazan, one of the main Tartar strongholds, in 1552, and Astrakhan, at the mouth of the Volga, in 1556. Ivan's name was a by-word for cruelty, in an age that knew the Borgias and the St. Bartholomew's Massacre; and in the latter part of his reign his orgies of bloodshed and lust seem to assume a clearly psychopathic character. One of the ferocious tyrant's whims, however, had important political and social consequences. This was the establishment of a force known as the *oprichina*, largely recruited from the lesser gentry, and endowed with unlimited power over the lives and property of all the Tsar's subjects. The emblem of this force consisted of a dog's head and a horse's tail, the first symbolizing the obligation to sniff out treason, the second the duty to sweep the land clear of rebellion. Besides inaugurating a general regime of violence, outrage and pillage the

oprichina turned with special vigor against the boyars, or old nobles, and by killing any of them who could be plausibly suspected of treason and confiscating their property helped to break up any possibility of the emergence of a powerful hereditary nobility as a counterpoise to the absolute power of the Tsar.

Besides carrying on Russia's traditional war against the peoples of the East (the early triumphs of Kazan and Astrakhan were somewhat offset later in Ivan's reign, when the Crimean Tartars sacked and burned Moscow) the Tsar endeavored to push westward and secure a foothold on the Baltic Sea. At first his troops overran Livonia, but ultimately the Swedes, Poles and Lithuanians pushed him out; and it remained for Peter the Great over a century later to secure the outlet on the Baltic. The bold Cossack Yermak, acting as a sort of mercenary captain for the wealthy Novgorod merchant family of the Stroganovs, crossed the Ural Mountains and reduced a large part of Siberia to submission, thereby opening up a new huge territory for Russian colonization.

By the end of the sixteenth century the outlines of the Russian state administration were already clear. The yoke which it laid on its subjects was an uncommonly heavy one; and medieval Russia well deserved its traditional adjective *mnogostradalnaya* ("much-suffering"). It has been estimated that between 1228 and 1426 Northern Russia sustained ninety civil wars, one hundred and sixty foreign wars, together with many harvest failures and innumerable fires. If the unification of the country and the concentration of authority in the hands of the Tsar eliminated many of the internal feuds the pressure of foreign war was never absent and placed an almost inconceivably heavy burden on the poor, landlocked, backward, isolated Muscovite state. As Kluchevsky writes:

"The Muscovite state was formed painfully and slowly. We now can scarcely understand and still less feel what sacrifices of the people's welfare it cost, how it pressed down on the existence of the individual." [3]

The state might be likened to a vast heavy pyramid, resting with almost intolerable weight upon the submerged serf class at the base. The trend was increasingly toward the servile state, the bound state, where the initiative of the individual was completely crushed beneath the omnipotent central state, embodied in the person of the Tsar. During the earlier centuries of Russian history the gentry enjoyed a good deal of freedom in moving from the service of one prince to that of another, and the peasants exercised

corresponding freedom in shifting from one landlord to another.

All this gradually changed under the overwhelming pressure of a central state that was obliged to extract the last bit of sweat and blood from its population in constant wars. Land was granted to the gentry only on condition of active military service and the peasants were more and more bound to the soil. A crude social theory developed to the effect that the peasant serfs were obligated to "feed" their landlord-master, who in his turn was supposed to serve the state.

The growth and intensification of serfdom was a major tendency in Russian history. A variety of causes contributed ultimately to bring about a situation where, at the end of the nineteenth century, after the French Revolution, thirty-four million people out of a population of thirty-six millions were reckoned as serfs, either of the state or of private owners. The military organization of the state was a primary factor in fastening the bonds of serfdom on the peasant masses. In response to the demands of the small landlords, who were unable to keep their serfs in free competition with the owners of larger estates, the restrictions on the peasant's freedom of movement were constantly extended; and the time for the reclamation of fugitive serfs was steadily lengthened. The fiscal exactions of the tax-collectors were so exorbitant that they drove free peasants to seek refuge in voluntary servitude to owners who would be responsible for their taxes; and in a typically medieval Russian paradox this practise was forbidden and people were commanded to remain free,—on pain of being flogged with the dreaded knout.

The administrative practises of the medieval Russian state were Asiatic in their cruelty and corruption. Torture was employed more ruthlessly and more extensively than in Western Europe. The pay of state officials and soldiers was habitually in arrears, and this led to frequent mutinies among the troops and to administrative extortions and abuses of all kinds.

But with all its defects the state survived, simply for lack of any available substitute. By sheer bulk and weight, combined with the inexhaustible capacity for suffering and endurance of the population, it expanded through conquest and colonization, more rapidly against the Mohammedan and pagan peoples of the South and the East, more slowly and painfully against the more advanced and developed Poles and Swedes in the West.

A very noteworthy feature in Russia's development was the

absence of any classes or institutions which could impose any check on the autocracy. Democratic institutions in the modern sense were, of course, absent in Western Europe during the Middle Ages. But in most European countries, in varying degrees, there were balancing forces, in the shape of the nobility, the clergy, the free cities, the landowning yeomanry, that placed some restrictions on the power of the sovereign and contained the germs of future representative institutions.

All this was notably lacking in Russia. The highest boyars, owners of thousands of serfs, were themselves only the first slaves of the Tsar. They possessed no security against sudden and arbitrary execution, accompanied with confiscation of their property. The Church, which in Western Europe represented a strong independent power, was completely subordinated to the Tsar in Russia. The Patriarch Nikon, who in the seventeenth century endeavored to assert the primacy of the Church, was sent into exile and the very institution of the Patriarchate was swept out of existence by the iconoclastic hand of Peter the Great. After the smashing of the independence of the trading cities of Novgorod and Pskov by Ivan III the Russian cities never emerged as autonomous communities. Few of them, indeed, attained any size or wealth, because of the country's slow economic development.

One finds in Russian history no parallel to the Barons at Runnymede, or to John Hampden refusing, on a point of principle, to pay an arbitrary tax. The Eurasian despotism caught perhaps some material reflections of the Renaissance and the Reformation, but entirely missed the spirit of these two movements, with their emphasis on human personality and individual judgment. The Muscovite state created a sense of popular strain and oppression which periodically expressed itself in destructive sweeping mass revolts that shook the governmental system to its foundations. But it did not promote or even permit the development of free creative forces that might have led Russia along lines of development similar to those of Western Europe. The whole course of subsequent events showed that the Russian autocracy could only be violently subverted; it could not be fundamentally modified in its character.

The "bound" Russian social order was subjected to more than one formidable shock. The danger of annihilation at the hands of the fierce Tartar warriors of the steppe may be said to have definitely passed after the fourteenth century, when the rise of the centralized Muscovite state coincided with the decline and degeneration of the

formerly invincible Tartars. But a new potentially explosive social force developed along the southern and southeastern marches of medieval Russia. Wild free communities of self-governing frontiersmen, the so-called Cossacks, grew up along the banks of the Don, the Ural, and the Dnieper. The Cossacks attracted soldiers of fortune from many countries, including the boldest and most enterprising of the fugitive serfs. Although they acknowledged the Orthodox faith and often served the Tsars in campaigns against Turk and Tartar, especially when there was a good chance of plunder, they were ruled by their elected atamans, not by the voevodas, or governors, whom the Tsars appointed as governors of provinces. While a propertied class with conservative sentiments existed among the Cossacks there was always a turbulent mass of rank-and-file warriors, ready to follow a popular leader not only against the Moslem but also on plundering expeditions with an element of social warfare into the realm of the Tsar. The Cossacks played a leading part in the three major upheavals which occurred in Russia before modern times: the so-called Troubled Times (1603–1613) and the uprisings of Stenka Razin (1670–1671) and Emilian Pugachev (1773–1775).

A dynastic and a social crisis, combined with foreign intervention, brought on the Troubled Times. The old line of the Moscow Grand Princes came to an end with the death of Ivan the Terrible's weak son, Fyodor, in 1598. An ambitious boyar, Boris Godunov, who is strongly suspected of having caused the murder of the youngest son of Ivan the Terrible, Dmitry, in order to pave the way for his own accession to the throne, was chosen Tsar. Several years of bad harvests predisposed the population to revolt; and a leader was found in the person of a Pretender, about whose identity historians are still in dispute, who gave himself out as the supposedly murdered Dmitry.

The Pretender was actively supported by Poland and entered Moscow after the sudden death of Boris Godunov in 1605. His short reign was terminated by assassination; and a period of almost indescribable confusion set in, with hordes of Cossacks plundering the country, Polish influences at work, endeavoring to reduce Moscow to the status of an appanage of the Polish Crown, and a widespread social war of rebellious peasants against the landlords further complicating the situation. Ultimately there was a revival of Russian national spirit; the Poles and Cossacks were driven off; and in 1613 Michael Romanov, first member of a dynasty which

was to reign in Russia for three centuries, was elected Tsar by a *Zemsky Sobor*, or National Assembly. The former political and social order was gradually patched up, although the seventeenth century is filled with riots, mutinies, local revolts, indicating that stability was not easily reattained.

The situation was further confused by a serious split in the Church. The Patriarch Nikon, with the aid and advice of ecclesiastical scholars, undertook to correct mistakes which had crept into the sacred books and the Church practises when they were transmitted to Russia from Constantinople. Many Russians, known as Old Believers, stubbornly refused to accept the Nikonite changes; and their resistance assumed political and social as well as religious significance. The Old Believers were active in movements of popular discontent, and their hostility to the state became intensified after the drastic innovating changes of Peter the Great, in which they saw the hand of Anti-Christ.

The formidable uprising headed by Stenka Razin in 1670–1671 indicated the weaknesses of the Muscovite state and, like the similar movement of Pugachev a century later, foreshadowed dimly the course of the Bolshevik Revolution and the subsequent civil war of 1917–1921. Razin was a Don Cossack who had acquired fame and followers by his raids on the coasts of Persia. Ultimately Razin and his wild followers turned against the Muscovite state, and swept up the Volga, calling on the peasants to rise against the landlords.

For a time the movement spread like wildfire. The troops in more than one instance passed over to the insurgents, whose ranks were swelled not only by rebellious serfs, armed with axes and pitchforks, but by the Tartars, Mordvians, Chuvashes and other non-Russian peoples of the Volga Valley, who found Razin's movement a convenient means of settling old scores of national oppression. At the height of Razin's success all the large middle and lower Volga towns, Samara, Saratov, Tsaritsin, Astrakhan, were in his hands, while insurgent bands penetrated provinces considerably to the west of the Volga, such as Penza and Nizhni Novgorod. All the horrors of future "Red" and "White" terrors were reproduced in this fierce insurrection against the serf state. In Astrakhan the voevoda was thrown from the top of the city tower and several hundred of the local aristocracy, officials and other members of unpopular classes were slaughtered. Public hangings, breaking on the wheel, cutting off of hands and legs were favorite methods of

pacifying the unruly serfs when the government forces gained the upper hand.

Razin was decisively defeated at Simbirsk and fled back to the Don, where the more conservative Cossacks arrested him and handed him over to the Tsar's representatives. He was publicly executed in Moscow for the edification of the populace and left behind only a memory, preserved in legends and folksongs. It is noteworthy that the reports of the Tsarist governors and commanders who were operating against the insurgents often speak of the unreliability of the local population, of the danger of mutiny among the troops. It was a thin layer of the population that upheld the Muscovite state. But the mass *jacqueries* of Razin and Pugachev could not subvert it. The deficiencies of the insurgents in arms, in training, in political ideas (both Razin and Pugachev put forward the idea of a "good" Tsar, who would kill the nobles and give land and freedom to the peasants) were too great. Clumsy and backward and corrupt as the state administration was, it always proved a little stronger in the long run than these wild tornadoes of death and destruction, emerging from the southeastern steppes.

The last major upheaval of this kind was headed by the Cossack Emilian Pugachev, who gave himself out as Tsar Peter III. It ran much the same course as Razin's movement, except that it covered a somewhat wider area. In addition to the familiar recruits of disorder, the Cossacks, serfs, minor nationalities and religious dissenters, Pugachev enlisted among his followers some of the first Russian proletarians, serfs who had been set to work in state mines and factories in the Ural region. Over 1500 landlords were killed during the Pugachev revolt, which ended with the capture and execution of its leader in 1775.

A hundred and thirty years elapsed between Pugachev's uprising and the next mass movement of revolt in Russia: the Revolution of 1905. More modern weapons and the gradual growth of modern means of communication strengthened the government as against the traditional sweeping uprisings on the outer marches of the empire. Moreover, the Cossacks were tamed; and, from a centre of insurrection they were transformed into a privileged military class of the population, endowed with land far beyond the average peasant's holding and trained to serve as cavalry in war and as a rough mounted police in the event of strikes and internal disturbances. When the last wave of peasant insurgence rolled over the country in 1917 the Cossacks were not in its vanguard.

Throughout the seventeenth century Western influences were gradually becoming stronger in the landlocked, Eurasian Muscovite state. Soldiers of fortune from various lands became instructors and officers in the Russian army. The number of foreign merchants and artisans increased and a special settlement, the *Nemetzkaya Sloboda* (literally German Freedom), grew up in the Russian capital.

The process of Westernization was driven forward at a furious pace by Peter the Great (1689–1725). It is significant that Peter grew up outside the medieval influence of the Kremlin. He narrowly escaped being murdered during a sanguinary riot of the *streltsi*, or oldfashioned troops of the guard, and during the regency of his ambitious half-sister Sofia he was brought up by his mother in the village Preobrazhensk, near Moscow. From his childhood he conceived hatred for the backward, primitive, medieval elements in Russian life, along with admiration for foreign achievements in warfare, science and technique.

A man of prodigious physical and mental energy and strong ungovernable passions (two of the most characteristic episodes in his life were the sentencing to death of his son, Aleksei, for suspected treason, and his own death as a result of a cold which he contracted while he was saving some sailors from drowning), Peter devoted his reign to the reorganization of Russia along Western lines. He invited large numbers of foreign experts, traders and mechanics to Russia; he shaved the beards off protesting boyars; he founded schools and built over two hundred factories, which were operated with serf labor. He won for Russia the long coveted outlook on the Baltic and emphasized the fundamental change which he endeavored to bring about in the country's outlook by establishing a new capital, St. Petersburg, on the banks of the Neva, near the sea, and removing the state administration from medieval, half-Asiatic Moscow. The first Russian newspaper was started in 1703 and the Academy of Sciences in 1725. The content of Peter's reforms has been summed up as follows: [4]

"The adoption of European technique and technical instruction, the encouragement of essential industries, the creation of a modern army and navy, the transformation of the theocratic monarchy into a secular absolutism."

Ministries, or, as they were called, "collegia," on the Swedish model were substituted for the oldfashioned Muscovite organs of administration; a Senate replaced the Council of Boyars. Peter,

the absolute autocrat, was notably democratic in his selection of advisers and associates; the pastry-cook's son, Menshikov, became his chief Minister and his wife, subsequently the Empress Catherine I, was a washwoman. There was a distinct anti-clerical streak in this extraordinary Tsar; he caricatured the rites of the Church in carouses with his boon companions and he suppressed the office of Patriarch. By introducing a system under which the holders of state offices automatically acquired titles of nobility Peter laid the foundation for a new bureaucratic class of the nobility which took its place along with the families that liked to trace their ancestors back to Rurik and the early Varangians.

Peter gave Russia a strong push toward the West. But he did not place his country in the general current of West European development or eliminate the dualism of Western and Eastern influences which is such a marked trait in the country's history. Some of his failures are attributable to the backwardness of the country, to the passive resistance of the people, who resented the Tsar's efforts to drive them rapidly in an unknown direction. Moreover, although he placed Western decorations on the structure of the Muscovite serf state, he did not change its essential character. The load on the enslaved peasants at the bottom of the social pyramid became heavier than ever as a result of the expenses connected with Peter's wars and administrative innovations. Admiring Western material achievements the Tsar never seems to have reflected that they were in no small degree the result of a far greater degree of individual initiative and freedom than Russia enjoyed. Peter's attempt to "square the circle" in this connection is eloquently analyzed in the following terms by Kluchevsky.[5]

"His beneficent actions were accomplished with repelling violence. Peter's reform was a struggle of despotism with the people, with its sluggishness. He hoped through the threat of his authority to evoke initiative in an enslaved society, and through a slave-owning nobility to introduce into Russia European science, popular education, as the necessary condition of social initiative. He desired that the slave, remaining a slave, should act consciously and freely. The inter-action of despotism and freedom, of education and slavery,—this is the political squaring of the circle, the riddle which we have been solving for two centuries from the time of Peter, and which is still unsolved."

Peter's reforms did not touch either the problem of serfdom or the problem of representative government. The last *zemsky sobor,* or national assembly, in Russian history was held during Peter's

reign in 1698. This was an institution which had first been convoked by Ivan the Terrible in 1566; it consisted of representatives
of the nobility, the clergy, the merchants and, in some cases, the
peasants. It met rarely and irregularly and exercised only consultative, not legislative functions; but even this modest germ of
popular representation disappeared from Russian history, and more
than two centuries elapsed between the last *zemsky sobor* and the
State Duma which was the result of the 1905 Revolution.

A feature of Russian development during the eighteenth century,
after the death of Peter, was an increase in the influence and privileges of the nobility. The basis of the peculiar Russian "social contract," under which the nobles were supposed to serve the state, while
the peasants "fed" the nobles, was completely destroyed in 1762,
when the nobles were exempted from the obligation of state service.
There was no idea at that time, however, of carrying out the logical
complementary step of emancipating the peasants. Catherine II,
the correspondent of the French Encyclopedists, who made the
reading of Voltaire popular among her courtiers, was quick to send
into Siberian exile A. N. Radischev, whose "Journey from St. Petersburg to Moscow" was a description of the misery of the people,
combined with a plea for the abolition of serfdom.

The institution of serfdom, involving as it did the unlimited
power of a small class of landed nobility over a vastly larger number
of peasant serfs, was a main cause of Russia's retarded development. As it could only be maintained by the most brutal methods
of flogging and torture it placed a brutalizing stamp upon the whole
Russian social order. A serf population was inevitably backward
and generally illiterate; and this exerted a paralyzing influence
on every branch of national life. And the serf system in Russia
was tightening just at the time when it was being loosened or
abolished in most European countries. As Professor Geroid Tan-
quary Robinson writes: [6]

"The eighteenth century saw a progressive degradation of the
peasantry, an intensive and extensive development of the servile system
which brought it to a place of vast importance in Russian life."

The free steppe lands of the south and southeast were brought
under the yoke of the central government; the Cossacks were
partly subdued, partly bought off; the philosophic Empress Catherine II through a series of decrees abolished freedom of movement
for the peasants in the newly acquired southern provinces from

the Dnieper to the Caucasus and thereby riveted the chains of serfdom still more tightly.

Serfdom remained intact through the reigns of Alexander I (1801–1825), whose early liberalism, imparted through a French revolutionary tutor, La Harpe, evaporated into reactionary mysticism in the latter part of his life, and Nicholas I (1825–1855). Indeed the state order created by Nicholas I, with its perfected espionage system, its savage public floggings and beatings, its fierce antipathy to any suggestion of progress or democratism (Nicholas is said to have written on a state document which contained the word progress: "This word must be deleted from official terminology"[7]) suggests nothing so much as an incarnate gendarme.

A noteworthy feature of the Russian state administration was its extreme secrecy. All meetings of the government departments were closed; the most important of them were definitely secret; it was considered a serious crime to report anything which went on at such meetings. In the Ministry of Foreign Affairs every paper, however unimportant, was marked "secret," so that documents whose secrecy was really essential had to be distinguished by other phrases, such as "only for the Minister" or "quite confidential." The state service was filled with "secret" or "very secret councillors."[8] And the power of the secret police, from the days of the *prikaz tainikh dyel* (Department for Secret Affairs) of medieval Russia down to the "Okhrana" of the last Romanovs was always very great.

Probably the most important event in Russian social history during the nineteenth century was the abolition of serfdom by Tsar Alexander II in 1861. Several factors had paved the way for this step. The advantages of free labor were becoming more evident; humanitarian feeling had been aroused by such works as Turgeniev's "A Sportsman's Sketches"; the backwardness and weaknesses of the old order had been exposed in humiliating fashion in connection with Russia's defeat by England and France in the Crimean War (1853–1855); the spectre of Pugachev still loomed on the horizon of the Tsar and the landlords. Alexander II frankly told an audience of nobles that it was better to abolish serfdom from above than to allow it to be abolished from below.

It was an ominous and, in the light of ultimate developments, a very significant circumstance that the peasants, who had remained quiet while the terms of the emancipation were being worked out in the government commissions, indulged in a flare-up of rioting after

the conditions of their liberation were made known. During the four months which followed the publication of the Tsar's manifesto of emancipation there were 647 recorded instances of peasant rioting.[9] In the village of Bezdna, in Penza Province, the troops fired on the peasant rioters and killed over fifty people.[10]

Under the terms of the emancipation the peasants, as a general rule, received only the land which they had cultivated as their own during the period of serfdom. Inasmuch as the general practise under serfdom had been that the peasant should work three days on his own land and three days on his master's these allotments were not sufficient for selfsupport, especially as the peasants were obliged to pay redemption dues extending over many decades.[11] It was not absolute lack of land, but rather primitive methods of cultivation that accounted for the poverty of the Russian peasants; but the chances of an emancipated serf, bound to pay his redemption dues, being able to acquire sufficient capital to improve his farming technique were slight indeed.

Moreover, while the Tsar freed the peasant from his landlord, the peasant remained bound to his village community, which he could not leave without permission. The powers of the community to dictate to the individual what crops he should plant and to make periodic redistributions of land remained in force; and this acted as a tremendous drag on individual peasant initiative. The motives of the government in retaining this community form of farming were partly fiscal, because the community could be made responsible for the arrears of taxes of any of its members, and partly social and political, since it was believed that the community would serve as a conservative and anti-revolutionary force. The advance of trade and of modern capitalist relations undermined the community organization; but the government itself gave encouragement to the individual farmer only after the 1905 Revolution.

So, while the emancipation ended the cruder outrages against human dignity of the era of serfdom, the lot of the Russian peasant remained distressingly hard. The amount of land which the thriftier and more hardworking peasants were able to buy from the less prosperous families of the country gentry did not keep pace with the growth of the population. The size of the average peasant holding shrunk from 13.2 desyatinas (a desyatina is 2.7 acres) in 1877 to 10.4 in 1905.[12] The number of cattle declined from 37.2 per hundred of population in 1880 to 30 in 1909.[13] Local famines in poor harvest years were not uncommon and in 1903 an agrarian

committee reported in the following terms to the Premier, Count Witte: "When the harvest is normal the peasant obtains thirty percent less nutriment than is physiologically required." All these facts indicate that the Russian peasant, even after the shackles of serfdom had been struck off, remained far behind his French or German brother in wellbeing; and this exerted a decisive influence both upon the psychology of the peasants and upon the final course of the Revolution.

Besides abolishing serfdom Alexander II modernized the courts and the conditions of army service and granted a limited amount of local selfgovernment to county boards known as *zemstvos*, in which the nobility played a dominant rôle. His reforms stopped short of granting a national constitution, however, and to some extent they were nullified or weakened in their effect by subsquent decrees withdrawing political cases from the jurisdiction of the ordinary courts and vesting wide authority in the country police chief, the *zemsky nachalnik*.

A profound force for change in nineteenth century Russia was the growth of industry, trade and railroad communication. Upon the accession of Alexander I at the beginning of the century Russia was a country of serf-owning nobles and peasant serfs, with a thin intermediate layer of government officials, traders and other city-dwellers. By the end of the century large-scale textile, metallurgical and mining industries had developed; the enormous distances of the country were spanned with a network of railroads; serfdom was only a memory; a middle class and an industrial working class were beginning to assert themselves. The rapid growth of Russian industry, especially during the second half of the nineteenth century, is evident from the following table: [12]

Date	Industrial Enterprises	Number of Workers	Value of Output
1765	262	38,000	5,000,000 rubles
1801	2423	95,000	25,000,000
1825	5261	202,000	46,000,000
1854	9944	460,000	160,000,000
1881	21,173	770,000	998,000,000
1893	32,483	1,400,000	1,760,000,000
1896	38,401	1,742,000	2,745,000,000

Between 1861 and 1870 the town population increased from 4,300,355 to 6,090,508, a growth of approximately 45 percent.[14] During the reign of Alexander III (1881–1894) the length of the railroad lines increased from 22,500 versts (a verst is about two thirds of a mile) to 36,662 versts.[15]

The richness of Russia's natural resources and the cheapness of labor contributed to an inflow of foreign capital and to a very rapid rate of progress in the development of many industries. This was especially true in regard to the southern iron and steel industry. Between 1886 and 1899 the Russian iron output increased by approximately five times. In its rate of building railroads Russia, as a result of its enormous size, outstripped other European countries.[16]

Foreign capital played a very important part in the development of Russian industry. It is estimated that about a third of the capital invested in Russian stock-companies in 1914 was of foreign origin. The inflow of foreign capital into Russia from 1905 until 1908 amounted to 370,700,000 rubles.[17] During the ten-year period 1904–1913 Russia placed bonds to the value of 3,235,700,000 rubles abroad. French investors bought heavily the bonds issued by the Russian Government (the Franco-Russian alliance, concluded in the reign of Alexander III, contributed to close financial relations between the two countries) and French capital was heavily interested in the Russian mining and metallurgical industries. So about 60 percent of the pig iron and about 50 percent of the coal produced in Russia on the eve of the War came from enterprise which were operating on French capital. British capital was largely invested in the Caucasian oil-fields and, to a lesser extent, in the textile industry of Northern Russia and in Siberian and Ural mining enterprises. Belgium and Germany made their contributions to Russian industrial development. All in all it is reckoned that 32.6 percent of the foreign capital invested in Russia was of French origin, 22.6 percent of British, 19.7 percent of German and 14.3 percent of Belgian.

This large-scale participation of foreign capital in Russian economic life possessed a double significance. It reflected the weakness of the Russian capitalist class and it helps to explain the material interest of Great Britain and France in the overthrow of the Bolshevik regime, which wiped out such large foreign investments through the simple processes of repudiating debts and confiscating property.

The Tsarist Empire, as it emerged into the twentieth century, was at once one of the largest and one of the weakest of the world's political entities. Spread out over half of Europe and a third of Asia it contained within its vast body many seeds of potential disintegration. Neither the forcible Westernization of Peter the Great, nor the reforms of Alexander II, nor the material changes

brought about through the infusion of modern capitalism had successfully solved the contradictions of the Eurasian state.

The peasant, often the son or grandson of a serf, still looked with hungry greed at the broad acres of the neighboring country squire. The young Russian industrial working class, with abundant grievances in the shape of long hours, low wages and bad housing conditions, denied the outlet of effective trade-union organization, possessed a far more violently revolutionary psychology than the corresponding class in Western Europe. The non-Russian nationalities represented another explosive force because of the policy of intolerant Russification and persecution of non-Russian languages which became especially marked during the reign of Alexander III. Extremist ideas which in the milder atmosphere of Western Europe were apt to remain in the realm of theory were caught up and held with fanatical earnestness by that part of the Russian intelligentsia which found the political repression and the social inequalities of the absolutist state quite intolerable. With so much combustible material inside its borders the Tsarist regime, which during the nineteenth century had expanded at the expense of weaker peoples, such as the Turks or the primitive Mohammedan states of Central Asia, was brought by historical destiny into clashes with more progressive and efficient state organisms, with Japan in the East and with Germany in the West. It only required the impact of these unsuccessful wars, with Japan in 1904–1905 and with the Central Powers in 1914–1917, to set in motion the greatest social revolutionary movement in history, whether measured by the number of people and the extent of territory affected or by the boldness and scope of the revolutionary objectives.

NOTES

[1] V. O. Kluchevsky, "Course of Russian History," Vol. II, p. 492.
[2] G. V. Plekhanov, "The History of Russian Social Thought," Vol. I, p. 131.
[3] Kluchevsky, *op. cit.*, Vol. II, p. 490.
[4] D. Mirsky, "Russia: A Social History," p. 183.
[5] *Op. cit.*, Vol. IV, p. 282.
[6] "Rural Russia under the Old Regime," pp. 32–33.
[7] Thomas G. Masaryk, "The Spirit of Russia," Vol. I, p. 113.
[8] M. N. Pokrovsky, "Russian History" (abridged edition), Vol. I, p. 141.
[9] Robinson, *op. cit.*, p. 86.
[10] Alexander Kornilov, "Modern Russian History," Vol. II, p. 66.
[11] Robinson, *op. cit.*, p. 94.
[12] Masaryk, *op. cit.*, Vol. I, p. 163.
[13] Masaryk, *op. cit.*, Vol. I, p. 120.
[14] S. Piontkovsky, "Sketches of the History of Russia in the Nineteenth and Twentieth Centuries," p. 128.
[15] Kornilov, *op. cit.*, Vol. II, p. 268.
[16] M. Tugan-Baranovsky, "The Russian Factory in Past and Present," pp. 269–273.
[17] Piontkovsky, *op. cit.*, 337–340.

CHAPTER II

PIONEERS OF REVOLUTION

WHILE the Russian state in the sixteenth, seventeenth and eighteenth centuries was shaken by elemental serf uprisings intellectual revolutionism in Russia begins only in the nineteenth century; and its first manifestation was the movement of the Decembrists, so called because their uprising occurred in December, 1825. This movement may be regarded as a belated and indirect Russian reaction to the French Revolution. Its leaders were young army officers who had seen something of Europe during the campaigns against Napoleon and who brought back with them dreams of constitutionalism and social reform.

In 1816 several officers of the Semyenov Guard regiment founded a society which was called "The Union of Salvation, or of the Faithful and True Sons of the Fatherland." Its original ideals were dreamy, mystical and not particularly hostile to the government; but it assumed a more revolutionary character after it was joined by Pavel Pestel, a young, energetic officer who was the strongest personality in the movement. Pestel believed that "the leading enterprise of our time is to be found in the struggle between the masses of the population and aristocracies of every kind, whether based on rank or on birth." [1]

There was a mutiny among the soldiers in the Semyenov regiment in 1820, as a result of harsh disciplinary measures; and, although there was no connection between the mutiny and the society, which had changed its name to "Union of Welfare," the leaders of the latter, in view of the increased suspicion and watchfulness of the government, decided to suspend activity in 1821. Two groups continued to function secretly, however, a Southern Society in which Pestel was the outstanding figure and a Northern Society, led by Guard officers, Nikita Muraviev, Prince S. P. Trubetzkoy and Prince Eugene Obolensky.

Of the two Societies the Southern, under Pestel's influence, was the more radical, although neither aimed at a fundamental social revolution. The ideas of the Decembrists are reflected in sketches

of proposed constitutions which were framed by Muraviev and Pestel.[2] Muraviev suggested the establishment of a constitutional monarchy on a federal basis, with thirteen states. He established a high property qualification for membership in parliament and proposed at first to liberate the serfs without land and in later drafts to give them very small land allotments. Such an arrangement, of course, would have left them in complete economic dependence upon their owners.

Pestel proposed to overthrow Tsarism by a *coup d'état* and to set up a military dictatorship as a prelude to the final establishment of a republican form of government. He was inclined to take more radical measures in alienating the land of large proprietors than was Muraviev, and he conceived his republic as a centralized, Russian national state, in contrast to Muraviev, who desired to grant more local autonomy. Pestel was willing to grant independence to Poland, but only on condition that Poland should adopt a similar form of government and be content with its ethnographic frontiers. He wished to deport the Jewish population of Russia to Palestine.

The members of the two societies obtained an uncommonly favorable opportunity to put their theoretical ideas into practise when a state of confusion in regard to the succession arose after the death of Alexander I in Taganrog on November 19, 1825. The legal heir to the throne, Alexander's brother Constantine, was unwilling to assume the crown and abdicated in favor of a younger brother Nicholas. The interchange of communications between Constantine, who was in Warsaw as Viceroy of Poland, and Nicholas in St. Petersburg led to delay and uncertainty; and on December 14, when the troops were supposed to swear allegiance to the new Tsar, the Decembrists persuaded one regiment of the Guards, the Moscow regiment, and several companies of Guard-Marines to come out on the Senate Square and refuse to take the oath to Nicholas. The soldiers announced that they considered Constantine the lawful Tsar and demanded a constitution.

Had the Decembrists acted promptly and decisively they might have carried out their *coup* successfully, because Nicholas was thrown into consternation by the unexpected resistance and for many hours took no effective measures to suppress it. But, despite their military profession, the Decembrists displayed singular incapacity for ruthless, decisive action; indeed this first appearance of the revolutionary intellectual in the Russian arena symbolized and foreshadowed the fate of that class in the revolutionary up-

heaval almost a century later. Except for the action of one of the Decembrists, Kakhovsky, in shooting the Tsar's envoy, General Miloradovitch, nothing was done to push on the revolt; there was no effective move to seize the enemy's cannon or the nearby Winter Palace; and when Nicholas finally made up his mind to act a few volleys of shells from his cannon dispersed the bewildered soldiers, most of whom thought that the "Constitutsia," for which they had been told to shout, was the wife of Constantine.

Pestel had been arrested by order of Alexander I; and a slight rebellion among the troops in the neighborhood of Kiev, inspired by the other leaders of the Southern Society, was easily put down. The new Tsar took an active part in questioning the prisoners and in endeavoring to unravel all the threads of the conspiracy. On July 12, 1826, five Decembrist leaders, Pestel, the poet Rileev, Muraviev-Apostol, Bestuzhev-Rumin and Kakhovsky, were hanged. Scores of other participants in the movement were exiled to hard labor in Siberia. Nothing was left of the Decembrist organization except a romantic halo which was perpetuated by Pushkin, Nekrasov and other poets, who paid tributes to the sufferings of the exiles and the fidelity of many of their wives, who forsook the pleasures and gayeties of life in St. Petersburg to share with their husbands the bleak hardships of Siberian exile. Typical of the sympathy which the Decembrists aroused in the small Russian educated class of their time is the ringing conclusion of Pushkin's "Message to Siberia,"[3] which was addressed to the exiles:

> The heavy-hanging chains will fall,
> The walls will crumble at the word;
> And Freedom greet you with the light,
> And brothers give you back the sword.

Despite the fact that the reign of Nicholas I has become a byword for iron reaction and merciless repression of independent thought Russia's cultural advance during the second quarter of the nineteenth century was truly remarkable. This age may be said to have witnessed the birth of modern Russian literature with the rich romantic poetry of Pushkin and Lermontov, the exuberant satires of Gogol, Griboyedov's moving drama "Grief from Thought," which reflected as far as censorship permitted the discontent of the educated class with the political and social and material backwardness of the country. The three masters of the Russian novel, Tolstoy, Turgeniev and Dostoevsky were looming on the horizon,

even though the regime of Nicholas did condemn Dostoevsky to death, commuting the sentence at the last moment to hard labor in Siberia.

Intellectual ideas filtered through from Western Europe; and German philosophers and French utopian socialists were eagerly if furtively discussed in the groups which formed around such men as Granovsky and Stankevitch. Two opposed currents of thought which exerted a definite influence on Russian social development made their influence felt. One of these currents of thought was represented by the Slavophiles, whose first outstanding thinker was Ivan Kireevsky. He saw in the Russian peasant the only true Christian and contrasted Russian humility with Latin pride. He exalted patriarchal, believing peasant Russia against the individualistic, urbanized, sceptical West. Another Slavophile, Khomiakov, was a champion of Russian Orthodoxy against Roman Catholicism and Protestantism. The Slavophiles idealized primitive medieval Russia and looked askance at the Westernizing innovations of Peter the Great. They were filled with a consciousness of Russia's mystical destiny, and one of their number, Prince Odoyevsky, expressed this element in the movement when he wrote:

"Western Europe is on the highroad to ruin. We Russians, on the contrary, are young and fresh and have taken no part in the crimes of Europe. We have a great mission to fulfill. Our name is already inscribed on the tablets of victory; the victories of science, art and faith await us on the ruins of tottering Europe."

The Westernizers, the philosophic opponents of the Slavophiles, had a very different conception of the relation between Russia and Europe. They believed that Russia needed not only Western technical progress, but Western ideas of constitutionalism, law and social progress. A leading exponent of this tendency was V. G. Byelinsky, the famous literary critic. In his letter to Gogol, who in his later years had become something of an Orthodox mystic, Byelinsky wrote in 1846: "Russia doesn't need Orthodox mysticism; she needs rights and laws in conformity with healthy understanding and justice. In a time and country when men sell men like cattle Gogol wishes to soothe our minds with empty sermons." Byelinsky contested the idea that the Russians are naturally religious; he conceded that they were superstitious, but was confident that civilization would drive this out.[4]

While the Slavophiles sometimes came into conflict with a suspicious and rigorous censorship they represented, in the main,

a conservative force in Russian development. The revolutionaries were practically all Westernizers. The sole traditional Russian institution which they desired to preserve was the *obschina,* or Russian peasant community, because they saw in the communal ownership of the village land the germ of a future socialist organization of society.

In contrast to earlier centuries, which witnessed mass movements of revolt without clearly defined ideas, the nineteenth century in Russia generated a multitude of revolutionary ideas, theories and personalities without arousing any genuine mass movement. If in the seventeenth and eighteenth centuries the masses rose in revolt with leaders from their own ranks, Stenka Razins and Pugachevs, in the nineteenth century there were many conspiratorial groups of potential leaders, but no widespread movement of the masses was perceptible until 1905. The three outstanding personalities of what may be called the pre-Marxian era of Russian revolutionary activity were Alexander Herzen (1812–1870), Mikhail Bakunin (1814–1876) and N. G. Chernishevsky (1828–1889).

Herzen, the illegitimate child of a Russian aristocrat and a German girl, was a rebel by instinct and sympathy from childhood. In his memoirs he tells how he and his kinsman Ogarev, returning from an evening walk in the outskirts of Moscow, embraced each other and vowed to devote their lives to revolutionary struggle, and the Decembrists were his boyhood heroes. Such a man was predestined for trouble under the regime of Nicholas I; and after several encounters with the police he went aboard in 1847 and remained an émigré until the end of his life. In the long line of Russia's émigré publicists (perhaps the first was a certain Prince Kurbsky, who from a safe retreat in Poland addressed a series of reproachful missives to Tsar Ivan the Terrible) Herzen was certainly one of the most eloquent. Turgeniev described his style as compounded of blood and tears; and there is an emotional swing about Herzen's writing that compensates for the frequent vagueness and occasional contradictoriness of his ideas.

Herzen was in Paris at the time of the 1848 Revolution and was repelled by the triumph of the middle classes and the suppression of the more radical groups. Believing that "the man of the future in Russia is the peasant" he hoped that Russia would reach socialism without passing through the intermediate stages of middleclass democracy and capitalism.

Herzen was at the height of his influence during the years which preceded the emancipation of the serfs in 1861. His magazine, "The Bell," published in London, enjoyed enormous surreptitious popularity among the Russian intelligentsia; it is said that even Tsar Alexander II and some of the highest state officials read it and were influenced by its criticisms. Herzen was by no means an uncompromising revolutionary and upon the occasion of the emancipation decision greeted the Tsar with the enthusiastic phrase: "Thou hast conquered, O Galilean." A characteristic specimen of his romantic style was his message to students who had been arrested and expelled from St. Petersburg University: [5]

"Where shall you go, youths, from whom knowledge has been shut off? Shall I tell you, Where? Give ear, for even darkness does not prevent you from listening,—from all corners of our enormous land, from the Don and the Ural, from the Volga and the Dnieper, a moan is growing, a grumbling is rising,—this is the first roar of the sea-billow, which begins to rage, pregnant with storm, after a long and tiresome calm. *V narod.* To the people.—That is your place, O exiles of knowledge."

This phrase "to the people," together with Herzen's theory that the way to socialism in Russia lay through the village community, exerted a profound influence upon the thought and activity of a whole generation of revolutionaries. Herzen's influence began to wane after 1863. His open support of the Polish insurrection in that year alienated moderate liberals who considered themselves Russian patriots while, on the other hand, a younger generation was growing up in Russia which regarded Herzen as too moderate and, indeed, outdated. There was a streak of moderation in Herzen, which did not accord with the mood of young extremists, and which finds expression in a letter to his friend Bakunin in 1869: [6]

"He who is unwilling that civilization should be based on the knout must not endeavor to secure liberty through the instrumentality of the guillotine."

In contradistinction to Herzen, who was a theorist and a passive observer, Mikhail Bakunin, the founder of Russian anarchism, was a man of prodigious personal activity, never so happy as when he was organizing a conspiracy or fighting on the barricades. The son of a small landowner with Decembrist connections, Bakunin left Russia in 1840, was outlawed by the government for refusing to obey an order to return and entered on an extraordinary

career as a cosmopolitan revolutionary. He participated in uprisings in Prague and Dresden, each of which earned him a death sentence, commuted in each case to life imprisonment; the Austrian Government turned him over to Russia, where he passed through a term of imprisonment in the dreaded Petropavlovsk fortress in St. Petersburg and was subsequently exiled to Siberia, whence he escaped and returned to Europe by way of America. Here he resumed his restless life, becoming a bitter opponent of Karl Marx in the First International, which was torn to pieces as a result of their dissensions.

Bakunin was the apostle of a simple creed of absolute destruction. The state, religion, the family and all the institutions connected with them must be annihilated if humanity was to be free. He was opposed in principle to all schemes for the reorganization of society, believing that the liberated masses by instinct would build up life along the lines which were most suitable. A programme which he drew up for the "Union of Socialist Democracy," which he created in 1868, contains the following passage: [7]

"The Union declares itself atheistic. It desires the final and complete destruction of classes, the political, economic and social equality of individuals of both sexes; it desires that land, tools of labor and capital of any kind should become the collective property of all society and be utilized only by workers, *i.e.*, agricultural and industrial associations of workers."

On another occasion, emphasizing his political and personal hostility to Marx, whom he regarded as a "Pan-German," Bakunin wrote: [8] "On the Pan-German standard is written: maintenance and strengthening of the state at any cost. On our social revolutionary standard, on the contrary, is inscribed with letters of fire and blood: destruction of all state, annihilation of bourgeois civilization, free organization from below by means of free unions, organization of a lawless mob of common laborers, of all liberated humanity, creation of a new human world."

Bakunin was inclined to Pan-Slavism and felt more at home with Latin peoples, such as Italians and Spaniards, than with Germans and English. He saw as the driving revolutionary force not the educated skilled worker, already tainted with "bourgeois" traits, but the utterly poverty-stricken classes, and he looked with favor on bandits and criminals.

Bakunin's passionate philosophy of rebellion made a strong impression on the Russian students who were beginning to attend

Swiss universities, and filtered into Russia through them and through other sources. One of his disciples, Nechaiev, who came to him from Russia and whose character represented an almost psychopathic combination of fanaticism and charlatanism, founded a secret society among the Moscow students, all the members of which were obliged to obey his commands blindly. When one of the members of the society, Ivanov, seemed unreliable, Nechaiev had him murdered in 1869. This murder led to the discovery and break-up of the group.

More significant as a revolutionary thinker than either Herzen or Bakunin was N. G. Chernishevsky, who approached the Marxian viewpoint in regard to capitalism more closely than any of the other advocates of what might be called Russian peasant socialism. Some of his criticisms of capitalism, for its absence of plan and for its ministering primarily to the needs of the propertied minority of the population, have a distinctly modern note.[9] At the same time he looked with favor on the peasant communal organization, in which he saw a means of saving Russia from class struggle and the development of a proletariat. Another point in which he deviated from a strictly Marxian materialistic conception of social forces was the rôle which he assigned to human understanding as a moving power. "We perceive nothing on earth higher than human personality," he wrote on one occasion,[10] a sentiment which would have always been in sharp contrast with the realities of Russian life.

Chernishevsky was the descendant of a long line of priests and received theological training, to which his reaction was distinctly negative. He emphasized utilitarianism as the proper foundation of ethics; and his novel "What to Do," while it is a work of negligible literary value, exerted a profound influence on the shaping of the Nihilist younger generation of the sixties. Chernishevsky was always inclined to stress the importance of social, as against political change. So in his diary for the year 1848[11] we find the following outburst:

"I do not like those gentlemen who say: Liberty, Liberty and do not destroy a social order under which nine tenths of the people are slaves and proletarians; the important thing is not whether there is a Tsar or not, whether there is a constitution or not, but that one class should not suck the blood of another."

As editor of the radical magazine "The Contemporary" up to the time of his arrest in 1862 Chernishevsky wielded enormous

influence. He possessed an extremely comprehensive mind, and his interests embraced the natural as well as the social sciences. In another country his career might have resembled that of John Stuart Mill or the French Encyclopedists. But the Russian political atmosphere has never been favorable to "critically thinking personalities," to use the phrase of a later revolutionary theorist, Peter Lavrov. The government looked with increasing disfavor on the radical ideas which found expression, even in masked and censored form, in "The Contemporary." Moreover, although Chernishevsky was an extremely discreet man, who left little written evidence of illegal activity, his biographer Steklov is most probably correct when he writes: [12] "There is no doubt that Chernishevsky was acquainted with all the revolutionary enterprises of his time, that he knew about all the manifestations of the current revolutionary movement and participated at least morally in many of them."

Chernishevsky was arrested in 1862 and was sentenced to lifelong exile in Siberia. His powers of thought and writing contracted under the hard conditions of exile and when he was finally allowed to return to Russia and live first in Astrakhan, later in his native Saratov, he was already a broken old man. His memory lived in the radical student circles; and no semi-legal *vecherinka,* or evening where forbidden thoughts were canvassed under the disguise of a social gathering, was complete without a toast to Chernishevsky and his ideals.

Protest under the iron police regime of Nicholas I was almost entirely restricted to the field of thought. Only two associations of a semi-political character were discovered in the course of his reign; both were of negligible scope and were promptly suppressed. One was the Union of Cyril and Methodius, an Ukrainian nationalist organization in which the poet Shevchenko was an active figure; it was put down in 1847. The other was the circle of the Petrashevtsi, so called after its leader, M. B. Butashevitch-Petrashevsky, an amiable and well-meaning if somewhat eccentric disciple of the French utopian socialist Fourier. Petrashevsky built a communal dwelling for his serfs; but they failed to respond to this peculiar idea of their *barin* (master) and burned it down at the first opportunity.

The circle was nothing but a discussion club for "advanced ideas," although a pledge, meaningless under the circumstances and distinctly perilous in view of the contemporary police regime,

was exacted of every member of the circle "to take full and open part in the uprising when the executive committee of the society should decide that the time for rebellion has come.[13] A government spy attended many meetings of the circle, and as a result of his denunciations the members were arrested and received the customary sentences of exile at hard labor in 1849.

The accession of Alexander II and the hopes which were aroused as a result of the emancipation of the serfs led to new ferment in the minds of the educated classes, and especially of the students, out of whose ranks came most of the revolutionaries of that period. In the summer of 1861 appeared three proclamations under the signature "Great Russian," which called for the grant of more land to the peasants and for the holding of a national constituent assembly, threatening that more violent means might be employed if these concessions were not made peacefully. And later in the year the watchful gendarmes confiscated a revolutionary appeal, couched in much stronger and more uncompromising language, addressed to the peasants, the authorship of which is commonly ascribed to Chernishevsky. The name "Land and Liberty," which became famous as a characterization of the most influential revolutionary group of the seventies, was first used in connection with a shortlived radical group which sprang up in 1862 with the participation of the emigrants Herzen and Ogarev.

The student Zaichnevsky was the author of a violent programme of revolution, published in 1862, after his arrest, under the name "Young Russia." Zaichnevsky proclaimed the extermination of counterrevolutionaries in the following vivid terms: "Kill the members of the Tsar's party unsparingly, as it doesn't spare us now; kill them on the squares, if the scoundrels venture to appear there; kill them in their homes; kill them in the narrow alleys of the towns; kill them on the broad streets of the capital, kill them in the villages. Remember that whoever is not with us is against us; whoever is against us is our enemy and enemies must be exterminated by all means. But do not forget at every new victory and in every battle to repeat: Long live the Russian social and democratic republic."

A successor to "Young Russia" was a student group headed by Ishutin which assumed the melodramatic name "Hell" and advocated regicide in the event that the government did not yield to demands for a popular constitution. Ishutin also conceived the idea that a dictatorship of his society would be necessary after

the revolution was completed, so as to control the leaders of the movement and prevent them from forgetting its principles. It was under the influence of these ideas that Ishutin's cousin, Karakozov, made an unsuccessful attempt on the life of Alexander II in 1866.[14]

Not one of these student circles of the sixties reached any large popular audience. But the ideas of the revolutionaries flowed into the broad stream of the movement that culminated in the following century and extremism, impatience with half-measures, eagerness to leap from the backward political and social conditions of the autocracy straight into the presumptive socialist paradise recur in later phases of revolutionary development. This Russian extremism was a product of several factors. First of all it was an inevitable psychological reaction to the absolutist "extremism" represented by the Tsarist regime. Then Western theories of social change seemed to acquire greatly intensified explosive force when they reached the young, ardent Russian intelligentsia, which really only came into existence in the nineteenth century. Finally Russians of all classes have always been singularly deficient in such typically middleclass virtues as thrift, prudence and moderation. The maxims of Benjamin Franklin's Poor Richard would have made equally little impression on a young aristocrat gambling away the family property at the card-tables, on the peasant spending a large part of his scanty income on vodka or on the fiery young student, willing to risk lifelong imprisonment or exile for the sake of drawing up a theoretical revolutionary blueprint, quite incapable of practical realization.

While the solid political structure of Tsarism was not shaken by the surreptitious student proclamations of the sixties, this decade witnessed important social and intellectual changes, at least among the educated classes. The patriarchal family was breaking up as more and more women insisted on the right to study in the universities and to lead independent lives. Not a few of these women students became propagandists of revolutionary ideas; the relatively high percentage of women participants is a feature of the Russian revolutionary movement.[15]

It was in the sixties that the so-called nihilist emerged as a common intellectual and social type among the Russian youth. Nihilism has been defined as "an outburst of materialism and democratism with a strong pessimistic shade." [16] Its spiritual progenitors were Darwin, Buckle, Comte, Herbert Spencer, Feuer-

bach. Its literary embodiment is the figure of Bazarov in Turgeniev's "Fathers and Sons." The nihilists worshipped science,
despised æstheticism and anything that savored of prettiness and
affectation. They were deliberately rough in dress and manners.
Prince Kropotkin gives the following sympathetic description of
nihilism: [17]

"The nihilist declared war upon what may be described as 'the conventional lies of civilized mankind.' He refused to bend before any
authority except that of reason, and in the analysis of every social institution or habit he revolted against any sort of more or less masked
sophism. He broke, of course, with the superstitions of his fathers, and
in his philosophical conceptions he was a positivist, an agnostic, a Spence-
rian evolutionist, or a scientific materialist. . . . Art was involved in the
same sweeping negation, and the criticisms of art which Tolstoy, one of the
greatest artists of the century, has now so powerfully formulated, the
nihilist expressed in the sweeping assertion, 'A pair of boots is more important than all your Madonnas and all your refined talk about Shake-
speare.'
"Marriage without love and familiarity without friendship were equally
repudiated. The nihilist girl, compelled by her parents to be a doll in a
Doll's House, and to marry for property's sake, preferred to abandon her
house and her silk dresses. She put on a black woolen dress of the plainest
description, cut off her hair, and went to a highschool, in order to win her
personal independence there.
"The nihilist carried his love of sincerity even into the minutest
details of everyday life. He discarded the conventional forms of society
talk, and expressed his opinions in a blunt and terse way, even with a
certain affectation of outward roughness."

Nihilism was partly a form of protest against the extreme repression of Russian life. It was also an indication that the educated class was no longer recruited solely, or even principally, from
the nobility. Representatives of the newly developing middle class
and also of the largely illiterate masses were making their way into
highschools and universities and taking part in political activity.
This is very noticeable in the revolutionary movement of the
seventies, when one finds among the revolutionists, side by side
with Prince Kropotkin and Sofia Perovskaya, who was a colonel's
daughter, the serf's son, Zhelyabov, the outstanding organizer
of the "People's Will" group, and the weaver, Peter Alekseev, whose
speech at one of the political trials produced a profound impression,
and Stepan Khalturin, whose skill as a carpenter gave him an
opportunity to place a bomb in the diningroom of the Tsar's
palace.

Revolutionary activity in Russia began to assume broader forms of expression in 1872, when the movement to "go to the people" began. Hundreds of young men and women from aristocratic and wealthy homes put on homespun clothes and went into the peasant villages, sometimes settling there as teachers or doctors. The purpose of the pilgrimage was twofold: to spread knowledge and education and to carry on propaganda for socialist ideas. The impetus to this movement came partly from students who had returned from Zürich, where they had imbibed socialist ideals from such emigrants as Bakunin, Lavrov and Tkachev, the apostle of a kind of Russian Jacobinism. In St. Petersburg a socialist group developed around Nicholas Tschaikovsky. The impulse to "go to the people," even with the certainty of hardship and the likelihood of arrest and imprisonment, also reflected the growing sense of social obligation among the more idealistic of the educated Russians. This mood finds expression in Kropotkin's question: "What right had I to these highest joys [scientific research in the problem of the ice-cap] when all around me was nothing but misery and struggle for a mouldy bit of bread, when whatsoever I should spend to enable me to live in that world of higher emotions must needs be taken from the very mouths of those who grew the wheat and had not bread enough for their children?" [18]

The practical results achieved by this mass pilgrimage to the villages were negligible. The peasants, as a general rule, listened with suspicious mistrust to the strange talk about socialism, equality and liberty from people of another class. In some cases the peasants themselves handed the ardent young agitators over to the police; and the latter often betrayed themselves by their inexperience and their transparent disguises. Hundreds of arrests were made; the magnitude of the repression could be measured by the "trial of the fifty" in Moscow in 1877 and the "trial of the hundred and ninety-three" in St. Petersburg in 1877–1878.

In 1875 and 1876 the revolutionaries who escaped arrest gathered in St. Petersburg and discussed plans of future action. The movement acquired a more organized, more conspirative character, and from 1878 it was known under the name "Land and Liberty," from the title of its underground newspaper. "Land and Liberty" may be considered the first Russian revolutionary party. The first workers' demonstration in Russia occurred in 1876, when Plekhanov, later a famous Marxian theorist, addressed a mixed crowd of workers and students at the Kazan Cathedral, in St.

Petersburg. The meeting was quickly dispersed by the police. In the same year another member of the "Land and Liberty" group, Stefanovitch, organized a secret society among the peasants of the Chigirin district near Kiev by showing the peasants a forged decree of the Tsar, instructing them to drive away the officials and landlords and seize the land.

With the passing of time the struggle between the autocratic government and the group of picked revolutionaries assumed fiercer and fiercer forms. On January 24, 1878, a young woman named Vera Zasulitch fired at and wounded the chief of the St. Petersburg police, Trepov, who had ordered the flogging of a political prisoner, Bogolyubov; and so great was the popular sympathy that the jury acquitted her and a crowd protected her from the gendarmes who wished to re-arrest her as she was leaving the courtroom. Later in the year the well-known revolutionary Stepniak-Kravchinsky cut down with a sword the head of the state espionage service, General Mezentsev. The Government on its side began to hang all revolutionaries who were implicated in acts of actual violence.

The growing terrorist mood led to a split in the ranks of the "Land and Liberty" party in the summer of 1879. The terrorist wing of the party organized itself under the name "People's Liberty" and set as its main goal the killing of the Tsar, the symbol of the autocratic state. The members of the "Land and Liberty" group, who discounted the importance of individual terrorism and laid more stress upon agitation and propaganda among the peasants, created a new party under the name of "Black-Earth Redivision" [19] The difference was one of tactics rather than of fundamental principle, and the relations between the two factions remained quite fraternal.

The programme of the "People's Liberty" group may be summarized as follows: [20] overthrow of the autocracy, establishment of a socialist order, based on the existing peasant communal land ownership, popular government, the simultaneous realization of a democratic and a socialist revolution, under the slogan, "The land to the people, the factories to the workers."

The members of the "People's Liberty" group were not socialists in the Marxian sense. They regarded as the basic social problem not the struggle of the working class against the capitalist class, but the struggle of the entire toiling population against the autocracy. Once this "colossus with clay feet" was overthrown they

believed that a socialist order could easily be established as a result of what they regarded as the instinctive preference of the peasant masses for communal land ownership. The slight development of industry and the absence in Russia of such clearcut economic class lines as existed in West European countries, with their greater wealth and more extensive trade and industry, favored this ideology.

After several daring but unsuccessful efforts to assassinate the Tsar by blowing up his train and by placing a bomb in the diningroom of the Winter Palace the terrorist goal was achieved on March 1, 1881. As the Tsar was driving along the Catherine Canal in St. Petersburg one of the revolutionists, Rysakov, hurled a bomb under his carriage. The Tsar was unhurt, but as he paused to inquire after members of his escort who had been wounded and to question Rysakov another revolutionary, Grinevitzky, threw a second bomb, mortally wounding the Tsar and perishing himself as a result of the explosion.

The assassination had been carefully planned by the Executive committee of the "People's Liberty"; a few picked revolutionaries had been selected from the forty-seven volunteers who offered to take part in an attempt on the Tsar's life. A mine had been laid on one of the main streets, the Sadovaya, in case the Tsar should drive along it. At first it seems surprising that an autocratic sovereign with an army and secret police at his disposal could not suppress and finally fell before a secret society with some five hundred members.[21]

There are several factors that may be mentioned in explanation. The leaders of the "Land and Liberty" were no ordinary men and women. In the majority they were young people of exceptional gifts and great moral and physical courage. Most of the men were of outstanding physical strength and dexterity.[22] The police organization of the time, while ruthless, was incompetent. Moreover, the revolutionaries enjoyed a good deal of sympathy and passive support from the more liberal members of the educated classes, who did not approve of terrorism, but detested the autocracy.

There is something at once tragic and heroic about these individual pioneer revolutionaries, who were doomed to fall in the unequal struggle with the autocracy, because the time was not ripe for any mass movement of revolt. The day of victory of the "Land and Liberty," the day of the assassination of the Tsar, also

marks the beginning of the dissolution of the organization. Shortly after the assassination the government succeeded, with the aid of spies and *agents provocateurs,* in capturing almost all the leaders of the "Land and Liberty." Five of those mainly implicated in the assassination, Zhelyabov, Mikhailov, Rysakov, Kibalchikh and Sofia Perovskaya, were executed and many others were exiled or shut up in the grim fortress of Schlüsselburg, from which they were only released after the Revolution of 1905.

Even before the physical break-up of the organization a sense of the futility of terrorism was beginning to oppress its members. Vera Figner, a member of the group, tells in her reminiscences how a suggestion to utilize the unexploded mine for an attempt on the life of the new Tsar, Alexander III, was voiced at a conspirative meeting of the revolutionaries and was dropped for utter lack of support. The revolutionaries had believed that they were striking at Tsarism by killing a Tsar. But the state machine functioned as before, uninjured by the bombs and bullets of the terrorists. The new Tsar, Alexander III, with his Procurator of the Holy Synod, Constantine Pobiedonostsev, a staunch believer in Nicholas I's triple formula, "Orthodoxy, autocracy, nationalism," enforced a regime of iron repression and considerably restricted some of the half-hearted concessions in the field of local self-government which had been made by Alexander II.

The eighties were a period of apathy and depression for the Russian revolutionary intelligentsia. This was attributable not only to the stern repressive measures of the government, but to the fact that the revolutionary objectives had become confused and unclear. The infiltration of Marxian ideas and the progress of capitalism were breaking up the old theories of peasant socialism. Terrorism had lost its romantic glamor. Tolstoy's theories of pacifism and nonresistance to evil corresponded with the mood of many intellectuals.

One of the few revolutionary flashes during the reign of Alexander III was an effort to assassinate him on March 1, 1887, six years after the death of his father, by a group of St. Petersburg students who considered themselves the continuators of the "Land and Liberty" tradition. The watchful police seized the conspirators before they could carry their plot into execution; and five of them were hanged. One of the five was a brilliant young man named Alexander Ulianov, son of a district school inspector in the Volga town of Simbirsk. At his trial Ulianov made no effort to

deny his guilt, but used the courtroom as a tribune from which to defend the right of the freedom-loving intellectual to employ terror in the struggle against a regime that crushed not only socialist but even general cultural propaganda.

"Terror," Ulianov declared before the Tsarist judges, "is the sole form of defense that is left to a minority, strong only in spiritual force and in the consciousness of its rightness against the consciousness of the physical force of the majority . . . Among the Russian people there will always be found scores who are so devoted to their ideas that it is no sacrifice for them to die for their cause." [23]

The news of Alexander's fate deeply affected his seventeen-year-old brother Vladimir, who in his highschool days was already a revolutionary by conviction. Thirty years later this younger brother, known to history under his pseudonym Lenin, was to be the main architect of the social revolution that replaced the autocracy of the Romanovs with the dictatorship of the Soviets.

The first Marxian socialist organization may be considered the group "Liberation of Labor," which was formed outside of Russia in 1883 by former members of the "Land and Liberty" and "People's Liberty." Its leaders were Plekhanov, Axelrod, Deutsch and Vera Zasulitch, among whom Plekhanov was the outstanding theoretician. Plekhanov and his associates went over to the Marxian viewpoint in their interpretation of Russian developments and expressed a number of ideas which subsequently figured in the ideology of the Russian Social Democratic movement. Among these ideas were the leadership of the working class in the struggle against Tsarism, the acquisition of power by the working class as the goal of the revolutionary movement, and the union of the working class with the peasantry, especially with the poorer peasants.[24] The members of the "Liberation of Labor" translated some of the works of Marx into Russian and helped to smuggle this forbidden literature across the frontier. Their ideas influenced the Social Democratic discussion circles which existed in Russia in the eighties under the leadership of the Bulgarian Blagoev and others, although the views of these circles often represented a mixture of Marxism with peasant socialism.

The last decade of the nineteenth century witnessed a distinct relivening of the revolutionary movement. The circles, which recruited their members largely from the educated classes and especially from the university students, expanded and endeavored to carry on more intensive propaganda activity among the workers.

The very rapid growth of industry during this decade strengthened the theoretical position of the Marxian Social Democrats, who contended that Russia must pass through the normal stages of capitalist development, although the *narodnik,* or peasant socialist, viewpoint still had its champions, including the famous literary critic N. K. Mikhailovsky. In 1894 the young Lenin, still an obscure figure in the surreptitious Marxist discussion circles, published illegally his first major political work under the title "Who Are the 'Friends of the People' and How Do They Fight with the Social Democrats?" It was couched in the sharply polemical tone that always marks Lenin's theoretical discussions and was directed against the *narodniki.*

The group of St. Petersburg revolutionaries in which Lenin was active until his arrest at the end of 1895, in 1896 assumed the name "Union of Struggle for the Liberation of the Working Class"; and similar "Unions" sprang up in Moscow, Kiev, Ekaterinoslav, Ivanovo-Vosnessensk and other cities. The situation was becoming ripe for the establishment of actual political parties, so far as these could function under the conditions of Tsarist repression.

The revolutionary movement was especially pronounced in the crowded, poverty-stricken Jewish Pale of Settlement in western and southwestern Russia; and in 1897 the "General Jewish Workers' Union in Lithuania, Poland and Russia," subsequently known as the Bund, was founded at a congress in Vilna. Both in the leadership and in the organized rank-and-file of the revolutionary movement in Russia there was a notably high percentage of Jews: a circumstance which is easily understandable in view of the systematic anti-Semitism of Tsarist policy, which denied Jews, as a general rule, the right to live in a large part of the Empire, excluded them from the state service, limited their right of entrance to high schools and universities and occasionally tolerated, or even directly instigated, fierce mob attacks on the Jews which were known as pogroms. Not only the Jews, but other more literate non-Russian nationalities, notably Letts, Poles, Finns, Georgians and Armenians, contributed more than their proportionate share of recruits to various forms of the revolutionary movement; and here again the methods of compulsory Russification employed by the Government provoked this nationalist reaction.[25]

The first Congress of the Russian Social Democratic Labor Party, which later split into its Bolshevik and Menshevik wings,

was held in Minsk, with the participation of the Bund, on March 14, 1898. The delegates assembled, adopted a Party name, discussed plans for publishing an all-Russian newspaper, issued a manifesto—and were promptly arrested as they dispersed to their homes. As often happened the police were well informed about this supposedly secret revolutionary congress; and it was followed by a wave of arrests which somewhat checked the growth and activity of the Social Democratic movement. The manifesto, ironically enough written by Peter Struve, who subsequently performed a complete turn to the right in his political views, passing from Marxism to liberalism and ultimately to monarchism, contained one striking passage which accurately reflects the subsequent Bolshevik viewpoint: [26]

"The farther one goes to the East of Europe the weaker, baser and more cowardly becomes the bourgeoisie and the larger cultural and political tasks fall to the lot of the proletariat. On its strong shoulders the Russian working class must bear and will bear the cause of conquering political liberty. This is necessary, but only as the first step toward the achievement of the great historic mission of the proletariat: the creation of a social order in which there will be no place for the exploitation of man by man. The Russian proletariat will cast off from itself the yoke of the autocracy in order with all the greater energy to continue the struggle with capitalism and with the bourgeoisie until the final victory of socialism."

The young Social Democratic movement was soon faced with a heresy in the shape of the so-called "economism," a viewpoint which found expression in the "Credo" of Mme. Kuskova and coincided to some extent with the revisionist conception of Marxism advocated in Germany by Eduard Bernstein. The "Credo," which was published in 1898, put forward the theory that the workers should concentrate on trade-union activity and effort to improve their material conditions, leaving to middleclass liberals the political opposition to the Government. This suggestion evoked hot criticism from the Social Democratic leaders; and the controversy over "economism" was subsequently forgotten in the more prolonged disputes between Bolsheviki and Mensheviki.

The newspaper *Iskra* (The Spark), the first number of which appeared in Stuttgart, Germany, in December, 1900, became a rallying point for the Russian Social Democrats in the first years of the twentieth century. Its board of editors included three veterans of the seventies, Plekhanov, Axelrod and Vera Zasulitch, and three men of the younger revolutionary generation,

Lenin, Martov and Potresov; and for a time Leon Trotzky was a member of the board. It led a peripatetic existence, moving from Stuttgart to Munich, then to London, finally to Geneva. Edited abroad, it was safe from the raids of the Tsarist police; and it was smuggled into Russia in considerable quantities. Although not one of Lenin's five associates ultimately shared his Bolshevik viewpoint his forceful personality impressed itself on the *Iskra;* and it carried on lusty polemics against the "economists," the Socialist Revolutionaries and the emerging Liberal opposition to the autocracy, which had its own foreign organ, the *Liberation,* which was published in Stuttgart.

The character of the future Communist Party is foreshadowed to no small degree in a remarkable pamphlet which Lenin published in 1902 under the title, "What Is to Be Done." Here he expressed views on Party organization which were radically different from those which prevailed in the Social Democratic parties of Western Europe. He laid stress on the development of a class of professional revolutionaries who should hold the strings of Party leadership in their hands. "An organization of revolutionaries," wrote Lenin, "must above all and mainly include people whose profession consists of revolutionary activity. This organization must be not very broad and as conspirative as possible. . . . Give us an organization of revolutionaries—and we shall turn Russia upside down." [27]

Along with this stress on the small picked band of professional revolutionaries as the backbone of the Party Lenin logically associated the idea of the maximum degree of centralization and discipline within the Party. He had no patience or tolerance for the waverer, the temperamental rebel against Party discipline, the champion of freedom of thought and criticism. "We go," he wrote, "along a precipitous and difficult path, firmly grasping each other by the hand. We are surrounded on all sides by enemies and we must almost always go under their fire. We united by a freely accepted decision in order to fight with enemies, and not to retreat into a neighboring swamp, the inhabitants of which blamed us because we formed a special group and chose the way of struggle and not the way of compromise." [28]

The differences of opinion which finally resulted in a definite split in the Social Democratic ranks were foreshadowed at the second Party Congress, which was held in July and August, 1903. The first sessions were in Brussels; when the Belgian police began

to create difficulties for the delegates it was transferred to London. Of the forty-three delegates only three or four were workers. The Social Democratic Party was still a party for but not of the proletariat.

The nervous strain that was a natural result both of underground work in Russia and of the isolated poverty-stricken life of the Russian revolutionary emigrant was very evident in the behavior of the delegates. Krupskaya tells how Lenin was so agitated that he could scarcely eat or sleep.[29] The most trivial point was apt to arouse embittered and long controversial speeches. While representatives of the organizations that grouped themselves around the *Iskra* were in the decisive majority among the delegates (the representatives of the Bund withdrew when the claim of their organization to be the exclusive representative of the Jewish working class was rejected) differences arose between the adherents of Lenin and an opposition that was led by Julius Martov, later an outstanding leader of the Menshevik Party.

A characteristic difference was about the conditions of eligibility for Party membership. Lenin desired the formula that the member must personally participate in one of the Party organizations, while Martov preferred the looser qualification: "giving the Party regular personal coöperation under the guidance of one of its organizations." The significance of this difference in phrasing was that Martov was willing to smooth the road for Socialist sympathizers who were unwilling to take the risks involved in formal membership in the Party, whereas Lenin, committed to the idea that the Party must be an organization of picked revolutionists, wished to impose a harder test.

Martov was victorious on this particular point; but as Lenin carried the majority of the Congress with him on practically every other important question his adherents came to be known as Bolsheviki (from the Russian word for majority), while their opponents were called Mensheviki (from the word for minority). The actual numerical strength of the two factions varied from time to time (at the Stockholm Congress in April, 1906, the Mensheviki had the majority, while at the London Congress in the following year the factions were about equal in number and the balance was held by national organizations of Lettish, Polish and Jewish Social Democrats) and would be difficult to establish with certainty at any time because of the impossibility, under Russian conditions, of conducting free and open voting. Generally speaking, the Bol-

sheviki were stronger in the industrial regions of northern and central Russia and of the Urals, and they elected the six deputies chosen by workingclass constituencies for the Fourth Duma. The Mensheviki were stronger in South Russia, and also in Georgia, where their Party combined moderate socialism with strong nationalism.

With the aid of his majority at the Congress Lenin desired to reorganize the editorial board of the *Iskra*, retaining as editors Plekhanov, Martov and himself and excluding Axelrod, Potresov and Vera Zasulitch. In the past Martov had generally been on Lenin's side in questions of tactics and Plekhanov in questions of theory, so that Lenin could hope after this reorganization to dominate the policy of the *Iskra*.[30] However, the victory was a Pyrrhic one, so far as the *Iskra* was concerned because Plekhanov soon broke with Lenin, who thereupon withdrew from the *Iskra*, which then passed over to the Mensheviki.

Differences which at the Second Congress were at least to some extent personal and temperamental hardened into opposed political and economic theories with the passing of time. Both Bolsheviki and Mensheviki accepted Marx as their basic authority. But they differed about the proper application of Marxian theory to Russian conditions. The Mensheviki contended that Russia, because of its industrial backwardness, because of the small percentage of the working class in the population, was ripe only for a "bourgeois" or liberal democratic revolution, which would sweep away autocracy and by establishing freedom of speech, assembly, trade-union organization, etc., create conditions which would make possible the ultimate realization of a socialist organization of society, when Russia had made the necessary cultural and industrial progress. The Mensheviki, and notably Plekhanov, regarded the peasants distrustfully as a potentially reactionary force and favored a certain measure of collaboration with the non-socialist liberal opposition parties.

Lenin also held the view that a democratic revolution must precede a socialist revolution in Russia. But his conception of how a "democratic revolution" should be achieved differed widely from that of the Mensheviki. He saw as the ally of the proletariat, the class which both parties theoretically exalted, not the middle-class liberals, but the rebellious peasantry. His formula was: "Democratic dictatorship of the proletariat and the peasantry." [31] "With all our strength," he wrote on September 1, 1905, when the revo-

lutionary movement of that year was in full course, "we shall help the peasantry to make the democratic revolution, so that it will be easier for us, the Party of the proletariat, to pass over as quickly as possible to the new and higher task of the socialist revolution."

Still a third tendency in Russian Marxism was represented by Leon Trotzky, who, with a small group of followers, stood aloof from both Bolshevism and Menshevism. In contradistinction to the Mensheviki Trotzky favored the direct seizure of power by the working class, without coöperation with the middleclass liberals. But he was not satisfied with Lenin's theory of "the democratic dictatorship of the proletariat and the peasantry." He believed himself that the Russian Revolution could succeed only if it served as a spark for the ignition of revolutions in economically more advanced countries. Otherwise the revolutionary government would fail as a result of the backwardness of the country and the conservatism of the peasants.[32]

A non-Marxian force in the revolutionary movement was represented by the Socialist Revolutionaries, who emerged as a Party almost simultaneously with the Social Democrats.[33] The theory and practise of the Socialist Revolutionaries contain many traits of resemblance with the *narodnik* movement of the seventies. While the Socialist Revolutionaries were not blind to the changes in Russian life which had been brought about by the rapid development of capitalism in Russia during the last quarter, and especially during the last decade of the nineteenth century, they regarded the peasantry, rather than the industrial working class, as the main moving force for the revolutionary movement and placed the nationalization of the land and the confiscation of the landlords' estates for the benefit of the peasantry in the forefront of their demands. They also differed with the Marxian parties in advocating and practising individual terrorism. Within their Party and subject to its Central Committee, but quite independent in its activities and strictly secret in make-up, was the so-called Fighting Organization, the avowed purpose of which was to organize political assassination. It came into existence under the direction of Gregory Gershuni in 1902; its leader after the arrest of Gershuni was the extraordinary provocator, Evno Azev.

Among the main victims of the systematic and successful terror organized by the Fighting Organization were the Grand Duke Sergei, uncle of the Tsar, von Plehve, Minister of the Interior, Sipiagin, Minister of Education, and Bogdanovitch, Governor of

Ufa Province. After each assassination the Fighting Organization published a statement explaining and glorifying the deed. Typical is the phrasing of the statement published after the killing of Sipiagin:

"We consider it not only our right, but our sacred duty, notwithstanding all the repulsion which such means of struggle inspire in us, to answer violence with violence and to pay for the spilled blood of the people with the blood of its oppressors. The crack of the bullet is the only possible means of talking with our ministers, until they learn to understand human speech and listen to the voice of the country.

"We do not need to explain why Sipiagin was executed. His crimes are too notorious, his life was too generally cursed and his death too generally greeted." [34]

Although the largest of the revolutionary parties, the Socialist Revolutionaries, probably because of the looseness and vagueness of their programme, ultimately proved to possess the least cohesion. There was no Lenin to place an iron yoke of discipline on this inchoate organization, which included in its ranks all types of members, from mild democrats to champions of thoroughgoing agrarian upheaval.

Two parties of relatively slight significance in the revolutionary movement were the Trudoviki, or Laborites, and the People's Socialists. The Trudoviki were not dissimilar to the Socialist Revolutionaries in viewpoint and outlook, but they kept within the bounds of Tsarist legality and were therefore able to take an open part in elections. The People's Socialists stood somewhere between leftwing Cadets and rightwing Mensheviki and had a numerically small following, chiefly in the academic and professional classes.

The late appearance of organized middleclass liberalism on the Russian scene was a major factor in determining the ultimate course of the Revolution. In Western Europe, as a general rule, the middle classes acquired constitutional rights and some administrative experience before the socialist workingclass movement became organized. But the Constitutional Democratic, or Cadet, Party, the organization of middleclass liberalism in Russia, was established only in 1905, when Tsarism was shaken by the first big revolutionary shock, seven years after the first Congress of the Social Democratic Party.

This belated political expression of liberalism is attributable partly to Russia's retarded economic development, partly to the Tsarist regime of repression. There were always middle-of-the-road

liberals in Russia in the nineteenth century who disliked autocracy without being able to subscribe to the programmes of the revolutionaries. But their possibilities of action and expression were narrow and limited. When Nicholas II succeeded Alexander III on the throne in 1894 he roughly rebuked as "senseless dreams" the suggestions of a delegation of the Tver *zemstvo* that some consultative functions in matters of general administration might be accorded to the *zemstvos*.

It was from the progressive *zemstvo* circles that the impulse came for the establishment of the journal *Liberation,* under the editorship of Peter Struve. The first number of this journal, which was published in 1901 in Stuttgart, expressed the ambition of "uniting all those groups of Russian society which cannot find an outlet for their feeling of indignation either in class or in revolutionary struggle." [35] In 1903 a "Union of Liberation" was formed among the readers of this journal; and the Cadet Party was the result of negotiations between this Union and an organization of *"Zemstvo-*Constitutionalists" and formally came into existence in the autumn of 1905.[36]

The Cadet Party was the sole non-socialist political organization which possessed vitality and survived the fall of Tsarism in 1917. Its programme called for the establishment of a constitutional monarchy, for the introduction of civil liberties, and the abolition of race discrimination, for reformist labor legislation and for the alienation of privately owned land for the benefit of the peasants, provided that fair compensation was paid to the owners. The character of the Cadet Party was affected by changing circumstances. It was much more radical in 1905, when there was a general popular upsurge against Tsarism, than it was in 1917, when all the parties farther to the right practically disappeared and the Cadets found themselves obliged to defend private property and the capitalist system against the onrush of social revolution.

Eighty years elapsed between the romantic, ill-executed conspiracy of the Decembrists and the 1905 Revolution. During this whole period there was an uneven struggle, rising and falling in intensity, between individuals and small groups with revolutionary ideas and an autocratic regime with origins rooted far back in the Middle Ages. Every conceivable weapon was used, from the bomb and bullet of the terrorist to clandestine circulation of propaganda. A definite type of "professional revolutionist," accustomed to living under a false passport, to moving backward and forward be-

tween the obscure émigré cafés of Geneva and Paris and the conspirative centres in Russia, to dodging the police in every way while he pursued his appointed task of distributing forbidden pamphlets or fabricating bombs, had emerged and reappeared in generation after generation. The familiar cycle of secret agitation, arrest, exile, return to seditious activity in another place under another name was known to many a revolutionist. Hundreds of "circles" had followed the usual development of growth from small beginnings, extension of activity, betrayal by a spy or traitor, break-up with wholesale arrests by the police.

Beneath the routine exterior of Russian life strange things were occurring. No one who saw a sign "Wholesale Caucasian Fruitshop" displayed on one of the Moscow boulevards in 1906 and 1907 suspected that in the basement of the "shop" was the printing-press of the Bolshevik Central Committee, busily employed in turning out its incitements to overthrow of the existing order. The proprietor and the shop assistants were all trusted revolutionists.

In the same way a "wealthy Englishman" who engaged a sumptuous apartment in Petrograd in 1904 and settled there with his wife, a valet and a cook aroused no suspicion on the part of the police. The "Englishman" was the Socialist Revolutionary terrorist, Boris Savinkov; the members of his household belonged to his group; and the climax of their enterprise was the assassination of the Minister of the Interior, von Plehve.

An extraordinary game of hide-and-seek, a game in which the stakes might well be life and death, was continually being played between the revolutionists and the police. Any Russian returning to his country from abroad might have bundles of the *Iskra* sewed up in a breastplate or concealed in a trunk with a double bottom. The police not infrequently placed its own agents in the revolutionary ranks. Evno Azev, a man of repulsive personality, greedy and coldblooded, but endowed with iron nerve and supple cunning, for years played the extraordinary double rôle of head of the Fighting Organization of the Socialist Revolutionary Party and agent of the Tsarist secret service, impartially betraying his comrades and employers alike. Roman Malinovsky, head of the small group of Bolshevik deputies in the Duma, a man who enjoyed the complete confidence of Lenin, was exposed as a provocator and ultimately shot after the Revolution.

One of the most extraordinary and picturesque personalities of the Revolution emerged in the wild Caucasus, with its traditions

of banditism, blood-feuds and tribal loyalties. This was the Armenian Ter-Petrosian, better known under the nickname of Kamo. His life was a long novel of amazing adventures, daring raids, hairbreadth escapes.[37] On June 23, 1907, the much frequented Pushkin Street in Tiflis was rocked with a series of bomb explosions. Dead and wounded lay about in pools of blood. Kamo and a group of his associates had made off with 250,000 rubles which were being transported under guard to the Tiflis State Bank. The money was sewed up for a time in the couch of the manager of the Tiflis Observatory and ultimately found its way abroad to replenish the Bolshevik Party funds. This was only the most striking of a series of "expropriations" which were carried through in the Caucasus by Kamo, who was a disciple and lieutenant and fellow-townsman of the Caucasian Bolshevik Djugashvili, who under the name of Stalin was to succeed Lenin as the leader of the Communist Party and the actual head of the Soviet state. Kamo was repeatedly arrested and effected some of the most daring escapes in the history of the revolutionary movement. He was condemned to death, but a lucky accident in the shape of the friendliness of the prosecuting attorney, who delayed the promulgation of the sentence until an impending amnesty became effective, saved his life. After surviving a thousand dangers of the pre-revolutionary and civil war periods he perished in an accident in Tiflis in the summer of 1922, when an automobile collided with the bicycle on which he was riding. Kamo himself was scrupulous in devoting the proceeds of his raids to the Party funds; for himself and his associates he took only a bare expense allowance. But not all expropriators were above suspicion in this respect; and the "expropriations," which were much more commonly practised by real or self-styled Socialist Revolutionaries and Anarchists than by Social Democrats, gave an opportunity for a criminal fringe to form around the revolutionary movement and also gave the authorities an opportunity, which they were not slow to exploit, of court-martialling and executing genuine revolutionists as bandits.

The conditions under which a revolutionist lived, whether he was doing underground work in Russia or participating in the emigrant circles abroad, were admirably calculated to produce fanatics, saints, heroes, inquisitors and neurotics. In this grim crucible were being forged future Red administrators and managers of socialized industry, future commanders of the Red Army and officials of the Cheka.

NOTES

[1] Masaryk, "The Spirit of Russia," Vol. I, pp. 95ff.

[2] For summaries of the constitutions of Muraviev and Pestel see Kornilov, "Modern Russian History," Vol. I, pp. 205–208, and M. Balabanov, "Sketch of the History of the Revolutionary Movement in Russia," pp. 15–17.

[3] Translation by Max Eastman.

[4] See Masaryk, *op. cit.*, Vol. I, pp. 237ff. and 336ff., for an outline of the Slavophile and Western conceptions.

[5] Cited in Kornilov, *op. cit.*, Vol. II, p. 208.

[6] See Masaryk, *op. cit.*, Vol. I, pp. 404ff.

[7] Vyacheslav Polonsky, "The Life of Mikhail Bakunin," p. 95.

[8] *Ibid.*, p. 109.

[9] U. Steklov, "Life and Activity of N. Chernishevsky," p. 59.

[10] Masaryk, *op. cit.*, Vol. II, p. 34.

[11] See introduction to "Diary of N. G. Chernishevsky," p. viii.

[12] *Op. cit.*, pp. 91–92.

[13] I. Poltavsky, "The Heroic in the Russian Revolution," Vol. I, p. 155.

[14] Balabanov, *op. cit.*, p. 55.

[15] Alfons Tun, in his "History of Revolutionary Movements in Russia" (Soviet edition), p. 119, shows that about a fifth of the revolutionary agitators who were arrested between 1870 and 1875 in Russia were women.

[16] Tun, *op. cit.*, p. 87.

[17] Peter Kropotkin, "Memoirs of a Revolutionist," pp. 297–299.

[18] *Ibid.*, p. 240.

[19] It derived this name from its demand that the peasants should receive the good "black-earth" land which had remained with the landlords at the time of the emancipation settlement.

[20] See "The 'People's Liberty' in Documents and Reminiscences," p. 25.

[21] Tun, *op. cit.*, p. 191.

[22] "The 'People's Liberty' in Documents and Reminiscences," p. 22.

[23] See "Alexander Ilyitch Ulianov and the Case of March 1, 1887," pp. 342, 343.

[24] Popov, "Sketch of the History of the All-Union Communist Party," p. 2.

[25] The Social Democratic newspaper *Proletarian* in September, 1906, gave the following figures of the number of dues-paying Social Democrats: Russians, 31,000; Poles, 26,000; Letts, 11,000; Bund, 30,000. See Masaryk, *op. cit.*, Vol. I, pp. 173ff.

[26] See full text of the manifesto in P. Lepishinsky, "The First Congress of the All-Union Communist Party," pp. 26–28.

[27] "What Is to Be Done," p. 84.

[28] *Ibid.*, p. 7.

[29] "Reminiscences of Lenin," p. 73.

[30] See Leon Trotzky, "Lenin," p. 60.

[31] Popov, *op. cit.*, p. 111.

[32] A clear exposition of Trotzky's differences with the Bolsheviki and the Mensheviki is to be found in his "Die Russische Revolution 1905," pp. 222–232.

[33] The first organizing congresses of the Social Revolutionist Party were held in Voronezh and Poltava in 1897. See Balabanov, *op. cit.*, p. 176.

[34] See "The Party of Socialist Revolutionaries and Its Predecessors," p. 118.

[35] Balabanov, *op. cit.*, p. 182.

[36] V. Stalni, "Cadets" (in series, "Parties Which Were in Russia"), p. 12.

[37] For a detailed account of Kamo's career see the article by his widow, S. T. Medvedeva Ter-Petrosian, "Comrade Kamo," in the magazine *Proletarian Revolution*, No. 8–9, for 1924.

CHAPTER III

THE 1905 REVOLUTION AND THE WORLD WAR

EIGHTY years elapsed between the abortive conspiracy of the Decembrists and the 1905 Revolution. During this period revolutionary agitation was never entirely extinguished, although it varied considerably in intensity. But until 1905 the struggle against the autocracy was predominantly an affair of individuals and small groups. It was only in that year that the Russian masses, the object of so much revolutionary plotting and theorizing, were stirred into action on a large scale under the triple impact of unsuccessful foreign war, domestic hard times and the ceaseless urging of the revolutionary parties.

Several events preceded and foreshadowed the storm of 1905. The rapid expansion of Russian industries during the nineties was succeeded by a period of depression, and industrial conflicts became sharper and more numerous. The year 1903 witnessed a noteworthy expansion of the workingclass movement in scope and in intensity. A strike in the Baku oil-fields in the summer of 1903 rapidly spread to Tiflis, Batum and other Caucasian towns. At the same time there were strikes in Odessa, Kiev and other South Russian cities. Two relatively new features of these strikes were the putting forward of political demands, such as the granting of a democratic constitution, and the holding of extensive street demonstrations, in which university students often joined. The underground propaganda of the revolutionary parties was beginning to reach the workers.

That the rebellious working class would find a more or less unconscious ally in the villages was indicated in the spring of 1902, when poverty-stricken peasants in some districts of Kharkov and Poltava Provinces raided the estates of the landowners, robbing and in some cases destroying fifty-four manor-houses in Poltava and twenty-eight in Kharkov.[1] Student disorders, assassination of government officials by Socialist Revolutionary terrorists, a growing demand for liberal reforms among the more progressive country

gentry and professional classes—all added to the worries of the Government and created an increasingly tense atmosphere. The Minister of the Interior, von Plehve, saw a desirable outlet from the situation in a "little victorious war" [2] ; and a brusque, uncompromising attitude on the part of Russian diplomats and administrators in connection with points of dispute in Manchuria contributed to the outbreak of the Russo-Japanese War in February, 1904.

The higher Russian civil and military officials entered upon this war, which was destined to prove neither little nor victorious, in a spirit of overweening selfconfidence, that was only matched by the country's woeful unpreparedness. The Tsar habitually referred to the Japanese as "monkeys" and felt that victory was assured when he distributed images of Saint Seraphim among the troops. The commander-in-chief, General Kuropatkin, and a former War Minister, General Vannovsky, disputed as to whether one Russian soldier was equivalent to one and a half or two Japanese.

Notwithstanding these arrogant expectations the Russian army and navy went from defeat to defeat. In the last days of August and the first days of September the Russian forces were defeated at Liao-Yang; Port Arthur fell on January 15, 1905; the Russian army was decisively beaten at Mukden in a prolonged battle that lasted from February 24 until March 9; and the final blow came when the Russian fleet, which had cruised halfway around the world, was wiped out by the Japanese in the Battle of Tsushima on May 27 and 28. The disastrous war was brought to a conclusion by the Peace of Portsmouth on September 5, which ceded to Japan Russia's possessions and interests in South Manchuria and the southern half of the island of Sakhalin. Every new defeat lowered the prestige of the Government in the eyes of the educated classes and intensified the unrest among the masses. Far from averting the revolutionary outburst the war with Japan accelerated it and greatly intensified its force.

The Tsar made his first concession to the liberal opposition when, under the influence of the Liao-Yang defeat, he appointed the mild Prince Sviatopolk-Mirsky Minister of the Interior on September 8, 1904; and the first All-Russian Zemstvo Congress, which was held in St. Petersburg in November of the same year, put forward eleven demands, calling for the legal establishment of civil liberties, the abolition of race and class discriminations and, most significant of all, the creation of a representative assembly with legislative functions. This last demand was adopted against

the votes of a substantial conservative minority which desired an assembly with purely consultative functions. The Zemstvo programme became the central point of discussion at a number of banquets and informal meetings.

The first outstanding signal of the revolutionary turn which developments were taking was "Bloody Sunday" on January 22, 1905. Carrying on the tradition of the Moscow police official Zubatov, who endeavored, unsuccessfully in the long run, to build up nonsocialist unions under the encouragement and protection of the police,[3] a priest named Georgi Gapon had built up an extensive association among the workers of St. Petersburg. Gapon was not a police provocator in the ordinary sense of the term; he cherished the hope that the Tsar would insure the loyalty of the workers by relieving their grievances. Gapon's movement was connected with liberal and radical intellectuals, who helped to phrase a petition to the Tsar in which old-fashioned expressions of fealty and obedience were strangely blended with modern demands for a constitution. The petition began as follows:

"Lord. We workers, our children, our wives and our old helpless parents have come, Lord, to seek truth and protection from you. We are impoverished and oppressed, unbearable work is imposed on us, we are despised and not recognized as human beings. We are treated as slaves, who must bear their fate and be silent. We have suffered terrible things, but we are pressed ever deeper into the abyss of poverty, ignorance and lack of rights. Despotism and arbitrariness throttle us and we choke. We have no more strength, O Lord. The limit of patience is here; for us that terrible moment has come when death is better than the continuance of the most unbearable torments."

The petition proceeded to denounce the government officials and "capitalist exploiters of the working class," put forward constitutional demands and contained the prophetic phrase: "If Thou wilt not answer our prayer we shall die here on the Square before Thy palace."

Gapon himself was doubtful about the wisdom of bringing large masses of workers onto the streets of the capital to present this petition but yielded to the pressure of his lieutenants, who in turn were being urged to act by the masses of the members of the association. So on January 22 a huge procession of St. Petersburg workers, some with their wives and children, bearing not red flags but ikons and portraits of the Tsar and singing not the Internationale but religious and patriotic songs, moved toward the Winter Palace.

The authorities had mobilized large forces of troops under the command of the Tsar's uncle, the Grand Duke Vladimir; and when the demonstrators refused to obey orders to disperse and go home volleys of rifle fire were poured into them while Cossacks charged with their whistling nagaikas, or whips. The casualties of Bloody Sunday are estimated at from two hundred to fifteen hundred. Whatever the number may have been the idyllic conception of the Tsar as the father of his people had received a shattering blow.

The immediate effect of Bloody Sunday was an intensification of unrest, which found its most frequent expression in strikes. Throughout the whole year 1905 there were continual stoppages of work; the total number of strikers reached the figure of 2,865,145, an enormous number if one considers that the total number of industrial workers in Russia at that time was less than two million. Many workers, of course, participated in several strikes. 64.4 percent of the strikers were involved in political strikes: another symptom of the spirit of the time.[4] The wave of strikes reached classes that were ordinarily out of reach of labor propaganda, such as housemaids and cabmen. There was an active movement to organize the brain workers of the country, and these groups were ultimately organized in a so-called Union of Unions.

The next spectacular event after Bloody Sunday was the mutiny on the cruiser *Potyemkin,* one of the most powerful ships of the Black Sea Fleet. This occurred on June 14, and commenced when the ship's officers proposed to shoot the ringleaders in a protest of the sailors against eating spoiled meat. The firing-squad refused to shoot; some of the officers were thrown into the sea and the insurgent warship sailed into the harbor of Odessa, where a large strike was in progress, flying the red flag. The loyalty of the whole Black Sea Fleet was in serious doubt and one other vessel joined the *Potyemkin* in its mutiny. However, irresolution and uncertainty about the next steps to be taken undermined the revolutionary morale of the sailors, and the *Potyemkin* finally sailed off to Rumania, where its crew surrendered to the authorities. The Russian navy was anything but reliable during 1905; and the month of November witnessed two other mutinies, in the naval bases of Kronstadt, near St. Petersburg, and Sevastopol, in the Crimea. The latter was under the leadership of a naïve idealist, Lieutenant Schmidt, who despatched the following message to the Tsar: "The glorious Black Sea Fleet, preserving devotion to the Tsar, demands

from you, Sire, the immediate convocation of a Constituent Assembly and will no longer obey your ministers." [5] Schmidt's assurance of devotion did not save him from execution when the mutiny was suppressed. Both in 1905 and in 1917 the Navy proved far more turbulent and more quickly responsive to revolutionary agitation than the Army. This is partly attributable to the very severe discipline, partly to the fact that a larger proportion of skilled workers, already affected by "dangerous thoughts," found their way into the Navy than into the Army.

Two noteworthy features of the 1905 Revolution were the very wide popular participation in the movement and the lack of clearly defined leadership. Especially up to the granting of the Constitution of October 30 the movement had the active support and sympathy of the majority of the educated middle classes and of a not inconsiderable number of landowners and industrialists. [6] Employers often encouraged their workers to take part in political demonstrations and paid them for days of absence. White-collar employees passed resolutions which were little less radical than those of the industrial workers.

While this broad popular character gave the movement scope and sweep and goes far to explain the hesitations and vacillations of the Government, which felt very little firm ground under its feet, the lack of generally accepted leadership and a clearcut programme was a main cause of the final defeat. The revolutionary movement embraced classes with very different ultimate objectives. The lawyer, the liberal businessman or landowner desired a constitutional regime on the model of Western Europe. The professional revolutionary dreamed of a far more sweeping social revolution. The worker thought of higher wages and shorter hours; the peasant, of the broad acres of his neighboring landlord; the soldier or sailor, of better food and milder discipline. No nationwide leader or party emerged to forge a practical and successful programme of action out of this crucible of varied discontents.

The announcement of the creation of a consultative assembly, the so-called Bulygin Duma, to be elected on a narrow franchise, in August failed to still the growing unrest. Nationalist and peasant disturbances, especially in the Baltic Provinces and the Caucasus, added to the general feeling of instability. When Count Witte, Russia's outstanding statesman of the period, returned to St. Petersburg at the end of September after signing the Peace of Portsmouth he found a state of affairs that seemed almost desper-

ate, from the standpoint of the existing regime. Witte's reactions to the situation in the early fall are vividly mirrored in the following phrases in his "Memoirs":

"All Siberia was in full confusion . . . Poland was almost in open uprising . . . In the Caucasus whole counties and cities were in a state of complete insurrection . . . Odessa was also completely revolutionized."

There were grave worries as to the mood of the beaten army, which was now to return from Manchuria. European Russia was largely denuded of troops. The governmental apparatus seemed half paralyzed. Its more restrictive laws and regulations were flouted without being formally repealed. The most violent speeches were delivered in the halls of the universities, which had been granted autonomy. What may be considered the climax of the victorious upswing of the Revolution occurred in October, when a railroad strike, beginning on October 20, rapidly spread all over the country until three quarters of a million railroad workers had stopped work. The discontent of the railroad workers had been aroused over a question of pension rights; but the strike assumed a definitely political character, with demands for free elections, constituent assembly and an amnesty for political prisoners. On October 23 the railroad strike began to turn into a general strike, which tied up the whole life of the country. Not only did the factories cease to function, but shops closed, streetcar lines no longer ran, lawyers refused to accept cases and jurors to sit in courtrooms.

The government was thunderstruck and helpless in the face of this mass demonstration. The Minister of the Interior, Trepov, reported to the Tsar that he disposed of enough reliable troops to crush an armed uprising, but that he could not reopen railroad service, even between St. Petersburg and Moscow.[7] Communication between St. Petersburg and nearby Peterhof, where the Court was in residence, could only be maintained on special government boats. Faced with this situation the Tsar made a reluctant gesture of conciliation, appointed Count Witte, the most supple and most capable of the available conservative statesmen, Premier and issued a decree promising an extension of the electoral franchise for the Duma, the institution of civil liberties and the vesting of legislative authority in the Duma.

Curiously enough this triumph of the revolutionary movement, the extortion of a constitution from the autocracy, viewed in retrospect, marks the beginning of a turn in the tide in favor of

the old regime. The granting of a constitution, as Witte had shrewdly calculated, drove the beginnings of a wedge between the liberal and the socialist forces in opposition. The old order still had its card of the anti-Semitic pogrom to play, the army had not gone over to the people, and while a number of formidable explosions of revolutionary energy were still in store, they were too disconnected and unorganized to be successful.

On the evening of October 26th thirty or forty delegates, some of them workers from St. Petersburg factories, others representatives of revolutionary parties, met in the hall of the St. Petersburg Technological Institute. This deserves to be remembered as an historic date; it was the first session of the Soviet (the Russian word means simply council) which not only played a major rôle in the further development of the 1905 movement, but furnished the political form which prevailed after the Bolshevik Revolution of 1917.[8] The initiative for the formation of this Soviet came from the Menshevik group in St. Petersburg.[9] The organization rapidly grew in numbers and authority and became a recognized organizing centre for the revolutionary and labor movement not only in St. Petersburg, but all over Russia. Its general basis of representation was one delegate for every five hundred workers, and it also included representatives of revolutionary parties. Its first president was the nonparty Jewish attorney Khrustalev-Nosar; after his arrest the Soviet was headed by a committee of three, one of whom was Leon Trotzky, until it was completely suppressed.

The Soviet during its brief existence (all its leading members were arrested on December 16) exercised a considerable measure of informal authority. It set the dates for the beginning and end of general strikes, granted or refused the petitions of citizens who wished to send telegrams when the telegraph lines were not functioning, issued manifestoes and appeals. The St. Petersburg Soviet did not possess a definite party shade, and included in its membership impartially Bolsheviki, Mensheviki, Socialist Revolutionaries and nonparty workers. Even among the more actively revolutionary workers a considerable number were nonparty, because only a few thousand of the 300,000 St. Petersburg workers belonged to either the Bolshevik or the Menshevik organizations.[10]

It is interesting to note that Lenin first appraised the significance of the Soviets with a certain amount of reserve, fearing that their loose nonparty character might interfere with their effective functioning. Toward the end of 1905 he characterized the Soviet

as "not a workers' parliament and not an organization of proletarian administration, but a fighting organization for the achievement of definite ends." It was only in March, 1906, that he recognized the Soviets as "organizations of power, despite all the embryonic, unorganized, scattered elements in their make-up and functioning." [11]

The Soviets of 1905 were numerous, if shortlived. They existed in St. Petersburg, Moscow, Kostroma, Saratov, Samara, Tver, Odessa, Kiev, Rostov, Baku, Novorossisk, Ekaterinoslav, Krasnoyarsk, Irkutsk, Vladivostok, and many smaller towns and special factory settlements.

It is significant of the wide sweep of the 1905 upheaval that two of the most actively revolutionary of the provincial Soviets were located far away from the capital in remote parts of the country, in the Black Sea port, Novorossisk, and the Siberian town, Krasnoyarsk. The Novorossisk Soviet deposed the local governor, nominated its own officials and established its own courts. Its power lasted for two or three weeks in December. The Krasnoyarsk Soviet, which rose and fell at about the same time (the fate of the provincial Soviets was sealed when the government crushed the armed uprising in Moscow at the end of the year), went even further in taking over all the functions of administration. A distinctive trait of the Krasnoyarsk and of other Siberian Soviets was the inclusion of soldier representatives, along with the workers. Siberia gave the government no little cause for concern, especially because it was the route by which the army must return from Manchuria. At one time the railroad and telegraphic communications were so completely in the hands of the insurgents that the government was obliged to communicate with its generals in Manchuria through London and Peking. Two armored trains, one under the command of General Meller-Zakomelsky starting from Russia, the other under the command of General Rennenkampf from Manchuria, moved along the Trans-Siberian Railroad from its two ends and reestablished order with the aid of summary court-martials and executions.

The first counterstroke to the constitution of October 30 was a bloody wave of pogroms all over the country. These massacres were reported from over a hundred places and the number of persons killed, according to revolutionary historians,[12] amounted to 3,500 or 4,000. The most sanguinary pogroms occurred in Odessa, with its large Jewish population, and in Tomsk, in Siberia, where many people were burned alive in a public building. The general setting

for these outbreaks was quite standardized. Rumors would circulate in a town that a pogrom was impending, and peasants would come from the surrounding countryside with carts to take away the booty. A patriotic procession, with pictures of the Tsar and ikons and singing of the national hymn, would be organized, with the active coöperation of the police. It was not difficult, as a rule, to pick a quarrel with passers-by, and when other means failed a provocator could always fire a shot, which would promptly be interpreted as an attack by Jews and serve as a signal for an assault on the Jewish quarter, accompanied by every kind of outrage and violence. The troops and police were passive in such outbreaks, or turned their arms against the revolutionary selfdefense organizations. Count Witte discovered that government printing-presses in the department of secret police were being used for the publication of pogrom appeals, and no serious effort was ever made to apprehend or punish the leaders of the pogroms. The main wave of pogroms occurred in the weeks immediately after the granting of the constitution; but there were earlier outbreaks, notably in Nizhni Novgorod, in the summer.[13]

While the pogroms were mainly directed against the Jews they also occurred in towns outside the Pale of Settlement, where few or no Jews resided, and in such cases the victims were intellectuals or workers suspected of revolutionary sympathies. Up to 1905 the Tsarist Government had never organized any active popular propaganda on its own behalf. The formidable growth of the revolutionary movement in that year inspired efforts on the part of monarchist sympathizers to create mass parties or organizations which would support the Tsar. The most successful organization of this type was the Union of Russian People, headed by Dr. Dubrovin. It put forward the idea of a patriarchal Tsar, regarded all non-Russian inhabitants of the Empire as "lesser breeds without the law" and described the Jews as the source of all Russia's woes.[14] It endeavored to win support among the masses by denouncing bureaucrats, urging that more land be given to poorer peasants and indulging in phrases about "equalizing the position of all toiling classes." It looked back to medieval Russia as its ideal and desired the restoration of the Patriarchate and the holding of a Church Council.

Enjoying the active support of the police and the Church, the Union of Russian People acquired a mass following, especially among the classes which were most sensitive to Jewish competition,

such as hand artisans and small traders, among the petty officials and, to a lesser extent, among the peasants. Depending, as it did, to a very large extent on official favor the Union of Russian People flourished mainly during the years when its services in carrying out pogroms were most appreciated by the authorities. After the Revolution had been definitely suppressed the government, distrusting the somewhat nondescript mob which had assembled under the banners of the Union of Russian People, preferred to rely more on the conservative propertied classes; and the Union of Russian People disintegrated and played no further significant rôle. By its very nature the Tsarist regime was incapable of creating a broad popular movement of a Fascist type.

Events crowd on each other so fast in the last quarter of 1905 that it is often difficult to decide whether the revolutionary curve was rising or falling. Just at the time when city mobs were rioting against Jews and revolutionaries a wave of destructive peasant revolt swept the country and gave the most convincing proof of the existence of a powerful subversive force in the rural districts.

There had been considerable unrest in the rural districts during the early part of 1905; but at that time the peasant movement in the main assumed peaceful forms: strikes of agricultural laborers, illegal cutting of timber which belonged to the state and the landlords, etc. On August 13 and 14 a surreptitious gathering of peasant delegates, with a few representatives from revolutionary parties, meeting near Moscow, declared itself "the Constitutional Assembly of the All-Russian Peasants' Union" and adopted a programme calling for the abolition of private property in land, which was to become "the common property of the whole people." [15]

By November a new, more widespread and violent upsurge of peasant rebellion had gone so far that the reactionary General Trepov, who for some time was Minister of the Interior, exclaimed to Count Witte: "I am a landlord myself and I will gladly give away half my land, because I am convinced that this is the only means by which I can keep the other half." The autumn peasant disorders were especially intense in the Province of Saratov, where every night the horizon was lit by the flames of burning manor-houses. The movement was strongest in the central provinces of Tambov, Kursk and Voronezh, in the Volga Provinces of Saratov, Samara and Simbirsk and in some Ukrainian provinces, such as Kiev, Chernigov and Podolia. Altogether over two thousand estates were looted and gutted and losses of the landlords in the ten provinces

most affected were estimated at 29,000,000 rubles.[16] This agrarian outburst was in a very full sense a class movement and took not the slightest account of the political view of the landlords. The estate of the Zemstvo Liberal fared no better than that of his Monarchist neighbor. The causes of the movement, the most formidable outbreak since the days of Pugachev, were analyzed quite accurately by Admiral Dubasov, who led punitive expeditions which "pacified" the peasants of Kursk and other Provinces and later put down the Moscow insurrection. Writing about the situation in Kursk in November Dubasov declared:

"The main cause of the movement which has arisen here is the long acute land question. The peasants think the source of all their hardships is the lack of land; the landlords have much land and the peasants decided to burn out the landlords and seize their land. Active propaganda aroused them to do this; local people carried on agitation, together with some new arrivals; the signal was the manifesto of October 30, because the peasants expected land, but didn't get it." [17]

Agitation doubtless played its part: the returned soldier who had picked up new ideas in the towns, the local schoolteacher who might be in sympathy with Socialist Revolutionary ideas, could easily stir up a whole village in a year of such general turmoil and unrest as was 1905.

A second and more radical congress of the Peasants' Union opened in Moscow on November 19. The mood of the delegates was naturally influenced by the stormy upheaval that was proceeding in the villages. Repeating the earlier demand for the nationalization of the land this congress added a proviso that land should belong only to those who actually tilled it, without the use of hired labor. Evidently under the influence of the revolutionary parties, the peasant delegates enlarged their agrarian programme with political demands such as the convocation of a constituent assembly and boycott of the elections to the Duma. A delegate from the turbulent Saratov Province aroused applause when he cried: "If we endure they will beat us, and blood will be spilled. Blood is suffocating us now. If we revolt blood will also be spilled, but out of it will rise the sun of freedom." [18]

Neither the fiery speeches of peasant delegates nor the looting and destruction of peasant mobs, however, could decide the fate of the Revolution. The peasant movement was far more spasmodic and unorganized than the urban revolutionary movement headed by the extremist parties and the Soviets. The peasant insurrection

still showed considerable signs of vitality during the first half of 1906. After this it ebbed away as a result of the stern repressive measures of the government and the decline of the revolutionary movement in the towns.

It was in the cities, and especially in St. Petersburg and Moscow, that the decisive struggles of the 1905 Revolution were waged during the last two months of the year. The greatest strength and solidarity was displayed by the revolutionary labor movement at the time of the October general strike. This was also the period of greatest unanimity in the popular movement against the government. On November 15 the St. Petersburg Soviet called a second general strike as a protest against the court-martialling of naval mutineers in Kronstadt and against the declaration of martial law in Poland and parts of Russia. While this strike was quite widespread in the capital and won at least a partial victory, since the government agreed to try the mutineers in a civil court, the response in the provinces was much less hearty than had been the case in October. The Soviet encountered a definite repulse when, in response to the demands of the St. Petersburg workers, it endeavored to enforce a general eight-hour working day. The employers responded with lock-outs; and by the end of November the Soviet was obliged to call off its campaign. On December 9 the government felt strong enough to arrest the President of the Soviet, Nosar. On the 15th the Soviet, together with the Social Democratic and Socialist Revolutionary Parties, the Peasants' Union and the Polish Socialist Party, issued an appeal to the population to refuse to pay taxes, to withdraw deposits from savings banks, demanding payment in gold, and to demand all wage payments in gold. The appeal also contained a warning that the debts which the government contracted "during its open and unconcealed war against the people" would not be paid. The appeal led to considerable financial results; withdrawals from savings banks exceeded deposits by ninety million rubles during December. On December 16, at the moment when it was discussing plans for a new general strike and armed uprising, the entire executive committee of the Soviet was arrested.[19]

The last decisive battle of the Revolution was at hand. St. Petersburg, cowed by the presence of the Guard regiments and the memory of Bloody Sunday and deprived of its leaders through the arrest of the outstanding members of the Soviet, remained quiet. But the workers of Moscow took to the barricades. On December 19 the Moscow Soviet, in which the influence of the Bolsheviki

was predominant, declared a general strike for the next day; and this strike soon developed into an armed uprising. For several days the outer parts of the city were in the hands of the insurgents; the governor-general Dubasov despatched urgent messages to St. Petersburg for reinforcements. Only on the 28th of December, after a week of sniping and guerrilla fighting in the streets, the government forces definitely gained the upper hand, when it became known that the Semyenov Guard regiment was on the way from St. Petersburg. Volunteer bands of the Union of Russian People began to appear as a counterweight to the revolutionary sharpshooters. On the 29th and the 30th the uprising was definitely crushed with the aid of heavy artillery bombardment of the Presna textile workers' region, which was a stronghold of the insurgents. At first sight it seems amazing that a force of armed insurgents which, according to Trotzky, did not exceed two thousand, could hold out for so long a time in a city with a garrison of 15,000. But the mood of this garrison was distinctly unreliable and Dubasov was afraid to send most of his soldiers into action. Moreover, the sympathy of the poorer classes was distinctly with the revolutionaries, who operated in small groups, in order to avoid exposing themselves to volleys of rifle fire or to artillery. The decisive factor in crushing the uprising was the despatch of the Semyenov Regiment from St. Petersburg; and this might have been checked if the December strike had been as generally supported in St. Petersburg as the two preceding ones and had tied up railroad communication between St. Petersburg and Moscow. Simultaneously with the Moscow uprising there was street fighting in other towns, including Rostov, Kharkov and Nizhni Novgorod; but these disturbances were put down with less difficulty than the revolt in Moscow.

Responding to a growing pressure for unity on the part of the rank and file membership the Bolshevik and Menshevik factions of the Social Democratic Party, which had held separate congresses in the spring of 1905 held a joint "unity" congress in Stockholm in April, 1906. The Mensheviki were in the majority here, with sixty-two delegates, against forty-nine of the Bolsheviki.[20] Among the factors which contributed to the victory of the Mensheviki in the election of this congress were the growing realization that the tactics of armed uprising to which the Bolsheviki were strongly committed had failed, at least for the time being, and dissatisfaction with the boycott of the election to the Duma, which Lenin had advocated in the belief that parliamentary activity would only dis-

tract the masses from the problem of preparing an armed uprising. Although the Mensheviki were temperamentally more tolerant than their opponents and did not exploit their majority as ruthlessly as the latter might have done, compromising with the Bolshevik views on some questions, the congress revealed more points of difference than points of agreement. Lenin at the congress stressed the need for armed uprising, while the Mensheviki advocated participation in the Duma. Lenin urged that nationalization of the land be included in the Party programme; the Mensheviki opposed this on the ground that such a measure would only strengthen the state which, they assumed, would be conservative. The unity which was formally realized at the Stockholm Congress was never really translated into practise, and the two groups really continued to exist as separate parties.

The situation in the revolutionary camp was further complicated by splits and differences of opinion which developed during the years of reaction in Russia. Some Mensheviki in Russia, the so-called "liquidators," favored the complete abandonment of underground and illegal activity and the adoption of a policy of carrying on such trade-union and educational work as was possible within the narrow limits which the Tsarist regime prescribed. Lenin, who reversed his original policy of boycotting the Duma elections when he realized that immediate chances of successful insurrection had vanished, was obliged to contend with an impatient group of his followers which wished to recall the Social Democratic deputies from the Duma. Another heretical group within the Bolshevik ranks departed from Marxian materialism and developed a tendency toward mysticism.

In Russia the steady trend after the defeat of the December uprising in Moscow was toward the restoration of the power of the government. When the first Duma met on April 10, 1906, the government had already felt sufficiently strong to curtail the rights and privileges of the new legislative body very appreciably. So a State Council, with an overwhelmingly conservative membership, was established as an upper chamber, co-equal in power with the Duma, while the government assumed the very important right to promulgate laws while the Duma was not in session. The Cadets emerged as the strongest party in the first Duma, with 177 members out of 524. Inasmuch as the groups to the left of the Cadets (the Laborites, or radical peasant deputies, together with the Social Democrats and Socialist Revolutionaries who were elected from regions

where the boycott tactics were not followed) numbered over 100 the Duma possessed a majority of the Left, committed to a programme of drastic agrarian reform which the government was not for a moment inclined to accept. On July 21, 1906 the Duma was dissolved; a number of its Cadet and Laborite members went to Viborg, in Finland, where Russian police regulations did not apply, and issued an appeal to the people to protest against the dissolution by refusing to pay taxes and to serve in the army. The Viborg Manifesto, like the appeal of the St. Petersburg Soviet in December, 1905, contained a warning that debts which might be contracted abroad without the consent of the people's representatives would not be acknowledged or paid.

The Viborg Manifesto, in the main, fell on deaf ears. The revolutionary flame had burned itself out. The military mutinies in ever turbulent Kronstadt and in Sveaborg, in Finland, and the few strikes of protest did not suggest the intensity of the movement in 1905. The Tsar dismissed Count Witte, who was inclined to coquette with liberalism, in May and later appointed as Premier the resolute and ruthless Saratov governor, Peter Stolypin, who ruled the country with a strong hand until he was assassinated in September, 1911.

One of Stolypin's first measures was to rid himself of the oppositionist Duma. The second Duma proved quite as intractable as the first from the standpoint of the government. On June 16, 1907, Stolypin dissolved the second Duma and simultaneously the police arrested all the Social Democratic deputies on whom it could lay its hands. A new election law, warranted to produce legislative assemblies of a satisfactory composition from the standpoint of the government, was promptly promulgated. Under the new law the representation of the non-Russian nationalities, Poles, Caucasians, Central Asians, was drastically reduced. At the same time the big landlords and the wealthy classes in the cities were given overwhelming predominance in the complicated indirect election system. In the first two Dumas 42% of the deputies were chosen by peasant electors, 4% by workers, 22% by city dwellers with tax and rental qualifications and 32% by big landowners. This was very far, of course, from equal suffrage; but Stolypin's change in the election law in 1907 shifted the balance much more heavily in favor of the propertied classes. Under the new regulations the landed aristocracy chose half the deputies in the Duma; the wealthy class in the cities 14%; the peasants 22%; the city middle class 12%;

and the workers 2%.[21] Under this system the troublesome Cadets and Laborites were reduced to small representation and the Social Democrats could only hope to elect a handful of deputies.[22] Parliamentary life in Russia represented the interplay of interests of a very small well-to-do minority of the population. The balance of power in the Duma first rested with the Octobrist Party (so called because its members took their stand on the constitution of October 30 and opposed further changes) and later passed to a combination of the more conservative Octobrists with groups still further to the right. This absence of a popular representative character condemned the Duma to a negligible rôle after the Revolution of 1917.

Besides restoring the essentially autocratic character of the state and crushing the last flickers of disorder with the aid of numerous executions (Stolypin evaded the absence of a death penalty in the ordinary Russian code by turning over offenders suspected of crimes of violence to courts-martial, which could mete out capital sentences) the new Premier launched a very important experiment in the agrarian field. The formidable peasant upheavals of 1905 and 1906 effectively disillusioned the government about the supposedly conservative character of the old-fashioned peasant communal ownership of the land. The spectacle of whole peasant communities marching with axes, pitchforks and combustible materials to the nearest landlord's estate was convincing enough in this respect. Unwilling to concede the radical demand for compulsory alienation of the land of the big estate-owners for the benefit of the peasants, the government preferred another scheme: to split the peasantry by giving the more energetic and well-to-do peasant households an opportunity to become small individual holders, freed from dependence on the commune. As early as 1904 Stolypin, while he was still governor of Saratov, had recommended this solution of the agrarian problem to the Tsar in a report which contained the following passage:[23]

"The Russian peasant has a passionate desire to level everyone, to bring everyone to one standard of living; and because it is impossible to raise the mass to the level of the most active and clever the best elements must be brought down to that of the inferior inert majority. Individual property ownership is the natural antidote to communal ownership. It is the guaranty of order, because the small proprietor is the basis on which stable conditions in the state can rest."

As Premier, Stolypin was able to give effect to his theory in two main laws, supplemented by a number of accompanying regulations.

The first of these laws, promulgated on November 22, 1907, broke up the compulsory communal life of the majority of the peasants by giving every member of a peasant community the right to demand his share of land in one consolidated holding. A second important decree of July 10, 1910, made it possible for any peasant commune to dissolve itself into an aggregate of individual holders by a majority vote of the members.

As a result 2,008,432 peasant households left the communes and became individual owners between 1907 and 1915.[24] This was 22% of the total number of members of the village communes; there were also 2,800,000 peasant families, mostly in the South and West, which owned their land on an individual basis before Stolypin's changes. Investigation into the results of this "wager on the strong," as Stolypin characterized his policy, is a complicated and difficult task. But it would seem that the main effects of this new agrarian policy were the strengthening of the very thin layer of peasants which formerly lived above the degraded poverty level of the masses of members of the communes and an increase in the number of peasants who lost all connection with landholding and were obliged either to seek their fortune as laborers in the towns or to become agricultural workers. Most of the sales of land were by peasants with very small holdings to peasants with holdings which were above the average. Another factor which was conducing to the emergence of a farmer class, with a higher standard of living, was the eagerness of the propertied nobility to sell their land after the numerous unpleasantnesses of 1905 and 1906. Between 1906 and 1911 the amount of land which was owned by the aristocracy in forty-seven provinces of European Russia diminished from 49,947,000 desyatinas to 43,205,000 desyatinas, or by more than eighteen million acres.[25]

Whether Stolypin's agrarian policy could have staved off violent social revolution in Russia by creating greater prosperity and a higher respect for property in the new class of individual proprietors is an interesting but necessarily speculative and debatable question. The experiment was limited in point of time, because it only got under way in the latter part of 1907 and was stopped with the outbreak of the War, since it was felt that large-scale reallotments of land should not take place at a time when so many peasants were at the front.

The fate of Stolypin's agricultural experiment was, of course, bound up with the larger problem whether Russia's political and

economic development, under normal conditions, could have proceeded without violent shocks and upheavals. In the years immediately after the defeat of the 1905 Revolution the labor movement in Russia was moribund. In 1905 there were 1,424,328 participants in political and 1,438,841 participants in economic strikes; the corresponding figures in 1910 were 3,777 and 42,846. These were times of profound depression for all the classes which had been active in the 1905 Revolution. The workers clung to their jobs, threatened with unemployment in view of the prevalent industrial stagnation; only the most stubborn of the revolutionaries carried on their activity during this period. Many of the rebels of 1905 turned their backs on revolutionary ideas; it was an epoch of suicides and of pornographic and semi-pornographic literature.

After 1910 the industrial situation began to mend; and the shooting of hundreds of workers by troops in a labor dispute in the remote Lena gold-fields of Siberia in April, 1912, was the signal for a wave of protest strikes and a relivening of the labor movement. In the summer of 1914, just before the outbreak of the War, large-scale strikes occurred in Baku and in St. Petersburg, accompanied in the latter city by clashes with troops and police. There is no convincing evidence, however, that the Tsarist regime at this time was confronted with a crisis of anything approaching the proportions of 1905; and every peasant who made a modest success out of his individual holding was an unconscious recruit for the propertied side of the barricade in any future social conflict.

Lenin called the 1905 upheaval a "dress-rehearsal" for the 1917 Revolution; and, despite its ultimately abortive character, the 1905 Revolution did reveal and foreshadow in an extraordinary way the moving forces of the successful movement of 1917: the mutinous armed forces, the turbulent workers, the landhungry peasants, the dissatisfied minor nationalities. It even revealed the form of organization which was predestined for the Russian Revolution by the failure of the middle class to conquer political liberty and the backwardness of the peasants: the Soviet of Workers' Deputies, acting, of course, under the guidance and prompting of the professional revolutionaries on whom Lenin set so much store. But the greatest of all forces for change and destruction, war, had to intervene before the revolutionary figures could again take their places on the stage. When Nicholas II signed the order for the general mobilization of the Russian army in 1914 he was uncon-

sciously signing his own death warrant and that of the system which he embodied.

Superficially it might have seemed that Russia was entering the War in 1914 under more favorable auspices than had existed when hostilities broke out with Japan in 1904. There was certainly in the beginning a much greater show of popular support. With the exception of the few Social Democratic deputies all the parties in the Duma supported the War. Even the spokesman of the Laborite group, the subsequent Premier of the Provisional Government, A. F. Kerensky, exhorted the peasants and workers "to defend our country and then set it free." A Jewish deputy Friedman vowed the loyalty of his people. Several outstanding individual revolutionaries such as the Anarchist Prince Kropotkin, the great Marxian theoretician Plekhanov, the "Grandmother of the Revolution," the Socialist Revolutionary Breshko-Breshkovskaya, took an unqualifiedly pro-war stand, motivated by the conviction that a German victory would mean a triumph of militarism and reaction. The fact that Russia was in alliance with democratic France and England was also a factor in attracting the support of the radical and liberal intellectuals, who had been, for the most part, indifferent or definitely defeatist in their attitude toward the Russo-Japanese War.

The War was definitely condemned by Lenin, Trotzky, Martov and other emigrant Social Democrat leaders of various shades of thought. While the Bolsheviki adopted Lenin's slogan that "the imperialist war must be turned into a civil war" the anti-war Mensheviki (some of the latter supported the War in so far as it was waged for national defense) stressed rather the necessity for immediate peace without annexations or indemnities. During the first months of the War, however, pacifist and revolutionary propaganda made little headway in Russia; and the formidable strike wave of the early part of the year completely subsided.

The actual course of events, however, fully justified the premonition of the conservative statesman, P. N. Durnovo, who, in a report submitted to the Tsar early in 1914 [26] predicted that "social revolution in its most extreme form" and "hopeless anarchy, the issue of which cannot be foreseen," would be the results of an unsuccessful clash with Germany. From the very beginning of hostilities the inferiority of the Russian military machine to the German in everything but sheer numbers was evident. Russia entered the World War, as it had entered every war in its history,

very badly prepared. At the outset Russia had sixty batteries of artillery against Germany's three hundred and eighty-one. Russia had one kilometre of railroad mileage to every hundred square kilometres of territory, as against Germany's 10.6.[27] The mobilization schedule called for 6,600,000 rifles over a three-year period; the actual need was for 17,700,000; and this large gap was only partially filled by extra production at the factories. Only 12 percent of the required 133,000 machine-guns were available on January 1, 1917.[28]

Some of these deficiencies were attributable to the bureaucratic inefficiency of the War Department; others were an unavoidable consequence of the industrial backwardness of the country, a circumstance which was enhanced by the fact that Russia was very largely blockaded. The German Fleet dominated the Baltic Sea and Turkey held the Dardanelles. Allied munitions were shipped to Russia through Murmansk, Archangel and Vladivostok; but here transport difficulties were a limiting factor.

Under these conditions military defeat, with all its inevitable consequences for the internal condition of the country, was very nearly a foregone conclusion. Any detailed description of Russia's participation in the World War lies outside the scope of the present work. The campaign that really shattered the morale and greatly reduced the fighting effectiveness of the Russian army was launched by the Germans in the spring of 1915. Before this drive, which was accompanied by a tremendous use of massed artillery, was finished the Russians had been obliged to evacuate extensive territory, including Russian Poland and a part of Galicia which had been overrun by the Russian armies earlier in the War. The Russian losses in this single operation totalled 1,410,000 killed and wounded and 976,000 prisoners. In general Russia's losses during the period of its participation in the War were far heavier than those of any other belligerent. They are estimated at from six to eight million dead, wounded and prisoners.[29] After the disastrous campaign of 1915 the Russian War Minister, General Polivanov, placed his sole reliance on "immeasurable distances, impassable roads and the mercy of St. Nicholas, patron of Holy Russia."[30]

Russia mobilized fifteen and a half million men during the War, in a vain effort to compensate for its lack of cannon and shells with sheer manpower. As a result of this enormous mobilization and of the heavy losses at the front the whole character of the Russian army was greatly changed. The old officers' corps, largely re-

cruited from the upper classes, had to be filled out with new members, drawn from the masses of the people. And it is difficult to exaggerate the revolutionizing effect on the hosts of peasant recruits of being suddenly thrown into contact with unimagined death-dealing implements of modern warfare and sustaining a series of overwhelming defeats, often accompanied by cases of clear incompetence and neglect on the part of the commanding officers. The peacetime Russian army was a fairly reliable bulwark of the government. The wartime army was a huge swollen mass, far more responsive to the mood of the civil population and far less reliable, from the standpoint of the existing regime.

As early as the summer of 1915 there were ominous symptoms in the shape of strikes and food riots, ending in bloodshed, in the textile towns of Ivanovo-Vosnessensk and Kostroma and in Moscow itself. At a cabinet session on September 28, 1915, the Minister of the Interior, Prince Scherbatov, expressed fear that an outbreak of disorder might occur at any moment in Moscow and complained of the lack of sufficient forces with which to put it down.[31]

During 1914 and 1915 several centres of organized public activity grew up in the shape of the Unions of Cities and Zemstvos and the War Industry Committee. Although the primary purpose of these organizations was to help the efficient prosecution of the War they almost inevitably turned into centres of criticism of the governing bureaucracy; and they were regarded with a suspicious eye by the secret police. A centre of political criticism was formed in September, 1915, with the organization of the Progressive Bloc, embracing about two thirds of the members of the Duma. The parties of the extreme Left and the extreme Right, for different reasons, remained outside the Progressive Bloc, which took its stand on a programme of mild reform, with a ministry made up of persons enjoying public confidence as its first demand.

The revolutionary groups were unable to carry on any extensive propaganda during the War, and the policy of the liberal opposition wavered between resentment at the growing irresponsibility and contempt for public opinion manifested by the government and fear of exciting a popular revolt that might go far beyond what its members regarded as desirable limits. Professor Milyukov continually endeavored to hold back his associates in the Cadet Party from precipitate action; at a conference of the Party in Moscow in the summer of 1915 he warned the delegates that "the strain is

so great that any carelessly thrown match may kindle a terrible fire. And God save us from seeing this fire. This would be not a revolution but a terrible Russian riot, senseless and pitiless. It would be an orgy of the mob." [32]

Milyukov's appraisal of public sentiment finds confirmation in the report of the chief of the Petrograd gendarme service for October, 1916.[33] The report declares that "a threatening crisis has already ripened" and describes how the man in the street is already saying "We are on the eve of big events, compared with which 1905 was child's play" while the workers are indignant over the rising cost of living and the peasants are beginning to talk politics as they have not done since the suppression of the 1905 Revolution. Most serious, perhaps, of all the symptoms of discontent which the watchful gendarmes had collected was the mood of soldiers at the front who were asking employees of the supply services whether it was true that there was famine in Moscow and Petrograd, that merchants were throwing soldiers' wives out of their homes, that the Germans had given the War Minister a billion rubies in return for a promise to starve as many of the simple people as possible.

As the Russian army, after General Brussilov's brilliant but tactically indecisive offensive against the Austrians in 1916 had ceased, settled down to the mud of the trenches the sense of hopelessness and bitterness in the country grew day by day. The middleclass intellectual or employee caught up and repeated rumors about the pro-German influences at the Court and about the sinister doings of Rasputin. Strikes multiplied among the industrial workers, despite the wartime restrictions, because of a rising cost of living that kept ahead of wage increases, at least for the majority of the laborers. The peasant grumbled more and more loudly over the depletion of able-bodied men and horses and over the difficulty of getting manufactured goods from the towns.

It is highly doubtful whether under any conditions the Russian political, economic and social organism could have stood such an ordeal as the World War. But the characters of the Tsar and the Tsarina accelerated and made inevitable the doom of the Romanov dynasty.

Nicholas II, whose personal misfortune it was to rule in a period of wars and profound social and economic changes, was less fit for the rôle of an autocrat than any sovereign since the mad Tsar Paul. He was a man of weak character, limited intelligence and

singular lack of initiative; indeed the most distinctive psychological trait of the last Tsar was his inability to react strongly to the most tragic and significant events. Even on the day after his abdication he could think of nothing more significant to write in his diary than: "I had a long sound sleep. Woke up beyond Dvinsk. Sunshine and frost . . . I read much of Julius Cæsar." The Tsar's weakness was not accompanied by humanitarianism or by a willingness to select strong and capable counsellors. Strongly impressed by the memory of his domineering father, Alexander III, the Tsar's first belief was that he must preserve the autocracy and hand it on to his descendants unimpaired, and he approved of the most ruthless punitive measures which were employed in suppressing the 1905 Revolution. And Count Witte seems to be correct in his observation that the Tsar disliked those whom he did not consider more stupid than himself.

The most amiable features in the character of Nicholas II, his complete devotion to his wife and children and his enjoyment of the simplest pleasures of family life, by an odd paradox became the most direct cause of his undoing. For his wife Alexandra, born a Princess of Hesse, stronger and more emotional in character than the Tsar, and even less competent, if that is possible, politically, became the real ruler of Russia in 1915–1916 and did more than anyone else to create an impassable chasm between the Tsar and those classes which would normally have been loyal to the monarchy.

Highstrung, almost hysterical in temperament, the Tsarina was a ready convert to the traditional Russian Court conception of the Tsar as an absolute autocrat; and, like many converts, she brought to her new faith a positively fanatical intensity. Her letters to the Tsar during the period of the War are full of adjurations to show his power, to arrest and deport the leading members of the Duma, whom she indiscriminately lumped together as traitors. "Be Peter the Great, Ivan the Terrible, Emperor Paul; smash them all," she writes in a letter of December 27, 1916; and in another letter, written just five days before the Revolution of March 12, she conveys even more strenuous advice to her consort:

"You have never lost an opportunity to show your love and kindness; now let them feel your fist. They themselves ask for this—so many have recently said to me: 'We need the whip.' This is strange, but such is the Slavonic nature—the greatest firmness, even cruelty and—warm love. They must learn to fear you; love alone is not enough." [34]

The influence of the Tsarina upon public administration became much more pronounced after the Tsar decided to take over the supreme command of the Russian armies from the Grand Duke Nicholas Nicholaevitch after the defeats of 1915. While his direction of military operations was purely nominal (the actual strategic decisions were taken by the Chief of Staff, General Alekseev) he frequently absented himself from the capital in order to visit the Stavka, or General Headquarters, which was located in Moghilev, in Western Russia. The Tsarina began to take a more and more active part in the state administration; and the Tsar seems to have welcomed this relief from the burdens of office.

While there is no concrete proof to justify the widespread rumors that the Tsarina was acting in the interests of Germany, her reactionary tendencies and political inexperience made her the worst possible adviser to the Tsar under the circumstances. The situation was further aggravated by the fact that the Tsarina had fallen under the psychical domination of a dissolute Siberian monk, Gregory Rasputin, who by general testimony possessed extraordinary hypnotic powers and who acquired almost unlimited influence over the Tsarina by his apparent ability to cure and heal her only son, the Tsarevitch Aleksei, who was afflicted with hæmophilia, a disease which exposed him to the imminent risk of dying from loss of blood as a result of any cut or wound. Although the lusty Rasputin possessed an uncommonly strong attraction for women and counted among his paramours more than one lady who was eminent in St. Petersburg society,[35] his hold on the Tsarina was attributable partly to his supposed healing powers, partly to a mystical faith on her part that here was a holy man, arisen from the common people. Throughout 1916 "Our Friend," as the Tsarina always calls Rasputin in her letters to her husband, appointed and removed ministers almost at will, and the more respectable representatives of the governing bureaucracy, such as the Foreign Minister Sazonov, were pushed out of office and replaced by nonentities and pliable tools of Rasputin, such as Stürmer and Protopopov. While there is no evidence that Stürmer was a German agent, as Milyukov broadly hinted in his famous "Stupidity or Treason?" speech in the Duma in the autumn of 1916, a feeling of complete irresponsibility was generated by the domination of Rasputin and his clique, which included a number of speculators and profiteers.

If Nicholas II took no measures to avert the impending up-

heaval it was certainly not for lack of warning. The British Ambassador, Sir George Buchanan, at the last audience which the Tsar granted him, on January 12, 1917, transgressed the rules of diplomatic etiquette by telling the sovereign: [36] "You have, sire, come to the parting of the ways, and you have now to choose between two paths. The one will lead you to victory and a glorious peace, the other to revolution and disaster." His kinsman, the Grand Duke Alexander Mikhailovitch, wrote to the Tsar in February: "Disaffection is spreading very fast . . . Strange though it may be, the government itself is the organ that is preparing the revolution." [37] The President of the Duma, Michael Rodzianko, a loyal monarchist, was unceasing in his appeals to the Tsar to cast off the influence of Rasputin and the "Court camarilla."

Conviction of the inevitability of some impending great change had penetrated very far into the ruling classes, as one may judge from an episode of the winter of 1916–1917 which is related in Rodzianko's memoirs.[38] In January, 1917, General Krymov, on leave from the front, told an excited audience of Duma members and other public men in Rodzianko's home that the whole army would greet the news of a *coup d'état* with joy. "The General is right," said the Cadet leader Shingarev. "A *coup d'état* is necessary. But who will dare to undertake it?" This was the fateful question to which the liberal and conservative opposition circles found no answer. Three men who were anything but revolutionaries by conviction or social position, Prince Felix Yussupov, the Grand Duke Dmitry Pavlovitch, and Purishkevitch, a conservative anti-Semitic member of the Duma, did organize the murder of Rasputin late in December.

But the dissatisfied politicians and army officers failed to organize a palace revolution. They had visions, no doubt, of the "terrible Russian riot, senseless and pitiless," which Milyukov had predicted in the event that the masses got fairly out of hand. So the Krymovs, Milyukovs, Rodziankos waited, with a vague sense of helplessness in the face of impending catastrophe, until an accidental push would reveal how thoroughly the outwardly imposing structure of the autocracy had decayed from within.

NOTES

[1] M. N. Pokrovsky, "Russian History" (abridged edition), Part III, p. 61.

[2] Sergei Witte, "Reminiscences: Reign of Nicholas II," Volume I, p. 262.

[3] Zubatov, who occupied the post of chief of political police in Moscow is credited with the observation that "the working class is a collective force of such power as revolutionaries have never possessed in the shape of a weapon, neither in the time of the Decembrists, nor in the period of the going to the people, nor at the

time of the student outbursts." (See Russian magazine, *Biloe,* The Past, Volume 4, 1917.) He organized conservative police-controlled unions in Moscow and among the Jewish workers of Odessa and Minsk. The Zubatov unions failed to achieve their purpose in times of crisis, however, because their members always went beyond the bounds which the police organizers set for them.

[4] Balabanov, "Sketch of the History of the Revolutionary Movement in Russia," p. 264. With the ebb of the revolutionary tide the number of strikers diminished to 1,108,407 in 1906 and to 740,074 in 1907.

[5] Pokrovsky, *op. cit.,* pp. 200–201.

[6] Leon Trotsky, in his "Die Russische Revolution 1905" pp. 138, 139), tells how he was invited, as a representative of the St. Petersburg Soviet, to a meeting in the salon of a radical Baroness, where the guests included Army and Navy officers, lawyers, journalists and other intellectuals, and the discussions centred around the question of proper revolutionary tactics.

[7] Witte, *op. cit.,* Vol. II, p. 10.

[8] From a strictly technical standpoint the first Soviet may be said to have been formed in the textile town of Ivanovo-Vosnessensk, in May, 1905. This body originated as a sort of enlarged strike committee, which subsequently guided the revolutionary movement in Ivanovo-Vosnessensk. See V. I. Nevsky, "Soviets and Armed Uprising in 1905," pp. 17ff. This Ivanovo-Vosnessensk Soviet, like the Kostroma Soviet, which was established in July, did not, however, possess the nationwide prestige and significance of the St. Petersburg organization.

[9] Martov, "Die Geschichte der russischen Sozialdemokratie," p. 138.

[10] Nevsky, *op. cit.,* estimates that there were about 6,000 members of both wings of the Social Democratic organization in St. Petersburg at the height of its influence in the autumn of 1905. A fair proportion of these, of course, were not manual workers.

[11] The first citation is from an article entitled "Socialism and Anarchism," in *New Life,* No. 21, of November 25 (December 10), 1905; the second from an article entitled "The Victory of the Cadets and the Problems of the Workers' Party."

[12] Pokrovsky, *op. cit.,* p. 194, and Trotzky, *op. cit.,* p. 109.

[13] See "1905: History of the Revolutionary Movement in Separate Sketches," Vol. II, pp. 238ff.

[14] V. Zalezhsky, "Monarchists," in series "Parties Which Were in Russia," pp. 25ff.

[15] Robinson, "Rural Russia Under the Old Regime," pp. 160ff.

[16] P. Maslov, "The Agrarian Question in Russia," Vol. II, p. 254.

[17] Pokrovsky, *op. cit.,* Part III, p. 270.

[18] Robinson, *op. cit.,* p. 171.

[19] Trotzky, *op. cit.,* p. 178.

[20] Since the norm of representation was one delegate per 300 members, the combined strength of the two wings of the Party at this time was probably in the neighborhood of 30,000 or 35,000.

[21] Otto Hoetzsch, "Russland," p. 121.

[22] In the fourth Duma, which was elected in the autumn of 1912, there were six Bolsheviki and eight Mensheviki, the latter including one Polish Socialist. Bolshevik candidates, however, were elected from all the large working class constituencies, the Mensheviki being chosen mostly from the Caucasus and from outlying parts of the country where nationalist dissatisfaction influenced the voting. One of the Bolshevik deputies, Roman Malinovsky, was a provocator and left the Duma group; the other five were arrested and exiled shortly after the outbreak of the War. One of their number, A. E. Badaev, gives an excellent account of the activity of the Bolshevik deputies in his book, "The Bolsheviki in the State Duma."

[23] Pokrovsky, *op. cit.,* Part III, p. 340.

[24] Piontkovsky, "Sketches of the History of Russia in the Nineteenth and Twentieth Centuries," pp. 330ff. Professor Robinson, in "Rural Russia Under the Old Regime," p. 270, estimates that peasant and holdings increased from 160,875,000 desyatinas in 1905 to 170,461,000 desyatinas at the end of 1914, while the land owned by the nobility decreased from 49,768,000 desyatinas to 39,558,000 desyatinas. There was thus a steady drift of land away from the nobles to the peasants.

[25] Piontkovsky, *op. cit.,* p. 359.

[26] Printed in the Soviet magazine, *Red Earth,* No. 6, 1922.

[27] Lieut.-General N. N. Golovine, "The Russian Army in the World War," pp. 32ff.

[28] *Ibid.,* pp. 127ff.

[29] Russian statistics on almost all subjects are proverbially unreliable and contradictory. The Russian General Staff on May 15, 1917, estimated the losses of the army at 619,631 killed and mortally wounded, 2,561,005 wounded, 34,736 gassed, 155,434 missing and 2,919,059 prisoners and 294 officers who perished in captivity, making a grand total 6,292,159 losses of all kinds. General Golovine considers this estimate too low, especially as regards the number of killed, and after weighing figures derived from other sources estimates the Russian losses as follows: 1,300,000 killed, 4,200,000 wounded (of whom 350,000 died), 2,500,000 prisoners, total 8,000,000.

[30] Michael Florinsky, "The End of the Russian Empire," p. 228.

[31] Frank A. Golder, "Documents of Russian History," p. 142.

[32] "The Bourgeoisie on the Eve of the February Revolution," p. 62.

[33] *Ibid.*, pp. 127–135.

[34] "The Correspondence of Nicholas and Alexandra Romanov," Vol. V, pp. 189 and 208.

[35] A very detailed record of Rasputin's debaucheries, as chronicled by the secret police agents who were set to watch him, may be found in "The Red Archives," selected and edited by C. E. Vulliamy, translated by A. L. Hynes, pp. 25–56.

[36] Sir George Buchanan, "My Mission to Russia and Other Diplomatic Memories," Vol. II, pp. 43ff.

[37] "Nicholas II and the Grand Dukes," pp. 117–122.

[38] See the translation of Rodzianko's memoirs in Golder, *op. cit.*, pp. 116–117.

CHAPTER IV

THE AUTOCRACY COLLAPSES

The collapse of the Romanov autocracy in March 1917 was one of the most leaderless, spontaneous, anonymous revolutions of all time. While almost every thoughtful observer in Russia in the winter of 1916–1917 foresaw the likelihood of the crash of the existing regime no one, even among the revolutionary leaders, realized that the strikes and bread riots which broke out in Petrograd on March 8 would culminate in the mutiny of the garrison and the overthrow of the government four days later.

The Tsarina was not distinguished by political perspicacity; and it is not surprising that she should write to her husband, who was at the Headquarters of the General Staff in Moghilev, on March 10, when the capital was in the grip of a general strike: "This is a hooligan movement, young people run and shout that there is no bread, simply to create excitement, along with workers who prevent others from working. If the weather were very cold they would all probably stay at home. But all this will pass and become calm, if only the Duma will behave itself." [1]

But it was not only the Tsarina who failed to see the impending storm. The Socialist Revolutionary Zenzinov declared: "The Revolution was a great and joyous surprise for us, revolutionaries, who had worked for it for years and had always expected it." [2] The Menshevik Internationalist Sukhanov observes: "Not one party was prepared for the great overturn." [3] The Bolshevik worker Kaourov, who took an active part in the Revolution, testifies that on March 8 "no one thought of such an imminent possibility of revolution." [4] As for the leaders of the Duma, they might whisper among each other about the possibility of a palace *coup d'état;* but the last thing they desired was an uncontrolled movement from below.

Wartime circumstances alone made any effective guidance of a mass uprising impossible. The men who afterwards distinguished themselves in the Bolshevik Revolution were either living abroad, like Lenin and Trotsky and Zinoviev, or in prison or in Siberian exile, like Stalin, Kamenev and Dzerzhinsky. The more prominent

leaders of other revolutionary parties were also absent from Petrograd in the decisive days. The Bolshevik members of the Duma had been exiled to Siberia in the first months of the War, and the Menshevik members of the War Industries Committee were arrested by the zealous Minister of the Interior, Protopopov, early in the year. There was a skeleton underground Bolshevik organization in Russia; but its activities were narrowly circumscribed by lack of experienced professional revolutionaries, lack of funds, and the all-pervading espionage. Indeed most of the members of the Bolshevik Petrograd Party Committee were arrested at a critical moment in the development of the movement, on the morning of March 11.[5]

So the police measures for the protection of the Tsarist regime were almost perfect. At first sight and on paper the military measures seemed equally imposing. Petrograd had a huge garrison of about 160,000 soldiers. To be sure the fighting quality of this garrison, as subsequent events were to prove, was in inverse ratio to its size. The original Guard regiments had been sent to the front (a grave strategic error, from the standpoint of the internal security of the old regime); and the troops quartered in Petrograd consisted mainly of new recruits, untrained, housed in crowded barracks, often poorly fed.[6]

But the Tsarist authorities did not rely primarily on the unwieldy garrison for the suppression of any possible uprising. The Minister of the Interior, Protopopov, proposed to operate against insurgent throngs first with police, then with Cossack cavalry units, bringing troops into operation only in the last resort. An elaborate plan for the suppression of disorder in the capital had been submitted to the Tsar in January.[7] A combined force of 12,000 troops, gendarmes and police was created for this specific purpose; and a military commander was appointed in each of the six police districts into which the city was divided.

Military preparations, therefore, had not been neglected, even if there were serious omissions, quite consistent with the frequently slipshod character of Tsarist administration, in paying little attention to the morale of the troops in the capital and in selecting as commander of the Petrograd Military District, General Khabalov, a man of little experience in commanding troops in actual military operations. The unforeseen circumstances that upset all the governmental calculations were the stubbornness of the demonstrators and the ultimate unreliability of the garrison.

The atmosphere of Petrograd was so charged with discontent in this third winter of an unsuccessful war that very slight causes were sufficient to bring about a formidable explosion. There had been intermittent strikes throughout January and February. Although there was not an absolute shortage of bread poor transportation and faulty distribution made it necessary for the workers and their wives, in many cases, to stand in long queues for bread and other products. The poorer classes of the city were not apathetic from actual hunger; but they were angry and annoyed at the growing cost of living and the other deprivations which the War brought with it. Something of a sense of crowd psychology, of a sense of massed power must have developed also, from the noteworthy growth in the number of industrial workers up to approximately 400,000 as a result of the presence of many war industry plants in the capital.

The movement that was to end in the overthrow of the Romanov dynasty started on March 8, which is observed by Socialist parties as Women's Day. After speeches in the factories crowds of women poured out on the streets, especially in the workingclass Viborg section of the city, clamoring for bread. Here and there red flags appeared with inscriptions: "Down with Autocracy." There were occasional clashes with the police; but the day passed off without serious conflicts. Almost ninety thousand workers struck and fifty factories were closed. A circumstance that enhanced the militant mood of the demonstrators was a lockout at the large Putilov metal works. The workers of this plant were proverbially turbulent, with a long record of strikes; and when a wage dispute had come up in one department the management on March 7 declared a general lockout. So a coincidence of three factors—the dissatisfaction with the food situation, the celebration of Women's Day and the Putilov labor dispute, which let loose over twenty thousand workers for active participation in the demonstration—combined to give the first impetus to the Revolution.

The movement gained in scope and intensity on March 9, when the number of strikers was estimated at 197,000. There was a concerted drive by the workers to reach the central part of the city. Although the police guarded the bridges over the Neva, which was to some extent a boundary between the workingclass and the governmental parts of the city, it was relatively easy to cross the river on the ice, and meetings and demonstrations were held in the centre of the capital. An ominous symptom for the government

appeared: the Cossacks showed little energy in breaking up the crowds. So a Cossack squadron rode off, amid loud cheers, leaving undisturbed a revolutionary gathering on the Nevsky Prospect, the main boulevard of Petrograd; [8] and the police reports of the day note an incident on Znamenskaya Square, when the Cossacks responded with bows to the applause of a throng which they did not disperse.

Attacks on the police became more common on this second day of the movement, the mobs using as weapons lumps of ice, cobblestones, heavy sticks. However, firearms were not used in suppressing the disorder and there was still no general conviction of an impending crisis. The British Ambassador, Sir George Buchanan, telegraphed to Foreign Minister Balfour: "Some disorders occurred to-day, but nothing serious." [9]

The 10th witnessed to a large extent a repetition of the events of the 9th, but on a larger scale. The strike became general; newspapers ceased to appear; the students in the universities abandoned their studies. The numbers both of the demonstrators and of the forces employed by the government increased; and there was a longer casualty list on both sides. Although there was still no mutiny, insubordination and passivity on the part of the troops, especially of the Cossacks, were more noticeable. On Znamenskaya Square a Cossack even cut down a police lieutenant, Krilov, with his sabre. The instinctive strategy of the crowd adapted itself to the mood of the troops. While there were fierce attacks on the police (by this time the police in the riotous Viborg district no longer ventured to appear on the streets, but were barricaded in their stations) there was an attempt to conciliate the troops and to avoid provoking them.

So far as there was organized leadership in the movement it aimed at winning over the troops, rather than at arming the workers. So the Bolshevik Shlyapnikov, one of the three members of the Bureau of the Central Committee of the Party, tells how he opposed the more hotheaded workers who continually demanded arms, or at least revolvers: "I decisively refused to search for arms at all and demanded that the soldiers should be drawn into the uprising, so as to get arms for all the workers. This was more difficult than to get a few dozen revolvers; but in this was the whole programme of action." [10]

These three days of turmoil naturally affected the national and local legislative bodies, the Duma and the Petrograd City Council;

and speeches were made demanding the appointment of a ministry responsible to the Duma. The Laborite deputy and radical lawyer Alexander Kerensky, destined to play a leading part in subsequent months, attacked the government so sharply in the Duma on the 9th that the Tsarina expressed a fervent desire that he should be hanged. These speeches, however, had little effect on the movement, because the War Minister forbade their publication, and after the morning of March 10, newspapers ceased to appear as a result of the general strike.

General Khabalov on March 10 received a peremptory telegram from the Tsar worded as follows: "I command you to suppress from to-morrow all disorders on the streets of the capital, which are impermissible at a time when the fatherland is carrying on a difficult war with Germany." This imperial order caused a sharp change in the tactics of the Petrograd authorities. Hitherto the use of firearms had been avoided. On the night of the 10th Khabalov gave his subordinate officers instructions to fire on crowds which refused to disperse after warning. This was the decisive stake of the old regime. If the troops obeyed, the revolutionary movement would be crushed. If they did not obey . . . But this alterna-' tive was apparently not considered very seriously.

As a further sign of resolute action the police on the night of the 10th arrested about a hundred persons suspected of holding seditious views, including five members of the Petrograd Committee of the Bolshevik Party. On the surface the course of events on the 11th, which was a Sunday, represented a victory for the government. There was firing on the crowds in four separate places in the central part of the city; and on Znamenskaya Square the training detachment of the Volinsky regiment used 'machine-guns as well as rifles, with the result that about forty persons were killed and an equal number were wounded. Toward evening there was an outburst of rebellion in one company of the Pavlovsk regiment; but it was put down with the aid of other troops, and the ringleaders were imprisoned in the fortress of Peter and Paul. The government, which was headed by Prince Golitzin as Premier, apparently felt in a stronger position, because in the evening it adopted a decision to dissolve the Duma, thereby breaking off the half-hearted negotiations which had hitherto been carried on with the President of the Duma, Rodzianko, about possible coöperation between the Ministry and the Duma.

Rodzianko decided to try the effect of a personal appeal to the

Tsar and despatched a telegram containing the following gravely warning phrases: "The situation is serious. There is anarchy in the capital. The government is paralyzed. It is necessary immediately to entrust a person who enjoys the confidence of the country with the formation of the government. Any delay is equivalent to death. I pray God that in this hour responsibility will not fall on the sovereign."

But neither this telegram, nor the still more urgent message which Rodzianko sent on the following morning, when the mutiny of the garrison was an accomplished fact, produced any impression on Nicholas II. Rodzianko's second telegram described the growing revolt and ended: "The situation is growing worse. Measures must be adopted immediately, because to-morrow will be too late. The last hour has come, when the fate of the fatherland and the dynasty is being decided."

After reading this message the Tsar impatiently remarked to his Minister of the Court, Count Fredericks: "This fat Rodzianko has written me some nonsense, to which I will not even reply." [11]

There is a double significance in these last urgent appeals of the President of the Duma to the Tsar and especially in his instinctive employment of the phrase "The situation is growing worse," at a moment when the revolution was moving to victory. Like the great majority of the members of the Duma Rodzianko, who was himself a well-to-do landowner, desired to see the monarchy reformed, but not abolished. All Rodzianko's actions in these turbulent days were motivated by two factors: his hope, up to the last moment, that the Tsar would save himself and the monarchical principle by making necessary concessions, and his fear that the revolutionary movement would get out of hand.

The decisive hour of the Revolution struck on the morning of March 12, when the centre of attention shifts from rebellious workers with sticks and stones and bottles to insurgent soldiers with rifles and machine-guns. The firing on the crowds on Sunday, the 11th, was the snapping point in the frail cord of discipline that held the garrison of the capital. The mutiny that was to transform the prolonged street demonstrations into a genuine revolution started in the very unit which had inflicted the heaviest losses on the demonstrating crowds: the training detachment of the Volinsky regiment. During the night the soldiers discussed their impressions of the day's shooting and agreed that they would no longer fire on the crowds. When Captain Lashkevitch appeared in the barracks of

the detachment on the morning of the 12th he was greeted with shouts: "We will not shoot." He read the telegram of the Tsar, demanding the suppression of the disorders; but this only aggravated the situation. Ultimately Lashkevitch either was shot by the insurgent soldiers or committed suicide; and the troops poured out into the streets under the command of Sergeant Kirpichnikov, one of the many obscure leaders of this unplanned upheaval. They soon aroused the soldiers of the Preobrazhensky and Litovsky regiments, who were quartered in nearby barracks.

Quickly brushing aside the resistance which some officers of the Moscow Regiment endeavored to offer and gaining new recruits among the soldiers of the Moscow regiment for their ranks, the swollen mass of soldiers made for the Viborg District, where they quickly fraternized with the throngs of workers and joined them in hunting down the police and breaking into arsenals, where the workers quickly secured the desired arms.

Khabalov, a weak and incompetent man at best, was thunderstruck as the news of one mutiny after another poured in on him. He formed a supposedly loyal force of six companies under the command of Colonel Kutepov, but it simply melted away as soon as it came into contact with the revolutionary mobs. This largely psychological process of "melting away" recurred, incidentally, whenever there was an attempt to send "reliable" troops against the revolutionary capital. It explains why a movement without organized leadership was nevertheless invincible. This breakdown of normal military discipline cannot be attributed to any single precise cause. It was a compound of many things: war-weariness, hatred of the hard and often humiliating conditions of Russian army service, responsiveness to the general mood of discontent in the country,—all explosive stuff that was ignited by the stubborn demonstrations of the working-class population of Petrograd.

There are two features of the March Revolution that strike the observer again and again. There is the lack of planned leadership, and there is the action of the soldiers independently of their officers. The latter, with very few exceptions, simply disappeared during the decisive hours of the uprising. This fact inevitably exerted a profound effect on the subsequent morale and psychology of the soldiers, who followed leaders from their own ranks, often sergeants and corporals.

Khabalov, with the rapidly thinning remnant of his loyal troops, took refuge in the Winter Palace, where his forces on the afternoon

of the 12th were reduced to "fifteen hundred or two thousand men, with a very small reserve of bullets." [12] At the insistence of the Grand Duke Michael, the Tsar's brother, the Winter Palace was evacuated and the last defenders of the old regime took refuge in the neighboring Admiralty, whence they quietly dispersed on the following morning.

So the city passed completely into the hands of the revolutionaries. The accounts of many eyewitnesses of the upheaval are pervaded with a spirit of chaotic exaltation. The monarchy had fallen; and in the masses of the population there were few who mourned it. Vast throngs gathered to watch the burning of the large District Court building and the adjoining prison; and the Tauride Palace, where the Duma held its sessions, was a magnet for endless throngs of soldiers, workers, students and curious spectators of all classes. Red bands and ribbons appeared as if by magic; and trucks filled with soldiers raced through the city, with their guns levelled against non-existent enemies. Except for the police, who were given short shrift when they were discovered hiding in garrets or firing from roofs on the crowds, the Revolution, although tumultuous, was, in the main, good-natured. There were relatively few excesses, surprisingly few, if one considers that common criminals were released indiscriminately with political offenders in the prisons which were stormed by the mobs. Class lines had not begun to assume their subsequent sharpness. An atmosphere of vague, formless good-fellowship was prevalent; and the nationalist speeches of Shulgin or Rodzianko evoked the same hearty "Hurrah" as the exhortations of the revolutionary orators. The great mass of the mutinous soldiers scarcely realized what they were doing and were uncertain whether in the end they would be treated as heroes or as criminals.

The anonymous host of workers in collarless blouses and soldiers in grey uniforms overthrew the Romanov dynasty, with its three centuries of absolute rule behind it. But the rebellious mass had nothing concrete to put in the place of the old order. The efforts to form a new government inevitably revolved around the Duma, which, despite its lack of representative character and the timidity which it displayed in its dealings with the monarchy, was the sole national assembly in existence at the time of the Revolution.

The members of the Duma on the morning of the 12th found themselves confronted with a difficult dilemma. On one hand was the Tsarist order to dissolve; on the other were the first echoes of the formidable mutiny of the garrison. Even with this last cir-

cumstance in view the Duma did not venture to defy the Tsar's order and place itself definitely at the head of the revolutionary movement. It accepted formally the decree of dissolution and moved from its customary hall of assembly into another chamber of the Tauride Palace, where it could be technically regarded as a gathering of private citizens. At the same time the delegates adopted a resolution not to leave Petrograd and commissioned the Council of Elders to elect a Temporary Committee, the functions of which were somewhat narrowly defined as the restoration of order in the capital and the establishment of relations with public organizations and institutions. The Temporary Committee included representatives of all parties in the Duma except the extreme Right and the Bolsheviki, whose deputies were in Siberian exile.

Before the members of the Temporary Committee were chosen Rodzianko made another effort, with the coöperation of the Tsar's brother, the Grand Duke Michael, to obtain the concession of a responsible ministry from the Tsar. Michael communicated with the Chief of Staff, General Alekseev, informing him of the seriousness of the situation and suggesting that either Prince G. Lvov, head of the All-Russian Union of Zemstvos, or Rodzianko himself should be placed at the head of the ministry. When Alekseev laid this suggestion before the Tsar the latter coldly replied that he thanked the Grand Duke for his advice, but that he knew himself how to act.[13] A message from the Premier, Prince Golitzin, pointing out that affairs had taken a catastrophic turn and imploring the Tsar to relieve him of office elicited a reply, extraordinarily unrealistic under the circumstances which prevailed in Petrograd at the time, demanding the most vigorous measures for the suppression of the uprising and characterizing as impermissible any change in the composition of the Cabinet. The seriousness of the situation was greatly underestimated in the Stavka. As late as 1.45 in the afternoon of the 12th, when the capital was already almost entirely in the hands of the revolutionaries, War Minister Byelaev sent an absurdly optimistic telegram to the effect that the disturbances in some military units were being suppressed and that tranquillity would soon be restored.[14]

While it was decided on the 12th to send General Ivanov with a force of Cavaliers of St. George (recipients of the highest Russian military decoration) to pacify Petrograd, Ivanov took his commission rather lightly, sending his adjutant to buy provisions in Moghilev, which he proposed to take to friends in the capital. And

there was no haste in sending troops from the fronts nearest to Petrograd, the northern and western, to reinforce Ivanov, because serious importance was not attached to the events in the capital.[15]

Throughout the few decisive days of the Revolution there was a noteworthy time-lag between the Duma and the popular movement, on one hand, and between the Tsar and the Duma, on the other. If the Duma was always behind the street crowds of Petrograd the Tsar, in his decisions, was still further behind the Duma. By the time the Tsar, on the evening of March 14, had reached the conclusion that he should commission Rodzianko with the formation of a ministry (reserving for himself, however, the appointment of War and Navy Ministers) a full-fledged provisional government was already functioning in Petrograd, and it had become too late to carry out the cherished dream of many of the Duma leaders: to save the monarchy by bringing about the abdication of Nicholas II in favor of his young son, with his brother Michael as Regent.

Events were rushing at whirlwind speed in the capital; and the Duma Committee, which set out in the afternoon with the modest functions of restoring order in the capital and establishing communication with public organizations and institutions, found itself by evening obliged to "take into its hands the restoration of state and public order and the creation of a government corresponding to the desires of the population and capable of enjoying its confidence."

When Rodzianko was still hesitating about the assumption of power the brilliant and outspoken conservative deputy of the Duma, V. V. Shulgin, offered a convincing argument in favor of prompt and decisive action: "If we don't take power, others will take it, those who have already elected some scoundrels in the factories."[16]

Whatever one may think of Shulgin's characterization of his political opponents, another force, a counterpoise to the Duma, had already come into existence in the shape of the Soviet of Workers' and Soldiers' Deputies. The rôle of the Soviet in the 1905 Revolution had not been forgotten, and it was quite natural that one of the first acts of the 1917 Revolution should be its revival. Early in the afternoon the members of the labor group of the War Industries Committee, who had been released from prison, together with the deputies of the Left parties in the Duma and some representatives of trade-unions and coöperatives constituted themselves a Temporary Executive Committee of the Soviet of Workers' Deputies and convened a session of the Soviet in the Tauride Palace on the

same evening. About two hundred and fifty delegates from factories and regiments were present at the evening session; and it was decided to fuse the representation of the workers and soldiers by creating a united organization under the name: Soviet of Workers' and Soldiers' Deputies. Although the Soviet was elected in rather haphazard fashion and suffered from the fact that most of the prominent leaders of the revolutionary parties were not in Petrograd it immediately began to assume some of the functions of power, creating a food commission to regulate the supply of the capital, organizing a workers' militia as a temporary substitute for the police and deciding which newspapers should be allowed to appear.[17] From the beginning the Soviet was closer to the masses and enjoyed more genuine authority than did the Duma.

Beginning with March 12 the halls of the Tauride Palace began to resound to the heavy tread of soldiers' boots; and the former seat of the predominantly aristocratic and middleclass Duma witnessed wave after wave of an inundation of the masses. The members of the Duma could scarcely make their way about amid the throngs which pressed into the Palace; and if few of them, perhaps, shared the bitterness of Shulgin, whose one desire, as he tells us. was for machine-guns to drive the hateful mob away, few members of the Duma felt altogether at ease among the raw masses which suddenly poured in on them.

An exception in this respect was Kerensky, who felt quite in his element, speaking everywhere, now saving an arrested Tsarist Minister from rough handling or possible lynching by a dramatic gesture, now rushing in to throw down before his perplexed colleagues a packet containing Russia's secret treaties or a sum of two million rubles which had been saved from some institution that was in danger of being plundered. The other outstanding figure among the Duma leaders in those days was Professor Paul Milyukov, leader of the Cadet Party, who seems to have contributed more than any other individual to the formation of the First Provisional Government. Strongly different in personality from the dashing, expansive, exuberant Kerensky, Milyukov was cold, precise, logical, slightly academic. At a time when many politicians could not orient themselves in the midst of the new chaotically changing conditions Milyukov retained to the full his powers of judgment; and it was no accident that he played the leading rôle in the negotiations which finally led to the support of the Provisional Government by the Soviet.

The leaders of the Soviet in its early days were rather accidental and haphazard figures; and it is significant that not one of them played a very distinguished part in the subsequent course of the Revolution. The large tumultuous mass of rank-and-file Soviet members, workers from factories and soldiers from the barracks, could feel and cheer, but was quite incapable of orderly deliberation; and the shaping of the Soviet decisions was in the hands of the Executive Committee, which first consisted of fifteen members, later enlarged by the inclusion of nine representatives of the soldiers, and ultimately still further supplemented when more of the revolutionary party leaders returned from prison and exile. The guiding figures in the Soviet in the first days of the Revolution were radical lawyers like N. D. Sokolov, journalists and publicists like Steklov and Sukhanov, while Chkheidze, the President of the Soviet, a Duma deputy of the Menshevik Party, was a Caucasian schoolteacher who spoke Russian with a heavy rasping Caucasian accent.

Party lines were rather obscure in the first period of the existence of the Soviet; but there were three marked tendencies in the Executive Committee.[18] The few Bolshevik members of the Executive Committee, with one or two allies from other left-wing groups, favored a temporary revolutionary government up to the election of a Constituent Assembly. The Bolsheviki had not yet reached their ultimate theory that the Soviets should be organs of power.[18a] At the other extreme were the advocates of a coalition government, in which the Soviet should have its representatives along with those of the middleclass parties. The majority, however, adhered to the idea that the Revolution was bourgeois in character, that it would be improper for socialists to take part in the Provisional Government, but that the Soviet should not take power itself. It should give grudging and very conditional support to the government for which the middleclass parties should have full responsibility. Of the three theories this last was perhaps least calculated to create a strong and stable government, especially in view of the influence which the Soviet enjoyed with the masses from the first days of its existence. This placed the Provisional Government from the start in the unenviable position of possessing responsibility without real authority. It corresponded, however, with the academic theories of the left-wing Mensheviki who predominated in the first Executive Committee, and it guided the subsequent course of events.

The Duma Committee on March 13 extended the scope of its authority by appointing commissars to administer the vacant min-

istries. A Military Commission under the presidency of Colonel Engelhardt was created for the double purpose of safeguarding the new regime against any attempts at restoration of Tsarism and endeavoring to restore some measure of order and discipline in the garrison of the capital. Arrests of former Tsarist Ministers and members of the police began, and the prisoners were brought to the Tauride Palace, whence a number of them were ultimately transferred to the Fortress of Peter and Paul. Some, including the hated Minister of the Interior, Protopopov, surrendered themselves for arrest voluntarily; and a feature of the Palace on this day was the appearance of long queues of police, eager to be arrested to save themselves from a worse fate at the hands of the revolutionary throngs.

The victory of the Revolution, already assured in Petrograd, became more evident throughout the whole country on the 14th. Moscow, second largest city in the country, passed into the hands of the revolutionaries much more bloodlessly than Petrograd, the situation being laconically summed up in a telegram which the governor-general, Mrozovsky, despatched to the Stavka at midday: "In Moscow there is complete revolution. The military units pass over to the side of the revolutionaries." [19]

Petrograd bore all the brunt of the fighting in the March revolution. The number of persons killed, wounded and injured was reckoned at 1315, of whom 53 were officers, 602 soldiers, 73 policemen and 587 other citizens of both sexes. [20] In the rest of the country the Revolution may almost be said to have been made by telegraph, practically without resistance and with serious excesses only in such naval centres as Kronstadt and Helsingfors, where the traditional hatred of the sailors for their officers flared up in a number of killings. Admiral Viren in Kronstadt and Admiral Nepenin in Helsingfors, together with a number of other officers, were put to death; and the sailors in Kronstadt, which from the beginning was a centre of extreme revolutionary sentiment, lodged the more unpopular officers in the local dungeons. A brigadier-general perished during a soldiers' demonstration in Penza and Governor Bunting was killed in Tver, where the overturn was marked by rioting and looting of liquor stores. [21] But such incidents were exceptional rather than typical. The change was accepted too easily and too generally to involve serious bloodshed.

The futility of any attempts to crush the revolutionary capital by sending troops from the front was already pretty obvious by

the night of the 14th. General Ivanov with his detachment of
Georgian Cavaliers arrived in Tsarskoe Syelo, only a few miles from
Petrograd, where the Tsarina was in residence at one of the Imperial
palaces with her children, who were suffering from measles. Ivanov
rather mysteriously obtained permission from the Duma Committee
to move with his troops over the last stretch of railroad line before
Tsarskoe Syelo—a fact which suggests that at least some of the
Duma leaders felt that a General with reliable troops might be an
asset in dealing with the turbulent workers and insurgent soldiers
of the capital. But, if there was any such calculation, it was doomed
to failure, because as soon as Ivanov's troops came into contact with
the revolutionized Tsarskoe Syelo garrison their "reliability" began
to dissolve; and the General, after a brief stay in Tsarskoe Syelo,
withdrew to Viritsa, where he remained until he received instructions
to return to the Stavka. Much the same experience befell some
troops which General Ruzsky sent from the northern front. As
soon as they arrived in Luga they began to fraternize with the local
soldiers and refused to proceed further. By the 15th the Stavka,
recognizing the uselessness of further efforts of this kind, issued
orders to stop sending troops from the front to Petrograd.

On the night of the 14th, in one of the rooms of the crowded,
noisy, smoke-filled Tauride Palace the radical lawyer, N. D. Sokolov,
suddenly elevated by the Revolution to the post of a Soviet leader,
sat at a writing desk, surrounded by a throng of soldiers. First
one soldier, then another threw out suggestions, all of which Sokolov
obediently wrote down. When the suggestions were exhausted the
paper received the heading: "Order Number One." [22] When the
monarchist Shulgin read the contents of this extraordinary document he exclaimed to himself, "This is the end of the army"; and
this view was widely shared in conservative military circles. Order
Number One certainly dealt a severe blow to traditional conceptions of military discipline, and its influence was profound and far-
reaching. At the same time it may be considered an effect as much
as a cause. The Petrograd garrison was completely out of hand
at this time; and the soldiers were the masters of the situation.
The contents of this collective handiwork of a group of soldiers
may be summarized as follows:

Committees were to be elected by the soldiers and sailors of all
companies, battalions and other military and naval units. Every
military unit was to obey the Soviet of Workers' and Soldiers'
Deputies in political demonstrations. Orders of the Military Com-

mission of the Duma were to be executed, except in cases when they contradicted the orders of the Soviet. The company and battalion committees must control all forms of arms and not give them out to officers, even on their demand. Soldiers, while obligated to maintain strict discipline in service, were to be given the same political and civil rights as other citizens outside of service. Standing at attention and compulsory saluting outside of service were abolished along with the sonorous titles, "Your Excellency," "Your Honor," etc. with which soldiers were formerly supposed to greet officers of the higher ranks. Officers were forbidden to use the familiar "thou" in addressing their soldiers.

Although this Order, according to the eyewitness Sukhanov, was written under the direct dictation of a group of soldiers, it corresponded closely with several resolutions which had been adopted at a session of the Petrograd Soviet; and it appeared in the Soviet official organ *Izvestia* under the signature of the Soviet. Its publication enhanced the popularity of the Soviet among the soldiers. While some parts of the Order might be regarded as harmless and reasonable modifications of the caste discipline of the old army the clause which took away the control of the arms from the officers could scarcely be reconciled with any kind of military efficiency; and the general spirit of the Order was permeated with distrust of the officers as a class. It was at once a symptom and a cause of the rapid disintegration of the military capacity of the Russian Army (already badly shaken by the disasters of poor generalship and inadequate preparedness which marked the conduct of the War) which set in after the March upheaval and was a main contributory factor in the leftward sweep of the Revolution.

Almost simultaneously with the publication of Order Number One the representatives of the Soviet reached a tentative agreement with the Duma Committee as to the conditions on which the Soviet would support the Provisional Government which the Duma Committee was now preparing to create. There was, of course, a wide gulf between the social and economic views of these two bodies; but there was a fairly wide common ground of agreement as to the establishment of democratic institutions and civil liberties. After prolonged discussion Milyukov, who proved a hard and stubborn bargainer on behalf of the Duma, persuaded the Soviet negotiators to abandon their original demands that army officers should be elected and that the Provisional Government should abstain from any action which would predetermine the future form of the state.

Milyukov still hoped that the monarchy could be saved through the abdication of Nicholas II. The points on which agreement was reached and which constituted the essential part of the declaration of the Provisional Government when it formally assumed office on March 16 were as follows:

Complete amnesty for all political and religious offenses. Freedom of speech, press, assembly, strikes and trade-union association. Abolition of all caste, religious and national limitations. Immediate preparation for the holding of a constituent assembly, chosen by the method of general, direct, equal, secret ballot, which should establish the form of government and the constitution of the country. Replacement of the police by a people's militia, with an elected administration, subordinated to the organs of local self-government. Election of local administrative bodies by direct, equal, general and secret ballot. No disarming and no removal from Petrograd of the military units which took part in the revolutionary movement. Abolition of all restrictions on the enjoyment by soldiers a general civil rights—on condition of the maintenance of the strictest discipline in service.

It is noteworthy that such really vital problems of the immediate future as the war and the land question were left unmentioned in the programme of the Provisional Government. Here the differences of viewpoint between the Soviet and the Duma Committee would have been too wide to be bridged over. Milyukov insisted that the Soviet should give some expression of support to the newly constituted government [23] and wrote himself some parts of the Soviet declaration, which appeared along with the programme of the Provisional Government on March 16, condemning illegal searches of private apartments, decline of discipline in the army, robbery and destruction of property. It cannot be said, however, that the statement of the Soviet Executive Committee about the Provisional Government was especially hearty in its assurances of sympathy and support. It is promised support only "in the measure in which the newborn government will act in the direction of fulfilling its obligations and struggling decisively with the old government." [24]

After assuring the indispensable support, or at least toleration, of the Soviet the Duma leaders proceeded to form the first Cabinet of the new regime. It was headed by Prince G. E. Lvov, a somewhat colorless liberal, head of the Union of Zemstvos, a man whose name, along with Rodzianko's, had often been mentioned as a suit-

able head of a "responsible government," had the Tsar ever been willing to grant one. Milyukov assumed the office of Minister for Foreign Affairs. The War Ministry was assigned to Guchkov, an active member of the Octobrist Party and a well-to-do Moscow merchant, who had been an advocate of military reform and modernization in pre-war years. Shingarev, a physician and a prominent member of the Cadet Party, became Minister of Agriculture and the Cadet Professor Manuilov, who had been persecuted on account of his liberal views, was appointed Minister for Education. A wealthy young Ukrainian sugar manufacturer, Tereschenko, filled the post of Minister for Finance; the progressive industrialist Konovalov, who had played an active part in the War Industries Committee, was Minister for Trade; the Left Cadet Nekrasov, Minister for Communication. The more conservative parties of the Duma had two representatives; State Controller Godnev and the Procurator of the Holy Synod, V. N. Lvov, who was subsequently to play a blundering rôle that helped to discomfit the conspiracy of General Kornilov. The Duma leaders were anxious to include representatives of the Soviet in the Cabinet; and offered the posts of Minister for Labor to Chkheidze and of Minister for Justice to Kerensky. Chkheidze, in conformity with the resolution of the Soviet Executive Committee, which by thirteen votes against eight had pronounced against the participation of its members in the new government, declined the suggestion. Kerensky, however, accepted the offer and simultaneously kept his footing in the Soviet by delivering a typical emotional speech, in which he declared, amid applause, that he could not let the representatives of the old regime out of his hands and that his first act would be the bringing back, with honor, of the exiled Bolshevik Duma deputies. Nothing was easier in those days than for a popular orator to win a rousing round of applause; and Kerensky, ignoring the frowns of some of the Soviet leaders, took the cheers of the more unsophisticated rank-and-file members as sanction for his action.

With a new government formed and a programme of adjustment, however fragile, concluded between the Duma and the Soviet, only one act in the revolutionary drama remained to be played: the elimination of the Tsar and the solution of the problem of future government. It was in Pskov, one of the oldest Russian cities, that the formal end of the sovereignty of the Romanov dynasty, which had endured more than three centuries, was destined to occur.

Disturbed by the illness of his children and by the growing re-

ports of serious disorder in the capital, Nicholas II left Moghilev early in the morning of March 13, with Tsarskoe Syelo as his destination. The Revolution had not yet spread over the whole country, and the imperial train reached the station of Malaya Vishera, about a hundred miles from Petrograd on the night of the 13th, without obstruction. Here, however, it was learned that the next stations were occupied by revolutionary troops and that the railroad authorities had instructions to direct the Tsar's train not to Tsarskoe Syelo, but to Petrograd. It was decided to proceed to Pskov, the headquarters of the Northern Front, where the Tsar probably hoped to find military support and perhaps to reach Tsarskoe Syelo by another route. The Tsar arrived in Pskov on the evening of the 14th. At first he was willing to appoint Rodzianko as head of a Ministry responsible to the Duma, reserving for himself the choice of the War and Naval Ministers.

But on the 15th events pointing to the climax of abdication fairly crowded on one another's heels. A conversation between General Ruzsky, commander-in-chief of the Northern Front, and Rodzianko made clear the extent of the upheaval in the capital and, incidentally, furnishes additional proof of Rodzianko's personally conservative sentiments as regards the monarchy. In the course of the conversation [25] Rodzianko, in response to Ruzsky's information about the Tsar's willingness to create a responsible ministry, replied that neither the Tsar nor Ruzsky understood what had happened.

"Such anarchy came on that it only remained for the Duma and myself to attempt to take the movement into our own hands, in order to avert such anarchy as would threaten the existence of the state. . . . The dynastic question is put sharply . . . There is a threatening definite demand for the abdication of the Tsar in favor of his son, with Michael Alexandrovitch as Regent. I communicate this to you with terrible pain, but what is to be done? . . . Power slips from my hands; anarchy reaches such proportions that I am compelled to-night to nominate a Provisional Government."

Meanwhile the highest army officers in the Stavka, the Chief of Staff, General Alekseev, and the Quartermaster-General, Lukomsky, had become convinced that only the abdication of the Tsar could save the monarchy and preserve authority and discipline in the army. On the morning of the 15th Alekseev communicated with the commanders of the various fronts, outlining the situation in the capital and urging them to join in an appeal to the Tsar to abdicate. The tones of the responses were varied; General Brussilov, leader

of the successful advance against the Austrians in the summer of 1916, was most outspoken in suggesting to the Tsar that abdication was the sole means of saving the situation, the dynasty and Russia's capacity to continue the war. At the other extreme General Sakharov, on the Rumanian Front, who had refused to express an opinion until he knew the views of all the other commanders, gave vent to strong expressions about the "bandit gang of people, called the Duma, treacherously exploiting a convenient moment for carrying out their criminal designs." But, having saved his monarchist face by this outburst, Sakharov also counselled acceptance of the demand for abdication. By two-thirty in the afternoon Alekseev was able to communicate to the Tsar, through Ruzsky, the opinions of Brussilov, of General Evert, the commander of the Western Front, and of the Grand Duke Nicholas Nicholaevitch, Viceroy of the Caucasus, all of whom favored abdication. Alekseev urged the Tsar to take a decision, on the grounds that delay threatened Russia with destruction, that it was impossible to vouch for the further maintenance of army discipline and that the interference of the army in internal politics would mean "the inevitable end of the war, Russia's shame and dissolution."

General Ruzsky, with Generals Danilov and Savitch, was promptly received by the Tsar in the presence of the aged Minister of the Court, Count Fredericks. Ruzsky read the telegrams of the various commanders and added his personal opinion that abdication was unavoidable. The Tsar was thunderstruck by this desertion of the highest generals, and was especially influenced by the telegram of the Grand Duke Nicholas Nicholaevitch. His decision to grant a responsible ministry had been taken slowly and reluctantly; his decision to abdicate was taken almost instantaneously. He addressed to Alekseev a telegram worded as follows:

"In the name of the welfare, tranquillity and salvation of my warmly beloved Russia I am ready to abdicate from the throne in favor of my son. I request all to serve him truly and faithfully."

A second telegram of similar content was addressed to the President of the Duma; but before the messages could be sent information arrived that two of the Duma leaders, Guchkov and Shulgin, would arrive in Pskov in the evening. The Tsar asked to have the telegrams back; but General Ruzsky, fearing a change of intention, did not return them, but merely delayed their despatch. The Stavka received the decisive news of the Tsar's decision after

three in the afternoon in the form of a telegram from Ruzsky, stating that the Tsar had decided to renounce his throne in favor of his son, with his brother Michael as Regent, and requesting that an act of abdication be framed. This was done, at Alekseev's request, by Quartermaster-General Lukomsky and the head of the diplomatic department of the Stavka, Bazili; and the projected manifesto was quickly despatched to Ruzsky.

Meanwhile the last forlorn efforts to save the monarchy were being made by the Duma leaders in Petrograd. Anxious to avoid and forestall any action by the Soviet, Shulgin and Guchkov, with the approval of the other members of the Duma Committee, slipped away in the afternoon in semi-conspirative fashion in a special train, consisting of an engine and a parlor-car, bound for Pskov. Simultaneously with their departure, on the afternoon of the 15th, Milyukov decided to test the effect of the proposed shift to constitutional monarchy in a speech before the mixed throng that crowded the Catherine Hall of the Tauride Palace.

Beginning with some popular phrases of denunciation of the old regime Milyukov announced the names and characteristics of some of the members of the new government. Here he was exposed to some heckling, one auditor shouting, "Who elected you?"—to which the speaker quickly retorted: "The Russian Revolution elected us." A reference to the Premier, Prince Lvov, as the representative of Russian organized society elicited the disparaging comment: "Propertied society." But the real storm burst out when Milyukov came to the question of the form of government and announced that after the Tsar's abdication or deposition the power would pass to Grand Duke Michael, as Regent, with Aleksei as the heir. There was much commotion, accompanied by cries: "That's the old dynasty." The popular discontent was not appeased by Milyukov's defense of the decision:

"We cannot leave without reply and without decision the question of the form of the state order. We conceive it as a parliamentary and constitutional monarchy. Perhaps others conceive it otherwise. But if we will dispute about this now, instead of deciding the question promptly, Russia will fall into a condition of civil war and the regime that has just been destroyed will rise again. We have no right to do this . . . But as soon as the danger passes and a stable peace is established we shall proceed to the preparation of the convocation of a constituent assembly, on the basis of general, direct, equal and secret balloting. The freely elected popular representative body will decide who expressed the public opinion of Russia more faithfully, we or our opponents." [26]

These arguments were far from convincing to the vast majority of the revolutionary Petrograd population; and Milyukov himself tells how late in the evening of the same day a throng of highly excited officers appeared in the Tauride Palace, insisting that they could not return to their regiments unless Milyukov repudiated his words. With a view to allaying the disturbance Milyukov gave the assurance that his statement represented only his personal opinion. This was really inaccurate, because the majority of the members of the Duma Committee favored the constitutional monarchical solution. But it was impossible to defend it against the waves of popular discontent.

It was a bad omen for the success of the mission of Shulgin and Guchkov that their improvised train was detained at Luga by insurgent soldiers and workers, who were only convinced with considerable difficulty that the journey of the Duma deputies pursued no counterrevolutionary ends.[27] As a result they arrived in Pskov with some delay about ten in the evening. They were immediately conducted into the salon-car of the imperial train and the Tsar in a Caucasian military uniform soon entered and greeted them. General Ruzsky, Count Fredericks and Major-General Narishkin, chief of the imperial military travelling office, were present at the interview. Guchkov, who together with Shulgin was still in ignorance of the Tsar's earlier decision to give up the throne, spoke at some length, depicting the turmoil in Petrograd, pointing out that "the extreme elements now regard me, Rodzianko and other moderate members of the Duma as traitors" and suggesting that Russia, the monarchical principle and the dynasty could be saved if the Tsar would transfer the burden of government to other hands.[28]

The Tsar accepted the proposal to abdicate with a readiness that surprised the delegates, but introduced an unexpected change in the original project by declaring that he wished to abdicate not only for himself, but also for his son, with whom he did not desire to be parted, because of his illness. During the afternoon the Tsar had talked with the court physician, Dr. Fedorov, who told him that the hæmophilia from which his son suffered was an incurable disease; and this was, in all probability, the dominant motive in inducing Nicholas II to alter his original decision.

Guchkov and Shulgin were somewhat confounded by this change of plan, but after brief hesitation they accepted the Tsar's decision. Guchkov proffered a project of abdication for the consideration of Nicholas II; the latter, however, preferred the text which had been

drawn up in the Stavka. Withdrawing for a short time he corrected this manifesto in order to provide that the succession should pass not to his son, but to his brother Michael, signed the document and, returning to the salon-car, handed to Guchkov the act which signalized the final departure of the Romanov dynasty from the Russian historical scene. It was worded in sonorous oldfashioned phraseology, of which the last paragraph is characteristic:

"In the name of the warmly beloved motherland we summon all faithful sons of the fatherland to fulfill their duty before him [the new Tsar], to obey the Tsar in the difficult moment of national trial and to help him, along with the representatives of the people, to bring the Russian state on the road of victory, prosperity and glory. May God succor Russia. Nicholas. Minister of the Imperial Court Count Fredericks. City Pskov. March 2, 1917.[29] 3 o'clock."

The manifesto was purposely predated by some hours in order to avoid the impression that it had been extorted from the Tsar by the Duma delegates. With a view to preserving the appearance of continuity in the government Nicholas II signed two further documents, one appointing Prince Lvov Premier, the other nominating as commander-in-chief the Grand Duke Nicholas Nicholaevitch. Both these documents were dated 2 P.M. The procedure was completed shortly before midnight.

Throughout the ceremony the Tsar preserved the curious masklike impassivity which characterized his behavior at critical moments. It was left to the brilliant monarchist publicist Shulgin to indulge in romantic laments over the fallen dynasty.

Guchkov and Shulgin promptly returned to Petrograd, where Shulgin delivered an improvised speech to a small casual crowd at the railroad station and elicited a few cheers with his proclamation of Tsar Michael II. Guchkov, however, went into the railroad workshops and encountered such a hostile attitude of the workers not only to the idea of a new Tsar, but even to the Provisional Government that he was glad to get out without physical injury. The last episode in the passing of the Tsarist regime occurred in the Grand Duke Michael's apartment on Millionaya Street in Petrograd on the morning of the 16th.

Most of the members of the Duma Committee gathered to learn his decision as to the acceptance of the throne. Curiously enough it was the veteran liberal Professor Milyukov who was still insistent for the assumption of the imperial title by the Grand Duke, while even such a convinced monarchist as Shulgin refused to take the

responsibility of advising Michael to endeavor to ascend the throne under such unfavorable circumstances.

Pale from sleepless nights, his voice hoarse and broken from endless speeches, Milyukov put forward his pleas for the preservation of the monarchy:

"If you decline, Your Highness, there will be ruin. Because Russia will lose its axis. The monarch is the axis, the sole axis of the country. Around what will the Russian masses rally? If you refuse there will be anarchy, chaos, bloodshed. . . ."

Kerensky presented the main argument on the other side: "You will not save Russia by accepting the throne. On the contrary. I know the sentiment of the mass of soldiers and workers. Bitter dissatisfaction is now directed just against the monarchy. Just this question will be the cause of sanguinary confusion. And this at a time when Russia needs complete unity. Therefore I appeal to Your Highness as a Russian to a Russian. I implore you in the name of Russia to make this sacrifice. If it is a sacrifice. Because I haven't the right to conceal the perils to which you will be personally exposed, should you decide to accept the throne. I cannot vouch for the life of Your Highness."

This last argument seems to have weighed heavily with the Grand Duke; for he took Rodzianko aside before making his decision and asked directly whether the latter could guaranty his life. The stout President of the Duma, sadly worn and depressed by the events of the last days, was obliged to answer in the negative, because, in his own words, "I had no reliable armed force behind me." [30] Then the Grand Duke returned to the general gathering and announced that under the circumstances he could not accept the throne.

Kerensky, whose sentimentality sometimes verged on buffoonery, burst out: "Your Highness. You are a noble man. I will say everywhere that you are a noble man." To this Milyukov adds the somewhat acid comment:

"The poetry of Kerensky was in poor harmony with the prose of the decision which had been taken. Behind it was felt not love and pain for Russia but only fear for himself."

It would have been an adventurous decision, indeed, to assert a claim to the throne before the excited throngs of workers and soldiers with red flags which were still demonstrating in the streets of Petrograd. And Michael was not of an adventurous nature. In England or Denmark he would have been an admirable constitutional monarch. In revolutionary Russia he was doomed to be

slaughtered, with many members of his family during the ferocious civil war in the Urals in 1918.

After his abdication Nicholas II returned to the Stavka in Moghilev. He made three requests of the Provisional Government: to remain in Tsarskoe Syelo until his family recovered, to travel then to Port Romanov, on the Murman Coast, evidently as a point of departure from the country, and to live in his favorite summer palace at Livadia, in the Crimea, after the end of the War. The amiable Prince Lvov in a cipher telegram dated March 19 granted the Tsar's requests as regards residence in Tsarskoe Syelo and transportation to Port Romanov. It was evidently the desire of the Provisional Government to permit the imperial family to find an asylum in England, because Foreign Minister Milyukov on March 21 asked the British Ambassador, Sir George Buchanan, for authorization to this effect; and this was conveyed by Buchanan on the 23d.[31]

Meanwhile the Soviet in its session of March 16 had decided to insist on the arrest of the former Tsar and the members of his family; and the Provisional Government, yielding to this pressure, issued a decree to the effect that the former Tsar and Tsarina should be deprived of liberty on March 20. The formal ceremony of arrest was carried out on the 21st at Moghilev; and the Tsar was escorted to Tsarskoe Syelo by a commission consisting of four members of the Duma. On the same day General Kornilov, the new commander of the Petrograd garrison, formally announced to the Tsarina at Tsarskoe Syelo that she must consider herself under arrest. The arrest of the former rulers did not necessarily conflict with the idea of sending them to England; indeed Kerensky expressly stated in a speech at Moscow on the 20th that the Tsar and his family would be sent to England.

But, as often happened in those days, the Provisional Government reckoned without the Soviet, which in turn was under the pressure of the masses of workers and soldiers which had anything but kindly feelings for the representatives of the fallen dynasty. Excited by the rumor that the Tsar would be sent abroad the Executive Committee of the Soviet on March 22 adopted a strongly worded resolution, proposing to occupy all the railroad stations with revolutionary troops, to arrest the Tsar and to imprison him in the bastion of the grim Fortress of Peter and Paul. This last resolution was not carried out; but the Soviet obtained from the Provisional Government a pledge that the former Tsar would not be permitted to leave the country without the special permission of the Executive

Committee. The members of the imperial family remained under arrest in their palace at Tsarskoe Syelo until they were transferred to the remote town of Tobolsk, in Siberia, in the summer. They were predestined victims of the subsequent rising tide of revolutionary passion.

The former Tsar's nomination of the Grand Duke Nicholas Nicholaevitch as commander-in-chief of the army remained as ineffectual as his abdication in favor of his brother Michael. As early as the evening of March 19 Prince Lvov, significantly commenting, "Events carry us along; we don't guide events," informed Alekseev that the tide of popular animosity to the Romanovs was too strong to make it possible for the Grand Duke to assume command of the army.[32] Alekseev, who was already dismayed by symptoms of declining discipline in the army and navy and especially by the appearance, in the immediate rear zone, of what he characterized as "undisciplined bands" of revolutionary agitators, argued strongly for the retention of the Grand Duke, in whose appointment he saw a guaranty for the discipline and unity of the army. But Lvov and Guchkov were adamant; and Alekseev himself very reluctantly, on account of his poor health and his pessimistic appraisal of the situation, agreed to take over the supreme command. The Grand Duke would indeed have been an impossible candidate in view of the fact that the Soviet had already passed a resolution calling for his arrest.

As a result of a misunderstanding the Grand Duke was not notified of the Government's change of intention; and on March 24 actually arrived in Moghilev and formally took over the command. He was quickly notified of the changed situation and was sent under house arrest to his Crimean estate.

The Romanov autocracy, with three centuries of traditional absolutism behind it, fell not as a result of any carefully planned conspiracy or *coup d'état*, but as a result of an unorganized, almost anarchical popular movement, the success of which was the measure of the inner weakness and decadence of the old order. So completely discredited was the fallen dynasty that during the subsequent civil war no outstanding leader of the anti-Bolshevik forces dared to write "Restoration of the Romanovs" on his banner. But although the old order had passed forever the outlines of the new were uncommonly vague in these confused and hectic March days. The Provisional Government was but a pale ghost of authority; the Soviet, although it possessed more real power, was still very uncertain both as to the extent of its strength and as to the use to

which this strength should be put. Vladimir Ilyitch Lenin, the man who was to impose on the Russian Revolution its final form, was still pacing the streets of dull, respectable, middleclass Zürich, conjuring up one scheme after another for crossing the inhospitable battle-fronts that separated him from his native country, which, as he instinctively realized, was ripe as never before for social upheaval on the grand scale.

NOTES

[1] "Correspondence of Nicholas and Alexandra Romanov," Vol. V, p. 128.

[2] See the Socialist Revolutionary newspaper, *Dyelo Naroda* (Cause of the People), No. 1, March 15, 1917.

[3] N. Sukhanov, "Memoirs of Revolution," Vol. I, p. 16.

[4] See Kaourov's article, "Six Days of the February Revolution," in the magazine *Proletarskaya Revolutsia* (Proletarian Revolution), No. 1 (13), 1923.

[5] Shlyapnikov, "The Year 1917," Vol. I, p. 99.

[6] See the informing brochure of E. I. Martinov, "The Tsarist Army in the February Revolution," p. 59.

[7] See the testimony of Protopopov in "The Fall of the Tsarist Regime," Vol. IV, p. 92.

[8] Shlyapnikov, *op. cit.*, Vol. I, p. 73.

[9] See the article "Diplomacy and Revolution," by Professor Storozhev, in *The Messenger of the People's Commissariat for Foreign Affairs,* No. 4–5, for 1920.

[10] Shlyapnikov, *op. cit.*, p. 86.

[11] See article by Alexander Blok, "The Last Days of the Old Regime," in magazine *Biloe* (The Past), No. 15, p. 28.

[12] See Khabalov's testimony in "The Fall of the Tsarist Regime," Vol. I, p. 203.

[13] General A. S. Lukomsky, "Reminiscences," Vol. I, p. 126.

[14] See article "February Revolution" in Volume XXI of magazine, *The Red Archives,* pp. 1–78. This article with its continuation in Volume XXII, pp. 3–70, gives a very complete picture of the developments in the Stavka, on the basis of documents taken from the Moscow Central Military-Historical Archives.

[15] Lukomsky, *op. cit.*, Vol. I, p. 125.

[16] Shulgin, "Days," reprinted in "February Revolution," in the series "Revolution and Civil War in the Narratives of White Guards," p. 99.

[17] Sukhanov, *op. cit.*, Vol. I, pp. 131ff.

[18] Shlyapnikov, *op. cit.*, Vol. I, p. 178.

[18a] Individual Bolsheviki, even at this early date, sponsored the idea that the Soviet should constitute a temporary government, up to the convocation of a constituent assembly. Shlyapnikov, *op. cit.*, pp. 193–194, cites the text of a resolution to this effect which was passed at a meeting of Bolshevik Party members in the Viborg District. But the Petrograd Committee forbade the circulation of this report and the official Bolshevik resolution, published in *Izvestia* of March 13, urges the creation of a provisional revolutionary government without mentioning the Soviet.

[19] See the text of Mrozovsky's telegrams in the previously cited article in Vol. XXI of *The Red Archives.*

[20] This estimate was made by the Statistical Department of the Petrograd City Council.

[21] Zaslavsky and Kantorowicz, "Chronicle of the February Revolution," Vol. I, p. 56.

[22] The best account of the origin of Order No. 1 is to be found in Sukhanov, *op. cit.*, pp. 262–267.

[23] Milyukov, "History of the Second Russian Revolution," Vol. I, pp. 47ff.

[24] See text of the Soviet declaration in N. Avdeev, "Revolution of 1917," Vol. I, p. 190.

[25] Lukomsky, *op. cit.*, Vol. I, p. 138.

[26] Milyukov, *op. cit.*, Vol. I, pp. 55ff.

[27] Martinov, *op. cit.*, p. 166.

[28] *Ibid.*, pp. 167ff.

[29] The manifesto was dated according to the old Russian calendar.

[30] See Rodzianko's article "The February Revolution and the State Duma," in "The Archive of the Russian Revolution," Vol. VI, p. 62.

[31] Sir George Buchanan, "My Mission to Russia and Other Diplomatic Memories," Vol. II, pp. 104ff.

[32] See *The Red Archives*, Vol. XXII, pp. 3–70.

CHAPTER V

FIRST STEPS OF THE NEW REGIME

THE Provisional Government that replaced the fallen autocracy was weak to the point of impotence. It was conspicuously lacking in all the means by which a state normally enforces its authority. The Tsarist regime was supported on tradition, on a bureaucracy that was often venal and inefficient but that still had acquired some administrative experience, on the army and police. The Provisional Government not only missed all these old supports of centralized authority, but failed to create any new ones.

It was not bound to the masses by ties of leadership in the revolutionary struggle. The Western ideals of parliamentarism, civil liberty, respect for private property on which the new regime took its stand had struck little root in Russia and appealed primarily to the very small educated minority of the population. Most important of all, the two agencies on which every government relies, in the last resort, to compel the obedience of refractory citizens, the police and the army, were in the highest degree unreliable, from the standpoint of the Provisional Government. The old police was so hatefully identified in the public mind with the Tsarist order that it could not be retained in the service of the new state. The old policemen, as a general rule, were dismissed and, if fit for military service, sent to the front. They were replaced by an inexperienced and undependable militia. The regiments of the Petrograd garrison which, by their mutiny, had overthrown Nicholas II had no enthusiasm or particular respect for Prince Lvov, Milyukov and the other members of the Provisional Government. The first desire of the Petrograd troops, as their subsequent conduct eloquently proved, was not under any conditions to be sent to the front. The second desire of most of them, as peasants, was to obtain a slice of the neighboring landlord's estate. The other garrisons in the rear quickly followed the example of Petrograd in throwing off the reins of discipline. And, while the disintegration of the armies at the front proceeded at a somewhat slower pace than that in the rear, there was no military unit that could be relied on to support the Pro-

visional Government in an effort to assert its authority, especially in the event of a clash with the Soviet.

Eloquent testimony to the complete helplessness of the Provisional Government in the first days of its existence is furnished by a letter which War Minister Guchkov despatched to General Alekseev on March 22.[1] "The Provisional Government," wrote Guchkov, "possesses no real power and its orders are executed only in so far as this is permitted by the Soviet of Workers' and Soldiers' Deputies, which holds in its hands the most important elements of actual power, such as troops, railroads, postal and telegraph service. It is possible to say directly that the Provisional Government exists only while this is permitted by the Soviet of Workers' and Soldiers' Deputies. Especially in the military department it is possible now only to issue orders which do not basically conflict with the decisions of the above mentioned Soviet."

If the Provisional Government represented little more than a shadow of authority in the capital, where the support of the workers and, even more important, of the armed soldiers, was always on the side of the Soviet, its influence was even fainter in the rural districts,[2] where the commissars whom it nominated to succeed the old governors possessed little power except that of persuasion, while the township and village committees elected by the peasants paid little attention to instructions from the centre. It is only against this background of virtual paralysis of central governmental authority that the rapid sweep of social revolution during the period from the downfall of Tsarism to the coming of Bolshevism is understandable. The extreme weakness of the central government was at once an effect and a cause of the four powerful currents that finally swept the Provisional Government into oblivion along with its Tsarist predecessor: the gigantic mutiny of the Russian Army; the drive of the Russian peasants for the long desired broad acres of the large estate owners; the growing demand of the workers, first for higher wages and shorter hours, then for control of industry; and the impulse of the non-Russian nationalities to assert their right to far-reaching autonomy, if not actual separation.

The full measure of the weakness of the Government and of the violence of subsequent upheavals was not visible at first. This was because the country in the early period of the new order was indulging in an orgy of sentimental speechmaking and fraternization, in which the sharper edges of class and party antagonisms were to some extent rubbed off. Broadly speaking there were three main trends

of opinion about the line which the development of the Revolution should take. All the parties to the right of the Cadets simply disappeared after the Revolution, with the result that the Cadets, who had been regarded as a liberal if not a radical party under Tsarism, now became a bulwark of conservatism. At their Party Congress in Petrograd, which was held from April 7 until April 10, the Cadets pronounced in favor of a democratic republic, despite the previous efforts of their leader, Milyukov, to save the dynasty during the March Revolution.

The first of the three trends, represented by the Cadets and by some very right-wing socialist groups, was that Russia should become a republic with a West European type of constitution, that the war should be carried on in agreement with the Allies and that basic social and economic changes should be postponed at least until the holding of the constituent assembly, if not until after the end of the War. At the other extreme the Bolsheviki, supported by a few of the more left-wing Socialist Revolutionaries, stressed the importance of drastic domestic innovations, such as the confiscation of the large estates, adopted an attitude of distrustful criticism toward the Provisional Government, supported every effort to curb and restrict the power of the officers in the army and called for a vigorous campaign against the war on the part of the working classes of all countries. Between these two extremes lay the position of the parties which dominated the Soviets during the first months of their existence, the Mensheviki and the Socialist Revolutionaries. This position, which acquired various shadings at different periods of time, was that the Provisional Government should be supported, with some reservations and with a certain amount of pressure and control from the side of the Soviet, that there should be an effort to enlist international workingclass support to force all governments to renounce imperialistic aims and thereby pave the way for a peace without annexations and indemnities, but that Russia should carry on the war, as a matter of national self-defense, until the conditions for a general peace were achieved.

The clay feet of the Provisional Government were only gradually recognized abroad. In the beginning the impression gained ground in foreign countries, partly as a result of a telegram sent out by the new Foreign Minister, Milyukov, that the Duma had played a much more spirited and active part in the Revolution than had actually been the case. There was also the belief, comforting to the Allied powers, but quite without historical foundation, that the Revolution

was a protest against the suspected pro-German influences at the Tsarist court and indicated a more vigorous prosecution of the war by Russia. The American Ambassador, David Francis, was the first diplomat to extend recognition to the Provisional Government on March 22; and the Ambassadors of England, France and Italy followed his example on the 24th.

The new regime was prompt in carrying out its programme of sweeping away the more oppressive restrictions of Tsarism. A manifesto promulgated on March 20 restored the Finnish constitution, which had been repeatedly violated with a view to Russifying the country under Nicholas II, and granted Finland full autonomy. On the 29th the independence of Poland was recognized. Inasmuch as all ethnographically Polish territory at this time was occupied by the forces of the Central powers this act had only declarative importance.

The Provisional Government on April 2 decided "to abolish all legal limitations on the rights of Russian citizens, based on faith or nationality." This decree primarily benefited the Jews, who were subjected to many discriminations under Tsarism in such matters as residence, ownership of property and right of entrance into high-schools and universities; other races also obtained the right to use non-Russian languages in business transactions. The death penalty was abolished on March 25; and courts-martial were eliminated, except in the region of the front, on the 26th. While such changes elicited no criticism, with the possible exception of muttered grumblings on the part of adherents of the old regime, there were other problems for which the Provisional Government was unable to find quick and easy solutions.

While news of the Revolution penetrated slowly into the log cabins and thatched-roof huts of the Russian villages, isolated cases of agrarian disorder in Kazan Province were reported as early as March 22, and on the 30th the Government found it desirable to issue an appeal to the people on the land question in which it declared that "the land question cannot be solved by means of any kind of seizure" and promised to collect preliminary material on agrarian problems for the use of the future popular representative assembly.[8] This appeal was later repeated in stronger form on May 4 when the Government, under the influence of the growing agrarian disorder, appointed a Main Land Committee, which was to collect material on which future agrarian legislation could be based, and local land committees, composed of representatives of

various classes and organizations, which were to mediate in cases of quarrels on land questions. At this time the Premier, Prince Lvov, and the Minister for Agriculture, A. Shingarev, issued an appeal with the following warning:

"A great disaster threatens our motherland if the population in the rural districts, without waiting for the decision of the Constituent Assembly, itself undertakes the immediate readjustment of land relations. Such arbitrary activities threaten general destruction. The fields will remain unsown and the harvest will not be reaped. Need and hunger will come to the country."

But reasons and arguments for delay were far more cogent to the city professor and agrarian expert, conscious of the complexity of the Russian land problem and of the difficulty of attaining a theoretically perfect solution, than to the bearded peasant in his sheepskin coat in the village. To the latter the new period of weak, almost non-existent authority seemed a marvellous opportunity to reverse the results of 1905 and to proceed to a new onset on the coveted land of the country gentry. Because of the isolation and ignorance of the peasants and because winter snow still covered the fields (agrarian movements in Russia habitually reached the greatest pitch of intensity during the sowing and harvesting seasons) the peasant was less active in the first weeks of the Revolution than the worker and soldier. But he remained, so long as his land hunger was unsatisfied, a powerful, perhaps a decisive if unconscious reserve force on the side of the advocates of extreme social revolution.

The first mutterings of agrarian upheaval created all the more anxiety for the Provisional Government because of the difficulty of feeding the swollen cities and the enormous army. This difficulty became so acute that the Provisional Government on April 7 proclaimed a state monopoly of grain, decreeing that all grain which was not required for the nourishment of the agriculturists and their domestic animals and for seed should be sold to state organizations at fixed prices.

The industrial workers also began to display considerable activity. The eight-hour day had been one of the unrealized objectives of the workers in the 1905 Revolution. Now, however, the relation of strength had changed decisively in favor of the workers. An agreement between the Petrograd factory-owners and the Soviet providing for the introduction of the eight-hour day and also for the establishment of factory committees, to be elected by the

workers, and of a system of arbitration for industrial disputes was signed on March 23. It was expedited in some cases by "direct action" on the part of the workers who simply refused to work more than eight hours at a number of factories. There was more opposition on the part of the Moscow industrialists; and in that city the Soviet on March 31 decided to introduce the eight-hour day without waiting for the decree of the Provisional Government.[4] This represented a substantial social gain for the workers, because in 1913 only 119,000 of Russia's 2,218,000 industrial workers enjoyed a working day of eight hours or less, while 1,351,000 worked ten hours a day or more.[5] Here and there, along with the agitation for a shorter working day, cases were reported of arrests of engineers by workers and of forcible removal from the factories of unpopular foremen.[6] Such developments could not yet be called typical; but the workers were already conscious of a new sense of power. The police guards who were formerly stationed at factories to maintain order had disappeared. The new militia was to a considerable extent recruited from workers. The old relations of private capitalism were not yet shattered; but they were becoming distinctly shaky.

By far the most urgent and serious problem which confronted the Provisional Government at the very outset was that of the War. This problem had two main aspects: the maintenance of discipline in the armed forces and the working out of conditions under which the prosecution of hostilities could command the support of the main representative body of the masses, the Soviet.

The central government, the generals and the officers never regained the hold on the army that was broken by the rebellion of the Petrograd garrison and some of its immediate sequels, such as the promulgation of Order Number One and the exemption of the Petrograd garrison from service at the front. A further blow to the authority of the officers and to the fighting capacity of the army was the Declaration of the Rights of Soldiers, which was adopted at a meeting of the Soldiers' Soviet on March 22 and published in *Izvestia,* the official organ of the Soviet, on March 28. This declaration took away from the officers the right to have orderlies; gave soldiers and officers the right to wear civilian clothes outside of service, deprived officers of the right to impose disciplinary punishments, abolished compulsory saluting and the political censorship of letters and literature and asserted the right of the soldiers to "internal organization," which was meant to authorize the elected committees which now grew up in the military units. A govern-

mental commission under the chairmanship of General Polivanov, which worked in close contact with the Soldiers' Soviet, subsequently gave legal sanction to many of these changes; but for the majority of the soldiers the published resolution of the Soviet was quite sufficient.

That the Tsarist military regulations were in some respects grossly humiliating to the soldier and that a thoroughgoing revision of these regulations was essential after the autocracy had given way to a democratic regime is scarcely open to dispute. Under the rules of service for 1913 the private soldier was forbidden to ride inside streetcars, to eat in public restaurants, except in the thirdclass buffets of railroad stations and passenger-boats, to receive books or newspapers without the permission of his commanding officers, to belong to any societies with political ends, to attend lectures or theatrical performances, unless permission was secured from a superior officer. Such regulations were not calculated to raise the dignity of the soldier in his own eyes or in that of the population; and, together with the brutal forms of corporal punishment which were sometimes practised in the old army, were naturally marked for elimination. But Order Number One and the Declaration of the Rights of Soldiers, in some of their provisions, went far beyond what the most liberal conception of army discipline would have regarded as compatible with military efficiency. They took the actual control of the troops out of the hands of the officers; and under such conditions even an army composed of more educated soldiers than the illiterate or semi-literate peasants who made up a large part of the Russian army could not have retained fighting capacity. The old general and the Socialist member of the Soviet might dispute as to whether the main responsibility for the break-up of the army rested on the old regime with its harsh and brutal discipline, its incompetent conduct of the War or on the Soviets with their newfangled conceptions of army organization; it is also debatable whether, if such organizations as the Soviets and the army committees had not existed, the mutiny of the soldiers might not have proceeded in more ferocious forms than it actually assumed. But only a blind optimism, accompanied by inexperience in military affairs, could have regarded the Russian army of 1917, where meetings were more popular than drill and any officer's order was apt to be questioned as "counterrevolutionary," as a force capable of offering serious resistance to the German and Austrian forces. A substantially accurate picture of the condition of the army is pre-

sented in the following expressions of General Alekseev's letter to War Minister Guchkov of April 29.[7]

"Discipline in the army is declining every day. . . . The authority of the officers has fallen, and there is no power to reëstablish it. The spirit of the officers' corps is falling more and more as a result of the undeserved insults and acts of violence which are inflicted upon officers, under the influence of their removal from actual power over their subordinates or the transfer of this authority to the soldiers' committees. . . . Pacifist sentiment develops in the armies. The masses of the soldiers don't admit the idea either of aggressive activities or of preparation for them. . . . Defeatist literature and propaganda have taken firm root in the army. . . . With great surprise I read the reports of irresponsible persons about the 'splendid' sentiment of the army. To what purpose? We don't deceive the Germans and for ourselves this is fatal selfdeception."

In retrospect it seems surprising that, in view of the hopeless state of the army, there was not a stronger movement in favor of a separate peace, which probably could have been obtained at this time on terms considerably less onerous than Germany prescribed in the following year at Brest-Litovsk. Nabokov, a Cadet who filled the post of administrative secretary in the Provisional Government, tells in his memoirs how he remarked to Guchkov early in April, after the War Minister had made a very pessimistic report: "If this is correct, then a separate peace with Germany is necessary." Guchkov did not agree with this proposition, but had no counter argument. Milyukov's view, according to Nabokov, was: "Perhaps something will be preserved as a result of the War; without the War everything would break up more quickly."[8]

The Cadets were so thoroughly committed to the idea of prosecution of the War in close union with the Allies that they could not change this orientation and merely attempted the task, quite foredoomed to failure, of attempting to restore discipline in an army that was rapidly turning into a mass of armed peasants, eager to return home and plunder the nearest landlord's estate.

As for the leaders of the Soviet, while they differed sharply with the Cadets in regarding the War as a capitalist and imperialist conflict which should be stopped as soon as possible by the combined efforts of the workers of all countries, they shrank from the responsibility of a separate peace. Moreover, it was almost a matter of honor with the Soviet leaders to deny or at least to minimize evidences of dissolution and break-up in "the revolutionary army."

The differing viewpoints of the Provisional Government, especially of its Foreign Minister, Milyukov, and of the Soviet

about War aims and about the emphasis which should be placed on various objectives of the conflict swiftly came to the surface. On March 27 the Petrograd Soviet, the leaders of which took the international significance of the Russian Revolution very seriously, issued a manifesto to the "peoples of the whole world," with the following appeal for concerted popular action for speedy peace:

"The time has come to begin a decisive struggle with the acquisitive aspirations of the governments of other countries. The time has come for the peoples to take into their own hands the questions of war and peace. In the consciousness of its revolutionary strength the Russian democracy declares that it will by all means oppose the acquisitive policy of the ruling classes and summons the peoples of Europe to decisive manifestations in favor of peace."

The spirit of this manifesto, which produced far more effect in Russia than in the foreign countries to which it was addressed, could scarcely be reconciled with Foreign Minister Milyukov's statement to representatives of the press on April 5 [9] that Russia looked to the coming peace conference for confirmation of its claims to "the Ukrainian lands of Austria-Hungary," to Constantinople and the Dardanelles, the acquisition of which had always been considered "an ancient national problem of Russia." Milyukov describes his own foreign policy in the following terms: [10]

"It was carried on in the spirit of traditional union with the Allies, excluding the thought that the Revolution could weaken the international significance of Russia by a sharp change of orientation and by a change of viewpoint in regard to agreements which had been concluded and obligations which had been assumed. . . . In all his declarations the Foreign Minister vigorously emphasized the pacifist aims of the liberating war, but always placed them in close connection with the national problems and interests of Russia."

Milyukov's conception of "pacifist aims" was decidedly not in harmony with that of the Soviet leaders; and a manifesto which the Provisional Government issued to the people of Russia on April 10, making concessions to both viewpoints, only postponed the first major crisis of the new regime, which occurred on the issue of Milyukov's foreign policy early in May. The manifesto of April 10 declared that "the aim of free Russia is not domination over other peoples, deprivation of their national possessions, violent acquisition of alien territory." At the same time the manifesto contained the more aggressive if somewhat obscure phrase, inserted by the Cadet Kokoshkin, that "the Russian people will not permit

that the motherland should come out of the great struggle humiliated and undermined in its vital forces."

The first weeks of the new regime were characterized by feverish organization and an endless flood of talk. Socialist parties and trade-unions, proscribed or barely tolerated under Tsarism, sprang into life and activity. With the long crust of censorship and repression broken, people of all classes felt the impulse to meet, discuss, pronounce speeches. The fullest liberty of speech and press had been decreed; and there was no power that could have enforced restrictions, even if any had existed. So meetings and speeches went on everywhere, at congresses of parties and organizations, on public squares and street corners.

The most significant development of this early stage of the Revolution was the emergence all over the country of Soviets of Workers' and Soldiers' Deputies. In general character and plan of organization the provincial Soviets followed Petrograd fairly closely, although the political complexion of local Soviets varied with circumstances. It is eloquently symptomatic of the numerical weakness and the political inexperience of the Russian middle class that it was able neither to find representation in the Soviets nor to create counter-organizations of its own of any popular weight or significance. By effectively barring the road to middleclass democratic evolution in Russian political life the Tsarist regime unconsciously but none the less surely paved the way for Bolshevism.

The Petrograd Soviet, as it was first constituted, was more like a mass meeting than a deliberative assembly. It had almost three thousand members; and the 160,000 soldiers of the garrison, as a result of the practise of allowing representation to every military unit, however small, had two and a half times as many deputies as the 400,000 workers of the capital. Later the rules of representation were changed and the rule was adopted of one representative to every two thousand electors, whether workers or soldiers.[11] The decisions of the Soviet were largely framed by the Executive Committee; but this body also grew to unwieldy size, and early in April its functions were largely delegated to a bureau of twenty-four members, an organization which included the more prominent representatives of all parties in the Soviet.

What was a typical day's work for the Soviet Executive Committee? The protocol of the session of April 6[12] gives a fair idea of the number and variety of problems, big and small, urgent and trivial, which came up for the decision of this improvised legislative

body. First there was a report about the discovery of a Tsarist police document recommending that efforts be taken to prevent a union of the Social Democratic parties. Then a decision was taken to send a commission to the southern provinces with a view to warding off the danger of pogroms. The third item on the agenda was a decision that the bakers of Petrograd must carry on their work without interruption. Then there was discussion of the case of a newspaper *The Kopeck,* which was crowded in its office because of the intrusion of the Soviet organ *Izvestia,* and a decision to open negotiations for the taking over of the Anichkov Palace for the use of the Soviet. Then it was decided to post up all over the city the decision of the central food committee that the bread ration should be fixed at one and a half pounds a day for people engaged in physical labor and a pound a day for others. There were reports about negotiations with the Provisional Government (the carelessly kept protocol does not state the subject of the negotiations) about issuing a newspaper for the soldiers, about some obscure point in connection with the Fortress of Peter and Paul, about a quarrel which arose between soldiers and workers over the distribution of white bread. And finally there was the reception of the endless delegations, from the Kamishlov garrison, from the Special Army, from the American Embassy (the character of this delegation is not explained), from four thousand soldiers' wives of Smolensk, and many others.

The sessions of the Executive Committee were held under exhausting and chaotic circumstances. They began about one in the afternoon and lasted until late at night; and it was seldom that the questions on the order of the day were satisfactorily solved. The lawyers, journalists, publicists and professional revolutionaries who predominated in the Executive Committee were mostly conspicuously lacking in the faculty of organization; moreover the sessions of the Committee were continually interrupted by the endless stream of delegates and delegations which poured in on the Soviet from all corners of the country. Debates were sketchy and imperfect; the most important decisions were sometimes taken by a purely accidental majority of votes. The delegates, with few exceptions, were physically exhausted; sleepless nights were the rule and regular meals were out of the question. The delegates were glad to snatch an occasional piece of bread and glass of tea.[13]

But, formless and disorderly as its sessions were, the Soviet more and more became the centre of Russian political life. It was

to the Soviet, not to the Provisional Government, that delegates swarmed with greetings, proposals, complaints. The more tough-minded and conservative members of the Government, such as Milyukov and Guchkov, were already probably contemplating the possibility of resignation. Some members of the Government were lulled by Kerensky's sentimental eloquence; and the weak and colorless Premier, Prince Lvov, consoled himself in the intervals between appeals to mutinous soldiers and rebellious peasants with such phrases as: "What a great happiness to live in such great days . . . The great Russian Revolution is really miraculous in its great tranquil progress." Although the conservative and prop-ertied classes would scarcely have agreed with this last state-ment, which becomes distinctly ludicrous in the light of later events, there was still no general thought of forcibly modifying the new order from the right. The energetic General Krimov, who had vainly recommended a palace revolution before the downfall of the dynasty, suggested to Lvov and Guchkov about the end of March that he should take one division of troops and "clear out Petrograd in two days, of course, not without bloodshed." [14] But several months were to elapse before General Kornilov would make a conspicuously unsuccessful attempt to put Krimov's idea into practise.

The Petrograd Soviet obtained more definite leadership and direction after the return from exile of Heracles Tseretelli, one of the Menshevik deputies of the second Duma whom Stolypin had arrested. Like the President of the Soviet, Chkheidze, Tseretelli was a Georgian. A brilliant orator with a clear and logical mind, Tseretelli was perhaps the strongest leader produced by the Soviet in its pre-Bolshevik period; and under his guidance the loose, vague, often uncoördinated resolutions and activities of the early period gave way to a more organized and definite policy, the main points of which were: prosecution of the War, combined with efforts to achieve peace on a democratic basis, and conditional support of the Provisional Government. The formula of conditional support was soon to give way to that of coalition, with representatives of the Mensheviki and Socialist Revolutionaries assuming a share of formal power and responsibility.

The first large test of Tseretelli's leadership came at the All-Russian Conference of Soviets, which opened in Petrograd on April 11. Tseretelli set forth the so-called "defensist" conception of the proper policy to be pursued in connection with the War. Expressing the hope that other peoples would soon follow the Russian example

and overthrow their governments or compel them to renounce annexationist designs, Tseretelli declared that until this happened it was a matter of honor that "the Russian Revolution should fight against the foreign enemy with the same courage which it showed against the internal forces." Opposing Tseretelli the Bolshevik spokesman, Leo Kamenev, called for the transformation of the Russian national Revolution "into a prologue to the uprising of the peoples of all the warring countries against the Moloch of war, the Moloch of Imperialism."

But the Bolshevik hour had not yet struck. When the typical interminable Russian speechmaking was over (no less than 102 delegates delivered addresses on the question) Tseretelli's resolution received 325 votes to 57 given for Kamenev's, while 20 delegates refrained from voting. The resolution was even stiffened by the inclusion of a clause about "preserving the capacity of the army for active operations." The Soviets were willing to pass warlike resolutions long after the will of the soldiers to carry them out had evaporated.

On the other major question which came under the consideration of the Conference the Bolshevik standpoint was better satisfied. Steklov, speaking on the relations between the Soviet and the Provisional Government, adopted such a hostile tone toward the latter and submitted such a sharply worded resolution about the need for constant vigilance and control that Kamenev withdrew the Bolshevik resolution on this question and accepted the one proposed by Steklov.

This Conference, held barely a month after the overthrow of the autocracy, offered striking proof of the spread of the Soviet idea among the workers and soldiers throughout the country. Among the 479 delegates were representatives of 138 local Soviets, seven armies, thirteen rear units and twenty-six front units.[15] This network of Soviets increased with the passing of time until every town of any size had its Soviet. The Conference itself hastened on the work of Soviet organization throughout the country, decreeing the organization of Soviets in places where they did not as yet exist, recommending that the Soviets of Workers' and Soldiers' Deputies, wherever possible, should be common rather than separate bodies and urging the Soviets to get in touch with peasant organizations. After the Conference the Petrograd Executive Committee took in representatives from the provincial Soviets, thus becoming an All-Russian body.

Although Petrograd to some extent occupied the leading and central rôle of Paris in the French Revolution the significance of the provincial Soviets should not be overlooked. Their existence made it impossible for the conservative classes to play off the provinces against revolutionary Petrograd. By assuming varied functions of authority they accustomed the people, even against the will and desire of the Mensheviki and Socialist Revolutionaries who dominated almost all the Soviets at the beginning, to look on the present flesh-and-blood Soviet, rather than on the future vague and somewhat unreal Constituent Assembly as the real organ of power.

While the majority of the provincial towns lagged behind Petrograd in the speed of their revolutionary development, there were conspicuous exceptions; and in several towns the authority of the local Soviet as the sole governing body was practised in the early months of the Revolution. A stronghold of extremism was Kronstadt, the island fortress near Petrograd, where no old regime officer could feel very secure as to his life and liberty. The Kronstadt Soviet raised a storm of nationwide excitement and protest when it declared on May 29: "The sole power in the city of Kronstadt is the Soviet of Workers' and Soldiers' deputies, which in all matters of state order establishes direct contact with the Petrograd Soviet of Workers' and Soldiers' Deputies." This declaration of local independence elicited a stern reprimand from the Petrograd Soviet; and after a wordy exchange of delegations and declarations (neither side in the controversy desired to resort to actual force) the Kronstadt representatives made some verbal concessions. These did not, however, alter the substance of the situation. The commissar of the Provisional Government in Kronstadt remained a mere figure-head; and the Kronstadt sailors remained reliable allies of any extremist outburst in Petrograd.

The Soviet in Krasnoyarsk, a Siberian town with active memories of 1905, also went very far in its pretensions to power. It introduced a rationing system, not only for food but also for manufactured goods, granted furloughs to soldiers, regardless of the protests of the commander of the military district, interfered in local labor disputes to the point of handing over to the trade-union sawmills and flour-mills where the employers refused to satisfy the demands of the workers.[16] Tsaritsin, on the Lower Volga, where the garrison was more than usually defiant of its commanding officers, was another early stronghold of Soviet power; and one finds

the local Soviet levying a contribution of dubious voluntariness for the benefit of the garrison on the well-to-do classes and confiscating and destroying shipments of wine and liquor on the ground that alcoholism was a source of public danger in the town. In some of the Ural factory settlements and in towns with a very strong predominance of industrial workers in the population, such as the textile centre, Ivanovo-Vosnessensk, the Soviet authority was far-reaching and effective long before there was any question of a Soviet regime on the national scale.

It is noteworthy that both in Kronstadt and in Tsaritsin the Soviets did not in the first month possess a majority of Bolshevik deputies. The mood and the degree of pressure of the masses were always more decisive in determining the activity of the Soviets than the party make-up of their membership.

During the first months of the Revolution the Bolsheviki were decidedly in the minority in the larger Soviets and at all national Soviet assemblies. Only a handful of votes were given for Bolshevik opposition proposals at the tumultuous sessions of the huge Petrograd Soviet of the early days of the Revolution. At the All-Russian Congress of Soviets in June only 105 of the 777 delegates who gave their Party affiliation described themselves as Bolsheviki.

There were several reasons for this weakness. The hard polemical spirit of Bolshevism was alien to the first period of the Revolution, when the popular mood was one of cheering indiscriminately for any resounding revolutionary generality. The large percentage of soldiers' representatives in the Soviets operated against the Bolsheviki, because the soldiers were considerably less permeated with Marxist teaching than the workers, and the delegates whom they sent to the Soviets were usually military clerks, ex-students, the best speechmakers among the sergeants, corporals and private soldiers—in the main people with a vague and hazy revolutionary outlook who felt more at home as Socialist Revolutionaries. The "Down with the War" slogan of the more radical Bolsheviki, while it corresponded well enough with the real desire of the masses of the soldiers, was too abrupt to become immediately popular. Patriotic and nationalist feeling did not disappear with one sweep of Revolution; it evaporated more gradually.

The Bolshevik official leadership up to the time of Lenin's return was affected by the prevalent sentiment and was distinctly inclined to conciliation and compromise with other left-wing groups in the Soviet. This was particularly marked after the return from

Siberian exile of three prominent Bolsheviki, Joseph Stalin, member of the Central Committee of the Party, Leo Kamenev, who belonged to the editorial board of the Bolshevik newspaper *Pravda* (The Truth) and the Bolshevik Duma deputy, Muranov. *Pravda,* which had been suppressed during the War, began to appear immediately after the Revolution under the editorship of V. Molotov, who was one of the three members of the Bureau of the Central Committee in Russia—an organization which endeavored to hold together and direct the activities of the small Bolshevik organizations which escaped the intensified police persecution of the War years.

Stalin, Kamenev and Muranov returned to Petrograd on March 25 and, resting on their superior status in the Party organization, carried out a sort of *coup d'état* in the editorial office of *Pravda,* formally announcing their entrance into the editorial board of the newspaper and the appointment of Muranov as a general director of *Pravda* in the issue of March 28.[17] The same issue contained a leading article by Kamenev entitled "Without Secret Diplomacy" which set forth views that were very different from Lenin's conception of Bolshevik policy in wartime.

"Our slogan is not disorganization of the revolutionary and revolutionizing army, not the empty 'Down with the War,' but pressure on the Provisional Government with the purpose of compelling it to come out immediately before the whole democratic world with an attempt to induce all the warring countries immediately to open up negotiations about means of stopping the World War. And until that time everyone remains at his fighting post. . . . When army stands against army it would be the most stupid policy to propose that one of them should lay down its arms and disperse to its homes. This would be a policy not of peace, but of slavery, which a free people would reject with indignation. No, it will remain staunchly at its post, answering bullet with bullet and shell with shell."

These sentiments could have been expressed by any Menshevik or Socialist Revolutionary in the Soviet with a moderate tint of internationalism and were not calculated to differentiate the Bolsheviki very sharply from the "Zimmerwaldists"[18] of other parties. Stalin, if one is to accept Trotzky's testimony,[19] was in favor of Tseretelli's proposal for a union of the Bolsheviki and Mensheviki. And Stalin, commenting on some of his own contributions to *Pravda* at this time, frankly observes:[20] "These articles reflect certain waverings of the majority of our Party on the questions of peace and the power of the Soviets which occurred, as is known, in March

and April, 1917. . . . It is not surprising that Bolsheviki, scattered by Tsarism in prisons and places of exile, and just able to come together from different ends of Russia in order to work out a new platform, could not immediately understand the new situation. It is not surprising that the Party, in search of a new orientation, then stopped halfway in the questions of peace and Soviet power. The famous 'April Theses' of Lenin were needed before the Party could come out on the new road with one leap. . . . I shared this mistaken position with the majority of the Party and renounced it fully in the middle of April, associating myself with the 'April Theses' of Lenin."

In the words of another Bolshevik, Ludmilla Stal, "All the comrades groped about in darkness until the arrival of Lenin." [21]

From the moment when the news of the Revolution reached him in Zürich, Lenin was consumed with feverish desire to return to Russia. He had long sensed the possibilities of war, especially of unsuccessful war, as a means of revolutionizing the masses. The problem of returning to Russia was difficult, for a man of Lenin's well-known revolutionary anti-war views, because the Allied powers controlled the travel routes and were disinclined to facilitate the return of Socialists who were not regarded as patriotic. Finally, as a result of the mediation of Fritz Platten, secretary of the Swiss Socialist Party, Lenin, with his wife Krupskaya, his close associate Zinoviev and a number of other Bolsheviki and a few members of other revolutionary parties, made arrangements to travel through Germany in a sealed car. By mutual agreement no communication was permitted with the Russians during their journey across Germany en route to neutral Sweden; the only obligation which the *émigrés* undertook was to urge on the Russian Government the release of an equal number of interned German civilians.

Lenin arrived at the Finland Station in Petrograd late in the evening of April 16. Some prominent Party members met Lenin at Beloostrov, the frontier station between Finland and Russia; and he asked them whether he would not be arrested after his arrival. This idea recurred in one of his speeches soon after his arrival in the capital and indicates at once how much he mistook the mood of spineless tolerance that dominated the existing regime and how firmly he was convinced that his own mission in Russia was to bring not peace but a sword.

Lenin was received with a good deal of popular celebration; around the station one could see a guard of honor from the Kron-

stadt sailors; companies and detachments of soldiers at attention; throngs of workers from the Sestroretzk arms factory and other plants. The commander of one of the groups of sailors, Maximov, expressed the naïve hope that Lenin would enter the Provisional Government.

Chkheidze, on behalf of the Soviet, greeted Lenin with carefully weighed words: "Comrade Lenin, in the name of the Petrograd Soviet of Workers' and Soldiers' Deputies, we greet you in Russia. But we suppose that the main problem of the revolutionary democracy is the defense of our Revolution against any attacks on it, whether from without or from within. We suppose that for this end not disunion but consolidation of the ranks of the whole democracy is necessary. We hope that you will pursue these objectives along with us."

Lenin's emphatic and uncompromising reply to this greeting was delivered in the course of a short speech from an armored car to the audience of workers, soldiers and sailors which gathered outside the station:

"I am glad to greet in you the victorious Russian Revolution . . . The robbers' imperialist war is the beginning of civil war in all Europe. . . . Any day may come the crash of European imperialism. The Russian Revolution, which you have carried out, has laid the foundation for it and opened a new epoch. Long live the worldwide socialist revolution!"

Lenin was mistaken in his estimate of the chances of international revolution. But in turning contemptuously away from the moderate leaders of the Soviet and addressing himself to the masses he was following a sure instinct of revolutionary leadership. He gauged admirably not the present but the future mood of the workers and soldiers who had gathered to meet him.

And he dealt unsparingly and resolutely with what he regarded as symptoms of wavering and weakness in the ranks of his immediate followers. His first words when he met Kamenev were of sharp rebuke for the tone of the *Pravda*. From the station he went to the Bolshevik headquarters in the palace of the Tsar's former favorite ballet-dancer, Ashesinskaya, which had been seized by a detachment of soldiers attached to an armored-car division in the first days of the upheaval and was used as a central Bolshevik Party office until government troops occupied it after the abortive July revolt. Here he delivered a speech before a Party gathering which first announced a complete break with many of the policies

that had been followed up to his arrival. In his speech he called for the change of the Party name to "Communist"; proclaimed that the Soviets should be the sole organs of power; and repeated his slogan of world revolution.

On the following day he emphasized these ideas in a speech before an audience of Social Democrats of all shades at a conference in the Tauride Palace which had been called with the idea of uniting the Bolsheviki, Mensheviki and smaller Social Democratic groups. His reception was predominantly hostile; the prominent Menshevik Soviet leader Bogdanov characterized his ideas as "the ravings of a madman"; another participant in the meeting, Goldenberg, suggested that Lenin was a candidate for the throne of the Anarchist Bakunin; the editor of *Izvestia,* Steklov, who ultimately came down on the Bolshevik side of the fence after protracted wavering, predicted that Lenin would soon renounce his theories after he had become more acquainted with Russian realities.[22]

It is not surprising that Lenin's programme of action should have seemed little more than a doctrinaire dream to the representatives of the Soviet majority. The Soviets of Workers' and Soldiers' Deputies were loose, embryonic bodies, still devoid of firm organization. The Soviets of Peasants' and Farmhands' Deputies, to which he proposed to turn over the confiscated lands of the estate-owners, were scarcely in existence. His declaration that only the left wing of the Zimmerwald anti-war Socialist conference could be regarded as truly revolutionary seemed to reduce the number of true Socialists to microscopic dimensions, because the majority of Socialists in all countries outside of Russia rejected the Zimmerwald anti-war platform altogether and stood for national self-defense.

But Lenin's ideas, which found more precise expression in his "April Theses," which called for "no support to the Provisional Government, explanation of the complete falseness of all its promises . . . no parliamentary republic (a return to this from the Soviet of Workers' Deputies would be a backward step), but a republic of Soviets of Workers', Farmhands' and Peasants' Deputies in the whole country . . . confiscation of all landlords' estates, nationalization of all land, with the establishment of a model farm under the control of Soviet Farmhands' Deputies on every large estate . . . establishment of a single national bank . . . elimination of the army, police, official class . . . pay to all of-

ficials not above the average earnings of a skilled worker" proved more potent in the end, unrealizable as they were in some details, than the politic reservations and maneuverings of the moderate leader of the early Soviets. The opposition within the Party was overcome and Lenin was the unquestioned leader at the Party Conference which was held from May 7 until May 12. His very first speeches completely destroyed any idea of union between Bolsheviki and Mensheviki.

Lenin's arrival in Russia is a major date in the development of the Revolution. Without his driving, extremist leadership, it is at least conceivable that the explosive mood of the masses would have evaporated in a series of disconnected, local outbursts. In Lenin the masses found a leader after their own mood—not their mood of April, but their mood of October and November. The hard, extreme, dogmatic viewpoint which Lenin enunciated from the moment of his arrival on Russian soil alienated a considerable part of the Social Democratic intelligentsia. But it won for the Bolsheviki the allegiance first of the workers, more slowly of the soldiers.

Into the formless and inchoate mass which Russian society represented in the first weeks of the Revolution Lenin's sharp, bitter words cut like a knife, revealing and inspiring class antagonism and class hatred. The revolutionary honeymoon when any orator could elicit the applause of almost any crowd was coming to an end. The epoch of clearcut class struggle was approaching.

NOTES

[1] Shlyapnikov, "The Year 1917," Vol. II, p. 236.

[2] Milyukov ("History of the Second Russian Revolution," Vol. I, p. 69) uses the phrase "vanishing of authority in the provinces."

[3] N. Avdeev, "The Revolution of 1917," Vol. I, pp. 101–102.

[4] E. Ignatov, "The Moscow Soviet of Workers' Deputies in 1917," pp. 52–53.

[5] "Statistical Collection of the Years 1913–1917, Vol. VII, Part I, of the works of the Central Statistical Department."

[6] The workers of the "Provodnik" factory in Moscow arrested five engineers on April 5, on the ground that the factory was not working for the defense of the country. A delegation of the Union of Engineers appealed to the Executive Committee of the Soviet on April 7 on account of the continual abuse of the managing and technical personnel of the factories by the unorganized workers. See Avdeev, op. cit., pp. 117 and 122.

[7] The full text of the letter is cited in Shlyapnikov, op. cit., Vol. III, pp. 74–77.

[8] V. Nabokov, "The Provisional Government," pp. 67ff.

[9] Avdeev, op. cit., p. 117.

[10] Milyukov, "History of the Second Russian Revolution," Vol. I, p. 84.

[11] Zaslavsky and Kantorovitch, "Chronicle of the February Revolution," Vol. I, p. 146.

[12] "The Petrograd Soviet of Workers' and Soldiers' Deputies: Protocols of Sessions," pp. 67–71.

[13] See V. B. Stankevitch, "Reminiscences: 1914–1919," p. 39. Stankevitch was a member of the Executive Committee.

[14] General A. I. Denikin, "Sketches of Russian Turmoil," Vol. I, p. 73.

[15] Zaslavsky and Kantorovitch, *op. cit.*, Vol. I, p. 154.

[16] "Sketches of the History of the October Revolution," Vol. II, p. 210.

[17] See Shlyapnikov, *op. cit.*, Vol. II, pp. 179ff. Shlyapnikov's testimony possesses special value because he was himself at this time a member of the Bureau of the Central Committee.

[18] Russian anti-war Socialists were often called Zimmerwaldists, because a conference of anti-war Socialist groups was held in the Swiss town of Zimmerwald in September, 1915.

[19] "The History of the Russian Revolution," Vol. I, p. 304.

[20] Stalin, "On the Roads to October," p. viii.

[21] See "The Petrograd General City and All-Russian Conferences of the Russian Social Democratic Labor Party (Bolsheviki)," p. 12.

[22] Sukhanov, "Memoirs of the Revolution," Vol. III, pp. 37ff.

CHAPTER VI

VLADIMIR ILYITCH LENIN: GENIUS
OF REVOLUTION

VLADIMIR ILYITCH LENIN was a supreme genius of revolutionary leadership. In Maxim Gorky's apt phrase, "Lenin was a man who prevented people from leading their accustomed lives as no one before him was able to do." [1] The magnitude of the social revolution which he led to victory speaks for itself. And far more significant, perhaps, than Lenin's ability to drive on the masses, unleashed after the collapse of Tsarism, to the final act of seizure of power by the Soviets (this was, after all, not so difficult under the conditions of 1917) was his subsequent success in building up a new type of state and a new social and economic order. Whatever one may think of the Russian Bolshevik Revolution or of the Soviet state which grew out of it, the political greatness of the main architect of these sweeping changes is scarcely open to question.

The Russian Revolution was in no small degree the result of the contact of two potentially explosive forces: the socially revolutionary teaching of Karl Marx and the peculiar conditions of Eurasian Russia, where the primitive mentality of the poverty-stricken masses, the repressive traditions of autocracy, the absence of a moderating powerful middle class and the numerous sharp jagged edges of social, economic and racial antagonisms made the soil singularly propitious for a literal application of Marx's more violent theories. And Lenin, in whom Western education and assimilation of Western economic and philosophical theory were strangely and strikingly blended with some very characteristic Russian psychological traits, absolute faith in his convictions, intolerance of opposition, contempt for compromise, was the indispensable incarnate link between Western revolutionary theory and Russian revolutionary practise.

It becomes increasingly doubtful with the passing of years whether the Russian Revolution was, as Lenin believed, a prelude to similar upheavals in other countries. Yet the political system of government which he sponsored in Russia, a system which might

121

be paradoxically described as a popular dictatorship, a system under which the ultimate source of power is a single party, monopolizing all the agencies of instruction and propaganda and ruthlessly and systematically extirpating the faintest symptoms of organized political opposition, has found conscious or unconscious imitation in two large European countries, even though Italian Fascism and German National Socialism would certainly have excited Lenin's fiercest denunciation. And on the economic side the Soviet system, with its virtually complete elimination of private profit-making enterprise, with its enormous extension of the functions of the state, remains distinctive, an inevitable object of favorable or unfavorable comparison with the systems of other countries.

One must go back a full two centuries in Russian history before a personality among the rulers of the country fit to stand comparison with Lenin can be found. Peter the Great, with his hatred and contempt for old customs and traditions, his determination to force Western attributes on the country at any cost, was an obvious forerunner of Lenin. And if the philosophic historian Kluchevsky had lived until the time of the Bolshevik Revolution and had been able to write a commentary on Lenin and his methods he might have seen the same effort to "square the circle," the same accompaniment of "beneficent actions with repelling violence" that he noted in the case of Peter. But the furrow which Lenin dug into the body of Russia's historical development was far deeper than that of Peter. Lenin destroyed more, created more, affected the lives of a far greater number of people.

This greatest figure in the long line of Russian revolutionaries led a much less exciting and externally dramatic personal life than many of his predecessors and contemporaries. In Lenin's life there are no terrorist exploits, no hairbreadth escapes from prison or exile, no periods, trying to health and nerves, of solitary incarceration or of imprisonment at hard labor. He passed through the apprenticeship of arrest, imprisonment and exile which fell to the lot of almost every revolutionary of any prominence; but his treatment in prison and exile was not harsh or inhuman.

Vladimir Ilyitch Ulianov was born in the sleepy little provincial town of Simbirsk, on the Volga, on April 22, 1870. (The name Lenin, under which he subsequently became known, is a pseudonym which he first adopted when he published his book on revolutionary tactics, "What to Do," in 1902.) His father, Ilya Nikolaevitch, was

Lenin at the age of three

Lenin at the Red Square, speaking at Sverdlov's funeral

an inspector of schools who in the later part of his life obtained the patent of nobility which was automatically granted to state officials who had reached a certain grade in the service. His mother, Marya Alexandrovna Blank, was the daughter of a poor doctor.

The Ulianov household was that of a typical provincial intellectual; and, as not infrequently happened in such families, the children all developed revolutionary views as they grew up. Alexander, the oldest brother, a student in the University of St. Petersburg, was executed for taking part in a conspiracy against the life of Alexander III.[2] Vladimir's younger brother Dmitry and his two sisters, Marya and Anna (another sister, Olga, died while still a young woman), entered the ranks of the Bolsheviki along with Vladimir.

Vladimir's father died in 1886 and on May 20 of the following year his brother Alexander was executed. The death of his brother, to whom he was strongly attached, made a deep impression on Vladimir and hardened his revolutionary convictions, although he reached the conviction that the romantic individual terrorism of the "People's Liberty" group, of which his brother was one of the last members, had no place in Marxist revolutionary strategy. In the same year, 1887, Vladimir was graduated from the Simbirsk highschool with a gold medal for proficiency in his studies. By a curious coincidence the director of the highschool, Kerensky, was the father of Lenin's future political adversary.

Vladimir entered Kazan University in the summer of 1887. In December of the same year he was expelled for taking part in student demonstrations of protest. For some time the doors of the Russian higher educational institutions were closed to him and he was also refused permission to continue his studies abroad. From 1887 until 1893 Lenin lived in the Volga towns of Kazan and Samara, spending his summers on a small farm which his mother owned. This was a period of study and preparation for his future revolutionary work. He read Marx and Engels, Plekhanov and Kautsky and he also took a keen interest in the development of Russian agrarian conditions. In 1891 he was finally permitted to take examinations in the law department of the University of St. Petersburg and in the following year he received his certificate as an assistant attorney. He practised law very little, however; and from 1893, when he moved from Samara to St. Petersburg, his attention was primarily devoted to revolutionary activity.

Lenin's first major political pamphlet, issued illegally and only partially preserved, was entitled "Who Are the 'Friends of the People' and How Do They Fight Against the Social Democrats?" and appeared in 1894. It was a polemical assertion of the Marxian viewpoint about the inevitability of capitalist development in agriculture, directed against the populist theorists who saw in the Russian village communal system of land ownership an embryonic form of socialism which might be preserved without passing through the capitalist process of dividing the peasants into rich and poor, landowners and land laborers. This pamphlet ended with the phrase, quite expressive of Lenin's entire subsequent outlook on the character of the Russian Revolution:

"The Russian worker, rising at the head of all the democratic elements, will overthrow absolutism and lead the Russian proletariat (together with the proletariat of all countries) along the direct road of open political struggle to the victorious Communist Revolution."

Lenin first went abroad in the spring of 1895 and got in touch with the leaders of the Marxist "Liberation of Labor" group, Plekhanov, Axelrod and Vera Zasulitch. Axelrod, despite the fact that he was subsequently a Menshevik and a bitter political opponent of Lenin, seems to have had a prophetic sense of his future destiny, because, in describing his first impression of Lenin, he observed:

"I felt then that I had to do with the future chief of the Russian Revolution. He was not only an educated Marxist,—of these there were very many,—but he knew what he wants to do and how it is necessary to do this. He smacked of the Russian land." [3]

It was indeed this capacity for knowing what he wanted and how it should be done that differentiated Lenin from the great majority of the dissatisfied Russian intelligentsia, who saw in some form of socialism a remedy for the evils of autocracy and capitalism, and marked him as the future leader of the Revolution.

Lenin, with many other members of the revolutionary group with which he was associated in St. Petersburg, was arrested in December, 1895. His prison experience was relatively mild, and he was able to write a large part of his work, "The Development of Capitalism in Russia," during his period of confinement. Early in 1897 Lenin was exiled for three years to Siberia, where he lived in the village Shushenskoe, in the district of Minusinsk. He lived here freely, renting rooms in a peasant's house, carrying on correspondence with Russia, continuing his polemic with the populists,

attacking the new heresy of "economism" (belief that the workers should concentrate on efforts to improve their material condition, through trade-union organization, leaving political struggle to other classes), giving legal advice to the neighboring peasants.

In July, 1898, Lenin married Nadyezhda Konstantinovna Krupskaya, with whom he had already become acquainted in the Marxist circles of St. Petersburg. Krupskaya was a not unfamiliar type of woman revolutionary, serious self-effacing, entirely devoted to the Social Democratic movement, with which her husband's personality was so closely associated. Completely identified with Lenin in her views and interests, Krupskaya was his loyal and indispensable comrade and helpmate throughout his life. She assisted him in everything, from carrying on illegal correspondence from abroad with the Party organizations in Russia to seeing that he obtained the necessary rest and recreation after a particularly stormy émigré conference.

After completing his term of exile Lenin went abroad in the summer of 1900. He was already convinced that a central organ was needed as a rallying point for the scattered Social Democratic groups and circles throughout the country and that such an organ could only be published outside of Russia. The first period of Lenin's emigration and his emergence as a leader of the Bolsheviki after the definite split of the Social Democratic Party into Bolshevik and Menshevik factions have already been described.[4]

Lenin returned to Russia in November, 1905. Although the Revolution had already met its first checks the concessions which the Tsarist Government had made in October were still largely in effect and a certain amount of legal political activity was possible. Living first in St. Petersburg, then in Finland, where there was greater security against molestation by the police, he directed the activity of the Bolshevik organization, laying the greatest stress on the necessity for armed uprising and hoping for a new upward turn in the movement for some time after the Tsarist Government had definitely regained mastery of the situation. Convinced of the hopelessness of a speedy revival of revolutionary activity, Lenin left Russia. When he arrived in Geneva he burst out, in a moment of profound pessimism: "I feel as if I had come here to lie down in my grave."[5]

This second period of life in exile, from 1908 until 1917, was a severe test even for Lenin's strong willpower and faith in the ultimate triumph of his cause. This was especially true of the years

up to 1911, when news of reviving labor unrest in Russia began to bring some measure of new hope to the revolutionaries in exile. In Russia the old regime seemed to have successfully withstood the tempest of 1905. The Social Democratic movement had broken up into several quarrelling groups. Apart from the difference between Bolsheviki and Mensheviki there were sectarian groups within both the Bolshevik and the Menshevik organizations. The gloomy atmosphere of émigré life was made still more depressing by the arrival of new political refugees from Russia, often people with shattered health and nerves whose chances of earning a living abroad were slight. It proved impossible to guard the most important secrets of the Bolshevik organization from the hosts of spies and provocators in the service of the Tsarist Government.[6]

There were moments, no doubt, when even Lenin's iron will faltered, when he doubted whether "he would live to see the next rise of the tide."[7] But in the main he was saved from pessimism and despair by his noteworthy capacity for devoting himself wholly to the necessary task of the immediate moment, however small it might appear in comparison with the recent struggles of 1905. Soon after his arrival in Geneva he writes to Gorky, plying him with detailed practical questions about means of smuggling copies of the new Bolshevik émigré newspaper, *Proletarian,* into Russia with the aid of Italian ships and sailors. And in another letter to Gorky, written in 1910, after frankly declaring that "emigrant life is now a hundred times more difficult than it was before the Revolution of 1905," Lenin adds: "The development of the Party and the Social Democratic movement goes ahead through all the devilish difficulties of the present situation."[8]

In the summer of 1912 Lenin moved from Paris, where he had maintained his headquarters for several years, to Cracow, in Austria, in order to be closer to the Russian frontier. Cracow was a post of vantage, from the standpoint of revolutionary activity, not only because of its geographical proximity to Russia, but also because the Austrian authorities were not unkindly disposed toward enemies of Tsarist Russia. So the local police did not interfere with Lenin's conferences and meetings with Party members who slipped across the border, and Tsarist secret service agents could not expect in Austria the same coöperation which they sometimes found in allied France.

It had proved possible to start a Bolshevik newspaper, *Pravda* (The Truth) in St. Petersburg; and despite many confiscations

and suppressions *Pravda* succeeded in prolonging its existence until the outbreak of the War. From Cracow Lenin contributed regularly to *Pravda* and guided its policy. He also gave instructions to the group of six workers whom the Bolsheviki had elected as deputies to the Duma. When a member of the group, Badaev, asked him how to discuss a complicated legislative project offered by the Cadets, Lenin laughed and said:

"Just get up and curse the bourgeoisie. You were sent to the Duma so that the voice of the workers should be heard there." [9]

Lenin had no belief in the possibility of the development of a labor political movement, wedded to peaceful and constitutional means, under Tsarist conditions, nor, indeed, would he have regarded such a movement as desirable. The Bolshevik deputies were in the Duma to "curse the bourgeoisie," to serve as a centre of agitation, to help the illegal movement as far as possible by utilizing their parliamentary immunity from arrest.

Immediately after the outbreak of the War Lenin was arrested in the village of Poronino, not far from Cracow, where he was living at that time. The Austrian Social Democrat Victor Adler intervened on his behalf, pointing out to the Government that Lenin was an irreconcilable enemy of Tsarism; and he was soon released and permitted to go to Switzerland, where he lived in Berne and Zürich until the outbreak of the Revolution gave him the opportunity to return to Russia.

The influence of the War on the development of Lenin's system of revolutionary thought can scarcely be overestimated. It strongly affected both his personal psychology and his theories. As Gregory Zinoviev, his close associate and coeditor of the newspaper which he published in Switzerland during the War, observed: [10]

"Lenin was never especially tender toward the bourgeoisie. But from the beginning of the War he displayed toward the bourgeoisie a concentrated and intensified hatred, as keen as a sharpened sword."

So the battlefields of France and Flanders perhaps made their indirect contribution to the executions of the Cheka.

Although Lenin had long regarded the West European Socialist parties as tainted with opportunism he had not anticipated the submissive falling in line with the national War policies of the majority of the Socialists in all countries. At the outset of the War he expressed the belief that the German Social Democrats would vote against War credits, while Zinoviev predicted that they

would refrain from voting. Neither anticipated that the German
Social Democrats would vote for the credits.

Once the first shock of stupefaction was over, Lenin's conclusions about the duty of every international Socialist were sharp
and clearcut. The Second International of the Socialist parties
had perished from opportunism; long live a revolutionary Third
International. The War was a product of capitalism and imperialism. The revolutionary reply to it must be not agitation for
peace, but an effort to "turn the imperialist war into a civil war."
Lenin despised the pacifist almost if not quite as much as he did
the pro-War Socialist. In his mind pacifist agitation, even if it
had any chance of success, was futile unless it was an integral part
of an effort to sweep away the capitalist social and economic
order. As he wrote in the *Sotzial-Demokrat* for November 1,
1914: [11]

"War is not an accident, not a 'sin,' as Christian priests think (who
preach patriotism, humanity and peace no worse than the opportunists), [12]
but an unavoidable stage of capitalism, just as normal a form of capitalist
life as is peace. . . . Refusal of military service, strike against war and
such things are mere stupidity, a pale and cowardly dream of unarmed
struggle with the armed bourgeoisie, a sigh for the annihilation of capitalism without desperate civil war or a series of wars. Propaganda for class
struggle also in War is the duty of a Socialist; work directed to the transformation of the war of the peoples into civil war is the sole Socialist work
in the epoch of the imperialistic armed clash of the bourgeois classes of all
nations. Down with preachers' sentimental and silly sighs for 'peace at
any price.' Up with the standard of civil war! Imperialism has placed at
stake the fate of European culture: after the present War, unless there is
a series of successful revolutions, other wars will soon follow; the tale of
'the last War' is an empty, harmful tale."

In his attitude toward Russia's participation in the War Lenin
was a thoroughgoing defeatist. "Russians cannot 'defend their
fatherland' except by desiring the defeat in any War of Tsarism
as the lesser evil for nine tenths of the Russian population," he wrote
on one occasion; [13] and he said to one of his companions in emigration, Shklovsky: "He is no Socialist who in the time of imperialist
war doesn't desire the defeat of his own government, doesn't fight
with his own chauvinists, with the imperialism of his own bourgeoisie and government."

Lenin's defeatism was not attributable to any dislike of his
own people. As he wrote during the early months of the War:
"Is the feeling of national pride alien to us, Russian class-conscious

proletarians? Certainly not. We love our language and our mother-land."

In desiring the defeat of Tsarism he was simply living up to his own conception of the duty of every Socialist: to desire and work for the defeat of his own government and to transform the war of nations into a war of classes. With a view to promoting this end he took an active part in the conferences held by anti-War Socialists in Switzerland at Zimmerwald in 1915 and at Kienthal in the following year. Only the Italian and Swiss parties, among the West European Socialists, sent official delegates; the other delegates at the conference were mostly representatives of small dissident left-wing minorities. Yet both at Zimmerwald and at Kienthal Lenin was in disagreement with the majority viewpoint, in which he found too much pacifism and too little preparation for civil war. Quite characteristically he preferred an uncompromising maintenance of his own viewpoint to concessions which would have made for a greater measure of unity. As he wrote to Kollontai, the future Soviet woman ambassador, in connection with an international women's anti-war congress: "The thing I fear most at the present time is indiscriminate unity, which, I am con-vinced, is most dangerous and harmful to the proletariat." [14]

Few of the solid Swiss burghers of Berne and Zürich knew of the existence of the bald little Russian who spent his days looking up statistics on the development of colonial empires, composing theses about turning international war into civil war, carrying on polemics with other isolated Socialists who did not share his view-point. Had they known of him they would probably have regarded him as a man more pitiable and ludicrous than dangerous. Had anyone suggested toward the end of 1916 that within a year this obscure emigrant would rule the empire of the Tsars the sug-gestion would have seemed incredibly fantastic.

But Lenin had grasped, as no other political leader had done, the possible ultimate revolutionary implications of the world con-flict, with the unprecedented strain which it placed upon the social and economic order everywhere. While he exaggerated the probable aftermath of the War in Western Europe (his repeated predictions that European revolution was a matter of the near future went for nought) he estimated quite correctly the enormous forces of social upheaval which unsuccessful war would release in Russia.

Lenin cordially despised sentimental phrases, even if they were revolutionary phrases. His conviction that war would lead

to revolution was not a merely emotional reaction to the whole-sale slaughter; it was based on a set of economic convictions which obviously gained ground in Lenin's mind during the War years: that the War was a result of imperialist conflict, that the world had definitely reached the stage of imperialism, that imperialism was the final stage of capitalism, and that, therefore, the time was ripe for transition to socialism. "Imperialism," he wrote in 1916, "is the highest stage in the development of capitalism. Capital in the leading countries has outgrown the limits of national states, has replaced competition with monopoly and has created all of the objective prerequisites for the realization of socialism." The same idea recurs in his address at the first Congress of Soviets in 1917:

"Imperialism is the last stage in the development of capitalism, when it has reached the point of dividing up the whole world, and two gigantic groups have fallen into mortal struggle." [15]

Lenin characterized this stage of imperialism as "monopolist capitalism, parasitic or decaying capitalism and perishing capitalism." He saw the monopolistic feature in the increasing domination of economic life by a small number of great banks; the parasitic and decaying feature in the increasing number of people who lived by clipping coupons and in the economic exploitation of colonial peoples. And in the widespread growth of monopoly, the diminution of the earlier free competition, Lenin saw a proof that imperialism was not only the highest, but the last, the perishing stage of capitalism.

Another idea which Lenin expressed during the War years and which was destined to afford an increasing measure of consolation to Russian Communists as the prospects of international revolution grew dimmer was that, because of the inequality of political and economic development under capitalism, "the victory of socialism in the beginning is possible in a few capitalist countries or even in one capitalist country. The victorious proletariat of that country, having expropriated the capitalists and organized socialist production in its own country, would rise against the remaining capitalist world, attracting to itself the oppressed classes of other countries, arousing them to uprising against the capitalists, coming out, if necessary, even with armed force against the exploiting classes and their states." [16]

Up to the very eve of the Russian Revolution Lenin was not sure whether he would live to see the revolutionary Promised Land

on which his thoughts were so intensely concentrated. On January 22, 1917, he addressed a Socialist youth meeting in Zürich, where he interpreted the 1905 Revolution as the prologue to a greater up- heaval of European scope. "We of the older generation may not live to see the decisive battles of this coming revolution," he said as he concluded the lecture.[17] Only a few weeks later news of the Revolution in Russia arrived; and Lenin responded with the ardor of a prophet who feels that his hour has come. Burning with im- patience to reach the arena of revolutionary struggle, considering every sort of device to make his way across the fighting lines (among other schemes he considered engaging an airplane and disguising himself as a deaf-and-dumb Swede, in order to utilize a forged Swedish passport without revealing his ignorance of the language) Lenin revealed from the first precisely what his po- litical opponents, the liberals in the Provisional Government and the moderate Socialists in the Soviet, conspicuously lacked: a clear vision of the probable future course of development in Russia after the Tsarist regime had been overthrown, while the country was still endeavoring to carry on war. The following excerpts from the first of Lenin's "Letters from Afar," sent by a personal messenger from Switzerland and published in *Pravda* of April 3 and 4, reveal an accurate vision of the breakdown which would come as a result of the further prosecution of the War and of the way in which this breakdown could be exploited for revolutionary purposes:

"The first stage of the Revolution has ended. This first stage will cer- tainly not be the last stage of our Revolution. . . . The imperialist war with objective inevitability had to hasten extraordinarily and to sharpen in unprecedented fashion the class war of the proletariat against the bourgeoisie, had to turn into a civil war between hostile classes. . . . The government of Octobrists and Cadets, of Guchkovs and Milyukovs can give neither peace, nor bread, nor freedom. . . .

"The Russian working class has as its first ally the mass of the semi- proletarian and especially of the small peasant population of Russia, which numbers many millions and constitutes the enormous majority of the population. This mass must have peace, bread, freedom and land. This mass will inevitably be under the influence of the bourgeoisie and especially of the small bourgeoisie. . . . The stern lessons of the War, which will be all the sterner as Guchkov, Lvov, Milyukov and Company carry on the War more energetically, will unavoidably push this mass toward the proletariat, force it to follow the proletariat. Exploiting the freedom of the new order and the Soviets of Workers' and Soldiers' Depu- ties, we must endeavor to enlighten and organize this mass, first of all and above all."

Another of the "Letters from Afar," dated Zürich, March 24, 1918, throws interesting light on the new type of state which Lenin believed should emerge from the future revolution. He outlined here a scheme for the creation of a "militia" in the large cities, consisting of all able-bodied adult citizens of both sexes, each member serving one day out of fifteen. This militia not only would maintain public order, but would act as the executive organ of the Soviet. It would turn democracy from a fiction into a fact by bringing the whole mass of the population into active administrative work. For the functions of the militia would not be limited to the maintenance of order. It would see to it that "every worker improved his living conditions, that every family had bread, that no adult in a rich family should have a bottle of milk before the need of every child was satisfied, that rich apartments, abandoned by the Tsar and the aristocracy, should afford refuge to the poor and homeless." [18]

This idea of a general militia invested with such varied functions was never carried into practise, even after the Bolshevik Revolution. But in his insistence that the masses should assume direct executive powers, and that women should participate equally with men in the projected militia, Lenin was expressing ideas which one often finds in his writings on questions of administration. His often quoted phrase that "every cook must learn how to administer the state" is a terse summing up of his belief that the achievement of socialism depends upon the training of the masses for direct executive tasks.

One of the most important traits of Lenin's thought was the importance which he attached to the question of power in the new revolutionary state. For the new regime he claimed an authority no less absolute, no less unlimited, no less ruthless, should occasion demand it, than that of the fallen autocracy. Lenin's views in this respect were eminently in line with the main currents of Russian historical development and at the same time create a sharp line of demarcation between him and liberals or Social Democrats who believe in parliamentary institutions and civil liberties.

"The basic question of every revolution is the question of power in the state," Lenin declared on one occasion; [19] and his theories on the character of the state under socialism and under capitalism have placed an indelible imprint both on the course of the Revolution and on the subsequent shape of the Soviet regime. Starting from the premise that the state, under capitalism, is simply an engine for

the suppression of the working class by the ruling capitalist class, Lenin comes to the conclusion that the working class, after completing a successful revolution, must smash the capitalist state apparatus and create a new apparatus of suppression of its own, the primary purpose of which is to be the smashing of the resistance of the "capitalist-exploiters." Between the successful socialist revolution which would overthrow the rule of the capitalists and bring about the socialization of all the means of production and what Lenin looked forward to as the highest stage of human society, communism, where class lines would be completely obliterated, there would be an indefinite intervening period, during which the dictatorship of the proletariat would prevail. The philosophic extremism which is so characteristic of Russian political and economic thought finds striking expression in Lenin's trenchant phrase: "While there is a state there is no freedom. When there is freedom there will be no state." While he was willing to admit that "capitalist" democracy created more favorable conditions for the political and economic struggle of the working class than autocracy or feudalism, he did not recognize in his heart any fundamental difference between the state order represented by pre-revolutionary Russia and the state order represented by England or Switzerland. Every state, in his conception, is an agency of suppression and oppression, irrespective of minor variations in external features.

And Lenin did not for a moment believe that socialist revolution would lead to an extension of the "capitalist democracy," for which he had all the contempt of a Mussolini or a Hitler. "From this capitalist democracy, inevitably narrow, quietly excluding the poor and therefore hypocritical and false through and through, development doesn't proceed simply, directly and smoothly, 'to ever greater and greater democracy' as liberal professors and petty-bourgeois opportunists imagine. No. Development forward, *i.e.*, to communism, proceeds through the dictatorship of the proletariat, and cannot proceed otherwise, because there is no other means of crushing the resistance of the exploiting capitalists."

It is interesting to note that Lenin's main theoretical work on the problem of government under socialism, "The State and Revolution," was written in the late summer and early autumn of 1917, when he was still a proscribed man, living in hiding in order to avoid the execution of the warrant of the Provisional Government for his arrest. So his conception that an indefinite period of dictatorship would follow a socialist revolution was not a mere improvisa-

tion, dictated by circumstances arising after the seizure of power had been completed. It was an integral part, and a most significant part, of his general revolutionary outlook.

Lenin is, therefore, scarcely to be reproached with inconsistency if he denounced the death penalty under Kerensky and championed it as soon as he held the reins of power himself; if he attacked the Provisional Government for suppressing Bolshevik newspapers and took an early opportunity of suppressing dissident voices of criticism after the Soviet regime was in power; if he denounced army and labor discipline under the Provisional Government and upheld both under the Soviets. Thinking, as he did, almost exclusively in terms of classes, attaching supreme importance to the problem of where economic power was lodged, he assigned an extremely subordinate place in his scheme of things to civil and individual liberty. This would come, he was dogmatically convinced, when the final highest stage of communism was reached. Then the state would automatically disappear; human nature would be so completely transformed that no compulsion would be necessary and Marx's formula, "From each according to his abilities; to each according to his needs," would be realized.

Lenin was distinctly not a maker of Utopias. One searches his works in vain for any detailed sketch of the new order, to the ultimate achievement of which his life was devoted. Like Marx, whose teaching he accepted without reservation or modification, Lenin was distrustful and somewhat contemptuous of imaginative blueprints of life in future generations. To him the socialist theory of Marx was an indisputable dogma, an inescapable law of human development. But he permitted himself only such relatively dry and bare glimpses into the future as one sees in the following sentences:

"The expropriation of the capitalists will inevitably yield a tremendous development of the productive forces of human society. But how soon this development will go farther, how soon it will reach the point of breach with division of labor, of destruction of the contrast between mental and physical labor, of transformation of labor into the 'first necessity of life,'— this we do not know and cannot know."

In discussing the immediate problems of a socialist state there is a definite note of difference between Lenin's ideas before the Bolshevik Revolution and his views after experience had shown some of the practical difficulties and complications of state administration of economic life. At first he took a decidedly oversimplified view of these difficulties and complications.

"Capitalism has created instruments of accounting in the shape of banks, syndicates, postal service, consumers' coöperatives, unions of employees. Without big banks socialism would be unrealizable . . . A single biggest state bank with departments in every township, in every factory,—this is already nine tenths of the socialist apparatus." [20] On another occasion [21] he employed the sweeping, if somewhat indefinite formula:

"All society will be one office and one factory with equality of labor and equality of pay."

He anticipated that there might be passive resistance on the part of those employees who were connected with the capitalist class by social and economic ties. But this would be broken by cutting off the food supply of the refractory employees and with the aid of armed workers, "who are people of practical life, and not sentimental intelligentsia, and will not permit any jokes with them." [22] It was natural that Lenin's purely bookish knowledge of industrial and commercial life should have led him to overestimate and oversimplify the service which capitalism had rendered to the future socialist society through its development of increasingly large industrial, commercial and banking units. After the seizure of power the problem of bringing order out of the chaos into which Russian life had been precipitated by the double shock of war and revolution loomed up as increasingly formidable; and early in 1918 Lenin was already recognizing the necessity for shifting the centre of attention from expropriation to organization, accounting and control. The slogan which Lenin had emphasized in 1917, that no state official should be paid more than the average earnings of a good worker, was modified at this time, to permit the payment of high salaries to the more indispensable "bourgeois" specialists.

This was one of many instances when Lenin displayed his readiness to drop or change a familiar phrase or declaration of policy in order to meet an immediate practical necessity. Yet it would be a mistake to regard him as an opportunist, maneuvering to remain in power at any price. His strength of leadership is to be found largely in the fact that he believed in Marxian doctrine with all the intensity of faith that would have characterized an early Mohammedan or a seventeenth century Puritan. There could be compromises, adjustments, temporary concessions; but at no time was Lenin disillusioned in his faith in the basic tenets of Marxism, in his own interpretation of them.

The Communist historian Pokrovsky has pointed to foreshadow-

ings of Lenin's ideas in such obscure revolutionaries of the sixties and seventies of the last century as Zaichnevsky, who called for the dictatorship of a revolutionary party and the nationalization of factories and shops, and Tkachev, the "Russian Jacobin," who stressed the necessity for conspirative organization which Lenin himself recognized in his noteworthy tactical book, "What to Do." But there is no definite evidence that Lenin even knew of these Russian predecessors, still less that he was perceptibly influenced by them. His almost exclusive mentors are Marx and Engels; and many of his ideas are directly derived not so much from the monumental "Capital" as from shorter, polemical pamphlets and brochures, such as "The Communist Manifesto," "The Critique of the Gotha Programme," "The 18th Brumaire of Louis Bonaparte," etc.

Lenin did not possess a strikingly original or a pyrotechnically brilliant mind. Among his contemporaries Plekhanov surpassed him in breadth of historical judgment and erudition, Trotzky in brilliance of phrase and quick receptiveness to new ideas, Ryazanov in Marxian scholarship. One is sometimes struck by the simplicity of Lenin's world outlook, by his reduction of every problem to terms of Marxian class struggle. Take his definition of morality, for instance: [23]

"Morality is that which serves the destruction of the old exploiter's society and the union of all the toilers around the proletariat, which creates a new society of Communists. Communist morality is that which serves this struggle, which unites the toilers against any exploitation, against any small private property, because small private property gives into the hands of one person that which was created by the labor of all society . . . We do not believe in eternal morality and we expose the deceit of all legends about morality."

Lenin was quite intolerant of religion in any form; to him it was "a kind of spiritual cocaine, in which the slaves of capital drown their human perception and their demands for any life worthy of a human being."

Lenin's antipathy to religion was avowedly based on his conviction that it was an agency in the hands of the ruling capitalist class for diverting the attention of the masses from revolutionary activity. There was quite possibly a subtler psychological connotation in his uncompromising atheism; a feeling that in the new society which was to be created the individual should not have any otherworldly preoccupations. Lenin's hostility to religion was in

no sense a mere expression of dislike for the state-controlled Russian Orthodox Church. To him all forms of religion, the most rationalistic as well as the most ritualistic, were simply varieties of "opium for the people"; and he protested most vigorously against the tendency of Lunacharsky and other Bolshevik philosophic thinkers to introduce a mystical flavor into the pure Marxian materialistic theory.

It was the destiny of Lenin, the convinced disciple of Marx, to be the leader of a revolution in a country where many orthodox Marxian Socialists believed that a genuinely socialist reorganization of society was impossible, because of the relatively backward development of capitalist industry and the preponderance of small peasant proprietors among the population. Regarding the possibilities of a victorious social upheaval under the leadership of a party with a socialist programme Lenin's revolutionary instinct was surer than the learned dogmas of Kautsky and Martov. He realized that if the proletariat, the class on which he relied, was numerically weak in Russia, by comparison with Germany or England, the hostile "bourgeois" class was still weaker. In carrying the Revolution to success and in the subsequent civil war he recognized and took full advantage of two outstanding features of Russian life: the thirst of the peasants for land and the dissatisfaction of the non-Russian peoples of the former Tsarist Empire with Russian overlordship.

Lenin's historical greatness is to be found not in creative originality of thought, but in his unrivalled ability to transmute an existing system of economic and philosophic thought into a programme of militant action. He combined in truly extraordinary measure all the traits of character that are indispensable in a revolutionary leader. There was first of all the absolute dogmatic faith in his cause without which no one ever moved millions of followers into action. There was the bold sweep of tactical imagination, combined with an abiding layer of shrewd commonsense which was lacking in many of his lieutenants. Lenin immediately sensed the weakness of the Provisional Government and systematically set about to prepare its overthrow. As early as May he was writing: "The country of the workers and poorest peasants is a thousand times more to the left than the Chernovs and Tseretellis and a hundred times more to the left than we are" [24]—a phrase which was to receive repeated confirmation when workers' demonstrations and soldiers' mutinies took place almost in spite of Bolshevik efforts to

organize them and hold them in check. But when, soon after the Bolshevik Revolution had been carried out, Lenin was faced with the question of whether to sign the annexationist Brest-Litovsk Peace which the Germans demanded, he insisted, in the face of much opposition in the Party ranks, that the peace must be signed and a breathing space gained. He realized immediately that the Empire of the Hohenzollerns was a very different thing from the house-of-cards Provisional Government; it could not be knocked over by revolutionary phrases and clumsily armed workers.

Lenin had a keen sense for the breaking point in popular endurance. This was why he was able to lead the Party out of what must have seemed to many the hopeless dilemma into which war communism had plunged the country in the spring of 1921, by declaring the New Economic Policy.

While Lenin was not a cruel man in the sense that he took delight in the infliction of suffering he was quite pitiless and ruthless when the occasion demanded: another indispensable characteristic of the successful leader in revolution, as in war. Trotzky tells how he constantly spoke of the necessity for shooting, for revolutionary terror in the weeks immediately after the seizure of power, when organized terrorism had not yet gone into effect.[25] And to Gorky, who often came to him with petitions for the lives and liberty of intellectuals who had fallen into the hands of the Cheka, Lenin put the penetrating question:

"With what footrule do you measure the number of necessary and superfluous blows in a battle?" [26]

Lenin's personal life reflects the spare austerity, the single-minded concentration that are so characteristic of his writing and thought. No man of corresponding historical significance was so indifferent to the exploitation of his own personality. Absolute master of the allegiance of the Communist Party, of the workers who sympathized with the Revolution, he never strikes the personal note in his speeches and appeals. It is always in the name of communism, never in the name of Lenin, that he calls on his followers to fight and die.

The simple habits of the penurious years of exile remained after Lenin was installed in the Kremlin, wielding more actual power than any Tsar since Peter the Great. The small rooms where he lived and worked in the Kremlin are little more comfortably furnished than the bare quarters in the home of a Zürich shoemaker where he received the news of the downfall of the autocracy. Any-

thing in the nature of luxury or ostentation was quite alien to Lenin's tastes and character.

Physically the leader of the Russian Revolution was rather below average height, with a strong, stocky body (in contrast to many Russian émigrés Lenin took vigorous exercise in the form of mountain climbing and bicycling), a high forehead, a largely bald head, surrounded by a fringe of reddish hair, quick, darting eyes and a distinctly Mongolian cast of features. It is perhaps noteworthy that Lenin's father was a native of Astrakhan, the port near the mouth of the Volga where a multitude of Eastern peoples mingle with the Russians.

Lenin, despite his iron selfcontrol, was subject to strong nervous agitation; he gave up chess because it placed too great a strain on his nerves, and he was seldom able to sit out a play, while a wearing conference often left him almost prostrated. There was nothing of the Bohemian in Lenin's tastes and character; and his preferences in literature were almost as conventional as his ideas in politics and economics were revolutionary. He keenly enjoyed the Russian classical novelists and poets, Turgeniev and Tolstoy, Pushkin, Lermontov and Nekrasov; and looked with doubt and bewilderment on the raw, uncouth, experimental "proletarian" literature which made its appearance after the Revolution.

A good deal of Lenin's personality communicates itself to his style. One can readily believe his remark to Gorky that he never wrote any verses. His writing is unembellished, clear, forceful. He often set down his ideas on an important question in the form of theses, neatly arranged as to division and presentation of ideas. Lenin was an impatient and intolerant controversialist; such uncompromising phrases as, "He who doesn't understand this doesn't understand anything," and "Either this or that: there is no middle way," are characteristic of his writing. At the same time there is general testimony that he was extremely thoughtful and considerate in his personal relations with Party comrades. Not the least proof of his ability in handling individuals was his success in utilizing those two strong and discordant personalities, Trotzky and Stalin, throughout the civil war without permitting their personal differences to affect the course of operations.

As one contemplates Lenin's character, which absolute faith in his dogmatic system made at once passionate, hard and implacable, one feels that all the elements of blood and iron with which Tsarism for centuries had crushed opposition to its will had been somehow

transmuted into the personality of this invincible revolutionary, the avenger of the many who had fallen before him, from the aristocratic Decabristi to the humbler victims of the punitive expeditions of 1905. Lenin's way was not the way of many of the earlier rebels against autocracy; and the system of violence and repression, terror and espionage, that inevitably grew out of his own conception of the requirements of "the dictatorship of the proletariat" was the bitterest of disillusionments to many honest and courageous revolutionaries, especially of the intellectual classes. But it was for such a leader and for such a revolution that the whole course of Russian historical development had shaped the way.

Lenin staked his life on a mighty wager, a gigantic act of faith: that through the revolutionary destruction of the old social order, after an indefinite intermediate period during which propaganda would be combined with terror and repression, a final stage of unimagined human welfare and prosperity would emerge as a result of the abolition of private property and the creation of a universal communist psychology. To this belief he devoted his life; for this belief he laid down his life, as much as any Red Army soldier who fell on the steppes of South Russia or on the frozen marshes around Archangel. So Lenin the man becomes inevitably fused with the system which he brought into existence, on which the last judgment has obviously not been pronounced. He was the incarnate doctrine of militant Marxism, the revolutionary Word become flesh.

NOTES

[1] Maxim Gorky, "V. I. Lenin," p. 29.

[2] See Chapter II, p. 33.

[3] Karl Radek, "Portraits and Pamphlets," p. 21.

[4] See Chapter II, pp. 37–41.

[5] N. K. Krupskaya, "Memories of Lenin," Vol. I, p. 156.

[6] Krupskaya in "Memories of Lenin," Vol. II (English edition), p. 78, relates how she prevented one provocator from attending the Prague Conference of the Bolshevik Party in 1912, only to discover later that two other provocators had been present at the Conference.

[7] Krupskaya, "Memories of Lenin," Vol. II, p. 81.

[8] "Letters of Lenin to Gorky," pp. 8 and 38.

[9] See M. N. Pokrovsky, "The October Revolution," pp. 13–24.

[10] Emilian Jaroslavsky, "The Life and Work of V. I. Lenin," pp. 47ff.

[11] G. Zinoviev and N. Lenin, "Against the Tide," p. 29.

[12] "Opportunist" and "social compromiser" are familiar Bolshevik terms of disparagement for Social Democrats of more moderate views.

[13] Zinoviev and Lenin, "Against the Tide," p. 57.

[14] Krupskaya, *op. cit.*, Vol. II, p. 160.

[15] Lenin, "Collected Works," Vol. XIV, Part I, p. 311.

[16] *Ibid.*, Vol. XIII, p. 133. The question as to Lenin's views about the possibility of building up socialism in a single country acquires additional interest, because it subsequently became a main point of theoretical controversy between Stalin and Trotzky. Lenin does not seem to have believed, at least until very late in his career, that a complete and final victory of socialism in a single country was possible. It is

noteworthy that he says "the victory of socialism *in the beginning* is possible in a few capitalist countries or even in one capitalist country" (italics mine). On the other hand he categorically declared in January, 1918, (Vol. XV of his "Collected Works," p. 87), that "the final victory of socialism in one country is impossible." In the spring of the same year he asserted (Vol. XV, p. 287): "It is possible to be victorious finally only on a world scale and only by the common efforts of the workers of all countries." And it is only in one of the last articles which he wrote before his final breakdown that he asks whether the combination of state ownership of all big means of production, concentration of state power in the hands of the proletariat, the union of this proletariat with millions of small peasants, together with the development of coöperation, "doesn't constitute everything necessary for the building up of a complete socialist society" and answers his own question: "This is still not the building up of a socialist society, but it is everything necessary and sufficient for this building up." (See "Collected Works," Vol. XVIII, Part II, pp. 129–130.) So it would seem that Lenin, up to the very last weeks of his conscious existence, was inclined to place the ultimate fate of the Russian Revolution in some dependence upon the success or failure of the international revolutionary socialist movement. Whether he would have adhered to this view if his life had been prolonged for another decade is, of course, a matter of conjecture.

[17] Krupskaya, *op. cit.*, Vol. II, p. 198.
[18] Leninist Collection, No. 2, pp. 342–355.
[19] Lenin, "Collected Works," Vol. XIV, Part I, p. 24.
[20] *Ibid.*, Vol. XIV, Part II, p. 231.
[21] *Ibid.*, Vol. XIV, Part II, p. 380.
[22] *Ibid.*, Vol. XIV, Part II, pp. 380–381.
[23] *Ibid.*, Vol. XVII, pp. 323–324.
[24] *Ibid.*, Vol. XIV, Part I, p. 152.
[25] Leon Trotzky, "Lenin," pp. 133, 137.
[26] Gorky, *op. cit.*, p. 35.

CHAPTER VII

THE DEEPENING OF THE REVOLUTION

Viewed in retrospect the eight crowded tumultuous months that elapsed between the overthrow of the Tsar in March and the coming into power of the Bolsheviki fall into three main periods. The first period, which ended with the disorderly uprising of the Petrograd soldiers and workers in July, was one of steady deepening of the Revolution. After the suppression of the July uprising there was a very feeble and unstable reaction, which endured until General Kornilov made his unsuccessful attempt at a *coup d'état* in September. After that the tide of events flowed strongly and irresistibly up to the climactic seizure of power by the Bolsheviki in November.

What were the outstanding characteristics of the first period of the "deepening of the Revolution"? Loosening of discipline in the army, increasingly radical demands of the industrial workers, first for higher wages, then for control over production and distribution, arbitrary confiscations of houses in the towns and, to a greater degree, of land in the country districts, insistence in such non-Russian parts of the country as Finland and Ukraina on the grant of far-reaching autonomy.

Another symptom of the mood of the time was the tendency of the masses of workers and soldiers to slip from under the control of the Soviet, especially in Petrograd, which consistently set the pace for the forward march of the Revolution. Not only did the masses display more and more disregard for the instructions and exhortations of the Menshevik and Socialist Revolutionary leaders, but they were even inclined to brush aside the Bolsheviki, when the latter counselled caution and moderation. The atmosphere of Petrograd, with its huge inactive garrison and its swollen working-class population, which became more and more restive as the War dragged on with its accompaniment of food cards and high cost of living, was so charged with explosive material that any popular and effective speaker in a factory or a soldiers' barracks could gain a hearing when he called for a demonstration of protest.

The first crisis of the Provisional Government occurred on the 3d and 4th of May and was a direct result of a note on Russia's war aims which Foreign Minister Milyukov had despatched to the governments of the Allied powers. From the beginning Milyukov, with his stiff nationalism, had been at odds with the leaders of the Soviet, whose formula was: peace without annexations and indemnities. The Provisional Government decided, as a concession to Soviet sentiment, to transmit to the Allied governments the text of its appeal to the citizens of Russia of April 9, which expressly repudiated imperialist aims.

Milyukov agreed to transmit this declaration, on condition that it be accompanied by a note of explanation; and this note was approved by the whole Cabinet, including Kerensky, who had been the sharpest critic of Milyukov's unwillingness to go beyond very narrow limits in altering the phraseology of his diplomatic communications in deference to the peace aspirations of the Soviet.

The note was despatched on May 1; and on May 3, when the text became known, the storm of disapproval on the part of the workers and soldiers burst out. It was not so much the substance of the note as its tone and the fact that Milyukov's name had become a symbol of imperialism in the eyes of the majority of the Soviet adherents that accounted for the clamor which its publication aroused. The note emphasized such points as Russia's determination to carry on the War, in full agreement with the Allies, Russia's intention to observe the obligations contracted toward the Allies, i.e., the secret treaties; and the note even contained the assertion, diplomatically polite but factually distinctly inaccurate, that the popular desire to bring the World War to a victorious end had only been strengthened after the Revolution.

On the afternoon of the 3d the Finnish Regiment, armed and in full military order, appeared before the Marinsky Palace, where the Government maintained its residence, with streamers and placards calling for Milyukov's resignation. It was followed by a number of other regiments and military units, the total number of demonstrators amounting to twenty-five or thirty thousand. General Kornilov, commander of the Petrograd garrison, suggested to the members of the Provisional Government, which was in session, that force should be used; but the majority of the ministers opposed this, probably having a better intuition than Kornilov as to the shakiness of the force at his disposal; and the soldiers were persuaded to return to their barracks after speeches by some of

the Soviet leaders. In the evening there were further demonstrations of workers, soldiers and sailors, with slogans "Down with Milyukov," which clashed here and there with counter-demonstrations of supporters of Milyukov, who carried inscriptions: "Down with Lenin," "Hurrah for Milyukov."

During the night there was a prolonged conference between the members of the Provisional Government and the leading members of the Soviet. Prince Lvov declared that either the Government must possess the full confidence and support of the Soviet or it would withdraw. After a good deal of wordy interchange between the participants in the conference, Tseretelli, the dominant leader of the Soviet, modified his original demand for the despatch of a new note and agreed that the Government should issue an explanation of certain phrases in the note which were regarded as ambiguous. At the same time he promised support for the Provisional Government.

The initiator of the demonstration of the Finnish Regiment, as it turned out, was Fyodor Linde, a philosopher and mathematician who was serving in the regiment and who enjoyed great popularity and influence among the soldiers. Ironically enough this same Linde, subsequently sent to the front as a government commissar, was lynched by mutinous soldiers who refused to obey his commands. It not infrequently happened that men who were favorites of the crowd in the first stages of Revolution later suffered unhappy experiences at the hands of the masses whom they had stirred up. So the goodhearted, if somewhat softheaded, radical lawyer, N. D. Sokolov, who actually wrote Order Number One, was later severely thrashed by the rebellious soldiers of a regiment on the front which he was endeavoring to recall to discipline.

Despite the agreement between the Government and the Soviet leaders, disturbances recurred on a more serious scale on the 4th of May; and blood was shed on the streets of Petrograd for the first time since the overthrow of Tsarism. The working-class districts across the Neva and in outlying parts of the city were on the march; and their columns of demonstrators, among whom were armed men with rifles and revolvers, clashed with counter-demonstrations organized by the Cadet Party in Milyukov's behalf in the centre of the city. The workers were already little inclined to reckon with the leaders of the Soviet; when Chkheidze urged one throng of marchers from the proverbially turbulent Viborg District to return, on the ground that the Government had satisfactorily

explained the incident, the improvised leaders retorted that the workers themselves knew what to do, and the demonstration continued.[1] Fire-arms came into play in some of the clashes; several people, mostly soldiers, were killed and more were wounded.

The day furnished a new striking proof of the power of the Soviet and of the impotence of the higher military command. At three in the afternoon General Kornilov, learning of the approach of large crowds of workers, with banners bearing such inscriptions as "Down with the Provisional Government" and "Down with the War" gave orders to some military units to take up their position on the square outside the Winter Palace. The units turned to the Soviet for instructions; and, as a result of the remonstrances of the Soviet representatives, who insisted that the carrying out of the order would only complicate the situation and that they would be responsible for the maintenance of tranquillity, Kornilov withdrew his order.

The Soviet Executive Committee then issued an order to the effect that no military unit should come out on the streets (except for ordinary reviews) unless instructions to this effect were issued under the seal of the Executive Committee under the signatures of not less than two of the following seven Soviet leaders: Chkheidze, Skobelev, Binasik, Filippovsky, Sokolov, Liber, Bogdanov. While this step was largely designed to prevent irresponsible agitators from bringing armed military units onto the streets it amounted, of course, to a repudiation of the theoretical supreme military authority of the commander of the Petrograd garrison; and Kornilov, already disgusted with the highly insubordinate character of the Petrograd garrison, resigned his post and was assigned to command one of the armies on the southwestern front.

By the evening of the 4th the movement had passed its peak. The Soviet Executive Committee, by a vote of 34 to 19, decided to accept the explanation which the Government issued in connection with Milyukov's note, an explanation which was to be conveyed by Milyukov to the ambassadors of the Allied powers. This "explanation" repeated some of the more pacific phrases of the declaration of April 9 and declared that the reference toward the end of the note to "sanctions and guaranties of firm peace" meant limitation of armaments, international tribunals, etc.

In these May disturbances one can recognize two features which were repeated, in much more pronounced form, during the outbreak in July: first, the growing popularity of Bolshevik slogans and

ideas among the workers and soldiers of the capital; second, the ease with which a mass movement could slip out of the hands of the Bolshevik Party leadership and go farther than the leadership desired or intended. In summing up the conduct of the Bolsheviki during this first trial of strength with the Provisional Government Lenin was unsparing in his criticism of Party members who, in words and deeds, urged on the masses to more violent action than the circumstances warranted.

"The slogan 'Down with the Provisional Government' was adventurous," Lenin declared; "to overthrow that government now was impermissible, therefore we gave out the slogan of peaceful demonstrations. We desired to carry out only a peaceful reconnaissance of the forces of the enemy, but not to give battle, and the Petrograd Party Committee took a position a little more to the left, which, under the circumstances, is a grave offense." [2] Raskolnikov, a young Bolshevik officer who brought some of the Kronstadt sailors, always ready for rebellious action, to Petrograd at the time of the May demonstration, also refers to the overzealous attitude of some members of the Petrograd Committee, "who brought workers and soldiers on the streets without the knowledge of the Central Committee, throwing out the extremely responsible slogan, 'Down with the Provisional Government,' which really meant an appeal to the completely unprepared Party to overthrow the Provisional Government." [3]

The hotheads in the Petrograd Committee found a responsive voice in the Helsingfors Soviet, which promised "at any moment to support with armed force demands for the withdrawal of the Provisional Government."

The May crisis naturally led to the elimination of Milyukov. It had a much more important result: the reorganization of the original Cabinet on the basis of a coalition with the moderate parties of the Soviet and the inclusion of Socialist Ministers in the new Cabinet.

The majority of the members of the Provisional Government, conscious of the extreme weakness of their position, were quite willing to try the experiment of endeavoring to obtain more active support from the Soviet by associating some of its leaders with the work of government. Milyukov and Guchkov were opposed to the idea of coalition; but their careers as Cabinet Ministers were drawing to a close. Guchkov, broken in health and profoundly depressed by the visible breakdown of the fighting capacity of the

army, resigned as War Minister on May 13; and Milyukov quit the Cabinet about the same time when he discovered, to his indignation, that he had been transferred, without his own knowledge, to the post of Minister for Education in the projected reshuffling of the Cabinet.[4]

Opposition to the idea of coalition with the "bourgeoisie" was more stubborn and deepseated on the side of the Soviet; and the Executive Committee, after a long debate, rejected the proposal by the close vote of 23 to 22 at its session of May 12. The Bolsheviki and the left, "Internationalist" wing of the Mensheviki were opposed to coalition with non-Socialist parties on principles; and even among the Soviet delegates of more moderate views there was doubt and hesitation as to whether the assumption of formal governmental responsibility would not lead to a rapid loss of influence with the masses.

But the bloodshed on the streets of Petrograd was a powerful argument in favor of a change of regime; and on May 14, after Kerensky, who had always been an ardent advocate of coalition, had painted a dark picture of the increasing military and economic disorganization, the Executive Committee, by 44 votes against 19, reversed its earlier decision and decided to authorize its representatives to participate in the Cabinet. It laid down the following conditions for participation: active foreign policy, aiming at achievement of peace on the basis of selfdetermination of peoples without annexations and indemnities; preparation for negotiations with the Allies for revision of the War agreements; democratization of the army and strengthening of its fighting power; control over industry and transport, and over the exchange and distribution of products as a means of combating economic breakdown; protection of labor; an agrarian policy which would "prepare the passing of the land into the hands of the toilers"; imposition of financial burdens on the propertied classes; establishment of democratic local administration and the speedy convocation, in Petrograd, of the Constituent Assembly. While some of these points were scarcely acceptable to the dominant middleclass party, the Cadets, the phrasing of the Soviet programme was sufficiently elastic and indefinite to open up prospects of future political bargaining and adjustment. And the Cadets agreed to send representatives of their Party into the coalition ministry[5] on condition that there should be not less than four Cadet Ministers in the new Cabinet and that the Soviet programme should be modified by emphasizing in the new govern-

mental declaration the necessity for undivided authority in the hands of the government and for struggle against anarchy. They also desired some modification of the Soviet viewpoint on foreign policy; but here the Soviet standpoint prevailed; and the foreign political programme of the new government included the well-known Soviet formula: peace without annexations and contributions. On the other hand the Cadets received satisfaction through the inclusion in the declaration of a statement that the new government must be clothed with full power in order "to take the most energetic measures against anarchistic, illegal and violent actions." Moreover the Soviet programme contained one distinct concession to the nationalist viewpoint of the Cadets by setting forth as an ideal the preparation of the army for offensive as well as defensive operations.

Indeed the launching of a military offensive was perhaps the outstanding objective which the Cadets hoped to realize by entering into a coalition with the Socialist parties. In retrospect it is easy to realize that the offensive, which was actually carried out in July, was foredoomed to failure, in view of the demoralized condition of the army, and that it hastened rather than arrested the downfall of the Provisional Government. But at the time there was a general feeling among the conservative classes and, to a lesser extent, among the moderate parties in the Soviet, that an offensive, if victorious, would check the disintegration of the army. Another psychological motive that helped to make the preparation of an offensive palatable to the right wing of the Soviet, despite its outspoken views on the imperialist character of the War, was a growing uneasy realization that the appeals for an active peace policy issued by the Soviet were not being taken very seriously abroad and that the international prestige of revolutionary Russia was lowered by the prevalent impression of its weakness and disorganization.

The experiment in coalition government was formally inaugurated on May 18. Six Socialists were included in the new ministry. Kerensky took over the Ministry of War, left vacant by the resignation of Guchkov. Another Socialist Revolutionary, Chernov, became Minister for Agriculture; and a third member of this party, Pereverzev, Minister for Justice. The Mensheviki Tsereteli and Skobelev were respectively Ministers for Posts and Telegraphs and for Labor; and the Populist Socialist, A. V. Peshekhonov, was Minister for Food. The wealthy young Ukrainian sugar manufac-

turer, Tereschenko, replaced Milyukov as Minister for Foreign Affairs and performed with fair agility the difficult juggling task of not offending the Allied governments and yet keeping on good terms with the Soviet. Along with the six Socialists there were ten "capitalist ministers"; but actual decisions were often taken by an unofficial triumvirate, consisting of Kerensky, Tereschenko and Nekrasov, a left-wing Cadet who, in striking contrast to the stiff-necked Milyukov, pursued a policy of conciliating the Soviet sentiment so far as possible.

When the first Cabinet of the Provisional Government quit office it published a sort of political testament, full of phrases of mournful chiding, of which the following are typical: [6]

"As the basis of political administration the Provisional Government has chosen not violence or compulsion, but the voluntary subordination of free citizens to the government they have themselves created. It seeks support not in physical but in moral force. . . . Unfortunately, and to the great peril of liberty, the building of new social buttresses for strengthening the country is lagging far behind the process of dissolution called forth by the collapse of the old political order. . . . The elemental urge of individual groups and elements of the population, as represented by the politically least intelligent and least organized of these elements, to achieve their desires and obtain satisfaction of their demands by methods of direct action and seizure threatens to destroy internal unity and discipline and to create fertile ground for acts of violence stimulating hostility to the new order. . . . There rises before Russia the terrible vision of civil war and anarchy which will destroy liberty."

This manifesto might serve as a swansong not only for the first Cabinet of the Provisional Government, but also for its coalition successors. It would indeed have held true for any government which was unwilling or unable to use ruthless repressive force in the country with the traditions of Ivan the Terrible and Emilian Pugachev.

The leading figure not only in the new Cabinet but in the whole subsequent course of the Provisional Government was the new War Minister, Alexander Kerensky. This radical lawyer and Duma deputy of pre-revolutionary times possessed many qualities which were calculated to bring him to the top in the first period of frothy, exuberant revolutionary enthusiasm, before hard class and party lines had been formed. A flamboyant oratorical style, a quick sense for the theatrical and the popular, a revolutionism of a not too dogmatic or definite hue, quickness of movement and gesture which created an external impression of strength of char-

acter: all these traits helped to make Kerensky the idol of the heterogeneous mass of students, soldiers, office workers who cheered for the Revolution without understanding very clearly what it was all about. And just as some of Kerensky's traits predestined him for leadership in the early phases of the Revolution, other qualities, inability to think coldly and realistically outside the haze of his own glowing phrases, sentimentality that occasionally verged on hysteria and led to alternations between extreme optimism and extreme pessimism, capacity for selfhypnotism, marked him out for disastrous failure when the romantic illusions of national unity were shattered on the hard facts of class antagonism.

Kerensky's first effort was to restore the fighting capacity of the army. He was conscious of the difficulties of this task, because at a conference of army delegates which was held shortly before his appointment he burst out: "Is it really possible that free Russia is only a country of mutinous slaves? I grieve that I did not die two months ago, in the first hour of the Revolution." [7]

However, this mood, although it recurred more than once, did not characterize Kerensky's attitude toward his new office. Unlike his predecessor, Guchkov, who was fatalistically pessimistic from the beginning to the end of his career, Kerensky believed that it would be possible to restore discipline and fighting capacity by a combination of appeals to the soldiers with administrative measures which would reflect the new democratic spirit of the country. In his first order to the army and fleet he peremptorily refused to consider any resignations offered by high military officers. Endeavoring to create the impression that he would use a firm hand in dealing with generals who displayed reactionary tendencies, Kerensky relegated General Gurko, commander of the western front, to the reserve on account of his open criticism of the Declaration of the Rights of the Soldiers,[8] which the government officially promulgated immediately after Kerensky's accession to office.

The commander-in-chief, General Alekseev, was abruptly dismissed on June 4 and replaced by General Brussilov, leader of the Russian victorious offensive of 1916. Alekseev, like Guchkov, had been a profound pessimist as to the condition and future prospects of the army, while Brussilov was disposed to trim his sails to suit the prevalent democratic breeze and thereby incurred the contempt and hostility of the conservative majority of the high officers in the Stavka (General Staff).

While Kerensky felt it was necessary to issue the Declaration

of the Rights of the Soldiers he modified it in two points, restoring to commanders the right to use armed force against subordinates who failed to obey orders and giving to the commanders the right to appoint and remove officers of lower status without consulting the army committees.[9] These changes caused the Bolsheviki to term the document the declaration of the lack of rights of soldiers and to carry on a constant agitation against it.

Under Kerensky's regime commissars were assigned to every army by the government; their function was to raise the morale of the troops and to act, in many cases, as mediators and buffers between the oldfashioned generals and the newly elected soldiers' organizations. At the same time the network of committees which had developed in the military forces, from the companies up to the armies, was brought under a certain measure of state control; Kerensky hoped that the commissars and committees, both abhorred by the typical officer of the old school, would provide valuable and, under the circumstances, indispensable leadership for the wavering troops.

The War Minister set out on a tour of the front and made a series of flaming speeches, from which the following are typical excerpts:

"You are the freest soldiers in the world. Must you not show the world that the system on which the army is now based is the best system? . . . Our army under the monarchy accomplished heroic deeds; will it be a flock of sheep under the republic? . . . I summon you forward, to the struggle for freedom, not to a feast, but to death. We, revolutionaries, have the right to death."

At the time when Kerensky undertook his speechmaking campaign the morale and discipline of the Russian armies, while severely shaken, were not entirely destroyed. There were already some units where it was physically dangerous to speak in favor of war or offensive. But in the main the War Minister received a respectful and attentive hearing; and his speeches, with their mixture of revolutionary and patriotic phrases, usually met with temporary success. There were loud cheers, vows to maintain strict discipline, to die in battle for free Russia . . . Then, after Kerensky had gone away and the electrical effect of his eloquence had worn off, the old mutinous habits, as a general rule, would reassert themselves. The "persuader-in-chief," as Kerensky was scornfully called by the old officers, had really undertaken an impossible Sisyphus task.

The regular German propaganda, which could operate in bolder and more uncontrolled forms as a result of the lowered discipline, made a small contribution to the break-up of the Russian armies. The systematic agitation of the Bolsheviki, with the aid of their well developed Military Organization, was a more important factor. But if one seeks for the fundamental causes of the wellnigh complete evaporation of the will to fight in the Russian army of 1917 one finds them first in the general vague popular sense that old authorities and rules of conduct had lost their validity with the elimination of the Tsar, second in the halfhearted, irresolute, psychologically quite untenable attitude of the moderate Soviet parties toward the War. General Brussilov, looking back over the stormy events of 1917, utters a well justified criticism when he writes: [10]

"The position of the Bolsheviki I understood, because they preached: 'Down with the War and immediate peace at any price,' but I couldn't understand at all the tactics of the Socialist Revolutionaries and the Mensheviki, who first broke up the army, as if to avoid counterrevolution, and at the same time desired the continuation of the War to a victorious end."

If war, which demands the most fearful sacrifices from its participants, is to be waged with any prospect of success, it must be waged wholeheartedly, energetically, without reservations of any kind. But what was the Soviet attitude toward the War? If one looks through any typical resolution passed by the Menshevik and Socialist Revolutionary majority one finds an utterly negative characterization of the War as imperialistic, a demand that it be stopped as quickly as possible and an unobtrusive phrase or two, inserted at Kerensky's urgent demand, suggesting, with dubious logic and no emotional appeal whatever, that, pending a general peace, it would be a good thing if the Russian soldiers would continue to fight. Now it is the virtually unanimous testimony of every observer that only appeals from the Soviet (or from groups, like the Bolsheviki, which stood to the left of the Soviet) exerted any influence on the soldiers. The Cadet papers, with their exhortations to orthodox patriotism, were read, in the main, only by the officers. And it is not surprising that the average soldier who was literate enough to read through a Soviet pronouncement on the War reached the conclusion that there was nothing worth risking his life for and voted very decisively against the continuance of the conflict by refusing to obey orders to advance, by running away

to his native village and, in extreme cases, by killing his commanding officer.

While Kerensky was endeavoring to whip up enthusiasm for an offensive on the front his colleagues in the Cabinet were facing equally difficult problems of administration behind the lines. The process of the deepening of the Revolution went on; the coalition Ministry was unable to give the masses either peace or land; and during the latter part of May and the first part of June unrest and disturbance in a score of forms swept the country from end to end.

"Russia is turned into a sort of madhouse," wrote the indignant Cadet newspaper *Rech* on May 30; and the word anarchy is constantly found in the speeches of conservative Duma members and in the editorials of conservative and liberal newspapers. Excesses there undoubtedly were in abundance. As Sukhanov, a chronicler of the times who certainly cannot be accused of undue sympathy with the propertied classes, writes: [11]

"Lynchings, breaking into homes and shops, acts of violence against officers, provincial authorities, private persons, arbitrary arrests, seizures and acts of vengeance—were registered daily in dozens and hundreds. Burnings and lootings of manor-houses increased in the villages. There were not a few excesses among the workers—against the factory administrators, owners and foremen. . . . Masses of deserters appeared in the rear and on the front. Soldiers, without any permission, poured homeward in enormous floods. They filled up all the railroads, attacking, the officials, throwing out passengers. . . . And in the cities they overcrowded and destroyed the streetcars and boulevards, filled up all public places. There also one heard of drunkenness and disorder."

The wave of strikes continually rose higher. Just as in 1905 the impulse to strike reached the most backward and least organized groups of workers: laundresses, house-janitors, waiters in restaurants. A major industrial conflict developed in the coal mines of the Donetz Basin; and the Soviet was only able with great difficulty to stave off a general railroad strike, which would have been catastrophic in view of the War situation.

The representatives of labor and capital exchanged the usual recriminations in connection with these strikes. Delegations of industrialists besieged the Provisional Government, declaring that the granting of the large wage increases which were demanded would swallow up not only the profits but also the basic capital of their undertakings. The trade unions and factory committees retorted by pointing to the large War profits which had been regis-

tered in many industries and contrasting these with the low real wages of the workers.

To a certain extent both sides were right. The Russian workers, intoxicated with their new sense of power and quite unaccustomed to the routine patient close bargaining of Western trade unions, were certainly not restrained in their demands by any consideration for the financial welfare of the employing firms. At the same time prices were shooting up so rapidly (they had reached seven times the pre-War average before the end of 1917 [12]) that even large wage increases did not bring a satisfactory standard of living. Such factors as the continuation of the War, the chronically poor functioning of the transportation system, the post-revolutionary breakdown of labor discipline and the upsurge of peasant disturbances in the village,—all inevitably diminished both the available stocks of food and manufactured goods and the possibility of delivering them where they were most needed.

The Provisional Government endeavored to cope with the crisis in industry by decreeing heavier taxes on income and property, by establishing measures of state control over production and distribution, by creating conciliation commissions for the settlement of wage disputes. But Russia was poorly prepared for the type of state socialization to which every belligerent government was obliged to resort. There was no strong central power to compel respect and obedience for its decisions. Control over production was interpreted in many cases in a semi-syndicalist fashion; the workers themselves took over to a greater or less extent the administrative functions in the factories where they were employed. Not only did the Bolsheviki preach this slogan of direct "workers' control" to the growing army of their adherents, but the Soviet Executive Committee on June 1 passed a resolution recommending that the workers "create control councils at the enterprises, the control embracing not only the course of work at the enterprise itself, but the entire financial side of the enterprise." [13]

It can readily be imagined that a plunge into this kind of direct management or at least control of plants by workers without administrative or technical experience, often accompanied by acts of violence against the unpopular factory managers, engineers and foremen, was not calculated to raise industrial productivity; and the Food Minister Peshekhonov, at a session of the Soviet Congress which was held in June and July, outlined the dilemma which confronted his department in the following terms: [14]

"We cannot take grain by force, the peasants don't want to take money, they must be supplied with those city products which they need. But there isn't enough of these products; there is no iron, no leather. Productivity of labor must be raised."

In general the experience of office tended to make the Socialist Ministers more moderate in their views. The Menshevik Minister for Labor, Skobelev, who started out with promises to extract all the War profits from the capitalists, was appealing to the workers in July to reduce their wage demands and increase their output.[15] But this change of attitude on the part of a few intellectual leaders had not the slightest effect on the masses, who promptly suspected them of having been "bought up by the bourgeoisie." Old conceptions of patriotism, and the rights of property were dissolving rapidly in the crucible of social revolution. The Petrograd workers were no more inclined to listen to Menshevik and Socialist Revolutionary appeals for class coöperation than the soldiers on the front were disposed to respond to the urgings of Emile Vandervelde, Albert Thomas, Arthur Henderson and other Socialists who came from the Allied countries in the hope of persuading Russia to remain in the War.

The leadership of the industrial workers in the revolutionary capital was passing definitely into the hands of the Bolsheviki. As early as April 26 the workers of the Old Parviainen metal factory passed a strongly worded resolution demanding, among other things, the retirement of the Provisional Government, "which only slows up the Revolution," the ending of the War, the organization of a Red Guard, "the requisitioning of all food products for the needs of the masses and the establishment of fixed prices on all objects of consumption" and the seizure of all privately owned land by the peasant committees.[16] This was considered an unusually violent declaration at that time; but during May and June more and more factories went over to the Bolsheviki, passing similar resolutions and sending Bolsheviki as their representatives in the Soviet. A significant although little noted date in the history of the Revolution is June 13, when the Workers' Section of the Petrograd Soviet passed, by 173 votes to 144, a resolution with the Bolshevik formula that power should be in the hands of the Soviets.[17] This indicated that the Bolsheviki had already gained a majority among the workers' representatives, although the Soviet as a whole did not go over to them until September, because the Socialist Revolutionaries and the Mensheviki received more sup-

port in the Soldiers' Section. Shortly afterwards an election to the municipal council of the Viborg District of Petrograd, the most definitely proletarian part of the city, gave the Bolsheviki 37 members out of 63.

Although the Bolsheviki obtained majorities in a large number of Soviets only in the autumn their dominant position at the Petrograd factories was indicated when a conference of representatives of the Petrograd factory committees, elected directly by the workers, and holding its sessions about the middle of June, consistently passed Bolshevik resolutions by large majorities. By June Bolshevik influence was already very pronounced in many of the regiments of the Petrograd garrison, and also among the sailors of the Kronstadt naval base.

The Bolshevik forces were notably strengthened by the return to Russia on May 17 of Leon Trotzky, who had already proved his capacity as a revolutionary leader in the days of the 1905 Soviet. A brilliant, bitter man, with a wide stock of erudition, a quick receptivity to new ideas and great oratorical capacity both for arousing the masses to enthusiasm and for annihilating his opponents with withering satire, gifted, as his subsequent achievement in creating the Red Army proved, with boundless energy and great executive ability, Trotzky was to play in the Revolution a rôle second only to that of Lenin. Indeed this son of a Jewish farm colonist (Trotzky's real name was Bronstein) complemented in many ways the son of the Russian Volga inspector of schools. Trotzky added the element of fire and brilliance to Lenin's cold inflexible logic and willpower. Whereas Lenin, even before his retirement into hiding after the July disturbances, rarely appeared at the Soviet and was largely engrossed in problems of direct Party leadership, Trotzky, almost from the moment of his arrival, was a constant speechmaker and soon established himself as one of the outstanding personalities of the Soviet.

Trotzky was not a member of the Bolshevik Party at the time of his arrival in Russia. Self-assured and temperamental, he had always previously rebelled against Lenin's conception of the requirements of iron Party discipline; and during the 1905 Revolution and after it, Lenin and Trotzky had repeatedly crossed controversial swords on points of doctrine and tactics. While Trotzky had shown himself far more militant than the average Menshevik in 1905, his special theory of the permanent revolution, *i.e.*, that a Russian revolutionary government would inevitably come into con-

flict with the peasantry and could only hope to survive if similar revolutions occurred in industrially more advanced countries, set him apart from Lenin; and in 1912 he endeavored, unsuccessfully, to unite all the factions of the Russian Social Democracy except the adherents of Lenin on a common platform.

From the moment of the March Revolution, however, there was no important divergence in the views of Lenin and Trotzky. They were in full agreement that the only answer to the imperialistic war was a violent workingclass revolution, that the Provisional Government must give way to a regime based on the Soviets. Some time elapsed between Trotzky's arrival in Russia and his formal entrance into the Bolshevik Party; but this was attributable to his desire to bring into the Bolshevik ranks a small group of personal adherents in Petrograd, the so-called inter-district group. That Trotzky was immediately accepted as a full-fledged Bolshevik is evident from the fact that he received one of the highest numbers of votes cast for candidates elected to the Party Central Committee at the Party Congress in August. In one of his first speeches on May 20 Trotzky summed up his position in words practically identical with those which Lenin had employed in the preceding month: "All power to the Soviets; no support to the Provisional Government."

Another factor that weakened and embarrassed the Government was the rapid development of centrifugal tendencies in Finland and in Ukraina. By June the Finnish Socialists were protesting against the presence of Russian troops in Finland; and in July the Socialist Party introduced in the Finnish Seym, or Diet, a project according to which the Seym should be the sole authority in Finland, except in questions of war and foreign affairs, in which some shadowy traces of authority were left to the Provisional Government.

Even graver was the situation in Ukraina, where the territory and population affected by the new nationalist movement were much larger. Ukraina included the fertile grain lands of South Russia, along with Russia's main coal field, the Donetz Basin, and rich iron reserves. It had a population of some thirty millions. While there were more Russians and Jews, taken together, than Ukrainians in the towns, the village population of this southern part of Russia was predominantly Ukrainian, especially in the five western and northwestern provinces of Ukraina, Kiev, Chernigov, Podolia, Volhynia and Poltava; and the group of Ukrainian intel-

lectuals who conceived the idea of creating an autonomous Ukrainian state found their main supporters in the more literate peasants and especially in the village intelligentsia of teachers, doctors, cooperative workers, etc.

Soon after the March Revolution the Ukrainian movement created a representative body in the Central Rada, which consisted of delegates from various Ukrainian parties, trade-union, coöperative and other associations. Sensing the weakness of the central Government the Rada gradually extended the scope of its pretensions. In May it put forward four demands to the Provisional Government: [18] that Ukrainian autonomy should be recognized by a special act of Government; that a separate administrative unit should be created out of twelve provinces with an Ukrainian population; that the office of commissar for Ukrainian affairs should be instituted and that a special Ukrainian military force should be created. As the Provisional Government hesitated to grant these demands the Rada took a more decisive tone and on June 16 appealed to the Ukrainian people to organize and proceed to the immediate laying of the foundation of an autonomous social order in Ukraina. About the same time an Ukrainian military congress met, in spite of Kerensky's prohibition, and received with jeering laughter the news that he had finally decided to permit the congress. On June 23 a representative of the Rada, at a ceremonial meeting on the Sofia Square in Kiev, before the monument of the seventeenth century Ukrainian Cossack hero, Bogdan Khmelnitzky, read the first "Universal," or message to the Ukrainian people, which urged the local communities of Ukraina to get into close touch with the Rada, not to reëlect officials who were out of sympathy with the Ukrainian cause and to pay money contributions to the Rada. The "Universal" was very far from a declaration of independence or complete separation; it recognized the right of the future All-Russian Constituent Assembly to confirm laws for Ukraina; but it marked a distinct step forward toward the virtual establishment of the Rada as the supreme authority in this wide area of South Russia.

The first Congress of Soviets, which met in Petrograd on June 16, faced a sorry balance-sheet of the first month's experiment in coalition. Class contradictions had not been mitigated by the entrance of Socialist representatives into the Government; on the contrary, as delegates to the Congress were soon to learn, the coalition had rather promoted a swing toward the Bolsheviki among the

soldiers and workers of the turbulent capital. No real progress had been made toward a concrete solution of any of the major problems which the Revolution had placed before the country: war and peace, the land question, the aspirations of the non-Russian nationalities, the creation of any generally respected state authority.

Several incidents which occurred on the eve of the Congress cast a vivid light on the prevalent disorganization and melting away of central authority. The Kronstadt Soviet had grudgingly and obviously only formally withdrawn its claim to be the sole power in that naval base. Admiral Kolchak, the forceful commander of the Black Sea Fleet and subsequent White dictator in Siberia, who had maintained authority and discipline longer than any other naval commander and for a time had established a working agreement with the sailors' committees, had resigned as a result of a conflict with the Sevastopol Soviet. A group of Anarchists had entrenched themselves in the Durnovo villa, in the Viborg District, and vied with the Bolsheviki in stirring up agitation against the Provisional Government. On one occasion a group of these Anarchists occupied the premises of a newspaper, *Russkaya Volya,* which they proposed to confiscate, but were finally ejected.

As was the case in the April Conference of Soviets the Bolsheviki and their occasional allies of the Left, the Mensheviki Internationalists, were in a very definite minority at the Soviet Congress. There were 1,090 delegates, of whom 822 possessed the right to vote, the remainder being present in a consultative capacity. Of 777 delegates who declared their Party membership 285 were Socialist Revolutionaries, 248 were Mensheviki, 105 Bolsheviki, 32 Mensheviki-Internationalists and 73 Socialists without being adherents of any party, while the remainder were divided among smaller parties and groups. The sharp contrast between the make-up of the membership of the Congress and the mood of the Petrograd workers and soldiers is accounted for by the fact that the political swing to the Left in the armies and in the provinces, from which the majority of the delegates were elected, was slower and more irresolute than in Petrograd.

There was a significant interjection on the second day of the Congress. When the leader of the moderate wing of the Soviet, Tseretelli, declared: "There is no political party in Russia which at the present time would say: 'Give us Power,'" Lenin called out from his seat: "Yes, there is." When his own turn came to speak Lenin put his ideas into strong uncompromising phrases which

excited the dismay and angry rejection of the moderate Socialist intellectuals, but which closely reflected the sentiment of the workers of the Viborg District or of the soldiers of the more mutinous Petrograd regiments:

"How is the breakdown to be explained? By the pilfering of the bourgeoisie. There is the source of anarchy. The Bolshevik Party is ready at any moment to assume full power. . . . Publish the profits of the capitalists, arrest fifty or a hundred of the biggest millionaires. . . . The War can only be ended by further development of the Revolution."

And a few days later, discussing the question of Russia's allies, he said: "They say that we cannot get on without the financial support of England and France. But this 'supports' us just as a noose supports the man who is being hanged. Let the Russian revolutionary class say: 'Down with this support; I do not recognize the debts contracted from French and British capitalists, I appeal for the uprising of all against the capitalists.' "

Within a week after its opening the Congress of Soviets faced a more formidable challenge than Lenin's uncompromising speeches. The boiling discontent of the workers and soldiers (the latter were particularly dissatisfied with Kerensky's interpretation of the Declaration of the Rights of the Soldier) led up to a decision by the Bolshevik Party organization to call for a huge street demonstration on June 23. Many of the military units desired to take part in this demonstration in armed formation.

The decision to call this demonstration evoked no little difference of opinion among the Bolshevik leaders. Tomsky counselled against it on the ground that it was impossible to foresee what would happen if hundreds of thousands of people, some of them with guns in their hands, poured out on the streets at a time when the tide of class hatred was running very high. Kalinin suggested that the workers did not have as definite grievances as the soldiers. Stalin, on the other hand, was strongly in favor of the demonstration, arguing: [19] "Since we are an organization which enjoys influence we must stir up the sentiment of the workers . . . It is our duty to organize this demonstration; it will be a review of our forces. At the sight of the armed soldiers the bourgeoisie will hide."

The decision to hold the demonstration was definitely adopted on June 21 at a conference of representatives of the Central and Petrograd Party committees, the Military Organization and the trade-unions and factory committees. Among the slogans which

were authorized for the occasion were: "Down with the ten capitalist ministers," "All power to the All-Russian Soviet of Workers', Soldiers' and Peasants' Deputies," "Reëxamine the Declaration of the Rights of the Soldier," "Down with anarchy in industry and the capitalists who declare lockouts," "Time to end the War. Let the Soviet declare just conditions of peace," "Neither separate peace with Wilhelm nor secret treaties with French and British capitalists" and, finally three words in which the Bolsheviki in 1917 were apt to sum up their programme: "Bread. Peace. Freedom."

There is no reason to believe that Lenin or any of the more responsible Bolshevik leaders regarded the proposed demonstration as a means of effecting a *coup d'état*. Conditions for this were still far from ripe, because while the Bolsheviki at this time were quite possibly strong enough to seize power in the capital such a move would in all probability have shattered in the end on the resistance of the provinces and the army. Kerensky notes that the farther away the troops were from the "poisonous" atmosphere of Petrograd the less, as a general rule, they were under Bolshevik influence.[20]

However, more aggressive designs were cherished by those Bolshevik leaders who were closer to the rank-and-file of the workers and soldiers. Smilga suggested at a session of the Central and Petrograd Committees that, if events should come to a clash, the demonstrators shouldn't abstain from seizing the post and telegraph offices and the arsenal.

Latzis, subsequently a prominent figure in the Cheka, notes in his diary for June 22 that he had agreed with Semashko, an influential Bolshevik agitator in the First Machine-Gun Regiment, and Rakhia, a Finnish Bolshevik, that "in case of necessity we should seize the station, the arsenal, the banks, the post and telegraph offices, supported by the machine-gun regiment."

What would have happened if the demonstration had taken place is, of course, conjectural. The Executive Committee of the Petrograd Soviet, having learned of the proposed demonstration on June 22, the day before it was supposed to take place, refused to permit it. At first the Bolshevik leadership refused to submit to this prohibition, merely proposing to emphasize the peaceful character of the demonstration. Later in the day the news of the impending demonstration reached the All-Russian Soviet Congress, which passed a resolution forbidding any street manifestations for three days and stigmatizing anyone who disobeyed this order as

"an enemy of the Revolution." The Bolshevik delegation to the Congress began to waver and question the advisability of disobeying a decision of the All-Russian Soviet representative body.

Lenin himself apparently did not make up his mind until almost the last possible moment. A relatively trivial point seems to have tipped the scale; when Lenin suggested at a session of Party leaders late at night that it was too late to eliminate the appeal for the demonstration from the *Pravda* a participant in the conference, Danilov, replied that "with one and a half printers" he could make the necessary changes.[21] Shortly after this the Central Committee decided to call off the demonstration, to eliminate the appeal from the *Pravda* and to send Party agitators to the factories and barracks to persuade the workers and soldiers not to come out. Many delegates of the Congress of other parties also took part in this difficult mission of persuasion.

It proved considerably harder to restrain the demonstrators than to arouse them. Even Bolshevik speakers sometimes found it difficult to get a hearing, while representatives of the more moderate parties were often greeted with hostile shouts, such as, "We are not your comrades."

The proposed demonstration was called off; but the circumstances which paved the way for it did not change; it would only be a matter of some three weeks before the bloodshed which was only threatened on this occasion would actually occur. On the 24th Tseretelli accused the Bolsheviki of having conspired against the Soviet majority and called for their disarmament; Kamenev challenged Tseretelli to have him arrested. The incident ended, as was usual when anything depended for decision on the Menshevik-Socialist-Revolutionary bloc, with a watery resolution of censure for the Bolsheviki, considerably milder than Tseretelli desired.

The Bolsheviki had their revenge for the prohibition of their demonstration eight days later when, on July 1, the Soviet Congress authorized a demonstration as an expression of confidence in the Soviets. The demonstration was a triumph of Bolshevism. Of the three or four hundred thousand marchers only a minority displayed the somewhat neutral slogans which the Congress had recommended: "Democratic republic," "General peace." The great majority marched under the Bolshevik banners which had been prepared for the 23d of June and laid away with so much reluctance. Only three small detachments, the Bund, the extreme right-wing Socialist group "Unity" and the Cossacks, displayed streamers calling for

confidence in the Provisional Government; and these were quickly torn up or voluntarily withdrawn. It is noteworthy that the Soviet Congress did not dare to appeal for open support of its own policy of coalition with the propertied classes.

After the demonstration of July 1 some Bolsheviki suggested to Lenin that nothing now remained for the moderate parties to do except hand over power. Lenin was more coldly realistic. "Power is not handed over; it is taken by arms," he declared.[22]

On the same day when the workers and soldiers of Petrograd were demonstrating with such vigor against the War and against the existing regime the long expected and long delayed offensive of the Russian army began on the Galician front. Kerensky despatched a message to Prince Lvov, announcing that "the Russian revolutionary army had gone into attack" and asking that the regiments which took part in the attack should be rewarded with red banners and the special name: "Regiments of the 18th of June" (the date of the commencement of the offensive, according to the old Russian calendar). The Nevsky Prospekt, Petrograd's main boulevard, which on July 1st had witnessed the march of the workers and soldiers, filled up on the 2nd with demonstrators of a different type: groups of people celebrating the beginning of the offensive, singing nationalist songs and carrying portraits of Kerensky.

But the offensive was foredoomed to failure. From the beginning there were cases of wavering, of flat refusal to obey orders, to follow up initial successes.[23] Some local successes were achieved at the beginning, thanks to three factors: the vast numerical superiority of the Russians, the elaborate and careful artillery preparation and the chronically weak morale of the Austrian troops who occupied a considerable sector of the hostile front. The 7th and 11th armies, during the first days of fighting, took over 18,000 prisoners; and still more important victories were won by the 8th army of General Kornilov, which broke through the Austrian lines on a twenty mile front, occupied the old town of Galich on the 10th and Kalusz on the 11th of July, taking over 10,000 prisoners.

But as soon as reserves of German shock troops came up and struck at the Russian forces the advance turned into retreat and then into disorderly rout, accompanied by an extraordinary amount of burning, pillage, rapine and outrages, all of which reflected the low morale of the army and the wellnigh complete breakdown of discipline. The figure of desertions was prodigious; in one night the "Battalion of Death" (these detachments were special voluntary

shock units organized by officers and by the few soldiers who desired to continue fighting) detained about 12,000 deserters in the outskirts of Volochisk.[24] Tarnopol, the main town which the Russians held in Galicia, was given up without a struggle on July 24 and by the end of the month the Russian armies, no longer actively pursued by the enemy, had rolled back in disorder to the Russian state frontier.

The old generals had regarded the chances of success in the offensive with considerable scepticism from the beginning; and one may suspect a note of malicious satisfaction in their reports of the poor showing of the "revolutionary" army. But the commissars and committees attached to the armies, recruited from men who, like Kerensky, had believed in the possibility of replacing the old discipline with a new wave of enthusiasm, also emphasized the point that the Russian defeat was not an ordinary military reverse, but a sheer collapse and rout. So the telegram of the Committee of the Southwestern Front reads as follows: [25]

"The majority of the units are in a state of ever growing disintegration. There is already no question of authority and subordination. Persuasion and argument have lost force. They are answered with threats, sometimes with shooting. Some units leave their positions at will, not awaiting the approach of the enemy. There were cases when an order to move quickly for support was debated for hours at meetings, so that the support was delayed for days. . . . The situation demands extreme measures. . . . To-day orders to shoot at the fugitives were given by the commander-in-chief of the Southwestern Front and by the commander of the Eleventh Army with the agreement of the commissar and committees."

Attempts at offensive operations on the Western and Northern fronts were made some time after the main campaign had been launched in Galicia. They were much feebler than the original thrust in Galicia and led to no success whatever. But as they did not provoke any serious counter-attack these fronts remained temporarily stationary, although the Germans occupied Riga with little resistance on September 3.

Both conservative nationalists and pro-War Socialists had, for different reasons, looked to the offensive as a way out of the crisis in which the country was involved. The conservatives hoped that the miracle of a victorious ending of the War would put an end to the rising tide of social upheaval. Men like Kerensky and his associates with varying hues of revolutionism, Savinkov, Stankevitch and Voitinsky, hoped that the offensive would raise Russia's interna-

tional prestige and force both Germany and the Allies to take its peace programme more seriously.

But all these hopes were destroyed when the first vigorous German counter-attack turned the Russian armies into a fugitive mob, more dangerous to the civilian population than to the enemy. The way out of the crisis through successful war was closed. The process of "deepening" the Revolution, even though it was on the eve of a temporary repulse and check, was bound to go on unless the government could somehow meet the challenge of the simple Bolshevik popular slogan "Peace, land, bread" or unless a "strong man" could somehow create order out of chaos. And it was in the direction of this hypothetical strong man that the eyes of Russia's propertied classes began to turn more and more during the summer months.

NOTES

[1] V. B. Stankevitch, "Reminiscences, 1914–1919," p. 58.

[2] "Sketches of the History of the October Revolution," Vol. II, p. 191.

[3] *Ibid.*, p. 190.

[4] P. N. Milyukov, "History of the Second Russian Revolution," Vol. I, p. 111.

[5] D. O. Zaslavsky and V. A. Kantorovitch, "Chronicle of the February Revolution," Vol. I, p. 267.

[6] A. Kerensky, "The Catastrophe," pp. 139–141.

[7] *Ibid.*, p. 185.

[8] Regarding this Declaration see Chapter V, pp. 105–106.

[9] Kerensky, *op. cit.*, pp. 186ff.

[10] A. Brussilov, "My Reminiscences," p. 214.

[11] N. Sukhanov, "Memoirs of the Revolution," Vol. IV, p. 136.

[12] G. Y. Sokolnikov and Associates, "Soviet Policy in Public Finance," p. 80.

[13] "The Revolution of 1917: Chronicle of Events," Vol. II, p. 174.

[14] *Ibid.*, Vol. III, p. 27.

[15] Ariadna Tyrkova-Williams, "From Liberty to Brest-Litovsk," pp. 189ff.

[16] "The Workers' Movement in 1917," p. 133.

[17] "The Revolution of 1917: Chronicle of Events," Vol. III, p. 242.

[18] Milyukov, *op. cit.*, Vol. I, p. 157.

[19] "Sketches of the History of the October Revolution," Vol. II, pp. 227ff.

[20] Kerensky, *op. cit.*, p. 168.

[21] See the recollections of S. Danilov in Vol. III of the collection entitled, "About Lenin."

[22] See N. Podvoisky's article in *Pravda* of April 23, 1920.

[23] Stankevitch, *op. cit.*, p. 79.

[24] "The Dissolution of the Army in 1917," p. 181.

[25] "The Revolution of 1917: Chronicle of Events," Vol. III, p. 173.

CHAPTER VIII

JULY DAYS: THE REVOLUTION CHECKED

THE forward sweep of social revolution in Russia between March and November, 1917, did not proceed in an unbroken upward curve. After the first four months of steady "deepening" of the Revolution, expressed in increasing disregard on the part of the masses of workers and soldiers for the authority, not only of the Provisional Government, but also of the Soviet, in seizures of land on the countryside and confiscations of houses in the towns, in the evaporation of the authority of the army officers, the swing to the left experienced a definite, although not, in the long run, a decisive check as a result of the disorderly and planless demonstrations and riots which have gone into history under the name of "the July Days."

While the fundamental social factors in Russian life in 1917 (the war-weariness of the soldiers, the landhunger of the peasants, the growing impulse of the workers to dispossess the capitalists in a very positive and literal fashion) were all on the side of the Bolsheviki there was one element in the situation which even such a master of revolutionary strategy as Lenin could not control. This was the tendency of many of the military units and most of the large factories in Petrograd to run far ahead of the country as a whole in their demands and in their actions. When the Petrograd workers and soldiers came out on the streets with the slogan "All power to the Soviets" the Bolsheviki were confronted with a difficult alternative. If they stood aside from the movement they ran the risk of losing their influence on the masses and seeing the element of organized leadership vanish altogether or pass into the hands of Anarchists and individual agitators. If they associated themselves with a movement that had many features of armed revolt they exposed themselves to the consequences of defeat if the movement failed. In the popular demonstrations of May and June the Bolshevik leaders maneuvered with sufficient skill to retain their authority and prestige with the masses without committing themselves to any rash and untimely programme of out-and-out insurrection. But

166

they were not so fortunate in July, when the explosive force from below was much stronger.

The storm that burst on July 16 and 17 had many ominous preliminary rumblings of thunder. On July 5 the Bolshevik delegates in the Vtsik (the All-Russian Soviet Executive Committee, which was the highest national Soviet authority between congresses) warned that body that the workers of the huge Putilov metal works were likely to strike any day, "which would inevitably cause an outbreak on the part of the majority of the workers and soldiers." Hitherto the Bolsheviki had restrained them, but there was no guaranty that this would continue. On July 6 the representatives of seventy-three factories and a number of labor organizations met at the Putilov works and resolved to press economic demands. At the same time they observed that higher wages would not compensate for rising prices and therefore demanded control of production, together with power in the hands of the Soviets. The strike wave which had begun in June was still in full swing and created in the minds of the workers a constant mood of nervous irritation.

There were equally strong symptoms of discontent and unrest among the military units. Many soldiers who had reached the age of forty had been furloughed from the front for field work earlier in the year. To their intense dissatisfaction they were recalled to the trenches for the offensive. On July 3 and 4 these "forty-year" soldiers demonstrated in Petrograd under such slogans as: "They asked us to sow more grain: so let us harvest it." In Astrakhan, Eletz and other provincial towns the recall of these unwilling veterans provoked riots.

There was also grave trouble in the First Machine-Gun Regiment, always a stronghold of Bolshevism. This unit held a meeting on July 4, decided to send to the front only ten detachments instead of the thirty which had been required by the military authorities and passed a strongly worded resolution to the effect that "if the Soviet will threaten our regiment and other revolutionary regiments with dissolution, even by means of using armed force, we shall not hesitate, in response to this, to dissolve by armed force the Provisional Government and the organizations which support it." In this resolution one gets a clear hint of the hostility to the Menshevik-Socialist-Revolutionary leadership of the Soviet which already characterized the attitude of many of the Petrograd workers and soldiers. This attitude, of course, did not chime in very well with the popular Bolshevik slogan, "All power to the Soviets"; and

much of the amazing confusion and disorganization of the July Days is attributable to the fact that the demonstrators were trying to force power on men whom they did not respect or trust.

With a view to preventing unauthorized outbursts among the soldiers of the garrison the Military Organization of the Bolsheviki on July 5 published in the newspaper *Soldatskaya Pravda* (Soldiers' Truth) an appeal to soldiers and workers not to believe orders to demonstrate in the name of the Military Organization. The appeal continued: "The Military Organization does not summon to a demonstration. Comrades, demand from every agitator or orator who is inciting to demonstration in the name of the Military Organization credentials with the stamp of the Organization, signed by its president and secretary."

In cases where regiments were quartered in factory districts the workers and soldiers not infrequently exercised an inflammatory effect upon each other. So we read in the diary of a Bolshevik leader in the Viborg District, Latzis, the following entry: [1]

"July 3—an ominous day. The workers of the Rosenkranz factory go to the Moscow and Machine-Gun Regiments and invite them to come out. Much energy had to be employed to pacify the passions that had been stirred up. One got the impression that neither the workers nor the soldiers can be held back."

On July 8 delegates from the Grenadier Regiment at the front came to Petrograd and told the reserve battalion of this regiment that violence was being employed at the front, that Czech troops with machine-guns were driving the Grenadiers into the offensive. A week later, on the 15th, the 1st Machine-Gun Regiment organized a farewell meeting for some units which were departing for the front. Trotzky and Lunacharsky addressed the meeting, urging Soviet power as the sole way out of the War, while spokesmen for the regiment, Zhilin and Lashevitch (the latter a resolute Bolshevik commander in the civil war), declared that the soldiers would give their lives only for the Revolution. The meeting protested against the alleged violence which had been used in dissolving the Grenadier Regiment.

In such a heavily charged atmosphere only a small incident was needed to provoke an explosion. While it is difficult, even on the basis of accounts of participants and archive materials, to say with precise certainty what did precipitate the July Days there is reason to believe that the resignation of four Cadet Ministers from the

coalition Cabinet on July 15 was a not unimportant factor. The immediate cause of their resignation was dissatisfaction with the concessions which Kerensky, Tseretelli and Tereschenko had made to Ukrainian autonomist demands after negotiations with representatives of the Rada in Kiev. Apart from the Ukrainian question, the Cadets were undoubtedly dissatisfied with the failure of their Socialist colleagues in the Ministry either to exert an effective moderating influence upon the workers or to restore discipline in the army.

The breakdown of the coalition through the withdrawal of the representatives of the sole substantial middleclass party from the Cabinet furnished an additional argument to the advocates of "All power to the Soviets." While the Mensheviki and Socialist Revolutionaries in Vtsik and the Petrograd Soviet began to discuss ways and means of forming a new workable government (Tseretelli was apparently in favor of carrying on the Cabinet without appointing successors to the Cadet Ministers, merely turning over their Ministries to suitable temporary administrators) the soldiers and workers were on the march to insist that the Vtsik declare itself the supreme power in the country.

The initiative for the outbreak came from the turbulent machine-gunners. A meeting of their company committees on the morning of the 16th spontaneously spoke out for an armed demonstration. Messengers were sent to other regiments, inviting them to participate. Throughout the day there was something of a race between envoys of the Bolshevik Military Organization, eager to stave off a movement for which no adequate political preparation had been made, and the impatient machine-gunners.[2] By late afternoon the Military Organization thought it had won the battle of argument; but at 6:30 it was learned that the regiment, along with the Moscow, Grenadier and 180th, was marching to the Bolshevik headquarters in the Palace of Kshesinskaya. Two ordinarily popular and influential Bolshevik speakers, Lashevitch and Kuraev, were booed down when they attempted to persuade the soldiers to return to their barracks; and at the same time the Bolshevik leaders in the Palace of Kshesinskaya learned that workers had come out on the streets under the slogan: "All power to the Soviets."

Earlier in the day Stalin, on behalf of the Bolshevik Central Committee, had assured the Vtsik that the Bolsheviki would not undertake any demonstration.[3] But the pressure from below was too strong; and it was decided to take under control the movement

which could not be stopped and to urge the workers and soldiers to proceed to the Tauride Palace, where the Vtsik and the Executive Committee of the Petrograd Soviet held their sessions and to present their demands in an orderly organized fashion. Lenin was not in Petrograd at the time (the best proof that there had been no serious effort on the part of the Bolsheviki to organize a *coup d'état*); when he returned on the morning of the 17th from the country house in Finland where he had been recuperating after a slight illness he approved the tactics of the Central Committee and the other Bolshevik organizations.

So, far from planning the July outbreak, the Bolsheviki were rather dragged into assuming the leadership, so far indeed as there was any leadership. Among all the major episodes of the Revolution this July outbreak is perhaps the most confused and chaotic. Masses of soldiers poured through the main streets of the capital, firing wildly at non-existing enemies and fleeing in panic if they thought they were being fired on; hosts of workers from the big munition and metal plants surrounded the Soviet headquarters, determined that the Mensheviki and Socialist Revolutionaries should take power, whether they wanted it or not. Ordinary criminals and German agents doubtless added their share to the general upheaval; undisciplined crowds repeatedly broke into houses and stores; and, under pretense of searching for weapons or for snipers, took away whatever they liked. Sukhanov, an eyewitness of the July Days, sums up the spirit of the affair in the phrase: "Excitement, with a coloring of rage, but not of enthusiasm." [4]

Soon after it had learned that a demonstration was under way the Vtsik issued an appeal, reminding "the comrades soldiers" that "not one military unit has the right to come out with arms without the command of the commander-in-chief of the troops, acting in full agreement with us" and characterizing those who violated this decision as "traitors and enemies of the Revolution." The time had passed, however, when Petrograd soldiers and workers paid much attention to such appeals; and waves of demonstrators intermittently besieged the Tauride Palace with demands that the Soviets assume power until late at night, when the movement broke up.

Meanwhile the Bolsheviki had won a tactical success in the Workers' Section of the Petrograd Soviet, which voted in favor of the assumption of governmental power by the Executive Committee of the Workers', Peasants' and Soldiers' Soviets. The Mensheviki

and Socialist Revolutionaries, being in the minority, left the assembly. The remaining Bolshevik deputies decided to elect a commission of fifteen, which was to be commissioned to act in the name of the Workers' Section. It is doubtful whether this commission was elected; and it certainly played no significant rôle in the subsequent developments. Practically all the Bolshevik representatives, both in the Vtsik and in the Petrograd Soviet, retired to their Party headquarters or went to the barracks and factories with a view to organizing the continuation of the demonstration on the following day.

It is difficult to say which side was more disgusted: the demonstrators because of the refusal of the Soviet majority to assume power or the Soviet leaders with the unruly mobs which were trying to force them to take a step which they considered unwise and unjustified. The spirit of the masses was pretty accurately expressed by a worker who, if we may believe Milyukov,[5] shook his fist on the following day at the Socialist Revolutionary Minister for Agriculture, Chernov, and angrily shouted: "Take power, you son of a bitch, when they give it to you." The Vtsik left no doubt as to its own sentiments when, late on the stormy night of the 16th, it issued a resolution containing the following phrases:

"Some armed military units have come out on the streets, attempting to master the city, seizing automobiles, arresting at their will individuals, operating with threats and violence. Coming to the Tauride Palace with arms in their hands, they demanded that the Executive Committees assume all power. Proposing power to the Soviets they are the first to attack this power. The All-Russian executive organs of the Soldiers', Workers' and Peasants' Deputies reject with indignation every attempt to bring pressure on their free will. It is unworthy to attempt by means of armed demonstrations to impose the will of some parts of the garrison of one city upon all Russia. . . .

"These actions are equivalent to treason to our revolutionary army, which is defending on the front the conquests of the Revolution. Whoever in the rear attacks the free will of the legitimate organs of democracy is plunging a dagger into the back of the revolutionary army."

Although the night of the 16th witnessed a good deal of tumult and disorder, including, according to rumor, an attempt to kidnap Kerensky at the station, which failed because he had already left for the front, the movement only reached its peak on the 17th. On this day the Bolshevik Central Committee had called for "a peaceful organized demonstration" on behalf of the assumption of power by the Soviets.

A formidable character was imparted to this demonstration, which turned out in practise to be neither peaceful nor organized, by the arrival of some 20,000 armed Kronstadt sailors, who disembarked in the morning and marched to the Palace of Kshesinskaya, where Lenin, who had now returned to Petrograd, greeted them with a short, reserved speech, in which he expressed confidence that the slogan "All power to the Soviets" would conquer in the end, "notwithstanding temporary zigzags," and told the sailors that tremendous firmness, restraint and watchfulness were required of them.[6] Evidently the Bolshevik leader did not believe that the hour had come to make the decisive stroke for power, although in a conversation with Bonch-Bruevitch on this same day he expressed the belief that armed uprising must come "not later than autumn." [7]

The demonstration of the Kronstadt sailors had much the same background as that of the Petrograd military units. On the afternoon of the 16th delegates from the Machine-Gun Regiment, together with some Anarchists, arrived in the naval base. A meeting was held on Anchor Square, the main assembly place of Kronstadt, and one of the newly arrived Anarchists aroused the passions of the turbulent and emotional sailors to a high pitch when, after denouncing the Provisional Government for persecuting the Anarchists, he cried out: "Comrades, your brothers' blood is now perhaps already flowing. Will you refuse to support your comrades? Will you refuse to come out in defense of the Revolution?"

The efforts of the young medical student, Roshal, a popular Bolshevik leader, to pacify the crowd completely failed; and after Midshipman Raskolnikov, another prominent member of the local Bolshevik organization, had conferred by telephone with Zinoviev in Petrograd it was decided that the Kronstadt sailors should proceed to Petrograd, armed and in full order, to take part in the demonstration on the following day.

Throughout the 16th and most of the 17th the situation of the Provisional Government and of the Soviet was weak and helpless to the last degree. There had not been time for response to the urgent appeals which were sent out for aid to the nearest fronts; and those regiments in Petrograd which were not actively participating in the demonstration remained passively in their barracks and showed no inclination to come to the Government's defense. As Sukhanov says,[8] "any group of ten or twelve men could have arrested the Government," the members of which were in session at the unprotected apartment of Prince Lvov, the Premier. Milyu-

kov confirms this picture of the defenselessness of the authorities against the armed mobs of tens or even hundreds of thousands which were surging through the main streets of the city.[9] "There was a moment," he writes, in describing the events of the 17th, "when the position of the Government seemed hopeless. The Preobrazhensky, Semyenov and Ismailov regiments, which did not join the Bolsheviki, informed the Government that they maintained 'neutrality.' On the Palace Square, for the defense of the Staff, were only invalids and a few companies of Cossacks. The troops from the outskirts of Petrograd, summoned by the commander-in-chief, General Polovtzev, could only appear by evening. Until they arrived the order of Polovtzev to the military units to 'proceed immediately to the restoration of order' remained a dead letter." Two influential Ministers, Nekrasov and Tereschenko, seem to have suddenly vanished and gone into hiding.

The Soviet, which was much more the objective of the demonstrators than the headquarters of the Government, was equally powerless, until late in the evening. As Voitinsky, an outstanding "defensist" among the Soviet leaders, subsequently reported: [10]

"At one time we had absolutely no forces. At the entrances to the Tauride Palace were only six men, who could not have held back the mob. The armored automobiles were the first unit to come to our aid."

So the city was really at the mercy of the demonstrators; and if there had been any concrete design to arrest the Cabinet Ministers, occupy the strategically important buildings of the city and generally carry out a *coup*, it could scarcely have been thwarted. But there was no such design, with the result that the demonstration, although it was certainly violent in many ways, finally evaporated for sheer lack of a definite goal. There was a good deal more bloodshed on the 17th than on the preceding day; and it is roughly estimated that about 400 persons were killed and wounded on the two days, many of them as a result of wild and accidental shooting.[10a]

As the Kronstadt sailors marched through the main streets of Petrograd they were fired on, or thought they were fired on, in several places. They promptly broke into houses from which shots were supposed to have come and killed with scant ceremony anyone whom they suspected of shooting. The following excerpts from an official report of the Executive Committee of the Petrograd Soviet [11] convey an idea of the characteristic incidents of this wild, chaotic day:

"At three in the afternoon Kantorovitch communicated that five people were killed and twenty-seven wounded before his eyes on Sadovaya Street. He explained the firing by the hysteria and nervousness of the mob, which marches with loaded rifles and fingers on the triggers and begins to shoot at the least panic. . . .

"On Liteiny Prospect the glass was broken in many shops and the street car cables were torn up. In many houses the Kronstadters carry out searches on the pretext that they have been fired on. If anyone is found he is pulled out on the street and lynched."

Here and there clashes occurred, with some loss of life, between the few Cossack patrols (with the aid of which General Polovtzev endeavored to guard the main buildings and offices) and insurgent soldiers and sailors. The peak of the demonstration was reached late in the afternoon when the Kronstadt sailors, along with large masses of workers, surrounded the Tauride Palace and demanded an accounting with the unpopular moderate leaders of the Soviet. The Anarchists had a good deal of influence among the sailors; and there were cries for the Minister of Justice, Pereverzev, who had ordered the raid on the Anarchist headquarters in the villa of Durnovo. Tseretelli appeared and told the crowd that Pereverzev had resigned and, in any case, was not responsible to a mob. This increased the indignation; and when the Socialist Revolutionary Minister of Agriculture, Chernov, endeavored to deliver a speech he was met with hostile cries, and some sailors seized him and pulled him into a nearby automobile.

Chernov would probably have been roughly handled, perhaps even lynched, if Trotzky, who enjoyed great popularity among the sailors, had not opportunely appeared and rushed to the rescue of his political opponent. Addressing the Kronstadters as "the pride and beauty of the Revolution" Trotzky spoke energetically against unnecessary and unprovoked arrests and dramatically ended: "Let anyone who is for violence raise his hand." The sailors were completely subdued by Trotzky's eloquence and energy; no one raised his hand or even opened his mouth, and Trotzky, triumphantly declaring with a wave of his hand, "Citizen Chernov, you are freed," invited the badly frightened Minister to get out of the automobile and return to the Soviet assembly hall.[12]

Shortly after this a combined session of the All-Russian Central Soviet Executive Committee and of the Executive Committee of the Soviet of Peasants' Deputies opened in the Tauride Palace, with the roaring mobs outside. A delegation of ninety representatives from fifty-four factories demanded a hearing; and four spokes-

men of the delegation, in varying phrases, voiced the demand that the Soviets should assume power.

"It is strange when one reads the appeal of the Vtsik: workers and soldiers are called counterrevolutionaries. Our demand—the general demand of the workers—is all power to the Soviets of Workers' and Soldiers' Deputies . . . We demand the retirement of the ten capitalist Ministers. We trust the Soviet, but not those whom the Soviet trusts. Our comrades, the Socialist Ministers, entered into an agreement with the capitalists, but these capitalists are our mortal enemies. . . . The land must pass immediately to the peasants, before the Constituent Assembly."

This strong language of the impatient proletarians awakened no response in the Soviet leaders, who were watching with not unnatural apprehension the arrival of wave after wave of angry demonstrators and were uneasily calculating how soon troops from the front or from the loyal units in Petrograd would come to relieve what was for them almost a state of siege. After a typically Russian interminable debate the viewpoint of the Soviet majority was registered in a resolution written by the Socialist Revolutionary Gotz. Its main point was that a plenary session of the Executive Committees of the Soviets of Workers', Peasants' and Soldiers' Deputies should meet in two weeks to discuss the question of organizing a new government. Meanwhile the present government must remain in power.

Two more striking incidents occurred before the end of the more violent phases of the demonstration coincided with the belated arrival of troops ready to defend the Soviet majority. The first of these incidents illustrates the strange confusion of these July Days. The 176th Regiment, quartered in Tsarskoe Syelo, a village in the neighborhood of Petrograd, had made a long march on a rainy day with the definitely Bolshevik intention of demanding that all power be vested in the Soviets. When it arrived at the Tauride Palace the Menshevik leader Dan greeted it, congratulated the soldiers on their devotion to the Soviet and actually had guards from this Bolshevik regiment posted around the Tauride Palace in order to defend the Menshevik and Socialist Revolutionary Soviet deputies against the intermittent intrusion of the other Bolshevik soldiers and workers who were clamoring for Soviet power on the streets.

The composure of the delegates was further disturbed by the arrival at the Palace of a host of workers from the large Putilov plant. They behaved very aggressively and demanded Tseretelli,

for whom they apparently had special aversion. He was not to be found. One of the workers, brandishing a rifle, leaped up on the speakers' platform and delivered a somewhat incoherent but vehement speech in the following terms.[13]

"Comrades. Shall we, workers, put up with treachery very long? You gathered here, you discuss, make deals with the bourgeoisie and the landowners. You are betraying the working class. The working class won't endure this. We, Putilovites, are thirty thousand strong. We'll get what we want. No bourgeoisie. All power to the Soviets. We have a tight grip on our rifles. Your Kerenskys and Tseretellis will not crush us."

Chkheidze, who, as a Georgian, was perhaps not unused to gunplay, showed more selfpossession in the face of this tirade than most of the other delegates. He gravely handed the excited worker a Soviet manifesto, urging the demonstrators to go home, on pain of being considered traitors to the Revolution. The worker, not knowing what to do, took the manifesto and stumbled off the platform. The incident was over. But in this minor episode, as in the broader panorama of the whole July upheaval, there is a definite foreshadowing of the later phase of the Revolution when the Russian masses would throw over their early leaders entirely and drive through to their goals: peace and land.

As Tseretelli was ending a speech at the long night session of the Soviet the trampling of soldiers' boots could be heard outside the Palace. At first the delegates wondered whether another mutinous regiment had come to present its demands; but their apprehensions were quickly relieved when they learned that this was the Ismailov Regiment, which had decided to come to the defense of the Soviet. A military band blared out the Marseillaise; and the Soviet delegates joined in singing it with a sense of wholehearted relief which they had scarcely experienced when the sans-culottes of the Russian Revolution, the workers from the Viborg District and the Kronstadt sailors, had been angrily demanding that they assume power earlier in the day.

The tide had turned even more decisively than the Soviet delegates realized at the moment. A packet of documents supposed to prove that Lenin and his associates were German agents had been released for publication by the Ministry of Justice. The character and probability of these documents will be analyzed later. Their immediate tactical effect was striking. The delegates of the "neutral" Preobrazhensky Regiment, as soon as they were told of the docu-

ments, agreed to come out actively against the demonstrators.[14] The announcement that Lenin was a "German spy" was calculated to have a far greater propagandist effect, especially on the ignorant soldiers, than any finespun political and economic arguments against his indubitably popular slogans of ending the War, seizing the land and "robbing what had been robbed."

That the forces of extremism were in retreat was clearly evident by the morning of the 18th. The Bolshevik organ, *Pravda,* called off the strike and demonstration. Most of the Kronstadt sailors, the most formidable fighting force at the disposal of the insurgents, had returned to their naval base on the night of the 17th. Only two or three thousand remained with their leaders, Raskolnikov and Roshal, with the idea of defending the headquarters of the Bolshevik Military Organization, the Palace of Kshesinskaya, and the adjoining Fortress of Peter and Paul, which had been occupied by insurgents during the disturbances of the preceding days. Acts of violence, which had mainly occurred on the side of the demonstrators on the 16th and 17th, now became more common on the part of the upholders of the Government. So, early on the morning of the 18th, an officer, with a small guard of soldiers, raided the office of *Pravda,* ransacked files, smashed up furniture and office equipment and arrested some of the employees. A newly established Bolshevik printing-shop, "Labor," was also raided and demolished. The habit of arbitrary arrest, common ever since the Revolution, continued; but now the victims of the arrests were persons suspected of Bolshevism. During the 18th loyal troops cleared the streets of the capital of the remnants of the insurgent demonstrators.

The last strongholds of the armed Bolshevik forces, the Palace of Kshesinskaya and the Fortress of Peter and Paul, were occupied without resistance or bloodshed by the government forces on the morning of the 19th. The active young midshipman Raskolnikov, the subsequent commander of the Red Volga flotilla during the civil war, had been appointed commandant of the Kshesinskaya Palace; and at first "interpreting his duties in a broad way, a Kronstadt way," to borrow Trotzky's expression,[15] he sent out requisitions for artillery to sympathetic military units and ordered a small warship to enter the mouth of the Neva. These warlike preparations were soon abandoned, however; and after some argument as to the retention of their arms, the remaining Kronstadt sailors agreed to give them up and to return peacefully to Kronstadt.

This marked the end of the July disturbances, which Lenin aptly

characterized as "something considerably more than a demonstration and less than a revolution." In some respects it suggested that "playing at insurrection" which Lenin himself, like Marx, most strongly condemned. The coming out on the streets of large masses of armed soldiers and sailors, the seizure of the Fortress of Peter and Paul, the exchanges of shots with government patrols, Raskolnikov's order for a small warship and artillery—all this did not fit in very well with the pattern of a peaceful and orderly demonstration of citizens desiring to express their views; such features of the July Days were needlessly provocative unless there was, as there certainly was not, a definite intention on the part of the Bolshevik leaders to oust the Provisional Government by force. In politics as in physics action provokes reactions, and a violent and riotous outbreak is almost certain to inspire intensified repression from a government which survives it.

The responsibility for this "playing with insurrection," however, did not rest with Lenin and his associates, but with the turbulent masses whom they could not check and whom they could barely hold under some semblance of control by joining in the movement. The question arises whether, since the Bolsheviki could not afford politically to repudiate and stand aside from this mass movement, they should have endeavored to turn it into an organized seizure of power, to have done in July what they subsequently did in November. So far as Petrograd alone was concerned, it is difficult to see any force that could have stopped an out-and-out *coup* on the evening of the 16th or during most of the 17th.

But the weak response which the Petrograd outbreak elicited in the provincial centres is perhaps the strongest proof that Lenin was correct in risking the effects of a period of anti-Bolshevik repression, the inevitable sequel to a violent demonstration without a definite end, rather than placing his stake on a stroke for power in July. There were echoes of the July Days in Ivanovo-Vosnessensk, Nizhni Novgorod, Kiev, Astrakhan and other towns; but only in Ivanovo-Vosnessensk, an overwhelmingly workingclass textile town with a long record of revolutionary activity, was there something in the nature of a conscious assumption of authority by the local Soviet, which established a censorship over telegraph and telephone messages. In Nizhni Novgorod a fight between some junkers (as officers in training were called in Russia) and soldiers led to the temporary installation of an impromptu soldiers' committee as the controlling force in the town. This was a short-lived affair, however,

and in Kiev, Astrakhan, Taganrog and other towns where disturbances occurred they were little more than evanescent riots. There
is every reason to believe that the armies at the front and the
great majority of the cities and towns throughout the country would
have repudiated a seizure of power by the Bolsheviki in Petrograd;
and the capital, isolated from the rest of the country, would scarcely
have held out.

The July demonstration had a peculiar repercussion in the Baltic
Fleet, which was stationed at Helsingfors. The assistant Naval
Minister, Captain Dudarev, despatched a message to Admiral
Verderevsky, commander of the fleet, that not one ship should leave
Helsingfors contrary to orders, and added: "Don't hesitate to sink
such a ship with the aid of a submarine." In the main it was the
big ships of the line that were most under Bolshevik and Anarchist
influence, while the submarines were still held more within the bonds
of discipline. Dudarev also asked Verderevsky to send four ships to
Petrograd; but the Admiral not only professed inability to do this,
but showed Dudarev's telegram to members of the Centrobalt, the
sailors' committee attached to the Baltic Fleet. Dudarev's order
aroused great indignation; and a delegation of sailors set out for
Petrograd on a torpedo-boat with the intention of arresting both
Dudarev and his chief, Naval Minister Lebedev. By the time they
reached the capital, however, the political atmosphere had changed
very sharply to their disadvantage; and the members of the delegation were themselves lodged in jail, while Kerensky gave orders to
dissolve the existing Centrobalt and elect a new one.

There were other factors besides the publication of the accusations of treachery and espionage against Lenin and his associates
that mark out the July Days as a distinct, if temporary setback to
the upward revolutionary curve. The disastrous defeat on the front
which closely followed the riots in Petrograd inspired a panicky
sentiment and helped to reconcile the Mensheviki and Socialist
Revolutionaries to the adoption of stronger repressive measures
than they had yet been willing to authorize. The memory of the
menacing hosts of Kronstadt sailors and Putilov workers also exerted
a distinctly sobering effect on the political views of the moderate
members of the Soviet.

But it was the denunciation of the Bolsheviki as German agents
that contributed most to creating a popular sentiment that made it
possible to drive the Bolshevik Party leadership into semi-under-
ground conditions for a period of almost two months. What were

the origin and the credibility of these accusations? The circumstances under which they were produced are calculated at once to arouse suspicion. On July 17, when matters looked bad for the Provisional Government, the Minister for Justice, Pereverzev, authorized the action of two journalists, Alexinsky and Pankratov, in making up a sort of communiqué based on incomplete and unsifted material at the disposal of the Ministry. The communiqué had a distinctly favorable political effect, as has been observed, when it was shown to the delegates of the Preobrazhensky Regiment, who resolved forthwith to abandon their neutral attitude; and on July 18 a small newspaper, *The Living Word*, published it, the larger newspapers following the example of *The Living Word* on the following day.

The material which was alleged to incriminate Lenin was based on the testimony of two men. The first was Ermolenko, a former police agent, who, after being captured by the Germans in the War, was, according to his own statement, sent across the lines for the purpose of carrying out sabotage activities, for a consideration of 38,000 rubles and thirty percent of the value of any damage he might cause. Reporting to the Russian General Staff in Moghilev, Ermolenko told them this story, adding that he had been told in the German General Staff that Lenin and Yoltukhovsky (an Ukrainian separatist) were Germany's agents in Russia. Ermolenko was mysteriously handed fifty thousand rubles in the street in Moghilev and drifted off to the East Siberian town of Blagoveschensk. Thence he was recalled to Petrograd; but apparently his imagination was exhausted, and he could add no further details.

Obviously neither Ermolenko's character nor his self-confessed activities created any presumption of truth for his story, which was unsupported by a shred of documentary evidence. The other witness whose testimony was used in the statement regarding Lenin's alleged German connections was a merchant, Z. Burstein, whom the chief of the Intelligence Department of the General Staff, Prince Turkestanov, characterized as a shady character, who deserved no credence.[16] Burstein testified that there was a German espionage organization in Stockholm headed by Parvus (Gelfand),[16a] who maintained financial connections with the Bolsheviki Ganetzky and Kozlovsky. It was further alleged in the statement that the military censorship had revealed "an uninterrupted exchange of telegrams of a political and financial character between German agents and the Bolshevik leaders." Here again the evidence is intrinsically

weak; and the arrest of Kozlovsky and of a woman named Sumenson, a relative of Ganetzky, and an investigation of their accounts and foreign financial transactions revealed that Ganetzky and Mme. Sumenson had been carrying on a lively contraband trade in medicaments; but brought out nothing about any financial dealings with the German General Staff.

From the beginning the accusations did not command any great degree of credence in informed circles. The Ministers Nekrasov and Tereschenko were indignant at the publication of such incomplete material; apparently they had hoped that something more positive might be learned through arresting Ganetzky on his next trip into Russia. One of the men who prepared the documents for publication, an ex-Bolshevik named Alexinsky, had a bad reputation as an irresponsible backbiter and slanderer, and had been refused admission to the Soviet for this reason. There is a significant passage in the communication which Kerensky addressed from the front to Prince Lvov as soon as he learned of the July disorders which suggests that political rather than judicial considerations prompted the publication of the material. After "categorically insisting" on "the decisive suppression of treacherous outbursts, the disarming of rebellious units and the trial of the instigators" Kerensky ends: "It is necessary to hasten the publication of the information in our hands," [17] a phrase which in all probability refers to the documents which were calculated to discredit Lenin and the Bolsheviki.

The Soviet leaders at first urged the newspapers not to publish the allegedly incriminating documents; and after the publication had taken place urged a suspension of judgment until a commission appointed by the Soviet to investigate the whole affair had submitted its report. This commission, however, never seems to have functioned;[18] and while the idea of Lenin as a "German spy" could scarcely have commanded belief even among political opponents who knew the iron fanaticism and personal incorruptibility of his character it did have a considerable, although transitory, effect among the masses, especially among the soldiers; and some of the irreconcilable anti-Bolshevik Russians cling to the idea of the Bolsheviki as German agents up to the present time.

Lenin, Zinoviev and Kamenev repudiated the accusations in a letter published in Gorky's newspaper *New Life* (*Pravda* had been closed down at this time) of July 24. They pointed out that as early as 1915 the Bolshevik newspaper *Social Democrat* had denounced Parvus as a "renegade, licking the boots of Hindenburg."

The authors of the letter also asserted that they had never had any dealings with Mme. Sumenson or even seen her and that they had "never received a kopeck from Kozlovsky or Ganetzky, either personally or for the Party." Lenin also repudiated Ganetzky as a Party comrade in a special leaflet which he issued on July 19,[19] in which he asserted: "Ganetzky and Kozlovsky are not Bolsheviki, but members of the Polish Social Democratic Party. The Bolsheviki received no money either from Ganetzky or from Kozlovsky."

It must be said that the tone of this leaflet in regard to Ganetzky does not altogether harmonize with a letter which Lenin wrote to Ganetzky in March[20] addressing him as "Dear Comrade," setting forth fully his views on revolutionary tactics and, finally, urging Ganetzky "not to spare money on communications between Peter [Petrograd] and Stockholm." Just what money Ganetzky was supposed to use is not clear; but it would be quite unreasonable to leap at the conclusion that, because Lenin regarded Ganetzky as a suitable intermediary for the establishment of communication between Sweden and Petrograd, there was any substance in the insinuations of such disreputable witnesses as Ermolenko and Burstein.

In the last analysis Lenin's life record as an international revolutionary is the best possible proof that he could never have accepted the rôle of paid agent of a government which he regarded as just as imperialistic, just as worthy of destruction as any other. There is a sense, of course, in which Lenin objectively aided the German military cause. By his presence in Russia and his agitation against the War and against the Provisional Government he made no inconsiderable contribution to the disintegration of the Russian army and thereby to the relief of the Central Powers from the pressure of the Eastern front, which had been quite formidable as late as Brussilov's offensive in 1916. It was with this expectation, no doubt, that the German military authorities decided to permit Lenin and other extreme revolutionaries to pass through Germany.

Lenin, on his part, believed that he was pushing forward a revolutionary movement which would ultimately sweep away not only the Provisional Government in Russia, but also the Kaiser's regime in Germany and the "bourgeois" governments of England and France. He was no more an "agent" of the German Government than the German extreme revolutionary, Karl Liebknecht, was an "agent" of England or France, although under similar circumstances it is quite conceivable that the Allied military leaders, without in the least sympathizing with Liebknecht's social views, might

have given him the same kind of coöperation that the German military leaders accorded to Lenin, simply on the assumption that his activity would be calculated to weaken the enemy.

An order for the arrest of Lenin, Zinoviev and Kamenev was issued on July 19. Lenin therefore had to choose between the alternatives of going into hiding and of submitting to arrest and trusting that the court would vindicate him. The first alternative involved the risk of strengthening the popular suspicion; the second, the danger, as Stalin suggested in discussions of the question, that Lenin might be murdered without being brought to trial. Moreover, from prison Lenin could not direct the activity of the Party as he could from an unknown hiding place.

After some hesitation Lenin with his intimate associate, Zinoviev, decided to go into hiding, justifying their action on the grounds that the Minister for Justice, Pereverzev, had admitted that he published the allegedly incriminating documents in order to stir up the soldiers against the Bolsheviki, that "there are no guaranties of a fair trial in Russia at the present moment," that "all the accusations against us are a simple episode of civil war." [21] Lenin successfully eluded the search for him which was instituted by the officers of the Provisional Government. First he hid in the loft of a shed which belonged to a Bolshevik laborer near Sestroretzk, about twenty miles from Petrograd. After spending some time in a still more secluded refuge, a hut in a hayfield, he was smuggled over the administrative frontier between Russia and Finland in the guise of a locomotive stoker and lived first in Helsingfors, then in Viborg, nearer Petrograd, until the very eve of the November Revolution.

Lenin not only anticipated but somewhat exaggerated the reaction which would follow the July Days. "Now they are shooting us up," he said to Trotzky on July 18. "For them it is the most favorable moment." A certain reaction undoubtedly occurred after the July riots; but it was of a feeble and halfhearted character. At no time in its career did the spineless Provisional Government apply repressions remotely comparable with those which followed the unsuccessful radical rebellions in Paris in 1848 and 1871, or the coming into power of the Italian Fascisti or of the German National Socialists, or of the Bolsheviki themselves.

Under the influence of the July repulse Lenin decided that it was expedient to discard, or at least to put in cold storage, his former slogan: "All power to the Soviets." His reasoning on this point was as follows: [22]

"This slogan was correct in the irretrievably past period of our Revolution, from March 12 until July 17. This slogan has clearly ceased to be correct now . . . The slogan of the passing of power to the Soviets would now sound like Don Quixotism or mockery . . . The substance of the matter is that it is already now impossible to take power peacefully. . . . No force except the revolutionary proletariat can achieve the overthrow of the counter-revolutionary bourgeoisie. . . . Soviets can and must appear in this new revolution, but not the present Soviets, not organs of compromise with the bourgeoisie, but organs of revolutionary struggle against it. . . . The Soviets *now* are helpless against the victorious counterrevolution. The slogan of the passing of power to the Soviets can be understood as a 'simple' appeal for the passing of power to the present Soviets, and to say this, to appeal for this would now mean to deceive the people. There is nothing more dangerous than deceit."

Lenin had no more respect for the "constitutional" rights of Soviets than for those of a parliament or a constituent assembly. He valued the Soviets primarily as a springboard to the absolute and unlimited state power which he always considered a major prerequisite for the realization of his social and economic theories. So he was quite prepared to make his revolution, if possible, against the will of Soviets where the Mensheviki and Socialist Revolutionaries were in the majority, just as he was prepared, after the Bolshevik Revolution, to put into effect administrative and electoral methods which would effectively prevent any backward swing of the pendulum, any new conquest of the Soviets from the Bolsheviki by other parties. Ordzhonikidze, one of the Bolshevik leaders of the Caucasus, recalls that Lenin said about this time: "Now it is possible to take power only by means of armed uprising, which will come not later than September or October. We must transfer our main attention to the factory committees. They must be organs of uprising." [23]

In actual practice this strategic shift to the factory committees, in which the Bolsheviki had a large majority from the beginning, was not necessary, because of the rapid swing to the left of the Soviets after the failure of General Kornilov's attempted *coup*. It was, however, quite characteristic of Lenin's revolutionary tactics that he was ready to cast aside one potential weapon of uprising for another, as soon as the first one revealed signs of becoming blunted.

Kerensky became Premier, following the resignation of Prince Lvov, on July 21; and during the next few weeks the reaction after

the July Days made itself felt. Kamenev and Kollontai, Lunacharsky and Trotzky were arrested (the last named after a characteristic message to the Provisional Government, in which he demanded to be placed on the same footing as Lenin, Zinoviev and
Kamenev in being subjected to arrest). Some of the more unruly
regiments, including the machine-gunners, were broken up. Searches
for arms were carried out in places like the Sestroretzk arms factory,
which were regarded as strongholds of Bolshevism. On July 25 the
Provisional Government restored the death penalty at the front.
Other decrees imposed restrictions on the press and forbade citizens
to keep weapons in their possession. Even proverbially insurgent
Kronstadt had been sufficiently tamed to permit the arrest of its
local prominent Bolsheviki, Raskolnikov, Roshal and Remnev.
There was nothing in the way of violent or extreme terrorism; there
seems to have been only one Bolshevik, a newspaper vendor named
Voinov, who was actually killed on the streets by government
troops during the post-July reaction. An external appearance of
tranquillity was restored; threatening armed demonstrations ceased;
a few of the more turbulent regiments were dissolved; orders to
troops to entrain for the front were enforced with a little more
vigor.

But beneath the surface the relation of forces was only slightly
changed. If a number of the more prominent Bolshevik leaders
were in hiding or in prison the rank-and-file Party agitators were
still at work in the factories. The trade-unions and large plants
continued to pass Bolshevik resolutions. On the front also the
death penalty was a matter of theory rather than of application.
As Denikin observes regarding the Southwest Front during the
period between the July disturbances and the Kornilov affair: [24]
"Shaken in the July days, the Southwest Front gradually began to
come to itself. But not in the sense of real recovery, as it seemed
to some optimists, but of the return approximately to that condition
which existed before the offensive."

The Sixth Congress of the Bolshevik Party (the first to be held
after the Revolution) was held in the second week of August.
Lenin guided its deliberations and helped to frame its resolutions
from his underground retreat. The Congress was held somewhat
surreptitiously, "half legally," in Petrograd and changed its meeting place in order to escape the surveillance of the government
agents. Yet the mood of the reports and discussions was far from
pessimistic. According to Sverdlov, one of the most active Party
organizers, the numerical strength of the Party had grown from

80,000 members, enrolled in seventy-eight local organizations, in April, to 200,000 members, enrolled in 162 organizations, at the time of the Congress. The Party naturally had its greatest strength in the industrial centres of the country. So Petrograd reported 41,000 members, the Moscow Region (including the fringe of industrial towns surrounding Moscow) 50,000, the Ural mining and industrial territory 22–25,000, etc. Volodarsky, who, like not a few other active Bolsheviki, had returned from America after the overthrow of Tsarism, declared that the Petrograd Party membership within four months had grown from 16,000 to 36,000.[25] (The figure, cited earlier, of 41,000 probably refers to the whole Petrograd Region.) The Mensheviki, on the other hand, had only 8,000 members. While the other rival party, the Socialist Revolutionaries, had a larger numerical following than the Mensheviki the influence of the Bolsheviki on the workers was greater. So, at the Triangle factory, where the Socialist Revolutionaries had from three to five thousand members, the Bolsheviki had eleven out of sixteen representatives in the Soviet.

The most important practical theme of discussion at this Party Congress was about the attitude toward the slogan: "All power to the Soviets." One group, headed by Sokolnikov, was inclined to abandon any hope of achieving power through the Soviets; Sokolnikov even expressed the opinion that the political rôle of the Soviets was finished. Nogin, a leading Moscow Bolshevik, argued on the other hand, that the slogan should be retained, on the ground that a new revolutionary outbreak was soon inevitable, in view of the situation at the front and in the country, and that the Bolsheviki could find support only in the Soviets when this outbreak came. The resolution finally adopted by the Congress discarded the slogan in favor of the vaguer formula, "dictatorship of the proletariat and the poorest peasantry," the pertinent phrases in the resolution reading as follows: [26]

"The Soviets live through a painful agony, disintegrating as a result of the fact that they did not take all the state power into their hands at the right time. . . .

"At the present time peaceful development and the painless passing of power to the Soviets have become impossible, because power has already in fact passed into the hands of the counterrevolutionary bourgeoisie.

"The correct slogan at the present time can only be the complete liquidation of the dictatorship of the counterrevolutionary bourgeoisie. Only the revolutionary proletariat, on condition that it is supported by the poorest peasantry, has the power to fulfill this task."

While the Bolsheviki were thus laying strategic plans to take advantage of the next upsurge of revolutionary sentiment among the masses the shadowy Provisional Government was endeavoring to clothe itself with more of the attributes of real power. Distrusted by the army officers, the industrialists, the middleclass liberals as too weak and irresolute, too much under Soviet influence, distrusted equally by even the moderate leaders of the Soviet as insufficiently sound in the socialist faith and too prone to compromise with the propertied classes, Kerensky still remained the indispensable keystone of any government. No one else was so widely known; no one else was so tolerable both to the Soviets and to the more conservative classes.

Although a renewal of the experiment in coalition was the only feasible sequel to the decisive rejection, by the Mensheviki and Socialist Revolutionaries, of the Bolshevik proposal that the Soviets should assume power themselves, it was far from easy to find a platform sufficiently broad for the prospective coalition partners to stand on comfortably. For over two weeks after his appointment as Premier, Kerensky wrestled with the problem of creating a new Cabinet. The difficulties seemed so insuperable that he took the extreme step of resigning all his offices on August 3. Inasmuch as there was no politically available substitute candidate, he was recalled as a result of a general agreement among the political leaders of various parties that he should choose the members of his Cabinet as he saw fit.

The new Cabinet, as it was finally formed on August 6, showed a slight preponderance of Socialists over non-Socialists. But the Socialist members were mostly men who stood distinctly on the right wings of their parties; the most radical was Chernov, the Socialist Revolutionary Minister for Agriculture. As the Cadet leader, Professor Milyukov, observes, "the real preponderance in the Cabinet definitely belonged to the convinced supporters of bourgeois democracy." [27] This was partly attributable to the fact that Kerensky deliberately chose Mensheviki and Socialist Revolutionaries who would not be too tightly bound by their party doctrines, partly to the sobering effect which power and responsibility, together with the riotous July Days, doubtless exerted upon the psychology of many Socialist Ministers.

The new Cabinet was not greeted with any excess of optimism in any quarter. The Soviet Executive Committees promised to support the new government on condition that it carried out a declaration

which had been issued by its predecessor on July 21, promising to propose to the Allied powers a conference on War aims, to convene the Constituent Assembly by the end of September and, without prejudice to the right of the Constituent Assembly to decide the land question, to carry out agrarian measures inspired by the conception that "the land should pass into the hands of the toilers." Very different points were emphasized by the Cadets: prosecution of the War in full union with the Allies, restoration of discipline in the army, strong and authoritative government without interference from the Soviets and other unofficial bodies. Milyukov, speaking at a Cadet Congress, recommended the support of the new coalition government by the somewhat gloomy argument that "not only does catastrophe threaten us; we are already in the whirlpool." And at the end of his speech the Cadet leader voiced a thinly disguised threat: "If it turns out that we have to do not with a declining influence of the Soviets and of socialist utopianism, if the spirit of Zimmerwald, which has already subsided and has been eliminated in the recent statements of Ministers, is resurrected, if the Bolsheviki again appear in the streets of Petrograd, then we shall talk in a different tone."

Another feature of the swing to the right which followed the July disturbances was a hardening in the attitude of the central government toward the demands of Finland and Ukraina. A virtual declaration of independence, promulgated by the Finnish Seym (parliament) evoked from the Government not only a denial of its constitutional legality, but the dissolution of the Seym on July 31, with an order to hold new elections in the autumn. A stiffer attitude was also adopted in regard to the demands of the Ukrainian Rada. Kiev, incidentally, had lived through its own peculiar edition of the July days. An Ukrainian substitute for the First Machine-Gun Regiment, a regiment of Ukrainian troops named after a national hero, the Hetman Polutbotko, seized the city fortress and other public buildings, with the avowed intention of proclaiming the Rada the supreme power in Ukraina. While the Rada was perhaps not as hostile to its champions as the Soviet Executive Committee was to the Kronstadt sailors and to the mutinous units of the Petrograd garrison, it regarded the outbursts as at least untimely and premature; and ultimately the turbulent soldiers were induced to give up their conquests and return to their barracks without bloodshed. Just as in Petrograd the outbreak was accompanied by a good deal of hooliganism and robbery.

The check and repulse which the more extreme revolutionary forces experienced as a result of the July demonstration gave to the conservative classes a sense of increased strength, a very illusory sense, as subsequent events were to prove. The Duma had lost all legal significance since the March Revolution. But groups of its members continued to meet in "private conferences," where fulminations against anarchy and lawlessness were the regular order of the day. At one of these conferences the Duma deputy Maslennikov expressed his sentiments in the following unrestrained terms: [28]

"The population is loafing and thinks only of how it can best rob someone. Our valiant army is turned into a horde of cowards. . . . It was thanks to the Duma that the Revolution was made; but in that great tragic historical moment a handful of crazy fanatics, adventurers and traitors, calling themselves the Executive Committee of the Council of Workers' and Soldiers' Deputies, attached itself to the Revolution. . . . Take Order No. 1. What was this: an act of madness or an act of vileness? . . . I recommend that we ask the President to convene all the members of the Duma not in some private, underground conference, but in an actual session of the Duma. I recommend that we demand that the whole Government appear there and report on the condition of the country. And then the Duma will point out to this Government what to do."

Maslennikov's idea of reviving the Duma was recognized as utopian even by his colleagues. But the cry for "strong government" proceeded more and more insistently from factory-owners who felt that their plants were slipping from under their control, from land-owners who knew that peasants were swarming onto their estates, from army officers who saw the soldiers whom they commanded turning into mutinous mobs, to a greater or less extent from all who had a stake in the private property system which was likely to be swallowed up in the rising tide of social revolution.

If one indulges in retrospective reconstruction of Russia's situation in the summer of 1917 it is easy to see that the sole chance of survival of the numerically weak middle class lay in pursuing a policy of conciliation toward the more moderate Soviet parties, in driving a deeper cleft between the right-wing members of the Soviets and the Bolsheviki and, above all, in agreeing to satisfy the two imperious popular demands which simply could not be effectively resisted, in the long run, by any Government: peace and land.

But the political leaders of the well-to-do classes and of the middle and professional classes which made up the backbone of the

Cadet Party thought differently. The very idea of the breach with the Allied powers which a separate peace or even a suspension of hostilities would have involved seemed to them monstrous and impossible. With a kind of ostrich-like blindness to the huge agrarian revolution that was already under way in the villages, a revolution which simply could not be checked by the meagre physical force at the disposal of the Government, they believed that it was good strategy to postpone any fundamental treatment of the agrarian question until the meeting of a Constituent Assembly, the date of which they were not anxious to expedite. Faced with insoluble dilemmas, such as the effort to wage war with soldiers who would not fight, or endeavoring to hold back the charge onto the landlords' broad acres of hosts of illiterate or semi-literate peasants with appeals to the sovereign rights of the Constituent Assembly, the spokesman of middleclass Russia began to look more and more hopefully to a miracle, or, more concretely, to a dictator, to a strong man on horseback. And when, on July 31, it was announced that General Brussilov had been replaced as Commander-in-chief by General Kornilov it seemed to many Russians of the old school that the desired dictator was already in plain sight.

NOTES

[1] *Proletarskaya Revolutsia* (Proletarian Revolution), No. 5 for 1923, p. 10.

[2] N. Podvoisky, in *Krasnaya Letopis* (Red Chronicle), No. 7 for 1923, p. 100.

[3] "The Revolution of 1917: Chronicle of Events," Vol. III, p. 308.

[4] N. Sukhanov, "Memoirs of the Revolution," Vol. IV, p. 411.

[5] P. N. Milyukov, "History of the Second Russian Revolution," Vol. I, p. 244.

[6] F. Raskolnikov, "Kronstadt and Peter in 1917," p. 123.

[7] V. Bonch-Bruevitch, "At the Fighting Posts of the February and October Revolutions," p. 81.

[8] Sukhanov, *op. cit.*, Vol. IV, p. 399.

[9] Milyukov, *op. cit.*, Vol. I, p. 243.

[10] "The Revolution of 1917: Chronicle of Events," Vol. III, p. 151.

[10a] The round approximate figure of 400 is given by Shlyapnikov and by some other investigators of the July Days. An official commission of inquiry reported that 29 were killed and 114 wounded during the disturbances. It seems doubtful, however, whether all the casualties in such a tumultuous affair could have been revealed and registered.

[11] A. Shlyapnikov, "The Year 1917," Vol. IV, p. 277.

[12] Raskolnikov, *op. cit.*, pp. 129–130.

[13] Sukhanov, *op. cit.*, Vol. IV, pp. 430, 431.

[14] Milyukov, *op. cit.*, Vol. I, p. 246.

[15] L. Trotzky, "The History of the Russian Revolution," Vol. II, p. 64.

[16] "Sketches of the History of the October Revolution," Vol. II, p. 334.

[16a] Parvus (Gelfand) was a Left Menshevik, a theoretical sympathizer with Trotzky in the Revolution of 1905. Later he emigrated to Germany and joined the Social Democratic Party there. He acquired a substantial fortune by means of speculation and during the War was a confidential agent of the Imperial Government.

[17] Shlyapnikov, *op. cit.*, Vol. IV, p. 279.

[18] According to Sukhanov the first commission which was appointed to investigate the charges against Lenin consisted of five members, all of whom were Jews.

As it was feared that anti-Semitic circles would be sceptical about a vindication of Lenin, pronounced by such a commission; it was proposed to change its make-up; but in the end the whole matter was apparently allowed to drop.

[19] V. Lenin, "Collected Works," Vol. XIV, Part II, pp. 6–9.

[20] "Leninist Collection," Vol. II, pp. 368–372.

[21] The letter of Lenin and Zinoviev was published in the Kronstadt organ of the Bolsheviki on July 28.

[22] Lenin, "Collected Works," Vol. XIV, Part II, pp. 12–18.

[23] "About Lenin" (a collection of reminiscences), p. 102.

[24] A. I. Denikin, "Sketches of Russian Turmoil," Vol. II, p. 199.

[25] "Protocols of the Sixth Party Congress," pp. 35–36.

[26] "The Sixth Congress of the Bolsheviki," pp. 49–50.

[27] Milyukov, *op. cit.*, Vol. II, pp. 44, 45.

[28] "The Revolution of 1917: Chronicle of Events," Vol. III, p. 194.

CHAPTER IX

KORNILOV AND THE FAILURE OF COUNTERREVOLUTION

GENERAL LAVR KORNILOV, whose mission it was to head the unsuccessful counterrevolutionary movement against the Provisional Government was a picturesque personality, full of Eastern color. Son of a Siberian Cossack, Kornilov's slanting eyes, slight, erect figure and Mongolian physiognomy suggest that in his veins flowed the blood of some Oriental people. Much of his early military service had been spent in Russian Central Asia and in the Far East; he knew a considerable number of Asiatic tongues and felt himself more at home with Asiatics than with Europeans. His personal bodyguard consisted of Tekintsi, Turcoman warriors from Central Asia, whose devotion to him as their military chief was enhanced by his knowledge of their language.

Kornilov's career as a soldier revealed him as a man of distinguished personal courage, but not as a very capable commander of large military units. During the retreat of the Russian armies from Galicia in 1915 Kornilov became separated from the division which he was commanding and was taken prisoner. Subsequently he escaped from an Austrian prison and made his way back to Russia. After the Revolution he was for a time commander of the Petrograd garrison; but he soon became irked by the low level of order and discipline in this organization and, at his own request, was transferred to the command of the Eighth Army, on the Southwestern Front. Kornilov's troops won the greatest individual measure of success during the short-lived Russian offensive in early July; and, when advance had given way to retreat and rout, Kornilov was promoted to the post of Commander-in-chief of the Southwestern Front. This was followed at the end of July by his appointment as Supreme Commander-in-chief.

Kerensky's decision to place so much potential military power in the hands of a man whom he soon came to distrust and to regard as a dangerous competitor for power may occasion surprise. It must

be remembered, however, that Kerensky was of an impulsive nature, quick to make and to withdraw responsible appointments, and a change in the command, after the pitiful failure of the offensive, seemed imperative. Brussilov, who of all the old Tsarist Generals had gone farthest in his efforts to adapt himself to revolutionary phraseology, had not succeeded in restoring the army's will or capacity to fight. Perhaps Kornilov, a younger man, with a reputation for great energy and iron will, might be more effective.

Two other factors helped to bring about Kornilov's appointment. On July 29th Kerensky had presided over an important military council at the Stavka, in Moghilev, which was attended by the commanders of European fronts, with the exception of Kornilov, who was detained by military exigencies, and by several other high military authorities. Most of the oldfashioned generals at the conference attacked the revolutionary innovations in the army, lock, stock and barrel; and the outspoken General Denikin, the future leader of the White movement in South Russia, delivered an impassioned speech, in which he did not mince words in attacking the Provisional Government and accused it of "trampling our banners in filth." By contrast the message which was received from Kornilov, suggesting that commissars and committees in the armies had their functions, but should be placed under definite limitations, sounded to Kerensky liberal and progressive. Furthermore Kornilov had a valuable political friend and guarantor in the person of Boris Savinkov, Commissar of the Southwestern Front, whom Kerensky was now selecting as the active administrator of the War Department, of which the Premier himself was the nominal head. Savinkov was a veteran member of the Fighting Organization of the Socialist Revolutionaries and had taken an active part in some of the spectacular terrorist plots in Tsarist days. As was the case with many members of his Party, however, Savinkov's "socialism" apparently did not go beyond a tolerably liberal republicanism. A stronger and more resolute character than Kerensky, Savinkov was a fervent believer in the restoration of order and discipline in the army and was convinced that General Kornilov, supplied with proper political guidance, could be a useful instrument in achieving this end.

So the appointment of Kornilov as successor to Brussilov took place; and Savinkov at the War Ministry and Captain Filonenko, who assumed the office of Chief Commissar attached to the Stavka, became the unofficial *liaison* agents who endeavored to inspire more

political discretion in Kornilov and more administrative firmness in Kerensky and, in general, to make it possible for the strongly contrasted and discordant personalities of the Premier and the Commander-in-chief to work in harmony. There was indeed a profound difference and an almost instinctive antagonism between the wordy, gesticulating lawyer-politician, Kerensky, and the stern simple soldier Kornilov, whose political and social ideas were of the vaguest and most limited character, and whose subsequent flowery appeals were written for him by his adjutant, Zavoiko, an expansive landowner with a strong streak of irresponsible adventurism in his make-up, who bears a considerable share of the responsibility for the uncommonly clumsy preparation of the subsequent *coup*.

Had Kerensky been a revolutionary of the uncompromising type and had Kornilov been an out-and-out monarchist, anxious to replace the Romanovs on the throne, the appointment of the latter would never have taken place, or at least the irrepressible conflict between the two men would have burst out much sooner than it actually did. But as a matter of fact the desires and objectives of the Socialist Revolutionary Premier and of the Cossack General ran along parallel lines to a certain extent. Kerensky, like Kornilov, wished to see an army where the soldiers would obey orders instead of debating them. Kornilov, on his part, a man of humble origin, had no desire to set up a monarchy. The points of difference that proved insuperable and led to the final clash were Kerensky's distrust of Kornilov's ambition and of the methods by which he proposed to create a strong government and to restore discipline in the army and Kornilov's contempt and dislike for Kerensky as an irresolute talker. But much of the confused and contradictory record of the period which immediately preceded Kornilov's open defiance of the Provisional Government is only understandable on the assumption that Kerensky, in his own way and with substantial modifications of emphasis and method, was aiming at goals which were not so very different from those of Kornilov himself. Moreover, Kerensky probably always had at least something of a premonition that by destroying Kornilov he would be simultaneously cutting the ground from beneath his own feet.

Kornilov's first act after being informed of his nomination was a clear indication that politically he was destined to be a more difficult figure to handle than his predecessors, the sick and discouraged Alekseev and the complaisant Brussilov. He despatched a telegram to the Provisional Government declaring that he could accept the

appointment and "bring the people to victory and to a just and honorable peace" only on the following four conditions:

(1) Responsibility before his own conscience and before the whole people.

(2) Complete noninterference in his operative orders and, therefore, in the appointment of the higher commanding staff.

(3) Extension of the measures which had recently been adopted at the front (presumably the reintroduction of the death penalty) to all places in the rear where army reinforcements were stationed.

(4) Acceptance of the proposals which he had sent by telegraph to the conference in the Stavka on July 29.

Even Kornilov's friend and admirer, Denikin, remarks[1] that the first of these demands would have created "a form of sovereignty of the Supreme Command that would have been very original, from the standpoint of state law." The Government at first took Kornilov's demands rather lightly, attributing the first point, which in strict logic implied the establishment of an independent dictatorship, to his unfamiliarity with political phraseology. However, a second incident followed quickly after the first; Kornilov strenuously objected to the appointment of General Cheremisov as Commander-in-chief of the Southwestern Front and threatened to resign if the nomination were not cancelled. Kerensky on this occasion was inclined to accept Kornilov's resignation; but the influence of Savinkov prevented this and both incidents were quickly settled. Cheremisov, who was one of the generals who endeavored to smooth their careers by keeping up good relations with Soviet circles, was dismissed; and Kornilov accepted the interpretation placed on his first point by Filonenko, who suggested that "responsibility before the whole people" implied responsibility before its authorized organ of representation, the Provisional Government.

Throughout Kornilov's political career one notices these alternations of strongly phrased demands and quick withdrawals and concessions. In all probability this is not attributable to outright hypocrisy, although Kornilov subsequently revealed that he was by no means devoid of guile. It was rather a case of complete inexperience in politics and ready susceptibility to the suggestion of the last adviser. Quite characteristic in this connection was Kornilov's conduct in sending, under Savinkov's influence, a relatively moderate set of demands to the conference in the Stavka and of shortly afterwards assuring Denikin of his agreement with all the latter's demands for the abolition of commissars and committees.

These initial misunderstandings left behind an undercurrent of suspicion that affected all Kerensky's later relations with Kornilov. This suspicion was not dissipated by the two personal meetings of the Premier and the Commander-in-chief which occurred in Petrograd on August 16 and August 23. On the first occasion Kornilov arrived with a memorandum outlining measures which he regarded as necessary for the restoration of fighting capacity at the front and in the rear. His mentors, Savinkov and Filonenko, looking over the memorandum, found it politically unacceptable and suggested that he leave it with them for working over and modification. This he agreed to do; but in the course of his interview with Kerensky he showed the latter the memorandum, which the Premier later characterized [2] as "setting forth a number of measures, the vast majority of which were quite acceptable, but they were set down in such form and with such arguments that the publication of the memorandum would have led to unfavorable results."

Kerensky seized this opportunity of sounding out Kornilov's political sentiments.[3] Hinting vaguely at the possibility of a military dictatorship he warned the General in the following terms: "Suppose I should withdraw, what will happen? You will hang in the air; the railroads will stop; the telegraph will cease to function." To Kerensky's questioning as to whether, in Kornilov's opinion, he should remain at the head of the state the Commander-in-chief gave the somewhat reserved reply that, although Kerensky's influence had declined, nevertheless, as the recognized leader of the democratic party, he should remain at the head of the Government.

Another incident on the occasion of this visit to Petrograd made a strong impression on Kornilov and very possibly predisposed him to listen to the counsels of his more adventurous friends. While he was reporting on the military situation at a session of the Cabinet Kerensky and Savinkov warned him to show discretion in discussing the question of where an offensive might be undertaken. They explained this warning by telling him that some of the Ministers (apparently there was a special insinuation against the Socialist Revolutionary Minister for Agriculture, Chernov) were in close touch with the Executive Committee of the Soviet, among the members of which were German agents. This was calculated to strengthen in Kornilov's politically very primitive mind the conviction that not only the Bolsheviki, but also the members of other parties in the Soviet were traitors and German agents, and that they exercised an impermissible degree of influence upon the Provisional

Government. Indeed it is questionable whether Kornilov ever understood that there was any distinction between the Bolsheviki and the more moderate Socialist parties which at that time constituted the majority in almost all the Soviets.

In the words of General Denikin: [4] "Kornilov became a banner. For some of counterrevolution, for others of the salvation of the Motherland."

His visit to Petrograd, followed as it was by rumors about his differences with the Government and about his drastic programme for the restoration of discipline, stirred up the passions both of his sympathizers and of his opponents. A càmpaign was launched against him in the press of the Left and voices were heard to the effect that he should be replaced by General Cheremisov. Conservative and military organizations rallied to his support. So on August 19 the Council of the Union of Cossack Troops flung down the gauntlet to the Provisional Government with the unequivocal declaration that "General Kornilov cannot be removed, because he is the true people's leader and because, in the opinion of the majority of the population, he is the sole general who can re-create the fighting power of the army and bring the country out of its very difficult situation," followed by the undisguised threat: "The Council regards it as a moral duty to state to the Provisional Government and to the people that it repudiates its responsibility for the behavior of the Cossack troops at the front and in the rear in the event of the replacement of General Kornilov."

The Union of Cavaliers of St. George (holders of the highest Russian military decoration) and the Union of Officers hastened to associate themselves with this militant declaration of the Cossack leaders. A gathering of public men of predominantly conservative sentiments in Moscow despatched to Kornilov a telegram, under the signature of Rodzianko, to the following effect: [5]

"In this threatening hour of heavy trial all thinking Russia looks to you with hope and faith."

Not one of these organizations, with the exception of the Cossacks, represented any mass numerical support; and the Cossack leaders, as subsequent developments would show, reflected very imperfectly the sentiments of the rank-and-file Cossack troops. But Kornilov, who, as several witnesses agree, was almost naïvely susceptible to flattery, very naturally had his head turned to some extent as a result of all these glowing tributes.

Throughout the month of August the air was thick with rumors

of plots; and when Kornilov returned to the Stavka from Petrograd Filonenko sent with him his assistant von Vizin with instructions to see to it that Kornilov should not engage in any untoward political activity, under the influence of the Staff. It is impossible to know precisely at what moment Kornilov began to consider seriously the advisability of placing himself at the head of an attempt at a forcible change in the existing regime. But his first overt act seems to have occurred on the 19th or the 20th of August, when his Chief of Staff, General Lukomsky, was surprised to receive an order to concentrate the Third Cavalry Corps (made up of Cossack units) and the so-called Savage Division (cavalry recruited from the mountain tribes of the Caucasus) in the neighborhood of the towns Nevel, Novi Sokolniki and Veliki Luki, within convenient railroad striking distance of Petrograd and Moscow. Lukomsky suggested to Kornilov that such a region of concentration was of little value as a means of strengthening the Northern Front, but was quite convenient for the eventuality of a blow at Petrograd or Moscow and asked the Commander-in-chief to tell him frankly what was in his mind. This Kornilov promised to do.[6] The circumstances of Kornilov's second visit to the capital were even more strained than those of his first visit. Some of his friends strongly advised him not to leave Moghilev, suggesting that Kerensky might arrest him. It required all the pleadings of Savinkov and Filonenko, accompanied by reminders that they had defended Kornilov against his enemies and critics in Petrograd, to persuade the Commander-in-chief to make the second visit. And when Kornilov finally set out he took along a bodyguard of Tekintsi with two machine-guns. When he went to pay his official call on Kerensky in the Winter Palace he took his fierce Central Asian warriors along; and passers-by in the corridors of the Palace could witness the piquant spectacle of the Turcomans with the two machine-guns waiting in the vestibule and ready to rush to the assistance of the General at his first call for help.

The main occasion for the interview which took place with this extraordinary background was the consideration of Kornilov's military program. It had been revised and softened in its phrasing by Filonenko; but the latter simultaneously added proposals for the militarization of the railroads and of the War industries. Kornilov handed this memorandum to Kerensky; and the latter, seeing the new demands for the militarization of the railroads and War industries, asked time for further consideration, simultaneously

expressing dissatisfaction that his assistant, Savinkov, should have signed such a document without his consent. At the close of the interview Kornilov told Kerensky that he had heard rumors about his impending removal from his post and bluntly advised the Premier, assuming there were any basis for these rumors, not to carry out any such intention.[7]

The memorandum was further discussed with Kornilov at a session of the familiar "inner circle" of the Government, consisting of Kerensky, Nekrasov and Tereschenko; and in the end Kornilov's original memorandum was found preferable to Filonenko's edited and amplified version. Kornilov, however, received only vague assurances about the precise time of carrying out his recommendations; and even after Kornilov's memorandum, as a result of the insistence of the Cadet Minister Kokoshkin, had been formally discussed at a regular Cabinet session, the decision, adopted after hot debate, remained decidedly indefinite: [8]

"To recognize in principle the possibility of applying various measures, including the death penalty in the rear, but to carry them out only after the discussion in legislative order of each concrete measure, according to the circumstances of time and place."

Kornilov returned to the Stavka thoroughly disgusted with what he regarded as the weak temporizing of Kerensky and frankly outlined to Lukomsky the real purpose of the cavalry concentration which had excited the latter's suspicion.

"It's time to hang the German supporters and spies, with Lenin at their head," Kornilov burst out in conversation with Lukomsky,[9] "and to disperse the Soviet of Workers' and Soldiers' Deputies so that it would never reassemble. You are right. I am shifting the cavalry corps mainly so as to bring it up to Petrograd by the end of August and, if a demonstration of the Bolsheviki takes place, to deal with these traitors as they deserve. I want to commit the leadership of this operation to General Krimov. I am convinced that he will not hesitate, in case of necessity, to hang every member of the Soviet."

This was plain soldierly speaking. Kornilov intended to make short work of the Bolsheviki and of the Soviet. But as regards the political side of his projected move he was more uncertain. He told Lukomsky that he did not intend to come out against the Provisional Government and hoped to come to an agreement with it, although he was prepared to strike at the Bolsheviki on his own

account, if he did not reach an agreement with Kerensky and Savinkov.

"I want nothing for myself," Kornilov concluded. "I only want to save Russia and I will obey unconditionally a cleansed and strengthened Provisional Government."

Here was the main outline of the Kornilov plot. The political side had been sketchily filled in; and here a good deal depended upon the expansive Zavoiko, whose favorite diversion was shuffling and reshuffling the ministerial portfolios in the Cabinet which would emerge after the *coup*.

A striking interlude in the development of the Kornilov affair was the Moscow State Conference, which was held from the 25th until the 28th of August. The idea of such an assembly of the "live forces of the country," to use a phrase much in vogue at the time, had commended itself to the Provisional Government shortly after the resignation of Prince Lvov as Premier. A noteworthy weakness of the Provisional Government throughout the whole course of its career was the absence of any generally recognized national assembly on which it could lean. The Vtsik could not serve as such a body, because only the Bolsheviki had favored the assumption of power by the Soviets and the non-Socialist part of the population would not have acknowledged the Soviets as representative bodies.

The Moscow State Conference was not conceived in any way as a legislative assembly; it was rather designed to be a large scale consultative body, where representatives of every class and profession could find expression. Among the 2,414 delegates who took part in the sessions of the Conference the largest delegations were from members of the four Dumas (488), from the coöperatives (313), from the trade-unions (176), from commercial and industrial organizations and banks (150), from municipalities (147), from the Executive Committee of the United Soviets of Workers', Soldiers' and Peasants' Deputies (129), from the Army and Navy (117) and from the Soviets of Workers' and Soldiers' and of Peasants' Deputies, each of which received 100 places.[10] There was an effort to balance the Conference carefully between the Right and the Left; and it was a symptom of the post-July reaction that the organizations of the propertied classes were granted representation out of all proportion to their numerical weight in the population.

The Bolsheviki denounced the State Conference as a counter-revolutionary gathering from the beginning and took no part in it.

They had some representatives in the delegation of the Vtsik; but Chkheidze, the President of the delegation, refused to permit them to carry out their intention of reading a declaration denouncing the Conference and then walking out of the place of assembly as a demonstration; and as a result of this the Bolshevik delegates absented themselves altogether. On the day of the opening of the Conference, however, the delegates received convincing proof that Bolshevism was very much alive, even if its voice was not heard in the ornate opera-house where the Conference was held. A one-day general strike of protest, initiated by the Bolsheviki and effectively carried out by the workers, despite the fact that the Moscow Soviet had voted against it by a narrow majority, was in full swing. The delegates could not ride on the streetcars or take tea in the restaurants.

This was regarded as an annoying interlude; but the tendency at the time was to underestimate the strength of the Bolsheviki. Popular attention was concentrated on what was felt to be the inevitable impending clash between Kerensky and Kornilov. So great was the apprehension that the large Conference in historic and ancient Moscow might be utilized by the conservative forces for the proclamation of a change of government that the Moscow Soviet, with its Menshevik-Socialist Revolutionary majority, decided to give Bolshevik agitators free access to the barracks where the soldiers of the garrison were quartered for a period of three days.[11] Reacting nervously to the rumor of a monarchist plot the authorities placed the Grand Dukes Paul and Michael Alexandrovitch under house arrest and arrested some other persons. This was apparently a completely false scent; the prisoners were soon released for lack of evidence against them; and Kerensky later expressed the opinion that an imaginary plot had been deliberately conjured up to divert attention from the actual plot in the Stavka. The Moscow Bolshevik newspaper offered the following comment: [12] "To arrest a pair of brainless puppets from the Romanov family and leave at liberty the military clique of the army commanders with Kornilov at the head—that is to deceive the people."

The State Conference was conceived as a rallying point of national unity. Its failure in this respect was dismal and complete. Not only were the considerable masses of workers and soldiers who were already following the banner of Bolshevism outside its pale; but from the very moment of its opening the participants split into two hostile and irreconcilable camps. Indeed the spectacle which

was represented by the sessions of the Conference in the opera-house that had often witnessed performances of "Boris Godunov" and other epic operas of Russia's past had many elements of historical drama.

On the right side of the auditorium sat representatives of the old propertied and military classes, assembled for what was destined to be their last dress-parade. There one could see bemedalled generals and officers, some in picturesque Caucasian uniforms, solid representatives of the business and financial world, professors and publicists of Cadet sympathies, many of whom had been regarded as dangerously advanced in Tsarist days, but who instinctively found themselves on the side of the Right in a country that was experiencing the first tossings of social revolution. On the Left side there were, to be sure, no typical figures of the July Days, no Kronstadt sailors, eager to wipe out the bourgeoisie, no grimy workers from the Putilov Factory Red Guard, nervously fingering their unfamiliar rifles. But there sat the flower of the self-styled "democratic forces" of the country: leaders of the moderate Socialist parties, trade-union organizers, radical lawyers and journalists and, last but not least, a fair sprinkling of the lieutenants, sergeants, corporals and private soldiers who represented the rank-and-file of the Army.

A stranger quite ignorant of the Russian language would have had little difficulty in sensing the spirit of the Moscow Conference; when the Left burst into applause the Right was stonily silent, and *vice versa*. There was something at once pathetic and futile in the clashing of these two groups, both of which within three months would be thoroughly submerged by the rising tide of Bolshevism.

Kerensky sat symbolically in the precise centre of the stage and throughout the Conference pursued his increasingly difficult task of political tightrope walking, endeavoring to balance himself between the Right and the Left. On this occasion he was undoubtedly the favorite of the Left side of the Conference, as the representatives of the Right saw their hero in Kornilov.

Kerensky's speech at the opening of the Conference on the afternoon of August 25 [13] was mainly directed against the suspected conspirators of the Right, although, for the sake of balance, there was also a threat against the Bolsheviki.

"Let all those who already once attempted to raise armed hands against the people's power [a clear reference to the July Days] know that such an attempt will be crushed with iron and blood.

▲ **PLEASE DETACH HERE BEFORE MAILING** ▲

Still more let those plotters beware who think the time has come to overthrow the revolutionary government, relying on bayonets [an even clearer hint to his enemies on the Right] . . . Here, in attempts at open attack or hidden plots is the limit of our patience. And anyone who transgresses that limit will meet a power which in its repressive measures will make the criminals remember what was under the old autocracy."

The rest of Kerensky's speech conformed to a familiar pattern: loud phrases which covered up feeble and irresolute actions and an almost painful effort to placate both sides of his audience which could scarcely have satisfied either. So he paid a tribute to the courage of the Russian officers and recalled that he had proposed to the Provisional Government a partial restoration of the death penalty, but dampened the welcome which the latter statement evoked on the Right by sounding a warning that "no one should dare to present to us any unconditioned demands on this point." A gloomy note pervaded the speech; one finds such phrases as "The state lives through an hour of mortal danger . . . Hungry cities, ever more disorganized transport." The speech was full of carefully balanced reproaches: so he simultaneously denounced the fall in the productivity of the workers and the refusal of the propertied classes to support the Government.

On the following day Kornilov arrived in Moscow and was greeted by his sympathizers with a maximum of pomp and ceremony. A guard of honor, recruited from the military schools of the city, was drawn up at the station and met the Commander-in-chief with bands playing and banners flying; deputations from a number of conservative groups and military organizations were waiting to welcome Kornilov as he stepped out of his car and passed through the double line of his Turcoman guards. The well known Cadet orator Rodichev pronounced a speech of welcome, ending: "We believe that at the head of the revived Russian army you will lead Russia to victory over the enemy and that the slogan, 'Long live General Kornilov'—now a slogan of hope—will become a cry of people's triumph. Save Russia and the grateful people will crown you." There were loud hurrahs and Kornilov was showered with flowers. Later he proceeded to the Chapel of the Iberian Virgin, the most famous shrine in Moscow, which Tsars habitually visited before their coronation, and prayed before its reputedly wonder-working ikon.

In the evening there was an acrid interchange of opinion be-

tween Kerensky and Kornilov about the contents of the speech which
the General was to pronounce on the following day. Kerensky insisted that Kornilov should restrict himself to military and strategic
questions, while Kornilov retorted that he would speak as he wished.
Actually, however, the speech which had been prepared for the
General was not so uncompromising or defiant as to provoke a
breach with the Government. It had been written by Commissar
Filonenko and, while it hinted broadly at the necessity for applying
drastic measures in the rear as well as at the front, it did not directly
attack the Government and Kornilov even declared that he was not
an opponent of the army committees, merely demanding that
they should not interfere in operative orders. Kornilov's appearance
on the platform at the session of August 27 was the signal for a
storm of ovation from the Right, during which the Left remained
demonstratively silent. It was significant for the fate of the future
attempted *coup* that the soldiers' representatives remained sullenly
seated, which made them a target for taunts and abuse from the
conservatives. Kornilov emphasized such points as the tremendous
fall of productivity in munition factories and hinted that further
military reverses would be the inevitable consequence of a continuation of the Government's lax policies, remarking: "We must not
permit that order in the rear should be the consequence of our loss
of Riga and that order on the railroads would be reëstablished at the
price of yielding Moldavia and Bessarabia to the enemy."

A more outspoken champion of the conservative viewpoint was
General Kaledin, Ataman (elected governor) of the territory inhabited by the Don Cossacks. He aroused loud cheers from the seats
of the Right when he boasted that the Cossacks, just because they
had never known serfdom, were not intoxicated by the new liberty
and that the Cossack regiments had no deserters; and a chorus of
approval from the Right, mingled with hisses and protests from
the Left, greeted his sweeping proposal that "all Soviets and committees must be abolished, both in the army and in the rear." [14]

Kaledin found his opponent later in the course of the Conference
when a young Cossack officer, Nagaev, elected as a delegate from the
Caucasian Front, contested Kaledin's right to speak in the name of
"twelve Cossack territories" and urged the General "not to tear
off the Cossacks from the people." Nagaev's declarations that the
rank-and-file Cossacks would not follow Kaledin's anti-Soviet slogan
elicited lively applause on the Left and much indignation on the
part of a group of officers who were sitting in a box. Someone in

the box called out "German marks," and the auditorium was filled with cries of protest. Kerensky intervened; and, when no one responded to the demand that the man who uttered this insinuation should give his name, declared: "Lieutenant Nagaev and all the Russian people who are present here are quite satisfied with the silence of a coward."

As the Conference dragged on, with scores of orators expressing the varied views of political parties, nationalities, social classes and religious organizations, it became increasingly evident that no united concrete decisions would be taken as a result of its labors. The few conciliatory gestures which marked the Conference, such as the public handshaking of the Soviet moderate leader, Tseretelli and the prominent industrialist, Bublikov, could not obliterate the dominant impression that the country was divided into two irreconcilably hostile camps. And there was something at once tragic and futile in this continual sniping between the two camps, one consisting of representatives of the propertied classes, the other of moderate Socialists, because both the contending groups were predestined to speedy obliteration at the hands of Bolshevism. If most of the participants in the Conference felt that the issue of power lay between Kerensky and Kornilov events would soon show that the real victor in the struggle for power would be Lenin.

A curious sense of impending collapse seems to have pervaded the last scene before the curtain fell on the deliberations of the State Conference. In Kerensky's last speech banalities alternated with flights of hysterical rodomontade.[15]

"Let my heart become stone; let all the strings of faith in man perish, let all the flowers and wreaths of man dry up . . . I shall throw far away the keys of my heart, which loves men, I will think only about the state."

The atmosphere of sentimental bathos was intensified when a woman's voice cried: "You cannot do that; your heart will not permit it."

So great was the Premier's nervous exhaustion and loss of self-possession that he had to be applauded into stopping his rambling speech; and when he absentmindedly started to walk off the stage he had to be recalled to bring the Conference to a formal conclusion.

The Moscow Conference was only an interlude in the development of Kornilov's plot. It certainly did not bring the General any closer to Kerensky; and the homage which the conservative classes

paid him was calculated still further to turn the head of the un-sophisticated Kornilov and to strengthen his belief that he was the man of destiny whose mission was to save his country by in-stituting a strong government. How far such veteran Duma political leaders as Rodzianko and Milyukov directly encouraged Kornilov in his adventurous scheme is difficult to say. There is certainly reason to suspect that they looked not unkindly on a military dic-tatorship as a temporary remedy for the country's difficulties. Kornilov was much more directly under the influence of his adjutant Zavoiko, who played the rôle of publicity agent for the General, issuing in a large edition a short popular biography of Kornilov; and after the Moscow Conference two other men, Aladin, a former Laborite Duma Deputy who had lost all trace of radicalism, and Dobrinsky, a Red Cross official, who made a doubtful claim to great influence among the Caucasian mountaineers, began to play sub-sidiary rôles in the General's circle of intimate counsellors.

By the beginning of September the military side of the plot was fully worked out. Quartermaster-General Romanovsky, one of the main participants, on September 3 signed an order to distribute hand-grenades among the three cavalry units with which it was proposed to envelop and seize Petrograd from the south: the Savage Division, concentrated near Dno, the First Don Cavalry Division, near Pskov and the Ussuri Division, near Veliki Luki.[16] This order was a clear indication that these units were designed not for service on the front, against the Germans, but for street fighting in Petro-grad. About the same time orders were given to insure a ten days' reserve of food and forage for these divisions. While these three divisions were to move from the south, the Fifth Caucasion Cavalry Division, concentrated between Viborg and Byelo-ostrov, was to move in a southeastern direction and close in on the capital from the north. The capital was to be subjected to a regular military occupation, the river Neva being the line of division between the sections to be taken over by the troops arriving from the south and those coming in from the north. A definite date for this operation was fixed: "as soon as news is received about the beginning of dis-orders in Petrograd and not later than the morning of September 14."[17]

There was special significance in this alert anticipation of dis-orders in Petrograd. It was believed that the stricter measures for restoring discipline in the army which the Government would soon proclaim would provoke some demonstration of protest on the part

of the Bolsheviki, and very probably on the part of the Soviet as well. Moreover the fact that September 9 (August 27, by the old Russian calendar) marked the lapse of six months since the occurrence of the Revolution, which took place on February 27, Old Style, aroused the belief in the ranks of Kornilov's sympathizers that some sort of Bolshevik outbreak would occur on this day and would serve as a pretext for decisive repressive measures.

In Petrograd itself two patriotic conservative organizations, "The Union of Military Duty" and "The Republican Centre," were ready to give Kornilov active support; in the Stavka it was understood that two thousand armed men could be counted on in the city; and Kornilov gave orders that officers should be sent from Petrograd to the front, under various pretexts, in order to give these auxiliaries training and instruction.[18] While the members of these organizations in Petrograd took their strength very seriously and were prepared to provoke and simulate Bolshevik outbursts, in case no real disorder occurred and subsequently "to seize armored automobiles, to arrest the Provisional Government, to arrest and execute the more prominent and influential members of the Soviet, etc.,"[19] their actual capacity for action, as subsequent events proved, was practically non-existent.

While a *coup d'état*, under the thin pretext of protecting the Provisional Government against a hypothetical attack from the side of the Left, was thus being prepared in the Stavka, Kerensky, in his eternal wavering between Right and Left policies, had veered rather definitely toward the Right. A series of explosions in munitions factories in Petrograd and Kazan during the last week of August suggested that German agents were at work and that discipline and watchfulness at these strategic enterprises were badly relaxed. Riga was on the verge of surrender; it actually fell on the night of September 2; and these events, combined with the impressions which he had brought away from the Moscow State Conference, had apparently convinced the Premier that he could hold his slipping power only by adopting a firmer line of policy in military affairs. So, on August 30, he informed Savinkov, whom he left in charge of the War Ministry, despite their former differences of opinion, that he was prepared to accept Kornilov's memorandum of August 23 as the basis for new military legislation. This concession, which Savinkov promptly communicated to the Stavka, did not, however, retard the military preparations which were being made there. Kerensky was cordially distrusted and despised by

conservative officers of the old school, and his expressed willingness to accept Kornilov's recommendations was probably interpreted as a sign of weakness.

Immediately after the fall of Riga [20] Kornilov telegraphed to Kerensky a request that all troops in the Petrograd district should be directly subordinated to him. (Hitherto the Petrograd district had been under a general directly responsible to the Provisional Government.) Kerensky, however, refused to agree to this, insisting that the city of Petrograd and its environs should remain in direct subordination to the Government. Kerensky cherished a lively apprehension that, if the Petrograd garrison were turned over to Kornilov, "we could have been eaten up at any time." [21]

The development of the plot now took an extremely curious turn; and Kerensky was very nearly placed in the anomalous position of a conspirator against himself. On September 5 Savinkov, always an advocate of rapprochement between Kerensky and Kornilov, arrived in the Stavka and laid before Kornilov the following requests of Kerensky:

(1) To liquidate the Union of Officers, because some of its members were reported to be involved in a plot.

(2) To liquidate the political department attached to the Stavka, for the same reasons.

(3) To convince Kornilov that the city of Petrograd should be excepted from the status of direct subordination to the Commander-in-chief which was to apply to the Petrograd district.

(4) *To ask Kornilov for a cavalry corps, which was to enforce martial law in Petrograd and to defend the Provisional Government against any attacks, especially from the side of the Bolsheviki.* (My italics.)

Kornilov and his associates must have been pleasantly surprised indeed by this last request, which amounted to a legal sanction of the very operation which they had been planning to carry out conspiratively. Kerensky himself, when the whole Kornilov affair was subsequently a matter of judicial investigation, was decidedly vague in his testimony as to why he wanted a cavalry corps. Apparently he was convinced, on the basis of the reports of some foreign intelligence service, that there was danger of a repetition of the July Days, possibly in combination with a German landing in Finland. Moreover, he probably wanted to be prepared for any opposition on the part of the Soviet to his programme. Of course he did not realize that he was playing into the hands of conspira-

tors who, if their plans succeeded, would certainly not leave him at the head of the Government.

Kornilov, overjoyed at finding his scheme promoted from such an unexpected source, agreed with Kerensky's other requests and did not raise any objection when Savinkov asked him not to appoint General Krimov, who bore the reputation of being a monarchist, as head of the cavalry corps and not to send the Savage Division, the officers of which were considered politically unreliable, to Petrograd. Actually Kornilov made no change in his dispositions, which contemplated both the employment of Krimov as Commander of the expedition and the utilization of the Savage Division. Savinkov, if we may trust Lukomsky's testimony,[22] employed as strong language as Kornilov himself might have used about the necessity for smashing the Bolsheviki and the Soviet also, if it should solidarize itself with them. Lukomsky, who was by far the ablest man among Kornilov's immediate associates, distrusted the intentions of the Government; but Kornilov himself seems to have derived from his talk with Savinkov a comforting conviction that the more energetic members of the Government were on his side and that Kerensky himself could easily be won over or swept aside, as circumstances might require.

The Kornilov affair might well have taken a much more serious turn if the movement of cavalry on Petrograd had proceeded with the Government's full sanction and authorization. But, almost immediately after Savinkov had departed for Petrograd, Kornilov received another visitor, Prince V. N. Lvov (not to be confused with the Prince G. Lvov who was the first Premier in the Provisional Government), who was destined to play the rôle of evil genius of his conspiracy.

V. N. Lvov, who for a time had filled the post of Procurator of the Holy Synod in the Provisional Government, was a goodhearted, somewhat weakheaded man, of moderate conservative views, whose bustling, officious character made him prone to undertake commissions which a more discreet and experienced politician would have hesitated to accept. After the Moscow State Conference, Lvov came to the conclusion that the position of the Provisional Government, in its present form, was untenable, because it had lost the support of so large a part of the propertied and educated classes. And when his friend, Dobrinsky, who belonged to the circle of "advisers" who fluttered about Kornilov, let slip some hints that plans were brewing in the Stavka for a change in the composition of the

Provisional Government, Lvov felt it was a duty of patriotism and friendship to go to Kerensky and expound the situation to him. The first of three interviews in which Lvov, quite unconsciously, was to tear up the threads of a conspiracy which he by no means fully understood occurred on the evening of September 4 in Kerensky's office in the Winter Palace. Lvov spoke at some length of the weak position of the Government and suggested that it should be reorganized along broader lines, through the inclusion of representatives of the more conservative political groups. This sort of advice was familiar enough; but what excited Kerensky's interest and suspicion was that Lvov mysteriously gave himself out as the representative of "important social groups," "possessing real strength."

There is a good deal of discrepancy in the subsequent testimony of Kerensky and Lvov as to the precise reply of the Premier to the hints and proposals of Lvov. Kerensky stated that he "did not consider it possible to refrain from further discussions with Lvov, expecting from him a more exact explanation of what was in his mind." Lvov, on the other hand, asserted that he had obtained from Kerensky permission to turn to various political groups with suggestions for the reorganization of the Government on broader lines. It seems most probable that Kerensky encouraged Lvov to sound out the groups which he professed to represent, hoping in this way to learn more of what might prove to be a formidable plot, and that Lvov considerably exaggerated and overstepped the bounds of his commission.

The second of the three fateful interviews occurred in Moghilev. Received by Kornilov late on the evening of the 6th Lvov told the Commander-in-chief that he had Kerensky's authorization to learn Kornilov's demands. The arrival of a man of Lvov's political standing, representing himself as Kerensky's personal envoy, so soon after the visit of Savinkov convinced Kornilov that Kerensky was ready to capitulate and that conspirative methods were no longer necessary. So when Lvov, at Kornilov's request, called on him again on the morning of the 7th the General put forward the two following requests: declaration of martial law in Petrograd and the handing over of all military and civil authority to the Commander-in-chief, whoever he might be. Kornilov added that he could not vouch for the lives of Kerensky and Savinkov anywhere in Russia and invited them to come to the Stavka, simultaneously suggesting that Kerensky might be Minister for Justice and

Savinkov Minister for War. A further talk with the boastful and garrulous Zavoiko, Kornilov's adjutant and political adviser-in-chief, left Lvov in no doubt that it was proposed not only to remove Kerensky from power, but also to assassinate him at the first convenient moment. The personnel of the new Cabinet was being freely discussed in the Stavka.

Hurrying back to Petrograd Lvov had his second talk with Kerensky in the Winter Palace on the evening of the 8th. The Premier was amazed as Lvov set forth Kornilov's demands. Kerensky urged that these be put in writing. This Lvov did, outlining as the three demands: the declaration of martial law in Petrograd, the transfer of all power to the Commander-in-chief and the resignation of all members of the Cabinet. At the same time he communicated to Kerensky Kornilov's invitation to come to Moghilev, but added a warning that it would be dangerous to accept this invitation.

A thousand lurking suspicions must have found sudden confirmation in Kerensky's mind as he heard Lvov's communication, which was all the more surprising because Savinkov had just reported optimistically about Kornilov's readiness to coöperate with the Government. The possibly fatal mistake which he had made in ordering a concentration of reactionary cavalry units in Petrograd loomed large before his eyes. His first lawyer's instinct was to obtain proof, with witnesses, of the correctness of Lvov's words.

In the presence of a companion, Virubov, Kerensky got into direct touch with Kornilov from the War Ministry. Lvov was supposed to be present at this interview, but was late, and Kerensky impersonated him[23] in the conversation, which was carried on by means of the Hughes telegraphic apparatus. Kerensky first asked whether he should act "according to the information given him by Lvov," and when he received an affirmative answer he assumed the rôle of Lvov and asked whether "it is necessary to carry out that definite decision about which you asked me to inform Kerensky personally," to which Kornilov replied that he desired Lvov to convey to Kerensky his "urgent request to come to Moghilev." Kerensky, revelling in the web of mystification, assured Kornilov that he hoped to leave Petrograd for Moghilev on the following day and ended the interview with the words: "Goodbye, we shall soon see each other." It is significant that Kerensky avoided any direct reference to the demands which Kornilov had communicated to him through Lvov. He was interested now not in explana-

tions or in possibilities of reconciliation, but only in destroying his rival as quickly as possible.

Still playing his part of an examining lawyer, Kerensky took Lvov (who had arrived just when the conversation with Kornilov had ended) with him to the Winter Palace, where Assistant Police Chief Balavinsky was concealed as a witness. Kerensky made the unsuspecting Lvov repeat the whole story and at the end of it dramatically placed him under arrest. The unfortunate Lvov was not only compelled to go to bed with two guards posted in the neighborhood; but found his sleep hopelessly disturbed because Kerensky, pacing up and down in an adjoining room, sang snatches from operatic airs without intermission.[24]

After describing the situation which had arisen to Nekrasov and Savinkov, rejecting the plea of the latter for direct negotiations with Kornilov and asking the advice of military experts about the technical possibilities of resisting Kornilov's troops, Kerensky, about four A.M. on the 9th, convoked a Cabinet session. The Ministers, astounded at the news, conferred on Kerensky unlimited powers of action in dealing with the emergency and proffered their resignations. The Cadet Ministers, who, if they did not directly sympathize with Kornilov's undertaking, were certainly opposed to a decisive and uncompromising deposition of the General on whom they had placed such great hopes, followed up their resignations by staying away from their offices for the duration of the crisis. The others, after Kerensky had refused to accept their resignations, continued to carry on their functions. After this session of the Cabinet Kerensky addressed to Kornilov the decisive telegram, which announced the final breach:

"I order you immediately to turn over your office to General Lukomsky, who is to take over temporarily the duties of Commander-in-chief, until the arrival of the new Commander-in-chief. You are instructed immediately to come to Petrograd."

Some reflection of the flurry in the mind of the Premier may be seen in the fact that the telegram bore no number and was signed simply "Kerensky," although the dismissal of the Commander-in-chief was supposed to require a decree of the Provisional Government.

Kornilov, after his talk with Kerensky, retired on the night of the 8th confident that his plans would meet no further opposition. He was correspondingly surprised, on the following morning,

to receive Kerensky's curt telegram of dismissal and immediately decided to remain at his post. His Chief of Staff, Lukomsky, refused to obey Kerensky's instructions to take over the command, and despatched a message to the Premier in which he declared that "for the sake of Russia's salvation you must go with General Kornilov, and not against him." Lukomsky refused to assume responsibility for the army, even for a short time, and informed the commanders of the various fronts of his decision and of the general situation.

Kerensky sent out an order to stop all troop movements toward Petrograd; Kornilov countermanded this order and instructed the cavalry units to proceed toward the capital according to plan. So the issue of civil war was fairly joined. In the first days the prevalent mood in the Stavka was one of confidence. General Krasnov, who was to command the Fifth Caucasian Cavalry Division, one of the units involved in the expedition, was assured before he left Moghilev that "No one will defend Kerensky. This is only a promenade." [25] And Prince Trubetzkoy, chief of the diplomatic department attached to the Stavka, summed up as follows in a telegram to Foreign Minister Tereschenko on September 10 what he regarded as the points in favor of Kornilov's success: "The whole commanding staff, the overwhelming majority of the officers and the best fighting units of the army are for Kornilov. On his side in the rear are all the Cossacks, the majority of the military training schools and also the best fighting units." Along with this Prince Trubetzkoy characterized as the mood of the masses "indifference that submits to the blow of the whip." [26]

Had it been merely a question of defending Kerensky, Kornilov might have encountered little resistance. But Prince Trubetzkoy, living in the secluded atmosphere of the Stavka, most fundamentally misjudged the mood of the masses when he anticipated from them an attitude of passive indifference. Among the city workers, and the poorer classes generally, among the soldiers there was still a large residue of the mood of fierce discontent that had boiled over in the July Days. Kornilov's challenge to the Provisional Government, his effort to set up a military dictatorship was just the stimulus that was needed to turn this mood into one of vigorous, active resistance. From the very beginning the attempted *coup* was doomed by the cloud of sabotage and propaganda which enveloped it. Railroad workers refused to operate or delayed the despatch of the trains

which carried the Kornilov troops. Telegraph operators declined to transmit the messages of Kornilov's generals. At every station the Kornilov troops found themselves surrounded by impromptu propagandists, workers and soldiers of the local garrisons, who rapidly undermined their morale by pointing out that they were being sent against the legal Government and urging them not to fight: an uncommonly popular appeal to the staunchest Russian troops in 1917. As Milyukov says: [27] "The issue was decided not so much by the troop movements, by the strategic or tactical successes of the Government or Kornilov detachments as by the sentiment of the troops . . . Bloodshed did not take place, for the simple reason that no one wanted to shed blood and sacrifice himself, on either side."

A lively war of words between Kerensky and Kornilov developed on the 9th. Savinkov, who was naturally one of the most active advocates of agreement, vainly endeavored to persuade Kornilov to give up his post as a means of paving the way to further discussion and removal of misunderstanding. Kerensky issued a rather temperately worded manifesto (its mildness probably reflected the influence of some of his counsellors, such as Tereschenko, who were still hoping for a compromise solution) in which he declared that Kornilov had despatched Lvov to him with the demand for the handing over of all military and civil power, ordered Kornilov to turn over his command to General Klembovsky, Commander of the northern front, proclaimed a state of martial law in Petrograd and urged all citizens to maintain order and tranquillity.

Kornilov responded with a much more violently worded telegram, characterizing the first part of Kerensky's manifesto as "a complete falsehood," inasmuch as he had not sent Lvov to Kerensky, but Lvov had come to him as Kerensky's spokesman. "So," Kornilov continued, "a great provocation, which placed the fate of the fatherland at stake, was carried out." Kornilov's declaration, written in a style of oldfashioned sentimentality by his literary aide, Zavoiko, urged all Russians "to pray the Lord God for the greatest miracle, the salvation of the native land" and ended:

"I, General Kornilov, son of a Cossack peasant, say to everyone that personally I desire nothing, except the preservation of Great Russia, and I vow to bring the people, by means of victory over the enemy, up to the Constituent Assembly, at which it will itself decide its fate and choose the form of its new state life. I cannot betray Russia into the hands of its

ancestral enemy, the German race, and make the Russian people slaves of the Germans and I prefer to die on the field of honor and battle, so as not to see the shame and destruction of the Russian land.

"Russian people, the life of your motherland is in your hands."

While such an appeal was calculated to strike a responsive chord in the heart of an oldfashioned officer, landowner or priest, its propagandist effect among the masses could scarcely have been great, even if it could have been widely distributed. War and victory were not popular slogans in Russia at that time; and the workers and soldiers were inclined to see the enemy in the "bourgeoisie" and not in the Germans.

Kornilov received the unanimous support of the commanders of the four European fronts. General Klembovsky declined the offered post of Commander-in-chief with the observation that he "considered any change in the higher command extremely dangerous." [28] From the southwestern front the blunt, outspoken General Denikin, the future outstanding leader of the White cause in the civil war, sent to Kerensky a telegram with the following sharp and unambiguous phrases: "Seeing in Kornilov's removal a return of the Government to the method of systematic destruction of the army and, consequently, of destruction of the country, I consider it my duty to inform the Provisional Government that on this road I will not go with it." Denikin took this occasion to remind the Premier that he had already accused the Government of having "destroyed the army and trampled our fighting banners in the mud." General Baluev, on the western front, and General Sherbatchev, on the Rumanian front, also expressed solidarity with Kornilov.

This support by the highest Generals was, of course, infinitely less significant than it would have been in a country where ordinary army discipline prevailed. Not one of these commanders of fronts was in a position to send to Kornilov's aid a company, to say nothing of a corps or division of troops. Denikin, the most active and energetic of them, could do no more than place a guard at the telegraph station in Berditchev, where his headquarters were located; and by September 11 the committee of the southwestern front felt itself strong enough to place Denikin, his Chief of Staff, Markov, and some of his other associates under arrest. [29]

In Petrograd Government circles, however, the weakness of Kornilov's position was not immediately grasped; and the representations of the Generals, combined with exaggerated rumors about

the progress of Kornilov's military units strengthened the hands of the advocates of some sort of face-saving compromise. The 10th was a day of nervous conferences of the Ministers. The Cadet leader, Paul Milyukov, was especially active in endeavoring to find a solution which would not permit Kornilov to be crushed. As late as the evening of the 10th Milyukov was urging, in a conference at the Winter Palace, that Kerensky should resign his office in favor of General Alekseev, to whom Kornilov might be expected to submit. Such a "compromise" would have been a victory for Kornilovism, if not for Kornilov, because Alekseev, while a much more cautious and discreet man, certainly shared Kornilov's views as to the necessity for a drastic restoration of discipline and for a generally more conservative turn of governmental policy. Even Kerensky's closest political friends were wavering: Tereschenko suggested that "both Kerensky and Kornilov should obtain satisfaction at the price of mutual sacrifices," and Nekrasov, who seems to have considerably overestimated Kornilov's chances of military success, also advised Kerensky to retire.

At this moment, however, according to Milyukov's account,[30] Kerensky received a sudden access of moral reinforcement. A delegation from the Soviet appeared, demanding the uncompromising suppression of Kornilov's movement. The idea of a compromise Premiership of Alekseev vanished. Another effort at mediation failed when Tereschenko, on the 11th, politely declined a tender of good offices as mediators in the conflict which the British Ambassador, Sir George Buchanan, made on behalf of the representatives of all the Allied powers and the United States on the evening of the 10th. Sir George accompanied the offer with the statement that it was made "with the sole object of averting civil war and serving the interests of Russia and her allies."[31] Tereschenko replied that Kornilov's attitude made it impossible for the Government to make terms with him. By the 11th the balance of forces had visibly changed to Kornilov's disadvantage.

The effect of Kornilov's move on the Petrograd Soviet was that of an electric shock, awakening that organization to new life and to a unanimous will to resistance. The Mensheviki and the Socialist Revolutionaries were quick to forget the unpleasant memories of the July Days in facing the immediate menace of an occupation of the revolutionary capital by Krimov and his Caucasian and Cossack cavalry. There was a general feeling that the Kornilov officers would make small distinction between members of the

various revolutionary parties when the hangings began. And it was a Menshevik, Weinstein, who proposed formal coöperation with the Bolsheviki at the session of the Vtsik on the evening of September 9.

According to Weinstein's proposal, which was accepted, a "Committee for Struggle with Counterrevolution," consisting of three Bolsheviki, three Mensheviki, three Socialist Revolutionaries, five representatives of the Vtsik and the Executive Committee of Peasants' Deputies and two representatives each from the trade-unions and from the Petrograd Soviet, was created. The Bolshevik spokesman, Sokolnikov, promised the coöperation of his Party; its influence on the soldiers and workers was indeed indispensable to the successful organization of the masses.[32]

The Bolshevik tactics at this important turn of events (summed up by Lenin in the phrase: "We will fight with Kornilov, but we will not support Kerensky")[33] revealed a high measure of finesse and flexibility. Exploiting to the utmost the opportunity for winning the masses away from the more moderate Socialist parties, they made all possible use of the possibilities for legal action which were extended to them and did not compromise themselves by any premature and ill-judged effort to overthrow the shadowy Provisional Government, which, with tongue in cheek, they were defending.

Their greatest success, perhaps, was in securing the approval of the Committee for Struggle with Counterrevolution for the creation of an armed workers' militia. This was little more than a legalization and rearming of the Red Guard which had been to some extent repressed and driven underground after the July Days. Within a few days some 25,000 recruits were enlisted in this organization, and the Bolshevik Military Organization succeeded in supplying them not only with rifles, but also with machine-guns.[34]

While the Bolsheviki were the main driving force in organizing the masses, Kerensky, with his usual instinct for balancing between Right and Left, entrusted the defense of Petrograd to two men who had only recently been earnest advocates of Kornilov's military programme, Savinkov, who was appointed military governor, and his assistant, Filonenko. Savinkov took measures to assure the food supply and the railroad communication of the capital and simultaneously kept an eye on the Bolsheviki, sending back to Kronstadt 2,000 sailors who had arrived on their own initiative

and who impressed him as undesirable champions of the Provisional Government.

The Committee for Struggle with Counterrevolution inaugurated a nationwide campaign for resistance to Kornilov, encouraging the creation of similar local committees in all important towns, sending instructions to the garrisons of the neighboring towns and to the strategically important railroad and post and telegraph workers. The outskirts of Petrograd were an armed camp. True, the military quality of the Petrograd troops, if one may credit the testimony of Filonenko and of the Commander of the Moscow garrison, Verkhovsky, who had preserved his loyalty to the Provisional Government, was very low [35] ; the chances of resistance to a powerful, well organized attack of disciplined troops would have been slight.

But the whole political and social background simply excluded the possibility of any such attack. Kornilov's warriors, so formidable in the imagination of nervous Ministers, simply melted away, like their predecessors, the force which Nicholas II despatched against Petrograd under General Ivanov.

From a purely military standpoint the preparation of the *coup* was very incompetent and reflects little credit on the capacity of many of Kornilov's officers who were responsible for making the plans. The Savage Division, one of the main units involved, consisted of only 1,350 horsemen and was short of 600 rifles, 1,000 lances and 500 spears. The units were not provided with field telegraph apparatus, and were consequently exposed to loss of communication both with the Stavka and among themselves. Kornilov himself, instead of taking the field with his troops, remained in Moghilev.

The fate of the units which took part in the affair was much the same, with minor variations. The Savage Division, under the command of Prince Bagration, reached the railroad station Viritsa, about twenty-four miles from Tsarskoe Syelo, on the evening of the 10th. Here its progress was checked because the railroad line was torn up. On the following day a Mohammedan delegation, organized by the Soviet, arrived in Viritsa. It included among its members a grandson of the national hero of the mountaineers of the East Caucasus, Shamil. The exhortations and arguments of this delegation, voiced in the varied guttural tongues of the Caucasian tribesmen, quickly shook the confidence of the troops in their officers; on the 12th Prince Bagration ordered the cessation of any hostile activity of his soldiers against the troops of the

Provisional Government (actually no bloodshed had occurred). And on the 13th a delegation of the Caucasian warriors in their picturesque native costumes appeared in Petrograd with vows of loyalty to the Provisional Government and expressions of regret for having been misled.

The Cossack regiments which were to coöperate with the Savage Division had much the same experience. Wherever they moved they were surrounded by zealous propagandists, who slipped in among them, despite the efforts of the officers to prevent this and used such arguments as:

"Comrades, Kerensky freed you from the officer's stick, gave you freedom; and do you want to crawl before the officer again? . . . Kerensky is for freedom and the happiness of the people. Kornilov is for discipline and the death penalty. Are you really for Kornilov? . . . Kornilov is a traitor to Russia and goes to lead you into battle in defense of foreign capital. He got much money for this, and Kerensky wants peace." There was no lack of agencies of propaganda: the Soviets, the station committees, the garrisons which were stationed in towns like Yamburg, Narva and Luga. Moreover, partly as a result of the poor technical preparation of the whole affair, partly because of the vigorous and deliberate sabotage of the railroad workers, the cavalry force by September 12 was in a hopelessly scattered and disorganized state, dispersed along eight railroad lines and poorly supplied with food and forage.[36] The authority of the officers had almost disappeared; the actual power was in the hands of the soldiers' committees, which hastened to offer assurances of submission to the Provisional Government. The generals and higher officers had no alternative except to follow their example.

The collapse of the enterprise was so evident that General Krimov himself went to Petrograd; and after an interview with Kerensky, who accused him of deliberate mutiny, withdrew to the apartment of one of his officers and shot himself through the heart.

The other forces which were supposed to coöperate in making the *coup* successful proved quite impotent. The leaders of the Petrograd patriotic societies proved to be charlatans and adventurers. When the time for action came they either disappeared altogether, in some cases taking with them the funds of the organizations, or were found carousing in restaurants. The Committee for Struggle with Counterrevolution raided the Astoria

Hotel, a favorite rendezvous of officers, and made fourteen arrests; but the precaution was almost superfluous.

The Don Cossack Ataman Kaledin, on whose support Kornilov had relied, and to whom he addressed a personal appeal, was threatened with arrest by the Soviet of Voronezh, a town lying near the frontier of the Don Territory and hastened back to his capital, Novo-Cherkassk, by a circuitous route, avoiding the larger railroad centres. The loyalty of the majority of the Cossacks was a sufficient guaranty for Kaledin's safety in Novo-Cherkassk; but he was in no position to exert any influence outside the frontiers of the Don Territory.

It now only remained to clear up the centre of the frustrated *coup*, Moghilev. On September 12 Kerensky himself assumed the office of Commander-in-chief, appointing as his Chief of Staff General Alekseev. The latter's assumption of office under Kerensky is explained by his desire to make the liquidation of the abortive *coup* as painless as possible for its participants. After some long-distance conversations with Kornilov and Lukomsky [87] Alekseev proceeded to Moghilev and on September 14, after being insistently prodded by Kerensky, who himself was being urged by the Soviet to show no leniency toward the conspirators, he formally arrested Kornilov, Lukomsky, Romanovsky and Colonel Pluschevsky-Pluschik. Members of an investigating commission arrived on the following day and carried out further arrests. This commission, which consisted of representatives of various public organizations, headed by a judicial investigator, Shablovsky, was decidedly indulgent in its attitude toward the arrested prisoners; as Lukomsky testifies: [38] "After the first examinations which the members of the commission carried out it was evident that they were all very well disposed toward us." Instead of pressing on the investigation with a view to a speedy trial the commission carried on its work in very leisurely fashion. Meanwhile the prisoners were transferred from Moghilev to a monastery in the neighboring town of Bikhov, where they were joined by Denikin, Markov and other persons arrested in Berditchev, who narrowly escaped being lynched by the enraged mob. After the Bolshevik Revolution the Generals were able to flee from Bikhov, and played a prominent part in the civil war in South Russia.

The Kornilov plot collapsed without the firing of a shot and without bloodshed,—except for such local excesses as the drowning of ten officers suspected of sympathy with Kornilov in Viborg and

the shooting of four naval officers of the warship *Petropavlovsk* by sailors who were infuriated by the refusal of the officers to sign a pledge of loyalty to the Provisional Government. But its significance was far-reaching in the extreme. Quite probably an ultimate victory of Bolshevism was predetermined by the entire political, economic and social condition of Russia in 1917. But Kornilov's futile, clumsy thrust for power facilitated and expedited this victory. It was no accident that the two most important Soviets in the country cast their first Bolshevik majorities immediately after the Kornilov affair: Petrograd on September 13 and Moscow on September 18.

Several of Kerensky's acts during this period indicate that he foresaw clearly enough the likelihood that the threat from the Right was likely to be followed by a threat from the Left. When a soldier in the delegation of the Savage Division began to talk about the necessity for pitiless punishment of the counterrevolutionary officers Kerensky interrupted and sharply rebuked him: "Don't speak in such a tone. Your duty now is to obey your officers; and we shall do ourselves whatever is necessary." [39]

Equally symptomatic were his desperate efforts to create a new coalition with the Cadets, despite the obvious sympathy of many of the latter with Kornilov, and his concentration near Petrograd of the Fifth Caucasian Cavalry Division under General Krasnov, who had been one of Kornilov's active lieutenants.

But the time was past when Kerensky could save his position by maneuvers of this kind. The stream of social revolution was in full tide; the last dykes had burst with the abortive resort to violence of the military and propertied classes. But before describing the last agony of the Provisional Government it seems advisable to give an outline of the three major movements of social upheaval which gripped the country throughout 1917 and which furnish at once a background and an explanation for the more spectacular events in Petrograd. These movements are the huge mutiny of the army, the violent seizure of the estates by the peasants and the upsurge of the industrial workers, beginning with wage demands and ending with definite trampling under foot of the employers' rights of ownership.

NOTES

[1] General A. I. Denikin, "Sketches of Russian Turmoil," Vol. II, p. 194.
[2] A. Kerensky, "The Kornilov Affair," p. 37.
[3] *Ibid.*, p. 52.
[4] Denikin, *op. cit.*, p. 195.

[5] P. N. Milyukov, "History of the Second Russian Revolution," Vol. II, p. 113.

[6] General A. Lukomsky, "Reminiscences," Vol. I, pp. 223ff.

[7] Milyukov, *op. cit.,* Vol. II, pp. 107, 108.

[8] Kerensky, *op. cit.,* p. 62.

[9] Lukomsky, *op. cit.,* Vol. I, pp. 228, 229.

[10] "The State Conference," p. xxiv.

[11] E. Ignatov, "The Moscow Soviet of Workers' Deputies in 1917," p. 307.

[12] Leon Trotzky, "The History of the Russian Revolution," Vol. II, pp. 202, 203.

[13] "The State Conference," pp. 3ff.

[14] *Ibid.,* pp. 74ff.

[15] *Ibid.,* p. 307.

[16] E. I. Martinov, "Kornilov: An Attempted Military *Coup,*" pp. 76, 77.

[17] See Krimov's secret order in the Archives of the October Revolution, "The Kornilov Affair," No. 26.

[18] Lukomsky, *op. cit.,* Vol. I, p. 232.

[19] Milyukov, *op. cit.,* Vol. II, p. 171, citing the testimony of one of the participants of the Petrograd organizations, Vinberg, in his book, "A Prisoner of Monkeys."

[20] Trotzky suggests that Kornilov deliberately surrendered Riga to the Germans. That he endeavored to exploit the fall of the city for his conspiratorial purposes is obvious. But the initiative for the Riga operation came from the Germans; and it is certainly doubtful whether any kind of successful defense could have been organized, in view of the condition of the Russian army at that time.

[21] Kerensky, *op. cit.,* p. 82.

[22] Lukomsky, *op. cit.,* Vol. I, p. 236.

[23] Archive of the October Revolution. "The Kornilov Affair," No. 25.

[24] Milyukov, *op. cit.,* Vol. II, p. 214.

[25] P. N. Krasnov, "On the Internal Front," reprinted in "The October Revolution" (in series Revolution and Civil War in the Memoirs of the Whites), p. 19.

[26] Kerensky, *op. cit.,* p. 144.

[27] Milyukov, *op. cit.,* Vol. II, p. 263.

[28] Archive of the October Revolution: "The Kornilov Affair," No. 9.

[29] Denikin, *op. cit.,* Vol. II, p. 215.

[30] Milyukov, *op. cit.,* Vol. II, p. 254.

[31] Sir George Buchanan, "My Mission to Russia and Other Diplomatic Memories," Vol. II, pp. 181ff.

[32] N. Sukhanov, "Reminiscences of the Revolution," Vol. V, pp. 290ff.

[33] V. I. Lenin, "Collected Works," Vol. XIV, Part 2, p. 95.

[34] Martinov, *op. cit.,* p. 113.

[35] *Ibid.,* p. 134.

[36] Krasnov, *op. cit.,* pp. 34, 36.

[37] Kornilov displayed some duplicity in these discussions. At the same time when he was negotiating with Alekseev for a peaceful surrender he was sending to Krimov a message instructing him to "act independently in the spirit of the instructions which I gave you, if circumstances permit." See "The Kornilov Affair," No. 27, item 193, in the Archive of the October Revolution.

[38] Lukomsky, *op. cit.,* Vol. I, p. 258.

[39] Vera Vladimirova, "The Revolution of 1917" (Chronicle of Events), Vol. IV, Supplement 33.

CHAPTER X

THE MUTINY OF THE RUSSIAN ARMY

The Russian military authorities during the World War called fifteen and a half million men to the colors. This enormous mobilization of manpower is estimated to have taken about half the younger able-bodied male peasants from the rural districts. At the time of the Revolution Russia had about nine million men under arms, including the garrisons and training-camps in the rear; the strength of the armies in the field declined from 6,900,000 to 6,000,000 between January 1 and September 1, largely as a result of the vast increase in desertion after the overthrow of the Tsarist regime.[1]

Perhaps the most significant fact about the Revolution of 1917 is that between spring and autumn this great host, the largest ever put into the field by any country, was transformed into "an enormous, exhausted, badly clothed, badly fed, embittered mob of people, united by thirst for peace and general disillusionment." [2] The ultimate complete loss by the Provisional Government of control over its armed forces predetermined and made possible the scope and success of the social upheaval throughout the country. There was small chance of saving the estate of the country landlord from pillage and confiscation, of protecting the town factory owner or merchant from the demands of the mob when the Government was equally lacking in reliable troops and in reliable police.

And the socially revolutionary effect of the breakdown of authority and discipline in the army was positive as well as negative. It was not merely that the Government could not call on the troops with any effect to maintain order. The overwhelming majority of the private soldiers were peasants. They were as eager to share in the spoils of the private estates as were their fellow-villagers at home. The backward flow from the front to the country districts, first of a broadening trickle of deserters and finally of millions of largely "self-demobilized" soldiers, was a mighty force in stimulating the agrarian revolution and in stirring up the placid

223

backwaters of Russian life, which knew and cared little about the stormy events in Petrograd.

Of course such an immense military machine as the Russian army did not cease to function abruptly on any one day. Researches in the archive documents and in the published reminiscences of soldiers and officers reveal definite shadings of differentiation in the behavior of various units. These shadings are at once military, geographical and social. The troops which were farthest away from what Kerensky calls the "poisonous" atmosphere of Petrograd [3] were, on the whole, slower to succumb to extremist agitation against the Provisional Government and for immediate peace. (This was a bad omen, incidentally, for the fate of the Government when it would be obliged to fight for the capital.) The morale of the infantry, largely made up of raw, poorly trained peasant recruits, evaporated much more rapidly and irretrievably than that of the traditionally conservative cavalry or of the artillery and motor units, where there was a higher proportion of educated middleclass officers and soldiers.

In the case of the Navy the Baltic Fleet, which was in close contact with the electrically surcharged atmosphere of Petrograd, adopted a Bolshevik position much more rapidly and uncompromisingly than the Black Sea Fleet, where an energetic commander, Admiral Kolchak, the future White dictator of Siberia, was able to keep up a fair measure of order and discipline for some months after the Revolution. In the Navy, especially in the Baltic Fleet, there seem to have been proportionately more murders of officers than was the case in the Army. This was partly attributable to the differing conditions of the two branches of service (it was more difficult for a naval officer to escape from an enraged mob), and is also explained to some extent by the circumstance that the naval officers were almost entirely of the pre-War aristocratic type, especially hateful to their men, whereas in the Army the officers' corps had been greatly changed in social composition by the heavy casualties, with the result that many of the new officers were of plebeian origin.

The mutiny of the Russian armed forces was a protracted and varied process. Sometimes it assumed relatively mild forms: refusal to obey orders or to go into the trenches, desertion. Sometimes it found expression in the lynching and beating of officers and commissars. The disintegration of the old army was cumulative and progressive in character. In the first weeks after the Revolu-

tion there was a vague feeling that the old disciplinary bonds had snapped, that the officer no longer possessed the authority that had been taken as a matter of course in Tsarist days.

Then there was an effort, at first spontaneous, later more organized, to replace the fallen prestige of the officer through new agencies of "democratic discipline," committees elected by the soldiers and commissars, appointed at first by the Petrograd Soviet, later by the Provisional Government. The collapse of the summer offensive proved the futility of endeavoring to re-create the fighting capacity of the army by such methods. But the committees and commissars were preserved (indeed it would have been impossible to abolish them) and there was an effort to stiffen discipline by introducing the death penalty at the front, which had been abolished in the early period of the Revolution. This measure remained largely a paper threat and was, therefore, less effective than might have been expected.

The complete and ignominious collapse of the Kornilov attempted *coup* had a most disastrous effect on the position and prestige not only of the officers, but also of the commissars and committees; and during the weeks which preceded the Bolshevik seizure of power the tide of soldiers' revolt was rising higher and higher, ruthlessly brushing aside the feeble resistance which the moderate Socialists, who occupied most of the commissarial posts and still controlled the central army committees, which had definitely ceased to represent the sentiment of the masses of soldiers, could offer. And when the decisive moment of the fight for power came in Petrograd Kerensky could rally to his support only a pitiful handful out of the six million soldiers who were on Russia's farflung fronts: a few military students, a few women, whose enlistment had been one of the curiosities of the "democratization" of the army, a few hundred Cossacks.

Such, in main outline, is the picture of the revolt of Russia's huge army, a revolt that was largely spontaneous, headed often by unknown leaders who have left no traces or scant traces behind them, a movement that provided at once the background and the explanation for the still greater process of social upheaval that was rising with torrential force all over the country. One may now fill in this sketch with more concrete details.

The internal condition of the Russian army at the time of the Revolution was far from satisfactory. At a conference of the commanding generals of the various fronts in the Stavka at the

end of December, 1916,[4] General Ruzsky spoke of Riga and Dvinsk as "the misfortune of the Northern Front, especially Riga. These are two nests of propaganda." General Brussilov spoke of disturbances in the Seventh Siberian Corps, including refusal to go into attack and the killing of a captain, after which several men were shot and order was restored. General Evert mentioned disorders in one regiment of the Third Army, in connection with the giving out of sugar, which led to the shooting of seven men.

In general the food and transportation difficulties which contributed so much to the creation of a revolutionary mood among the civilian population were beginning to be reflected in the supply of the army; and this was accompanied, of course, by the lowered morale that was the natural result of two and a half years of largely unsuccessful warfare. It is a debatable speculative question whether the Russian army would have broken down in 1917, even if the Tsarist regime had survived, or whether the extraordinary stolid endurance of the Russian soldier would have sustained the burdens of another campaign. But the abrupt revolutionary change; the disappearance of the Tsar; the new flood of talk and discussion; the assurance that the new government stood for liberty, a conception that to the average peasant soldier was inseparably associated with peace and land—all this made the loss of the fighting capacity of the army quite inevitable. A conference held in the Stavka on March 31[5] recorded in a secret protocol the sharp change for the worse in the morale of the country's armed forces:

"The Baltic Fleet has lost its fighting capacity and there is no hope of quickly bringing it into order. . . .
"The army is living through a sickness. It will be possible to adjust the relations between officers and soldiers probably only after two or three months. . . .
"It is necessary to go over to defense on all the fronts, until order is restored in the rear and the necessary reserves are organized.
"The most energetic measures must be taken to reduce the number of eaters on the fronts."

Another symptom of the changed mood is to be found in the letters written by soldiers at the front. The military censor of the Fifth Army registered in early February three enthusiastic letters to one that could be classified as pessimistic; in the latter part of March and the first part of April the proportion had altered to four to three.[6]

If five Generals commanding various fronts despatched to the War Minister on March 31 an optimistic telegram asserting that "the armies wish to attack and can attack," one finds a much more realistic note in the message of General Dragomirov, commander of the Fifth Army, to General Ruzsky, commander of the Northern Front, dated April 1.[7] Declaring that "arrests of officers do not cease," that "demands for elected commanders are put forward more and more definitely by unknown agitators," that "proclamations about the beating of officers have appeared" and that "all the thoughts of the soldiers are turned to the rear," General Dragomirov professes inability to carry out a regrouping of troops which has been ordered, because the officers have no means of compelling the obedience of the soldiers.

A foreign military observer attached to the Russian army, the British General Knox, on returning from a visit to the Northern Front at the end of April, told the British Ambassador of "the deplorable state of affairs at the fronts. Units have been turned into political debating societies; the infantry refuses to allow the guns to shoot at the enemy; parleying in betrayal of the Allies and of the best interests of Russia takes place daily with the enemy, who laughs at the credulity of the Russian peasant soldier."[8] Friendly meetings between Russian and German soldiers were not uncommon; the Russians sometimes gave bread in exchange for cigarettes.

Two members of the Duma, Maslennikov and Shmakov, who visited the front immediately after the Revolution and made a second trip in the latter part of April, report[9] a distinct deterioration in will to fight during the intervening period. They tell of "extreme speeches" at soldiers' meetings, accompanied by demands that the Russian Government's treaties with the Allies should be published, "as a guaranty that we are not fighting for the imperialist and capitalist ambitions of our Allies." In some cases the soldiers of the infantry cut the telephone communications of the artillery observation points and threatened to bayonet the artillerists, if they opened fire on the Germans. Summing up their impressions the Duma members report:

"The soldiers are no longer eager for battle; the talk is only of defense, and even so with fear of protecting mythical French and British capital. The rear is already considerably infected with this propaganda. Our gallant artillery and the Cossacks are not affected by this propaganda. . . .

"The officers, the majority of whom urge war until victory, do not meet sympathy, and agitation against them falls on prepared soil.

"It is significant that the most suspected officers are, in most cases, the best in the military sense. This is explained by the involuntary fear that good officers may compel the troops to attack."

Another member of the Duma, Mankov, wrote to Rodzianko from the front on May 23 about the continuation of fraternizing and about the threats of the infantry against the artillery, in case there should be any firing. Mankov added: "The position of the officers is a torment; on May 6 [10] an officer of the Volchansk Regiment shot himself. His soldiers had refused to carry out an order about replacing their comrades and threatened him with violence."

The outstanding feature of the post-revolutionary Russian army was the farflung network of committees which sprang up everywhere, like mushrooms: company committees, regimental committees, army committees, front committees. They were authorized immediately after the Revolution by the famous Order Number One [11]; and the Provisional Government subsequently endeavored to define their character and functions. But the movement to form committees was so spontaneous and widespread that their origin cannot be attributed to any individual or organization.

There was a good deal of variety in the methods of election of the committees. On the Southwestern Front, for instance, the Front Committee consisted of representatives only of the army organizations; on the Western Front workers' and peasants' deputies participated, along with the soldiers, in electing the committee. In some cases officers and soldiers were represented in the same committee; in others they had separate organizations. [12]

Very detailed regulations about the committees are to be found in an order issued by General Alekseev on April 12 and by War Minister Guchkov on April 29. [13] The fact that Alekseev and Guchkov, neither of whom could be regarded as holding radical views, found it necessary to legalize and sanction the committees is the best proof that they seemed quite indispensable, however distasteful they might be to the more conservative officers. The committees, according to Alekseev's order, were to be chosen by companies, regiments, divisions and armies; and one third of their members were to be officers and two thirds soldiers.

Guchkov's order prescribed a somewhat different method of election. Members of regimental committees were to be chosen

separately by soldiers and by officers, and one fifth of the members were to be officers. The functions of the regimental committee were outlined by Guchkov in the following terms: "To control the supply department of the unit; to take legal measures in the event of abuse and exceeding of authority by responsible persons in the unit; to settle misunderstandings between officers and soldiers; to look after the maintenance of discipline and order in the regiment; to prepare for the elections to the Constituent Assembly."

Actually, by the very force of circumstances, the committees not infrequently went beyond the functions which were legally assigned to them. They were a sort of buffer between the higher officers and the often refractory soldiers; and the officer who could not get along with the committee usually found his position impossible.

It is almost amusing to read the contradictory reproaches levelled against the committees by conservative generals and by Communist historical writers. The typical General sees in them mischiefmakers who irreparably destroyed the old army discipline. The Communist regards their members as wolves in sheep's clothing who deceived the soldiers and made possible the prolongation of the War.

In reality the typical army committee, making allowance for some traces of military psychology, was not very different in political viewpoint and physiognomy from the typical Soviet. In its membership one would find the less aristocratic junior officer, who had entered the army during the War, and the more educated type of noncommissioned officer or soldier, with a liberal sprinkling of "army intelligentsia": doctors, clerical workers, etc. Few if any of the committees had a Bolshevik majority; the majority of the members who professed any political faith were Socialist Revolutionaries.

Some of the committees were extremely loyal, from the standpoint of military discipline; Vilenkin, the President of the Committee attached to the Fifth Army, declared that the purpose of the committee was to create such an atmosphere of discipline that any unit would arrest the committee at the first command of its officer. Others were more combative and clashed continually with officers of the old school. One of Kerensky's chief aides, the army commissar Stankevitch, frankly recognizing that the committee system was bound to shake up the whole military system, ob-

serves: "There was not a regiment which would not have arrested its officers if the committees had not opposed. Therefore the commanding officers themselves insisted on the creation of committees, seeing their salvation in them." [14]

This is only partly true; conservative Generals of the type of Denikin were implacable enemies of the committees throughout. But the committees probably did function as a brake on the unruly soldiers rather than as a force making for disobedience to orders; and there would have probably been even more cases of lynching of officers if the committees had not existed. The Generals and the officers were divided into two camps in their attitude toward the committees. The more realistic of them, sometimes, perhaps, motivated by personal ambition and by desire to win favor with the new Government, endeavored to work in harmony with the committees; and weaker and more timid officers were inclined to shuffle off all responsibility, not only for the discipline and morale of the troops, but even for their operating orders, onto the committees.

At the same time there was a die-hard type of commander who refused to accept the new order and was in constant conflict with the committees. It was among officers of this type, of course, that Kornilov found his strongest supporters and sympathizers. In the last analysis neither the General who tried to coöperate with his committee nor the General who adopted an attitude of stiffnecked opposition could do anything effective to stop the process of disintegration which had set in. The forces, summed up in the slogan "Peace and Land," that were working for the break-up of the old army were far too strong to be checked either by conciliation or by any force which was at the disposal of the army commanders.

Centrifugal nationalism was another element that contributed to the dissolution of the army. Lettish and Czecho-Slovak units (the latter formed out of Austrian soldiers of Czech origin who had been captured or had deserted) had existed at the time of the Revolution. Under the pressure of the growing nationalism of the non-Russian parts of the country Ukrainian, Polish and other national corps and regiments began to be formed. This led to a good deal of confusion in transferring soldiers from one part of the army to another. Moreover, following the example of the Ukrainian political leaders in Kiev, the chiefs of the new Ukrainian army units displayed more and more tendency to pay scant regard to the orders of the Provisional Government, to regard their forces

as the nucleus of a future independent national army. On the Caucasian front the three dominant nationalities of the Trans-Caucasus, the Georgians, Armenians and Azerbaidjan Tartars, began to form national units, each keeping a distrustful eye on the arming of its neighbors.

During the spring and summer there were efforts to counteract the disorganization of the army as a whole by encouraging the formation of shock units, recruited from volunteers and from those soldiers who were willing to assume special obligations. The initiative for this idea apparently came from a military student named Batkin; and it met with the hearty sympathy of General Brussilov.[15] Most of the other higher commanders were sceptical about its possibilities. A special committee was formed for the creation of a "volunteer revolutionary army" and its recruits took an oath, among other things, "to obey all orders without question, to go into attack ahead of everyone, not to surrender, not to drink anything alcoholic, to believe that my death for the motherland and for the freedom of Russia is happiness and justification of my oath." A number of women's battalions were organized, and one of them took part in the offensive on the Western Front.[16]

Neither the formation of shock units, nor the appearance of the women's battalions, however, stemmed the tide of disorganization to any appreciable degree. Had there been a rising wave of patriotic enthusiasm for the prosecution of the War such experiments might have had some moral effect. But with the current running strongly in the other direction the members of the shock units found themselves isolated, faced with the indifference and often with the hostility of the other troops. Few people cared to risk their lives under such conditions, or to undertake attacks when there was little prospect of support from the other troops; and the "volunteer revolutionary army" in the end simply evaporated without leaving a trace.

A vivid picture of the break-up of the army and of the curative measures which were proposed by the leading commanders is to be found in the record of the deliberations of a secret military council, held at General Staff Headquarters, in Moghilev, on July 29.[17] At this time the offensive had dismally failed; the Government had reintroduced the death penalty at the front and was showing more inclination to adopt more severe repressive measures. The council was convened by Kerensky; and two other civilians were present, the Commissar of the Southwestern Front, Savinkov,

and Foreign Minister Tereschenko. The other participants were all military officers of high rank, including Brussilov, who was then Commander-in-chief; his Chief of Staff, Lukomsky; the Commander of the Northern Front, Klembovsky; the Commander of the Western Front, Denikin. Kornilov was absent, but sent in recommendations by telegraph.

The longest, most impassioned and most uncompromising speech delivered at the council was that of General Denikin, who put forward the maximum programme of the oldfashioned officers without mincing words. He started out with a gloomy description of conditions on his front, where "disobedience, debauchery and robberies prevailed among the troops." He cited cases where regiments which had promised to go into attack after hearing a speech by Kerensky or receiving a red banner, changed their minds and flatly refused to attack when the hour of action came. He sharply criticized the army committees for changing officers and cited Alekseev's characterization of the Declaration of the Rights of the Soldier as "the last nail driven into the coffin of our army." He pointed out that courts-martial had practically ceased to exist, because the Declaration abolished the old courts, which consisted exclusively of officers, and the soldiers boycotted the new "disciplinary courts," in which both officers and soldiers were supposed to take part.

"The officers are in a terrible position," declared Denikin, his voice shaking with emotion. "They are insulted, beaten, murdered. There is only one honest way out for the officer; and that is death." He proposed ten measures for the reëstablishment of discipline, including the annulment of the Declaration, the removal of the commissars and committees, the restoration of the disciplinary powers of the officers, the creation of picked units to support the authority of the officers and to employ force against refractory soldiers, the introduction of the death penalty in the rear as well as at the front. Reaching a peroration Denikin cried, turning to the representatives of the Provisional Government: "You dragged our glorious banners in the mud. Now raise them up, if you have any conscience."

Instead of resenting this sharp insinuation Kerensky rushed over to Denikin and, with a typical theatrical gesture, insisted on shaking hands with him and thanking him for his honest expression of opinion.

Klembovsky, who followed Denikin, was less oratorical, but

equally pessimistic. "The Northern Front is in a condition of dissolution. Not a single officer's order is fulfilled without begging and humiliation before soldiers. Fraternizing goes on everywhere; if machine-guns are turned against the fraternizers mobs of soldiers throw themselves on the guns and make them useless. . . . The Twelfth Army could not help the Fifth with an artillery demonstration because the soldiers refused to permit the opening of fire."

Klembovsky made the further significant remark that "the better the army committee the faster its authority falls in the eyes of the soldiers" and ended on a note of sceptical pessimism:

"What can help? The death sentence? But can you really hang whole divisions? Courts-martial? But then half the army will be in Siberia. You don't frighten the soldier with imprisonment at hard labor. 'Hard labor? Well, what of it?' they say. 'I'll return in five years. At any rate I'll have a whole skin.' "

Kornilov's telegram, sent from his headquarters, called for the application of the death penalty at the front and in the rear, for the prohibition of Bolshevik meetings and literature, for an acknowledgement of mistakes in dealing with officers, who had shown the greatest courage in recent battles, for the restoration of the officer's right to inflict summary punishment upon soldiers under his command. (This right had been taken away as a result of the Declaration of the Right of the Soldier). In regard to the committees and commissars Kornilov did not go so far as Denikin. Acting, no doubt, under Savinkov's influence, he proposed to strengthen the authority of the commissars, who were to confirm such death sentences as might be imposed. As for the committees, they were to be restricted to dealing with questions of the supply and internal life of the units, and were to be strictly forbidden to interfere in operative orders or in the personnel of the officers. Savinkov endorsed Kornilov's suggestions, with the exception of the restoration of the disciplinary powers of the officers, which he characterized as premature.

Faced with a phalanx of old Generals, Kerensky's speech was defensive and apologetic. He endeavored to shift responsibility for measures which had excited especially bitter criticism to his predecessor, Guchkov, who had dismissed a considerable number of high commanders, and to General Polivanov, head of the commission which had worked out the much attacked Declaration of the Rights of the Soldier. In reply to Denikin he said:

"Should the maximum programme of General Denikin be ac-

cepted we could anticipate great disorders. Personally I am willing to resign, to recall the commissars and to suppress the committees. But I am convinced that in such a case complete anarchy and a massacre of officers would start in Russia to-morrow."

Tereschenko asked what he could inform the Allies as to future military coöperation. Brussilov gave him the cold comfort of a suggestion that small operations might be possible on the Southwestern and the Caucasian Fronts; but emphasized the point that these should not be counted on. After some discussion as to whether Petrograd was in serious danger (the consensus of opinion was that the capital was reasonably safe, not because of any effective military forces at the disposal of the Government, but because the Germans could not spare enough troops to effect its capture) and an exchange of opinions as to how the Petrograd garrison could be broken up and distributed among the fronts, the council broke up. The majority of its participants signed a resolution which coincided closely with the opinions expressed in General Kornilov's telegram. A sense of futility must have brooded over the whole conference. The Generals might relieve their feelings by heaping reproaches on the Government; but the more intelligent of them must have realized that it was a question not of lacking will but of lacking power to bring about any drastic restoration of discipline.

The collapse of the offensive created a panicky mood which made it possible for the Government, without serious opposition from the Soviets, to announce the reintroduction of the death penalty at the front. But in practise this turned out to be little more than a paper scarecrow. As Commissar Stankevitch says: "I don't know of one case when the military revolutionary courts inflicted a death sentence. It was equally difficult to pick out anyone who had transgressed the bounds and under these conditions to find anyone who would assume responsibility for the death of a living man. And it was a grave question whether it would have been easy to find executioners." [18]

So-called military-revolutionary courts, consisting of three officers and three soldiers, were instituted by a decree of the Provisional Government dated July 25. Cases were to be decided by a majority of votes, with acquittal in the event of the votes being evenly divided. But, on account of the reasons outlined by Stankevitch, and because of the general mood of the army, these courts functioned very feebly, and one can find no evidence that they ever

inflicted capital sentences. On the other hand the sentiment of the soldiers became increasingly impatient.

"Our Provisional Government attacks the Bolsheviki very much," one reads in a typical soldier's letter of August.[19] "But we front-line soldiers don't find any fault with them. Earlier we were against the Bolsheviki, but now, after the Provisional Government has promised so long to give freedom to the poor people, and hasn't given it, we are little by little passing over to the side of the Bolsheviki."

So, even in the period which was relatively most favorable to the assertion of the Government's authority, the period between the July Days and the Kornilov Affair, it does not appear that any progress was made in regaining control of the army. Behind the lines there was, if possible, less discipline than at the front. Station-masters and railroad employees repeatedly complained of acts of violence committed by drunken bands of deserters or of soldiers on leave, who compelled them to operate trains regardless of schedule limitations. The rear garrisons were in many cases out of hand; and cases of plundering and food riots became more common toward autumn. Desertion assumed larger and larger proportions; on September 8 the Stavka reported that 12,500 deserters had been detained in the town of Venden and 3,500 in the neighboring district, that 3,000 had been detained in the town of Valk, while great numbers were in Pernov and in Pskov.[20] One wonders what troops could have been found to guard these deserters and what could have been done with them.

How far was the break-up of the old army attributable to Bolshevik agitation and propaganda? Lenin had always attached great importance to armed force as a decisive factor in revolution; and from the first days of the Revolution the Bolsheviki concentrated a good deal of attention on the soldiers and sailors. The main agency of the Party in this connection was its Military Organization,[21] which was especially influential in the regiments of the Petrograd garrison. The Military Organization edited a newspaper, *Soldatskaya Pravda* (Soldiers' Truth), which was especially designed for soldier-readers. It was later supplemented on the Riga front by another newspaper entitled *Okopnaya Pravda* (Trench Truth).

Soldatskaya Pravda endeavored to link up its readers as closely as possible with the Military Organization, urging them to write letters and articles describing life in the trenches. It carried on

agitation for the seizure of the landlords' estates by the peasants, for organized fraternizing at the front, for "making the soldier the master in all regimental, company, division and other committees."

The Military Organization also maintained a soldiers' club in Petrograd where delegations from the front were entertained and efforts were made to implant Bolshevik ideas in the newly arrived soldiers. In the first weeks of the Revolution some conservative newspapers endeavored to stir up antagonism to the workers among the soldiers, contrasting the hard life of the soldiers in the trenches with the demands of the workers for shorter hours and higher pay. The Bolsheviki and the other Soviet parties counteracted this by organizing visits of soldiers' delegations to the factories and meetings with workers.

In July the Military Organization reckoned 26,000 members, organized in forty-three front and seventeen rear organizations. In all probability its numerical strength increased after that time. The significance of the Military Organization in the development of events in Petrograd was very considerable; in the summer demonstration it was able to call out some regiments of the garrison; subsequently it played a considerable rôle in organizing detachments of the Red Guard in the factories and in smoothing the way for passive if not active support of the Bolshevik stroke for power in November by practically all the units of the Petrograd garrison.

But in the breakdown of the whole army the rôle of the Bolsheviki seems to have been relatively subsidiary. They did not possess enough Party members or resources to organize effectively every regiment of the predominantly peasant army. What they were able to do, through their agents in the various armies, was to sense the mood of the troops, and to insure the benevolent neutrality of the front at the time when the decisive struggle for power was taking place in Petrograd and Moscow.

If the condition of the army, from the standpoint of its commanders, had seemed gloomy enough at the council in July, it became quite hopeless after the collapse of Kornilov's ill conceived adventure. Stankevitch, a keen and observant eyewitness, summed up the post-Kornilov situation in the following terms: [22]

"The authority of the commanders was destroyed once for all. The masses of soldiers, seeing how a General, Commander-in-chief, had gone against the Revolution, felt themselves surrounded by treason on all sides and saw in every man who wore epaulettes

a traitor. And whoever tried to argue against this feeling also seemed a traitor."

Indeed Kornilov's move was fatal not only to the conservative officers who supported it, but also to the moderate commissars and committees. In the Fifth Army the Committee even found it necessary to ask for the protection of an armored-car division. The reports of commissars during the weeks between the Kornilov Affair and the Bolshevik Revolution bristle with accounts of unpunished and unpunishable excesses. So the commissar of the Western Front, Zhdanov, reporting for the week which ended on September 20, announced that in the 191st Tambov detachment the commander, two captains and two ensigns had been deposed by the soldiers' committee, while in the 24th Siberian Regiment a hand-grenade had been thrown into the quarters of the commander of the regiment and two officers, who were deafened as a result. This practise of throwing bombs and grenades into officers' quarters, incidentally, became a very popular sport during the last weeks of the Provisional Government. About the same time Sokolov, commissar of the 42nd Corps, on the Northern Front, described the murder of Lieutenant Smerechinsky and Ensign Vildt by the soldiers of the third company of the 34th Infantry Regiment. "The soldiers explained the murder by the counterrevolutionary tendency of the officers, but the main cause was dissatisfaction with the serious attitude of the officers toward service and their refusal to permit absence on leave." [23]

The following excerpts from a secret official report on the sentiment of the army from October 28 until November 12 [24] convey an excellent idea of various manifestations of the spirit of the disintegration at its height:

"In the 141st Regiment of the 12th Army a plan was worked out for movement to the rear, and it was decided to kill the company commanders, if they opposed, and then to apply to the battalion and regimental commanders, to demand a special train and to go to Pskov. . . . In the region of the 432nd Regiment trade with the enemy has begun; the trenches are decorated with white flags; and music is being played. . . . In the 227th Regiment of the Special Army Ensign Baranov was killed before the eyes of the commander and officers; a private soldier of the 43d Regiment of the 7th Army with two rifle-shots killed a second lieutenant of the 123d Regiment; when there was an attempt to arrest him the soldiers resisted and the murderer hid. . . . In the 4th Cyclist Battalion (Special Army) the commander of the 3d Company and the manager of the supply department were removed and soldiers were elected in their places; the commit-

tee of a hospital train deposed the senior doctor, the manager of supplies and a nurse and elected new persons. . . . The committee of the units of the Staff of the 11th Army decided to requisition the horses of the officers, to search departing officers and take away their arms and to transfer the officers to common living quarters."

On November 3, just four days before the Bolshevik Revolution, the President of the Executive Committee of the Western Front, Kozhevnikov, sent out a frantic appeal to the Premier, to the Vtsik and to various army organizations, beginning, "The source of all the miseries which the country lives through is the War, begun by the imperialists of all countries," and declaring that the War must be ended as soon as possible, on the basis of no annexations, no contributions, and selfdetermination of peoples. To judge from its phrasing this appeal was framed not by Bolsheviki, but by Mensheviki and Socialist Revolutionaries; but this fact makes it all the more impressive as a proof of the hopelessness, not only of going on with the War, but of rallying the troops to fight against the Bolsheviki, who were promising the masses what the majority of them certainly wanted: peace and land.

The wave of disorder was equally marked in the distant Caucasus. The commissar of the Caucasian Front, Donskoy, in a message of October 15, recounted a soldiers' riot, accompanied by disorderly firing and looting in Kutais, the beating half dead of the assistant commandant of the Tiflis station, the killing in Ekaterinodar by soldiers of a Cossack officer and the beating in Erzerum (then occupied by Russian troops) of an officer named Kuchapov by Cossacks of the Second Sappers' Brigade and gloomily added: "The wave of anarchy rises irresistibly." [25]

The situation in Russia itself during this last agony of the Provisional Government may be judged from Stankevitch's characterization: [26]

"The Stavka was occupied with the problem of maintaining public safety in the rear and in the whole country. News continually arrived of terrible robberies, pillaging of estates, demolition of railroad stations, etc. No measures yielded positive results, because the troops on guard were as unreliable as the troops which committed the disorders, and often themselves took part in the rioting."

The Russian sailors, a very small force numerically, by comparison with the land troops, went much the same way as the soldiers. In fact, as might have been expected, in view of the greater activity of the Navy in 1905, the sailors, especially in the Baltic

Fleet, were perhaps more definitely revolutionary than their comrades on land. The naval base at Kronstadt, as we have already seen, was one of the early strongholds of Bolshevism; and the whole Baltic Fleet was a hotbed of opposition to the Provisional Government. There were waverings; the larger warships, in the main, were more revolutionary than the torpedo-boats; and here and there a vessel would pass a pro-War resolution even in the summer of 1917. But the Baltic sailors in an overwhelming majority were on the side of the Bolsheviki by autumn; and this fact would probably have been even clearer if the seizure of power in Petrograd had not proceeded so easily that little aid from naval auxiliaries was required.

The course of events in the Black Sea Fleet, stationed far away from Red Petrograd, was somewhat different. Whereas the Baltic sailors started out by killing some unpopular officers and imprisoning a good many more, there were no excesses or disorders in Sevastopol, the base of the Black Sea Fleet; and at first the central committee elected by the sailors functioned in close coöperation with the commander of the Fleet, Admiral Kolchak. The Black Sea Fleet even despatched a large delegation to agitate throughout the country for prosecution of the War.

But the general tendency to throw off the old authority and discipline ultimately reached the Crimean waters of the Black Sea. The departure of the delegation took away some of the sailors and junior officers who were most inclined to work hand in hand with Kolchak. The latter resented the action of the committee in arresting General Petrov, an official of the port who was accused of speculating in leather. Other quarrels came up over the appointment and removal of commanders. By June 19 the sailors had reached the point of disarming the officers. Kolchak hurled his sword into the sea rather than surrender it and resigned his command.[27] He was summoned to Petrograd and sent on a naval mission to America. The Fleet drifted more and more to the Left, despite the fact that the Bolsheviki only obtained a majority in the sailors' committee some time after the November Revolution; and during the winter months the sailors fully equalled the sanguinary record of their Baltic fellows.

Viewed in retrospect this greatest mutiny in history, this complete break-up of the old Russian army, was an integral part of the downfall of the Tsarist system. Given the poor morale of the army after two and a half years of mainly unsuccessful fighting under

conditions of extreme physical hardship, the sudden relaxation of all the old disciplinary bonds, which in itself was an inevitable result of the Revolution, could have only one result: the evaporation of fighting capacity and a growing impatience of the peasant soldiers with the Government which gave them neither peace nor land.

As is often the case with mass movements of revolt from below, the mutiny of the Russian armed forces was to a considerable extent anonymous. While the names of a few influential anti-War agitators, Ensign Krilenko, later for a short time Bolshevik Commander-in-chief and now Soviet Commissar for Justice, the soldier Romm, Captain Dzevaltovsky, have been preserved, it is hard to determine in many cases who incited this or that act of rebellion and mutiny. The soldiers' revolt at the front went hand in hand with the peasant revolt in the villages; both were sweeping movements of social upheaval which were destined to change forever old social relations; both went forward irresistibly under the slogan: "Land and Peace."

No armed force and no administrative power at the disposition of the Provisional Government could have stopped this immense movement of millions of war-weary soldiers, of whom some wanted to turn their weapons against the officer, the landlord, the "boorzhui," as all people of property and education were apt to be called in Russia in 1917, while the majority simply wanted to go home. A Government endowed with sufficient prescience to recognize from the beginning the physical impossibility of compelling the army to fight and of withholding the large estates from the landhungry peasants might conceivably have mitigated the violence of the social revolution and somewhat deflected its course by taking immediate steps to bring about a cessation of hostilities and by adopting prompt and drastic measures for parcelling out the large estates. But the Government, faced with the spectre of the Allies and provided with a convenient pretext for postponing agrarian decisions by the impending Constituent Assembly, took no positive steps, and the revolt of the masses ran its appointed course.

Indeed it is one of the ironies of Russian history that just the classes which stood to lose most from a thoroughgoing social revolution obstinately clung to policies which made such an upheaval inevitable. By refusing to give up the utopian formula "War to the victorious end" the Russian propertied and middle classes assured themselves revolution to the bitter end.

NOTES

[1] Lieut. Gen. N. N. Golovine, "The Russian Army in the World War," pp. 106f.

[2] "The Dissolution of the Army in 1917," p. 143. While this was a specific characterization of the 12th Army it would apply well to practically all the Russian forces at that time.

[3] A. Kerensky, "The Catastrophe," p. 168.

[4] "The Dissolution of the Army in 1917," p. 7.

[5] Ibid., pp. 10, 11.

[6] "Soldiers' Letters of 1917," pp. 8–11.

[7] "The Dissolution of the Army in 1917," pp. 30–32.

[8] General Sir Alfred Knox, "With the Russian Army, 1914–1917," p. 613.

[9] "The Dissolution of the Army in 1917," pp. 50–56.

[10] Ibid., p. 57.

[11] See p. 86.

[12] S. E. Rabinovitch, "The Struggle for the Army in 1917," p. 82.

[13] The full texts of these orders are published by A. Shlyapnikov, "The Year 1917," Vol. III, pp. 313ff.

[14] V. B. Stankevitch, "Reminiscences, 1914–1919," p. 83.

[15] "The Dissolution of the Army in 1917," pp. 64ff.

[16] Gen. A. I. Denikin, "Sketches of Russian Turmoil," Vol. I, Part II, p. 139.

[17] The full protocol of this secret War council is published in the magazine, Krasnaya Letopis (Red Chronicle), No. 6, for 1923, pp. 9–64.

[18] Stankevitch, op. cit., pp. 97–98.

[19] "Soldiers' Letters of 1917," p. 91.

[20] "The Dissolution of the Army in 1917," p. 113. The towns mentioned are in Esthonia and Latvia and in the northwestern part of Russia.

[21] See N. Podvoisky's article, "The Military Organization of the Russian Social Democratic Labor Party," in Red Chronicle, No. 6, for 1923, pp. 64–97. Podvoisky was himself a prominent member of the Organization.

[22] Stankevitch, op. cit., p. 122.

[23] "The Dissolution of the Army in 1917," p. 117.

[24] Ibid., pp. 143ff.

[25] Ibid., pp. 132, 133.

[26] Stankevitch, op. cit., p. 129.

[27] For descriptions of Kolchak's ultimately unsuccessful effort to maintain discipline in the Black Sea Fleet from diametrically opposed viewpoints, see V. K. Zhukov, "The Black Sea Fleet in the Revolution of 1917–1918," pp. 44–74, and M. I. Smirnov, "Admiral Kolchak in the Time of Revolution in the Black Sea Fleet," in Istorik i Sovremennik, Historian and Contemporary, Vol. IV, Berlin, 1923.

CHAPTER XI

THE PEASANT UPSURGE

SIDE by side with the mutiny of the Russian army marched a second great social revolutionary movement: the seizure of the landed estates by the peasantry. Indeed these two movements have much in common and proceed with very similar rhythm. Both the desire of the soldiers to cease fighting and the desire of the peasants to possess themselves of the land of their richer neighbors had behind them an ultimately irresistible measure of mass support. Both movements were largely anonymous, so far as leadership was concerned; the peasants who stirred up their fellow-villagers to march on the nearest landlord's estate, armed with axes, pitchforks and whatever homemade weapons came to hand, are even more difficult to identify than the army agitators who first defied the officers and persuaded the other soldiers to do likewise.

The soldiers' mutiny and the peasants' upsurge coincide very closely in their tempo of development, in their moments of check and hesitation, in the climactic sweep of their final stages. At the moment when the typical peasant soldier had reached the point of refusing to salute his captain or of failing to carry out an order to move into the trenches, his brother in the village was declining to pay the customary rent and pasturing his cow on the landlord's meadows. By the time the soldiers had reached the point of lynching unpopular officers and commissars and deserting from the front in hordes the peasants were burning and sacking the manor-houses, and sometimes killing their inmates.

The peasant was certain to be a pivotal figure in the Russian Revolution. More than four fifths of the pre-war population of the Russian Empire lived in the villages. Once the iron bands which held the Tsarist structure together were suddenly struck off, the mood of the peasants could not fail to exert a powerful influence on the course of events. And that mood in 1917 could be summed up in two words: Peace and Land.

One cannot understand the course of the Russian social upheaval and subsequent developments unless one bears in mind that

the Russian peasant, as a result of a very different social and economic background, possessed a different psychology from that of the small landed proprietor in France or Germany, to say nothing of the American farmer. As Professor Florinsky says: [1]

"The sacred right of private property, so passionately defended since the Bolshevik Revolution by Russian opponents of socialism, was, until 1906, very nearly an empty sound for the masses of the Russian people."

Viewed in retrospect one of the most fateful decisions in Russian history was made by Tsar Alexander II when he left the peasant, whom he had freed from serfdom, under the power of the *obschina*, or village community. The periodic land redistributions, the control which the community exercised over the crops, the difficulty of buying additional land, were all calculated to discourage individual initiative and the development of the keen sense of private ownership that grows up with the possession of a separate homestead. The autocratic power wielded by the patriarchal head of a Russian peasant family also repressed the spirit of economic individualism.

Only after the widespread peasant outbursts against the landed gentry in 1905 the Government, during Stolypin's Premiership, deliberately adopted a new policy of breaking up the peasant communal method of farming and encouraging the development of a new class of well-to-do individual proprietors. What Stolypin's policy might have achieved in the course of a generation is an interesting speculation; very possibly a new, solidly established farmer class would have acted as an effective brake on extreme revolutionary tendencies. But the War prematurely ended this belated effort to give the Russian peasant a sense of property ownership.

Professor Robinson estimates [2] that about a tenth of Russia's thirteen or fourteen million peasant households had been settled on individual holdings as a result of Stolypin's measures; but these new proprietors were a raw and unfledged class, often regarded with envy and dislike by the majority of their neighbors, who remained in the traditional *obschina*. They proved quite ineffective as a force to stem the tide of agrarian revolution.

The majority of the Russian peasants were wretchedly poor at the time of the Revolution. It was not so much an absolute lack of land (many German and French peasants led a tolerably comfortable existence on land allotments that were no larger than the Russian average, although there was definite overcrowding in certain dis-

tricts of Central Russia and of Western Ukraina) as poor methods of cultivation,[3] absence of crop diversification, insufficient numbers and poor quality of livestock that kept the Russian peasant on a low material standard of existence.

The causes of agrarian distress were numerous and varied. But the peasant, inasmuch as he thought about the matter at all, saw one cause for his troubles: the landlord, to whom he was obliged to pay rent,[4] or whose fertile large estate formed a contrast to the little strips of peasant land around the village where the Russian peasants, in the great majority of cases, lived. And he saw one remedy: to grasp for himself as large a share of the country squire's land as he could. Liberal professors might point out that the nobility, as a class, by 1914 already owned less than a quarter of the amount of land possessed by the peasants; that the distribution was steadily altering in favor of the peasants; [5] that the chaos and destruction involved in a violent seizure of land would considerably outweigh any possible benefits which the peasants might obtain from it. Deep in the hearts of many of the peasants, nourished sometimes by the quiet talk of a village teacher or doctor or *zemstvo* employee with radical ideas, was the conviction that they had been cheated at the time of the Emancipation; that when they were released from bondage they should have been given, if not all their former masters' land, at least a much larger share than they actually received.

The War inflicted a number of blows, direct and indirect, on Russian agriculture. It took out of the villages perhaps twelve million able-bodied peasants and over two million horses. By 1916 the planted acreage had declined 8.4 percent in European Russia, and in the fertile North Caucasus, which was especially hard hit by the loss of manpower and by the closing of the export market, the decline amounted to 23.8 percent.[6] The peasants found a ready market for their products; indeed the needs of the gigantic army and the swollen cities were supplied with increasing difficulty; and the Government itself began to carry out a larger and larger share of the grain purchases. But the peasants were receiving a more and more dubious equivalent for their products; the rubles which were flowing off the printing-press in growing quantity were able to buy less and less as goods became scarcer and more expensive. The differential among the peasant families tended to become sharper, because those who had lost all their more robust workers as a result of mobilization were at an increasing disadvantage by comparison with their neighbors.

As might have been expected, in view of the backwardness and ignorance of the peasants and the enormous expanse of the Russian countryside, the agrarian movement was slower in getting under way than the soldiers' mutiny at the front or the working-class drive in the towns. During the first weeks of the Revolution one finds a record of scattered, sporadic outbreaks. On March 26, for instance, a landowner in Tula Province named Butovitch reports disturbances among the peasants and War prisoners (the latter were often employed as laborers on Russian farms); the peasants forbid the prisoners and day laborers to work on the estate. In Ryazhsk County, Ryazan Province, the peasants "demand the turning over to them of the estate of Prince Trubetzkoy, which they want to manage themselves." At the station Inza, in Simbirsk Province, a mob kills a big landowner, Gelahert, whose German name is apparently responsible for his fate. Reports come in, especially from Western and Southwestern Russia, of sacking of estates and burning of manor-houses; these, however, are exceptional.[7]

As early as March 29 the Moscow Agricultural Soviet informed the Minister for Agriculture, Shingarev, that agrarian disorders had begun, and on the same day a regional conference of the Socialist Revolutionaries in Petrograd adopted a resolution to the effect that land could only be confiscated by decision of the Constituent Assembly and that "socialization of the land cannot be confused with arbitrary seizure of it for personal advantage."[8] On the following day the Government worked out an appeal to the population on the land question, warning them that "it cannot be solved by any kind of seizure."

But the masses of the peasants thought otherwise. Feeling their way a little cautiously until they could see whether the new regime had any punitive detachments of Cossacks at its disposal, but moving with increasing boldness as they sensed the helplessness of the central government, they began to encroach on the estates in a score of ways. Cattle were pastured on the estate meadows; wood was cut without payment or permission in the landlord's forest; rent for leased land was left unpaid or was fixed at a nominal sum; thefts, large and small, from the landlord's stables and granaries were committed with impunity. A favorite practise was to prevent prisoners or laborers from working on an estate by threats of violence; then to take the land into the charge of the local land committee on the ground that it was not being cultivated.

Murders of the country gentry and destruction of their homes,

common enough in autumn, were unusual in the spring. Much more characteristic was the process of squeezing and harassing which a woman landowner, Pelagea Oznobishina, of Ranenburg County, Ryazan Province, describes in considerable detail in the course of a long complaint to the Minister for Agriculture.[9]

First there were threats against the managers of her farms. Then hay was forcibly requisitioned by the peasants at low fixed prices. Later the head of the local township committee, one Bulanov, appeared with some companions at the estate and took twenty-seven horses out of the stable. Here apparently the peasants felt that they had gone too far and perhaps received a reprimand from the shadowy local authorities: for the horses, after an interval of time, were returned. But then rye was requisitioned at a low price, which Oznobishina refused to accept. There was also a proposal to make a raid on her stock of bricks; and when she obtained two policemen from the town of Ranenburg there was such an outcry among the peasants that the policemen were withdrawn.

"So now," she writes, "we are completely at the mercy of the local population, and my two sons, who could give us some defense, are now at the front, and here, at the estate, are my two grandchildren, three and four years old, whose fate frightens me more than my own."

She adds that "the whole county is now affected by such disorders, which compel the majority of the landowners to abandon their estates and move into the town."

The Minister for Agriculture doubtless sympathized with this distressed country gentlewoman; but her case was only one of thousands which poured in on him; and there was no military or police force that could protect every country estate against the onsets and encroachments of the hostile neighboring peasants.

Oznobishina repeatedly mentions township and county committees which are encouraging and abetting the peasants in their assaults on her property rights. One of the most striking features of the year 1917 was the speed with which the masses, after the overthrow of Tsarism, created new forms of organization. The city workers had the Soviets and the factory committees. The army was covered with a network of organizations, representing units varying in size from a company to several armies on one of the fronts. And the peasants, despite their political ignorance and their high percentage of illiteracy, also found their representative organizations in the shape of *volost,* or township, committees, which

often assumed the functions of local government; peasant Soviets, which supplemented the township committees, and land committees.

The latter were instituted by the Provisional Government early in May. A Main Land Committee was formed in Petrograd, and provincial, county and township committees, elected by the local organs of administration, were set up all over the country. The Main Land Committee was supposed to collect information on the agrarian situation and to work out a project for land reform, while the local land committees were to function as agencies of conciliation in settling disputes and misunderstandings in the country districts. In practise the Main Land Committee, which was of unwieldy size and which included in its membership representatives of the most irreconcilable views, from Bolsheviki to landowners, turned into a futile debating society and exerted little influence on the course of agrarian development. The local land committees, on the other hand, were often pace-makers in the cause of expropriating the landlords.

The provincial peasant organizations, pressed on by the masses, often adopted very radical decisions about the land questions, quite inconsistent with the repeated appeals of the Provisional Government to the population to do nothing until the Constituent Assembly was convened. The Kazan Soviet of Peasant Deputies on May 26, for instance, decided that all land owned by the state, by landlords, by churches and monasteries and by city dwellers, along with all livestock and machinery belonging to landlords, should be transferred to the possession of the township committees.[10] Division of the land was frowned on, because this would prejudice the rights of the soldiers at the front. The township committees were simply to administer the land for the benefit of the peasants until the Constituent Assembly adopted final agrarian legislation. The Assistant Minister for the Interior, Leontiev, threatened the Kazan Soviet of Peasants' Deputies with legal pains and penalties; but the Soviet stood its ground, insisting that its decision reflected the will of the people. Other provinces in the neighborhood of the Volga were not behind Kazan. A provincial peasant congress in Penza at the end of May adopted a similar decision about the transfer of privately owned estates to the township committees. A harassed government commissar in April reports from Lenin's birthplace, Simbirsk:

"Throughout the province landlords and their managers are expelled and arrested by decisions of township and village committees; workers are removed; land is seized; arbitrary rentals are

fixed; a movement of the peasants who remain in the communal organization against individual holders has begun." [11]

While this ferment was proceeding and deepening all over the country a national Congress of Soviets of Peasant Deputies was held in Petrograd from May 17 until June 10. The Socialist Revolutionary Party, which had always concentrated its attention upon the peasantry, at that time commanded the allegiance of those peasants who knew or thought about politics at all; and of the 1,115 delegates at the Congress 537 were Socialist Revolutionaries, while there were only fourteen Bolshevik delegates. [12] The Socialist Revolutionaries dictated the resolutions of the Congress and predominated heavily in the Executive Committee, which was elected and remained as a permanent representative body after the Congress had dispersed. The Executive Committee created a number of departments; and the success of the Socialist Revolutionaries in the election for the Constituent Assembly was in some measure attributable to the energetic propaganda which was carried on in the country districts under the auspices of the Executive Committee.

Perhaps the most accurate index of what was passing in the minds of the traditionally "dark people," the Russian peasantry, in the first months of the Revolution is to be found in the model *nakaz,* or resolution, based on 242 resolutions which had been made up by peasant gatherings and were brought to the Congress by delegates. The *nakaz* is doubly significant because it served as a basis for the Land Law which the Soviet promulgated immediately after its accession to power; indeed many of its phrases were incorporated bodily in the Soviet decree. The central point of the *nakaz* is to be found in the following decisive words: [13]

"The right of private property in land is abolished forever; land can be neither sold nor bought nor leased nor pledged nor alienated in any way. All land . . . is taken over without compensation as the property of the whole people and passes over to the use of those who work on it. . . . The right of using the land is enjoyed by all citizens (without distinction of sex) of the Russian state who desire to cultivate it with their own labor, with the help of their family, or in a coöperative group, and only so long as they are able to cultivate it. Hired labor is not permitted."

These ideas, a compound of Socialist Revolutionary philosophy and of the practical desires of the poorer peasants, who saw in private ownership and unequal distribution of land a constant threat of poverty and exploitation, are encountered again and again in

the innumerable village, county and provincial peasant meetings of the period. This programme would certainly have gained a majority of suffrages among the Russian peasants at that time.

Despite the fact that it was politically controlled by the Socialist Revolutionaries, the Congress gave Lenin a hearing; and he delivered a long speech expounding his ideas on agrarian policy. The bearded peasants in the gathering must have listened, in the majority, with distinct approval to the stocky, bald little man with the formidable reputation when he urged them to take over the landlords' estates without compensation and to make an end of private property in land. Other points in his speech,[14] the demand that all power should pass to the Soviets, the call for the special organization of farmhands and of the poorest peasants, the suggestion that a model farm should be set up on every large landlord's estate, must have inspired headshaking and muttered disagreement. For what the average peasant really envisaged as a result of the agrarian upheaval was freedom from the burden of the landlord's rent, a slice of the landlord's rich fields and a cow or a horse from the landlord's stock. The idea that the state should step into the landlord's boots was far indeed from the desire of the insurgent peasantry.

In a resolution which was adopted at one of its last sessions the Congress voiced the familiar demand for the taking over of all state, church, and privately owned land (the peasant holdings, of course, would not be included in this category, except in the case of peasants who had climbed up to the position of small landowners) "for equalized toiling use without any purchase." At the same time arbitrary and unorganized seizures of land by the peasants were condemned.

On every question except land the Executive Committee elected by the Congress of Peasant Soviets was rather moderate in its views. It severely condemned the Bolshevik demonstration in the July Days; adopted a definitely defensist attitude in regard to the War, supported the idea of a coalition government to the end and was violently hostile to the Bolshevik overturn in November. In October, when the tide of agrarian revolution was rising higher every day, the Executive Committee submitted a project under which all private estates were to be transferred to the land committees, pending a final decision of the land problem by the Constituent Assembly. But the Government took no decisive action until it was swept away.

At first sight it might have seemed that the Socialist Revolution-

ary Party, with its monopolistic position of political leadership among the peasants, who constituted the vast majority of the Russian population, was destined to play the leading rôle in post-revolutionary Russia. Two circumstances, however, offset the apparent numerical support of the Socialist Revolutionaries and condemned that party to political defeat and ultimate extinction. First, only a small percentage of the Russian peasants were sufficiently educated to take any intelligent interest in politics or to distinguish between the claims of rival parties. Second, there was a great discrepancy between the standpoint of the Socialist Revolutionaries who took part in coalition governments and that of the Socialist Revolutionaries in the villages who often took an active part in the peasant Soviets and land committees.

Right-wing Socialist Revolutionaries of the type of Kerensky and Savinkov were inclined to postpone any fundamental agrarian legislation until the meeting of the Constituent Assembly. The Minister for Agriculture, Chernov, was more radical, more alive to the realities of the situation in the country districts. But his hands were tied by the restraints of coalition. The Cadets would never have participated in a government which openly flouted the rights of private property; and up to the very last gasp of the Provisional Government Kerensky was insistent on keeping some representatives of the Cadets, the party of the propertied classes, in his Cabinet. As a result the agrarian legislation of the Provisional Government was meagre and inadequate. A law which was passed in the spring gave local food committees the right to take over unused land and to requisition unused machinery and working animals. On July 25 a decree prohibited any land deals which were not expressly sanctioned by the provincial land commissar. The purpose of this decree was "to stop land speculation, to prevent fictitious dealings in land, sales to foreigners, etc." [15]

But such measures were of no avail in checking the roaring conflagration which was spreading in the villages and which was destroying forever old land deeds, the old civilization based on the rule of the country gentry, and the entire agrarian system. And the peasants, whether they considered themselves Socialist Revolutionaries or not, became increasingly impatient with the dilatoriness of the Government in taking any steps to take the land away from the landlords.

The situation was only aggravated by a feeble display of energy on the part of the Government in checking agrarian disorders and

excesses after the suppression of the July demonstration had created an illusory sense of strength and stability. The Menshevik Minister for the Interior, Tseretelli, on July 31 sent out a circular to the provincial authorities worded in part as follows:

"You are obligated to suppress most decisively any attempts to stir up anarchical confusion. No arbitrary seizures of property and land, no acts of violence, no appeals for civil war and violation of military duty are permissible."

In conformity with the spirit of these instructions the authorities, in the few cases where they were strong enough to do so, arrested members of the land committees which had been most zealous in carrying out the demands of the peasants, which, of course, clashed very definitely with the property rights of the landlords. On August 14 the Executive Committee of the Soviet of Peasants' Deputies discussed the "unceasing arrests of representatives of the peasant Soviets in the rural districts," which were described as "an offensive of the counterrevolutionary groups." [16] On the same day Chernov expressed prophetic apprehension that such arrests would be followed by "disturbances and disorders, possibly accompanied by bloody excesses."

It would have taken a Government equipped with the Tsar's military and police powers and headed by a Premier with Stolypin's ruthlessness to have crushed the agrarian movement that had developed by the summer. The sporadic arrests of radical land committees, the occasional sending of troops into the more disturbed areas merely irritated the peasants without frightening them into submission. And in the autumn a distinct change came over the character of the peasant movement; it became at once less organized and much more violent. The single month of October (old style)[17] witnessed 42.1 percent of all the cases of sacking and destruction of country homes reported for the whole eight months after the overthrow of the Tsar. In the month of June, when the influence of the various peasant committees and organizations was at its height, there were 120 cases of organized action to 100 cases of unorganized violence. By October the proportion of organized actions of the peasants had sunk to fourteen percent.[18]

The spread of the peasant upsurge was rapid. The thirty-four counties affected by it in March increased to 174 in April, to 236 in May, to 280 in June and to 325 in July. Broad as the movement was its degree of intensity was quite uneven. The hotbed of the peasant

insurrection was the block of provinces south and southeast of Moscow which made up the Central Agricultural and Middle Volga Regions. Of 5,782 cases of agrarian disturbance in European Russia which were registered by the police in 1917, 2,908, or more than half, fall to the share of the eleven provinces (Tambov, Voronezh, Orel, Kursk, Tula, Ryazan, Penza, Saratov, Simbirsk, Nizhni Novgorod and Kazan) of those two Regions. Altogether there were forty-eight provinces in European Russia. The reason for the special intensity of the movement in these provinces seems to be the widespread prevalence of the leasehold system in this part of Russia. The *pomyeschik,* or country squire, who parcelled out his land among the neighboring peasants for rental was, in the eyes of the latter, simply a parasite who had to be driven out as quickly as possible. It is noteworthy that these same regions of Central Russia and the Volga furnished the largest number of cases of agrarian violence during the 1905 Revolution.

In Western Russia and in Ukraina, where the *pomyeschik* was more apt to cultivate the land himself, the agrarian movement was apparently somewhat less violent (there were relatively more cases of seizure of estates than of burning and destruction); but the landlords were driven out, in the end, just as effectively. On the other hand, in regions where landlordism was exceptional, such as the northern provinces and the Urals, few cases of disorder were reported. The peasant movement of 1917 was primarily a drive of the peasantry against the *pomyeschik* class. Among the cases of agrarian disturbance, violent and peaceful, 4,954, overwhelmingly the largest number, were directed against landlords, as against 324 against the more well-to-do peasants, 235 against the Government and 211 against the clergy. It is noteworthy that the richer peasants, as a general rule, did not stand up for the landlords and did not share their fate at this stage of the Revolution. On the contrary, it not infrequently happened that the village "kulak," or well-to-do peasant, realizing on one hand that he would be exposed to unpleasant experiences if he did not go along with his aroused fellow-villagers and feeling at the same time that, with his larger stock of machinery and working animals, he would reap the main benefit from the dividing up of the squire's land, took an active part in the spoliation of the neighboring estate.

Apart from resentment at the Government's ineffective attempts at repression and from the natural momentum with the passing of time, the upswelling of the peasant movement in the autumn of

1917 is explained by the arrival of more and more soldiers, demobilized and "self-demobilized," in the villages. The soldiers brought with them from the front a smattering of Bolshevik agitation and a habit of violence; and they often played a leading rôle in pushing aside hesitating local peasant leaders and spurring on the villagers to more decisive action. The peasant V. G. Lisov, a native of Nikolaevsk County, Samara Province, recalls: [19]

"More and more soldiers came to us from the towns and from the trenches,—some of them wounded, some of them demobilized. They brought more news and stirred up the revolutionary sentiment of the peasantry."

Lisov's own father came back from the front just at the time when the peasants were beginning to cut down the landowners' wood and urged them to cut it down and "not to wait until the Constituent Assembly tells you to do this." From cutting down the wood it was a fairly easy step to dividing up all the privately owned land; and, as Lisov remarks:

"We all still called ourselves Socialist Revolutionaries; but in fact we fully carried out the programme of the Bolsheviki."

Another eyewitness describes a typical episode in what was perhaps the most stormy region of Russia, Tambov Province.[20] Here, in Yaroslavka Township, Kozlov County, the movement had begun with strikes for higher wages among the farm laborers. During the summer the peasants got into the habit of going with sacks to rob the landlord's fields. One September evening the landlord Romanov fired at a crowd of peasants and hit two of them. On the next evening there was hot debate in the village, which was called Sichevka. Some wanted to divide up the estates and take over the farm buildings in an organized orderly way. But the poorer peasants, who were in the majority, were in favor of burning up everything. This was the only way, they contended, in which it was possible to get rid of the *pomyeschiks* for good. This advice prevailed, and at ten in the evening a huge mob set out for the house of Romanov, pulled him out of bed in his nightshirt (what became of him is not clear) and set about the work of plunder and destruction, which the narrator describes as follows:

"The signal of the fire was caught up by other villages. The peasants of Yaroslavka went to rob and burn the manor-house of Aleksei Nikolaevitch Davidov, the peasants of Tidvorka and Ekaterinino burned the homes of Ushakov and Komarov; the village Bashovka burned out Volosatova-Zaeva, and in the night of Sep-

tember 7 a sea of flames seized all the manor-houses of our township. The experimental farm was burned; the blooded stock were cut up and there was drunkenness up to loss of consciousness. It was the poor peasants, not the middle-class ones and the more prosperous, who were active in the looting and burning. On the morning of the 8th mobs moved along the roads to the villages with the stolen property: one carried grain, another a bed; others drove cattle and took along broken chairs."

In this particular case, perhaps because the excesses were so violent, there was short-lived retribution; troops arrived from the town of Kozlov and there were arrests among the ringleaders. But after the Bolshevik Revolution the peasants were free to work their will as they chose,—until the new proletarian regime showed that it possessed decidedly more teeth and claws than the Provisional Government and the worker at the head of a food requisitioning detachment became as hated a figure in the village as the pre-War *pomyeschik.*

Some idea of the varied antagonisms, social and national, that found expression in the agrarian revolution may be gained by looking through the police records of rural disorder for Samara Province in the month of June.[21] Here are some Mohammedan villages which are trying to take away land from Russian small holders. Immediately after this is an indignant report from the local committee of the Cadet Party that "the Samara Peasants' Congress has worked out and carried into effect rules about the rights of enjoying land, based on the seizure of land, livestock and machinery and the elimination of the landowners." Some small peasant holders, of the village Pestravki, probably beneficiaries of the Stolypin reform, appeal, most probably in vain, for defense against the more numerous inhabitants of surrounding villages, who propose to take away their special holdings and make them take their ordinary share of the communal land. In the estate of one Mordvinov, in Bugulma County, the peasants are apparently on the warpath; the owner declares that "they have taken away laborers, purposely spoiled water in the well, stolen and smashed articles of domestic use."

Later in the year these central police reports are full of cases of wholesale sacking and burning and frequent murders. Curiously enough not all the peasant violence expends itself on the landlords. Not infrequently one reads how the peasants of some district, having plundered and gutted a local "nobleman's nest" to their hearts

content, turned around and lynched, apparently with the best of conscience, some army deserter or tramp who had been caught stealing horses. In short the peasants' complete contempt for the property rights of the landlords was accompanied by a keen attachment to their own: a circumstance which was to influence in no small degree the course of events during the civil war.

The measures which the Provisional Government took to meet the autumn upswing of the peasant movement, which in many places had reached the stage of small-scale insurrection, were inevitably futile. Commander-in-chief Kerensky issued a typical pompous military order, dated September 21, forbidding the peasants to take other people's land, cattle and machinery, to cut wood which did not belong to them, to interfere with the hiring of agricultural laborers and threatening them with various legal penalties if they persisted in doing so. It was about as effective as King Canute's proverbial order to the waves to recede. The Minister for the Interior, Nikitin, addressed an appeal to the Government commissars in provinces and towns to "rally the healthy elements of the population for struggle with the increasing anarchy, which is steadily leading the country to destruction" and to "fill up the police with selected reliable people." [22] This order, which was issued on October 23, the very day when the Bolshevik Central Committee was taking the final decision for armed uprising, was also a feeble defense against the stormy waves of popular upheaval that were battering the fragile edifice of the Provisional Government from every side. One suspects that there was little desire among "the healthy elements of the population" to go into battle against rural and town mobs. On November 3, just four days before the Provisional Government was overthrown, Nikitin again urged the commissars to make every effort to combat anarchy, using cavalry detachments where these were necessary. But the Provisional Government no longer had enough reliable troops to save its capital, much less to restore order all over the vast Russian countryside, already heaving in the last stages of a fundamental social overturn.

The accession to power of the Soviet regime and the prompt promulgation of a Land Law which was based not so much on Lenin's theoretical Marxist ideas as on the popular demands voiced in the resolutions of peasant assemblies put an end to the discrepancy between the policy of the central authorities and the peasant practise on the spot. Out of the chaos, much of it senseless and barbarous, that prevailed in many places in 1917, some kind of order

began to evolve; and it is estimated that about half the land in Russia was redivided according to the new principles in 1918. The varied fortunes of civil war led to brief restoration of the landlords here and there; but the final victory of the Soviets sealed forever the doom of the old landed aristocracy. In appropriating confiscated land the peasants were guided by a kind of inverted feudal principle: whatever belonged to the *"barin,"* or master, now belonged to the peasants who had worked for him or had rented land from him. The allotment of land between villages proceeded, in the main, according to this principle. In allotting land to the peasant households the usual rule was that each household received land in proportion to the number of its members. This remained in force until the decision of the Soviet Government to introduce state and collective farming made a new farreaching change in all Soviet agricultural relations.

The broad general result of the wholesale peasant land seizure of 1917 was a sweeping levelling in Russian agriculture. The big latifundia, even the small estate, ceased to exist. On the other hand landless or nearly landless peasants obtained larger allotments. How this worked out in practise may be seen from the example of two townships, Kandeev. in Penza Province, and Abdulov, in Tula Province: [23]

DISTRIBUTION OF SOWN AREA

Classes of Holdings	Kandeev Township		Abdulov Township	
	1917	1920	1917	1920
Up to 2 desyatinas	8.82%	3.09%	6.46%	4.12%
2–4 desyatinas	12.38	16.98	15.44	15.95
4–6 desyatinas	9.50	29.74	22.64	26.20
6–8 desyatinas	10.71	25.02	19.58	26.65
8–10 desyatinas	16.59	14.26	14.27	17.67
10–16 desyatinas	26.94	10.21	14.95	7.52
16 and higher	15.06	0.70	6.66	1.39

In other words, the effect of the upheaval was to parcel out much the greatest part of the land in small holdings ranging from five to twenty-seven acres. The *pomyeschik*, with his estate of hundreds or thousands of acres, was annihilated; the peasant small holder, owning fifty or a hundred acres, was, as a general rule, pulled down to the general level of his fellow-villagers. The new system did not promise high agricultural productivity; but it reflected and embodied the feeling of envy and bitterness which the mass of

Russia's poverty-stricken peasants cherished not only for the country squire, but for the fellow-peasant who by superior industry, thrift or cunning had pushed ahead.

So the peasant cottages, the log cabins of the North and the clay huts with thatched roofs of the South rose up and wiped out the manor-houses of the country gentry, sparing neither the stately mansions of the higher aristocracy nor the simpler homes of the lesser proprietors. The movement was ferocious and elemental, undiscriminating and irresistible. It wrought a tremendous amount of havoc and destruction. The most varied symbols of Russian rural civilization, libraries and old prints and miniatures, blooded stock and experimental stations, were looted and destroyed with equal abandon. In reading accounts of the wilder excesses one recalls the phrase about "the Russian rebellion, senseless and pitiless."

Pitiless the Russian agrarian revolution was; but, from the peasants' standpoint, it was by no means senseless. The flowering of aristocratic landlord culture had cost them too dearly in toil and sweat. And the very fierceness and brutality which marked their upsurge are in some measure an indictment of the social and economic system which they swept away. It had built no adequate protective dykes; it had not given the peasantry enough education, enough sense of a stake in the land, enough feeling for property to insure itself against a violent collapse.

Any shrewd observer of Russian conditions who weighed the lessons of the agrarian disorders of 1905 could have foreseen that a breakdown of central power and authority was almost certain to bring an even greater upheaval in its train. A generation of Stolypin individualism might have created a second line of conservatism in the villages in the shape of a landowning farmer class; but the few years which elapsed between Stolypin measures and the outbreak of the War, which led to their suspension, could not raise any large part of the peasants out of the state of poverty where they were ready converts to any agitator of agrarian revolt.

The importance of the peasants' attitude, from the standpoint of the Bolsheviki, can hardly be overestimated. In almost any other country a Government menaced by extremist revolutionaries could turn for support to the propertied peasant or farmer class. There was obviously no support for the Provisional Government in the Russian villages during September and October, 1917. And it was not the least sign of Lenin's genius as a revolutionary leader that

he sensed the mood of the peasantry and the force and reality behind the agrarian revolution. Behind the moderate and anti-Bolshevik resolutions of the Executive Committee of the Peasants' Soviet he could see the mobs of enraged villagers, who cared little whether the country was governed by Bolsheviki or by Socialist Revolutionaries; but who were firmly determined to burn out the neighboring *pomyeschik* at any cost.

The mutiny of the army and the peasant upsurge, both of which had reached their high points in the autumn, paralyzed the Provisional Government. But neither of these movements would have necessarily overthrown it. The peasant in the village could not see beyond the nearest estate. The peasant in the trenches was more familiar with political slogans; but he, too, thought only of getting home to share in the spoils; he felt no impulse to march on Petrograd. For the decisive spearhead of their final thrust against the Kerensky regime the Bolsheviki relied neither on the soldiers nor on the peasants, whose benevolent neutrality, of course, was of the highest importance, but on the class of city workers on which from the beginning they had concentrated their propaganda. And this class, as will be shown in the next chapter, had gone through its own process of radicalization during the summer and autumn of the revolutionary year, 1917.

NOTES

[1] Professor Michael Florinsky, "The End of the Russian Empire," p. 193.

[2] Professor Geroid T. Robinson, "Rural Russia under the Old Regime," p. 225.

[3] According to Professor A. A. Kaufman ("The Agrarian Problem in Russia," Vol. II, p. 9), Russia's pre-War average yield of wheat was 28 poods (a pood equals 36 pounds) per desyatina (a desyatina equals 2.7 acres), as against 50 in the United States, 70 in France, 77 in Germany, 111 in Belgium and 124 in England. The Russian yield of oats was 29 poods, as against 63 in the United States, 61 in France and 74 in Germany.

[4] Professor P. I. Lyashenko estimates that about 135,000,000 acres of land were rented annually by the peasants for a payment of over 315,000,000 rubles (about $160,000,000). See "Agrarian Revolution," Vol. II, p. 57.

[5] See the tables of Professor Robinson, *op. cit.*, pp. 268, 270.

[6] "Agrarian Revolution," Vol. II, pp. 17, 41.

[7] "The Peasant Movement in 1917," pp. 3ff.

[8] "The Revolution of 1917: Chronicle of Events," Vol. I, p. 100.

[9] A. Shlyapnikov, "The Year 1917," Vol. III, pp. 346–352.

[10] *Ibid.*, Vol. III, p. 353.

[11] *Ibid.*, Vol. III, p. 148.

[12] "Agrarian Revolution," Vol. II, pp. 116, 117.

[13] The full text of this resolution is published in *Izvestia of the All-Russian Soviet of Peasant Deputies*, Nos. 88, 89.

[14] N. Lenin, "Collected Works," Vol. XIV, Part I, pp. 156–174.

[15] "The Revolution of 1917: Chronicle of Events," Vol. III, p. 330.

[16] See the newspaper *Dyelo Naroda* (Cause of the People), of August 1 (14), 1917.

[17] All computations of agrarian disorders by months are according to the old Russian calendar, which is thirteen days behind the West European.

[18] The main source of detailed information about the peasant upheaval of 1917 is the police record of agrarian disorders, which has been published in Russian under the title: "The Peasant Movement in 1917." Generalized data, based on these reports, are to be found in the introduction to the above mentioned book, written by Y. A. Yakovlev and in the contribution of I. Verminichev to the work "Agrarian Revolution," Vol. II, pp. 170ff.

[19] "1917 in the Village," pp. 287–292.

[20] *Ibid.*, pp. 68–72.

[21] "The Peasant Movement in 1917," pp. 102ff.

[22] *Ibid.*, pp. 420, 421.

[23] "Agrarian Revolution," Vol. II, p. 220.

CHAPTER XII

THE REVOLT OF LABOR

KARL MARX, the recognized prophet of revolutionary socialism, saw in the proletariat, or industrial wage-earning working class, the force which would blow asunder the capitalist system and create the new socialist order.

"Among all the classes that confront the bourgeoisie to-day, the proletariat alone is really revolutionary," we read in the "Communist Manifesto," published by Marx and his collaborator, Friedrich Engels, in the stormy year 1848. "Other classes decay and perish with the rise of large-scale industry, but the proletariat is the most characteristic product of that industry." And in his major work, "Capital," Marx forecasts the doom of the existing economic regime in the following terms: [1]

> "While there is a progressive diminution in the number of the capitalist magnates, there occurs a corresponding increase in the mass of poverty, oppression, enslavement, degeneration and exploitation; but at the same time there is a steady intensification of the wrath of the working class—a class which grows ever more numerous, and is disciplined, unified and organized by the very mechanism of the capitalist method of production. Capitalist monopoly becomes a fetter upon the method of production which has flourished with it and under it. The centralization of the means of production and the socialization of labor reach a point where they prove incompatible with their capitalist husk. This bursts asunder. The knell of capitalist private property sounds. The expropriators are expropriated."

In one sense Russia did not seem to fulfill Marx's specifications for successful socialist revolution. For capitalism had taken root there later than in Western Europe; and the Russian proletariat was at once less technically developed, less organized and disciplined and less numerous, in proportion to the general population, than the industrial wage-earning class in most European countries. In round numbers about three million people were employed in industry and approximately a million in transportation in 1913. Even when families are reckoned in, these figures represented a small percentage of the Empire's population of about 180,000,000.

But there were other elements in the situation which marked out the Russian working class for a leading rôle in the Revolution. If Russia's proletariat was weak in numbers the capitalist class and the middle class were relatively even weaker, because many workers were employed in enterprises established not by domestic but by foreign industrialists and capitalist groups. Moreover, Russia was the only large country in Europe where a radical workingclass movement could count on the passive support of the majority of the peasantry, who were still too poor to have developed the conservative political and economic views that usually go with the ownership of land.

Finally, the conditions under which the Russian workers lived were calculated to make them considerably more revolutionary, considerably more indifferent to the consequences of smashing up established social and economic conditions, than were their fellows in America or England, Germany or France. Among the most important of the factors which determined the status, living standards and psychology of Russia's working class were the late development of modern capitalist methods of production, the continual pressure on the labor market of pauperized peasants who sought work in the towns, the retention by many workers of some connection with the land and the absolutist character of the Tsarist system. All these factors made for poor living conditions and a low subsistence level of wages.

The early stages of the capitalist system are always painful for the workers; and Russia, during the two generations which followed the abolition of serfdom in 1861 and the gradual emergence of capitalist relations, experienced many of the hardships and abuses which were already outlived in other countries. There was always a reserve army of peasants, unable to subsist in the villages and ready to accept work at low wages; and the living standard of the industrial worker was further depressed by the fact that many workers, especially in the textile industry which grew up in Moscow and in a number of neighboring towns, were peasants who kept their land allotments in the villages, to which they returned in the summer, who looked on their factory work as a source of subsidiary earning and were slow to develop the habit of organized struggle for higher pay and better living conditions.

The autocratic character of the government had a double effect: it repressed and retarded the development of the workers' movement, and made it potentially much more revolutionary. Trade-

unions, except those which existed under the patronage of the police, were forbidden until 1905; and during the period between the subsiding of the 1905 Revolution and the World War trade-unions led a semi-legal existence and were apt to be closed by the authorities on any small pretext, and active trade-union workers were always under the eye of the local police and were not infrequently sent into exile. The result was that Russia could scarcely be said to have possessed a trade-union movement in 1917. The sobering and essentially conservative influence of old traditions of collective bargaining, of the existence of trade unions with comfortable reserve funds and an assured place in society was conspicuously absent.

The average monthly earning of the Russian industrial worker in 1913, according to the data of the factory inspectors, was 22 rubles.[2] Nominally this was a little over eleven dollars. The real wages of the Russian worker were somewhat higher, because basic foodstuffs in Russia were definitely cheaper than in most other countries. A pound of rye bread, for instance, cost about two kopecks (approximately one cent) in the Moscow Province during the period 1900–1905; a pound of meat of the best quality cost a little less than twelve kopecks; a pound of meat of poor quality a little less than eight kopecks.[3] Moreover, the average wage was dragged down by the large numbers of poorly paid women and children, especially in the textile industry; a skilled metal worker or miner might earn from fifty to a hundred rubles a month.

But, with all these qualifications, the living standard of the workers was very limited; and long hours generally went with low wages. In 1897 a law forbade a working day in excess of eleven and a half hours; but it was largely nullified for lack of effective provision for enforcement. The length of the working day did show a tendency to contract [4] but the ten hour day was common in 1913. Bad housing was general; many textile workers were housed in crowded barracks, where they were subjected to a strict disciplinary regime.

"If the worker goes to the factory from the barracks, they search him; if he goes from the factory to the barracks they search him; if he comes home from the street to the barracks, again there is search and examination," writes a correspondent about life in these barracks in 1905.[5] Another correspondent from the factory of a certain Berg, in Tver Province, describes conditions in the barracks as "worse than prison," while in the Morozov factory in Bogorodsk, near Moscow, mounted guards ride about with whips. True, condi-

tions in the textile mills of the Moscow Province were among the most backward; in Petrograd and in Poland barrack life was not common.

But, although there was a modest amelioration of conditions after the 1905 Revolution, the Russian worker had little to look forward to, for himself or his family. His chances of moving into another social class were slight. His opportunities for recreation were scanty.

Among Russian workers at the time of the Revolution one can distinguish two main types. The masses of the unskilled and slightly skilled laborers, especially the women and the peasants who came to the factories to earn a few extra rubles, were ignorant and backward, sometimes illiterate or barely literate. But among the workers who had received a little education, who had perhaps picked up a leaflet which a Socialist agitator had circulated in the factory, there was a class of potential revolutionaries. The Tsarist Minister, Prince Svyatopolk-Mirsky, in a report dated 1902, notes the emergence of such a class in the following terms: [6]

"In the last three or four years out of our good-natured Russian yokel has developed a peculiar type of half-literate intellectual, who thinks it is his duty to reject religion and the family, to despise the laws and not to obey the authorities."

These "half-literate intellectuals" were practically all convinced Socialists; only Social Democrats stood any chance of election to the few seats which were reserved for workingclass representatives in the Duma. Here and there in pre-War Russia there were no doubt exceptionally fortunate workers who had more or less reason to be satisfied with their lot; and of course large masses of the workers never thought about political or social ideas at all except possibly in times of great revolutionary stress and upheaval. But in the main the bleakness and poverty of Russian workingclass life promoted among those workers who were best able to speak and influence the others an extremism that was bound to come to the surface as soon as the restraints of Tsarism were removed. In the light of the background of the Russian working class it is easy to understand why, from the first days of the Revolution, there was little sentiment in favor of class coöperation, of negotiated agreements with the employers, and a great readiness to listen to the Bolshevik speakers who supported their more extreme demands and urged them not to be content with shorter hours and higher wages, but to take the

factories out of the hands of the owners by means of a system of workers' control.

Two other factors contributed considerably to the swing of the Russian workers to the Left. Two extremes had always prevailed among Russian industrial enterprises. Along with small, primitively equipped plants and workshops were big new factories, employing tens of thousands of workers and fitted out with modern machinery, often built with the aid of foreign capital.[7] In these big plants, where large masses were drawn together, the sparks of revolutionary agitation spread with special rapidity. The huge Putilov works, for instance—its number of workers swelled to 35,000 as a result of War orders—was always a leader in the demonstrations in the capital.

Another feature of 1917 was the pouring back into Russia of thousands of people who had emigrated to America, England and other countries for political or economic reasons. Along with such outstanding leaders as Lenin and Trotzky, Zinoviev and Bukharin, many obscure and unknown emigrants who had worked in mines and factories, on boats and in sweatshops returned to their native country. Almost all these returned emigrants were radical Socialists; and they often played a considerable part in stirring up their more sluggish countrymen.

The mood of the workers in 1917 was determined not only by past labor conditions, but by immediate War conditions. According to the estimate of the distinguished economist, S. N. Prokopovitch, the War in 1917 was taking forty or fifty percent of Russia's national income.[8] This could scarcely fail to mean a reduced standard of living all around. The breakdown of transportation, important cause of the fall of the old regime, became intensified under the Provisional Government. During the first seven months of 1917, 980,000 fewer cars were loaded than in the corresponding months of the preceding year, while the percentage of locomotives which were out of commission reached the unprecedented figure of 25 on August 1, 1917. The productivity of the individual worker declined by about thirty percent in the metal industry, by almost fifty percent in the Donetz coalmines. The output of sugar fell from almost two million tons, in pre-War years to one million tons in 1917. Although the prices which the state paid for cotton in 1917 were almost trebled, by comparison with 1916, the failure of transportation and the resultant shortage of bread impelled the natives of Turkestan, the main cotton region of the country, to substitute wheat

for cotton. A reversion to barter economy was visible in the tendency of some factories to exchange manufactured goods directly with the peasants for food.

The harvest of 1917, while it was not catastrophically bad, was definitely unsatisfactory; it amounted in European Russia to a little less than fifty million tons of the main grains, as against an average pre-war yield of over sixty-two million tons.[9] The realization of this harvest was made more difficult because of the peasant disorders, because of the poor transportation, and because the best crop yields were obtained in parts of the country which were far away from Moscow and Petrograd, in the provinces around the Black Sea and in Western Siberia. The bread ration for city dwellers, fixed at one pound a day in the spring, was subsequently reduced to three quarters of a pound and was cut to half a pound in Petrograd and in Moscow shortly before the Bolshevik Revolution.

The country was drowning in a sea of inflation; and repeated increases in money wages brought no real improvement in the workers' lot, because prices shot up equally fast, or a little faster, and many articles simply disappeared from the market and could only be bought by profiteers at surreptitiously paid fantastic prices. The estimated value of the ruble on the London Stock Exchange was 56.2 kopecks in February, 27.3 kopecks in October. Inside the country the purchasing power of the ruble, which was 27 kopecks on the eve of the March Revolution, had shrunk to six or seven kopecks at the time of the Bolshevik Revolution.[10]

There was a sharp contrast in the movements of real and of nominal wages. While the workers' earnings in paper rubles rose steeply throughout 1917, an inconsiderable gain in real wages during the first half of the year, by comparison with the last half of 1916, was followed by a sharp drop in real wages during the last half of 1917, as is evident from the following table: [11]

	Nominal Monthly Wages	Real Wages (Calculated in Rubles of Pre-War Buying Power)
First half 1916	36 rubles	21.7 rubles
Second half 1916	45 rubles	18.7 rubles
First half 1917	70.5 rubles	19.3 rubles
Second half 1917	135 rubles	13.8 rubles

So in every way the stage was set for vigorous and aggressive action on the part of the industrial workers after the March Revolution. There was the mood of bitterness generated by memories of class oppression. There were the queues and the shortages, all

the elements of irritation that came with the increasing collapse of national economic life. There was the unaccustomed new flood of radical speechmaking, the complete helplessness of the Provisional Government.

As was the case with the soldiers and the peasants, the workers' movement advanced toward its ultimate goal through a series of stages. At first there is a period of intensive organization, accompanied by minor conflicts over wages and hours. Then strikes become more frequent and more bitter; the slogan of workers' control becomes more widespread; and there are occasional practical applications of it by arresting unpopular factory-owners, engineers and foremen and by forcibly keeping open plants which the owners desire to close. And in the end the workers' industrial movement becomes to some extent fused with the Bolshevik political movement for assumption of power by the Soviets.

Trade-unions sprang up all over the country with mushroom rapidity after the overthrow of the old regime. An All-Russian Trade-Union Conference, held in Petrograd in July, reported 1,475,429 members; and this figure had increased to 2,252,600 by the end of the year.[12] The trade-unions of Petrograd, which had enlisted 200,000 members in May, counted 450,000 by October.[13]

No single Party dominated this Trade-Union Conference, and the All-Russian Trade-Union Council which it elected contained representatives of the three revolutionary parties, Bolsheviki, Mensheviki and Socialist Revolutionaries. The stronghold of Bolshevism was not the central trade-union organization, but the factory committees, which were elected directly by the workers at each factory. It was a general psychological characteristic of the year of upheaval, 1917, that all the bodies which were in closest touch with the masses were most extreme in their demands; and the factory committees were no exception to this rule. The first conference of factory committees, held in Petrograd in June, adopted by an enormous majority the Bolshevik programme of workers' control; and it was to these bodies that Lenin thought of turning for support when efforts to capture the Soviets from within seemed to have failed. The factory committees maintained contact with the trade-unions; but they had their own central organization and exercised a good deal of independence.

The first serious defeat which the workers sustained in 1905 was the failure to obtain the eight-hour day. And the clearest proof that the Revolution of 1917 was destined to have a different issue

from its predecessor was the general adoption of the eight-hour day in the spring of 1917. In Petrograd the eight-hour day was adopted by agreement between the Soviet and the local association of factory-owners on March 23. In Moscow, where some employers were obstinate, the Soviet took matters into its own hands and decreed the change, with scant regard for legal niceties, on March 30. There was significance in the difference of procedure in the two cities. The Petrograd industrialists, whose plants were technically more advanced, had always been readier than their Moscow colleagues to concede shorter working hours.

What happened to industrial discipline in Russia during 1917 was not dissimilar to what happened to military discipline, although the refusal of the workers to toil was, of course, not so absolute as the refusal of the soldiers to fight. But there was a tremendous revolt against the pre-revolutionary harsh factory regime, with its labor spies, bullying foremen and ever watchful police; and the revolt, however justified and understandable it may have been in many cases, made efficient production impossible. Unpopular engineers and foremen were ridden out of the factories in wheelbarrows and there were some cases of beating and even of murder, although in general there was more organization and selfcontrol among the workers than among the soldiers and the peasants. Productivity of labor declined sharply, partly because of the general substitution of payment by day or hour for piecework, partly because of incessant strikes, partly because the workers were quick to leave their benches to listen to an agitator's speech, to attend a meeting or to march in a demonstration behind the red flag. A vicious circle developed, because the lowered productivity reduced the amount of fuel and manufactured goods and lowered the capacity of transportation; and this, in turn, adversely affected the food supply and provided a new excuse for lower productivity.

The workers, of course, had their grievances; they could point to the rising cost of living, which nullified the effect of wage increases, to the speculation and profiteering which were rife and which the Government could not check; and they were quick to accuse the employers of deliberate "sabotage" in the sense of closing plants for which there was an adequate supply of fuel and raw material, with the design of creating unemployment and starving the workers into submission. A well-known industrialist, P. P. Ryabushinsky, addressing a congress of businessmen in Moscow on August 16, let slip a phrase about "the bony hand of hunger,"

which "would grasp by the throat the members of the different committees and Soviets" [14] and bring them to their senses. This phrase obtained wide circulation and had an effect not unlike that of Marie Antoinette's "Let them eat cake."

How far the closing of some plants [15] was a deliberate effort to bring the workers to what the employers considered a more reasonable frame of mind and how far it was attributable to shortage of fuel and raw material and to impossible conditions, arising from the complete breakdown of factory discipline in some places, is difficult to determine. The entire economic situation made for conflict, and strikes and lockouts were the weapons naturally employed by both sides. The Provisional Government endeavored to intervene, to set up conciliation commissions, to set fair wage rates on a basis of arbitration; but, while it was able to stave off the frequently threatened railroad strike that would have been a major economic catastrophe under the circumstances, it was unable to coerce either labor or capital effectively; and the ground was paved for the Bolshevik Revolution by a continual series of strikes, large and small, which grew in intensity and seriousness with the passing of time.

Among the major strikes were that of the Moscow leather workers, which began at the end of August and was not fully settled at the time of the Bolshevik Revolution, and that of the textile workers of the Ivanovo-Vosnessensk and Kineshma Districts, which was also in progress at the time of the Revolution. There were continual clashes in the Donetz Basin, the main coal region of the country; and at the time of the Revolution this part of the country was threatened by a general strike which seemed likely to assume aspects of civil war, since the miners violently objected to the presence of Cossacks from the neighboring Don Territory, who had been sent to maintain order in the coal mines.

What were the demands of the strikers? The Moscow leather workers held out for a six-hour day on the eve of holidays, for a two weeks' annual vacation with pay, for pay on a time, not a piecework basis, for higher wages and for a system under which the factory committee could protest and refer to arbitration any dismissal of a laborer. The Ivanovo and Kineshma textile workers put forward similar demands, also insisting on a "minimum living wage," on maternity vacations for women workers and on the abolition of the system of fines. They also demanded a more definite workers' control over the hiring and discharge of laborers, proposing that no

worker should either be taken on or be dismissed without the consent of the trade-union.[16]

These demands could be parallelled in nonrevolutionary trade-union movements of other countries. What was more significant for the mood of the Russian workers on the eve of the Bolshevik Revolution was a resolution adopted by a delegates' meeting of the striking Moscow leather workers on October 29, which demanded:

"The transfer of all power into the hands of the Soviets.

"The immediate sequestration of plants where agreements between workers and employers were not concluded. . . .

"After October 29 the factory committees immediately proceed to practical measures for the preparation of the sequestration; they register and seal up goods, machines, etc."

This resolution was soon followed by a decisive decree of the Moscow Soviet, dated November 5, which was revolutionary from two standpoints: it assumed legislative power for the Soviet and it deprived the employers of the right of engaging and discharging employees. The main clauses of this decree were as follows: [17]

"The taking on and the dismissal of workers are carried out by the management of the factories with the agreement of the factory committee. In the event that the latter does not agree the matter is transferred to the consideration of the regional Soviet of Workers' Deputies, the decision of which is obligatory for both sides. Until the final decision both the engagement and dismissal are regarded as invalid.

"The engagement and dismissal of employees are carried out with the consent of the employees' committee.

"This measure is obligatory for all enterprises of the city of Moscow. Against persons guilty of violating it the Soviet of Workers' and Soldiers' Deputies will apply the most vigorous punitive measures, including the arrest of such people."

This, of course, was on the eve of the establishment of the Soviet regime. But even earlier there were many cases when the workers went far beyond the bounds of ordinary strikes and pretty effectively deprived the employers of real control of their factories. A conference of factory committees in the metal plants of Kharkov, for instance, decided on July 9 "to satisfy the demands of the workers with their own revolutionary power," adding: "If the factory owners within the course of five days refuse to satisfy these demands the directors are to be removed from the enterprises and are to be replaced by elected engineers." When the management

270 THE RUSSIAN REVOLUTION

of the Helfferich-Sade factory, in the same city, wanted to close the plant in connection with a labor dispute in September, the factory committee decided that work should be carried on under the direction of a special commission. And at the large locomotive factory in Kharkov more forceful measures were used. The harassed Kerensky on October 3 received a telegram from the plant to the effect that "the director and all the administrative personnel of the factory have been arrested by the workers. The local military and civil authorities are completely inactive." How often that last sentence must have been used during 1917, when formal legality and the rights of private property were at a very great discount!

The rough, hardbitten miners of the Donetz Basin were quick to exploit the loosening of all old bonds that came with the March Revolution. In the spring and summer mine Soviets and workers' meetings were ordering payments of disputed wages, regardless of the wishes of the administration, and deciding whether horses should be given to engineers. The mine-owners besieged the Provisional Government with futile remonstrances and complaints. By autumn some of the mine Soviets were proclaiming their dictatorship and a communication addressed to the Premier and the Minister for Trade and Industry by a mine-owners' association painted the following picture of a growing wave of excesses and of driving the owners of the mines away from their property: [18]

"In the Bokovo-Khrustalsk region of the Donetz Basin, at the mine of the company 'Russian Anthracite,' . . . the manager of the mine, engineer Pechuk, was beaten up at a session of the local Soviet of Workers' Deputies at the initiative and following the incitement of the President of the Soviet, Pereverzev. In the same region, at the Mikhailov mine of Donchenko, the same Pereverzev arrested one of the owners of the mine, Yakovlev. . . . In general there are searches of the homes of employees of the mines in the Bokovo-Khrustalsk region, and the employers are terrorized and have left the mines. From other regions of the Donetz Basin come reports of increasing excesses, beating and robbing of the mine-owners, and everything that is going on indicates that this anarchical and riotous movement is spreading broadly in the Donetz Basin. The local authorities are completely inactive."

And a list of workers' "excesses," compiled by a newspaper,[19] indicates that the engineer, like the army officer or the landlord, sometimes received short shrift from mobs of enraged workers:

"At the Lisva factory the engineer Lepchukov was killed with a shot in the back.

"At the Sulinsk factory, at the demand of the workers, the managing director of the factory, engineer Gladkov, was arrested for refusing to increase wages by a hundred percent.

"In Makeevka, at the factory of the company, 'Russian Mining and Metallurgical Union,' a worker in the foundry fired two shots at the chief of the foundry, a French citizen, the engineer Remy.

"At the factory of the Nikopol-Mariupol Company a mob of workers beat up the engineer Yasinsky and took him out on a wheelbarrow.

"At the Alexandrovsk factory of the Briansk Company in Ekaterinoslav Province the assistant director, Beneshevitch, the chief of the railroad department, Shkurenko, and some employees have been removed.

"At the factory of the Novorossisk Company in Yuzovka the workers have cut off electrical lighting in the apartments of the senior employees and the factory management."

So, all over the country, the masses of workers were in revolt, and this found expression in a great variety of ways, from cutting off electricity to outright murder. The revolt was distinctly one of the factory laborers. Where employees are mentioned they are usually objects of the excesses, rather than participants in them. This was quite understandable, because in Russia, even more than in other countries, there was a sharp social line of distinction between the manual workers and the white-collar workers.

In the face of this rising storm of proletarian revolt the Provisional Government fumbled helplessly, just as it did with the equally pressing problems of the War and of the outburst of agrarian disorder. It had no means of repressing or punishing acts of violence. And it lacked the will, or the ability, or both, to combat the growing economic chaos with energetic measures of state control and regulation. The wartime organization of industry in Germany and in England found no parallel in Russia. One reason for this, no doubt, was that the propertied classes were unwilling to submit to effective regulation by a Government which showed little power to maintain order.

Shadowy organizations, an Economic Council and a Main Economic Committee (the former consisting of representatives of the Government and of various public organizations, the latter of representatives of the various Ministries) came into existence, de-

bated and tried to find means of averting strikes and lockouts and directing distribution into effective channels. A state coal monopoly was instituted. Sixty percent of the textile goods remaining after the needs of the army had been satisfied were bought up and distributed through the Ministry for Supply. But in the main the Government did little to halt the clear drift of Russian economic life toward catastrophe.

The factory committees were as energetic as the Government was inactive. By autumn a situation had arisen where scarcely any step could be taken against their will. The Government at this time had worked out a plan for relieving Petrograd of as many enterprises as could conveniently be transferred elsewhere. There were genuine economic reasons in favor of such a step, because Petrograd was tremendously overcrowded and was remote from sources of food and raw material. There was also an element of political calculation in the scheme; the large workingclass population of the capital, now largely under Bolshevik influence, was a constant threat to the security of the Government.

The factory committees not only opposed this scheme in general, as "counterrevolutionary"; but often interposed objections to the transfer of individual plants on grounds which made a strong appeal to the masses of the workers. So, when the management of the factory "Russian Renaud," proposed to move to Ribinsk, the factory committee sent agents to that town, who brought back unfavorable news about food, housing and wage conditions prevailing there, with the result that a general meeting of the workers in the factory authorized the committee "to take all necessary measures to keep the factory in Petrograd." [20]

Closings of plants became increasingly common in the autumn of the year, partly because the Treasury had become less generous in financing War orders, partly because employers were in many cases inclined to give up, at least temporarily, the attempt to operate factories, in view of the growing extremism of the labor demands. But the workers were not in a mood to submit passively to unemployment. In almost every case a proposal to shut down a factory encountered the vigorous resistance of the factory committee, which would often carry out an examination of the financial position of the undertaking, and of its resources in fuel and raw material and point out ways in which production could be carried on. When the big "Naval" shipbuilding works in Nikolaev proposed to dismiss half its employees in the autumn the workers' organizations immediately

characterized this as "an act of resistance of the bourgeoisie" and proposed to send delegates to the places from which the plant received its raw material, to get into touch with the committees of factories which supplied the "Naval," and meanwhile to stop the dismissals.[21]

One cannot overestimate the psychological effect of this widespread and increasing intervention of the workers in the management of the factories. There is little evidence to show that it yielded beneficial economic results. The Russian workers, in the mass, were much less educated and technically trained than workers in the United States, England and Germany. And, even apart from this consideration, management of factories directly by their workers has never proved practicable on a large scale, in the Soviet Union or anywhere else. Individual authority and responsibility are as necessary in a factory as in an army.

Indeed Lenin himself, as an orthodox Marxian socialist, certainly did not look with favor on such an heretically syndicalist idea as operation of factories directly by the workers employed in them as a permanent arrangement. He welcomed the factory committees, which broke down discipline in industry, as he favored the army committees, which broke down discipline in the army, not because he was an advocate of anarchy or of pacifism, but because he believed that what he regarded as the capitalist state and industrial organization must be smashed before a new socialist organization could be set in its place.

And if the activity of the factory committees was scarcely calculated to arrest the process of economic breakdown, it had, from the Bolshevik standpoint, some very positive political benefits. It thoroughly destroyed in the minds of the workers any respect for the rights of private ownership. It accustomed the more energetic workers who naturally pushed to the fore in the factory committees to the idea of giving orders instead of taking them. Not a few commanders of the Red Army, not a few future "red directors" of Soviet industrial enterprises came out of the training school represented by the factory committees in 1917.

During and after the Kornilov affair the economic movement of the workers became largely fused with the political drive for the establishment of the Soviet regime. The railroad and telegraph workers played a large part in thwarting Kornilov's attempted *coup* by hampering the movements of his troop trains and refusing to transmit his telegrams. The union of metal workers assigned a

large sum of money for the use of the committee to combat counter-revolution and placed its staff of employees at the disposal of the committee. The chauffeurs' union offered all its cars for use against Kornilov and the printers' union urged its members to cease printing the more conservative newspapers.

When the Bolshevik Revolution came most of the trade-unions were on the side of the Bolsheviki and coöperated actively in overthrowing the Provisional Government. The office of the Petrograd Council of Trade-Unions was the headquarters of the Military Revolutionary Committee, which guided the Revolution in Petrograd, and the parallel committee in Moscow had its base in the building occupied by the Moscow union of metal workers. A conspicuous exception to the general rule was the printers' union, which was under Menshevik leadership and maintained an oppositionist attitude for some years under the Soviet regime.

The workers' movement of 1917 reached its climax when the Soviet Government, about three weeks after its accession to power, promulgated on November 27 a decree which accorded to the general practise of workers' control the force of law.[22] This decree pretty effectively ended private capitalist operation of industry in Russia. It established workers' control over "production, the purchase and sale of products, the keeping of these and also over the financial side of the enterprise." All business correspondence was to be controlled; all account books were to be opened to the inspection of the workers' committees which were to exercise the supervision; commercial secrets were abolished. Employers and control committees alike were held responsible for theft or damage to factory property. Such a system was quite incompatible with the private operation of industry. Hoping for a speedy fall of the Soviet regime, the factory-owners of Leningrad endeavored, with some temporary success, to enlist the coöperation of the engineers and the white-collar employees in making the control purely informative, so that business could be carried on as formerly.[23] But as time went on the drive against private ownership became still more intense, and by the summer of 1918 private operation of large-scale plants had practically come to an end in the territory under Soviet control. The vague and inchoate "workers' control" was gradually replaced by a system of nationalization and state operation; but this process belongs to a future period of the history of the Revolution.

The wresting of Russia's industrial enterprises out of the hands

of their owners was the third major event of a socially revolutionary upheaval that was also marked by the break-up of the army and by the seizure of the landed estates by the peasants. Of the three movements it was the most positive and decisive, from the standpoint of the success of the Bolshevik Revolution. For, while the average soldier simply wanted to leave the trenches and go home, and the average peasant could see no farther than the nearest "nobleman's nest," which was to be looted and burned, the majority of the active-minded workers in the autumn of 1917 were in favor of the slogan "All power to the Soviets" and supplied the basis of mass support on which every successful revolution must rest.

There is much matter for reflection in the double circumstance that a revolution which appealed primarily to the industrial working class was victorious in Russia in 1917, and that no such revolution has achieved permanent success anywhere else. This would seem to point to certain special and peculiar features of Russian working-class development. And the Russian worker in 1917 was in a special position. His standard of living was somewhere between that of a Chinese or Indian coolie and of a West European worker. And Russia's experience would suggest that the greatest measure of social dynamite is stored up in a proletarian class that has emerged from the wellnigh complete illiteracy and backwardness of the East without yet attaining the standard of living that holds good for the corresponding class in the West. The predestined standardbearer of the social revolution according to Marx proved to be neither the miserable, half-naked, rice-fed coolie of Shanghai or Bombay nor the skilled mechanic of Essen and Birmingham, but the Petrograd metal worker or the Donetz miner, sufficiently literate to grasp elementary socialist ideas, sufficiently wretched to welcome the first opportunity to pull down the temple of private property.

NOTES

[1] Karl Marx, "Capital" (Everyman edition), Vol. II, p. 846.

[2] S. G. Strumilin, "Wages and Productivity of Labor in Russian Industry, 1913-1922," p. 6.

[3] A. Nikolaenko, "The History of the Working Class in Russia," p. 155.

[4] In 1889 the average length of the working day in industry was 13 to 13.5 hours; in 1904 it was 10.7 hours; in 1913, 9.87 hours. See Joseph Freeman, "The Soviet Worker," p. 10.

[5] Nasha Zhizn (Our Life), No. 72, for January 27, 1905.

[6] "The Proletariat in the Revolution of 1905–1907," p. 6.

[7] S. O. Zagorsky, "State Control of Industry in Russia During the War," p 10.

[8] S. N. Prokopovitch, "National Economy in the Days of Revolution," p. 4.

[9] Ibid., pp. 30, 31, 37ff.

[10] Z. Lozinsky, "The Provisional Government in Struggle with Industrial Breakdown," in *Proletarskaya Revolutsia* (Proletarian Revolution), No. 69, p. 155.

[11] *Ibid.*, p. 148.

[12] "The Workers' Movement in 1917," p. 85.

[13] "The Revolution of 1917: Chronicle of Events," Vol. IV, pp. 275, 276.

[14] *Ibid.*, Vol. III, p. 248.

[15] Apparently 768 enterprises, employing 165,372 workers, closed between the 1st of March and the end of September (old style). See the newspaper *Torgovo-promishlennaya Gazeta* (Commercial-Industrial Gazette), No. 213, and the magazine *Promishlennost i Torgovlya* (Industry and Trade), Nos. 42–43, for 1917.

[16] "The Workers' Movement in 1917," pp. 170–186.

[17] E. Ignatov, "The Moscow Soviet of Workers' Deputies in 1917," pp. 347, 348.

[18] "The Workers' Movement in 1917," pp. 229, 230.

[19] See the newspaper *Russkoye Slova* (Russian Word), No. 234.

[20] See the newspaper *Rabochii Put* (Workers' Way), for October 3.

[21] *Ibid.*, for October 11.

[22] "The Decrees of the October Revolution," Vol. I, pp. 93ff.

[23] A description of this ultimately futile attempt of the employers is to be found in an article by B. Freidlin, entitled "The Struggle of the Employers Against Workers' Control in 1917," published in the magazine *Borba Klassov* ("Struggle of Classes"), No. 6–7, for 1931, pp. 21–27.

CHAPTER XIII

ON THE EVE

ALTHOUGH Kornilov's *coup* collapsed without the firing of a shot, its political consequences were momentous. It achieved results which were precisely the reverse of those which the General and his advisers had hoped for and expected. It gave the turbulent and dissatisfied masses just the blow that was necessary to arouse them to violent revolutionary action. It knocked the feeble underpinning of confidence completely from under the Provisional Government.

Although he seems to have seriously underestimated the strength of the Bolsheviki up to the end, Kerensky was not blind to the fact that, once the menace from the Right had disappeared, there would be a more serious threat from the Left. He tried to carry on the old policy of balancing himself between the conservative and radical forces in the country. While he made concessions to the Left by summoning a Democratic Conference, from which representatives of the propertied classes, who had been so numerous at the Moscow State Conference, were excluded, by appointing as War Minister Verkhovsky, who, as Commander of the Moscow garrison, had denounced Kornilov's adventure from the first, and as Naval Minister Admiral Verderevsky, who was popular with the moderate Socialists, he simultaneously endeavored to create a new coalition government, in which both the Cadets and the representatives of finance and industry would be represented.

But the possibilities of effective maneuvering of this kind were slight. Hitherto the Provisional Government owed whatever stability it possessed to the fact that the great majority of the Soviets accorded it formal support. But immediately after the Kornilov affair the Soviets began to slip out of the hands of the Mensheviki and the Socialist Revolutionaries. On September 13 the Petrograd Soviet, by a vote of 279 to 115, with 51 abstentions, adopted a Bolshevik resolution, with the familiar demands for immediate peace negotiations, confiscation of the large estates and introduction of workers' control in industry. Attendance at this session had been thin and a more decisive test of strength took place on the 22nd,

when the Mensheviki and Socialist Revolutionaries in the presidium
of the Soviet offered their resignations. A clever political trick of
Trotzky, who had been released from prison on the 17th, helped
to turn the tide in favor of the Bolsheviki: [1] he pointed out that
Kerensky was still formally a member of the presidium and introduced into the voting the element of confidence or lack of confidence
in Kerensky, who was anything but popular among the rank-and-
file soldiers whose votes decided the issue. The Bolsheviki won
a second and decisive victory, with 519 votes against 414, and 67
abstentions.

From this moment the Petrograd Soviet, which enjoyed a good
deal more authority in the capital than the Provisional Government,
was in the hands of the Bolsheviki. On October 8 Trotzky was
elected President of the Soviet. With his usual sense for the dramatic he recalled his former election to the same office in 1905, on
the eve of the suppression of the Soviet and the arrest of its
leaders by the soldiers of the Ismailov Regiment. "But now," he
declared triumphantly, "the Ismailov Regiment is entirely different.
We feel ourselves much firmer now than then." [2]

Lenin was still in hiding, still liable to arrest. But the two
strongest Soviets in the country (Moscow followed Petrograd's ex-
ample and "went Bolshevik" on September 18) were in the hands
of Lenin's Party. And Petrograd and Moscow did not stand alone.
As early as September 14 the Bolshevik newspaper *Rabochii*
(Workers) announced that 126 Soviets had requested the Soviet
Central Executive Committee, or Vtsik, to take over power. The
Vtsik, elected at the first Congress of Soviets and dominated by
Mensheviki and Socialist Revolutionaries, had no intention of
complying with this request; but the mood of the local Soviets was
none the less significant. On September 18 a Congress of Soviets
in the radical centre of Siberia, Krasnoyarsk, revealed a Bolshevik
majority; on the following day a message from Ekaterinburg, the
main city of the Urals, announced that power had passed into the
hands of the Soviets in this important mining and industrial region.
In the large Briansk factory, in Ekaterinoslav, in Ukraina, the
workers were passing a resolution to the effect that "we cannot recognize the Provisional Government." The same swing of the pendulum
to the Left was visible in the Volga towns, in the Donetz Basin.
It was no longer possible to assume, as it had been in the summer,
that the more conservative provinces would oppose a revolutionary
stroke in Petrograd.

Still more significant, because closer to the nerve centre of the Kerensky regime, was the trend in the Baltic Fleet and in Finland. On September 23 a Regional Congress of Soviets in Finland adopted Bolshevik resolutions by big majorities. The Socialist Revolutionaries who were elected to the congress were almost all members of the left wing of the Party, which was now growing steadily in strength and often voted and acted with the Bolsheviki.

The Baltic Fleet, always a pacemaker in agitation against the Provisional Government, took a stand of sharpest opposition after the Kornilov affair. Its attitude toward its nominal Commander-in-chief, Kerensky, was pungently expressed in a published resolution of a congress of the Baltic Fleet, which contained the following sentences: "We demand the removal from the ranks of the Provisional Government of the political adventurer, Kerensky, as a person who, by his shameless political trickery in favor of the bourgeoisie, disgraces the great Revolution, and, along with it, the whole revolutionary people. To you, betrayer of the Revolution, Bonaparte Kerensky, we send our curses."

Bonaparte was not a historically accurate epithet for Kerensky; but after this resolution, which was passed on October 16, there was little doubt on which side of the barricades the sailors would be when the decisive struggle for power came. Even the peasants of the Petrograd District, usually political adherents of the Socialist Revolutionaries, caught the infection of the Red capital and elected a Bolshevik as their representative in the Democratic Conference.

The Bolshevik upsurge can be traced not only in the Soviets, where workers and soldiers predominated, but in local elections which were held under the system of universal suffrage. A startling shift of sentiment is revealed by comparing the election figures for the ward councils of Moscow for July and for October: [3]

	July	October
Socialist Revolutionaries	374,885 (58%)	54,374 (14%)
Mensheviki	76,407 (12%)	15,887 (4%)
Bolsheviki	75,409 (11%)	198,320 (51%)
Cadets	108,781 (17%)	101,106 (26%)

Although these figures would not hold good for the whole country (the subsequent election for the Constituent Assembly showed that the majority of the peasants were still inclined to vote for the Socialist Revolutionaries), they are very symptomatic for the mood of the larger towns on the eve of the Bolshevik stroke for power. One notices the big falling off in the total vote, attributable to the

disillusionment of many voters with the results of the Revolution, the large increase in the Bolshevik vote, the relative stability of the Cadets, who rallied around them all those who felt a stake in the existing property system, the tremendous decline of the buffer parties, the Mensheviki and the Socialist Revolutionaries. It was the sort of political situation that points to an early decisive solution.

The voting reflected the internal disorganization of the moderate Socialist parties. The Menshevik organization in Petrograd, which had formerly counted 10,000 members, was in a state of virtual paralysis by October; ward meetings attracted only twenty or twenty-five participants.[4] The Socialist Revolutionaries, who had gained so many new recruits immediately after the Revolution, were now hopelessly divided among themselves. While a right-wing minority in the party still adhered to Kerensky the growing left wing, headed by Kamkov, Karelin and Maria Spiridonova, and especially strong in Petrograd, adopted a position little different from that of the Bolsheviki on questions of land and peace. The bulk of the party, followers of Chernov, the former Minister for Agriculture, occupied a position somewhere between the two extremes. Meanwhile the workingclass supporters of the party melted away; almost every day during the autumn one can find in the Bolshevik newspapers statements of groups of Socialist Revolutionaries who had passed over to the Bolsheviki.

So on every side the ground was crumbling from beneath Kerensky's feet. The political parties which had supported, or at least tolerated, his government were rapidly losing their influence with the masses. The Soviets were transformed by their Bolshevik majorities into potential instruments of insurrection. A large part of the armed forces were in a state of active or passive mutiny; every day brought new evidence of the hurricane that was sweeping the countryside. The vicious circle of inflation, with rising prices nullifying wage increases and goading the workers into more and more frequent strikes, was in full swing.

It was against this gloomy background that the Democratic Conference, one of Kerensky's last improvisations, opened its sessions in the Alexandrine Theatre in Petrograd on September 27. About 1200 delegates assembled,[5] the largest representation being accorded to Soviets of Workers', Soldiers' and Peasants' Deputies, to municipal and county legislative bodies, to coöperatives and trade-unions. The propertied elements were entirely excluded, so that the balance of forces was very different from what it had been at the Moscow

State Conference. The right wing was now represented by the cooperators, while a vociferous Bolshevik left wing, recruited largely from Soviet and trade-union organizations and from soldiers' and sailors' units, shouted dissent and interpolations whenever Kerensky made a controversial statement. If the shadow of Kornilov brooded over the Moscow Conference, with its liberal representation of bemedalled officers and old Duma political leaders, the spectre of Lenin loomed large before the Democratic Conference. Arguing with his critics of the Left, Kerensky declared that he should be reproached for the reintroduction of the death penalty at the front only when he actually confirmed a death sentence: a statement that was taken as a sign of weakness rather than of humanitarianism and that excited ridicule rather than sympathy. And one young soldier shook his fist at Kerensky and called him "the sorrow of the motherland."

Any spectator at the Democratic Conference who could have looked back to the cruelties of Tsarism and looked forward to the ruthless terrorism that would be practised in the name of the proletariat could scarcely have escaped a sense of national pathos and tragedy in the failure of this and similar assemblies, in which Russia's thin layer of a humane and civilized intelligentsia was heavily represented, to give any kind of effective leadership out of the crisis. For the first and perhaps the last time in its history Russia during the period of the Provisional Government enjoyed almost unlimited freedom of speech and press; for the first and probably for the last time a leading rôle belonged to the radical and liberal intelligentsia, which in all its mental and emotional make-up was equally alien to Tsarism and to Bolshevism.

But, at the Democratic Conference, as on many other occasions, this intelligentsia, with all its admirable qualities, showed itself quite incapable of authoritative leadership and united, resolute action. A Socialist Revolutionary, Minor, implored the assembly to take a unanimous decision in favor of a coalition government, predicting that otherwise "we will begin to cut to pieces. " "Whom?" inquired voices from the floor, and Minor, with a certain prophetic vision, replied: "We will cut each other to pieces." [6]

The audience listened in gloomy silence; but when the vote was taken it was evident that it could agree neither on a coalition government nor on any other way out of the crisis. Indeed this vote on the outstanding political question of the day, whether a new government should be based on a coalition of the moderate Socialist

and the propertied elements, revealed a wellnigh hopeless confusion of thought. Kerensky for some time had wished to re-create a coalition government; but, in view of the strong opposition in Soviet circles to further common action with the Cadets, some of whom had been obviously sympathetic with Kornilov, he had postponed final action until the meeting of the Democratic Conference, carrying on meantime with a rump Cabinet which included himself, Foreign Minister Tereschenko, the Minister for the Interior, Nikitin and the Ministers for War and the Navy, Verkhovsky and Verderevsky.

The question of approving the principle of coalition came up before the Democratic Conference on October 2. By a narrow margin, 766 to 688, the Conference expressed itself in favor of it. But this resolution was promptly stultified when an amendment to the effect that the Cadets should be excluded from the coalition was carried by 595 votes against 493. So strong was the dislike and distrust for the Cadets that a considerable number of delegates who favored the idea of coalition in general could not bring themselves to favor joint action with the Cadets. But, since the latter constituted the sole non-Socialist Party of any size or significance, the formula, "coalition without the Cadets" was simply an empty absurdity. And when it was put to a vote it was overwhelmingly defeated, 813 to 183. The Conference had thus proved unable to pronounce any clear judgment for or against coalition and the final outcome of the matter was that Kerensky went ahead with the creation of a new coalition Cabinet which included two of his personal friends among the Cadets, the Moscow physician Kishkin and the industrialist Konovalov, and also a well-known Moscow manufacturer, Tretyakov. The Petrograd Soviet promptly denounced the new Cabinet as "a government of civil war," and refused it any support and declared that the coming Congress of Soviets would create "a truly revolutionary government." [7]

The Democratic Conference found a successor in the shape of the so-called Council of the Republic, a body which included fifteen percent of the number of delegates elected to the Democratic Conference, with additional representation for the propertied and non-Socialist parties and groups which had been excluded from the Democratic Conference. The purpose of the Council of the Republic was to be a deliberative and consultative body which should carry on until the repeatedly postponed Constituent Assembly should meet. It included 550 members, of whom 156 belonged to the non-

Socialist groups, and held its sessions in the luxuriously appointed
Marinsky Palace.

Two observers of very different views, the Cadet Professor
Milyukov and the left-wing Menshevik Sukhanov, testify to the extremely high calibre of this pre-parliament. The various parties
sent their best representatives; the flower of the Russian intelligentsia was gathered within the walls of the Marinsky Palace. But
the Council of the Republic might be likened to a head without a
body; it had no effective following in the country; the real currents
of political life were flowing elsewhere, in the dirty, crowded, chaotic
Soviet headquarters in the Smolny Institute; in the mass meetings
at the Cirque Moderne and in other assembly-halls where Trotzky
and other Bolshevik orators were arousing the masses with fierce
denunciations of "the government of civil war"; in the barracks
and factories, where the atmosphere was becoming more and more
surcharged with electricity.

The Bolsheviki played the part of a left-wing opposition in the
Democratic Conference. By a vote of 72 to 50 their delegation resolved to participate in the Council of the Republic, to the great
disgust of Lenin, who was already throwing the whole weight of
his authority on the side of organizing an armed uprising and seizure
of power and who believed, not without reason, that a policy of
dallying in consultative bodies was calculated to paralyze the will
to action. But on October 20, when the Council of the Republic
held its first session under the presidency of an intellectual Socialist
Revolutionary, Avksentiev, the leftward swing was already so strong
that the Bolshevik delegation decided to walk out of the stillborn
assembly on the day of its opening. There was some fear that the
53 Bolshevik delegates would mark their exit by some form of noisy
demonstration; but Trotzky reassured a questioner with the statement that there would be only "a little pistol shot." [8] The "pistol
shot" was the reading of a declaration, in which the Government
was denounced for irresponsibility and the Council for helplessness [9] and the withdrawal of the Bolsheviki was heralded by salvoes
of Trotzky's rhetorical artillery:

"The Provisional Government, under the dictation of Cadet
counterrevolutionists and Allied imperialists, without sense, without
force and without plan, drags out the murderous war, condemning
to useless destruction hundreds of thousands of soldiers and sailors
and preparing the surrender of Petrograd and the throttling of the
Revolution. . . . We, the delegation of Bolsheviki, say: we have

nothing in common with this Government of treason to the people and with this Council of complicity in counterrevolution . . . All power to the Soviets! All land to the people! Long live an immediate, honest, democratic peace! Long live the Constituent Assembly!"

There was an element of unconscious irony in this last cheer for the Constituent Assembly, which the Bolsheviki would disperse with bayonets almost as soon as it met. But during the early months of the Revolution the Left parties were eager for an early convocation of the Constituent Assembly, while the Rights were for delay. The demand for the Constituent Assembly was still a useful trump card in Bolshevik agitation.

The majority of the delegates watched the departure of the Bolsheviki with a sigh of relief at the thought that the sessions would now be less turbulent, and then relapsed into the familiar academic debates about how to restore the fighting capacity of the Army (which was already passing more and more definitely under Bolshevik influence) and how to get peace in agreement with the Allied powers, which, intent on the prosecution of the War and buoyed up by the accession of the United States, were inclined to regard Russia as a parasite and its peace demands as a nuisance.

The moderate socialists had always been pathetically eager to grasp at any straw, however dubious, which seemed to promise an ending of the War on the basis of international agreement. An immense amount of talk and preliminary preparation was expended on the proposed Stockholm Conference of representatives of all the Socialist parties, a Conference which never took place at all, because the governments of the Allied countries refused passports to the delegates. Now there was a new hope: a conference of the Allied powers, to be held in Paris in November. The Soviet Executive Committee selected the Menshevik Skobelev as its representative,[10] to accompany Foreign Minister Tereschenko to this conference. It worked out a very detailed set of instructions,[11] including such farflung proposals as the neutralization of the Suez and the Panama Canals, the granting of civic rights of Rumanian Jews and the establishment of autonomy for Turkish Armenia, apparently quite oblivious of the certainty that these theoretically idealistic suggestions were bound to suffer shipwreck at the first encounter with the real War aims of the Allied powers, as embodied in the secret treaties. A cold statement by the British Foreign Minister, Balfour, that the conference proposed to discuss not the objectives of the War, but the

best means of prosecuting it, was calculated to dampen the ardor of the sponsors of Skobelev's mission; and the Council of the Republic spent one of its last sessions listening to Professor Paul Milyukov, the former Cadet Foreign Minister, denounce Zimmerwald and pacifism, amid the interjections and counter-cheers of the left-wing Mensheviki in the assembly. Meanwhile the Russian soldiers, of whom not one in ten thousand had heard of the meeting of obscure revolutionaries and pacifists in Zimmerwald, were quitting the War in their own very effective way.

When the Bolsheviki demonstratively walked out of the Council of the Republic they served clear notice of future extra-constitutional activity. But the necessary prelude to an attempt to overthrow the Government was an enormous volume of propaganda, calculated to arouse the masses to the fighting revolutionary pitch. And, especially after the formation of the coalition Government, Petrograd became a seething caldron of Bolshevik agitation. In the large assembly-halls one could hear the outstanding orators of the Party: Trotzky; Lunacharsky, the literary and dramatic critic who was to become Commissar for Education; Alexandra Kollontai, a radical feminist who would be the first woman Commissar and the first woman Ambassador. In the factories and in the barracks the rank-and-file Party agitators held forth on the same themes in simpler language.

The main points of the Bolshevik propaganda crusade were as follows.[12] The coalition Government was denounced as a group of irresponsible usurpers, sympathizers with Kornilov, who might be expected to renew Kornilov's attempted *coup*. It was suggested that this "Government of treason to the people" would deliberately surrender Petrograd to the Germans. Use was made of an indiscreet contribution of the former President of the Duma, Rodzianko, to the Moscow newspaper, *Utro Rossii,* in which he spoke of the military danger to Petrograd and observed that he would be very glad if the central Soviet institutions were destroyed, since they had brought nothing but evil to Russia.[13] A proposal of the Government to evacuate Petrograd and move to Moscow, a project that was quickly dropped because of the storm of criticism which it aroused, even among the moderate Socialists, furnished more ammunition for the Bolshevik speakers. And finally there was the argument, extremely popular with the soldiers of the garrison, who disliked nothing so much as the idea of being sent to the front, that any transfers of troops must be regarded with suspicion, as pursuing

counterrevolutionary ends. All this led up to the slogans, increasingly popular among the masses: "Peace, land to the peasants, workers' control in industry, all power to the Soviets."

The military threat to the capital had become more real as a result of the appearance of a German squadron in the Baltic in the middle of October. Troops were landed on the islands Dago, Oesel and Moon, outside the Gulf of Riga, and the Russian Fleet joined battle. The central organization of the Baltic Fleet put out a flowery appeal to the proletarians of the world, in which the following sentences are characteristic: [14]

"Attacked by superior German forces our fleet perishes in the unequal battle. Not one of our ships evades the struggle, not one of our sailors goes vanquished to the land. The slandered Fleet fulfills its duty before the great revolution. We vowed to hold the front firmly and to guard the approaches to Petrograd. We keep this vow. We keep it not at the command of some pitiful Russian Bonaparte, who is ruling by the mercy and long-suffering of the Revolution. We go into battle not in the name of carrying out the treaty of our rulers with the Allies, who have bound with chains the hands of Russian freedom. We go to death with the name of the great Revolution on lips that do not tremble and in the warm hearts of the fighters. We send to you a last flaming appeal, oppressed of the whole world!

"Lift the banner of insurrection! Long live the world revolution! Long live the just general peace! Long live socialism!"

The sailors, inspired, perhaps, by some vague sentiment of militant revolutionism, offered more resistance than was customarily shown by Russian forces during 1917, but were unable to prevent the Germans from occupying the islands. The larger scheme of an offensive against Petrograd did not enter into the German plans, however, and the revolutionary situation in the capital continued to develop without the complications which a foreign attack would have created.

Behind the turbulent panorama of Petrograd was the directing brain of the master strategist of revolution, Vladimir Ilyitch Lenin. There is no period in Lenin's life when his stature as a leader and his capacity to grasp accurately the basic facts of a new and changing political situation appear so vividly as in the few weeks which elapsed between the Kornilov affair and the Bolshevik stroke for power. He recognized immediately that Kornilov's defeat was Bolshevism's opportunity, that the failure of the attempt to create a

dictatorship of the Right opened wide the door to a dictatorship of the Left.

During this momentous period Lenin showed himself greater as a strategist than as a tactician. Living in hiding first in Helsingfors, then in Viborg, nearer Petrograd, and only moving to the capital on October 20, dependent for his information on newspapers which reached him with some delay and on clandestine meetings with trusted members of the Party, it was only natural that his judgment should be faulty in connection with some of the details of the projected uprising. He was convinced, for instance, that success was more certain in Moscow than in Petrograd and recommended that the uprising should begin in Moscow. Actually, Petrograd fell into the hands of the Bolsheviki almost without a struggle, while days of sanguinary fighting were needed to conquer Moscow. He seems to have been precipitate with his suggestion that the uprising should have begun at the time of the Democratic Conference [15] and in his single-track insistence on the organization of insurrection at the earliest possible moment he was somewhat too contemptuous of the expediency of linking up the uprising with the meeting of the Second Congress of Soviets, with its assured Bolshevik majority.

But these were minor miscalculations of detail, which could be and were corrected in the development of the action. Lenin's indisputable claim to greatness as a revolutionary leader lies in the fact that he realized immediately after the collapse of Kornilov that the time for action had come, that he drove home this view in political arguments of iron logic, shot through with revolutionary passion, and that he never relaxed his pressure on the Party Central Committee, some of whose members were hostile, while others were lukewarm in regard to his insistence on armed uprising, until the opposition was crushed and the Party organization had swung into line behind his proposals. Incidentally the whole cast of Lenin's political thought and the salient traits of his personality are reflected with amazing vividness in the letters and pamphlets which he published in rapid succession at this time: "The Bolsheviki Must Take Power," "Marxism and Insurrection," "Can the Bolsheviki Hold State Power?" "The Crisis Is Ripe," etc.

As a general rule Lenin does not aim at or achieve special effect in his style. But there is genuine eloquence in the rugged, hard, metallic ring of many of the sentences in these appeals for uprising. What could be stronger, simpler or more decisive than the opening

sentence in his letter, addressed to the Central Committee and to the Petrograd and Moscow Committees of the Party: "Having obtained the majority in the Soviet of Workers' and Soldiers' Deputies in both capitals [16] the Bolsheviki can and must take the state power into their hands." Or what could be a keener psychological appraisal of one of the main conditions of successful revolution than the following excerpt from "Marxism and Insurrection": "An insurrection must rest on a turning point in the history of a growing revolution, when the activity of the leading ranks of the people is greatest and when the waverings in the ranks of the enemies and of the weak, halfhearted, undecided friends of the revolution are greatest."

These two letters were read and discussed at a session of the Party Central Committee on September 28. They must have produced something of the effect of an exploding bomb. For Lenin outlined not merely theoretical arguments for an armed seizure of power, but a definite plan of action. The Bolshevik delegates were to read a declaration, setting forth their demands in clear and unmistakable language and to leave the Conference, transferring their work to the factories and barracks. After this there was to be an uprising: "We must, without losing a moment, organize a staff of insurgent detachments, distribute forces, send loyal regiments to the most important points, surround the Alexandrine Theatre, occupy the Fortress of Peter and Paul, arrest the General Staff and the Government," etc.

These letters met a very chilly reception. By a vote of six to four, with six sustaining, the Central Committee decided that only one copy of the letters should be kept. Instead of deciding to withdraw the Bolshevik delegation from the Democratic Conference and sound the tocsin of insurrection among the workers and soldiers it was decided "to take measures so that no outbreak should take place in the barracks and in the factories." [17]

But time and the increasingly revolutionary atmosphere were on Lenin's side. On October 12 he reinforced his views with another article, "The Crisis Is Ripe," which begins with the gross misconception that "we are on the threshold of a world proletarian revolution" but proceeds with a thoroughly sound analysis of Russia's internal condition, emphasizing such points as the peasant uprising that was flaming up on the countryside, despite the fact that Kerensky, a Socialist Revolutionary, was at the head of the Government; the falling off from the Government of the Finnish troops and

the Baltic Fleet; the general testimony that the soldiers will fight no longer; the swing toward Bolshevism reflected in the Moscow municipal election.

Shortly before this Lenin had written a long letter to Smilga, head of the Regional Soviet Committee in Finland and an ardent advocate of insurrection, suggesting that Kerensky's regime could be overthrown with the aid of combined action by the troops in Finland and the sailors of the Baltic Fleet. It is noteworthy that during this critical period of preparing for the supreme risk of uprising Lenin showed scant regard for the strict requirements of Party discipline. He went over the head of the Central Committee on more than one occasion, sending copies of his letters and messages to the more important local Party organizations, the Petrograd and Moscow Party Committees, getting into direct contact with the men whom he regarded as most reliable partisans of insurrection, seeing to it that extra copies of his appeals got into the hands of the more active local Party workers. Trotzky declares [18] that at one time in the middle of October Lenin proffered his resignation as a member of the Central Committee, "in order to leave himself freedom of agitation in the lower ranks of the Party and at the Party Congress." The resignation was not accepted and the incident was apparently quickly closed. But it is symptomatic of Lenin's spirit of restless driving, of fear that the opportunity for successful uprising would be lost. Between the 16th and the 20th of October he sent a letter directly to the members of the Petrograd and Moscow Committees of the Party, the general content of which is summed up in the following phrases:

"To wait is a crime. The Bolsheviki have not the right to await the Congress of Soviets, they must take power immediately. . . . To delay is a crime. To await the Congress of Soviets is a childish play at formality, a shameful play at formality, treachery to the Revolution."

No picture of Lenin's thought at this time would be complete without reference to his remarkable pamphlet, "Can the Bolsheviki Hold State Power?" It is largely devoted to a refutation of the arguments advanced in Maxim Gorky's newspaper, *Novaya Zhizn* (New Life), which occupied a position somewhat to the left of the Mensheviki and somewhat to the right of the Bolsheviki, to the effect that the Bolsheviki could not hold power even if they captured it.

"After the Revolution of 1905, 130,000 landlords governed Rus-

sia. And cannot 240,000 members of the Bolshevik Party govern Russia in the interests of the poor and against the rich? . . . The state, dear people, is a class conception. The state is an organ or machine of violence of one class against others. While it is a machine of tyranny of the bourgeoisie over the proletariat there can be only one proletarian slogan: destruction of this state. And when the state will be proletarian, when it will be a machine of tyranny of the proletarian over the bourgeoisie, then we will be completely and unreservedly for firm authority and for centralism. . . . A real, deep, people's revolution is an incredibly tormenting process of the death of an old and the birth of a new social order, of a new way of life of tens of millions of people. Revolution is the sharpest, fiercest, most desperate class war and civil war. Not one great revolution in history was achieved without civil war. . . .

"And when the last unskilled laborer, every unemployed, every cook, every impoverished peasant sees,—not from the newspapers, but with his own eyes,—that the proletarian power does not grovel before the rich, but helps the poor, that it does not shrink from revolutionary measures, that it takes surplus products from the idlers and gives them to the hungry, that it forcibly settles the homeless in the apartments of the rich, that it compels the rich to pay for milk, but does not give them one drop of milk until the children of all poor families are adequately supplied, that the land passes to the toilers, the factories and banks under the control of the workers, that immediate and serious punishment awaits the millionaires who hide their riches,—when the poor see and feel this, then no power of the capitalists and kulaks, no power of world finance capital, that has stolen billions, can conquer the people's revolution. On the contrary, it will conquer the whole world, because the socialist upheaval ripens in all countries."

If to this fierce gospel of class war one adds the touch of bitter scorn with which Lenin in this pamphlet refers to an engineer, a former Bolshevik, who had raised the objection that the workers in Russia were too ignorant and backward to make a successful revolution ("He would be ready to recognize the social revolution if history led up to it as peacefully, tranquilly, smoothly and accurately as a German express train approaches a station; the conductor opens the doors of the car and announces: 'Station Social Revolution; everyone get out' "), one has a good psychological insight into the mood of the man who would soon drive Kerensky from his unstable seat of power.

Gradually but surely Lenin's slogan of revolution broke through the crust of inertia and hesitation which it had originally encountered. The tactics of demonstrative withdrawal which Lenin had vainly recommended for the Democratic Conference were applied, as we have seen, by the Bolshevik delegates in the Council of the Republic. And the hour of definite decision struck at a session of the Central Committee which may fairly be called historic on the evening of October 23.

With considerable stealth and secrecy twelve members of the Party Central Committee, of whom two, Lenin and Zinoviev, were still liable to arrest, gathered in the apartment of Sukhanov, one of the editors of *Novaya Zhizn*. His wife was a Bolshevik in sympathy and took care that her husband was absent on the evening of the meeting. No one has given us a full-length description of the proceedings; only the main points of Lenin's speech, which naturally dominated the occasion, were noted down and preserved.[19] There was eager and passionate discussion until late into the night, with intervals for refreshment in the shape of tea and sausage sandwiches.

Lenin began his speech on a reproachful note which reflected his weeks of struggle to obtain agreement with his view about the necessity for immediate insurrection. He pointed out that from the middle of September there had been indifference to the question of uprising. This was not to be permitted, "if we take seriously the slogan of seizure of power by the Soviets." It was high time to turn attention to the technical side of the question. The indifference of the masses could be explained by the fact that they were tired of words and resolutions.

Lenin emphasized the point that the political situation was quite ripe for the seizure of the power. It was only a matter of technical preparation. He aimed another shaft at those who were inclined to hesitate and procrastinate, observing: "We are inclined to consider the systematic preparation of an uprising as something in the nature of a political sin. To wait until the Constituent Assembly, which will clearly not be with us, is senseless, because this would mean a complication of our problem."

The main contributions to the discussion, so far as one can judge from the existing records, were made by Sverdlov, who declared that in Minsk, the headquarters of the Western Front, a new Kornilov affair was being prepared, and that the town was being surrounded by Cossack units, and by Uritzky, who gave a somewhat pessimistic

picture of the situation in Petrograd. "We passed a large number of resolutions, but there is really no action. The Petrograd Soviet is disorganized, there are few meetings." Uritzky declared that there were 40,000 rifles in the hands of the workers, but that this was inadequate, while no great hope could be placed in the garrison after the July Days.

In the end the Central Committee passed a resolution of the following content, which clearly set the course of the Party on an armed seizure of power:

"The Central Committee recognizes that both the international position of the Russian Revolution (mutiny in the fleet in Germany as an extreme manifestation of the growth all over Europe of the world socialist revolution, then the menace of a separate peace between the imperialists with the object of strangling the Revolution in Russia) and the military situation (the unquestionable decision of the Russian bourgeoisie and of Kerensky and Company to surrender Peter [Petrograd] to the Germans) and the gaining of a majority by the proletarian party in the Soviets,—all this, taken in connection with the peasant uprising and with the turn of popular confidence toward our Party (elections in Moscow), finally, the clear preparation of a second Kornilov affair (removal of troops from Peter, bringing up of Cossacks to Peter, surrounding of Minsk by Cossacks, etc.)—all this places armed insurrection on the order of the day.

"So, recognizing that armed insurrection is inevitable and that the time is quite ripe for it, the Central Committee proposes to all Party organizations to be guided by this and from this standpoint to consider and solve all practical problems (the Congress of Soviets of the Northern Region, the withdrawal of troops from Peter, the demonstrations of the Moscow and Minsk people, etc.)."

This resolution, which marked a crossing of the political Rubicon, so far as the question of insurrection was concerned, was adopted by a vote of ten to two. Curiously enough the two dissidents, Lenin's old associates in exile, Zinoviev and Kamenev, were elected as members of the Political Bureau of seven members (the others were Lenin, Trotzky, Stalin, Sokolnikov and Bubnov) which was selected from members of the Central Committee at the suggestion of Dzerzhinsky. The task of this Bureau was defined as "political leadership"; but as an organization it seems to have played little part in the stirring events of the following weeks.

The reconstruction of historical facts is sometimes made more difficult by the subsequent antagonism between Trotzky and Stalin. Trotzky asserts that a definite date, October 26, was set for the uprising at the session of the Central Committee; Stalin denies this. If any such date was set it was not kept; and while the resolution

of October 23 gave the active advocates of uprising in the Party ranks a distinct advantage, it was still possible for the more wavering members to construe it as a general piece of instructions, the practical application of which might be postponed indefinitely.

Opposition within the Central Committee was not altogether silent. Not content with voting against the resolution, Zinoviev and Kamenev on October 24 addressed a long appeal against it to several of the leading Party organizations. Beginning with the statement that "an armed uprising means to put at stake not only the fate of our Party, but also the fate of the Russian and the international Revolution" Zinoviev and Kamenev argued that, with correct tactics, the Bolsheviki could obtain a third or more of the seats in the Constituent Assembly and that the type of state to be aimed at was "the Constituent Assembly plus Soviets." They advanced as arguments against insurrection the war-weariness of the soldiers and the absence of serious prospects of revolutionary success in other countries and conjured up a terrifying, but, as events proved, a quite unreal picture of the forces at the disposal of the Government in Petrograd: "Five thousand Junkers [students in officers' training courses], eager (as a result of their class situation) and able to fight, the Staff, the soldiers of the shock brigades, a considerable part of the garrison, much of the artillery that is located around Petrograd. Moreover, the enemy with the aid of the Vtsik will almost certainly try to bring troops from the front." [20]

The conclusion at which Zinoviev and Kamenev arrived was that there should be no effort to seize power by violence, but only an attempt to strengthen the influence of the Party by peaceful means. Their resistance to Lenin's insistent demand for insurrection was stubborn and continued up to the eve of the uprising. It came out again at an important conference of members of the Central Committee, the Petrograd Committee, the Party Military Organization, the trade-unions and factory committees on October 29. Here Zinoviev argued [21] that the Bolsheviki could not count on the railroad and telegraph workers, that the influence of the Vtsik was still quite strong, that "our enemies have an enormous organizing staff," that "the sentiment in the factories is not what it was in June" (Zinoviev apparently believed that it had changed for the worse from the Bolshevik standpoint) and that in general it would be advisable to wait for the convocation of the Constituent Assembly before undertaking any decisive steps. Kamenev supported him and offered his

resignation from the Central Committee when the Conference, by a vote of 19 to 2, with four abstentions, adopted Lenin's resolution, calling for "intensified preparation of an armed uprising." Their attitude provoked a merciless verbal lashing from Lenin, who was never a mild controversialist and whose rage at seeing two of his old comrades oppose the Revolution in which he saw the crowning victory of his life work may readily be imagined. In his "Letter to Comrades," published in three successive issues of *Rabochii Put*, he called Zinoviev and Kamenev "heroes of parliamentary illusions and parliamentary cretinism." [22] With bitter sarcasm he replied to their argument that the defeat of Bolshevism would be a blow to the international revolutionary movement:

"We will judge as the Scheidemanns and Renaudels: [23] it is more reasonable not to rise up, because, if they shoot us down, the world will lose such splendid, reasonable, ideal internationalists. We will show our good sense. We will pass a resolution of sympathy with German rebels and reject uprising in Russia. This will be real, reasonable internationalism."

He characterized the peasant uprising as the "biggest fact in contemporary Russia" and declared that such a factual argument for insurrection was "stronger than a thousand pessimistic evasions of a confused and frightened politician." And in typical hard simple phrases he repeated for the hundredth time his summons to immediate action: "Hunger does not wait. The peasant uprising did not wait. The War does not wait."

Although Zinoviev and Kamenev were the outstanding opponents of the uprising they were by no means without sympathizers among the Party leaders. Rykov and Nogin, two outstanding figures in the Moscow organization, held similar views. And, although Zinoviev and Kamenev alone voted against Lenin's resolution at the meeting on October 29, a compromise resolution, offered by Zinoviev, suggesting that no violent action be taken until the Bolshevik delegates to the impending Congress of Soviets had been consulted, collected six votes, with fifteen participants in the conference opposed and three abstaining,—a familiar device of people who desired to sit on the fence.

In retrospect the rightness of Lenin's strategy is obvious. There can be little doubt that if the Bolsheviki had not struck for power approximately when they did their opportunity would have passed. There would have been some way out of the Government's state of helpless paralysis. The meeting of the Constituent Assembly, in

which the Bolsheviki, as the later voting showed, could not have gained a majority, would have been a barrier against a violent *coup.* Moreover, the impatient masses would soon have tired of passing resolutions. The Bolsheviki could not have counted on holding their masses of supporters in the Viborg District or the turbulent sailors of Kronstadt over a long period of inaction.

But the impotence of the Government is more evident in retrospect than it was at that time. It is easy to understand the mentality of those Bolsheviki who hesitated to stake everything on an uprising. After all, the July Days had been a fiasco. Red Guard units had been springing up like mushrooms at the factories; but these hastily armed workers were still raw and untrained. The soldiers of the Petrograd garrison were so accustomed to a life of loafing about the streets of the capital that they could scarcely be expected to put up a vigorous fight for anything. Even the mood of the masses was susceptible of various interpretations. So Shlyapnikov, an old underground Party worker, now head of the metal workers' union, declared at the session on October 29 that, while Bolshevik influence prevailed in his trade-union, the idea of a Bolshevik outbreak was not popular; rumors of such an outbreak even provoked panic. Skripnik, who, as a representative of the factory committees, was more in touch with rank-and-file workingclass sentiment, retorted that everywhere there was a desire for practical results; the leaders were more conservative than the masses. This same Skripnik, the hot revolutionist of 1917, took his own life in the summer of 1933, when the juggernaut of the centralized Soviet state rolled too heavily over his native Ukraina.

While the Bolshevik leaders were working out the plans for revolt, life in Petrograd in the grey, chilly, wet autumn days went on its hectic, nervous, uncertain course.

"In the factories the committee-rooms were filled with stacks of rifles, couriers came and went, the Red Guard drilled. . . . In all the barracks meetings every night, and all day long interminable hot arguments. On the streets the crowds thickened toward gloomy evening, pouring in slow voluble tides up and down the Nevsky,[24] fighting for the newspapers. . . . Hold-ups increased to such an extent that it was dangerous to walk down side streets . . . On the Sadovaya one afternoon I saw a crowd of several hundred people beat and trample to death a soldier caught stealing. . . . Mysterious individuals circulated around the shivering women who waited in queue long cold hours for bread and milk, whispering that

the Jews had cornered the food supply—and that while the people starved the Soviet members lived luxuriously . . .

"At Smolny there were strict guards at the door and the outer gates, demanding everybody's pass. The committee-rooms buzzed and hummed all day and all night, hundreds of soldiers and workmen slept on the floor, wherever they could find room. Upstairs in the great hall a thousand people crowded to the uproarious sessions of the Petrograd Soviet. . . .

"Gambling clubs functioned hectically from dusk to dawn, with champagne flowing and stakes of twenty thousand rubles. In the centre of the city at night prostitutes in jewels and expensive furs walked up and down, crowded the cafes."

This is how John Reed, American radical journalist and future Communist, now buried in Moscow's place of honor, under the Kremlin Wall, in the Red Square, summed up an eyewitness panoramic impression of the Russian capital on the eve of the Bolshevik *coup*.[25] For the masses of the people life was steadily becoming harder; the luxurious living of a small class of lucky speculators simply accentuated the general poverty, distress and bitterness.

Meanwhile routine and inertia seemed to dominate the actions of the Government. The growing conviction in the Allied capitals that Russia need no longer be treated as an equal partner in the War is reflected in a hectoring note which was jointly presented by the British, French and Italian Ambassadors on October 9. The note hinted very plainly that the Allied Governments would be obliged to cease rendering aid in arms, munitions and material if the Russian Government did not show more resolve "to employ all proper means to revive discipline and true military spirit among the fighting troops." Kerensky was annoyed by this forcible remonstrance[25a] and conveyed to the American Ambassador, David Francis, his grateful appreciation of the fact that America had not associated itself with the note. The latter had, of course, no effect in arresting the disorganization of the Army.

Early in November Kerensky, in turn, aroused sharp criticism in the Allied countries, especially in England, by giving out an interview in which he characterized Russia as "worn out," suggested that "the Allies should take the heaviest part of the burden on their shoulders" and querulously asked: "Where is the great British Fleet, now that the German Fleet is out in the Baltic?"[26] In this same interview Kerensky, more prophetically than he realized him-

self, suggested that it would take years for the Russian Revolution to develop fully.

What was the attitude of the Government, of the conservative classes and of the moderate Socialists toward the impending Bolshevik blow? As reflected in the newspapers and in the reminiscences of the time it was a curious compound of panicky apprehension and of overconfidence. It cannot be said that the Bolsheviki took power by means of a conspiratorial surprise. A member of the Bolshevik Central Committee, Sokolnikov, was quite accurate when he remarked that "we are openly preparing an outbreak." [27] As early as October 7 *Ryetch,* the Cadet organ, was speaking of the threat of "a cannibal triumph of the Lenins on the ruins of Great Russia." Mensheviki in the Petrograd and Moscow Soviets directly asked Trotzky and other Bolsheviki whether an armed outbreak was under consideration: a question which naturally elicited evasive replies.

As the period which remained before the decisive day, November 7, dwindled from weeks to days, the chorus of the non-Bolshevik press became shriller. Along with the recognition of the danger of a Bolshevik uprising there was a general profession of confidence that it would be crushed. *Ryetch* on November 3 was writing: "If the Bolsheviki venture to come out they will be crushed without difficulty." The Menshevik *Rabochaya Gazeta* wrote of the "isolation of the Petrograd proletariat and garrison from other social classes." The more left-wing *Novaya Zhizn* asserted that only the party of Kornilov could benefit from an armed uprising. [28]

Kerensky was apparently resorting to artificial stimulants in the last weeks of his regime [29] and had fallen into a state of fatalistic apathy which was somewhat symbolic of the prospects of the Provisional Government. Despite the critical situation in the capital, he went off to the Stavka from October 27 until the 30th and professed a desire to take a long trip to the Lower Volga. In the last days of October the Cadet Minister Konovalov began to press for more information on the measures which the Government was taking for selfdefense and on October 27 succeeded in obtaining a report from the Chief of Staff of the Petrograd Military District, General Bagratuni, which merely convinced him that no real measures had been taken. Yet only four or five days before the Bolshevik uprising Kerensky, in response to the questions of a prominent Cadet, Nabokov, about the danger of such an uprising and the means of coping with it, said: "I could pray that such an uprising would take

place. I have more strength than I need. They will be finally smashed." [30]

The sweep toward inevitable clash of the Bolsheviki, still insufficiently conscious of their strength, and the Government, distinctly unconscious of its weakness, moved at an accelerated pace during the last days of October and the first days of November. An issue of major importance, which had considerable effect on the final timing of the outbreak, was the holding of the second national Congress of Soviets. The convocation of this Congress was overdue, since the first Congress, held in June and July, had decided that a second should be convened within three months. But the old Central Executive Committee, with its predominance of Mensheviki and Socialist Revolutionaries, had little desire to call a new Congress, which, in view of the pronounced swing to the left in the local Soviets and in the army organizations, was almost certain to return a Bolshevik majority. Various arguments were advanced against the new Congress; it was suggested, among other things, that it would divert attention from the impending election to the Constituent Assembly.

But the Bolsheviki were insistent that the Congress be held; and, partly as a means of insuring that the Congress, which the reluctant Vtsik had finally convoked for November 2, would be held, partly in order to review the revolutionary situation in the area in the immediate vicinity of Petrograd, the Bolsheviki convened a Congress of Soviets of the Northern Region, which opened in Petrograd on October 24, with 150 delegates from twenty-three places. Finland, the Baltic Fleet, the local Soviets and garrisons of the strategic railroad centres around the capital were well represented and the sentiment of the Congress was overwhelmingly Bolshevik in sentiment. A resolution proposed by Trotzky and containing the militant sentence, "The hour has come when the question of the central government can be decided only by a resolute and unanimous coming-out of all the Soviets," was carried without one vote in opposition and with only three abstentions. The Lettish delegate, Peterson, promised forty thousand of the Lettish sharpshooters, who were subsequently to be an important element in the newly formed Red Army, as a defense for the impending Congress of Soviets. This mobilization of revolutionary forces from a ring of towns and fortresses around Petrograd foreshadowed the failure of any attempt to put down the projected uprising by bringing forces from the front.

The broad forces making for the success of the Bolshevik revolt were the overwhelming popular demands for peace and land, combined with the more or less conscious desire of the workers to take control of industry and to make life as unpleasant as possible for people of wealth and property. In Petrograd, which, as the capital, was inevitably the decisive point of the uprising, the Bolshevik leaders cleverly exploited two local issues: the holding of the Second Congress of Soviets and the mood of the Petrograd garrison. The latter by the autumn of 1917 was about the most unwarlike body of men in uniform that could well have existed. Its fighting mood, from the Bolshevik standpoint, was not as promising as that of the Kronstadt sailors or of the Red Guards. But the soldiers of the garrison could be aroused to a man in resistance to any attempt to send them to the front.

This sentiment of the soldiers explains the rapid and easy success of the Military Revolutionary Committee in wresting the garrison out of the control of the Provisional Government. Up to the latter part of October there had been nothing that could function as a staff of leadership for the uprising. This serious deficiency was remedied when, on October 22, the Bolsheviki caught up a Menshevik proposal in the Executive Committee of the Soviet and expanded and modified it in such a way as to discomfit its authors. The Mensheviki had proposed the creation of an organ of coöperation between the Soviet and the Staff of the Petrograd District, which should take measures to insure the defense of Petrograd, and which should be informed in the event of any transfer of units from the capital.

When this proposal had been worked over by the Bolshevik majority in the Executive Committee it came out in much more extended and ambitious form. The Committee was to be created by the Executive Committee of the Soviet and was to include representatives of a considerable number of workers', soldiers' and sailors' organizations. It was to decide which forces might not be withdrawn from Petrograd, to register all the personnel of the garrison of Petrograd and towns in the neighborhood, to take account of supplies and foodstuffs, to work out a plan for the defense of the city. Along with the Military Revolutionary Committee was to be a Garrison Conference, with representatives of all military units. The Garrison Conference was a valuable aid in determining the sentiment of the different regiments; and the whole Military Revolutionary Committee, in the form in which it was finally organized, was a thinly disguised staff for the guidance of the insurrection.

The Menshevik minority in the Soviet protested against it vigorously but vainly.

The moderate Socialists boycotted the Committee, a circumstance which merely made its work easier. Of its sixty-six original members (the figure fluctuated from time to time) all were Bolsheviki, with the exception of fourteen Left Socialist Revolutionaries and four Anarchists. A Left Socialist Revolutionary, Lazimir, was placed at the head of the Bureau of the Committee, with a view to giving it the appearance of a Soviet, not a purely Party organization. But the moving spirit in it was Trotzky, and his most active associates were men who, for the most part, were closely connected with the Military Organization of the Party: Podvoisky, Antonov-Ovseenko, Sadovsky, Mekhonoshin, Lashevitch. There was not one figure among them of extensive experience in military command: the Revolution was destined to win not by any subtle strokes of military strategy, but by sheer weight of mass support and by the weakness of its opponents.

The Military Revolutionary Committee pursued a shrewd tactical line of moving toward the seizure of power while keeping up an appearance of "defending the conquests of the Revolution" against largely imaginary "counterrevolutionary attacks." It was aided in this by the psychology of the garrison, by the irresolute weakness of the Government and of the commander of the Petrograd Military District, Colonel Polkovnikov, and by the tradition of dual power which had existed since the Revolution and which made the interference of the Soviet in military matters a more or less normal and familiar matter. At times the Government seemed deliberately to shut its eyes to the approaching danger, to hope against all reasonable evidence that no revolt would take place. On October 27 Polkovnikov, in a press interview, declared his belief that the soldiers of the garrison would refrain from taking part in an outbreak, adding: "In any case we are ready." [31] Just at the time when Polkovnikov was making this reassuring statement the Moscow Regional Committee of the Bolshevik Party, after hearing the report of two of its leading members, Lomov and Yakovleva, about the decision of the Central Committee in favor of uprising, decided "to proceed to the organization of armed insurrection for the seizure of power" and to abandon the method of settling local conflicts with authorities of the Provisional Government by means of compromise. On the following day, when Polkovnikov, in two brief orders, spoke of "irresponsible armed outbreaks which are

being prepared on the streets of Petrograd" and asserted that he would employ "most extreme measures" against any breaches of order, it was already known that the workers of the nearby Sestroretzk arms factory had delivered five thousand rifles on an order signed by Trotzky, while ominous reports of the general swing toward Bolshevism poured in from all parts of the country.

In Kazan, the old Tartar capital on the Volga, the soldiers of the garrison had voted almost unanimously for a Soviet regime. In Baku, the large oil centre of the Caucasus, a meeting of the Soviet and of labor and army organizations voted, 238 to 55, for non-confidence in the Provisional Government and for the transfer of power to the Soviets. In Nikolaev, a town in South Ukraina, the Bolsheviki obtained thirteen seats out of fifteen in the reëlected Soviet Executive Committee. Even in the Kuban, with its Cossack population, where the local Cossack Government in Ekaterinodar had declared itself independent, in an effort to cut loose from the sinking ship at Petrograd, a Soviet Congress was held in Armavir and passed the usual Bolshevik resolutions. These are only a few of many indications that, in contrast to July, the swing toward Bolshevik slogans and action was nationwide and not confined to the capital.

The efforts of General Cheremisov, Commander of the Northern Front, acting in agreement with Kerensky, to bring about a transfer of some troops from Petrograd to the front played into the hands of the Military Revolutionary Committee. A conference of the regimental committees of the garrison, meeting in Smolny on the 28th, decided that not one unit should leave without the assent of the Petrograd Soviet. Cheremisov endeavored to take advantage of the sentiment of some of the soldiers at the front, who felt that the Petrograd garrison should have its share of the hardships of the trenches; and on October 30, at his invitation, a delegation of the Petrograd Soviet arrived in Pskov to discuss the question. No decision was reached; the Soviet delegates could be certain that resistance to Cheremisov's demand would assure them the hearty loyalty of the garrison. There was undoubtedly a political element in this demand for the transfer; the morale of the Petrograd troops was such that they would have weakened the front instead of strengthening it; and a telegram from Cheremisov to Kerensky and to the Chief of Staff, General Dukhonin, significantly observes: "The initiative for despatching the troops of the Petrograd garrison proceeded from you, not from me." [32]

It is not altogether easy to say at what moment the preparatory activity of the Military Revolutionary Committee passed into open revolt. But a big step in this direction was certainly taken on November 3. On this day the delegates of the regimental committees, after listening to a redhot speech by Trotzky, decided "to promise the Military Revolutionary Committee full support in all its steps," simultaneously passing another resolution to the effect that "the All-Russian Congress of Soviets must take power into its hands and guaranties the people peace, land and bread."

There were a few military units in Petrograd which could still be regarded as doubtful or hostile: the officers' training-schools, the three Cossack regiments, a force of cyclists in the Petropavlovsk Fortress, the Semyenov Regiment, which had put down the Moscow uprising in 1905. But, feeling itself supported by the vast majority of the large garrison, the Military Revolutionary Committee on the 21st felt strong enough to take the decisive measure of sending its own commissars to all the military units, pushing out the Government commissars and thereby assuming control of the armed forces of the capital.

This was too much even for Colonel Polkovnikov, anxious as he certainly was to avoid an armed clash. When three members of the Military Revolutionary Committee, Lazimir, Sadovsky and Mekhonoshin, called on him on the evening of the 21st and told him that they were appointed as commissars to supervise the Staff and that his orders would not be valid without the counter-signature of at least one of them, Polkovnikov replied that he did not recognize their authority and had no need of guardianship. In response to Mekhonoshin's suggestion [33] that his orders might be badly obeyed if he took this attitude Polkovnikov observed that the garrison was in his hands. After this, as Mekhonoshin says in his memoirs, "there was nothing to do but to return to Smolny and take corresponding measures."

One of these measures was the issue, on November 4, of a proclamation on behalf of the Military Revolutionary Committee which was little short of a declaration of war on the Provisional Government and on the Staff, which it accused of "having broken with the revolutionary garrison and with the Petrograd Soviet" and of "becoming a direct tool of counterrevolutionary forces" and added:

"The Military Revolutionary Committee repudiates any responsibility for the actions of the Staff of the Petrograd Military

District . . . Soldiers of Petrograd. The defense of revolutionary order against counterrevolutionary attacks rests on you under the guidance of the Military Revolutionary Committee. No orders to the garrison which are not signed by the Military Revolutionary Committee are valid."

This last sentence contained a challenge which even the feeble Provisional Government could not ignore and may be regarded as the first shot in the decisive struggle for power.

November 4 was observed as "the Day of the Petrograd Soviet." There was a tremendous outflow of the workers and soldiers and of the poorer classes generally to meetings which were organized all over the city. Originally the Cossack soldiers had proposed to hold a religious demonstration, a Procession of the Cross, on the same day; but this was called off, apparently at the desire of Polkovnikov, who was still eager to avoid anything that might precipitate street fighting.

The purpose of the Day of the Petrograd Soviet is authoritatively defined by Trotzky [34] as follows:

"The plan of the Military Revolutionary Committee was to carry out a gigantic review without clashes, without employing weapons, even without showing them. They wanted to show the masses their own numbers, their strength, their resolution. They wanted with unanimous numbers to compel the enemy to hide, to keep out of sight, to stay indoors. By exposing the impotence of the bourgeoisie beside their own masses they wanted to erase from the consciousness of the workers and soldiers the last hindering recollections of the July Days—to bring it about that having seen themselves the masses should say: Nothing and nobody can any longer oppose us."

As a final stimulant to the morale of the classes which sympathized with the impending upheaval the Day of the Petrograd Soviet, according to the testimony of a number of eyewitnesses, was eminently successful. Crowd passion reached an especially high pitch in the huge building of the People's Home. Here was the lure of Trotzky's magnetic, infectious eloquence:

"The Soviet regime will give everything that is in the country to the poor and to the people in the trenches. You, boorzhui,[35] have two coats—hand over one to the soldier who is cold in the trenches. You have warm boots? Sit at home; the worker needs your boots."

"Who will stand for the cause of the workers and peasants to

the last drop of blood?" Trotzky concluded; and the throng of thousands, as if hypnotized, all raised their hands. And Trotzky drove home his climactic exhortation:

"Let this voting of yours be your vow, with all your strength, at any sacrifice, to support the Soviet, which has taken on itself the great task of bringing the victory of the Revolution to the end, and of giving land, bread and peace." [36]

It was in this atmosphere of tense emotional fanaticism that the masses of "Red Peter" prepared for the plunge into the unknown venture of the Soviet regime, a regime that would indeed demand of them more sacrifices, perhaps, than Trotzky had even dreamed of when he summoned up his last reserves of eloquence to drive forward the revolutionary cause.

NOTES

[1] N. Sukhanov, "Reminiscences of the Revolution," Vol. VII, pp. 28ff.

[2] "The Revolution of 1917: Chronicle of Events," Vol. IV, p. 269.

[3] P. N. Milyukov, "History of the Second Russian Revolution," Vol. I, Part III, p. 80.

[4] *Novaya Zhizn* (New Life), for September 29 (October 11).

[5] The total number of delegates eligible to sit in the Conference was 1,775.

[6] Milyukov, *op. cit.*, p. 47.

[7] *Ibid.*, p. 75.

[8] Sukhanov, *op. cit.*, Vol. VI, p. 252.

[9] While the moderate Socialist parties were anxious to make the Government responsible to the Council, it remained merely a consultative body and the Government was regarded as independent in its decisions.

[10] See "The Revolution of 1917: Chronicle of Events," Vol. IV, pp. 235, 236, for the full text of Skobelev's instructions.

[11] *Ibid.*, Vol. IV, pp. 233–234.

[12] Sukhanov, *op. cit.*, Vol. VII, pp. 11ff.

[13] L. Trotzky, "The History of the Russian Revolution," Vol. III, p. 65.

[14] Antonov-Ovseenko, "In the Year '17," p. 245.

[15] V. I. Lenin, "Collected Works," Vol. XIV, Part II, p. 140.

[16] Petrograd and Moscow were often referred to as "the two capitals."

[17] "Protocols of the Central Committee of the Russian Social Democratic Labor Party," p. 65.

[18] Trotzky, *op. cit.*, pp. 136, 137.

[19] "Protocols of the Central Committee . . . ," pp. 99ff.

[20] "Zinoviev and Kamenev in 1917," pp. 35–44.

[21] "Protocols of the Central Committee . . . ," pp. 117ff.

[22] Lenin, "Collected Works," Vol. XIV, Part II, pp. 271–288.

[23] Scheidemann and Renaudel were leaders respectively of the nationalist wings of the German and French Socialist parties.

[24] The Nevsky Prospect was the main boulevard of Petrograd.

[25] John Reed, "Ten Days That Shook the World," pp. 40, 41.

[25a] Kerensky replied that he would try to prevent a false interpretation from being placed on the note, spoke of Russia's sacrifices, declared the Allies were ill advised in hesitating to send war material and concluded: "Russia is still a great power." The Russian Embassy in London was instructed to present a formal note of protest. See Sir George Buchanan, "My Mission to Russia and Other Diplomatic Memories," Vol. II, p. 193.

[26] "Foreign Relations of the United States: Russia: 1918," Vol. I, pp. 221, 222.

[27] "Protocols of the Central Committee," p. 121.

[28] Sukhanov, *op. cit.*, Vol. VII, pp. 45, 46.

[29] Milyukov, *op. cit.*, p. 78.

[30] See V. Nabokov's article, "The Provisional Government," in the magazine, *Archive of the Russian Revolution,* Vol. I, p. 36.

[31] "The Revolution of 1917: Chronicle of Events," Vol. V, p. 89.

[32] See the newspaper *Army and Fleet of Workers' and Peasants' Russia,* No. 18.

[33] *Proletarian Revolution,* No. 10, p. 87.

[34] Trotzky, *op. cit.*, Vol. III, p. 116.

[35] "Boorzhui" was a contemptuous term for anyone suspected of belonging to the well-to-do classes, very generally used in Russia in 1917. It was a corruption of the French "bourgeois."

[36] Sukhanov, *op. cit.*, Vol. VII, pp. 91, 92.

CHAPTER XIV

THE BOLSHEVIKI TAKE POWER

A VERY important strategic point in Petrograd was the Fortress of Peter and Paul, located on an island in the Neva. Its guns commanded the Winter Palace and its arsenal was a valuable prize for either side in a struggle for power. Garrisoned by a unit of cyclists which had been brought into Petrograd when the July disturbances were being repressed and by artillerists, the Fortress had been slow in coming over to the side of the Military Revolutionary Committee.

On November 5, when the breach with the Staff was an accomplished fact and the hour of decisive conflict was not far away, there was heated discussion among the leaders of the uprising as to how to secure possession of the Fortress. The impetuous Antonov wanted to take a reliable force of soldiers and occupy the Fortress, employing force if necessary. But Trotzky preferred to resort to more peaceful methods. Going over to the Fortress in the afternoon, he found one of the familiar soldiers' meetings in progress and took the first opportunity to address it. His words were as effective as bullets; the soldiers, who had been wavering anyway, came over to the side of the insurrection; and one of the Provisional Government's main strongholds had fallen without a struggle.

On the same day the Staff of the Petrograd Military District, painfully conscious of its own impotence, endeavored to reopen negotiations with the Military Revolutionary Committee. It agreed to accept the control which Colonel Polkovnikov had originally rejected, on condition that the Military Revolutionary Committee should annul its order characterizing the Staff as counterrevolutionary. The representatives of the Military Revolutionary Committee to whom this proposal was made withdrew without giving any definite answer.[1] As a conspirative stratagem, the Military Revolutionary Committee announced that "in principle" it accepted the proposal of the Staff. Actually it was intent only on putting the finishing touches to the plan of uprising.

The capture of the arsenal attached to the Fortress of Peter and Paul made it possible to furnish a liberal supply of guns to the Red

Guards, who, with the less numerous sailors, constituted the more active part of the forces of insurrection. The Red Guards were factory workers, who had been drilling and training with special vigor after the defeat of Kornilov. According to the most reliable sources,[2] about twenty thousand Red Guards were available for service on the eve of the uprising.

Forces of the Red Guard were organized at almost every factory, the smallest unit consisting of thirteen men, while the battalion, in which a number of these smaller units were included, consisted of five or six hundred. Commanders were elected. The Red Guard was at the disposal of the Petrograd Soviet and described its purposes and constitution in the following terms: [3]

"The workers' Red Guard is an organization of the armed forces of the proletariat for struggle with counterrevolution and defense of the conquests of the proletariat.

"The workers' Red Guard consists of workers who are recommended by Socialist parties, factory committees and trade-unions."

The Red Guard endeavored to organize its technical and hospital branches; working women offered their services as nurses. Judged by conventional military standards, the Red Guard was a very crude and amateurish organization, which could not have stood up against a much smaller number of trained soldiers. But it was effective enough as a force for the achievement of the Bolshevik Revolution because it had only the feeblest opposition to encounter. Almost all the units of the Petrograd garrison were favorable or at least neutral in their attitude toward the projected *coup*. And the conservative classes had created no volunteer organizations of their own to pit against the armed proletarians of the Viborg and other factory regions. The junkers, or military cadets, represented practically the only armed force on which the Government could place any reliance; and they were decidedly inferior to the Red Guards, both in numbers and in morale.

Smolny on the night of the 5th was a beehive of activity. Among the throngs of Soviet delegates, representatives of the Red Guard, couriers who were running in with news of the latest developments in the factories and the barracks one could see the leaders of the impending uprising: "Podvoisky, the thin, bearded civilian . . . Antonov, unshaven, his collar filthy, drunk with loss of sleep; Krilenko, the squat, wide-faced soldier, always smiling, with his violent gestures and tumbling speech; and Dibenko, the giant bearded sailor with the placid face." [4]

The Government had decided that it was time to put up some kind of fight for continued existence. A Cabinet meeting on the night of the 5th decided to close the Bolshevik newspapers *Workers' Road* and *Soldier* for instigation to uprising, to arrest immediately all those Bolsheviki who had taken part in the July disturbances and, after being released, had again taken part in anti-Government agitation, to initiate criminal proceedings against the members of the Military Revolutionary Committee. At the same time it was decided to bring up military units which were regarded as reliable from the outskirts of Petrograd: junkers from Oranienbaum, shock troops from Tsarskoe Syelo, artillery from Pavlovsk.

On the morning of the 6th the Provisional Government attempted to carry out some of its decisions and to take further military precautions. A Government commissar, with a detachment of junkers, appeared in the printing-shop of the Bolshevik newspapers at 5.30 A.M., presented the order for their closing, broke up the type and confiscated 8,000 copies of the newspapers. On the same morning the cruiser *Aurora,* which was stationed in the river Neva in uncomfortable proximity to the Winter Palace, was ordered to put out to sea on a training-cruise.

A women's battalion appeared at the Winter Palace and took its place with the junkers who, along with a few Cossacks, were the main defenders of this headquarters of the Government. Detachments of junkers were posted in Government institutions, at the stations and at the bridges; and the latter were raised in an effort to isolate the workers' quarters across the Neva from the central part of the city. The telephones in Smolny Institute were disconnected.

The Military Revolutionary Committee was not slow to strike back. It bestowed on the soldiers of the Lithuanian Regiment and of the Sixth Reserve Sappers' Battalion "the honorable duty of guarding revolutionary printing-shops against counterrevolutionary attacks" and by eleven in the morning the newspapers were again able to appear. The order to the *Aurora* to put to sea was promptly countermanded by the Military Revolutionary Committee, and the cruiser, the crew of which was entirely in sympathy with the uprising, helped to drive away the junkers who were posted at the Nikolaevsky Bridge and on the following day made its contribution to the capture of the Winter Palace.

While the Government was being worsted in these minor but significant first tests of strength with the Military Revolutionary

Committee, Kerensky rushed off to seek support from the Council of the Republic. He described the activity of the Military Revolutionary Committee, spoke of the tolerance of the Government, and demanded that the country should support him in decisive measures. With the lawyer's instinct that never left him during his tenure of office he endeavored to make out a case of treason against Lenin by citing excerpts from one of the latter's appeals to insurrection which had appeared in *Workers' Road*. "So," Kerensky continued, "I must define the condition of a part of the population of the city of Petrograd as a condition of insurrection."

As Kerensky was speaking a member of his Cabinet, Konovalov, handed him the latest order of the Military Revolutionary Committee, which was being circulated among the troops of the garrison and which read as follows:

"Danger threatens the Petrograd Soviet. During the night counterrevolutionary plotters attempted to call up junkers and shock battalions from the suburbs. The newspapers *Soldier* and *Worker's Road* have been closed.

"We order you to put the regiment into a state of military preparedness and to await new orders. Any delay or non-execution of the order will be regarded as treason to the Revolution.

For the President, Antonov
Secretary, Podvoisky

Kerensky characterized this as "an attempt to arouse the mob against the existing order and to open the Russian front before the serried regiments of the iron fist of Wilhelm." Declaring that the Government intended to put down the uprising with decisive measures, Kerensky demanded in conclusion that "the Provisional Government should receive from you to-day a reply as to whether it can fulfill its duty with confidence in your support."

After a long intermission, during which the various parties and groups discussed their attitude, the Council reassembled. The last ballot in this stillborn institution was a victory for its left wing. By a vote of 113 to 102, with 26 abstentions, the Council adopted a resolution offered by the left-wing Menshevik, Martov, which was very far from being the expression of unconditional confidence that Kerensky had desired. The Cadet and Cossack delegates voted against Martov's resolution; the right-wing Socialists abstained. Martov's resolution severely censured the impending armed outbreak, predicting it would lead to the break-up of the Constituent Assembly and the destruction of the Revolution. But it spoke out

for "an immediate decree transferring the land to the administration of the land committees and a decisive move in foreign policy, with a proposal to the Allies to proclaim conditions of peace and begin peace negotiations." Finally the resolution proposed that a committee of public safety should be set up in Petrograd, consisting of representatives of the municipal council and of the organizations of the revolutionary democracy, which should act in contact with the Provisional Government.[5]

So the Council of the Republic placed itself on record as believing that the only way to defeat the Bolsheviki was to take over two thirds of their programme,—the parts relating to land and peace. So strong was the feeling on this score that the Menshevik, Dan, and the Socialist Revolutionary, Gotz, taking with them the unwilling President of the Council, Avksentiev, a Socialist Revolutionary of the right wing, who did not sympathize with the resolution, went to Kerensky and urged on him the necessity of immediately placarding the streets of Petrograd and sending telegrams throughout the country to the effect that the Provisional Government stood for peace, land and a speedy convocation of the Constituent Assembly. Kerensky, who was in a state of extreme nervous exhaustion, was highly irritated at the phrasing of the resolution and at first declared that the Government would resign the next day.[6] This threat was apparently allowed to drop; but the Premier definitely rejected the appeal of Dan and Gotz, asserting that the Government required no outside advice, and would cope with the uprising itself. The Provisional Government, on the eve of its last agony, thus experienced a political breach with the parties, the Mensheviki and the Socialist Revolutionaries, which had hitherto given it fairly consistent, if sometimes grudging support.

An authoritative session of the Central Committee of the Bolshevik Party was held on November 6, with a view to working out the last details of the uprising.[7] Lenin was not present; eleven members of the Central Committee took part in the conference. Zinoviev was also absent; but Kamenev, despite his opposition to the uprising, was present and took an active part in the discussion; at his suggestion it was decided that no member of the Central Committee on this day should leave Smolny without the special permission of the Central Committee.

Various members of the Central Committee were assigned to special functions during the uprising: Bubnov was to establish con-

Painting by V. V. Khvosmenko

Lenin at the Smolny Institute

Painting by Grabar

Lenin giving military orders by direct wire

nection with the railroad workers, Dzerzhinsky with the postal and telegraph workers, Milyutin, an economist, was to organize food supply. Sverdlov, the hardworking, unobtrusive, indispensable future President of the Soviet Executive Committee, was to keep his eye on the Provisional Government and its orders. One of the two Moscow members of the Central Committee present, Lomov and Nogin, was to be despatched immediately to Moscow, so that revolutionary activity in the two main cities would be coördinated. At Trotzky's suggestion it was decided to establish a reserve base in the Fortress of Peter and Paul, in the event that the Government forces should compel the evacuation of Smolny.

The purely military leadership of the uprising was in the hands of a triumvirate, Antonov, Podvoisky and Chudnovsky. It was originally planned to launch an attack on the Winter Palace on the night of the 6th with the combined forces of a detachment of Kronstadt sailors and the Red Guard of the Viborg District, supported by the *Aurora* and by some torpedo-boats which were expected to enter the Neva. There was an effort to assign to the more passive and lethargic regiments of the garrison such light and defensive tasks as keeping watch on the junker schools and on the barracks of the Cossack regiments, while the sailor and Red Guard units, the morale of which was rated more highly, were to represent the spearhead of the attack at the Winter Palace, where the stiffest resistance was likely to be encountered.

The uprising began earlier and ended later than had been anticipated. The first operation, entirely bloodless, like almost all the incidents which attended the seizure of power in Petrograd, was the forcible reopening of the closed Bolshevik newspapers. The attack on the Winter Palace, on the other hand, occurred much later than the scheduled time, because the Kronstadt sailors arrived many hours after they had been expected.

A last barrage of words preceded the clash of arms. Trotzky, addressing the Petrograd Soviet on the night of the 6th boasted of the first victories of the Military Revolutionary Committee in forcing the republication of the Bolshevik newspapers and keeping the *Aurora* in the Neva, and characterized the Provisional Government as "a semi-government that awaits a sweep of the broom of history, in order to clear the way for a real Government of the revolutionary people. If the Government tries to exploit the twenty-four or forty-eight hours which remain at its disposition, in order to plunge a knife into the back of the Revolution, then we say that

the vanguard of the Revolution will answer blow with blow and iron with steel." [8]

After midnight the Vtsik, with its majority of moderates, held a meeting in which a considerable number of delegates to the Congress of Soviets took part. The Menshevik Dan, in the crushed, shapeless uniform of a military doctor, delivered a speech which might be considered the swansong of the moderate socialism which he represented, which was being swept out of power and influence by the impatient insurgent masses. "Counterrevolution," Dan asserted, with singular blindness to the realities of the immediate moment, "was never so strong as at the present moment. . . . The Black Hundred press enjoys more success in the factories and barracks than the Socialist press." Dan predicted that the provinces would cut off the bread supply of the capital and that any government organized by the Bolsheviki would be overthrown by popular discontent. Dan's views were those of the majority of the members of the Vtsik, but they found scant sympathy among the largely Bolshevik Soviet delegates; and when he asserted that "only over the corpse of the Vtsik will the bayonets of the hostile sides clash" there was a disrespectful interpolation: "That corpse has been dead for a long time." Trotzky was on his feet immediately after Dan had finished, declaring that the policy of the Mensheviki and Socialist Revolutionaries had led to their political bankruptcy and calling on the Soviet delegates for resolute action: "If you do not waver, there will be no civil war, because our enemies will immediately capitulate, and you will occupy the place which belongs to you of right,—the place of masters of the Russian land."

As John Reed was leaving this meeting he met Zorin, one of the fairly large number of Bolsheviki who had returned to Russia after a period of immigrant life in America, with a rifle slung over his shoulder.[9]

"We're moving," Zorin said. "We've pinched the Assistant Minister of Justice and the Minister of Religions. They're down cellar now. One regiment is on the march to capture the Telephone Exchange, another the Telegraph Agency, another the State Bank. The Red Guard is out . . ."

Indeed during the night of the 6th and the early morning of the 7th the insurrection had made decisive progress. Two of the main railroad stations, the Nikolai and the Baltic, were occupied about 2 A.M. At 3.30 the *Aurora* cast anchor near the Nikolai Bridge and put out a landing party of sailors, who chased away the

junkers who had been guarding the bridge. At daybreak some torpedo-boats from Helsingfors entered the Neva. At six o'clock a squad of forty soldiers, acting under the orders of the Military Revolutionary Committee, took over the State Bank; at seven a detachment of the Keksholm Regiment occupied the central telephone station and disconnected the telephones of the Winter Palace and the Staff. About the same time a Bolshevik patrol appeared at the Palace Bridge, in close proximity to the headquarters of the Government.

The most striking feature of the Bolshevik overturn in Petrograd was its relative bloodlessness. Both the March Revolution and the July disturbances cost far more lives. At first sight it seems amazing that the decisive act, the seizure of power in the capital, in a social upheaval that was to bring ruin and suffering to some classes of the population and that was subsequently to lead to a civil war of great bitterness and ferocity on both sides should have been accomplished with so little resistance. There was a noteworthy absence of disorderly rioting and looting; theatres and moving-picture houses remained open as usual. The discipline and the lack of bloodshed on November 7 were, of course, a result of several causes: the careful preliminary work of the Military Revolutionary Committee in getting a firm grip on the garrison, the overwhelming superiority of forces at the disposal of the insurgents, the confusion and low morale in the camp of the Government's adherents.

The hours of Kerensky's last night as Premier in the Winter Palace, were, as he tells us himself,[10] long and painful. They were largely spent in vain efforts to conjure up non-existent forces that would defend the Provisional Government. As the futility of these attempts became increasingly clear a sense of agonizing helplessness seems to have grown in the Premier's mind. Immediately after his unsatisfactory interview with the leaders of the left wing of the Council of the Republic, Gotz and Dan, Kerensky received a delegation from the representatives of the three Don Cossack regiments which were quartered in the capital. The delegates asked Kerensky for assurances that this time Cossack blood would not be shed in vain and that the rebels would be decisively smashed, and, after Kerensky had tried to paint his conduct during the July Days as that of a strong ruler, they assured him that their regiments would go into action. Apparently, however, the regiments thought otherwise; and all the aid that came from them was a series of telephone messages to the effect that they "were getting ready to saddle their horses."

The Cossacks were discouraged by the evident lack of infantry support; and the prevalent mood of disgust with the War and the Provisional Government had affected even these traditional upholders of law and order to the point where, while unwilling to fight on the side of the Bolsheviki, they were also disinclined to take up arms against them.

Efforts to call Socialist Revolutionary Party forces to the rescue of the Government were also unavailing; the number of Socialist Revolutionaries who were willing to fight for Kerensky at this time would scarcely have made a corporal's guard. While Kerensky rushed back and forth between disconsolate talks with his Ministers in the Winter Palace and equally disheartening conferences with the officers in the Staff of the District, which was located very near the Winter Palace, on the opposite side of the huge Palace Square, the news about the progress of the uprising was becoming more and more alarming.

About ten in the morning Kerensky decided that his only hope was to make his way to the front and return at the head of reinforcements. One of his adjutants requisitioned a car which belonged to Secretary Whitehouse, of the American Embassy; and Kerensky made off in this car, which carried the American flag and, aided by this disguise, slipped through the numerous Bolshevik patrols which were already active in the city.[11]

After Kerensky's departure Konovalov became Acting Premier, and another Cadet member of the Cabinet, Kishkin, was appointed commissar for the restoration of order in Petrograd. Kishkin promptly dismissed Colonel Polkovnikov, on the ground of incompetence and irresolution, and appointed as military commander the Chief of Staff of the District, General Bagratuni. There was, of course, no possibility of "restoring order in Petrograd" with the scanty forces (between 1,000 and 2,000 soldiers) at the disposal of Konovalov and Kishkin; there was only the faint hope of holding out in the Palace until Kerensky should return with troops from the front. Had the Military Revolutionary Committee risked a bold push, the Palace might have been taken early in the day: for its heterogeneous defenders, the Women's Battalion, junkers from several training schools, a few War invalids and Cossacks, were halfhearted and very uncertain of themselves. But the forces of the Revolution were also in ignorance of their own strength, and of the weakness of their adversaries; and the decisive attack on the Palace was put off until evening.

At ten in the morning the Military Revolutionary Committee issued the following triumphant message:

"To the Citizens of Russia

"The Provisional Government is overthrown. State power has passed into the hands of the organ of the Petrograd Soviet of Workers' and Soldiers' Deputies—the Military Revolutionary Committee, which stands at the head of the Petrograd proletariat and garrison.

"The cause for which the people fought—immediate proposal of a democratic peace, abolition of landlords' property rights in land, workers' control over production, the creation of a Soviet Government—this cause is assured.

"Long live the Revolution of the workers, soldiers and peasants."

An interesting description of the main features of the Bolshevik *coup* by an opponent is to be found in a telegram which Colonel Polkovnikov despatched to the Commander-in-chief, General Dukhonin, on the night of the 6th, when the uprising was already in full progress:

"I report that the situation in Petrograd is threatening. There are no street outbreaks or disorders, but a systematic seizure of institutions and stations and arrests are going on. No orders are carried out. The junkers give up their posts without resistance. The Cossacks, notwithstanding a number of orders, have not come out of their barracks up to this time. Recognizing all my responsibility before the country, I report that the Provisional Government is in danger of losing its power, and there are no guaranties that there will not be attempts to seize the Provisional Government."

Polkovnikov was more successful in foreseeing than in averting the doom of the Provisional Government.

The only effort to take the offensive against the forces of the Military Revolutionary Committee was made at the initiative of Stankevitch, whom Kerensky had appointed commissar attached to the General Staff. He took a company of junkers from an engineering school and marched off with the idea of protecting the Marinsky Palace, where the Council of the Republic was in session. Hearing that armored cars were in the neighborhood of this Palace, Stankevitch changed his objective and endeavored to retake the central telephone station. Nothing came of this, however, except a wordy exchange with the Bolshevik soldiers in the telephone station, who refused to evacuate it. A few stray shots on the street, a passing armored car shook the dubious morale of the junkers; and Stanke-

vitch decided to raise the "siege" of the telephone station and return to the Winter Palace, whence he had come. He and part of the junkers got back safely; but another part of the company was surrounded and disarmed by Red Guards.

"Thus ended the sole attempt at active resistance to the Bolsheviki of which I know," writes Stankevitch.[12] And, if one excepts the subsequent defense of the Winter Palace, this statement seems to be quite correct.

Early in the afternoon the Marinsky Palace was surrounded by troops and the Council of the Republic was ordered to quit the building. Resistance was hopeless; and this pale consultative body dispersed, never to reassemble, after registering a formal protest against "the violence of the irresponsible elements, interrupting the work of the Council with the threat of bayonets." Throughout the afternoon the occupation of the capital, with the exception of a small area around the Winter Palace, went on steadily.

Lenin, who had been secretly living at the apartment of Forfanova, a woman Party member whose residence was conveniently located in the Bolshevik Viborg District, until he moved to Smolny on the 6th, made his first public appearance at a session of the Petrograd Soviet on the afternoon of the 7th. Greeted with loud applause, he began his speech:

"Comrades, the workers' and peasants' revolution, which the Bolsheviki always said must come, has been achieved." Then he spoke of the necessity for breaking up the old state machine and creating a new one, announced the liquidation of the War as one of the immediate problems and declared: "We shall acquire the confidence of the peasants with one decree, which will destroy the landlords' rights of property."

The international significance of the Russian Revolution, which bulked large in Lenin's mind at this time, found reflection in this first public address after months of hiding; he spoke of helping the world workers' movement, "which already begins to develop in Italy, England and Germany," and ended on the note: "Long live the world socialist revolution!"

The crowning military operation of the day, the attempt to capture the Winter Palace, began at 6.30, when two cyclists from the Fortress of Peter and Paul served an ultimatum on the Staff of the Petrograd Military District, demanding that the Palace be surrendered within twenty minutes. In the event of resistance there would be bombardment from the Fortress and from the *Aurora*

and other warships in the Neva. There was a hasty conference between Kishkin and his assistants, Rutenberg and Palchinsky, and the military men in the Staff, General Bagratuni, Quartermaster General Poradelov and others. The question of surrender was also discussed at a meeting of the Ministers in the Winter Palace.

The military men were inclined to emphasize the hopelessness of resistance; but the civilian Ministers decided to disregard the ultimatum and to leave it unanswered. Thereupon Poradelov and Bagratuni resigned their posts, and both fell into the hands of the insurgents, Bagratuni when he walked out of the Palace, Poradelov when the Red Guards, after the lapse of a supplementary ten minutes which had been added to the original period of twenty minutes, occupied the defenseless Staff headquarters with a rush. The problem of taking the Palace remained; there was delay in carrying out the threat of opening up a bombardment, because the gunners of the Fortress, who were not very sympathetic with the *coup* anyway, protested that the cannon were out of repair and that it would be dangerous to have them fired. It cost a good deal of time and running about by Antonov, the tireless member of the Military Revolutionary Committee, and Blagonravov, commandant of the Fortress, before naval gunners were procured to operate the cannon.

The morale of the defenders of the Winter Palace was decidedly shaky; during the day the junkers held meetings, argued, treated the speeches of Ministers who addressed them with scant respect.[13] Part of the garrison, consisting of veteran Ural Cossacks and junkers from an artillery school, slipped away fairly early in the evening. But a number of junkers remained; a plan of defense was worked out by Lieutenant-Colonel Ananiev, whom Kishkin appointed in the place of Bagratuni; piles of wood in the courtyard were thrown up as barricades.

Although the central telephone station was in the hands of the Bolsheviki the Government had the use of two telephones which were unregistered, and was thereby able to keep in touch with the city Duma and with organizations which sympathized with it, while it sent out appeals for help over a direct wire which connected it with the Stavka. One such appeal was sent out at nine in the evening and, after describing the demand for the surrender of the Palace and the Government's decision "to hand over power only to the Constituent Assembly," ended: "Let the country and the people reply to the mad effort of the Bolsheviki to raise an uprising in the rear of the fighting army."

Armored cars were brought up to the Square by the troops of the Military Revolutionary Committee; a close blockade was established. About nine a blank shot was fired from the *Aurora;* this was the signal for lively rifle and machine-gun fire which continued for about an hour. At ten the Women's Battalion essayed a sortie; a rumor had got about that General Alekseev was in the building of the Staff, and the women decided that he must be rescued. The only result of the sortie was that they fell into the hands of the besiegers. Wildly exaggerated stories of wholesale shooting and violation of the captured women subsequently gained circulation; actually there seem to have been a few cases of rape; [14] but there were no killings, and the women were sent back to the camp from which they had come to their luckless mission of defending the Winter Palace.

Like everything that happened on November 7 in Petrograd, the siege of the Winter Palace was conspicuous for its lack of bloodletting. Neither side wished to resort to extreme measures. The artillery bombardment, which began about eleven at night from the guns of Peter and Paul, inflicted little damage; most of the shots went wide of the mark and only a few windows on the river side of the Palace were smashed. The Palace is a huge building, with many entrances and winding passages; and many soldiers and sailors filtered in and tried to overcome the resistance of the junkers, partly by carrying on propaganda among them, partly by disarming them. There were numerous scuffles, again without the use of mortal weapons, in the corridors and picture galleries of the Palace. Late at night a piece of encouraging news reached the hardpressed garrison. A procession of the non-Bolshevik members of the city Duma, along with some other representatives of the Cadet and moderate Socialist parties, had set out to the Winter Palace, determined to save its defenders or to perish with them. But the procession was turned back by an unsympathetic patrol of sailors; more and more of the besiegers began to surge into the Palace. Whereas in the beginning the junkers had usually succeeded in disarming the sailors and Red Guards, now the reverse process set in. Kishkin, hoping to the last, called up another Cadet, Assistant Finance Minister A. G. Khrushov, and pleaded for reinforcements that would enable the Palace to hold out until morning when Kerensky might arrive with troops.[15] "What kind of a Party is it," cried Kishkin, "that cannot send us at least three hundred armed men?"

In this unanswered question was the deathknell of Russian

liberalism, represented by the Cadet Party, just as the deathknell of Russian radicalism was sounded by the failure of the Mensheviki and the Socialist Revolutionaries to oppose the Bolshevik upsurge with anything more effective than resolutions of protest. In Russia there were latent forces that would make the triumphant Bolsheviki in time fight hard for their easily won power. There were officers, there were peasants who would rise in angry disillusionment when the orgy of seizing the estates was succeeded by the era of requisitions. But the weak hold on the masses of the parties, liberal and moderate Socialist, which supported the Provisional Government was never illustrated so clearly as in this almost bloodless capture of the capital by the forces of Lenin.

Kishkin returned from his futile appeal for reinforcements to find the end of the defense at hand. The surging throng of invaders, led by Antonov and Chudnovsky, had reached the inner room of the Palace to which the Ministers had retired when the outer rooms seemed too much exposed to artillery fire. A last line of faithful junkers guarded the door of the room where the Ministers were sitting; but it was decided to surrender without further resistance. A slight figure, with a sharp face, a broad-brimmed hat, such as artists used to wear in Bohemian quarters, and a *pince-nez*, burst into the room and announced: "In the name of the Military Revolutionary Committee I declare you arrested." [16] This was Antonov-Ovseenko.

There were some cries in favor of lynching the Ministers; but Antonov, who more than once showed his ability to restrain mob excesses, quickly formed an improvised guard of twenty-five reliable men; and the arrested Ministers, who included all the members of the Cabinet except Kerensky and the Food Minister, Prokopovitch, were escorted across the Neva to the Fortress of Peter and Paul and consigned to its dungeons, which had held many illustrious state prisoners in Tsarist times. The journey to the Fortress was interrupted by accidental sporadic rifle fire, which caused the Ministers and their guards to lie down together on the bridge; but all the prisoners were brought to the Fortress safely in the end. The Socialist Ministers were soon transferred to the milder status of "house arrest"; the others were released after a comparatively short time. The Revolution had not yet reached its ferocious stage. The losses in the taking of the Winter Palace were negligible: five sailors and one soldier killed and a number slightly wounded among the assailants. [17] Apparently no one perished among the defenders

To the accompaniment of crackling rifle and machine-gun fire, punctuated by the occasional booming of cannon in the neighborhood of the Palace, the Second Congress of Soviets opened late that evening in Smolny. Its make-up was very different from that of the first Congress. John Reed [18] tells of the scornful remark of the girl at the office of the Credentials Committee of the Congress: "These are very different people from the delegates to the first Congress. See how rough and ignorant they look. The Dark People." M. Philips Price, a foreign observer, speaks of the predominance of young men from the Baltic Fleet and from the front at the Congress, most of the peasant delegates being soldiers. "Conspicuous by their absence," says Price, "were the middle-aged intellectuals, the old type of peasant with a long beard and the old Socialist Party leader." [19]

As a representative assembly of the whole country the Soviet Congress was, of course, decidedly imperfect. The hated bourgeoisie had no place there; and the rich grainlands of Southern and Southeastern Russia, where the opposition to Bolshevism would later be strongest, seem to have sent few representatives. But the Congress, with its mass of little known delegates, sent directly from factories and barracks, from trenches and warships, was a good crystallization of the dominant mood of the country at that moment: a fierce determination to get rid of the War and of the Provisional Government which was held responsible for it, to smash the big estate owners and somehow to strike out in the direction of a new social order.

As a result of the confusion which prevailed at the time no very accurate account either of the number of the delegates at the Congress or of their Party membership has been preserved. According to a reliable estimate, however, the Bolsheviki had about 390 delegates out of a total number of 650.[20] The dominant parties at the first Congress of Soviets, the Mensheviki and the Socialist Revolutionaries, had been reduced to a pitiful minority; there were not more than 80 Mensheviki of all shades, including representatives of the Bund, and not more than 60 Socialist Revolutionaries of the Right and Centre. Most of the remaining delegates were Socialist Revolutionaries of the Left, who had now definitely split off from the more moderate wing of the Party and, especially in Petrograd, worked hand in hand with the Bolsheviki, although they wavered occasionally and endeavored, without success, to act as a bridge between the Bolsheviki and the more moderate Socialist parties.

Most of their leaders were people of little note in the revolutionary movement, the most striking personality among them being the passionate, hysterical Maria Spiridonova, who had acquired nation-wide fame by shooting a general who was notorious for his ruthless repression of peasant disturbances.

The Congress opened at 10.45 in the evening under the presidency of Kamenev. The Mensheviki and Right Socialist Revolutionaries refused to accept places in the presidium, which had been elected in proportion to the numerical strength of the parties represented at the Congress. After Martov, leader of the Internationalist, or Left, wing of the Mensheviki, had proposed to open up discussion with all Socialist parties as to the best means of stopping the conflict (a proposal which was accepted without opposition and led to no result) the dissident minority of moderates fired off several verbal guns, as a prelude to walking out of its sessions. Kharash, member of the Committee of the 12th Army, wearing a captain's epaulettes, repudiated the Congress and all its works, and was seconded by Kuchin, representative of the Front Group, who characterized the seizure of power as "a stab in the back of the Army and a crime against the people," whereupon he was interrupted by shouts: "You lie." [21] Then Khinchuk, on behalf of the Mensheviki, and Gendelman, Socialist Revolutionary, announced the decision of these parties to leave the Congress. Several soldier delegates, Peterson of the Lettish Sharpshooters, Ghelshakh, Lukyanov, sprang up to answer Kuchin and Kharash, Lukyanov crying: "Kuchin and Kharash represent the opinion of little groups sitting in the Army and Front Committees. The men in the trenches are eager for the Soviets to take power."

Abramovitch, leader of the Bund, his eyes snapping behind thick glasses, described the present turn of events in Petrograd as a great calamity, announced that the Bund would leave the Congress and urged a decidedly unsympathetic audience to join the procession to the Winter Palace which was being organized by the city Duma.

Trotzky was then on his feet, declaring that what was happening was an uprising, not a conspiracy, and, with a typical contemptuous gesture and bitter phrase, characterized the delegates who were leaving the Congress as "so much refuse that will be swept into the garbage-can of history."

The upshot of all these recriminations was that the Mensheviki and Socialist Revolutionaries, after leaving the Congress, withdrew to the city Duma. After a futile effort to organize a march to the

Winter Palace as a demonstration of protest (a group of three or four hundred people, deputies of the Duma, members of the Menshevik and Socialist Revolutionary parties and prominent public men, did set out, but were turned back by a detachment of Bolshevik sailors) a Committee for the Salvation of the Country and the Revolution was formed. It included representatives of the Petrograd Duma, the old Soviet Executive Committee, the Peasant Soviet Executive Committee, the moderate Socialist parties, the Council of the Republic and the Front Committees. This Committee, for the time being, became the main anti-Bolshevik organized centre; and affiliated Committees were formed in Moscow and in other cities. The old Vtsik hastened to coöperate with the newly formed Committee, sending out a telegram to all Soviets and Army Committees to the effect that "the Vtsik regards the Second Congress of Soviets as not having taken place and regards it as a private conference of the Bolshevik delegates." The telegram characterized all the decisions of the Second Congress as illegal and urged all Soviets and Army organizations to rally around the original Vtsik.

While plans of opposition were being worked out in the city Duma the majority of the delegates to the Soviet Congress continued their session. The Left Socialist Revolutionaries remained in the Congress, although they decided not to participate in the new Government; the Mensheviki-Internationalists flitted back and forth like uneasy ghosts, now leaving the Congress, now returning with a utopian proposal for "Socialist unity." Before the Congress adjourned at six A.M. on the morning of the 8th it had heard several cheering pieces of news. The Winter Palace had fallen. The commissar from nearby Tsarkoe Syelo announced that the garrison was for the Congress and would guard the approaches to Petrograd. A representative of the Third Cyclist Battalion, which Kerensky had summoned from the Southwestern Front for the defense of Petrograd announced, amid a storm of applause, that the cyclists had decided not to support the Provisional Government. Still more important was the news from the Northern Front, the nearest to Petrograd and therefore the most important, from the standpoint of the immediate safety of the new regime. A Military Revolutionary Committee had been set up in Pskov, headquarters of the Front; Commissar Voitinsky, one of Kerensky's chief aides, had resigned.

While the Congress rolled on its course, the master strategist of the victorious uprising, Lenin, remained in the background, saving his strength for the next night, when the decisive decrees on land

and peace would be promulgated, perhaps resting from the "giddiness," which, as he once told Trotzky, the sudden leap to power inspired in him. For a short time Lenin and Trotzky lay side by side on covers and cushions in a little room in Smolny.[22] Lenin had been somewhat apprehensive up to the end that Trotzky, in his desire to adjust the time of the insurrection to the meeting of the Soviet Congress, might let slip the most favorable opportunity. Now he was reassured and he spoke to Trotzky in a tone of special cordiality. "What a splendid picture, the worker with the rifle warming himself at a bonfire next to the soldier. At last the worker has been brought together with the soldier."

Very few people in Petrograd indeed woke up on the morning of the 8th with a consciousness that the most fundamental social upheaval of modern times had taken place. Those non-Bolshevik newspapers which appeared (the Military Revolutionary Committee had stopped several newspapers which were regarded as especially hostile) denounced the usurpation and violence of the Bolsheviki, predicted the failure of their "adventure." A confused war of posters and proclamations set in. The Military Revolutionary Committee continued to function at high speed, sending its commissars everywhere, taking over control of the city police, ordering shops to remain open, threatening state employees who ceased to work with trial before revolutionary courts, issuing appeals to the Cossacks not to move against Petrograd, to the railroad workers to continue operating the trains. The death penalty at the front was abolished; the arrested members of the peasant land committees were ordered freed.

Meanwhile the other side was not inactive. The period of severe dictatorship and repression had not yet come; and, despite the suppression of some newspapers, the anti-Bolshevik organizations exercised a good deal of freedom in agitation. One newspaper, Volya Naroda (People's Will), published an order which Kerensky had issued in Pskov, declaring that "the disorders caused by the insane attempt of the Bolsheviki place the country on the verge of a precipice" and instructing "all chiefs and Commissars, in the name of the safety of the country, to remain at their posts, as I myself retain the post of Supreme Commander, until the Provisional Government of the Republic shall declare its will."

The "Committee for Salvation" put itself forward as the legal heir of the fallen Provisional Government in a proclamation "to the citizens of the Russian Republic" which read in part as follows:

"Preserving the continuity of the sole legal Governmental power, the Committee for the Salvation of the Country and the Revolution . . . takes the initiative in forming a new Provisional Government, which, basing itself on the forces of democracy, will conduct the country to the Constituent Assembly and save it from anarchy and counterrevolution. The Committee for Salvation summons you, citizens, to refuse to recognize the government of violence. Do not obey its orders.

"Rise for the defense of the country and the Revolution.

"Support the Committee for Salvation."

The Committee for Salvation was giving a lead to the general inclination of the white-collar workers in the Government departments to refuse to obey the new masters whom the Revolution had set up. Passive resistance to the commissars who were being installed in the offices became the order of the day. The banks were generally closed and prices in the stock exchange naturally dropped heavily. Some phases of life went on, however, as if nothing had happened: stores and restaurants remained open, streetcars continued to run, theatres went on playing.

The city became a vast sounding-board of rumor and gossip. Kerensky was supposed to be marching on Petrograd with an army from the front. There were vaguer reports of military action on the part of the Don Cossack leader, Kaledin. Tales of atrocities perpetrated against the captured junkers gained circulation; these were refuted, however, by an official investigating commission, headed by the Socialist Revolutionary Mayor Schreider.

Amid all the hurlyburly and confusion the Bolshevik leaders moved forward toward the consolidation of their power by the formation of a new Government and the promulgation of the two basic decrees, on peace and on land, which represented the best means of holding the allegiance of the masses.

The adoption of these decrees and the announcement of the make-up of the new Government took place at the session of the Soviet Congress on the evening of November 8, where Lenin was easily the dominant figure. This is how Lenin appeared to a keen and imaginative observer on the night of the Congress: [23]

"A short, stocky figure, with a big head set down in his shoulders, bald and bulging. Little eyes, a snubbish nose, wide generous mouth, and heavy chin; cleanshaven now, but already beginning to bristle with the wellknown beard of his past and future. Dressed in shabby clothes, his trousers much too long for him."

After a few unimportant preliminary speeches had been made Lenin rose and, after an ovation which lasted for several minutes

died away, proceeded to read a "proclamation to the peoples and governments of all the fighting nations," which proposed an immediate peace without annexations and without indemnities. The proclamation announced the abolition of secret diplomacy and the intention of the new Government to publish all the secret treaties, simultaneously denouncing all the clauses of the latter "which have for their object to procure advantages and privileges for Russian capitalists." The proclamation further proposed a three months' armistice and ended with a special appeal to the workers of England, France and Germany, expressing the hope that "these workers, by decisive, energetic and continued action, will help us to bring to a successful conclusion the cause of peace—and at the same time the cause of the liberation of the exploited working masses from all slavery and exploitation." After a brief discussion, in the course of which Lenin declared that the proclamation must be addressed to the Governments as well as to the peoples and that the Soviet proposals must not be given the form of an ultimatum, because the ignoring of the Governments would delay the conclusion of peace and the putting of the proposals in ultimative form would give an excuse for rejecting them, the proclamation was put to the vote and carried unanimously. One delegate tried to hold up his card as a sign of opposition; but there was such an outburst of indignation that he promptly put it down. Then the "Internationale" rang out: a common enough song in those days, but invested with a special significance after the reading of a proclamation which at least meant the end of the World War for Russia, although it would be rejected with scorn by the Allied Governments and would excite only a muffled and uncertain echo among the masses of the warring countries.

The next question on the order of the day was that of land. Lenin read a short decree abolishing landlord property in land "immediately and without purchase," transferring the administration of privately owned, Church and monastery land to land committees and Soviets of Peasants' Deputies and laying down as the guiding rule for future distribution of the land the principles set forth in the typical *nakaz*, or set of instructions, which the official organ of the Council of Peasants' Deputies had drawn up on the basis of 242 resolutions of local peasant assemblies. This *nakaz* provided for the complete abolition of private property in land, for the confiscation of all land which was privately owned, for the prohibition of the purchase and sale of land and for the use of

land only by persons who actually cultivated it with their own labor, hired labor being forbidden.

The Council of Peasants' Deputies was a body dominated by Socialist Revolutionaries, which bitterly opposed the Bolshevik Revolution. And Lenin's adoption of a peasant programme of agrarian change which was to some extent of Socialist Revolutionary origin was a masterpiece of political flexibility, of which a more stubborn doctrinaire would scarcely have been capable. For Lenin, as a Marxist, did not believe in the desirability or in the practicability of the system of equalitarian small holdings which the *nakaz* aimed to institute. But Lenin as a political leader understood the supreme importance of obtaining the support, or at least the benevolent neutrality, of the peasant majority of the population during the first months of the establishment of the new regime. In response to cries from the floor that the *nakaz* was made up by Socialist Revolutionaries Lenin set forth his position in the following words: [24]

"As a democratic Government, we cannot disregard the decision of the masses, even if we disagree with it. The peasants themselves will learn where the truth is when they apply the law in practise. Life itself is the best teacher; and it will show who is right; let the peasants solve this question from one end and we from the other. It isn't important whether the problem is solved in the spirit of our programme or in the spirit of the Socialist Revolutionary programme. What is important is that the peasants should be firmly assured that there are no more landlords in the villages. Let the peasants decide all questions, let them organize their own life."

This idea of letting the peasants settle their own affairs was scarcely in harmony with many subsequent phases of Bolshevik agrarian policy. But in this initial stage of the Revolution, when no force in the country could have stopped or greatly diverted the stormy course of the agrarian upheaval, Lenin's decision to give the peasants a free rein was a brilliant piece of political insight. It insured the new revolutionary power in the towns against any backfire from the villages, at least for a fair interval of time.

Lenin conceived the idea of the Soviet Land Law while he was living at the apartment of Forfanova, who was herself an agricultural expert by profession. On one occasion he asked for all the available copies of the *Izvestia of the Council of Peasants' Deputies* and studied them very intensively, working over them until late at night. In the course of this study he discovered the *nakaz,* based on the resolutions of 242 peasant gatherings and ex-

claimed: "There is our agreement with the Left Socialist Revolutionaries. We will take this as the basis of a land law and see if the Left Socialist Revolutionaries think of rejecting it." [25]

The other major decision which the Congress adopted before its members dispersed to their homes was the confirmation of the first Council of People's Commissars, as it had been decided to call the Ministers of the revolutionary regime. The Left Socialist Revolutionaries, while they continued to work in the Military Revolutionary Committee and did not leave the Congress, were unwilling to participate in a Government which did not include representatives of other Socialist parties, besides the Bolsheviki. So the first list of People's Commissars consisted entirely of Bolsheviki. It read as follows:

President of the Council—Vladimir Ulianov (Lenin)
Commissar for Internal Affairs—A. I. Rykov
    Agriculture—V. P. Milyutin
    Labor—A. G. Shlyapnikov
    For Military and Naval Affairs,—a committee consisting of V. A. Antonov-Ovseenko, N. V. Krilenko, and P. E. Dibenko.
    Trade and Industry—V. P. Nogin
    People's Education—A. V. Lunacharsky
    Finance—I. I. Skvortsov (Stepanov)
    Foreign Affairs—L. D. Bronstein (Trotzky)
    Justice—G. I. Oppokov (Lomov)
    Food—I. A. Teodorovitch
    Posts and Telegraph—N. P. Avilov (Glebov)
    President for Nationality Affairs—I. V. Djugashvili (Stalin)

The names of Lenin, Trotzky and Lunacharsky were greeted with special applause; the other Commissars were little known, except to a narrow circle of active veteran Bolsheviki. The post of Commissar for Transport was deliberately left open, in the hope of reaching an agreement with the Vikzhel, the Central Executive Committee of the Railroad Workers' Union, which was insistent on the formation of a broad all-Socialist Government, where the moderate parties would be represented. After electing a new Vtsik of 101 members, of whom 62 were Bolsheviki and 29 Left Socialist Revolutionaries, the Congress adjourned.

The new Government was immediately confronted with fighting problems. The success of the Revolution in various parts of the country was uncertain; centres of opposition were looming up in the Cossack territories of the Don and the Kuban and in Kiev, where power had been taken over by the Ukrainian Rada; the Stavka

was hostile; the issue of the struggle in Moscow was still undetermined. Closer at hand was the menace of the return of Kerensky, escorted by General Krasnov and his Cossacks. Out of the first welter of confused rumors about Kerensky's movements facts began to emerge. The former Premier, with Krasnov's Cossacks, had occupied Gatchina on November 9 and Tsarskoe Syelo, a short train ride from the capital, on the 10th.

The new men in charge of the War Ministry, Antonov, Dibenko and Krilenko, set to work energetically but found it difficult, amid the prevalent confusion, to see that the smallest order was actually carried out. There were extremely few troops who wished to fight (the occupation of Tsarskoe Syelo, where there was a garrison of 16,000, by a few hundred Cossacks was a vivid illustration of this) and there was a shortage of artillery. The best guaranty of the safety of Petrograd was the small force at Kerensky's disposal; but this was not known inside the city, and there was still harassing anxiety as to whether units might be shifted from the front. On the 10th there was a big outpouring of workers to dig trenches and set up barbed-wire entanglements on the outskirts of the city, in response to an order from the Military Revolutionary Committee.

On the morning of the 11th Petrograd awoke to sporadic bursts of rifle fire. There had been no incursion of Kerensky's troops into the city; but on the preceding night the junkers, under the leadership of Colonel Polkovnikov and apparently at the instigation of some of the more active members of the Committee for Salvation, had launched an uprising, taking some armored cars in one of the garages, seizing the Central Telephone Station, where they captured Commissar Antonov, who was on a round of inspection and had no idea that an insurrection had broken out. Despite these initial successes the uprising was quickly put down. On the preceding evening a Socialist Revolutionary named Bruderer, who had on his person a detailed plan of the insurrection, had fallen into the hands of a Soviet patrol; [26] and the discovery of the plan made it easy to throw Red Guards and sailors against the junker centres. The fighting was considerably bloodier than on the day of the Revolution; about two hundred were killed and wounded on both sides in the storming of the Vladimir junker school, which put up especially stubborn resistance.[27] Some of the junkers were thrown from the roofs of houses and lynched by the enraged Red forces, although Antonov kept his word to insure the safety of the

junkers who had arrested him in the Telephone Station when they were obliged to surrender.

Meanwhile negotiations had been set on foot for the creation of an all-Socialist Government. This had been the constant desire of the groupings which stood to the left of the parties which had participated in coalition Governments and to the right of the Bolsheviki, such as the Left Socialist Revolutionaries and the Mensheviki-Internationalists. A considerable number of prominent Bolsheviki, especially those who had opposed the idea of a seizure of power through insurrection, wished to see the basis of the Government broadened; and there was substantial popular sympathy with the idea of Socialist unity, as is evident from the resolutions in favor of this idea which were passed by the Petrograd Council of Trade-Unions and by the Viborg District Soviet.[28] The Vikzhel threatened to call a general railroad strike if fighting were not stopped in Petrograd and Moscow by the night of November 11 and added its pressure to the forces which were working for an all-inclusive Socialist Government.

At the initiative of the Vikzhel a conference of representatives of all the Socialist parties, of the Committee for Salvation and of various trade-unions opened on November 11, with a view to discussing means for the formation of a new government which would include representatives of the parties which had left the Congress of Soviets. These negotiations dragged on for some time, but led to no positive result. In the beginning the moderate Socialists were inclined to put their demands far too high, some of them demanding the dissolution of the Military Revolutionary Committee and the elimination of Lenin and Trotzky from any future Government. And after the victory of the Bolsheviki in Moscow and the definite dissolution of the tiny army with which Kerensky endeavored to retake Petrograd, the balance of power swung decisively to the Bolshevik side and Lenin, who was always on principle against concessions to the moderate Socialists, was able to crush the opposition of the more conciliatory members of his Party.

An element of quixotic futility entered into Kerensky's last act on the Russian political stage: his effort to return to power with the aid of troops from the front. After narrowly escaping arrest by the local Bolsheviki in Gatchina, Kerensky arrived in the ancient Russian town of Pskov, headquarters of the Northern Front, on the evening of the 7th. General Cheremisov, Commander of this Front, had already decided to quit the sinking ship of the Provi-

sional Government and had countermanded Kerensky's orders about sending troops to Petrograd. He received the fugitive Premier coldly and refused to support him.

But, as it happened, General P. N. Krasnov, Commander of the Third Cavalry Corps, which had participated in Kornilov's luckless adventure, was also in Pskov. He called on Voitinsky, Commissar of the Front, who greeted him with the enthusiastic ejaculation "God has sent you here just to-day" [29] and brought him in touch with Kerensky, who assured him very overoptimistically that "the whole Army stands for me against these Bolshevik scoundrels" and urged him to launch a drive against Petrograd. A typical oldfashioned officer of monarchist views and a sympathizer with Kornilov, Krasnov was certainly no admirer of Kerensky. But he considered it a matter of duty to strike a blow against the Bolsheviki and he agreed to set out with his 700 Cossacks against Petrograd, in the hope that reinforcements, especially infantry, would join him later. He felt nothing but ironical amusement when Kerensky, in his habitual grandiloquent style, said to him: "General, I appoint you commander of the army marching on Petrograd. I congratulate you, General."

Krasnov's corps was scattered about in a number of towns; and he was only able to entrain a part of it, some 700 men in all, at the town of Ostrov. Passing through Pskov by train at full speed in order to avoid a possible clash with the hostile soldiers who filled the station, the little force proceeded to Gatchina and occupied it without resistance on the morning of the 9th. If Krasnov encountered no resistance he also found no recruits, with the exception of a few officers of the aviation school, who repaired and operated a captured armored car and supplied two airplanes which dropped proclamations over Petrograd. On the following day, early in the morning, Krasnov advanced on Tsarskoe Syelo. Here there was a little shooting; but two shells from Krasnov's light artillery were sufficient to send the motley Red Guard force which had been sent out from Petrograd scurrying in flight. The regular garrison of 16,000 soldiers maintained sullen neutrality.

The occupation of places so close to Petrograd by a small force of relatively disciplined troops in the face of vastly superior forces which were nominally on the side of the Bolsheviki showed that the military strength of the new regime was still negligible. With a few regiments of reliable troops Krasnov could probably have entered Petrograd. But the significant fact of the moment was

that no such regiments made their appearance. Prominent political leaders, the restless ex-Terrorist and former War Minister Savinkov, the Socialist Revolutionary Gotz, Stankevitch and Voitinsky turned up at the headquarters of Kerensky and Krasnov; but there were no fresh troops. The Cossacks, whose morale had already been lowered by the Kornilov fiasco, began to murmur, to declare that they could go no further without infantry.

On the 11th, when the junker uprising occurred in Petrograd, Krasnov made no further movement. On the 12th, as a despairing last venture, he sent his Cossacks into action against the considerable Red forces which were massed on the Pulkovo heights, just outside the city limits. This time real resistance was shown; the sailors on the Bolshevik side displayed will and capacity to fight; the advance of the Cossacks was hindered by a marsh. Large Red forces began to appear on the flanks of Krasnov's diminutive force; the ammunition of the Cossacks ran low; the Tsarskoe Syelo garrison assumed an increasingly aggressive attitude, threatening to attack the Cossacks in the rear if they did not cease fighting. Faced with this combination of adverse circumstances, Krasnov gave the order to fall back on Gatchina. A retreat, in the growing atmosphere of lack of confidence among the Cossacks, was equivalent to the failure of the whole enterprise.

Trotzky is inclined to attribute much of the credit for the successful stand of the Red troops at Pulkovo to Colonel Walden, an old colonel who had often been wounded in battle, who assumed command and directed the flanking operations. "It couldn't have been that he sympathized with us," writes Trotzky, "because he understood nothing. But apparently he hated Kerensky so strongly that this inspired him with temporary sympathy for us." [30] The appointment of Captain Muraviev, a former organizer of shock units who was now swimming with the revolutionary tide, as commander of the heterogeneous Red troop units also helped to bring order into the defense of the capital. The main cause of Kerensky's defeat, of course, was the failure of any reinforcements to arrive from the front.

On the 14th the political and military leaders of the expedition discussed the situation. It was decided to propose an armistice, with the establishment of a demarcation line between the contending forces. But it was already late for such measures. Sailors were beginning to slip in among the Cossacks; and the familiar picture of loosening of traditional disciplinary ties was repeated. Kerensky

had never been popular either among the rank-and-file or among the officers; and suggestions that he should be arrested and handed over to the Bolsheviki found increasing favor.

At dawn on the morning of the 14th the gigantic sailor, Dibenko, one of the three directors of the War Commissariat, appeared in Gatchina with the Cossacks who had been sent over to the Red lines to negotiate an armistice. Dibenko found the ground well prepared for his propaganda and soon persuaded the Cossacks to sign an agreement under which they would deliver up Kerensky, while Dibenko agreed that Lenin and Trotzky would not be included in the Government.[31] There was not the slightest intention, of course, of adhering to this latter part of the "treaty"; Dibenko simply made this promise in order to facilitate the arrest of Kerensky. Krasnov warned the latter that danger was impending; and Kerensky, who had almost given himself up for lost and had been thinking of suicide as a preferable alternative to capture, found succor at the last moment. With the assistance of a Socialist Revolutionary, Semyenov, and a sympathetic sailor Kerensky disguised himself in a sailor's costume, slipped past the guard which had been posted at the single entrance to the palace and escaped into hiding,[32] ultimately to leave Russia on a false passport with the aid of the British diplomatic agent, Bruce Lockhart.

On November 15 a considerable number of Bolshevik troops entered Gatchina. Krasnov was arrested and brought to Smolny under guard. This was still a mild and careless period of the Revolution, so far as the treatment of political prisoners was concerned; and Krasnov was soon released and succeeded in making his way to the Don, where he became the leader of the Cossack anti-Bolshevik movement in the following spring.

The collapse of Kerensky's drive against Petrograd, which closely coincided with the victory of the Reds in Moscow, showed that the Bolsheviki were holding the power which they had taken on November 7. Their seizure of governmental authority was bitterly resented, of course, by the small propertied class and also by the great majority of the intelligentsia, of whom some clung to the utopian idea that Russia had to proceed with the War, while others resented the dictatorial methods of the new rulers and feared the consequences of a sweeping effort to introduce socialism in an economically and socially backward country like Russia. But one cannot read the records of the time without being impressed by the fact that the active masses of workers and soldiers were, in the

main, on the side of the *coup,* or at least regarded it with friendly neutrality. The floods of resolutions which emanated from the Committee for Salvation, from the deposed Vtsik, from the anti-Bolshevik political parties failed to rouse any battalions of soldiers, ready to fight against the new regime and for the Provisional Government.

The explanation of this is quite simple. The Russian soldier, who in four cases out of five was a peasant, simply could not be induced to oppose a Government that had inscribed Land and Peace on its banner. Months would have to pass before the "bony hand of hunger," as Ryabunshinsky had predicted, would grip the country and create a broad popular basis for counterrevolution. During the first period of their rule the Bolsheviki did not find it necessary to resort to systematic executions, although such acts as the lynching of General Dukhonin and the murder in a prison hospital of two Cadet leaders, Shingarev and Kokoshkin, are typical of the uncontrolled and unregulated mob violence which prevailed in many parts of the country. During the first months of its existence the Soviet regime, abhorrent as it was to the former ruling classes and also to the majority of the educated classes, was giving the masses pretty much what they wanted: to the soldier the right to quit the trenches, to the peasant the right to get what he could out of the spoliation of the landlord's estate, to the city worker an intoxicating sense of power over the hated "boorzhui."

NOTES

[1] *Cf.* Sadovsky's reminiscences in *Proletarian Revolution,* No. 10, for 1922, pp. 76, 77.

[2] Leon Trotzky, "The History of the Russian Revolution," Vol. III, p. 187; V. Antonov-Ovseenko, "In the Year 1917," p. 296, gives a detailed estimate of the forces of the Red Guard in various parts of the city.

[3] K. Ryabinsky, "The Revolution of 1917: Chronicle of Events," Vol. V, pp. 261ff.

[4] John Reed, "Ten Days That Shook the World," pp. 60, 61.

[5] Ryabinsky, *op. cit.,* p. 268.

[6] *Cf.* F. Dan's article "The History of the Last Days of the Provisional Government," in "October Revolution," in the series, "Revolution and Civil War as Described by the Whites," pp. 127ff.

[7] "Protocols of the Central Committee of the Russian Social Democratic Labor Party," pp. 141ff.

[8] Ryabinsky, *op. cit.,* pp. 268–270.

[9] Reed, *op. cit.,* p. 73.

[10] *Cf.* Kerensky's article, "Gatchina," in "October Revolution," pp. 169–179.

[11] David Francis, "Russia from the American Embassy," pp. 179, 180.

[12] V. B. Stankevitch, "Reminiscences, 1914–1919," p. 133.

[13] *Cf.* paraphrase of the narrative of Lieutenant Sinegub, one of the defenders of the Winter Palace, in "October Revolution," pp. 142, 143.

[14] The Petrograd city Duma sent a commission to Levashovo, where the Women's Battalion was stationed, to investigate the treatment of its members. One member of

the commission, Mme. Tyrkova, reported that the women had been taken to the barracks of the Pavlovsk Regiment, where some of them had been badly treated, but that at present most of them were in Levashovo, with the remainder in private homes. Dr. Mandelbaum, another member of the commission, reported three cases of violation, adding that none of the women had been wounded or thrown out of the windows of the Winter Palace. *Cf.* Reed, *op. cit.,* p. 337.

[15] Professor P. N. Milyukov, "History of the Second Russian Revolution," Vol. I, Part III, p. 232.

[16] Antonov-Ovseenko, *op. cit.,* p. 319.

[17] *Ibid.,* p. 324.

[18] Reed, *op. cit.,* p. 34.

[19] M. Philips Price, "My Reminiscences of the Russian Revolution," pp. 145ff.

[20] *Cf.* Y. Yakovlev, "Problems of the Second All-Russian Congress of Soviets" in *Proletarian Revolution,* No. 71, pp. 70, 71.

[21] Reed, *op. cit.,* p. 90.

[22] Trotzky, "Mein Leben," p. 314.

[23] Reed, *op. cit.,* p. 125.

[24] "The Second All-Russian Congress of Soviets" (under the editorship of Y. A. Yakovlev and M. N. Pokrovsky), p. 73.

[25] *Cf.* N. Krupskaya's article, "October Days," in *Bolshevik,* No. 20, for 1933, p. 56.

[26] S. A. Alekseev, "The October Revolution," p. 201.

[27] N. Sukhanov, "Reminiscences of the Revolution," Vol. VII, p. 286.

[28] Alekseev, *op. cit.,* pp. 217, 218.

[29] P. N. Krasnov, "On the Internal Front," in "October Revolution," p. 51.

[30] *Cf.* article, "Reminiscences of the October Revolution," in *Proletarian Revolution,* for 1822, No. 10, pp. 61–62.

[31] P. E. Dibenko, "Rebels," p. 90.

[32] *Cf.* Kerensky, "Gatchina," in "October Revolution," p. 202, and Alekseev, *op. cit.,* p. 193.

CHAPTER XV

THE REVOLUTION IN THE COUNTRY

PETROGRAD, of course, was not Russia. The Bolshevik seizure of power in the capital would have been nullified if the Provisional Government had found effective support in Moscow, in other procincial centres, most important of all, in the armies at the front. But the same causes which made for success in Petrograd operated, in the long run, to bring about the victory of the Bolshevik forces throughout the country, although the ease and the speed of the triumph in the capital were not duplicated everywhere.

The most stubborn struggle for power took place in Moscow, historic capital of medieval Russia. Here the preparation of the insurrection had been far less complete; measures which had been taken in Petrograd days in advance of the actual *coup* were only adopted in Moscow when news of the developments in Petrograd arrived. And for some reason the officers and junkers in Moscow displayed considerably more fighting spirit than the men of the same classes in Petrograd. Perhaps the ancient walls of the Kremlin and the cupolas of Moscow's hundreds of churches strengthened the will to fight against an upheaval that threatened to destroy everything that was old and traditional in Russia.

The Moscow Bolsheviki were in close touch with Petrograd by telephone and telegraph; moreover, a member of the Party Central Committee, Lomov, who had participated in the session of the Central Committee in Petrograd on November 6, was despatched to Moscow to insure coördinated action there. The Moscow Party Committee elected a "fighting centre," with five members and four substitutes, to direct the insurrection; and decided to raise in the Moscow Soviet the question of creating a military Revolutionary Committee, on the Petrograd model.

Feeling between the Bolsheviki and the moderate Socialist parties had been less bitter in Moscow than in Petrograd; and at the decisive session of the Moscow Soviet, which was held on November 7, there was a good deal of support, even among the Bolsheviki, for a compromise proposal, offered by the Mensheviki, that

a temporary administrative body should be constituted, with representatives of the Soviet, the city Duma, the trade-unions of railroad and postal and telegraph workers and the Staff of the Moscow Military District. But no agreement was reached on whether the Soviet or the Duma should have a majority in this proposed body, so that the proposal fell to the ground. And the Soviet gave the signal for battle when it adopted a Bolshevik resolution to create a Military Revolutionary Committee of seven members which was "to give all possible support to the Petrograd Military Revolutionary Committee." [1] The vote was 394 to 106, with 23 abstentions.

The anti-Bolshevik forces rallied around the Committee of Public Safety, which was created on the same day at a session of the city Duma. The most active figure in this Committee was the Mayor of Moscow, a right-wing Socialist Revolutionary named Rudnev; the military defense of the city against the Bolsheviki was in the hands of the commander of the Moscow District, Colonel Ryabtsev, who, like many officers of the Kerensky period, seems to have been inclined to compromise and irresolution and to have resorted to strong action only under considerable pressure from the Committee of Public Safety.

The Military Revolutionary Committee at first consisted of four Bolsheviki, two Mensheviki and one United Socialist (a group which stood somewhat to the left of the Mensheviki). The Mensheviki openly declared that they entered the Military Revolutionary Committee only to obstruct its work and soon withdrew from it altogether, as no one paid any attention to them. On November 8 a conference of representatives of the garrison units voted, 116 to 18, in favor of the seizure of power by the Soviets; in Moscow, as in Petrograd, not one regular regiment came out on the side of the Provisional Government. It is suggestive of the inferior preparation of the uprising in Moscow, by comparison with Petrograd, that this garrison conference was held so late; the Petrograd garrison was definitely under the control of the Military Revolutionary Committee much earlier.

So on the 8th and the 9th two rival authorities, the Military Revolutionary Committee and the Committee of Public Safety, disputed the mastery of Moscow; each appealed to the support of the population and pronounced the orders of the other null and void. There was no actual bloodshed, however, up to the evening of the 9th. As early as the 7th, troops of the 56th Regiment had taken over the guard of the central telegraph office on behalf of

the insurgents; Red Guards were busily arming in the workers' quarters on the outskirts of the city; and the Kremlin, which was of great strategic importance, both because of its central location and strength as a fortress and because of the arsenal it contained, was in the hands of a Bolshevik leader, Ensign Berzin, who easily won the allegiance of the soldiers of the guard.[2] Outside the Kremlin gates, however, were strong patrols of junkers, who prevented Berzin from carrying out his intention of supplying arms from the arsenal to the Red Guards.

There are varied estimates of the numbers of forces on the two sides. N. Muralov, a Bolshevik soldier who was one of the most active leaders of the Moscow uprising and who subsequently became military commander of the District, estimates that fifty thousand soldiers and armed workers were fighting on the Bolshevik side, with perhaps an equal number that might be described as benevolently neutral.[3] There were about ten thousand junkers, officers, armed students and volunteers on the side of the Committee of Public Safety. If one considers that all the heavy artillery was also on the side of the Bolsheviki it may seem surprising that the fighting in Moscow was so protracted.

But there were disadvantages which, especially in the first days, offset the numerical superiority of the insurgents. There were almost no trained officers to guide the operations. The anti-Bolshevik forces held the centre of the city; and communication between the outlying districts was poor and uncertain. The junkers were much better trained; it required time to bring the heterogeneous insurrectionary forces into action; and the mood of the garrison, like that of the soldiers in Petrograd, was not, in the main, very warlike. In Petrograd also the military leadership of the uprising was amateurish; but there all the centres of effective resistance had been paralyzed in advance. In Moscow a relatively small number of resolute men were able to dispute the possession of the city for a whole week.

On the 9th Colonel Ryabtsev entered the Kremlin and endeavored to persuade the soldiers to admit a guard of junkers. He was met with jeers and hostile cries and narrowly escaped rough handling before he got away. On the evening of the same day he decided to take the offensive and despatched a telephonic ultimatum to the Military Revolutionary Committee, giving it fifteen minutes in which to disperse and demanding at the same time the evacuation of the Kremlin, the postoffice and other public

buildings which had been occupied. In the event of noncompliance he threatened to open artillery fire on the headquarters of the Soviet, which were located on Tverskaya Street, about ten minutes' walk from the Kremlin.

Ryabtsev's threat excited considerable apprehension in the Military Revolutionary Committee, which had taken no adequate measures of defense. It was decided to ignore the ultimatum and to call a general strike. Ryabtsev did not carry into execution his threat to attack the headquarters of the Soviet; but during the night of the 9th and on the 10th the forces under his command won substantial victories. The junkers occupied the postoffice, the central telegraph and telephone stations, some of the railroad stations. On the morning of the 10th Ryabtsev called up Berzin, the Bolshevik commandant of the Kremlin, and told him that the uprising was suppressed, demanding the surrender of the Kremlin.

Berzin had been cut off from communication with the city; the troops in the Kremlin were not in the best of spirit; and he accepted the summons to surrender, on condition that the lives of the soldiers be spared. This promise was not kept, a number of soldiers being shot down by the enraged officers and junkers after they had occupied the historic fortress.

An irregular battle line was formed in the city. The forces of the Committee of Public Safety held the part of the city between the Moscow River and the circular boulevards, beyond which are the main workingclass quarters, which were in the hands of the insurgents, who also held the part of the city which lies on the opposite side of the Moscow River from the Kremlin. There was a good deal of symbolism in this topography of Moscow's civil war; in the junkers' territory were the government buildings, the university, the main theatres, the large shops—all the things that were to be smashed or profoundly changed as a result of the Revolution. On the other side of the barricades were the factory districts of Moscow, the Presnya, which had played such a big rôle in 1905, and several others.

The fighting went on for a week, with one day of an imperfect nominal truce. The junkers used armored cars, which drove through the streets and attempted occasionally, although without success, to force the evacuation of the building of the Soviet, which was in an exposed position, near the fighting line. The Red Guards dug trenches in the streets to obstruct the armored cars; and, repeating the tactics of 1905, sent small parties of snipers into the rear of

their opponents' positions. These snipers threw down hand-grenades and fired from the roofs of houses.[4]

The high point of Ryabtsev's success was reached on the 10th. After this the numerical superiority of the Reds began to make itself felt, and the junkers were gradually pushed back to a contracting area in the centre of the city. Artillery was brought into play; and, although it was clumsily used, inflicting more destruction on the city than on the enemy, it had some effect. The junkers were driven from the Tverskaya Street on the 11th.

The representatives of the Vikzhel, the railroad workers' union, succeeded in bringing about an armistice on the 12th by threatening to stop the transportation of troops which both sides expected from the front. Under the terms of the armistice the Military Revolutionary Committee and the Committee of Public Safety were to dissolve; and a government was to be formed, with representation from the Soviet, the Duma and other public organizations. The armistice was poorly observed, since communication with the outlying districts was defective; and isolated clashes took place in different parts of the city on the 12th. The Alekseev junker school, located in a hostile workingclass district, was compelled to surrender on this day.

Before midnight on the 12th, when the armistice expired, the Military Revolutionary Committee received encouraging news. Red Guards were coming from Mitishi, Serpukhov and other factory towns in the neighborhood. Two companies of Bolshevik soldiers were on the way from Minsk; the Tula munition workers were sending machine-guns.[5] In view of these circumstances, it was decided to denounce the armistice; and fighting was resumed with still greater bitterness on the 13th. The advantage was now clearly on the side of the Reds, who captured the postoffice, the telephone station and several of the railroad stations on the 13th. The increasing hopelessness of the military situation as it became evident that no reinforcements would arrive and the feeling among the junkers that they were "isolated from the rest of Russia"[6] hastened the inevitable end. Moreover, there were differences of opinion in the anti-Bolshevik camp. Most of the old officers had little enthusiasm for the Provisional Government, which they were nominally defending; some of the junkers, on the other hand, had Socialist sympathies and felt ill at ease with their conservative allies.

On the 14th one stronghold of the junkers after another fell into the hands of the Reds, who occupied some of the hotels in

the centre of the city and the building of the city Duma and trained cannon on the Kremlin. This bombardment of Russia's greatest historical memorial called forth remonstrances from some of the milder spirits in the Bolshevik ranks; Lunacharsky, who had heard exaggerated versions of the damage wrought by the artillery fire, resigned his post as Commissar for Education as a protest. His resignation, like many similar acts in those crowded days, was quickly withdrawn.

On the morning of the 15th a detachment of Red Guards carried the Kremlin by storm, blowing open the massive gates and quickly beating down the resistance of the exhausted junkers. The Bolshevik soldiers who had been held as prisoners since the Kremlin passed into the hands of Ryabtsev were released, and they promptly fell on a colonel and some junkers whom they accused of having shot some of their comrades and cut them down.[7] The old palaces and churches inside the massive battlements of the Kremlin, which had witnessed more than one sanguinary scene during medieval palace *coups,* looked down on a new burst of ferocious civil strife.

The Kremlin emerged from the struggle battered and scarred, with some injury to the mosaics and frescoes of the Uspensky and Blagoveschensky Cathedrals, but escaped any sweeping destruction of its more important historical buildings. Only the Little Nikolai Palace, which had been sometimes used for grand-ducal receptions, and which had served as barracks for the junkers, was both bombarded and sacked.[8]

On the morning of the 15th, Rudnev, on behalf of the Committee of Public Safety, addressed peace overtures to the Military Revolutionary Committee, expressing readiness to "liquidate the armed struggle against the political system which is established by the Military Revolutionary Committee, passing over to methods of political struggle." An armistice prevailed during the morning; in the afternoon there was a last flare-up of desperate fighting, which resulted in the destruction of a large house near the Nikitsky Gates, where the junkers had entrenched themselves, by artillery fire. At five in the afternoon a formal peace treaty was signed. Under its terms the Committee of Public Safety passed out of existence; the officers and junkers gave up all arms except those which were required for service; military activities were to cease immediately; prisoners on both sides were to be released; the Military Revolutionary Committee guarantied the freedom and safety of the junkers.

Five hundred who had fallen on the Red side were buried in a common grave on the Red Square, under the Kremlin wall. The burial was marked by a huge demonstration of workers and soldiers, who defiled through the Red Square with bands playing the revolutionary Funeral March.[9] The Whites, as the anti-Bolsheviki were already beginning to be called, buried their dead privately.

Moscow was the sole place in Central and Northern Russia where the Bolshevik seizure of power encountered serious, sustained and sanguinary resistance. The course of transfer of power to the Soviets varied from place to place, depending on such factors as the strength of the local Party organization, the proportion of industrial workers in the population and the mood of the local garrison. In factory towns, such as Ivanovo-Vosnessensk, "the Russian Manchester," and Vladimir, the taking over of power was bloodless and easy. In the Volga towns of Kazan and Saratov there were short fights with the junkers and adherents of the Provisional Government, which ended in victories of the local Bolsheviki. In nonindustrial provincial centres, such as Penza and Simbirsk, the setting up of a clearcut Bolshevik regime occurred slowly and was only completed in December.[10] The Ural and Siberian towns accepted the Soviet regime, in the main, without serious opposition, although remote Blagoveschensk, on the Amur River, was an exception in this respect. Here there was a miniature repetition of Moscow; the local junkers, under Socialist Revolutionary leadership, attacked the Soviet institutions and were only crushed after fighting had gone on for more than a week. This Blagoveschensk incident occurred in the latter part of December.

In Tashkent, the main city of Russian Central Asia, the 1st Siberian Regiment, united with armed workers from the local railroad workshops, overcame the resistance of the junkers and Cossacks and set up a Soviet regime, which was later destined to be a sort of Red oasis, surrounded by hostile Cossacks and primitive Asiatic tribesmen. In the Caucasus, Baku, the large oil centre, and Tiflis, the capital of Georgia, took opposite sides; a Soviet regime was decreed in Baku on November 15; in Tiflis the influence of the Georgian Mensheviki, who were much more nationalistic and much less radical than the Russian Mensheviki, was stronger, and a local Congress of Soviets passed a resolution in favor of combating anarchy in the Army and convening the Constituent Assembly at the appointed time.

The nationwide sweep of the Revolution was a natural result

of the conditions which had developed during the rule of the Provisional Government. The garrisons in the rear were, if possible, more turbulent than the units at the front. The combination of soldiers of the garrison with armed workers was almost invariably too strong for the local authorities, or for the Mensheviki and Socialist Revolutionaries, to resist. In places where the Bolsheviki already possessed a majority in the Soviet the transfer of power was simple. Where they were not in the majority the customary procedure was to create a local Military Revolutionary Committee, seize the government institutions and later hold new elections for the Soviet. It should not be imagined that the Soviet regime emerged generally in finished, working form; the confusion and uncertainty which prevailed in Petrograd during the first period of Soviet rule were naturally even more characteristic of many provincial centres. In some instances the city Dumas and zemstvos existed for weeks side by side with the Soviets. Central authority was extremely weak; and every Soviet acted very much according to its own pleasure. The town of Kursk declared itself a republic; Samara and other places created their own Councils of People's Commissars. But amid all the chaos there was a steady tendency to consolidate the Soviet authority; the huge stream of returning soldiers from the front supplied sufficient armed force to crush any resistance that might be offered.

After Kerensky's drive against Petrograd had failed and after Moscow was in the hands of the Red forces several centres of opposition to the new regime still remained. There was the Stavka in Moghilev, where General Dukhonin refused to recognize the authority of the Council of People's Commissars and where Socialist Revolutionary political leaders were gathering in the hope of finding support. There was Kiev, where the Ukrainian Central Rada had come off the victor in a peculiar three-cornered struggle between the forces which remained loyal to the Provisional Government, the Bolshevik soldiers and Red Guards and the troops of the Central Rada. There were the lands of the Don, Kuban and Orenburg Cossacks, where the elected chiefs, or Atamans, of the Cossacks, General Kaledin in Rostov and General Dutov in Orenburg, were still able to hold the local Bolsheviki in check.

Of these hostile centres Moghilev was the nearest to Petrograd and the one which the new Soviet rulers set out first to reduce. The position of the newly established Soviet regime was greatly strengthened by the fact that the armies on the fronts which were

closest to Petrograd, the Northern, with headquarters in Pskov, and the Western, with headquarters in Minsk, were most thoroughly permeated with Bolshevik propaganda. In the subsequent voting for the Constituent Assembly, while the Socialist Revolutionaries received somewhat more votes than the Bolsheviki in the whole Army, the Northern and Western Fronts, together with the Baltic Fleet, returned large Bolshevik majorities.

General N. N. Dukhonin, who was the actual Commander-in-chief of the Russian Army at the Stavka at the time of the Revolution (Kerensky was merely the formal occupant of this post) gave orders to various troop units to proceed to Petrograd as soon as appeals for help began to pour in from officials of the Provisional Government in Petrograd. But his orders were not executed; some of the units refused to move; others were stranded in railroad junctions and quickly "propagandized" by Bolshevik emissaries. Moreover, General Cheremisov, Commander of the Northern Front, threw up the cause of the Provisional Government as hopeless and as early as ten o'clock on the evening of November 7 countermanded all instructions for troop movements to Petrograd from his Front. In an exchange of communications with Dukhonin he endeavored to justify his conduct by making false statements to the effect that Kerensky had abdicated and wished to bestow the office of Commander-in-chief on Cheremisov.[11]

The Commander of the Western Front, General Baluev, was more loyal to the Provisional Government, but was quite helpless in the matter of despatching troops. On the very day of the Bolshevik *coup* the Minsk Soviet, with the aid of Bolshevik troops, took over power in this headquarters of the Western Front. The army Committee of the Front was still dominated by moderate Socialists, and it succeeded in bringing into the city some cavalry which still professed allegiance to the Provisional Government. An armed clash was avoided by the creation in Minsk, as the supreme authority, of a Committee for the Salvation of the Revolution, with representatives of all Socialist parties and of the Committee of the Front. This temporary retreat of the Bolsheviki, however, was turned into a strategic victory because the Committee for Salvation agreed to permit no troop trains to be sent through Minsk to Petrograd and Moscow.[12] That this promise was kept is evident from a telegram which Dukhonin sent to Kerensky on November 13, complaining that he encountered all sorts of obstacles from the Committees for Salvation on the Western and Rumanian

Fronts, which did not permit the transfer of troops.[18] There is similar testimony from General Malyanin, on the Western Front, who reported about the same time that the Committee for Salvation prevented the transfer of troops, while such important railroad junctions as Orsha, Vyazma and Gomel were falling into the hands of the Bolsheviki.

The arrival of an armored train from the front in Minsk on November 15 turned the balance of forces in favor of the Bolsheviki; the Committee for Salvation disappeared from the scene; and General Baluev was soon removed from his post and arrested. The Front and Army Committees were, as a general rule, re-elected; and this process, in view of the mood of the soldiers, led to the replacement of the former moderate Socialists by Bolsheviki.

Dukhonin, who on November 13 had signed a telegram demanding "the cessation of violent action and unconditional submission to the Provisional Government" on the part of the Bolsheviki, adding that the Army would support these demands by force, by the following day had become sufficiently convinced of the futility of further efforts to send forces against the capital to issue an order stopping the further movement of troops on Petrograd.[14] So the Stavka gave up the attempt to oppose the new regime by force of arms.

A new conflict, however, soon arose over the question of peace negotiations. On the night of November 20 the Soviet Government addressed to Dukhonin a communication instructing him to propose an armistice for the purpose of opening up peace negotiations. He was also instructed to keep the Government informed of the course of the negotiations and to sign an armistice only with its consent.

On November 22 Lenin, Stalin and Krilenko got into direct long-distance communication with Dukhonin. At first the latter endeavored to evade a direct reply to the demand that he initiate armistice proposals. He asked whether the Council of People's Commissars had received any reply to its decree on peace and to its appeal to the belligerent states, what was to be done with the Rumanian Army, which was included in the Russian Front, whether the armistice was to be separate or general. The Commissars (Lenin, Stalin and Krilenko) impatiently brushed aside these questions and insisted on a definite answer. Dukhonin finally declared that he could not carry out their request and that "the peace which is in-

dispensable for Russia can only be given by a central government."
Thereupon the Commissars dismissed him from his post "for non-
fulfillment of the instructions of the Government and for behavior
which brings unheard of sufferings to the toiling masses of all countries and especially to the Army." Dukhonin was ordered to carry
on the work of his post until an authorized representative of the
Government arrived in Stavka; Ensign Krilenko, the tireless agitator and active participant in the Revolution, was appointed
Commander-in-chief.

At the same time the Government issued an appeal to the soldiers
and sailors, urging the units in the trenches to select plenipotentiaries for peace negotiations and ending: "Soldiers. The cause of
peace is in your hands. Watchfulness, restraint, energy, and the
cause of peace will triumph." [15] On the 23d Krilenko set off for
the Stavka, with a convoy of sailors. He moved slowly, stopping
at Pskov and Dvinsk in order to remove generals and to solidify the
Bolshevik control of the Fronts.

Dukhonin's position in Moghilev became increasingly critical.
A conventional army officer, with a sense of duty and patriotism,
but with little political experience or imagination, he hesitated and
remained passive amid the streams of contradictory advice which
poured in on him from all sides. On November 23 the chiefs of
the Allied Military Missions, stationed at Moghilev, addressed a
note to Dukhonin reminding him of the inter-Allied Agreement of
September 23, 1914, to conclude no separate peace or armistice and
warning him that "any violation of the treaty on Russia's part will
have as its sequel the most serious consequences." This provoked
an immediate fiery retort from Foreign Commissar Trotzky, who
accused the Allied representatives of interfering in Russia's internal
affairs with the purpose of provoking civil war and declared that
the Council of People's Commissars did not consider itself bound
by Tsarist treaties.

The statement of the Allied missions, under the circumstances,
was an empty threat. There was much more serious significance in
a message which Dukhonin received on November 24 from General
Boldirev in Dvinsk, to the effect that Krilenko had arrived for
the purpose of initiating peace negotiations; Boldirev added: "Not
possessing force I cannot interfere with him; even the more tranquil
units in such cases will refuse to maintain neutrality." [16] Soon the
news arrived that Boldirev had been arrested. There was equally
discouraging information from the Western Front, where General

Baluev had been forced to resign on November 25 and the Military Revolutionary Committee had nominated Lieutenant Colonel Kamenshikov Commander of the Front. On the following day Quartermaster-General Malyavin, from the same Front, sent the following message, very characteristic for the position of the higher officers in those days:

"In view of the threat of violence which has been made to me, confirmed a second time in the presence of witnesses, I am obliged to cease performing my duties. . . . We are surrounded by troops. Whether they intend to guard us or to kill us is difficult to know. However, they let no one out." [17]

Moghilev itself was still quiet; it was a small town without a considerable workingclass population, and the Soviet had a majority of moderate Socialists. The local troops, a battalion of Cavaliers of St. George, two companies of "shock troops," and some Cossack and Tekintsi units seemed reasonably reliable. The 35th Corps in Vitebsk and the First Finnish Division, posted between Orsha and Moghilev, were also considered loyal, and it was expected that they would bar the way to Krilenko and his sailors.

Feverish but futile efforts were made to utilize the Stavka as the base of a new Government. Several prominent Socialist Revolutionaries, Chernov, Gotz and Avksentiev, came to Moghilev; and the General Army Committee on November 20 issued an appeal, proposing to take the initiative in forming a new Government and nominating Chernov as its head.[18] Chernov made a speech accepting the nomination; but shortly afterwards the Socialist Revolutionary, Semyenov, found Gotz wringing his hands, while Chernov, "apparently in the most complete moral and physical helplessness," lay on a couch with a compress on his head.[19] The proposal of the Army Committee had met with no effective response; the proposals to convene a Peasant Congress and a Congress of Army representatives in Moghilev were quietly dropped; in the end the Socialist Revolutionary leaders left the doomed Stavka and went back to Petrograd, still hoping that the voting for the Constituent Assembly might undo the Bolshevik regime.

Meanwhile the atmosphere in Moghilev was becoming more and more gloomy. Neither the 35th Corps nor the First Finnish Division took any steps to oppose Krilenko's advance. Signs of discontent began to appear among the soldiers in Moghilev; when an attempt was made to despatch some of the archives and docu-

ments of the Stavka to a safer place farther south the soldiers forcibly prevented the evacuation. The Generals in the Stavka, the members of the General Army Committee, felt the ground slipping from beneath their feet. In every messenger and chauffeur they suspected a Bolshevik agent; they were afraid to talk over the telephone, for fear that what they said might be betrayed.[20]

On December 1 the Allied military missions left for Kiev; and on the night of the same day the Executive Committee of the Moghilev Soviet, yielding to the insistent demands of the Left parties, decided that the Soviet should take over power in Moghilev and appoint a revolutionary committee. On the morning of the 3d Krilenko arrived with his sailors and occupied Moghilev without resistance. The sole anti-Bolshevik force in the town, the shock troops, had left on December 1, feeling that they were hopelessly outnumbered and, moreover, feeling little sympathy for the Socialists of the General Army Committee.

Dukhonin might have fled on the very morning of Krilenko's arrival; the Kerensky Front Commissar, Stankevitch, had succeeded in procuring an automobile; but Quartermaster-General Diederichs persuaded him to remain.[21] Dukhonin was brought as a prisoner to Krilenko's railroad car at the station. A mob of soldiers, sailors and peasants soon gathered on the platform, demanding that Dukhonin should be killed on the spot. Krilenko spoke strongly against any lynching; the mob began to disperse; but after Krilenko had left a burly sailor again aroused the crowd; Dukhonin was dragged out of the car and beaten to death.

This killing was the climax of the break-up of the old army. There was a special element of pathos in Dukhonin's fate, because the unfortunate General was not an active anti-revolutionist; he had no desire to be a leader of civil war. He had remained in Moghilev because, as he declared in a telegram to General Manikovsky, he felt he could only turn over his post "to a legally authorized person, nominated by the Senate." But no Commander-in-chief with the seal of the Senate appeared; instead there was the ferocious sailor, leading the bloodthirsty mob.

A Provisional Revolutionary Committee now took charge of the Stavka. On December 14 a ruling was published, "democratizing" the Army, making all officers elective, abolishing titles and epaulettes, transferring military authority to elected committees.[22] On December 24 forty-two delegates, representing all the Fronts, except the remote Rumanian and Caucasian, which dissolved some-

what more slowly, met in Moghilev, and created a Central Committee of the Operating Army and Fleet, with Krilenko as Commander-in-chief. The old Army melted away in a vast torrent of homeward moving demobilized soldiers; the new Red Army came into existence early in the following year.

Moghilev had been only a cardboard centre of opposition to the Bolshevik regime; it crumbled at the first pressure. Rostov and Kiev were more serious; they fell after a more protracted struggle. In Rostov, capital of the Don Cossack Territory, as in Ekaterinodar and Orenburg, the capitals respectively of the Kuban and Orenburg Cossack Territories, the local Cossack authorities, although they were none too firmly in the saddle, were able to survive the first shock of the November Revolution and to carry on independently of Moscow.

General Kaledin, the Don Cossack Ataman, became the main hope of the propertied and military classes of Russia. Political leaders of the more conservative type, such as Milyukov and Rodzianko, officers and junkers who were determined not to submit to Bolshevik rule, members of the aristocratic and well-to-do classes, businessmen and merchants, began to seek a refuge in Rostov from the proletarian storms of Petrograd and Moscow. Kornilov and the Generals who had been actively associated with his attempted *coup*, Denikin, Lukomsky, Romanovsky and Markov, escaped from Bikhov with the willing consent of their lenient guards on the night of December 1, thirty-six hours before Krilenko and his sailors, who might well have given them short shrift, entered the neighboring Moghilev. They too made their way to the Don, where they created what was destined to be in time the most formidable military challenge to the Soviet regime in the form of the so-called Volunteer Army.[23]

In Kiev, the political centre of Ukraina, the Revolution took a peculiar course because of the existence of an organized nationalist authority in the form of the Central Rada. The Kiev Soviet had passed a Bolshevik resolution on November 8; on the 10th the local junkers opened hostilities, making a raid on the headquarters of the Soviet and arresting the members of the Military Revolutionary Committee which had been elected. This was followed by an uprising in the workingclass district in the vicinity of the Kiev arsenal; after three days of street fighting the junkers and officers, learning that Bolshevik troops were on the way from the Front to Kiev, gave up the struggle and evacuated the city.

But after this the Rada, not the Bolsheviki, emerged as the master of the situation in Kiev. With some Ukrainian troops which were at its disposal, and which had remained neutral during the struggle between the Bolsheviki and the forces of the Provisional Government, the Rada took over the important public buildings and strategic points in the city. Later it succeeded in bringing up more Ukrainian military units and in disarming the Bolshevik forces. By December 3 the Rada felt sufficiently strongly entrenched to issue its Third Universal, which proclaimed Ukraina a People's, not a Soviet, Republic and declared the Rada the sole authority in Ukraina.

Actually the power of the Rada, shaky, like all state authority in this turbulent period, was restricted to the Western part of Ukraina, where nationalist feeling was strongest and where the industrial working class was relatively weak. In the more industrialized eastern and southeastern regions of Ukraina, where the Russian population was larger and Ukrainian nationalism had few roots, a rival authority grew up in the shape of an Ukrainian Soviet regime. The Soviet of Kharkov, the largest city in Eastern Ukraina, passed a resolution repudiating the authority of the Rada and demanding an All-Ukrainian Congress of Soviets on December 7.[24]

In view of Russia's vast distances, poor communications and multitude of races it is not surprising that the issue of the Revolution throughout the country dragged out for a longer time than would have been likely in a more compact and closeknit country. But within a month after the decisive blow in Leningrad the Bolsheviki had conquered the important Fronts and the Army General Staff and were in fairly effective control of the main towns and railroad centres of Northern and Central Russia and of Siberia. In the Southwest, where the Rada appealed to the repressed nationalism of the Ukrainians and in the Southeast, where the Cossack regions had not been subdued, there were clouds of danger and opposition. But between these two anti-Bolshevik centres there was already a wedge, in the shape of the Kharkov and Donetz industrial districts of Ukraina, where Bolshevik influence was paramount. And in Ukraina and in the Cossack regions alike there were landhungry peasants, turbulent returning soldiers from the front, sullen workers who were potential recruits for Bolshevism and who made the position of General Kaledin and of the Rada very unstable.

This nationwide sweep of Bolshevism did not mean that a hun-

dred and fifty million people of various races and languages had suddenly been converted to the ideas that more or less clearly animated the 300,000 organized Bolsheviki of that time. Over a large part of the country, especially in predominantly peasant provinces, the new regime was only skin-deep and could be overthrown, as subsequent events showed, by a very light tap of foreign intervention, combined with the forces of internal resentment and disillusionment. But the magic of the slogan "Peace and Land" was sufficient for the time being to carry the Soviet banner triumphantly from the factory quarters of Petrograd to the rolling steppes of Ukraina and the Far Eastern port of Vladivostok.

NOTES

[1] E. Ignatov, "The Moscow Soviet of Workers' Deputies in 1917," p. 352.

[2] *Cf.* O. Berzin, "October Days in Moscow," in *Proletarian Revolution*, No. 71.

[3] *Cf.* Muralov's article in *Proletarian Revolution*, No. 10, pp. 310–312.

[4] V. Karpov, "Year of Struggle," pp. 136–139.

[5] Vera Vladimirova, "A Year of Service of 'Socialists' to Capitalists," p. 60.

[6] Professor Paul Milyukov, "History of the Second Russian Revolution," Vol. I, Part III, p. 302.

[7] Y. Peche, "About the Struggle of the Red Guard in October," in *Proletarian Revolution*, No. 70, pp. 180ff.

[8] Ignatov, *op. cit.*, p. 398.

[9] John Reed, "Ten Days That Shook the World," pp. 256ff.

[10] *Cf.* article of V. Leikina, "October in Russia," in *Proletarian Revolution*, No. 46.

[11] *Cf.* article "The Stavka on October 25 and 26," in *Archive of the Russian Revolution*, Vol. VII.

[12] *Cf.* article of A. Kirzhintz, "October Days in White Russia," in *Proletarian Revolution*, No. 71, pp. 108ff.

[13] *Red Archives*, Vol. XXIII, pp. 171ff.

[14] G. Lelevitch, "October in the Stavka," pp. 32, 33.

[15] "Protocols of the Sessions of the Second All-Russian Central Executive Committee," pp. 54, 55.

[16] *Red Archives*, Vol. XXIII, pp. 208, 209.

[17] *Ibid.*, pp. 231, 232.

[18] Lelevitch, *op. cit.*, pp. 61, 62.

[19] Semyenov, "The Military and Fighting Work of the Socialist Revolutionaries," p. 8.

[20] V. B. Stankevitch, "Reminiscences, 1914–1919," pp. 147, 148.

[21] *Ibid.*, pp. 152, 153.

[22] Lelevitch, *op. cit.*, pp. 93, 94.

[23] *Cf.* Chapter XVII for a fuller account of the flight of Kornilov and his associates. The news of their escape excited great rage among the masses in Moghilev and was one of the causes of the lynching of Dukhonin.

[24] I. N. Lubimov, "The Revolution of 1917: Chronicle of Events," Vol. VI, pp. 206, 207.

CHAPTER XVI

FIRST STEPS OF THE NEW REGIME

THE Bolshevik Revolution perhaps affords the most striking illustration in all history of the reins of power in a large country falling into almost completely untrained hands. Of the new Commissars not one had any serious administrative experience. And there was no question of taking over an obedient, smoothly running apparatus of authority. The state officials, as a class, were bitterly hostile to the Bolsheviki and declared a protest strike as soon as the Commissars appeared to take over the offices. Keys to offices and safes were withheld or only surrendered under duress. The rooms and corridors of the big Ministries were empty; most of the officials remained at home. Only the humbler grades of employees, such as couriers and doorkeepers, showed any sympathy with the new rulers. Most of the officials followed the leadership of a strike committee, the so-called Union of Unions, which on November 18 issued an appeal to the population to "join our struggle for a generally recognized Government" against "the Bolsheviki, who rely on the brute force of bayonets."[1]

The employees of the State Bank stubbornly refused to pay out money to the new Government; the Government obtained its first advance of five million rubles on November 30, after which the employees of the State Bank went on strike as a protest. It was only on December 27 that the Soviet Government took physical control of all private banks, occupying the premises with armed guards of soldiers and sailors, while keys to the vaults and safe-deposit boxes were handed over to the commissar in charge of the State Bank.

The striking officials and employees received support from various sources, from the old Vtsik, which had refused to turn over its funds to its successor, from private bankers and businessmen. But with the steady tightening of state control over the disposition of funds (after the nationalization of the banks no one was permitted to draw out more than 250 rubles a week) the sources of support

351

dried up, and the strike, which was maintained until the meeting of the Constituent Assembly in January, gradually collapsed.

One of the most pressing problems which arose after the Revolution was the make-up of the Government. There was a considerable moderate wing in the Council of People's Commissars and in the Central Committee of the Bolshevik Party, which disapproved of the ruthless policy of suppressing "bourgeois" newspapers and which clung to the hope that an all-Socialist Government could be formed. Not all Bolsheviki possessed Lenin's complete contempt for liberty as an abstract conception or were able to discard, immediately after coming into power, their traditional attitude of favoring freedom of the press. But the collapse of Kerensky's movement against Petrograd and the sweep of the Revolution in the country played into the hands of the uncompromising Bolshevik leaders, such as Lenin and Trotzky.

On November 14 the Central Committee adopted a resolution to the effect that any further negotiations on the question of forming an All-Socialist Government should be carried on "only for the purpose of finally exposing the impracticability of this policy and of finally stopping further negotiations for a coalition government." [2]

Soon after this, on November 17, five moderate members of the Central Committee, Zinoviev, Kamenev, Rykov, Nogin, and Milyutin, resigned, declaring: "We cannot bear the responsibility for this fatal policy of the Central Committee, which is carried out against the will of a large part of the proletariat and the soldiers, who are eager for the speediest stoppage of bloodshed between separate parts of the democracy.[3] We resign office as members of the Central Committee, in order to have the right to express our opinion openly to the masses of workers and soldiers and to call them to support our slogan: Long live a Government constituted from Soviet parties. Immediate agreement on this condition." At the same time five members of the Government, Rykov, Nogin, Milyutin, Teodorovitch and Shlyapnikov, along with several minor commissars, laid down their offices and published a manifesto to the effect that the sole alternative to an all-Socialist Government was "the preservation of a purely Bolshevik Government by means of political terror," an idea which they repudiated.

It might have seemed that the resignation of five members of a small Central Committee and of five out of twelve members of the new Cabinet would portend a serious crisis. But Lenin, with his

keen sense for the realities of power, was not impressed by this demonstration on the part of his milder associates. He replied to it with a thundering manifesto, issued in the name of the Central Committee, and written by himself, in which he denounced the men who resigned as deserters and recalled that Zinoviev and Kamenev before the uprising had behaved as "deserters and strike-breakers." Lenin argued that the Left Socialist Revolutionaries had been offered places in the new Government and had declined and that the purely Bolshevik Government which had been created was unanimously ratified by the Congress of Soviets. He drew a contrast, not altogether accurate,[4] but oratorically effective, between "all those of little faith, all the waverers and doubters who let themselves be frightened by the bourgeoisie" and the "workers and soldiers, who have no shade of wavering," declared that "the great heroism of millions of workers, soldiers and peasants in Petrograd, in Moscow, on the front, in the trenches and in the villages threw aside the deserters with the ease of a railroad train throwing off chips" and ended:

"Let all the toilers be calm and firm. Our Party, the Party of the Soviet majority, stands resolute and united in defense of their interests, and behind our Party, as formerly, stand millions of workers in the towns, soldiers in the trenches, peasants in the villages, ready to achieve at any cost the victory of peace and the victory of socialism."[5]

Lenin's uncompromising attitude ended the last effort to reach any agreement with the Mensheviki and the Socialist Revolutionaries of the Right and Centre. In the future these parties would be treated with increasing severity, which would culminate in their virtual outlawry during most of the period of the civil war. But toward the end of November a temporary rapprochement was reached between the Bolsheviki and the Left Socialist Revolutionaries. The latter constituted the strongest party in a Peasants' Congress which was held in Petrograd in the last week of November. This Congress, which was hastily and irregularly elected, reflected the changed spirit of the time and was quite different in social make-up from the gathering of sober, well-to-do peasants and Socialist Revolutionary intellectuals which had met earlier in the year.

"To the right was a sprinkling of officers' epaulettes, and the patriarchal, bearded faces of the older, more substantial peasants; in the centre were a few peasants, non-commissioned officers, and

some soldiers; and on the left almost all the delegates wore the uniforms of common soldiers." [6]

Unlike the Congress of Soviets, this Peasants' Congress was not under Bolshevik leadership; and there was a good deal of hot debate, in which the principal figures were Lenin, Marie Spiridonova, emotional leader of the Left Socialist Revolutionaries, a slight, pale woman with spectacles and hair drawn flatly down, who had become a heroine in revolutionary circles because of the torment to which she was subjected after she had killed a Tsarist General, and Chernov, the former Minister for Agriculture of the Provisional Government, who still hoped to win support among the peasantry against the Bolshevik regime. Lenin emphasized the significance of the Land Law, which was drawn up in conformity with the desires of the peasants, and argued that the right of the workers to take over the factories was as indisputable as the right of the peasants to seize the land.

On November 27 an agreement was reached between the leaders of the Bolsheviki and of the Left Socialist Revolutionaries and the Peasant Congress, from which the more conservative delegates had seceded; the Peasants' Congress elected 108 delegates to the Soviet Executive Committee, which now became a formal representative organ of the peasants, as well as of the workers and soldiers. The delegates to the Peasants' Congress marched en masse to the headquarters of the Soviet, where the fusion of the two bodies was celebrated to the familiar accompaniment of revolutionary speeches and music.

Some time later, on December 22, the Left Socialist Revolutionaries agreed to enter the Government and received three places in the Soviet Cabinet, with Kalegaev as Commissar for Agriculture, Steinberg as Commissar for Justice and Proshyan as Commissar for Post and Telegraph. They left the Government again as a protest against the Peace of Brest-Litovsk; but maintained a loose working alliance with the Bolsheviki until the final breach, which resulted in their suppression, in the summer of 1918.

A noteworthy feature of the first weeks of the Soviet regime was the multitude of new decrees issued by the Government. In striking contrast to the Provisional Government, which had always seen an excuse for postponing a definite decision in the vastness or complexity of a subject, the Soviet authorities from the very beginning undertook to make pronouncements on the most vital questions: peace and land, rights of nationalities, control of industry

and finance. And, along with decrees on subjects of major importance, one finds in the first legislative acts of the Soviet Government a great quantity of regulations affecting the pettiest details of local administration. Together with measures of such outstanding importance as the decree on peace, the Land Law, the establishment of workers' control in industry, the nationalization of the banks, the definition of the rights of the peoples of Russia one finds decrees on such subjects as the taking over of the Petrograd Telephone Station by the Commissariat for Post and Telegraph, the uniting of some suburbs with the town of Bogorodsk, the assignment of 450,000 rubles (a sum of negligible value at this time) for the needs of the population of Kremenchug County, in Ukraina, which had suffered from a flood, the appointments and dismissals of officials.

In many cases the early Soviet decrees had declarative rather than immediate practical importance; Lenin was anxious to use a term of power which might be long or might be short in order to give as extensive a practical illustration of his policies as possible. Sessions of the Soviet Cabinet were held almost daily and usually lasted for five or six hours.[7] Subjects were brought up without preliminary preparation; speakers were limited to ten minutes; Lenin had a habit of sending scribbled notes on random pieces of paper to members of the Cabinet, asking for information on this or that point. Lenin presided regularly at these sessions, and the "points" in which he formulated his summary of the discussion were usually the basis of the subsequent decree.

Several organs of opposition to the Soviet Government continued to exist for some time after the November Revolution. An "underground Provisional Government," consisting of the assistant Ministers and of the Socialist Ministers who had been released from the Fortress of Peter and Paul, carried out shadowy functions for a time, meeting conspiratively at the apartments of sympathizers, holding discussions, passing resolutions. Kerensky from his hiding place communicated his resignation to this body.[8] The old Vtsik held some meetings; the Committee for Salvation existed for two or three weeks after the Revolution; the city Duma in Petrograd continued to be a forum for anti-Bolshevik speeches until it was dissolved at the end of November. But these organizations were helpless, because there was no armed force behind their speeches and resolutions. That the masses of the poorer classes in the large towns were on the side of the Bolsheviki during these first weeks of

the Soviet regime is scarcely open to question. Mme. Tyrkova-Williams, a prominent Cadet and a bitter opponent of the Bolsheviki, remarks in this connection, "The masses already looked upon the members of the Petrograd City Council as counterrevolutionaries," and tells how the workers who crowded into the galleries of the City Council during the last days of its existence shouted at the moderate Socialist members, who tried to pacify them by calling them "comrades": "What sort of comrades are we of yours? You are bourgeois, counterrevolutionaries. We will sweep all of you away with a dirty broom." [9]

This loyalty of the masses was not attributable to any improvement in material conditions after the Revolution. M. Philips Price, a foreign observer distinctly sympathetic with the Bolshevik viewpoint, describes the fall of his bread ration from half a pound to an eighth of a pound a day; other allowances included half a pound of sugar a month and a minute quantity of butter. Under the system of workers' control which was made legally effective on November 27, and which had actually been prevalent much earlier, something like anarchy prevailed in the industries. There was no common industrial plan and the factory committees had no higher authority to which they could look for guidance. Machinery was sold or bartered for raw material. Factory committees began to requisition railroad cars for their own needs.[10]

But, if the Bolsheviki could not give bread, they were stopping the War and they were giving the peasants a free hand with the land seizures. If they could do little to relieve the misery of the masses they were making the formerly well-to-do classes still more miserable: a fact of considerable psychological importance. For the Bolshevik Revolution brought out with unmistakable vividness the repressed hostile feeling, compounded of envy, hatred and mistrust, with which Russia's illiterate and semi-literate masses regarded the small propertied and educated class. Like the peasants' onslaught on the landlords, this feeling was ruthless, blind and undiscriminating. It did not spare the liberal or the moderate Socialist with a record of persecution under Tsarism. The ability of the Bolsheviki to exploit this feeling, to whip it up with the fierce eloquence of their leaders, Lenin, Trotzky, Zinoviev and others, who were seconded all over the country by a host of minor agitators, was a very strong factor in securing the maintenance of the Soviet regime, not only during the turbulent and uncertain first weeks,

when there was no effective organized opposition, but also under the far more severe test of intervention and civil war.

The Bolshevik leaders were quite conscious of the fact that their tenure of power depended largely on their success in bringing about peace. On November 26 three hastily chosen plenipotentiaries, Lieutenant Schneur (later exposed as an adventurer and a man who had offered his services to the Tsarist police) and two members of the Committee of the Fifth Army, with Krilenko's authorization approached the German lines near Dvinsk, protected by a white flag and a trumpeter, and were conducted to the German headquarters, where they proposed a meeting to discuss an armistice. Communication was established with the High Command of the German Eastern Front; and the latter proposed that a Russian delegation should proceed to Brest-Litovsk, a Polish town where the German High Command was stationed. December 2 was set as the date for the first meeting; in the meantime hostilities and fraternizing were to cease.

An invitation addressed by Trotzky to the representatives of the Allied powers to participate in the impending negotiations was ignored. A. A. Joffe, a Bolshevik, was selected as chief of the Soviet delegation, which also included the Bolsheviki Kamenev and Sokolnikov, the Left Socialist Revolutionaries, S. D. Mstislavsky and Mme. A. A. Bitzenko, a nonparty peasant as a representative of the Extraordinary Peasants' Congress and, in order to add the requisite proletarian tinge to the delegation, a worker, a soldier and a sailor, together with some military and naval experts. The Bolshevik Karakhan was secretary of the delegation.

The stiff German officers at Brest-Litovsk were doubtless horrified at the composition of this unusual peace delegation, with its professional revolutionaries, its worker, uncertain of the use of knife and fork at official banquets, and its peasant, chiefly interested in obtaining the strongest liquor obtainable. But they naturally welcomed the disappearance of Russia from the camp of their effective enemies and the negotiations for an armistice proceeded successfully, although General Hoffmann, a leading figure on the German side, who throughout the conference adopted a much more blunt and uncompromising tone than that of the civilian diplomats, took an early opportunity to attempt to put the Russians in their place. The Soviet delegates on December 4 suggested an armistice for six months, the evacuation of Dago, Oesel and Moon

Island by the German forces and an agreement that no troops should be moved from the Front.

Hoffmann indignantly retorted that such terms could only be proposed if the Central Powers were beaten and made counter-proposals which amounted to a flat refusal to evacuate the islands, an insistence on freedom of transferring troops and a demand that peace negotiations should follow the conclusion of the armistice.[11] On December 5 an armistice was agreed on, to last until December 17; a compromise formula which gave some satisfaction to the Russians, while leaving the Germans real freedom of action, was found in regard to the movement of troops. It was stipulated that only units which had received orders to be moved before December 5 should be shifted.[12] On December 15 a longer period for the armistice was established; it was to be effective from December 17 until January 14, 1918; and on December 22 the first session of the Peace Conference took place.[13]

Meanwhile a bleak winter was descending on Petrograd. Robberies were common, armed guards were posted in most of the large houses by the house committees. A peculiar form of disorder broke out in the form of the so-called "wine pogroms." Bands of the demoralized soldiers of the Petrograd garrison broke into liquor storehouses and drank themselves into unconsciousness. On December 15 the Vtsik appointed Blagonravov "extraordinary military commissar of Petrograd for combating drunkenness and pogroms" and decided to place military forces at his disposal and to commission him to destroy the stocks of wine and "to clear Petrograd of hooligan bands, to disarm and arrest all those who have disgraced themselves by participation in drunkenness and destruction."[14] Drastic measures, including in some cases the use of firearms, were required before the plundering and guzzling of the liquor stocks could be stopped.

Order of a kind was maintained during the first weeks of the Revolution by patrols of Red Guards. The need of a more centralized and specialized police force soon became evident; and on December 20 the veteran Polish Bolshevik, Felix Dzerzhinsky, a man with an extraordinarily long record of prison and hard labor for revolutionary activity, carried out Lenin's instruction and formed the organization which subsequently became so dreaded under the name of the Cheka, the Russian abbreviation for its official title: "All-Russian Commission for Struggle with Counter-revolution and Sabotage." As it ultimately developed, the Cheka

was second to few, if any, similar institutions in history in the ruthlessness of its terrorism and in its farflung network of espionage. But in the beginning its staff was small; its resources were limited; and the few death sentences which it passed were on bandits and ordinary criminals. It endeavored to mobilize the masses for spying out the work of counterrevolutionaries; one of its early appeals reads as follows: [15]

"The Commission appeals to all workers, soldiers and peasants to come to its aid in the struggle with enemies of the Revolution. Send all news and facts about organizations and individual persons whose activity is harmful to the Revolution and the people's power to the Commission for Struggle with Counterrevolution and Sabotage.

"The Commission proposes to all local Soviets to proceed immediately to the organization of similar Commissions. The resistance of enemies of the Revolution will be broken more quickly by general united efforts."

As the Government felt itself more firmly in the saddle it proceeded to aim one blow after another at the institutions of private property. The right of private ownership of large houses was abolished on December 6; such dwellings were transferred to the ownership of town Soviets, or Councils where Soviets did not exist; and the administration of the houses was placed in the hands of house committees, elected by the residents.[16] There was as yet no wholesale nationalization of industry; this would only come in the summer of 1918. But the Supreme Economic Council, a body charged with general management of the economic and financial affairs of the country and provided with the right of confiscating or sequestrating industrial enterprises, was decreed on December 15; and industrial enterprises which refused to submit to workers' control were generally taken over by the state.

Lenin had always attached great importance to the rôle of the banks in modern economic society. On December 27 banking was declared a state monopoly; all banks were nationalized, and the former private banks were fused with the State Bank. On the following day all proprietors of safes in banks were ordered to appear within three days and submit the contents to inspection. If they failed to comply with this order the contents of the safes were confiscated; all gold held privately was taken over by the state. Soon afterwards, on January 5, 1918, all payments of dividends and dealings in shares were declared illegal; and on February 10 a sweeping decree annulled all debts of the Russian Government. Foreign debts were repudiated "unconditionally and without any

exception." Citizens of the poorer classes who owned not more than 10,000 rubles of state loans were offered the doubtful financial advantage of an equal sum of a new state loan of the Soviet Government, the conditions of which were to be "specially defined." [17] The inflation of the currency, which had made great strides under the regime of the Provisional Government and was continued practically without limitation under the Soviets, was even more effective than confiscatory decrees in wiping out all money savings, while the nationalization of the land and the steady practise of confiscation and requisition in the towns made it impossible for people of wealth to transfer their money into any form of more tangible property.

Wages and salaries thus tended to become the sole source of available income; and the first steps of the new regime were in the direction of equalizing these to a very large degree. So the state ceased to pay pensions of any amount above three hundred rubles a month. Members of the Council of People's Commissars were restricted to salaries of five hundred rubles a month, if unmarried, with an extra allowance of a hundred rubles for each child; in the matter of apartments they were to be restricted to one room for each member of the family. [18] The Spartan intention of these measures is evident if one considers that at this time the ruble had perhaps a twentieth of its pre-war purchasing power. In actual practise the living standard of a Commissar was not determined exclusively, or even mainly, by his money salary; a good deal depended on the apartment which was allotted to him or on the organization of the store where he obtained his rations or of the restaurant where he took his meals. Lenin, Dzerzhinsky and Chicherin, the subsequent Commissar for Foreign Affairs, acquired a special reputation for austere living; and in general, although the new heads of the Government certainly did not share the extreme suffering and hunger which the years of civil war brought to the masses, Party ethics and sheer pressure of work seem to have checked, in the main, any lapse into gross luxury.

The provinces followed the lead of the central Government in carrying out what Lenin later called "a Red Guard offensive against capital." So on December 18 the Soviet of Ekaterinburg, in the Urals, "in view of its great need of resources," imposed a tax of 150,000 rubles on local capitalists. In Baku on the same day the city council, which was dominated by the Bolsheviki, decided to raise a forced "loan" of 5,000,000 rubles from the bourgeoisie. In

Samara, on December 25, the local Military Revolutionary Committee decided to let out of prison nineteen "capitalist hostages" who had agreed, after a term in prison, to pay the sums which were demanded of them. The Soviet of the town of Soroka, in remote Karelia, decided to take over some sawmills which belonged to the Brothers Byelaev and to forbid the managers of the factories to live in the region.

Other typical instances of measures of persuasion applied to refractory capitalists were the action of Antonov-Ovseenko, commander of the Red partisan army in the South, who had fifteen of the wealthiest men in Kharkov arrested and brought to his train, where he threatened to send them to the Donetz mines if they did not pay a million rubles which the workers were demanding as pay for the Christmas holidays,[19] and the decision of the Ural Territory Soviet to arrest the bureau of Ekaterinburg mineowners on January 9.

It was not only in the economic field that the old Russian world was being turned upside down. The Soviet Government displayed an insatiable desire for innovation. The Russian alphabet was pruned of letters and signs which were considered superfluous. The traditional Russian calendar, which was thirteen days behind the Western in its calculation of time, was discarded; after February 1, 1918, Russia officially reckoned its time according to the Western calendar.

The strict pre-War Russian marriage and divorce laws were swept away by two decrees, dated December 18.[20] According to these decrees only civil marriage was to be recognized by the state; children born out of wedlock were to be given the same rights as the offspring of marriages; divorce, which had formerly been difficult to obtain, was to be had for the asking by either party to a marriage. The new laws also emphasized the full juridical equality of men and women.

The complete separation of church from state and of school from church was decreed in a law promulgated on February 9, 1918. Under this law every Soviet citizen was free to profess any or no religion; no religious ceremonies were to be performed in connection with any state function; religious teaching was forbidden in public and in private schools where general subjects were taught, although citizens had the right to give and receive religious training privately. Churches and religious societies were denied the right to own property.

The courts also felt the sweep of the innovating broom. The old judges were removed from office and replaced by new ones, who were to be elected either by the Soviets or by popular vote.[21] Former laws were to be valid "only inasmuch as they are not abolished by the Revolution and do not contradict revolutionary conscience and revolutionary sense of right." This sweeping but somewhat vague reservation was supplemented by a provision to the effect that all laws which conflict with decrees of the Soviet Government, and with the minimum programme of the Social Democratic and Socialist Revolutionary Parties are annulled. Revolutionary tribunals, consisting of a president and six jurors, elected by the Soviets, were set up to deal with cases involving counterrevolution and sabotage.

One of the first striking cases to be tried before one of these Tribunals was that of Countess Sofia Panina, who was accused of refusing to turn over to the Bolsheviki 92,000 rubles of state funds which were in her possession in the Ministry for Public Welfare. Countess Panina's defense was that she did not regard the Bolshevik regime as a legitimate government. In pre-revolutionary days Countess Panina had been an active social worker and had founded a People's Palace, where many workers learned to read and write and took educational courses. One of the former students in this People's Palace, a workman named Ivanov, spoke in defense of the Countess and ended his address in homely Russian fashion: "For all that you did for me and for many of us I bow low to you." But the Tribunal was not moved by sentiment; it had received its instructions from the Bolshevik Commissar for Justice, Stuchka; and the verdict was that Countess Panina must remain in prison until the 92,000 rubles was surrendered. Ultimately some of her friends raised the money and procured her release.[22]

The foreign Embassies remained in Petrograd for some time after the Revolution, pursuing a policy of passive observation. There was no disposition to recognize the Soviet Government: dislike of its social and economic ideas, resentment at the abandonment of the Allied cause and indignation excited by the flippant, offhand repudiation of Russia's substantial foreign debts all weighted the scales against this. Moreover, in the early period of their regime the Bolshevik leaders were extremely neglectful of the distinction, on which they would later insist with meticulous care, between their foreign policy and their views on the desirability of promoting social revolution throughout the world.

"What sort of diplomatic work will we have?" said Trotzky, soon after his appointment as Commissar for Foreign Affairs. "I will issue some revolutionary proclamations to the peoples and then shut up the shop." [23]

Early in December Lenin and Stalin, as Commissar for Nationality Affairs, signed a flamboyant appeal to the Mohammedan peoples of Russia and of the East, in which, with a good deal of revolutionary phraseology, they urged the Mohammedans of India "to throw off the robbers and enslavers of your countries." Whether this appeal, which was supposed to be printed in a million copies in all Mohammedan languages, was actually circulated with any effect outside of Russia is doubtful. But it caused considerable annoyance to Sir George Buchanan, the British Ambassador, who declared in a press statement that "the attitude of the Soviet leaders is more calculated to estrange than to attract the sympathies of the British working classes." [24]

One naïve document of this infant period of Soviet diplomacy is sufficiently brief and sufficiently amusing to be worth citing in full:

"In view of the fact that the Soviet regime stands on the basis of the principles of international solidarity of the proletariat and brotherhood of the toilers of all countries; that the struggle against war and imperialism can lead to full victory only on an international scale,

"The Council of People's Commissars considers it necessary to come to the aid of the left, internationalist wing of the workers' movement of all countries with all possible resources, including money, quite irrespective of whether these countries are at war or in alliance with Russia or maintain a neutral position.

"For these purposes the Council of People's Commissars decides to assign for the needs of the revolutionary internationalist movement at the disposition of foreign representatives of the Commissariat for Foreign Affairs two million rubles.

"President of the Council of People's Commissars, V. Ulianov (Lenin)
"Commissar for Foreign Affairs, L. Trotzky" [25]

This conception of foreign diplomatic representatives as paymasters of the radical parties in the countries to which they were accredited was not calculated to hasten diplomatic rapprochement between Russia and other countries, apart from the other issues which caused the Allied powers to take a decidedly unfavorable view of the Soviet regime.

Trotzky was energetic in diplomacy, as in everything else; and non-recognition did not prevent him from taking vigorous action whenever circumstances seemed to permit it. So he obtained the

release of some Russians who had been interned in England by threatening to stop the departure of British residents in Russia. He raised a teapot tempest over the case of a certain Captain Kalpashnikov, a Russian officer in the service of the American Red Cross, who, through a misunderstanding, was suspected of shipping automobiles to Kaledin's headquarters in Rostov. He called on the French Ambassador, M. Noulens, to protest against alleged support of the Ukrainian Rada by French officers stationed in Ukraina.

These were minor incidents; a more serious complication arose on January 13, when the Rumanian Ambassador in Petrograd, M. Diamandi, and the members of the Rumanian Military Mission were arrested as a reprisal for the action of the Rumanian military authorities in surrounding and disarming some Russian troops in Rumania. All the members of the diplomatic corps joined in a protest on the following day and Diamandi was promptly released, the official Soviet Government communiqué stating that the purpose of his arrest, that of making a protest against Rumania's actions, had been achieved. Later in the month the Rumanian Ambassador and his staff were deported; this coincided with the occupation of the Russian province of Bessarabia by Rumanian troops. At the same time the Rumanian gold reserve, which had, unfortunately for the Rumanian Government, been transferred to Petrograd for safekeeping, was seized by the Soviet authorities, with the understanding that "it was to be preserved as the property of the Rumanian people and kept inaccessible to the Rumanian oligarchy." Nothing more has been heard of this Rumanian gold; it is perhaps regarded as an informal set-off for the Rumanian annexation of Bessarabia.

After military opposition to the Bolshevik regime in Northern and Central Russia had been crushed and after such bodies as the Committee for Salvation, the Petrograd City Council and the old Vtsik had faded away, the opponents of Bolshevism retained one faint hope. This was the convocation of the Constituent Assembly, the election of which had been fixed by the Provisional Government, after several delays, for November 25. In relation to the Constituent Assembly the Bolsheviki found themselves in a political dilemma. They had no intention of handing over the power which they had won through insurrection to this body; and Lenin had long proclaimed the theory that the Soviets, from which the propertied classes were excluded, represented a higher form of democ-

racy than the Constituent Assembly, which was to be chosen on the basis of universal suffrage.

On the other hand they had attacked the Provisional Government so much for postponing the meeting of the Assembly that it seemed politically inexpedient to cancel or delay the election after they had come into power. Lenin, who was always more uncompromising than some of his associates in his contempt for what he called "bourgeois" democracy, was strongly in favor of postponing the election.[26] On this point, however, he was overruled; it was decided to carry through the election and to allow the Assembly to meet, but to dissolve it if it showed any signs of refractoriness. As early as November 21 Volodarsky declared at a meeting of Communist leaders: "We may have to dissolve the Constituent Assembly with bayonets." [27]

Although the Vtsik had issued an appeal for freedom of election, the circumstances of the voting, which began in Petrograd on November 25 and continued for some time in other parts of the country, were naturally affected by the Bolshevik dictatorship and by the general confusion of the time. The Cadets especially labored under considerable disadvantages; their newspapers were suppressed; their meetings were held with difficulty; many of their leaders were arrested or were in hiding.

There was no wholesale falsification of the election returns, however; the best proof of this is the fact that the Bolsheviki received only about twenty-five percent of the recorded votes. No complete accurate record of the votes cast in this first, and last, election held in Russia under a system of universal suffrage and relative freedom of speech and press is available. But figures compiled by a Socialist Revolutionary, N. V. Svyatitzky, and accepted by Lenin as accurate, covering fifty-four out of the seventy-nine electoral districts, and all the fronts, give a fairly reliable picture of the trend of the voting.

According to these figures the Russian Socialist Revolutionaries polled 16,500,000 votes; the Bolsheviki, 9,023,963; Ukrainian and other non-Russian Socialist Revolutionaries, 4,400,000; the Cadets, 1,856,639; other conservative and middleclass groups and parties, Russian and non-Russian, about 2,750,000; moderate Socialist Democrats of all shadings, Mensheviki, People's Socialists, etc., about 1,700,000.

One could summarize the result more briefly by saying that about 62 percent of the votes were cast for moderate Socialists of

all kinds, mostly for the Socialist Revolutionaries, about 25 percent for the Bolsheviki and about 13 percent for the conservative and middleclass liberal parties. An undefined number of the Socialist Revolutionary votes were cast for Left Socialist Revolutionaries; but the lists of candidates had been made up before the Left Socialist Revolutionaries had formally broken away from the Party; and the combination of Bolsheviki and Left Socialist Revolutionaries still remained a minority in the Assembly.

But if the total vote was thus unfavorable to the Bolsheviki, an analysis of its distribution shows that the opposition majority in the Constituent Assembly was no real menace to the new dictatorship. The big Socialist Revolutionary vote was rolled up in the country districts, where the peasants voted partly from habit, partly because of the well organized agitation of the Executive Committee of the Council of Peasants' Deputies. Behind these votes there were no rifles.

The Bolsheviki, on the other hand, received a large preponderance of votes just in those places which were strategically most important, in Petrograd and in Moscow, in the fronts which were nearest to the capital, in the Baltic Fleet. As Lenin subsequently observed,[28] they had "an overwhelming preponderance of force at the decisive moment in the decisive points."

The Cadets received practically no support among the soldiers or among the peasants; but as a general rule they received more votes than the moderate Socialists in the large towns. In Petrograd and Moscow together, for instance, the votes were divided as follows: Bolsheviki, 837,000; Cadets, 515,400; Socialist Revolutionaries, 218,000; all others, 194,700.

While the Bolsheviki were taking measures to maintain their power at all costs, sending those delegates whom they elected to the Constituent Assembly on a round of agitation to factories and barracks, preparing reliable military units,[29] the prevalent mood among the Socialist Revolutionaries and among the radical and liberal intelligentsia who supported the Constituent Assembly was one of apathy and depression. The Socialist Revolutionary delegates who arrived in Petrograd, mostly inexperienced provincials, were dismayed at finding in Petrograd not a warm welcome as people's representatives, but an armed camp of their enemies.

The Assembly was not altogether neglected. A Committee for the Defense of the Constituent Assembly was formed and worked in contact with the Military Commission of the Socialist Revolu-

tionary Party in an effort to insure some measures of protection for the Assembly when it should open. The Military Commission brought a few Socialist Revolutionary soldiers from the front, tried with little success to recruit armed groups among the workers who still considered themselves Socialist Revolutionaries and carried on propaganda among two former Guards regiments, the Semyenov and the Preobrazhensky, which were showing symptoms of disaffection with the Bolsheviki.[30] But any prospect of obtaining support from the soldiers vanished when the Central Committee of the Socialist Revolutionary Party rejected the suggestion of having the regiments come out with arms on the day of the opening of the Assembly. The soldiers had nothing but contempt for the idea of an unarmed demonstration.

The Soviet Government announced on December 9 that the Assembly would open as soon as 400 deputies had arrived in Petrograd. The "underground" Provisional Government had set December 11 as the date for the opening of the Constituent Assembly; and on this day forty-three members of the Constituent Assembly, mostly Right Socialist Revolutionaries, went to the Tauride Palace, accompanied by a crowd of some ten thousand sympathizers, forced their way in and held an impromptu session, which was largely devoted to protests against the action of the Bolsheviki in arresting some members of the Constituent Assembly. The participants in the demonstration themselves seemed in doubt as to whether they had held a meeting of the Assembly or a private gathering; and the Soviet Government prevented any repetition of the incident by strengthening the guard at the Tauride Palace. On the same day the Council of People's Commissars, striking back at the demonstrators, declared the Cadets "enemies of the People" and their leaders subject to arrest and trial by revolutionary tribunals.[31] Two prominent Cadets, the former Minister for Finance, A. I. Shingarev, and F. F. Kokoshkin, were arrested and imprisoned in the Fortress of Peter and Paul. Later they were transferred to a hospital, where they were brutally murdered by a band of soldiers and sailors on the night of January 18. Both were men of conspicuous idealism; and on the eve of his murder by the representatives of the masses Shingarev was writing in his diary how in his student days he had been struck by class inequality in Russia, how he had decided to "go to the people" as a doctor and how he "would not hesitate to begin all over again, notwithstanding all the horrors the country has gone through."[32]

The commission which the Provisional Government had appointed to prepare and supervise the election to the Constituent Assembly was dissolved and the Bolshevik Uritzky was placed in charge of arrangements for its convocation. A clear exposition of the prospective Bolshevik attitude toward the Assembly was given in a series of theses on the subject, written by Lenin and published in *Pravda* of December 26. After expressing the opinion that "a republic of Soviets is a higher form of democratism than the ordinary bourgeois republic with a constituent assembly," Lenin declared that "the sole chance of a painless solution of the crisis which has arisen as a result of the lack of correspondence between the election to the Constituent Assembly and the will of the people, and the interests of the toiling and exploited classes . . . is an unreserved statement of the Constituent Assembly about recognition of the Soviet regime, and the Soviet Revolution, of its policy in regard to peace, land and workers' control, a decisive adherence of the Constituent Assembly to the camp of enemies of the Cadet-Kaledin counterrevolution." About the same time Uritzky, speaking at a session of the Petrograd Committee of the Bolshevik Party, summed up the situation as follows:

"Shall we convene the Constituent Assembly? Yes. Shall we disperse it? Perhaps; it depends on circumstances."

The atmosphere on the eve of the opening of the Constituent Assembly became more tense when shots were fired at Lenin as he was returning from a meeting on the evening of January 14. He was uninjured; Fritz Platten, a Swiss Socialist, who was in the automobile, was slightly wounded in the hand. There may have been some connection between this unsuccessful attack and a scheme which had been hatched by a few of the more militant Socialist Revolutionaries to kidnap Lenin and Trotzky and hold them as hostages,[33] a scheme which was given up when the Party Central Committee condemned it.

The first and sole meeting of the Assembly took place on January 18. Just as had been the case when the first Duma met in the spring of 1906, the newly elected legislators found themselves surrounded by hostile troops. The whole district around the Tauride Palace was heavily guarded; and soldiers and sailors with rifles, pistols and cartridge belts prominently displayed filled the building. A demonstration of sympathizers with the Assembly, among whom the middleclass intellectuals and office workers predominated, took place; but the unarmed demonstrators had little chance against

the armed Bolshevik soldiery and were dispersed after some shooting, in which, according to the Bolshevik estimates, seven or eight
persons were killed.

Just as a venerable Socialist Revolutionary named Shvetzov, as
the senior deputy, was on the point of opening the Assembly,
Sverdlov appeared on the platform, took away the presiding officer's bell from Shvetzov and opened the meeting in the name of
the Soviet Executive Committee. Sverdlov read a "declaration of
the rights of the toiling and exploited people," to which he invited
the Assembly to subscribe. Among its points were the vesting of
all power in the Soviets, the abolition of private property in land,
the attempt to achieve a general democratic peace, the cancellation
of state loans, the nationalization of the banks and the establishment of workers' control of industry.

However, there was a definite anti-Bolshevik majority in the
Assembly, as was shown when the moderate Socialist Revolutionary,
Chernov, was elected President, receiving 244 votes, as against
153 cast for Marie Spiridonova, the Left Socialist Revolutionary
whom the Bolsheviki supported. Chernov delivered a somewhat
flabby speech, in which he vainly endeavored to conciliate the
hostile Bolshevik part of the Assembly by emphasizing his anti-war
views and his desire for the transfer of the land to the peasantry.
The Georgian Menshevik Tseretelli made a more substantial address, in which he asked what were the concrete results of the effort to organize industry along socialist lines and, in response to
an interpolation, "Sabotage," retorted: "I want to warn you, citizens,
if you set out to achieve a socialist order, you bear witness to your
own incompetence if you attribute the failure of the socialist experiment to the sabotage of the bourgeoisie." [34] He emphasized
the disunion of the country, the destruction of civil liberties and
the hopelessness of obtaining a democratic peace in the midst of
anarchy and civil war.

But speeches, good or bad, strong or weak, were of no avail in
deciding the fate of the doomed Assembly. The soldiers and sailors
in the galleries were the deciding force; and they interrupted all
the Socialist Revolutionary speeches with hoots, jeers and hostile
interjections. When the Assembly refused to discuss Sverdlov's
declaration the Bolshevik delegates withdrew and decided not to
return.

The Assembly prolonged its session until almost five o'clock
on the morning of the 6th, adopting three legislative measures.

The first was a Land Law which closely copied the main features of the Soviet decree on the same subject. The second was an appeal to the Allied powers, in which regret was expressed that the negotiations with Germany had assumed the character of negotiations for a separate peace. The Constituent Assembly, however, sanctioned the armistice and proposed to carry on further negotiations itself. At the same time it proposed to coöperate in the convocation of an international socialist conference "for the purpose of realizing a general democratic peace." Finally, the Assembly proclaimed Russia a democratic federative republic.[35]

As Chernov was reading the decree on land the commandant of the Tauride Palace, an Anarchist sailor named Zheleznyak, stepped up to him and asked the delegates to disperse, "since the guard is tired." Chernov hastened to finish the reading of the decree and put it to a vote; it was carried without opposition. Then the delegates dispersed, Chernov having appointed noon on January 19 as the time for the opening of the next session. But this next session was never held. For on January 19 the All-Russian Soviet Executive Committee published a decree dissolving the Constituent Assembly, on the ground that it was serving "only as a cover for the struggle of bourgeois counterrevolution for the overthrow of the power of the Soviets." The decree was convincingly supported by the strong guard which barred all approaches to the Tauride Palace. Russia's brief experiment in democratic parliamentarism was ended.

"On our side were legality, great ideals and faith in the triumph of democracy.

"On their side were activity, machine-guns, weapons." [36]

This is how one embittered supporter of the Constituent Assembly reacted to its dissolution. No doubt this was the predominant sentiment among the radical and liberal intelligentsia. But the dissolution of Russia's first and sole freely elected parliament evoked scarcely a ripple of interest and protest, so far as the masses were concerned.

There were two main reasons for this popular indifference. First, the Bolsheviki, by seizing power and taking the decisions which the majority of the people wanted on the engrossing questions of land and peace, had robbed the deliberations of the Assembly of most of their interest. It was distinctly significant that the Assembly, in its three legislative acts, simply followed along the path which the Bolsheviki had marked out.

A second and more fundamental cause of the defenseless col-

lapse of the Assembly was the absence in Russia of any parliamentary tradition, of any widespread understanding, among the masses, of the significance of universal suffrage, free parliamentary debate, civil liberties and other things which, in Western countries, were the fruits of centuries of a process of struggle and evolution which had no parallel in Russia. The Constituent Assembly collapsed because it had no solid foundation, because Russia was conspicuously lacking in all the conditions which historical experience indicates as essential to the effective functioning of parliamentary democracy: general literacy; a numerous, well organized middle class, a long tradition of settling internal differences by peaceful methods; a keen sense of personal and property rights. Because Russia lacked these characteristics the alternative to Tsarism was not constitutional monarchy or liberal republicanism, but Bolshevism. And for just the same reason the alternative to Bolshevism, had it failed to survive the ordeal of civil war, the first shots of which were already being fired, would not have been Chernov, opening a Constituent Assembly, elected according to the most modern rules of equal suffrage and proportional representation, but a military dictator, a Kolchak or a Denikin, riding into Moscow on a white horse to the accompaniment of the clanging bells of the old capital's hundreds of churches.

NOTES

[1] *Edinstvo* (Unity), No. 180.

[2] "Protocols of the Russian Social Democratic Labor Party," p. 156.

[3] The term "democracy" was often used in Russia in 1917 to describe all non-bourgeois parties and groups, ranging from Bolsheviki to very moderate Socialists.

[4] In reality a number of workers' organizations in Petrograd expressed themselves as favorable to the idea of an All-Socialist Government.

[5] For the full texts of the resignations and of Lenin's reply *cf.* "Protocols of the Russian Social Democratic Labor Party," pp. 157–163.

[6] John Reed, "Ten Days That Shook the World," p. 297.

[7] Leon Trotzky, "Mein Leben," p. 329.

[8] *Cf.* article of A. Demyanov, "Notes on the Underground Provisional Government" in Vol. VII of *Archive of the Russian Revolution.*

[9] Ariadna Tyrkova-Williams, "From Liberty to Brest-Litovsk," pp. 328, 330.

[10] M. Philips Price, "Reminiscences of the Russian Revolution," pp. 206ff.

[11] *Izvestia,* Nos. 234–237, for 1917.

[12] *Novaya Zhizn* (New Life), No. 171.

[13] For the sake of narrative continuity the further course of the Brest-Litovsk negotiations is reserved for Chapter XVIII.

[14] *Izvestia,* Nos. 244, 246, for 1917.

[15] *Ibid.,* No. 252, for 1917.

[16] "Decrees of the October Revolution," Vol. I, pp. 163–168.

[17] "Collection of Decrees, 1917–1918," p. 18.

[18] *Pravda,* No. 195, for 1917.

[19] V. A. Antonov-Ovseenko, "Reminiscences of the Civil War," Vol. I, pp. 178, 179.

[20] "Decrees of the October Revolution," pp. 333–339.

[21] *Ibid.*, pp. 154ff.

[22] Tyrkova-Williams, *op. cit.*, pp. 385–389.

[23] Trotzky, *op. cit.*, p. 327.

[24] Sir George Buchanan, "My Russian Mission and Other Diplomatic Memories," Vol. II, pp. 233ff.

[25] *Izvestia*, No. 259, for 1917.

[26] Leon Trotzky, "Lenin," pp. 119ff.

[27] I. N. Lubimov, "The Revolution of 1917: Chronicle of Events," Vol. VI, p. 99.

[28] *Cf.* Lenin's article, "Elections to the Constituent Assembly and the Dictatorship of the Proletariat," in his "Collected Works," Vol. XVI, pp. 439–459.

[29] With a view to insuring the dispersal of the Constituent Assembly by force of arms, if necessary, Lenin ordered the transfer to Petrograd of a Lettish regiment, consisting almost entirely of workers. He feared that peasant soldiers might not be fully reliable in such an emergency. *Cf.* Trotzky, "Lenin," p. 122.

[30] *Cf.* the article of Boris Sokolov, "The Defense of the Constituent Assembly," in Vol. XIII of *Archive of the Russian Revolution.*

[31] *Izvestia*, No. 239, for 1917.

[32] Tyrkova-Williams, *op. cit.*, pp. 364, 365.

[33] *Cf.* Sokolov in *Archive of the Russian Revolution.*

[34] "The All-Russian Constituent Assembly," in the series, "1917 in Documents and Materials," p. 40.

[35] *Ibid.*, pp. 112, 113.

[36] Sokolov, *op. cit.*

CHAPTER XVII

CIVIL WAR BEGINS

WITH their power firmly established in northern and central Russia, the Soviet leaders in December decided to crush the two main centres of opposition to their regime in the Don and in Ukraina. On December 13 Lenin commissioned Antonov-Ovseenko, the fiery ex-officer and revolutionary who had played such an active part in the seizure of power in Petrograd, to take charge of operations against the Cossack General Kaledin and his "abettors," a phrase which was meant to apply to the Ukrainian nationalists.[1]

Antonov immediately went to the Stavka and subsequently established headquarters in Kharkov. Kaledin was regarded as the most immediate and dangerous enemy; and Antonov's plan of campaign was to cut off the Don from Ukraina and to utilize the Black Sea sailors in diversion operations in Kaledin's rear. At his disposal was a loosely organized, ill-disciplined force of six or seven thousand troops, with thirty or forty cannon and a few dozen machine-guns.[2] This "army" was divided into several partisan detachments, which kept in irregular touch with one another; the soldiers were mainly recruited from the Baltic sailors and the more adventurous of the Petrograd and Moscow Red Guards, with a very small number of soldiers of the old army who still had some stomach for fighting.

The military quality of this motley force was very low; Antonov, in his own account of his campaign, repeatedly cites instances when units refused to obey orders to advance or fled at the first volley of hostile shots. However, discipline and morale were equally lacking on the other side; and sheer weight of numbers (the original six or seven thousand were reinforced and increased by new Red Guard levies and by an accession of strength from local insurgents in the regions where fighting took place) was calculated in the end to insure victory for the Reds.

Although Antonov's first blows were directed against Kaledin, relations between the Soviet Government and the Ukrainian Rada were becoming increasingly strained. On December 17 the Soviet

Government despatched an ultimatum to the Rada, presenting four demands and declaring that, if no satisfactory reply was received within forty-eight hours, "the Council of People's Commissars will regard the Rada as in a condition of open war against the Soviet power in Russia and in Ukraina."

The demands were that the Rada should cease disorganizing the front by recalling Ukrainian units without previous consultation with the Soviet Commander-in-chief, that it should not permit troops to pass through its territory to the Don and the Urals without the consent of the Commander-in-chief, that it should coöperate with the revolutionary troops in fighting with Kaledin, and that it should cease disarming Soviet troops and Red Guards in Ukraina and restore the arms which had been taken away from them.[3]

The Ukrainian General Secretariat, as the Cabinet responsible to the Rada was called, despatched a sharp reply to this ultimatum, declaring that it was dishonest or contradictory for the Council of People's Commissars simultaneously to recognize Ukraina's right to selfdetermination and to impose its own form of political organization upon Ukraina. The General Secretariat asserted its right to create an Ukrainian front and to disarm military units which did not recognize its authority; justified its policy of permitting Cossacks to proceed to the Don through its territory by a reference to the right of the Don, the Ural and other territories to set up their own independent governments and proposed the organization of a federal all-Socialist Government.

Although this reply did not satisfy the Soviet demands, actual hostilities were delayed for a time and a representative of the Congress of Peasants' Deputies undertook to mediate between the Council of People's Commissars and the General Secretariat. Efforts at mediation came to nothing; the Ukrainian Bolshevik leaders fled from Kiev to the more hospitable atmosphere of Kharkov and here organized an Ukrainian Soviet Government on December 27; and the Council of People's Commissars on December 29 recognized this as the "real Government of the people's Ukrainian Republic."

The power of the Ukrainian Rada was brittle and its troops were unreliable. When Muraviev, a former Captain and organizer of shock battalions who had come over to the Bolsheviki, set out from Kharkov on a drive against the Rada he captured Poltava, the first large town on his route, with a loss of only one man killed.[4]

In general the characteristics of this early phase of the civil war were the small numbers of troops engaged, the lightness of the casualties, the ease with which both sides succumbed to panic, and the general atmosphere of confusion and disorganization. The country was war-weary to the last degree, and neither Reds nor Whites were able to muster large organized forces. Such fighting as occurred was almost exclusively along the railroad lines.

Although the nationalist slogans of the Rada possessed a considerable appeal to the Ukrainian middle classes and to the more educated peasants, the spirit of social upheaval was so strong at this time that the Ukrainian nationalist forces could not make a successful stand against the invading force of Muraviev, which pushed on from Poltava toward Kiev. One large town after another passed into the hands of the Bolsheviki as a result of local uprisings of the workers. So Ekaterinoslav was taken on January 10; Zhmerinka and Vinnitsa on January 23; Odessa on January 30; Nikolaev on February 4.

The forces of the Rada endeavored to drive back Muraviev at Kruti, a railroad station east of Kiev; but were defeated after a two-day battle on January 30. Meanwhile the workers of the Arsenal district in Kiev, among whom Bolshevik influence was strong, raised an uprising against the Rada in its capital. This was suppressed after several days of heavy firing and bombardment (Kiev suffered much more than the average Russian city during the vicissitudes of civil war), since Petlura's retreating troops, arriving in Kiev, gave the Rada supporters a decisive superiority.

But Muraviev's advance continued; and after several days of street fighting and bombardment this stronghold of Ukrainian nationalism was captured by the Reds on February 9. The Rada Ministers fled to Zhitomir. About the same time the Ukrainian delegation at Brest-Litovsk concluded a separate peace with the Germans, a move which paved the way for the German occupation of Ukraina and the expulsion of the Bolsheviki.

The Ukrainian Soviet Government took up its residence in Kiev; but during the short time when it was able to remain there it became clear that it was far easier to capture cities, with the aid of the Red Guards, than to organize passably efficient administration. Muraviev's ill disciplined troops committed many excesses; shooting and pillaging were common. At one of its first sessions the Kiev Soviet passed a strong resolution of protest against lynchings, shootings without trial and other outrages committed by the

Red troops, demanding that "those who disgraced themselves by the murder of unarmed people must be expelled from the socialist army and handed over to a revolutionary court." [5]

Kiev, incidentally, was not the only place which witnessed conflicts of this kind between the Red Guards, who included a considerable proportion of ruffianly and criminal elements, and the local Bolsheviki in the Soviets, who at this time were milder than they became later under the stress of prolonged civil war, accompanied by ruthless terrorism on both sides. There were similar protests against arbitrary executions in the Soviets of Rostov, after it was captured, and of Kharkov, where Antonov suggestively describes one member of his "revolutionary court" as "the uncompromising sailor Trushin, who regarded everyone with white hands as worthy of extermination." [6]

Apart from the excesses of the invading troops, the problem of governing Kiev was made more difficult by continual robberies (all the criminals had been released from the prisons during the protracted street fighting) and by the acute shortage of paper money, which bore especially hard on the workers. In an effort to cope with food difficulties the Soviet Government published an order for the requisitioning of all surplus food products, even "employing armed force, if necessary, in the struggle with speculation and malicious hoarding." [7]

But long before this or other decrees of the Soviet authorities could yield noticeable results a serious threat to Kiev appeared. News arrived that the Central powers had concluded a separate peace with the Rada, providing for the exportation of grain and other food products from Ukraina to Germany and for the destruction of the Soviet regime in Ukraina. Soon after this it was learned that a large German and Austrian force, along with the beaten troops of the Rada, was on the march to Kiev.

There was no possibility of successfully defending the city. Muraviev had moved off and was waging an indecisive war of ultimata and demonstrations with the Rumanians, who had occupied Bessarabia. The forces at the disposal of the Ukrainian Soviet Government were small in number, poorly armed and disciplined. A well equipped Czecho-Slovak corps, made up of Czech war prisoners and deserters from the Austrian army, decided to maintain neutrality in the German-Soviet conflict and to withdraw from the city. There were panicky features in the evacuation of Kiev; the Executive Committee of the Soviet leaped on the first train

"The Comrade was found"

for Poltava without convening the Soviet and without taking any measures to guard the rifles which were left in the building of the Soviet;[8] the bridge across the Dnieper River was prematurely dynamited before the Soviet troops had succeeded in crossing; only the fact that the explosion was not very effective saved them from being cut off. The Soviet leaders left Kiev on March 1 after a rule of less than three weeks; on the following day the grey-uniformed German troops marched into the city. The Rada was nominally reinstated; but actually the supreme power in Ukraina was the German Command, which methodically and systematically extended the occupation until it included the whole of Ukraina.

While the Soviet regime was being set up in Ukraina, only to fall under the pressure of the German invaders, Antonov's main forces had been thrown against the Don. In normal times this region, like the still more fertile Kuban territory, which lies to the south of it, would have been a substantial barrier to the triumph of extremist ideas. The Don and the Kuban were the most populous of the Cossack regions of Russia; and the Cossacks, far better provided with land than the Russian peasants and traditionally trained to military service in the Tsar's armies, were less susceptible to revolutionary agitation than any other part of the Russian masses.

But 1917 was far from a normal year. Even the Cossacks felt the general popular stirring and were more disposed to compromise with the Soviet regime than to fight it. Moreover, the Cossacks did not make up the entire population of the Don and the Kuban. Side by side with the Cossacks lived an approximately equal number of *inogorodni,* or outlanders—peasants who lived in the Cossack territories without enjoying equal rights as regards land ownership and local voting.[9] The Revolution gave these *inogorodni* an excellent opportunity to settle old scores with the Cossacks. While this southeastern part of Russia was mainly agricultural, its largest town, Rostov, had a workingclass population with a turbulent revolutionary reputation; and the workers in Taganrog and other places were also very definitely against the Cossack Government. Still another source of weakness in the position of Ataman Kaledin, the head of the Don Government, was the mood of the Cossack regiments which were returning from the front. Far from strengthening his position, these regiments proved indifferent, if not definitely hostile, to the traditional regime.

General A. S. Lukomsky[10] describes a typical incident when the 6th Don Cossack Regiment, after arriving in Novo-Cherkassk, the

Cossack capital, in good order, with its officers in full command and no soldiers' committee, promised to go to the front against the Bolsheviki, marched off after ceremonial prayers and greetings from the hard pressed Government, and promptly disintegrated and refused to fight "under the influence of agitators." The Don, as a citadel of anti-Bolshevism, was very shaky; and the fact that it did not fall sooner is attributable not to any forces which Kaledin was able to muster, but to the organization on its territory of the so-called Volunteer Army.

The founder of the Army was General Alekseev, former Commander-in-chief of the Russian armies, who slipped away from Petrograd shortly after the Bolshevik Revolution, arrived in Novo-Cherkassk on November 15 and set about what must have seemed at that time the almost hopeless task of creating a nationalist conservative army. Without funds, without a base or a clearly defined objective, Alekseev made slow progress, although his name attracted a few officers and junkers who were uncompromising in their hatred of Bolshevism.

The leadership of the Volunteer Army was considerably strengthened in December, when the five Generals who had been most actively implicated in the Kornilov affair, Kornilov, Denikin, Lukomsky, Markov and Romanovsky, made their way to the Don. At the time of the Bolshevik Revolution these Generals were imprisoned in Bikhov, near Moghilev. Kerensky's Investigating Commission had seen to it that they were not placed in difficult or unpleasant conditions; their guards sympathized with them and encouraged them to flee when Krilenko was approaching Moghilev. Kornilov took the field at the head of his mounted Tekintsi with the idea of making his way overland to Rostov. But after the Tekintsi had fallen into an ambush of Bolshevik troops and suffered losses their morale began to waver; they discussed whether they should save themselves by giving up Kornilov. The latter left the Tekintsi and continued his journey alone, reaching Novo-Cherkassk on December 19. The other Generals adopted different disguises and took out false passports: Lukomsky became a German colonist; Denikin a Polish official; Romanovsky an ensign; while Markov tried to put on the rough, cocksure manner of a private soldier of the time.[11]

All the Generals arrived in the Don without accident; the Bolsheviki had sent out orders to intercept them; but amid the general turmoil there was little effective control or espionage. They immediately joined General Alekseev in his effort to create a new

army. The situation on the Don, however, was much less favorable than they had expected. Although Kaledin heartily sympathized with the ideas of the newly arrived Generals, he was so afraid of being compromised by their reputation for counterrevolutionism that he suggested the advisability of their departure from the Don Territory, at least for a time; and Denikin, Markov and Lukomsky proceeded farther south, the former two to Ekaterinodar, the capital of the Kuban Territory, and the latter to Vladikavkaz. About the end of the year, however, they returned, in response to Kornilov's summons.

Kaledin faced a serious crisis in December, when a military revolutionary committee, which had been organized in Rostov, demanded the resignation of his Government. This was followed by armed conflict between the Black Sea sailors and Red Guards who supported the committee and Kaledin's Cossacks, under General Pototzky. The Cossacks had better military training, but fought with so little enthusiasm that the insurgents succeeded in disarming them, arresting General Pototzky and, on December 10, getting effective control of Rostov. Their success was shortlived, however, because the Volunteer Army units moved on Rostov from the neighboring Novo-Cherkassk and crushed the revolt, restoring the power of Kaledin's Government on the 15th.

The Volunteer Army grew up as a picked force of anti-Bolshevism. Emerging at a time when the outlook for a successful military movement against the Soviets was extremely dark, when the popular spirit was stormily revolutionary, it attracted into its ranks, in the main, only the bravest, the most reckless and the most embittered officers and aristocrats. Even among officers the response to its recruiting appeals was slack and weak; only a minority cared to risk their lives in what seemed a desperate enterprise. The total fighting strength of the Army in February, 1918, on the eve of the fall of Rostov, was only about three or four thousand men, divided among a number of units.[12] The fighting quality of the troops was very high; there was a large proportion of veteran officers, and many of the recruits came from families which had suffered very much at the hands of riotous mobs in city or village and were filled with a burning spirit of vengeance. But the supply with artillery and munitions was very inadequate and, however superior the Volunteers might be, man to man, to the Red Guards of that period, this could not compensate for their overwhelming numerical inferiority.

Denikin, one of the organizers and later the leader of the Volun-

teer Army, admits that from the beginning it bore a class character. Herein lay the secret of its ultimate defeat. Even at a later period, when the Bolshevik policy had aroused bitter discontent among the peasants and, to a lesser extent, among the workers, this class army, with its leadership so heavily drawn from reactionary officers and landlords' sons, was never able to win any real measure of popular support, except in the Cossack regions.

The ideals of the Volunteer Army were set forth in an appeal which its Staff issued early in January, 1918, calling for the "creation of an armed force which could be opposed to the impending anarchy and to the German-Bolshevik invasion." The appeal declared that, as its first direct goal, the Army would resist armed attack on Southern and Southeastern Russia "hand in hand with the valiant Cossacks, in union with the regions and peoples of Russia which are rising up against the German-Bolshevik yoke." The appeal also spoke out for the defense of civil liberty and the Constituent Assembly, although neither of these ideas commanded much respect among the oldfashioned officers who were the backbone of the Army.

Kaledin adopted a more sympathetic attitude toward the Volunteers after they had put down the Bolshevik uprising in Rostov and rejected all suggestions that they be removed from the Don Territory. He also endeavored to form partisan detachments of Don Cossacks, recognizing that the regular regiments were decidedly unreliable; and one of these detachments, under a young subaltern officer, Chernetzov, carried out a series of daring raids and held at bay for a time the Red Guard forces of the Donetz Basin miners. At the same time the Ataman endeavored to conciliate the non-Cossack population. About the middle of January an agreement was reached with representatives of the latter under which a new Government was to be set up, with an equal number of representatives of the Cossacks and non-Cossacks; the Government promised to release political prisoners and to relax the state of military emergency which had been proclaimed throughout the Territory. The Government also decided to send a delegation to Petrograd in order to persuade the Soviet leader to stop military action against the Don.

But this political maneuver was of no avail. Antonov's forces were concentrating at several points along the Don frontier. Kaledin's Government received a stunning blow when a conference of representatives of a number of Cossack regiments, meeting in the *stanitsa* [13] Kamenskoe on January 23, repudiated the existing Gov-

ernment of the Don Territory, elected a Military Revolutionary Committee, which declared itself the supreme authority in the Don and arrested Kaledin's local officers and officials. This was a breakdown from within, which made resistance to Antonov's Red Guard detachments difficult, if not impossible.

To be sure this Cossack insurrectionism was very far from full-blooded Bolshevism. The Cossack Military Revolutionary Committee showed little desire to organize the workers and peasants and attempted to conceal from the Cossack masses its association with Sirtsov, Shadenko and other local Bolsheviki.[14] But the united front of the Don Cossacks was broken; Antonov could now rely on aid against Kaledin from the insurgent Cossacks and send his main forces against Rostov along the southern seacoast, through Taganrog. Sivers, one of Antonov's chief lieutenants, was repulsed at first by the Volunteer Army; but on the same day, January 29, an uprising of the workers of the large Baltic Factory compelled the Kaledin troops to evacuate Taganrog; and early in February Sivers won a decisive victory at Matveev Kurgan.

Meanwhile Chernetzov, the most daring of Kaledin's partisan leaders, had been routed and captured by the insurgent Cossacks, who were headed by Golubov, an old warrior who had served in the Russo-Turkish War. Chernetzov was promptly put to death; even in this early phase the civil war was taking on a ruthless character; and the taking of prisoners, in clashes between the Volunteers and the Red Guards, was the exception, rather than the rule.

With Rostov threatened from several directions, with the last traces of his power crumbling away, Kaledin on February 11 delivered a last speech before the Cossack Krug, or legislative assembly, in which he described the hopelessness of the situation, and resigned his office. He then withdrew into a private room and shot himself through the heart.

The Ataman's dramatic suicide elicited a momentary flicker of fighting spirit among the Cossacks of the rich *stanitsas* of the southern Don, near Rostov and Novo-Cherkassk. A new Ataman, Nazarov, was elected; Cossack recruits began to appear in Novo-Cherkassk for the defense of the capital. The Volunteer Army still covered Rostov.

But the last efforts at resistance were shortlived. The Volunteers, while they fought with courage, skill and grim hatred for the Bolshevik forces which were attacking them, were handicapped by numerical weakness, by the lack of shells and ammunition and by

the necessity for utilizing part of their slender forces in order to hold down the restive workers of Rostov. The Cossack rally at Novo-Cherkassk was ephemeral. On February 24 Sivers' Red Guards fought their way into Rostov. The Volunteer Army made good its escape across the Don; Antonov's order to a Red partisan detachment which was operating on the other side of the Don to cut off the retreat by occupying the *stanitsa* Olginskaya was not carried out.

On the following day Golubov and his Red Cossacks occupied Novo-Cherkassk without resistance; Golubov burst into the building of the Krug and ordered its members to disperse. Nazarov had remained in Novo-Cherkassk, believing that an elected Ataman should not leave his post; along with other leaders of the Krug he was arrested. Some fifteen hundred Cossacks, under the leadership of General Popov, took refuge in the steppe country east and south of the Don, where cattle were driven during the winter months.

The month of February witnessed the extension of the Soviet regime to almost all the main centres of early opposition. Orenburg, where the local Cossack Ataman Dutov had held out for a time, was captured by workers' detachments from a number of neighboring towns on February 2. Still earlier, in January, the sailors of the Black Sea Fleet had crushed the attempt of the Crimean Tartars to establish a conservative nationalist government in the Crimea and had set up a Soviet regime in this southernmost peninsula of European Russia. Some very sanguinary episodes marked this sailors' dictatorship; for several days wild and uncontrolled terror raged in the streets of Sevastopol, when bands of sailors, completely out of hand, went about killing all the "boorzhui" on whom they could lay their hands, men, women and children.[15]

The sole organized anti-Bolshevik force which remained in European Russia was the Volunteer Army. There is something at once heroic, romantic and quixotic in the early adventures of this little force of some three or four thousand men, which included among its leaders two former commanders-in-chief of the Russian armies, Kornilov and Alekseev, and a large number of generals and officers with distinguished records in the World War.

After Rostov was evacuated the leaders of the Volunteer Army discussed the question where to begin new operations at several councils of war. A proposal to join the Don Cossacks in the steppes beyond the Don was rejected; and it was decided to turn south,

to the Kuban, where a local Cossack Government was still holding out in its capital, Ekaterinodar, although Red partisan detachments, recruited partly from soldiers returning from the Caucasian front, partly from Black Sea sailors and *inogorodni*, were already occupying many of the larger towns and railroad stations.

This expedition of the Volunteer Army, the hardships of which were greatly intensified by the unusually cold weather, later became known as the "icy march." An emblem of a crown of thorns, pierced through with a sword, was awarded to its survivors.

From the moment when they left Rostov the Volunteers were cut off from the outside world. They had no base, no regular commissariat for food and medical supplies; and the railroads in the territory which they entered were in the hands of their enemies. Hopes of arousing a broad popular anti-Bolshevik movement among the well-to-do Kuban Cossacks were disappointed. The general attitude which they encountered was one of cautious neutrality. The Soviet regime had not yet made itself odious to the Cossack masses through wholesale requisitions and through the plundering tactics of ill disciplined Red partisan detachments. Few Cossacks cared to cast in their lot with what seemed to be a desperate enterprise, and new recruits barely balanced the losses which were sustained in skirmishes which took place as the little army moved from *stanitsa* to *stanitsa*.

When the Volunteer Army reached Korenovskaya, within striking distance of Ekaterinodar, it received a piece of gloomy news. Surrounded by growing Bolshevik forces, and placed in much the same hopeless position as Kaledin had been on the Don, the Kuban Cossack Government had abandoned its capital and fled into the foothills of the Caucasus Mountains, south of the Kuban River. Ekaterinodar was in the hands of the Bolsheviki.

The Volunteer Army thereupon changed its line of march; instead of advancing farther on Ekaterinodar it turned southward, crossed the Kuban River and continued to fight its way from place to place among the Cossack *stanitsas* and the *auls,* or mountain villages of the Caucasian mountaineers. According to Denikin the *auls* had in many cases been laid waste by Bolshevik bands; and the Circassians welcomed the Volunteers as deliverers and furnished some recruits for the Army.

Kornilov received welcome reinforcements when he succeeded on March 27 in establishing contact with the forces of the Kuban Government, which were under the command of General Pokrov-

sky, a young officer of a type not unfamiliar on both sides in this early stage of the civil war, whom Denikin describes as "bold, ruthless, ambitious and unencumbered by moral prejudices." The Kuban army consisted of 2,500 or 3,000 cavalry and infantry, with some artillery.

Pokrovsky at first showed some reluctance to surrender his independent command; but on March 30 an agreement was signed by the leaders of the Volunteer Army and by the chief representatives of the Kuban Government, which recognized Kornilov as sole commander of the united army. It was decided to make an immediate attack on Ekaterinodar. Diverting the attention of the Reds by making a feint at crossing the Kuban in another place, the Volunteer Army, with its 9,000 men (including fugitives and wounded), its 4,000 horses and 600 carts, crossed the river without opposition with the aid of a primitive hand-operated ferry and a few fishing boats at Elizavetinskaya, somewhat to the west of Ekaterinodar.[16] Thence the Army advanced on the Kuban capital, and on April 9 the battle began.

The defense of the town was stubborn and bitter. The Reds had concentrated there some thirty thousand troops [17] under the command of two of the more prominent North Caucasian partisan leaders, Avtonomov and Sorokin, both junior Cossack officers who subsequently proved unreliable. A Congress of Soviets was taking place in Ekaterinodar at the time of Kornilov's attack; and, while some of the delegates returned home in a panic, others took up arms themselves or made the rounds of the trenches, cheering on the soldiers.

As against the superiority of the Reds in numbers and in artillery the Volunteers had the advantage of experienced leadership and military training (despite the fact that they were on the offensive they inflicted much heavier losses than they sustained). And the cupolas of Ekaterinodar's churches doubtless reminded many of the Volunteer officers of the golden domes of Moscow and inspired them with fierce determination to end their cheerless march from one remote village to another with a decisive victory.

Four days of hard fighting with varying success followed the attack. Here and there the Volunteers penetrated into the western suburbs of the town; but they were unable to break the resistance of the Reds, and their successes were temporary. When Kornilov summoned the other generals to a military council in the farmhouse which served as his headquarters on the 12th the general sentiment

was one of depression. As the smaller force the Volunteers had felt more keenly the attrition of the prolonged sanguinary fighting. Fifteen hundred wounded crowded their rough improvised field hospitals. The supply of shells and of bullets was running low. Many senior officers had been killed. Most of the Generals felt that the attacks should be given up. But Kornilov, with the grim obstinacy which was a feature of his character, insisted that Ekaterinodar must be stormed at any cost. Otherwise, as he said to Denikin after the council, "there is nothing for me to do but to put a bullet into my brain." [18]

It was agreed that the decisive attack should take place at dawn on April 13. But shortly before the appointed time Kornilov was killed by a shell which burst in his headquarters. A very poor politician, but a very brave man, he met a soldier's death.

After Kornilov's death there was no more thought of continuing the struggle for Ekaterinodar. The command of the Volunteer Army passed to Denikin, and a sullen but orderly retreat began. Avoiding the railroad lines, on which there were Bolshevik armored cars, and the large towns, Denikin brought his little army back to the frontier of the Don and Kuban Territories. Here it was safe from pursuit; the Bolshevik regime in the Don was already tottering to its fall and the Kuban Bolsheviki thought only of defending themselves against a possible German attack. The result of the "icy march" are summarized by Denikin as follows: [19]

The Army was on the march eighty days, of which forty-four were days of battle. It covered a distance of seven hundred miles. It set out with four thousand men and returned with five thousand, receiving a slight net reinforcement from the Kuban Cossacks. Its losses amounted to four hundred killed and over fifteen hundred wounded.

Despite the generally high military quality of its leaders and the desperate courage of its men, the Volunteer Army had failed to occupy the Kuban, just as it had proved unable to defend the Don, and for the same reason: the political and social atmosphere was still too unfavorable to any movement which smacked of counter-revolution. The poorer classes of the population, the non-Cossack peasants and the relatively few railroad and factory workers, were much more aggressive at this stage than were the well-to-do Cossacks. Indeed the younger Cossacks often returned from the front with a good deal of rebellious spirit and were often to be found in the ranks of such Red partisan leaders as Sorokin and Avtonomov.

While there were a few sporadic outbreaks in individual *stanitsas* the mood of the mass of the Cossacks was not yet ripe for acceptance of the leadership of the oldfashioned Generals of the Volunteer Army against the new regime. And even the most talented Generals could do little without soldiers.

Yet, although it had failed to find a new base in the Kuban, the Volunteer Army was by no means demoralized or discouraged. It had passed a very stern test of hardships and disappointments without falling to pieces. It still remained an embryo of future struggle against the Soviets, a magnet which attracted every officer, every military student, every landlord's son who dreamed of a restoration of "the good old days." And it was assured an opportunity to recuperate and to strengthen its forces undisturbed as a result of a favorable political change which had occurred in the Don.

The Soviet regime was naturally much shakier in agricultural regions with a strong Cossack population, such as the Don and the Kuban, than it was in parts of the country where the numbers of industrial workers and of Bolshevik Party members were proportionally larger. The military occupation of the main towns of the Don Territory did not bring about any great change in the life of the Cossack *stanitsas,* where the old officials remained, as a general rule, and officers were able to live and take part in the preparation of an uprising against the new authorities.[20] Golubov, the ambitious veteran Cossack who had occupied Novo-Cherkassk and dispersed the Krug, was offended because he was not made Ataman. Early in April he and his associates were implicated in resistance to the orders of the Soviet leaders in Rostov; a punitive expedition was sent against Golubov in Novo-Cherkassk; he fled and was shot. This episode was symptomatic of the changing attitude of some of the Cossacks who had taken part in the movement against Kaledin. In the middle of April Colonel Fetisov made a raid on Novo-Cherkassk and held this old Don Cossack capital four days. Fetisov was driven away; but during the month of April many of the *stanitsas* of the middle and lower Don joined in a general uprising, with the aid of General Popov, who had returned with his forces from his wanderings in the steppes beyond the Don. The main cause of this outbreak seems to have been the bad behavior of many of the Red Guard detachments, especially of those which fled before the Germans from Ukraina. I. Borisenko is a former Soviet official, and is therefore probably not guilty of exaggeration when he writes: [21]

"In the towns were dozens of different Red detachments. Most of them were disintegrating and addicted to banditism. They demanded much for their maintenance and refused under various pretexts to go to the front. Looting, theft, assaults and robberies increased."

The Don Cossacks were not predisposed to new social ideas in any case; and it required only a few outrages on the part of a wandering Red detachment to turn a *stanitsa* into an angry hornets' nest. As is usually the case in irregular guerrilla warfare, the Cossack uprising met with varying and uneven success. Some *stanitsas* were still inclined to side with the Reds; the coal miners of the Donetz Basin and the non-Cossack peasants of the territory supplied some reliable Red forces.

But the harassed Government of the "Don Soviet Republic," which had been proclaimed in Rostov in the vain hope that this assumption of independence would ward off an attack from the Germans who were already occupying Ukraina, was obliged to fight on two fronts, against the insurgent Cossacks on the east and against the invading Germans on the west. The Germans took Taganrog on May 1st; and the May Day demonstration in Rostov, where a paper "commune" had been established, with equal distribution of food, forced labor for the bourgeoisie and public works for the relief of the unemployed, was held to the ominous accompaniment of droning German airplanes overhead.

On May 4 Rostov was attacked by an unexpected enemy in Colonel Drozdovsky, who had created a small force, mainly recruited from officers and very similar in ideas and social composition to Denikin's Volunteer Army, and had marched seven hundred miles overland from the Rumanian Front to the Don. He was driven out of Rostov by superior Red forces on the 5th; but rendered valuable aid to General Denisov, commander of the anti-Bolshevik Don Cossacks, who had occupied Novo-Cherkassk on the 6th and was hard pressed by the Red Guard miners of the neighboring Alexandro-Grushevsk region. Rostov fell on May 8, when the German troops marched in, accompanied by some of Drozdovsky's forces and by a detachment of Denisov's Cossacks. On the 11th Alexandro-Grushevsk was taken, and the "Red" terror which had prevailed in Rostov and in other large towns during the period of the Soviet rule was succeeded by a pitiless "White" terror against the revolutionary miners, many of whom were shot, while others were immured alive in the mines.[22]

So the easy overrunning of the Don and Ukraina by Antonov's

motley Red Guards was quickly followed by the overthrow of the Soviet regime in both these regions. In Ukraina the Soviets fell directly as a result of German intervention; in the Don the dissatisfaction of the Cossacks contributed considerably to the change. This difference was reflected in the character of the two regimes which emerged after the downfall of the Soviets. General Skoropadsky, who became Hetman, or supreme ruler, of Ukraina, was a pure puppet, entirely dependent for support on the German-Austrian army of occupation. General P. N. Krasnov, who, after his unsuccessful drive on Petrograd with Kerensky, reappeared in the Don and was elected Ataman, obtained all the help he could from the Germans in the shape of munitions; but he was able to create a Cossack army which for a time drove the Bolsheviki entirely out of the Don Territory.

NOTES

[1] V. A. Antonov-Ovseenko, "Memoirs of the Civil War," Vol. I, p. 46.
[2] N. Kakurin, "How the Revolution Was Fought," Vol. I, p. 172.
[3] *Cf. Izvestia*, No. 244, for the full text of the ultimatum.
[4] Antonov-Ovseenko, *op. cit.*, Vol. I, p. 135.
[5] *Cf. Izvestia of the Kiev Soviet of Workers' and Soldiers' Deputies* of January 30 (February 12), 1918, No. 1.
[6] Antonov-Ovseenko, *op. cit.*, p. 55.
[7] Evgenia Bosch, "A Year of Struggle," p. 150.
[8] *Ibid.*, p. 162.
[9] In the Don, where the rural population was almost equally divided between Cossacks and *inogorodni*, the former owned seventy percent, the latter ten percent of the arable land. (*Cf.* I. Borisenko, "The Soviet Republic in the North Caucasus in 1918," Vol. I, p. 23.) The Kuban Territory in 1914 counted in its population 1,339,430 Cossacks, 1,646,901 *inogorodni* and 136,574 Caucasian mountaineers. Of the arable land the Cossacks owned 60 percent, the *inogorodni* 37 percent and the mountaineers 3 percent. The average Cossack household had about fifty percent more agricultural implements and about three times as many cattle as the average holding of the *inogorodni*. (*Cf.* G. Pokrovsky, "The Denikin System," p. 11, 13.)
[10] Gen. A. S. Lukomsky, "Reminiscences," Vol. I, pp. 295, 296.
[11] Gen. A. I. Denikin, "Sketches of Russian Turmoil," Vol. II, pp. 145, 146.
[12] *Ibid.*, Vol. II, pp. 200ff.
[13] The Cossack *stanitsa*, which had often been originally established as a military settlement, was usually much larger than an ordinary Russian peasant village; some of the larger *stanitsas* had populations ranging up to 20,000.
[14] *Cf.* Antonov-Ovseenko, *op. cit.*, Vol. I, pp. 200, 201.
[15] For a detailed description of the outburst of terror in Sevastopol, which lasted three days, February 22, 23 and 24, and cost the lives of 350 or 400 persons, *cf.* V. K. Zhukov, "The Black Sea Fleet in the Revolution of 1917–1918," pp. 145–161. As the author is thoroughly in sympathy with the Bolshevik cause his description of the terror is, in all likelihood, not exaggerated.
[16] Denikin, *op. cit.*, Vol. II, p. 282.
[17] I. Borisenko, *op. cit.*, Vol. I, p. 141.
[18] Denikin, *op. cit.*, Vol. II, pp. 294, 295.
[19] *Ibid.*, Vol. II, p. 345.
[20] *Cf.* the excerpt from General S. V. Denisov's "Memoirs," published in the volume, "The Beginning of the Civil War," in the series: "Revolution and Civil War in the Descriptions of the Whites," p. 90.
[21] Borisenko, *op. cit.*, Vol. I, p. 81.
[22] *Ibid.*, Vol. I, p. 103.

CHAPTER XVIII

BREST–LITOVSK: THE STRUGGLE FOR PEACE

THE peace negotiations at Brest-Litovsk represented at once one of the most vital and one of the most difficult problems of the new Soviet regime. It was a matter of life and death to win peace. The Bolshevik leaders and a comparatively small number of their convinced followers felt, of course, that there was a substantial difference between war in defense of the "capitalist" Provisional Government and war in defense of the Soviet Republic.

But the overwhelming majority of the Russian soldiers in the trenches were no more inclined to fight for Lenin than they were inclined to fight for Kerensky. Their sympathy for Lenin and against Kerensky was based on the belief that Lenin stood for peace and for giving land to the peasants. Peace, peace "without annexations and indemnities" if possible, but peace at any price, if necessary, was an indispensable condition of the survival of the Soviet Government; and no one saw this more clearly than Lenin, whose hard realistic mind was not intoxicated by the success of the Revolution in Russia and was not diverted by optimistic fantasies about the possible immediate spread of the revolutionary flame to Germany and Austria.

At the same time it was imperatively necessary to hold out as long as possible against German annexationist demands, to utilize the negotiations as a forum from which to proclaim to the world what the Soviet Government regarded as just peace conditions, to dispel, so far as circumstances would permit, the accusation that the Bolsheviki were German agents, to give the German and Austrian workers an opportunity to react to the course of the negotiations and to protest against excessive demands of their own Governments. The question how far the Soviet Government was morally obligated to resist the demands of the Central powers was to be a subject of major disagreement between Lenin, who believed from the beginning that it was necessary to sign even a bad peace, and many of his associates in the Party Central Committee.

Two worlds, the world of oldfashioned diplomacy and militarism

and the world of emerging revolutionism, met when the peace delegations held their first plenary session in Brest-Litovsk on December 22. The Soviet delegation had dropped its ornamental worker, sailor and peasant, who were taken along to the armistice discussions, and consisted of men of high education and culture: A. A. Joffe, the President, L. B. Kamenev, M. N. Pokrovsky, the Bolshevik historian, and L. B. Karakhan, the future Assistant Foreign Commissar, who acted as Secretary. The Left Socialist Revolutionaries had a typical representative: Mme. A. A. Bitzenko, who had made herself a heroine in revolutionary circles by killing a Tsarist official and serving a long term in prison and exile.

The main figures in the delegations of the Central powers were the German Foreign Minister, von Kühlmann, the Austrian Foreign Minister, Count Ottokar Czernin, and the German Major-General Max Hoffmann, who represented the German Supreme Command and more than once intervened brusquely in the discussions when he felt that the civilian negotiators were not showing sufficient energy and firmness. Count Czernin was the most conciliatory member of this triumvirate; Austria's psychological and physical need for peace and bread was second only to that of Russia itself, and Count Czernin was seriously afraid that a breakdown of the negotiations might lead to a collapse of the Dual Monarchy. But his influence on the course of affairs was slight; Austria was helplessly dependent on Germany for everything, from military support to assistance with food. The Bulgarian and Turkish delegates at the Conference played secondary rôles; both were anxious to obtain sanction for territorial expansion—Bulgaria at the expense of its Balkan neighbors, Rumania and Serbia, and Turkey in the Caucasus.

After demanding and obtaining consent for publicity in connection with the proceedings of the Conference, Joffe offered the following proposals as a basis for peace negotiations: [1]

1. No forcible annexations of territories seized in time of war are permitted. Troops in occupation of these territories are withdrawn from them in the shortest period of time.

2. The political independence of those peoples who were deprived of it during the present war is fully restored.

3. National groups which did not enjoy political independence before the war are guaranteed the possibility of deciding the question of their attachment to one or another state or of their state independence by means of a referendum. This referendum must be

organized in such a manner that complete freedom of voting will be assured to the whole population of the given territory, not excluding emigrants and fugitives.

4. In regard to territories which are inhabited by several nationalities the right of the minority is guarded by special laws, which guaranty it national cultural independence and, if possible, administrative autonomy.

5. No one of the belligerent countries is obligated to pay to other countries so-called "war expenditures"; contributions which have already been levied are to be returned. As for the compensation of private persons who have suffered from the war, this is to be made out of a special fund, created by means of proportionate contributions from all the belligerent countries.

6. Colonial problems are to be decided in accordance with the principles set forth in Points 1, 2, 3 and 4.

Joffe also suggested that such measures of pressure of strong on weak nations as economic boycott, naval blockade and discriminatory commercial agreements should be forbidden.

The negotiators of the Central powers were all apostles of *Realpolitik* and certainly had no intention of relaxing their grip on Poland and on the considerable part of Russia's Baltic Provinces which had been occupied in response to the moral exhortations of Russian revolutionaries who had behind them no serious armed force. But Kühlmann and Czernin believed that some diplomatic advantage might be gained by outwardly accepting the Soviet formulas. There was a faint chance that such a method would pave the way to peace negotiations with the Entente powers; there was also the possibility that the Bolsheviki, if they obtained the shadow of recognition of their theoretical principles, would be ready to surrender the substance of Russian territory, which they had no means of reconquering.

So, despite the private remonstrances and misgivings of the more downright and straightforward General Hoffmann, Kühlmann, in the name of the Quadruple Alliance (Germany, Austria-Hungary, Bulgaria and Turkey), delivered a very conciliatory reply to Joffe's proposals on December 25.[2] He declared that the delegation of the Quadruple Alliance was ready to conclude immediately a general peace without forcible annexations and without contributions. For the sake of conquests the Quadruple Alliance would not prolong the War a single day. He added, however, the significant reservation that the proposals of the Russian delegation could be

realized only if all the powers involved in the War bound themselves within a definite period of time to observe these same conditions. He renounced, on behalf of the Quadruple Alliance, any intention of forcibly annexing territories which had been occupied, and declared that the peace treaty should define the conditions of withdrawal of troops. He welcomed the Soviet proposal that colonies occupied during the War should be evacuated (a suggestion that would have benefited only Germany) and politely rejected as impracticable the application of Soviet ideas of selfdetermination to the native population of the German colonies.

At Joffe's suggestion it was decided to suspend the negotiations for ten days, in order to give the other belligerent powers an opportunity to participate in the negotiations. So far the course of the discussions had been unexpectedly harmonious. But on December 26 the blunt, outspoken General Hoffmann, who was not disposed to leave the Russian delegates in any doubt as to the firm intention of Germany to retain effective control of the territory which had been conquered, took advantage of the first opportunity at luncheon to tell Joffe that the Central powers did not regard it as forcible annexation if some parts of the former Russian Empire, such as Poland, Lithuania and Courland (all occupied at this time by the German forces) decided to secede from Russia and to unite with Germany or with any other state.

It is not altogether clear whether the Soviet delegates had been so naïve as to believe that their proclamation of international socialist peace principles would induce the German Supreme Command to give up its conquests. But Hoffmann's statement excited great indignation and for a day or two the atmosphere at the conference was strained and uncertain. There was some talk on the Russian side of breaking off the conference; and Count Czernin declared in conversation with Kühlmann and Hoffmann that he would open up separate peace negotiations, if the general negotiations broke down.[3]

Hoffmann, as much of a realist in his way as Lenin was on the other side, remained unmoved. He knew that Austria could always be browbeaten into submission. As for Russia, the masses were eager for peace, the army had fallen to pieces, the sole chance for the Bolsheviki to remain in power was to obtain peace. All this strengthened the Prussian General in his conviction that "the Bolsheviki must accept the conditions of the Central powers, however harsh they may be."[4]

Hoffmann's confidence was justified when the Soviet delegation reappeared in Brest-Litovsk and formal negotiations were resumed on January 9, 1918. Trotzky replaced Joffe as head of the delegation and henceforward was far and away the dominant figure in the negotiations on the Soviet side. A sterner atmosphere prevailed in this second phase of the negotiations. Trotzky isolated the members of his delegation from the Germans and forbade the former practise of dining with the representatives of the Central powers.

The Soviet delegation again raised the question of transferring the sessions of the conference from Brest-Litovsk and suggested that Stockholm would be preferable. This proposal was firmly and definitely rejected. General Hoffmann seized the first opportunity on January 9 to lodge a protest against the circulation of revolutionary appeals, "full of abuse of the German Army and the German Supreme Command" and signed by representatives of the Russian Government and of the Russian Army, addressed to the troops of the Central powers.

Representatives of the Ukrainian Rada were now participating in the negotiations; and the German and Austrian diplomats were quick to grasp the favorable opportunity of denying Trotzky's right to speak for all Russia and to drive a wedge between Kiev and Petrograd.[5] Ukraina was far richer in agricultural resources than Northern and Central Russia; and a separate peace with the Rada seemed to open up alluring possibilities, both political and economic, for the Central powers.

The Ukrainian delegates, conscious of the weakness of their Government's position before the rising wave of Bolshevism, were not hard bargainers, although in the beginning they put forward certain territorial demands, suggesting, as a compensation for food exports to hungry Germany and Austria, that Austria-Hungary should cede to Ukraina East Galicia and Bukovina, with their predominantly Ukrainian population, and that the Kholm district of Poland, should also be allocated to Ukraina. The Germans and Austrians refused pointblank to consider any cession of Austrian territory; but a compromise was arranged under which Kholm was to go to Ukraina (Hoffmann was quite willing to weaken Poland and Czernin felt that Kholm would be a cheap price for Ukrainian bread), while a special Crown Land within the Austrian Empire was to be created out of East Galicia and Bukovina.

Kühlmann on January 10 asked Trotzky whether his delegation was to be the sole diplomatic representation of Russia, and Trotzky

replied that he "had no objection to the participation of the Ukrainian delegation in the peace conference." [6] At this time the Bolshevik offensive against Kiev had not advanced so far that Trotzky felt inclined to deny the right of the Rada to represent Ukraina.

The second phase of the Brest-Litovsk negotiations resolved itself largely into a verbal duel between Trotzky and Kühlmann, ranging around the subject of how the principle of selfdetermination should be applied in the regions which were occupied by German troops. Trotzky adopted the viewpoint that only a free referendum, taken without the presence of foreign military forces, would constitute a genuine expression of popular will. Kühlmann refused to consider the withdrawal of the German troops and argued that the occupied districts had already declared their will through the resolutions of bodies which had been created under the regime of occupation. He also insisted that the Soviet Government, in view of its professed willingness to permit any part of the former Russian Empire to secede, if the majority of its inhabitants so desired, had no right to interfere in the arrangements which Germany might reach with the population of the occupied territories. Trotzky's reply to this was: [7]

"We defend not the possessions of Russia, but the rights of separate nationalities to free historical existence. We shall never in any case consent to recognize that all those decisions which are being taken, which have already, perhaps, been taken or will be taken in the near future, under the control of the German occupation authorities, through the medium of organizations which are created by the occupation authorities, or with their coöperation, or through institutions which are arbitrarily recognized as authoritative organizations,—that these decisions are an expression of the genuine will of these nationalities and can determine their historic fate. . . . We are revolutionaries, but we are also realists, and we should prefer to talk directly about annexations, rather than to replace their real name with a pseudonym."

While Kühlmann endeavored to put the German case in diplomatic phraseology General Hoffmann, in his occasional interventions, talked the plain language of superior force. So, on January 12, [8] he complained that "the Russian delegation talks the language of a victor, invading our country. The facts contradict this; victorious German troops are on Russian territory." Hoffmann furthermore undertook to give the Bolsheviki a lecture on ethics, declaring that "the Soviet Government is based exclusively on force, and anyone

who thinks otherwise is simply declared a counterrevolutionary and a bourgeois and outlawed." He cited as proof of his statement the armed dissolution of a White Russian Congress on December 30 and the employment of arms against the Rada. Finally he referred to the acts of such bodies as the Courland Popular Assembly, the Lithuanian Landrat, the municipal administration of Riga and others, which had repudiated all connection with Russia and appealed to Germany for defense.

Actually the bodies which Hoffmann mentioned could not reasonably be regarded as nationally representative. They were handpicked bodies of delegates elected by the landlords and by the wealthier classes in the towns, and they contained a disproportionately large number of delegates elected by the German racial minorities in the Baltic States. Equally little could be said for the popular basis of the Government which had been created under German-Austrian auspices in occupied Poland. This regime disappeared immediately after the breakdown of the German military power. The Soviet delegates were indefatigable in denouncing the unrepresentative character of the Polish and Baltic governmental bodies; several Socialists from Poland and the Baltic Provinces, including the brilliant and sharp-tongued Karl Radek, were attached to the delegation as "consultants on national questions."

Neither side in the wordy duel at Brest-Litovsk seriously expected to convince the other. Trotzky's policy was to play for time in the hope that some revolutionary sparks might be kindled in Germany and Austria. There were some rather faint and muffled responses to this policy; there were strikes and hunger demonstrations in Austria in mid-January; later in the month there were serious strikes in Berlin and in a number of provincial towns, such as Hamburg, Danzig and Kiel. These strikes aroused exaggerated hopes in Russia; but the discipline of the German Empire was proof against everything except definite military defeat, and the strike wave ebbed away without shaking the position of the Government.

Why the representatives of the Central Powers allowed the negotiations to drag on so long is less comprehensible. The military leaders were eager for a swift decision in the East which would free their hands for the projected great spring offensive on the Western Front. But the civilian diplomats hoped, by the exercise of some patience, to obtain a settlement which would not be too obviously a mere product of superior military force. The parallel discussions with the Ukrainian delegates raised questions affecting

the internal structure of Austria-Hungary and required time for solution.

By January 18, however, the patience of the negotiators of the Central powers, or at least of the German Supreme Command, had worn thin. At Kühlmann's invitation General Hoffmann, never loath to present an ultimatum, spread out a map of Eastern Europe on the table and pointed to a blue line, running north of Brest-Litovsk, as the future boundary of Russia. Hoffmann declared that territorial arrangements south of Brest-Litovsk would depend on the issue of negotiations with the delegates of the Ukrainian Rada. Hoffmann's line coincided precisely with the military line held by the German forces. It separated from Russia most of the territory now included in Poland, all Lithuania, western Latvia, including the city of Riga and the islands in Moòn Sound, inhabited by Esthonians. In response to an ironical question from Trotzky as to what principles guided the drawing of the line Hoffmann said: "The indicated line is dictated by military considerations; it assures the peoples living on this side of the line a tranquil organization of state life and the realization of the right to selfdetermination." [9]

Confronted with this semi-ultimatum Trotzky maneuvered for time by proposing a suspension of the negotiations for some days. Apart from the desire to test out the effect of the sweeping German demands on the German working class and on world public opinion, Trotzky felt that it was necessary to return to Petrograd in order to participate in the shaping of the fateful decision as to what should be done, if, as seemed quite probable, the Germans should put their demands in more imperative form after the resumption of the negotiations.

Now that the question of war or peace had become urgent, three main viewpoints, along with several minor shadings, had developed among the Bolshevik leaders. Lenin, supported by Stalin, Zinoviev, Kamenev and Sokolnikov, stood for the signature of peace after all the resources of delay had been exhausted. At the other extreme were Bukharin, Lomov and some other "left-wing" Communists, who were especially strong in the Moscow Party organization. They favored absolute refusal to sign an annexationist peace and the proclamation of a "revolutionary war." Trotzky's position was an intermediate one. He does not seem to have cherished any illusions about the possibility of resuming war. But he was anxious to play out to the very end the appeal to international workingclass solidarity. What he advocated was a sort of demonstration of

passive resistance: a refusal to sign peace on the terms of Hoffmann and Ludendorff, accompanied by a declaration that Russia no longer considered itself in a state of war and a demonstrative demobilization of the Russian army, which was already, to a very large extent, "self-demobilized."

There is an intoxication about successful revolution that makes retreat psychologically very difficult for the revolutionists. A period of only a little more than two months separated the seizure of power in November from the German demand for an annexationist peace, the signature of which seemed to many ardent Communists a betrayal of their international principles. It is not surprising, therefore, that even the weight of Lenin's personal authority was unable to bring about an immediate general acceptance of the necessity of agreeing to what he himself described as "a Tilsit Peace."

In his usual fashion Lenin had outlined his attitude toward the problem of peace in a series of "theses," or argumentative propositions, written on January 20, but only published on February 24, when the situation had become much more critical.[10] Lenin started out with the assumption that an interval of some months was necessary for the success of socialism in Russia, so that the Soviet Government might have a free hand in crushing the bourgeoisie and carrying out organizing work. He answered the criticism that acceptance of the German terms would be a breach with proletarian internationalism with the statement that workers who are obliged to accept unfavorable terms imposed by a capitalist do not betray socialism.

The socialist revolution in Europe must and would come; "all our hopes for the *final* victory of socialism are based on this conviction." But it would have been a blind gamble to try to determine precisely when the European, and especially the German, Revolution would come. The army could not resist a German attack; any attempt to continue the War, unless it was accompanied by a speedy revolution in Germany, would merely mean that the Soviet Government would be swept away and a still more onerous peace would be imposed upon its successor. To stake the existence of the Soviet regime on the possibility that a revolution might break out in Germany within a few weeks was "a risk which we have not the right to take."

Lenin's theses, bitterly realistic and quite unsentimental, failed at this time to command general support. At a discussion in which Bolshevik delegates to the Third Congress of Soviets participated

along with members of the Central Committee of the Party, fifteen votes were cast for his proposal to sign an annexationist peace, thirty-two for the slogan of "revolutionary war" and sixteen for Trotzky's idea: refusal to sign the peace, accompanied by a declaration that the state of war was ended.

Lenin again remained in the minority at a very important session of the Party Central Committee on January 24 which discussed the policy to be pursued at Brest-Litovsk.[11] Lenin repeated his arguments about the exhaustion of the army and the certainty that any attempt to prolong hostilities would lead to the overthrow of the Soviet Government. He resorted to a homely metaphor, declaring: "Germany is still only pregnant with revolution; and a quite healthy child has been born to us—a socialist republic which we may kill if we begin war." He characterized Trotzky's proposal as an international political demonstration which would hand over Esthonia to the Germans. "If the Germans begin to attack," he predicted, "we shall be compelled to sign any peace, and then, of course, the terms will be worse."

Bukharin spoke in opposition to Lenin, recalling how Kornilov's forces had been demoralized by propaganda, hopefully mentioning the strike in Vienna, arguing that the prospects of international revolution should not be sacrificed to the preservation of the Soviet regime. Trotzky followed, advocating his "no war and no peace" formula, urging that only such a procedure could test out the forces of resistance to militarism in Germany. Stalin supported Lenin's views, emphatically declaring, in contravention of the internationalist views of Trotzky and Bukharin: "There is no revolutionary movement in the West. There are no facts; there is only a possibility, and with possibilities we cannot reckon."

Lenin, who was himself strongly convinced that the Russian Revolution was closely linked up with the international movement, dissented from Stalin's outspoken formula, remarking that "there is a mass movement in the West, but the revolution there has not begun," and adding: "If we should believe that the German movement may develop immediately in the event of an interruption of the peace negotiations, we should be obliged to sacrifice ourselves, because the German Revolution in its force will be greater than ours." It was only Lenin's doubt about the likelihood of an immediate outburst of insurrection against the Kaiser that made him insist on the necessity of purchasing a longer term of life for the Soviet Government by signing the peace.

At the end of the session three propositions were put to a vote. Revolutionary war was rejected by eleven votes to two, with one abstention; only one vote was cast against Lenin's proposal to put off the signing of the peace by dragging out the negotiations as much as possible; finally, Trotzky's "no war and no peace" slogan obtained the sanction of the Central Committee by nine votes to seven. So Trotzky's subsequent action in refusing to sign the peace at Brest-Litovsk was authorized by the Central Committee, although it was opposed to Lenin's recommendations.

The Third Congress of Soviets, which, like the Second, had an overwhelming majority of Bolshevik and Left Socialist Revolutionary delegates, holding its sessions in Petrograd from January 23 until January 31, adopted a resolution approving the previous policy of the Soviet peace delegation and granting it practically a free hand in future negotiations. The peace negotiations in Brest-Litovsk were resumed on January 30, and Trotzky announced that the Soviet delegation now included two representatives of the Ukrainian Soviet Republic, Medvedev and Shakhrai.

The course of military operations at this time was definitely against the forces of the Kiev Rada; Kiev itself would soon fall into the hands of the Soviet troops.[12] But this circumstance did not affect the attitude of the Central powers. Their leaders realized that a few secondclass German and Austrian divisions could easily restore the Rada and drive the disorderly Red Guards out of Ukraina. On February 1 Count Czernin, in the name of all the delegations of the Central powers, announced the recognition of the Ukrainian People's Republic "as a free sovereign state, fully authorized to enter into international relations." On the same day Czernin's diary contains the following entry: [13]

"My design is to play the Petersburgers and the Ukrainians against each other and to come to a peace with at least one or the other of them."

Trotzky exhausted his batteries of sarcasm on "the non-existent Ukrainian Republic, the territory of which is restricted to the rooms which are assigned to their delegation in Brest-Litovsk." But the Ukrainian Rada at this moment was a useful pawn in the hands of the Germans and Austrians. Prodded by Ludendorff for quicker and more decisive action, Kühlmann promised a breach with Trotzky within twenty-four hours after the signature of peace with Ukraina.[14]

The drama at Brest-Litovsk was now approaching its climax. Apparently Trotzky wavered somewhat between the possibility of

obtaining peace, with perhaps a slight improvement of the original German terms, and plunging into the risks associated with his own policy of refusing to sign the peace. At any rate when Czernin talked with him on February 7 Trotzky admitted that Russia was too weak to regain the territory occupied by the Germans and laid stress on two points: the abandonment by the Central powers of a separate peace with Ukraina and the restoration of the Moon Sound Islands. About the same time Trotzky endeavored to sound out Kühlmann as to whether Riga and the Moon Sound Islands might be given back to Russia.[15]

Kühlmann, eager for a peace which would bear some sign of agreement rather than for a breaking off of the negotiations, took Trotzky's suggestion so seriously that he proffered his resignation rather than deliver an ultimatum which the Kaiser, greatly incensed over one of the revolutionary proclamations which the Bolsheviki were addressing to the German soldiers, had demanded. The proposed ultimatum would have required the cession of the whole of Latvia and Esthonia. Kühlmann's resignation was not accepted and the ultimatum was not delivered.

But peace by agreement did not come about. The Ukrainians signed a treaty with the representatives of the Central powers on February 9, thereby paving the way for an exchange of German military assistance against the Bolsheviki for Ukrainian exports of grain, eggs and other foodstuffs to blockaded and hungry Germany and Austria. And Trotzky, after some delay, rejected Kühlmann's suggestion to discuss a settlement on the basis of possible concessions in connection with Riga and the Moon Sound Islands. The impulse to make a spectacular appeal to world opinion, to test the possibilities of international workingclass solidarity, was too strong. Trotzky chose February 10, the day after the conclusion of the separate peace between the Central powers and Ukraina, as the occasion for formally breaking off negotiations. Always eloquent in moments of crisis, he announced his decision in a speech that made a profound impression upon the members of the hostile delegations in the council room: [16]

"We no longer desire to take part in this purely imperialistic War, where the pretensions of the propertied classes are clearly paid for with human blood. We are equally uncompromising in regard to the imperialism of both camps, and we are no longer willing to shed the blood of our soldiers in defense of the interests of one camp of imperialists against the other.

"In anticipation of that hour, which we hope is near, when the oppressed working classes of all countries will take power into their own hands, like the working people of Russia, we withdraw our army and our people from the War. . . .

"We refuse to sanction the conditions which German and Austro-Hungarian imperialism is writing with the sword on the bodies of living peoples. We cannot place the signature of the Russian Revolution beneath conditions which bring oppression, sorrow and misfortune to millions of human beings.

"The Governments of Germany and Austria-Hungary wish to rule lands and peoples by the right of military conquest. Let them do this openly. We cannot sanction violence. We withdraw from the War, but we are obliged to refuse to sign the peace treaty. . . .

"Refusing to sign an annexationist treaty, Russia, on its side, declares the state of war with Germany, Austria-Hungary, Turkey and Bulgaria as ended. At the same time the Russian troops are ordered to demobilize entirely on the whole front."

The bold and unique experiment of thus ostentatiously throwing down arms while at the same time refusing to sign an objectionable peace was launched. The German reply was swift and crushing. On February 13 the highest German military and civilian authorities, Hindenburg, Ludendorff, the Chief of the Naval Staff, the Chancellor, Hertling, the Vice-Chancellor and Foreign Minister Kühlmann met in council at Homburg.[17] The military men agreed that the situation in the East must be cleared up; otherwise a new front might arise and divisions which were needed in France would have to remain in Poland and the Baltic States. Moreover, Ukrainian grain was badly needed. It was decided, after a little half-hearted opposition on the part of the civilian participants in the council, to strike a brief hard blow, which would round out the German acquisitions in the East by advancing the line of occupation to the eastern boundaries of Latvia and Esthonia and which would bring in a quantity of booty in the shape of war material.

The original armistice had provided for a period of seven days' notice before the resumption of hostilities. The Germans interpreted Trotzky's refusal to sign the peace as an automatic denunciation of the armistice; and their advance began on February 18. Everything turned out as Lenin had foreseen. There was no refusal on the part of the German troops to march, and there was no organized Russian force to meet them. So complete was the disorganization of the Russian Front that there was little successful effort to carry out

such passive defensive measures as the blowing up of bridges or the removal and destruction of munition stocks.

The German Military Command announced on February 16 that the armistice would come to an end at noon on the 18th. On the morning of the 18th the Bolshevik Party Central Committee met to consider the new situation.[18] All the news was disquieting. German airplanes had appeared over Dvinsk; Prince Leopold of Bavaria, commander of the German Eastern Front, had broadcast a speech proclaiming that Germany's mission was to ward off the "moral infection" of Bolshevism; an offensive against Reval was expected at any moment. Lenin urged an immediate proposal to Germany to resume peace negotiations. Trotzky was in favor of holding out a little longer; the offensive might bring about a serious explosion in Germany. If this did not occur there would still be time to propose peace. Lenin was defeated on this issue by one vote; seven members of the Central Committee were against his proposal, while six voted for it.

This decision was reversed, however, on the evening of the same day. The Germans had already occupied Dvinsk and were advancing everywhere without meeting serious resistance. Lenin spoke passionately and bitterly, insisting that it was impossible "to play with war" and that the breakdown of the Revolution was inevitable, unless a clearcut decision were taken. If Esthonia, Latvia and Finland were given up the Revolution was still not lost.

Trotzky protested against the phrase "playing with war" and reminded Lenin that the latter had proposed "to feel out the Germans." Apparently, however, he believed that the demonstration had gone far enough, and by changing his vote he gave Lenin a majority for the proposal to make immediate peace overtures. A radio message was promptly despatched to Berlin, under the signatures of Lenin and Trotzky, protesting against the German troop movements, expressing readiness to sign peace on the terms proposed by the delegations of the Central Powers at Brest-Litovsk and promising to give without delay a reply to precise conditions of peace offered by the German Government.

This Soviet message was sent to Berlin on the 19th. For three anxious days no reply was received, while the Germans continued to advance. The Council of People's Commissars appealed to the workers, peasants and soldiers "to let our enemies know that we are ready to defend the conquests of the Revolution to the last drop of blood" and a second appeal, written by Trotzky, called for the de·-

struction of railroad communication, of food and munition stores, for the organization of workers' battalions to dig trenches, for the shooting of "enemy agents, speculators, bandits, hooligans, counter-revolutionary agitators and German spies." [19]

It is doubtful whether these appeals would have evoked any effective popular resistance if the Germans had endeavored to occupy Petrograd and Moscow. But such a large-scale operation, which would have involved the employment of considerable numbers of troops, did not enter into their plans. What the German Government and the German Supreme Command regarded as practicable and desirable was set forth plainly enough in the new peace conditions, which were received on February 22. They were considerably more unfavorable than the original conditions of Brest-Litovsk. The chief new demands were the evacuation of Latvia and Esthonia by Russian troops and Red Guards; the immediate conclusion of peace between Russia and the Ukrainian People's Republic and the withdrawal of Russian troops and Red Guards from Ukraina and Finland. All this pointed clearly to a German protectorate over Ukraina and Finland, combined with German annexation, in one form or another, of the Baltic Provinces.

The harsh new terms were accompanied by a sharp intimation that they must be accepted within forty-eight hours, that Soviet representatives must immediately set out for Brest-Litovsk and sign the treaty within three days. Ratification must follow within two weeks. There was to be no loophole for a repetition of Trotzky's former tactics of delay and evasion.

Lenin was heartily weary of what he called "the policy of the revolutionary phrase." At a session of the Central Committee on February 23 [20] he reinforced the German ultimatum with one of his own. For a revolutionary war an army was necessary and Russia had no army. Therefore the terms must be accepted. Otherwise he would withdraw from the Central Committee and from the Soviet Government.

This threat was of decisive importance. Trotzky and Dzerzhinsky, who were both unreconciled to signing the peace, agreed that it was unthinkable to organize successful resistance if a considerable part of the Party, headed by Lenin, was unwilling to coöperate. When the question of accepting the German conditions was put to a vote seven of the fifteen members present voted in favor of acceptance. Four irreconcilable members, Bukharin, Lomov, Uritzky and Bubnov, voted in the negative. Four others, Trotzky, Dzerzhin-

sky, Joffe and Krestinsky, abstained from voting. They would not support Lenin; but they would not assume the responsibility of causing his withdrawal from the Party and the Government.

In these last stages of the negotiations Trotzky had based some hope on military aid, at least of a passive character, from the Allies. The senior diplomats were all definitely anti-Bolshevik in senti-ment; but such men as Colonel Raymond Robins, head of the American Red Cross Mission in Russia, R. H. Bruce Lockhart, formerly British Consul in Moscow, who was playing the difficult and thankless rôle of an unofficial British diplomatic agent with vague and undefined powers, and Captain Jacques Sadoul, of the French Military Mission, believed in the stability of the Soviet regime and argued that a friendly policy on the part of the Allied Governments might keep Russia as at least a potential enemy of Germany. Some offers of limited and unofficial military coöperation apparently came from the French Military Mission; and at the height of the German offensive Colonel J. A. Ruggles, of the Amer-ican Military Mission, and Captain Sadoul had a meeting with Lenin, where it was agreed that, if the Germans advanced beyond Pskov, Allied troop units would assist in blowing up bridges and destroying war material.[21] About the same time Trotzky told Lock-hart that, if an Allied promise of support were forthcoming, he would sway the decision of the Soviet Government in favor of war.[22] In view of the closeness of the division in the Central Committee Trotzky might easily have carried out this assurance. But the British Government was unwilling to commit itself and Lockhart's inquiry went unanswered.

The question of the propriety of accepting military instructors and supplies from the "imperialistic" Allied Governments was hotly debated within the Party Central Committee on February 22 and Trotzky obtained a majority of one vote for his view that aid should be accepted, on condition that the Bolsheviki retained com-plete independence in foreign policy and gave no political promises. Lenin was not present at this session, but, characteristically enough, he agreed with Trotzky's practical view on this question and put himself on record with a scribbled note which read: "I ask to add my vote in favor of taking potatoes and arms from the bandits of Anglo-French imperialism."[23]

Even after the peace had been signed Trotzky seems to have kept in view the possibility of Allied military coöperation. On March 5, two days after the Treaty of Brest-Litovsk had been signed,

but before it had been ratified, Trotzky gave Robins a written statement [24] asking whether, in the event of a Soviet refusal to ratify the Peace or of a subsequent breach with Germany, "the Soviet Government could rely on the support of the United States, of Great Britain and of France in the struggle against Germany"; what would be the nature of this assistance; what would America do if Japan should occupy Siberia.

Lockhart talked with Trotzky on the same day and telegraphed to the British Foreign Office, recommending that aid should be extended to Russia on the ground that "if ever the Allies have had a chance in Russia since the Revolution the Germans have given it to them by the exorbitant peace terms they have imposed." [25]

The representations of Robins in Washington and of Lockhart in London did not lead to any positive results. President Wilson did, indeed, make two sympathetic gestures in Russia's direction. One was in his famous "fourteen points" speech, delivered on January 8, in direct response to an appeal from Edgar Sisson, representative of the Committee on Public Information in Russia, couched in the following terms: [26]

"If President will restate anti-imperialistic war aims and democratic peace requisites of America in thousand words or less, in short, almost placard paragraphs, short sentences, I can get it fed into Germany in great quantities in German translation, and can utilize Russian version potently in army and everywhere."

Wilson's reference to Russia in the sixth point of this speech was obviously designed to encourage the Soviet delegation at Brest-Litovsk to resist the German demands. It read as follows:

"The evacuation of all Russian territory and such a settlement of all questions affecting Russia as will secure the best and freest coöperation of all the nations in the world in obtaining for her an unhampered and unembarrassed opportunity for the independent determination of her own political development and national policy and assure her of a sincere welcome into the society of free nations under institutions of her own choosing; and, more than a welcome, assistance also of every kind that she may need and may herself desire. The treatment accorded Russia by her sister nations in the months to come will be the acid test of their goodwill, of their comprehension of her needs as distinguished from their own interests, and of their intelligent and unselfish sympathy."

Wilson's second gesture took the form of a friendly message to the Fourth All-Russian Congress of Soviets, which opened on

March 14 to discuss the ratification of the Peace of Brest-Litovsk. The message spoke of "the sincere sympathy which the people of the United States feel for the Russian people" and continued: "Although the Government of the United States is unhappily not in a position to render the direct and effective aid it would wish to render, I beg to assure the people of Russia through the Congress that it will avail itself of every opportunity to secure for Russia once more complete sovereignty and independence in her own affairs and full restoration to her great rôle in the life of Europe and the modern world."

The message had little immediate concrete significance, but it did seem to reflect a not unfriendly attitude on the part of Wilson toward the new regime. Whether from a sheer oversight on the part of the Soviet leaders or whether because of conviction that American and Allied aid was a mirage and an illusion, the Congress answered Wilson's soft words with a trumpet blast of uncompromising revolutionism,[27] "expressing to all the peoples which are perishing and suffering from the horrors of imperialist war its sympathy and its firm conviction that the happy time is not far away when the working masses of all bourgeois countries will overthrow the yoke of capital and establish the socialist order, which alone can assure a stable and just peace, and at the same time the culture and welfare of all the toilers."

The actions of the Soviet Government in quitting the War, repudiating Russia's foreign obligations and issuing appeals for world revolution had alienated the Allied Governments to such an extent that it is not surprising that proposals for collaboration with it fell on deaf and unfriendly ears. And indeed in retrospect it is difficult to see how the Allies could have effectively served their own cause by offering active military coöperation to the Soviet regime. The Russian masses obviously would not fight; the sending of small forces and quantities of war supplies would have been futile, while the despatch of a large expedition or the sending into a disorganized and chaotic country of considerable stocks of munitions would have been a risky adventure.

After the decision to accept the German terms had been taken by the Bolshevik Party Central Committee there was a good deal of discussion as to who should assume the onerous and undesired function of going to Brest-Litovsk to sign the Treaty. Trotzky refused to go; he had resigned as Commissar for Foreign Affairs and was preparing to devote his boundless energy to the new post, with

which his name will always be associated, of Commissar for War. A delegation headed by G. Y. Sokolnikov, a member of the Central Committee who had supported Lenin's attitude on the question of peace, proceeded to Brest-Litovsk and signed the Treaty on March 3. Sokolnikov ostentatiously refused to discuss or even to read with any care the terms of the document which was submitted for his signature, in order to emphasize the point that the Peace was a matter of pure dictation, not of agreement. The final text of the Treaty was made still worse from the Russian standpoint, by the insertion, at Turkey's request, of a new clause which provided for the evacuation of the Kars, Batum and Ardaghan districts of the Caucasus and the cession of this territory to Turkey.

To Russians who thought in nationalist terms the Brest-Litovsk Peace must have seemed the climax of the country's humiliation and misfortune. It swept away at one stroke the fruits of two centuries of expansion toward the West and South. It stripped the former Russian Empire of almost a third of its population; of almost eighty percent of its iron and ninety percent of its coal production, of about half its industrial plant and equipment. It threw Russia back from the Black and Baltic Seas.

From a revolutionary, as well as from a nationalist, standpoint the Treaty was a cause for bitter heartburning, with its clauses demanding the withdrawal of Russian troops from Soviet Ukraina and Soviet Finland and cessation of revolutionary agitation and propaganda both in Germany and Austria-Hungary and in Ukraina and Finland. The Left-Socialist Revolutionaries were strongly opposed to the Treaty and quit the Government on this issue. Bukharin and his "Left" Communists continued to fulminate against Lenin's peace policy in their organ, *The Communist*.

But Lenin, after forcing through the decision to sign the Peace by the threat of his resignation, pushed steadily on toward ratification. A Party Congress, attended by a small number of delegates, met on March 6, 7 and 8. Here Lenin repeated his familiar arguments. There was no army; it was impossible to hold out. "We should have perished at the least attack of the Germans; we should have been the prey of the enemy within a few days." He compared Russia's position with that of Prussia when Napoleon imposed the Peace of Tilsit; and offered some consolation to the more militant delegates by saying: "Yes, of course we break the Treaty; we have already broken it thirty or forty times." [28] Probably Lenin had in mind the giving of aid with arms and military instructors to the

Red Finns, which was, of course, a contravention of the terms of the Treaty.

Bukharin summed up the case for the critics of the Treaty: he argued that Lenin's theory of a "breathing-space" was unsound, because a short respite would not permit the reorganization of the railroads and the military training of the population. Bukharin also complained that the Peace compelled the Bolsheviki to renounce internationalist propaganda, "which is the sharpest weapon at our disposal."

The Congress upheld Lenin by 28 votes to 12, with four abstentions, passing a resolution to the effect that "the ratification of the most oppressive and humiliating Peace Treaty is necessary because of the incapacity of our army and because of the necessity of exploiting even the slightest possibility of obtaining a breathing-space before the assault of imperialism upon the Soviet Republic." The Brest-Litovsk Peace had called not only for the cessation of revolutionary propaganda against the Governments of the Central Powers, but also for the demobilization of the Russian army; and therefore it is understandable why the Congress resolution on war and peace, which called for general military training and ended with the declaration that "the socialist proletariat of Russia with all its forces and all the resources at its disposal will support the brotherly revolutionary movement of the proletariat of all countries" was kept secret for almost a year, until the breakdown of the German Imperial regime had made it possible to end the Brest-Litovsk Treaty. The final ratification of the Treaty took place at the Fourth Congress of Soviets on March 15 by a vote of 784 to 261, with 115 abstentions. Among the latter were 64 "Left Communists."

From the time of the Seventh Congress the official name of the Party was changed from Bolsheviki to Communists. This led, in some cases, to disastrous misunderstandings, because the politically unschooled peasants, confused by the change of name, began to declare that they were "for the Bolsheviki but against the Communists" when the "Communists" began to requisition their grain after the "Bolsheviki" had encouraged them to seize the land.

The Peace of Brest-Litovsk sounded the deathknell of the newly established Soviet regimes in Ukraina and in Finland. In Ukraina the small, poorly trained Red forces which had been able to overcome the still weaker troops of the Rada, proved quite unable to resist the regular German and Austrian armies. The defense of Ukraina was made still more difficult by the fact that every city

tried to defend itself independently, while separate regions in Ukraina also created their own Soviet Governments, with scant regard for any central authority. After occupying Kiev on March 3 the invaders pushed steadily on in eastern and southern directions, occupying Poltava on March 29, Kharkov on April 8, Odessa on April 13. On April 17 the Central Executive Committee of Ukraina decided to dissolve itself on the ground that Ukraina was entirely in the hands of the invaders.[29] A few flashes of courage and initiative on the part of Red detachments could not offset the generally slack discipline and the complete lack of trained military leadership. Some of the Red partisan bands withdrew into the Kuban, where their habits of marauding and requisitioning made them a nuisance rather than a help to the local Soviet Government. Other Red forces, under the leadership of K. E. Voroshilov, a Donetz metal worker, who subsequently became the Soviet Commissar for War, and a number of local partisan chieftains, fought their way across the hostile Don Territory, already bristling with insurgent anti-Soviet Cossacks, and established themselves in Tsaritsin, on the Lower Volga, which acquired the name of the "Red Verdun" because of its stubborn resistance to the attacks of the Cossack Ataman General Krasnov. The Germans also overran the Crimea and set up a conservative government there.

Once in full occupation of Ukraina the Germans hastened to turn the wheel of social revolution backward. Finding the Rada not sufficiently subservient, the German Command about the end of April dissolved it and placed a number of its leaders under arrest. At the same time a handpicked congress of landlords and substantial farmers proclaimed as ruler of Ukraina, with the old-fashioned title of Hetman, the Russian General Skoropadsky. His regime was completely dependent upon the bayonets of the German army of occupation and was popular only with the landlords and with the well-to-do classes in the towns. With a view to marking the separation of Ukraina from Russia, Skoropadsky carried out a regime of artificial Ukrainization in state documents and titles, although neither he nor the officers of his entourage were in any sense genuine Ukrainian nationalists.

Skoropadsky and the Germans created a kind of conservative law and order which was greeted with a sigh of relief by the harassed propertied classes and by the numerous refugees from Soviet Russia. But the workers, subjected to the rigors of a military occupation and denied the right to strike, were in a state of deep,

if repressed, discontent. And in the country districts peasan guerrilla bands soon began to appear, cutting off small parties o: foreign soldiers, raiding landlords' estates and killing their owners There were two causes of this widespread agrarian movement Skoropadsky endeavored to take the land which the peasants had seized away from them and to give it back to its former owners; and German military support for his regime was made dependent upon large exports of foodstuffs from Ukraina to Germany and Austria. Altogether the Central powers are officially reported to have extracted from Ukraina during the period of the occupation 113,421 tons of foodstuffs, mostly grain, together with eggs, butter, meat and sugar.[30] This was not sufficient to offset the Allied blockade or to stop the process of exhaustion through hunger; but it was enough to arouse considerable discontent among the Ukrainian peasants, who were paid for the foodstuffs which they were obliged to surrender in currency of doubtful value.

The Ukrainian Communists who had taken refuge in Soviet Russia kept up lively communication with the insurgents across the border; Lenin's promise to the delegates of the Party Congress that the Peace of Brest-Litovsk would be broken was fully carried out. Other radical parties were also active; some peasant bands were under the leadership of Ukrainian nationalists, and the Left Socialist Revolutionaries, faithful to the old traditions of their Party, carried out terrorist acts, such as the assassination of the commander of the German forces in Ukraina, General Eichhorn, and the blowing up of powder stores in Kiev and Odessa. While the Germans were able to crush a Bolshevik attempt to organize a widespread peasant uprising in August (the only serious outbreak at this time was in Chernigov Province, near the Russian border), the countryside was seething with discontent; and it was quite evident that Skoropadsky would fall as soon as the German bayonets were withdrawn.

Finland was also drawn into the orbit of German influence. This sparsely populated country of lakes and forests, with its standards of neatness and cleanliness that suggest Scandinavia rather than Russia, was torn by fierce social strife during the first months of 1918. So far as voting is any gauge the Finnish Reds and Whites were almost equal in numbers, a fact which made for a prolonged and stubborn struggle. The election to the Finnish Diet in the summer of 1917 resulted in a small non-Socialist majority, the Socialists obtaining between ninety and ninety-five seats out of 200. The Russian Revolution and the establishment of a Soviet

regime in Petrograd, only a short distance from the Finnish border, naturally had its repercussions among the Finnish workers, who began to organize their Red Guard detachments. The sympathies of the Russian soldiers and sailors in Finland were also distinctly against the "boorzhui." A non-Socialist Government, headed by Svinhufud, and supported by a small majority in the Diet, was formed; and the Russian Soviet Government, sympathetic, of course, with the Finnish revolutionaries, but anxious to avoid any appearance of Russian dictation in Finnish affairs, decided to recognize Finland's independence on December 31.

The atmosphere of class antagonism became increasingly bitter; and on January 26 Svinhufud's Government was overthrown as a result of a general strike and the action of the Red Guards. A Red regime was set up in the industrial southern and southwestern part of Finland, while the northern part of the country, with its predominantly peasant population, supported the Svinhufud Government. The most reliable military force of the Finnish Whites, in the beginning, consisted of young Finns who had gone to Germany during the War in the hope of being able to strike a blow against their country's traditional oppressor, Russia, and who returned to Finland as well armed and disciplined military units.

For several weeks the Finnish civil war went on without decisive victories for either side. In March, after the signing of the Treaty of Brest-Litovsk, Russian troops and warships which had been supporting the Finnish Reds were withdrawn, although the Soviet Government, which hastened to conclude a "treaty of friendship and brotherhood" with the Finnish Socialist Workers' Republic,[31] gave some aid in the form of munitions, military instructors and volunteers. The "White" Finnish Government concluded a peace treaty with Germany on March 7; and on April 3 a German expeditionary force, under General von der Goltz, landed in the rear of the Red lines at Hango. The arrival of the German troops determined the issue of the Finnish civil war.[32] One by one the towns in the hands of the Reds fell: Tammerfors on April 23, Helsingfors on April 27. On May 9 von der Goltz surrounded the Finnish Red Army in the neighborhood of Tavastgus and forced it to surrender. On the same day Viborg was captured; the leaders of the Finnish Government fled to Russia on icebreakers. A sanguinary White Terror was the climax of a bitterly fought civil war.

At Brest-Litovsk the Russian Revolution, flushed with its easy triumphal march over the territory of the former Tsarist Empire,

encountered embattled German militarism, and was obliged to retreat. The weapon of propaganda, effective enough against Kornilov and Kaledin, was of little avail against the gray-uniformed legions of Hindenburg and Ludendorff. It is a striking proof of Lenin's perspicacity and freedom from selfdelusion that he could reckon the chances against successful resistance to Germany just as accurately as a few months earlier he had calculated the chances in favor of the overthrow of Kerensky. Seen in retrospect the signature of the Peace was inevitable; the only alternative would have been a collapse of the Soviet Government. Yet this inevitable act was so intensely distasteful that it required a strong combination of willpower and tact on Lenin's part to push through the ratification of the Peace without bringing about a split in the Party.

The consequences of Brest-Litovsk would have been far more serious for the Soviet regime if Germany had not been on the eve of decisive defeat on the Western Front. There is no convincing evidence to show that the Bolshevik propaganda which filtered in among the German troops on the Eastern Front or the surreptitious communications which passed between the Soviet Ambassador in Berlin, Joffe, and the left-wing leaders of the German Social Democrats played more than a minor rôle in undermining German morale and hastening the final debacle. The German military Empire, and the Brest-Litovsk system for East Europe, which was one of its last diplomatic achievements, were broken on the battlefields of France. Had Germany emerged from the World War victorious or at least strong enough to bargain for a free hand in the East in exchange for territorial concessions in the West, it might well have gone hard with the Bolshevik Revolution. For the subsequent Allied intervention in Russia, feeble and halfhearted, intermittent and constantly thwarted by the cross-purposes and conflicting interests of its initiators, was a far less serious threat to Soviet existence than intervention of the type which Ludendorff and Hoffmann would probably have sponsored, if their system had survived the shock of military defeat.

NOTES

[1] "Peace Negotiations at Brest-Litovsk," edited by A. A. Joffe, pp. 7, 8.
[2] *Ibid.,* pp. 9, 10.
[3] Count Ottokar Czernin, "Im Weltkriege," p. 311.
[4] "Die Aufzeichnungen des Generalmajors Max Hoffmann," Vol. II, pp. 201, 202.
[5] Czernin's diary for January 6 has the significant note: "It is our interest

either to win the Ukrainians for our peace basis or to drive a wedge between them and the Petersburgites [Bolsheviki]." *Cf.* "Im Weltkriege," p. 316.

[6] "Peace Negotiations at Brest-Litovsk," p. 52.

[7] *Cf.* transcript of Trotzky's speech in the session of January 11 in his "Collected Works," Vol. XVII, Part I, pp. 26–28.

[8] "Peace Negotiations at Brest-Litovsk," pp. 94ff.

[9] *Ibid.,* pp. 126ff.

[10] The full text of these theses is published in Lenin's "Collected Works," Vol. XV, pp. 63–69.

[11] *Cf.* "Protocols of the Central Committee of the Russian Social Democratic Labor Party," pp. 199–207.

[12] *Cf.* Chapter XVII, p. 375.

[13] Czernin, *op. cit.,* p. 332.

[14] Erich Ludendorff, "Meine Kriegserinnerungen," p. 445.

[15] Hoffmann, *op. cit.,* pp. 213, 214.

[16] Trotzky, *op. cit.,* Vol. XVII, Part I, pp. 103, 104.

[17] Ludendorff, *op. cit.,* pp. 440ff.

[18] "Protocols," pp. 230ff.

[19] *Cf. Izvestia* for February 21 and 22.

[20] "Protocols," pp. 247–258.

[21] *Cf.* Louis Fischer, "The Soviets in World Affairs," Vol. I, p. 62. Fischer cites Chicherin as authority for his statement.

[22] R. H. Bruce Lockhart, "Memoirs of a British Agent," p. 229.

[23] "Protocols," p. 246.

[24] *Cf.* United States Congressional Record for January 29, 1919.

[25] "Russian-American Relations," edited by Cummings and Pettit, p. 82.

[26] Edgar Sisson, "One Hundred Red Days," p. 205.

[27] Professor Yuri V. Kluchnikov and Andrei Sabanin, "Recent International Policy in Treaties, Notes and Declarations," Part II, p. 135.

[28] *Cf.* "The Seventh Congress of the Russian Communist Party (Stenographic Report)," p. 29.

[29] Evgenia Bosch, "'A Year of Struggle," p. 184.

[30] Czernin, *op. cit.,* pp. 445, 446.

[31] Kluchnikov and Sabanin, *op. cit.,* pp. 120, 121.

[32] An adequate summary of the fighting in Finland, written by a Russian participant on the side of the Reds, is M. S. Svechnikov's "Revolution and Civil War in Finland."

CHAPTER XIX

THE SHORTLIVED "BREATHING–SPACE"

LENIN had insisted on the signature of the Peace of Brest-Litovsk because he was convinced that the very existence of the Soviet regime depended on obtaining a *peredishka,* or breathing-space. This breathing-space was shortlived; less than three months elapsed between the signing of the Brest-Litovsk Peace and the outbreak of hostilities with the Czecho-Slovaks which precipitated a more serious phase of the civil war. And this brief period of relative calm was marked by two problems which taxed to the utmost the fanaticism, energy and determination of the Bolshevik leaders: a growing crisis of food supply and a wave of disorderly excesses of various kinds all over the country: hunger riots, outbursts of looting by returned soldiers, professional criminals and "anarchists" who were often only robbers under a thin "ideological" disguise; mutinies among the Red Guards and among the newly recruited and unreliable Red Army soldiers.

Although he was one of the greatest of revolutionary leaders, Lenin abhorred disorder as a permanent state. "Our proletarian dictatorship aims at guarantying order, discipline, productivity of labor, accounting and control," he declared on one occasion, in the spring of 1918.[1] His writings and speeches during the "breathing-space" are saturated with the idea that the destructive part of the revolution has largely been completed, that the basic problem of the moment is to learn how to operate the nationalized factories, to achieve some measure of economic reconstruction. "Our work in organizing proletarian accounting and control clearly lagged behind the work of expropriating the expropriators," he wrote at this time; and he proclaimed the slogans, which must have sounded strange in the ears of many Red Guard partisan "expropriators":

"Carry out an accurate and honest account of money, manage economically, don't loaf, don't steal, maintain the strictest discipline in labor." He was willing to offer very high pay for the services of the biggest "bourgeois" specialists, although he was careful to

414

insist that this was a compromise, a retreat from "the principles of the Paris Commune and of every proletarian government, which demand the levelling of pay to that of the average worker." More than that, he was prepared to introduce piecework payment and "whatever is scientific and progressive in the Taylor System," in an effort to restore the falling productivity of labor.

When the so-called left-wing Communists who had opposed the conclusion of the Peace criticized Lenin's policy of economic moderation as likely to lead to state capitalism, he retorted that state capitalism would be a step forward for Russia. "In the transition from capitalism to socialism," declared Lenin, "our main enemy is the small bourgeoisie, its habits, its economic situation. The small proprietor more than anyone else is afraid of state capitalism, because he has one desire: to grasp, to get more for himself, to plunder, to smash the big landlords, the big exploiters . . . Only the development of state capitalism, only the careful arrangement of accounting and control, only the strictest organization and labor discipline will bring us to socialism. And without this there is no socialism." [2]

When workers' delegations came to him asking for the nationalization of their factories, Lenin at this time was in the habit of putting embarrassing questions to them. Did they know accurately what their factories produced, or what markets could be found for their products? Were they prepared to operate the factory efficiently if the state placed it in their hands? If they could not answer these questions satisfactorily Lenin would recommend that they make haste slowly and consent to an arrangement under which the capitalist would have a share in the management of the factory and would provide technical knowledge and experience for its operation.

Trotzky was inclined to strike the same note. In a speech which he delivered before a Moscow City Conference of the Communist Party on March 28, 1918,[3] he emphasized the need for "labor, discipline and order," urged that specialists be given a free hand in managing industry and suggested that the workers themselves should organize courts to try to punish sluggards and slackers in the factories.

It is possible that if there had been no civil war and no foreign intervention this clear recognition, on the part of the Soviet leaders, of the vital necessity of bringing some kind of order out of the economic chaos into which the country had fallen would have

given a different and a much more moderate turn to the economic development of the Revolution. Soviet Russia might have started on a basis similar to that of the New Economic Policy which was introduced in 1921 without passing through the intermediate phase of war communism.

At the same time it should not be forgotten that even Lenin's iron will and unquestioned authority as Party leader could make little headway against the prevalent confusion and disorganization in the early period of the Soviet regime. No matter how many decrees might be issued by the central government, every province, every town, every factory was to a considerable extent a law unto itself. Quite typical of the spirit of the time was the action in May of the "Council of People's Commissars" of the little town of Eletz in seceding from Orel Province and refusing to carry out the orders of the provincial food authorities.

And only a minority of the workers shared the mood of conscious socialist discipline which Lenin and Trotzky endeavored to inculcate. The majority were willing enough to throw out the capitalist owners of the factories, to confiscate the homes and other property of the rich. But when it was a question of settling down to hard work there was distinctly less enthusiasm. An anecdote of the time represents a worker as replying to the question, "What would you do if you were director of a factory?" "I should steal a hundred rubles and run away."

Quite apart from the will of the workers, they were often physically unable to labor with any real efficiency. "The bony hand of hunger," which the capitalist Ryabushinsky had predicted, certainly gripped the workers, along with the whole population, in the spring of 1918, even if it did not, as Ryabushinsky had expected, "bring them to their senses."

Eloquent testimony of how bad the situation had become is to be found in a circular telegram which Lenin and the Food Commissar, Tsurupa, despatched to all provincial Soviets and food committees, in May: [4]

"Petrograd is in an unprecedentedly catastrophic condition. There is no bread. The population is given the remaining potato flour and crusts. The Red capital is on the verge of perishing from famine. Counter-revolution is raising its head, directing the dissatisfaction of the hungry masses against the Soviet Government. In the name of the Soviet Socialist Republic, I demand immediate help for Petrograd. Telegraph to the Food Commissariat about the measures you have taken."

Petrograd was no exception. There were smaller places where the hunger was even greater and where desperate riots broke out. There were such riots in the middle of May in Koplino, a town just outside Petrograd, and in Pavlovsk Posad, east of Moscow. In the latter town a mob of enraged peasants set fire to the building of the Soviet and shot down and beat to death some of its members when they tried to escape. How desperate the situation was may be judged from the fact that the promise of a bread ration of a quarter of a pound a day was considered sufficient to pacify Koplino. On April 29 hungry crowds in the town of Rybinsk, on the upper Volga, surrounded the building of the Soviet, beat some of the members and tried to throw the President into the river and disarmed a small group of Red Army soldiers. A company of troops had to be called to disperse the mob. On May 15 there was a similar disturbance in Zvenigorod, where ten thousand peasants from neighboring villages gathered, smashed up the headquarters of the Soviet and arrested the President. Fifty soldiers, sent in an automobile from Moscow, restored order.[5]

The Soviet newspapers in the spring of 1918 are full of accounts of such spontaneous local outbreaks, which were often characterized by great brutality and were put down with equal ruthlessness by the Government. In the village Taldom, in Tver Province, a riotous mob, after demanding food from the Soviet, rushed to the home of the local food commissar, beat him to death before the eyes of his family and stuffed his mouth full of food cards.

As early as the end of March and the beginning of April small fights, no less ferocious than the big battles of a real war, were taking place between poor peasants and Red Army soldiers, on one side, and the more well-to-do peasants and *meshochniki* (bagmen) on the other. A laconic news item reads as follows: "In the village Smirnov, of Ryazan County, the poorest peasant youth decided to apply terror in their struggle with the kulaks [richer peasants]. After twelve kulaks had been killed the others yielded and said they would obey the Soviet Government."[6]

The Bolsheviki had taken Russia out of the World War. But they kindled the flame of an equally fierce class war in every Russian hamlet and village, systematically setting the poorest peasants against the more well-to-do, in an effort to squeeze out of the latter their hidden stocks of grain. As the pinch of hunger becomes tighter in the last months before the new harvest the Governmental decrees on food requisitioning become more sweeping and

relentless; the reports of riots and uprisings (all quickly suppressed because of the lack of unity and organization) become more frequent and more serious; one senses a mood of disillusionment not only among the peasants, but also among the city workers to whom the Bolsheviki always looked for their main support.

There were several reasons for this hungry spring. The Brest-Litovsk Peace had taken away from Russia one of its richest grain producing regions, Ukraina, together with seventy percent of its iron and steel production and ninety percent of its sugar industry. The Don territory also passed out of Soviet control in the spring. While there was undoubtedly surplus food in the Volga Provinces and in Siberia (the middle Volga was lost for several months and Siberia for a much longer period as a result of the successful anti-Bolshevik movement initiated by the Czechs at the end of May) the breakdown of transportation and the weak authority of the central Soviet Government made it extremely difficult to bring it over any great distances.

The railroad system, the weakness of which had been a factor in bringing about the fall of Tsarism, had been going from bad to worse since the Revolution. According to an estimate of the Supreme Economic Council, the body which the Soviet Government had created to manage the nationalized industries, the number of disabled locomotives increased from 5,100 on January 1, 1917, to 10,000 on January 1, 1918, so that by the latter date 48 percent of the Russian locomotives were out of commission. With hunger rife all over the country and with every local Soviet exercising wide independent authority, it was not uncommon for grain cars to be forcibly uncoupled before they reached their destinations. The transportation system was further debilitated because many loosely controlled and ill-disciplined Red Guard detachments seized trains and lived in the cars for months at a time, moving about more or less as it suited their fancy.

Then the Revolution brought about a virtual paralysis of normal goods exchange between city and village. The peasant was no longer obliged to sell his products in order to pay rent to his landlord or taxes to the state. Inasmuch as manufactured goods were scarce and the Soviet Government was unable to create an organization for distributing them effectively the peasants preferred to keep their grain, to make "samogon," or moonshine whiskey out of it, rather than to sell it to the state at fixed prices with which they could buy little or nothing in exchange. Incidentally,

this complete inability of the Soviet Government to give the peasants a normal equivalent in manufactured goods for their foodstuffs (an inability which persisted throughout the period of civil war and intervention, when the needs of the Red Army came ahead of everything else) was the basic cause of peasant dissatisfaction and sporadic revolts and finally led to the introduction of the New Economic Policy.

Formidable unemployment was another problem which confronted the new Bolshevik rulers of the country. The war industries, which had greatly swelled the city working class, were demobilized; and there was an acute shortage of fuel and raw material for the ordinary factories. It was estimated that by the spring of 1918 seventy or eighty percent of the Petrograd industrial workers had been thrown out of employment.[7] Most of them drifted back to their native villages; one of the ironical peculiarities of the first years of the Revolution which had been made in the name of the industrial proletariat was that a considerable part of the working class melted away as a result of the acute food shortage in the cities. Many went back to the villages; others joined the ranks of the bagmen who packed the overcrowded trains and, running the gantlet of the military and police forces with which the Soviet Government endeavored to suppress such "speculation," surreptitiously furnished those of the town dwellers who could afford to pay their high prices some food supplies over and above the extremely small rations which the Soviet authorities were able to dole out.

All these hardships had an unmistakable effect on the mood of the workers. A Soviet election in Sormovo, an industrial town near Nizhni Novgorod, in April gave a small majority to the Mensheviki and Socialist Revolutionaries; the workers had been incensed by the sudden reduction in their bread ration from forty pounds to ten pounds a month. Here, as most probably in all such cases, the Bolsheviki did not allow themselves to be disconcerted by an unfavorable election; they promptly created a new governing body, remaining in the Soviet for purposes of observation and propaganda.[8] As time went on, and especially after the beginning of the civil war, the Soviets lost their character as freely elected bodies; the dictatorship of the proletariat turned more and more into a dictatorship of the Communist Party. As early as the spring of 1918 Mensheviki and Socialist Revolutionaries were being expelled from membership in some provincial Soviets.

In some cases, especially in the Ural Territory, where the

workers themselves were sometimes small property owners, with cottages, gardens and farm animals, discontent with the food situation reached such a pitch that there were revolts in a number of factory and mining towns in May.[9] These revolts broke out more easily because the more active Bolsheviki among the workers were absent, fighting in the Red Guard detachments against the Orenburg Cossack Ataman Dutov.

If human misery were an infallible barometer of revolutionary action the Soviet regime could scarcely have escaped overthrow in 1918. If one excepts the soldiers in the trenches who were in danger of being killed in battle, the Russians of all classes were living under much greater sufferings and deprivations than had been sufficient to bring about the downfall of Kerensky.

But, as Russia's experience was to prove very conclusively, revolution is not an automatic reaction to a given amount of suffering. The spirit and character of the government in power, and of the forces in opposition to it, may be of decisive importance. The Provisional Government under Kerensky had been weak and flabby, unsure of itself, unable to take strong action in any direction. The popular movements of revolt against it were to a large extent co-ordinated and given driving force by a determined revolutionary organization, the Bolshevik Party, headed by a leader of genius, Lenin.

Very different was the situation in 1918. Lenin and his associates, even in the darkest days of hunger and chaos, were buoyed up by the fanatical strength of their convictions. They envisaged a European, if not a world, revolution breaking out at the end of the World War and coming to their aid. They possessed both the determination and the ability to apply ruthless measures against those who resisted them. For, even though there was a distinct cooling off in the sentiment of the workers, and still more so of the peasants, by comparison with the enthusiastic November days, there was always a nucleus of tested and hardened Communists, of workers and people of the poor classes generally to whom the revolution had brought opportunity and promotion, which could be relied on for support.

On the other hand, there was no leader, no common idea, no unifying force among the numerous discontented elements. The country sputtered like damp wood, but failed to burst out in a general conflagration of anti-Soviet revolt. The Bolsheviki held with a fair degree of security the main towns, the railroad lines, the more

effective weapons of modern warfare, such as artillery and machine-guns. Riotous workers, who were motivated by hunger, rather than by fundamental disagreement with Bolshevik ideas,[10] could usually be cajoled by an extra distribution of bread, combined with a few fiery revolutionary speeches by practised Bolshevik agitators. More stubbornly insurgent peasants, armed with hunting rifles and pitchforks, could be shot down with machine-guns.

There were, to be sure, a number of underground conspirative organizations, which aspired to lead an anti-Soviet movement. There was the Right or Moscow Centre, an organization of business-men, landowners and conservative and liberal politicians. It had a military department, which recruited members largely among officers, but really existed only on paper. There was the National Centre, which split off from the Right Centre in June, 1918, partly because its members disapproved of the Germanophile tendencies of the parent organization, partly because they favored a more liberal programme of reconstruction for the future non-Bolshevik Russia. If the Right Centre attracted its supporters mainly from the ranks of the former Tsarist bureaucracy, the National Centre was a rallying point for the Cadet Party. More to the left was the Union of Regeneration, in which the right-wing Socialists mingled with left-wing Cadets. Some measure of agreement was reached between the National Centre and the Union of Regeneration. The former agreed to abandon its demand for a dictator in favor of a directory of three persons, one Socialist, one Cadet and one military man. The Union of Regeneration, on its side, gave up the proposal for the convocation of the original Constituent Assembly, agreeing on the election of a new Assembly.

These underground anti-Bolshevik organizations, however, were quite unable to organize and lead any broad popular anti-Bolshevik movement. As Denikin, who was intimately acquainted with their inner history, writes:[11] "Without resources, without mutual confidence and clarity in their relations with each other and, most important of all, without real force, their work in the beginning proceeded indifferently, without bringing any results . . . They were leaders without the people."

A more serious secret threat to the Soviet regime in the spring of 1918 was represented by Savinkov's organization, "The Union for the Defense of the Motherland and Freedom." An old master in the art of conspiracy and dodging the police, Savinkov returned to Moscow from the Don, where the conservative officers looked

askance on this veteran Socialist Revolutionary terrorist, and built up an organization, consisting mainly of former officers, which, according to his own possibly exaggerated estimate, numbered 5,500 members. But they were scattered in Moscow and in thirty-four provincial towns and were too few in numbers to strike an effective blow independently. And between the officer who slipped away on a dark night to a secret meeting in the home of the doctor, Grigoriev, or of some other of Savinkov's lieutenants in Moscow, and the worker who listened more readily to the Menshevik speaker when his bread ration fell below an existence minimum and the peasant who pulled out gun, hoe or pitchfork and joined the mob that was attacking a requisitioning detachment there was no inner unity, no common slogan, no agreement as to what should take the place of the Soviet regime if it should be overthrown. The whole history of the struggle of the Soviet regime against its enemies is the record of a struggle of weakness against weakness, in which the Communists, thanks in large measure to their Party discipline, always retained a slight, but sufficient margin of superior reserve strength.

Some of the anti-Soviet agitation which was going on in the spring of 1918 was based on the appeal of returning to the old Tsarist times, which, however bad they seemed to the masses before the War, must have seemed enviable to some of the people who were unable to get a quarter of a pound of bread as a daily ration. One finds repeated references in the Soviet newspapers to a revival of the anti-Semitic propaganda of the "Black Hundreds." Public religious demonstrations of the Orthodox Church, especially the processions of the cross, when throngs marched through the streets, bearing ikons and crucifixes and headed by priests, not infrequently led to outbursts against the Soviets.

But, along with the current of opposition on the part of people, especially those who possessed any property before the upheaval, who felt that the Revolution had gone too far, the Soviet Government also had to face the hostility and disobedience of those who believed the Revolution had not gone far enough, who resented such features of the new Soviet policy as the substitution of a regular trained army for the Red Guards, the demand for order and discipline in the factories and on the railroads, the effort to repress individual acts of plundering and expropriation. The Bolshevik leaders had conjured up in the Russian masses a spirit which was easier to arouse than to suppress, a spirit which the hordes of

Stenka Razin and Emilian Pugachev would have understood, a spirit of fierce hatred for all authority and discipline, of determination to kill any "boorzhui" they might meet on the streets, to smash and destroy and pillage as they chose. One of the hardest struggles of the Soviet regime during the first period of its existence was with the excesses which the revolutionary spirit generated.

In Moscow, in Petrograd and in a number of provincial towns strong Anarchist groups made their appearance. Some of their members were idealists who were opposed in principle to any kind of human inequality or to any, even the mildest, exercise of organized state power. But many of these self-styled anarchists were adventurers and criminals, who were more inclined to loot than to work for a living. Proof of this is furnished by a statement which the newspaper *Anarchia*, organ of the Moscow Federation of Anarchist Groups, issued on March 16:[12]

"Lately an abuse has been noticed. Unknown individuals are taking away pocketbooks, making threats for the purposes of extortion, making searches and arrests in the name of the Federation.

"The Moscow Federation of Anarchist Groups announces that it does not justify any seizures whatsoever for the purposes of personal profit or, in general, of personal gain and that it will combat by all means such demonstrations of bourgeois spirit."

Such appeals had little practical effect; and robberies and murders by self-styled anarchists continued. Bands of the latter entrenched themselves in forcibly occupied Moscow mansions. The Cheka for some time had been contemplating stern action to repress these depredations; and when some anarchists seized the automobile of Colonel Raymond Robins, the American Red Cross representative, who was well liked by the Soviet leaders because of his friendly attitude, decisive measures quickly followed. On the night of April 11 armored cars, accompanied by armed detachments of the Cheka, drew up before the various anarchist headquarters and delivered to the inhabitants a five-minute ultimatum to surrender and to submit to disarming. In many cases the show of force was sufficient; here and there the anarchists resisted, with the result that about thirty of them and ten or twelve of the Cheka agents were killed in the subsequent fighting.[13] Several hundred arrests were made; those prisoners who were regarded, after investigation, as anarchists by conviction were released.

The backbone of armed hooliganism in Moscow was broken.

But in many provincial towns Soviet authority remained very weak, as is evident from the armed uprisings which broke out in large towns as well as in small ones during the spring of 1918. One of the most serious of these outbreaks took place in the Volga town of Saratov on the night of May 16. Some former front soldiers opened fire on the building of the Soviets; they were supported by some of the Red troops in the town, who had mutinied, demanding advance pay for three months and new clothing before departing for the front against Dutov's Cossacks. Right Socialist Revolutionaries took part in the uprising, putting forward such slogans as "Constituent Assembly" and "Reëlection of the Soviet." It was suppressed after two or three days of desultory shooting by the arrival of loyal Soviet troops from neighboring towns. Thirty people were killed and thirty-four wounded.

About the same time there was an outbreak of disorder in another Volga town, Tsaritsin, where the head of an Ukrainian Soviet regiment, Petrenko, incited his soldiers to revolt by telling them that the Tsaritsin Soviet was under bourgeois influence and that the Red officers were going about with epaulettes. Petrenko was driven out of one of the town railroad stations, which he had occupied, by other Soviet troops.

There was a flare-up of disorder in Samara, a third large town on the Volga, on May 17. As was often the case with the outbreaks at this time, it was spontaneous, rather than planned. A crowd had gathered; shots rang out and a woman and a girl were killed. A sailor then killed a representative of the local Extraordinary Staff, Autenfisch, who was suspected of firing the shots. This was the signal for a general riot, in which Anarchists, Left Socialist Revolutionaries and mutinous sailors took part, beating members of the Soviet, releasing prisoners from the city prisons and temporarily occupying the postoffice. The uprising was put down by Communist detachments; and the Samara Provincial Soviet Executive Committee, where Anarchists and Left Socialist Revolutionaries predominated, was summarily dissolved.

These numerous outbreaks of violent discontent were symptomatic and important, even though the Soviet regime possessed sufficient forces to suppress each one of them individually. They showed that the Bolshevik power, especially in the predominantly agricultural and trading regions of Eastern Russia and of Siberia, was on decidedly clay feet, that it could scarcely withstand the vigorous push of a strong organized hostile force. Such a force had not yet

crystallized among Russians. But the amazingly rapid and sweeping victories of the Czecho-Slovaks, which will be described in the next chapter, can only be understood if it is borne in mind that the local Soviets in many provincial towns were pale shadows of authority, without reliable armed forces at their disposal, and quite unpopular with considerable sections of the population.

Amid all the elements of turmoil and chaos during these first months of the Bolshevik Revolution, amid the secret meetings of underground anti-Soviet organizations, mutinies of unreliable Red Guards, efforts of some of the Allied diplomatic representatives to help and coördinate the anti-Soviet movement, it was the bony hand of hunger that furnished the most real cause of concern to the Communist leaders. An extremely large proportion of the speeches and decrees of this time are devoted to this ever more pressing problem. The fight for bread became a fight for the very existence of the Soviet regime.

The sole peaceful solution of this problem, of course, would have been to proffer the peasants a reasonable equivalent for their grain in the shape of city products. But this was out of the question because of the breakdown of industrial production, which, in turn, was attributable partly to the fact that the transition from capitalism to socialism was a good deal less simple than the Communist leaders had imagined before they seized power, partly to causes over which the Soviet Government had no control, such as the dismemberment of the country through the German occupation of Ukraina and the consequent disruption of supplies of raw material. The Mensheviki and Socialist Revolutionaries, along with many nonparty spokesmen, urged the raising of the fixed price of bread and free or, at least, freer trade as a means of relieving the situation. But the Communists would not agree to this, on the ground that higher prices would perhaps ease the position for those who still had an abundance of paper money, but would make the lot of the workers and the poorer classes still worse.

Finally a hard and ruthless policy was evolved, to meet a desperate situation. It was decided to wrest the surplus grain from the richer peasants by force, simultaneously splitting the village by bribing the poorest peasants to take the side of the city workers by offering them a share in the food products which would be taken from the richer peasants. One of the first appeals for such a policy is to be found in *Byednota* (Poverty), a newspaper published for circulation among the poorer peasants. The writer, speaking on behalf

of the city workers, addressed the poorer peasants as follows: "We will make with you a union of the hungry against the well-fed and will conquer or die with you." [14]

A month later this policy received official sanction in the shape of an extremely drastic law which threatened with imprisonment for ten years any peasants who held back surplus grain, called on "all toiling and unpropertied peasants" to "unite immediately for pitiless struggle with the kulaks" and granted to the Commissariat for Food extraordinary powers, including the right to apply armed force in the event of any resistance to requisitions and to dissolve any local food committees which disobeyed its orders.[15]

About the same time Sverdlov, President of the Central Soviet Executive Committee, addressing that body, summed up the Bolshevik agrarian policy in the following terms:[16]

"We must place before ourselves most seriously the problem of declassifying the village, of creating in it two opposing hostile camps, setting the poorest layers of the population against the kulak elements. Only if we are able to split the village into two camps, to arouse there the same class war as in the cities, only then will we achieve in the villages what we have achieved in the cities."

That this policy of setting the landless farm laborer and the utterly poverty-stricken small holder of the Russian village against their neighbors who perhaps had a horse and one or two cows apiece and who would themselves have been considered wretchedly poor by West European or American standards would lead to civil war of the most ferocious and sanguinary kind was obvious. Trotzky, addressing a Soviet and workers' meeting in Moscow on June 4, frankly declared: "Our Party is for civil war. The civil war rages around the question of bread. We, the Soviets, are on the offensive." When an interrupter ironically called out, "Long live civil war," Trotzky passionately shouted back: "Yes, long live civil war, in the name of bread for children and old people, for the workers and the Red Army, in the name of direct and merciless struggle with counterrevolution. Long live the drive of the workers in the village for bread and for union with the poor peasants." [17]

The die was cast. Russia was to be churned up with internal strife as it had not been since the Troubled Times. And side by side with the civil war which the Soviet rulers proclaimed against those peasants who still had food reserves, confident of victory if only because there were so many more hungry than well-fed people

in the country, a different kind of civil war, which would test to the utmost the capacity of the Revolution to defend itself, was bursting out as a result of the clash of the Czech Corps with the Soviets in Eastern Russia and in Siberia, which closely coincided with uprisings of Russian anti-Soviet organizations.

NOTES

[1] V. I. Lenin, "Collected Works," Vol. XV, p. 239.

[2] *Ibid.*, Vol. XV, pp. 235, 237.

[3] L. D. Trotzky, "How the Revolution Armed Itself," Vol. I, pp. 28ff.

[4] *Izvestia*, for May 11, 1918.

[5] *Znamya Truda* (Banner of Labor), for May 19, 1918.

[6] *Izvestia*, for April 2, 1918.

[7] *Ibid.*, for May 10. *Cf.* article by Khodorovsky, "Changes in Productive Forces and in the Labor Movement."

[8] *Znamya Truda*, for May 23, 1918.

[9] A. Anishev, "Sketches of the History of the Civil War, 1917–1920," p. 128.

[10] While there were a number of spontaneous strikes and riots among the workers, usually on the ground of extremely bad food conditions, there were few instances during the civil war when large masses of industrial workers took up arms against the Soviet regime for any long period of time. Two exceptions to this general rule were the rebellion of the workers of the Izhevsk and Votkinsk factories in the summer of 1918 and the revolt of the railroad workers in Trans-Caspia, which will be described in greater detail later.

[11] General A. I. Denikin, "Sketches of Russian Turmoil," Vol. III, p. 75.

[12] Cited by Professor E. A. Ross in his book, "The Russian Soviet Republic," p. 77.

[13] *Izvestia*, for April 13, 1918.

[14] *Byednota*, for April 9, 1918.

[15] The full text of this decree is published in *Izvestia,* for May 14.

[16] *Znamya Truda*, for May 16, 1918.

[17] L. D. Trotzky, *op. cit.*, Vol. I, pp. 71, 72.

APPENDIX

DOCUMENTS OF THE REVOLUTION
March 12, 1917–May 14, 1918

Telegram of the President of the State Duma, Rodzianko, to Tsar Nicholas II, of March 12, 1917

THE sessions of the State Duma, by order of Your Majesty, have been broken off until April. The last bulwark of order has been removed. The Government is completely powerless to suppress disorder. The troops of the garrison are unreliable. The reserve battalions of the Guard regiments are caught up by the revolt. They kill their officers. Joining the mob and the popular movement they advance to the building of the Ministry of Internal Affairs and to the State Duma. Civil war has begun and blazes up. Give orders immediately to summon a new government on the basis outlined to Your Majesty in my telegram of yesterday.* Give orders to abrogate your Imperial decree and to convoke again the legislative chambers. Proclaim these measures immediately by Imperial Manifesto. Do not delay, Sire. If the movement spreads to the army the German will triumph, and the fall of Russia, and with it of the dynasty, is inevitable. In the name of all Russia I implore Your Majesty to fulfill these suggestions. The hour which will decide your fate and that of the motherland has struck. To-morrow may be already too late.

(Published by Professor B. N. Storozev in the magazine, *Scientific News*, of The Academic Centre of the Commissariat for Education, Moscow, 1920.)

Order Number One

March 1 (14), 1917.

To the garrison of the Petrograd District. To all the soldiers of the Guard, army, artillery and fleet for immediate and precise execution, and to the workers of Petrograd for information.

The Soviet of Workers' and Soldiers' Deputies has decided:

1. In all companies, battalions, regiments, depots, batteries, squadrons and separate branches of military service of every kind and on warships immediately choose committees from the elected representatives of the soldiers and sailors of the above mentioned military units.

2. In all military units which have still not elected their representatives in the Soviet of Workers' Deputies elect one representative to a

---

* In the preceding telegram Rodzianko had urged the Tsar to create a ministry which would enjoy public confidence.

429

company, who should appear with written credentials in the building of the State Duma at ten o'clock on the morning of March 2.

3. In all its political demonstrations a military unit is subordinated to the Soviet of Workers' and Soldiers' Deputies and its committees.

4. The orders of the military commission of the State Duma are to be fulfilled only in those cases which do not contradict the orders and decisions of the Soviet of Workers' and Soldiers' Deputies.

5. Arms of all kinds, as rifles, machine-guns, armored automobiles and others must be at the disposition and under the control of the company and battalion committees and are not in any case to be given out to officers, even upon their demand.

6. In the ranks and in fulfilling service duties soldiers must observe the strictest military discipline; but outside of service, in their political, civil and private life soldiers cannot be discriminated against as regards those rights which all citizens enjoy.

Standing at attention and compulsory saluting outside of service are especially abolished.

7. In the same way the addressing of officers with titles: Your Excellency, Your Honor, etc., is abolished and is replaced by the forms of address: Mr. General, Mr. Colonel, etc.

Rude treatment of soldiers of all ranks, and especially addressing them as "thou," is forbidden; and soldiers are bound to bring to the attention of the company committees any violation of this rule and any misunderstandings between officers and soldiers.

This order is to be read in all companies, battalions, regiments, marine units, batteries and other front and rear military units.

PETROGRAD SOVIET OF WORKERS' AND SOLDIERS' DEPUTIES.

("The Revolution of 1917, Chronicle of Events," Vol. I., pp. 186–187.)

ACT OF ABDICATION OF NICHOLAS II

In days of great struggle with the foreign enemy, who for almost three years has endeavored to enslave our motherland, it has pleased the Lord God to send to Russia a new heavy trial.

The internal popular disturbances that have begun threaten to be reflected disastrously in the further conduct of the stubborn war.

The fate of Russia, the honor of our heroic army, the welfare of the people, all the future of our dear fatherland demand the prosecution of the war to a victorious end at any cost.

The ruthless enemy is straining his last forces, and the hour is already near when our valiant army, together with our glorious allies, can finally break the enemy. In these decisive days in the life of Russia we have found it a conscientious duty to help our people to close unity and the gathering of all their forces for the speediest achievement of victory and, in agreement with the State Duma, We have recognized it as good

to renounce the throne of the Russian state and to lay down the supreme power.

Not desiring to part with Our beloved son, We transfer Our succession to Our brother the Grand Duke Michael Alexandrovitch, and We bless him upon his accession to the throne of the Russian state.

We enjoin upon Our brother to direct affairs of state in full and inviolable union with the representatives of the people in the legislative assemblies on the bases which will be established by them, pledging in this an inviolable oath in the name of the warmly beloved motherland.

We summon all faithful sons of the fatherland to fulfill their sacred duty to it by obeying the Tsar in the difficult moment of general trial and to help him, along with the representatives of the people, to bring the Russian state out on the road of victory, prosperity and glory. May the Lord God help Russia.

Pskov, March 2 (15), 1917.

(*Izvestia* of the Committee of Petrograd Journalists, No. 8, March 16, 1917.)

ACT OF ABDICATION OF THE GRAND DUKE MICHAEL

A heavy burden has been imposed on me by the will of my brother, who has transferred to me the all-Russian imperial throne in a time of unparallelled war and popular disturbances.

Inspired, along with the whole people, by the thought that the welfare of our motherland is above everything, I have taken a firm decision to accept the supreme power only if this will be the will of our great people, whose right it is to establish the form of government and the new basic laws of the Russian state by general voting through its representatives in the Constituent Assembly.

Therefore, invoking the blessing of God, I request all citizens of the Russian state to obey the Provisional Government, which arose at the initiative of the State Duma and is endowed with all fullness of power, up to the time when a Constituent Assembly, convoked in the shortest possible time on the basis of general, direct, equal and secret voting, shall express the will of the people by its decision about the form of government.

March 3 (16), 1917, Petrograd.

(*Izvestia* of the Committee of Petrograd Journalists, No. 9, March 17, 1917.)

DECLARATION OF THE PROVISIONAL GOVERNMENT

CITIZENS

The Temporary Committee of members of the State Duma, with the coöperation and sympathy of the troops and the population of the

capital, has now achieved such a degree of success over the dark forces of the old regime that it can proceed to the firmer organization of executive power.

For this end the Temporary Committee of the State Duma nominates as ministers of the first public Cabinet the following persons, who have guarantied for themselves the confidence of the country by their past public and political activity. President of the Council of Ministers and Minister for Internal Affairs, Prince G. E. Lvov. Minister for Foreign Affairs, P. N. Milyukov. War and Naval Minister, A. I. Guchkov. Minister for Transportation, N. V. Nekrasov. Minister for Trade and Industry, A. I. Konovalov. Minister for Finance, M. I. Tereschenko. Minister for Education, A. A. Manuilov. Procurator for the Holy Synod, Vladimir Lvov. Minister for Agriculture, A. I. Shingarev. Minister for Justice, A. F. Kerensky. In its present activity the Cabinet will be guided by the following principles:

1. Complete and immediate amnesty for all political and religious cases, including terrorist attacks, military uprisings, agrarian crimes, etc.

2. Freedom of speech, press, union, assembly and strikes, with extension of political liberties to persons in military service within limits consistent with military technical conditions.

3. Abolition of all caste, religious and national discriminations.

4. Immediate preparation for the convention of a Constituent Assembly, which will establish the form of administration and the constitution of the country, on the basis of general, equal, secret and direct voting.

5. Replacement of the police by a people's militia with an elected administration, subordinated to the organs of local selfgovernment.

6. Elections to the organs of local selfgovernment on the basis of general, direct, equal and secret ballot.

7. The military units which took part in the revolutionary movement are not to be disarmed or removed from Petrograd.

8. Along with the maintenance of strict military discipline in the ranks and in military service: elimination for soldiers of all limitations in the enjoyment of the general rights which are granted to all other citizens.

The Provisional Government considers its duty to add that it does not intend to exploit military circumstances for any delay in the realization of the above outlined reforms and measures.

PRESIDENT OF THE STATE DUMA M. RODZIANKO.
PRESIDENT OF THE COUNCIL OF MINISTERS PRINCE LVOV.
MINISTERS: MILYUKOV, NEKRASOV, MANUILOV, KONOVALOV, TERESCHENKO, V. LVOV, SHINGAREV, KERENSKY.
(*Izvestia* of March 16.)

Declaration of the Executive Committee of the Soviet of Workers' and Soldiers' Deputies

COMRADES AND CITIZENS

The new government, created out of the socially active moderate layers of society, to-day declared all those reforms which it is bound to realize partly still in the process of struggle with the old regime, partly after the completion of this struggle. Among these reforms some must be greeted by wide democratic circles: political amnesty, the obligation to undertake the preparation of the Constituent Assembly, realization of civil liberties and elimination of national discriminations. And we suppose that in the measure in which the government which is coming into being will act in the direction of realizing these obligations and of decisive struggle with the old power,—the democracy must show it its support.

Comrades and citizens. The complete victory of the Russian people over the old regime is approaching. But for this victory immense exertions, exceptional restraint and firmness are still required. Disunion and anarchy cannot be permitted. All disorders, robberies, invasions of private apartments, stealing and spoiling of all kinds of property, senseless seizures of public institutions must immediately be stopped. The fall of discipline and anarchy destroy the revolution and the people's freedom.

The danger of a military movement against the revolution is not yet removed. In order to prevent this it is very important to insure the co-operative work of the soldiers with the officers. Those officers who prize the interests of freedom and of the progressive development of the mother-land must bend all their energies to establish common activity with the soldiers. They will respect in the soldier his personal and civil dignity, and will take account of the soldier's feeling of honor. The soldiers on their side will remember that the army is strong only in the union of soldiers with officers, that it is not right to stigmatize the whole officers' corps for the bad conduct of some officers. For the sake of the success of the revolutionary struggle there must be tolerance and oblivion for minor offenses against democracy of those officers who have joined that decisive and final struggle which you carry on with the old regime.

EXECUTIVE COMMITTEE OF THE SOVIET OF WORKERS' AND SOLDIERS' DEPUTIES.

(*Izvestia* of March 16.)

Appeal of the Petrograd Soviet to the Peoples of the Whole World, of March 27, 1917

COMRADES,—PROLETARIANS AND TOILERS OF ALL COUNTRIES

We, Russian workers and soldiers, united in the Petrograd Soviet of Workers' and Soldiers' Deputies, send you our flaming greeting and in-

form you of a great event: the Russian democracy has overthrown the old despotism of the Tsar and enters into your family as an equal member and a threatening force in the struggle for our general liberation. Our victory is a great victory of world freedom and democracy. The main pillar of world reaction and the "gendarme of Europe" is no more.

May the earth lie heavy on its grave. Long live liberty. Long live the international solidarity of the proletariat and its struggle for final victory.

Our cause is still not completely won; the shades of the old order have not yet dispersed, and not a few enemies collect their forces against the Russian Revolution. But nevertheless our achievement is enormous. The peoples of Russia will express their will in a Constituent Assembly, which will be convoked at a very near date on the basis of general, direct, equal and secret ballot. And it may already be predicted with confidence that the democratic republic will triumph in Russia. The Russian people possesses full political freedom. It can now say its weighty word in the internal selfdetermination of the country and in its foreign policy.

And, turning to all peoples, exterminated and ruined in the monstrous War, we say that the time has come to begin a decisive struggle with the acquisitive ambitions of the governments of all countries; the time has come for the peoples to take into their hands the decision of the question of war and peace.

Conscious of its revolutionary power, the Russian democracy affirms that it will oppose the acquisitive policy of its own ruling classes by all means and it summons the peoples of Europe to common decisive actions in favor of peace.

We also appeal to our proletarian brothers of the Austro-German coalition and, above all, to the German proletariat. From the first days of the War they convinced you that, by taking up arms against autocratic Russia, you were defending European culture against Asiatic despotism. Many of you saw in this the justification of the support which you showed to the War. Now this justification has ceased to exist; democratic Russia cannot be a menace to freedom and civilization.

We will firmly defend our own freedom against any reactionary attacks, from within and from without. The Russian Revolution will not retreat before the bayonets of conquerors and will not permit itself to be crushed by foreign military force.

But we appeal to you: cast off the yoke of your semi-autocratic regime, as the Russian people flung off from itself the Tsarist autocracy; refuse to serve as a weapon for conquest and violence in the hands of kings, landlords and bankers; and by vigorous united efforts we will stop the terrible butchery that is disgracing humanity and darkening the great days of the birth of Russian liberty.

Workers of all countries. Stretching out to you a brotherly hand

over mountains of brothers' corpses, over rivers of innocent blood and tears, over the smoking ruins of cities and villages, over the perishing treasures of culture, we call you to restore and strengthen international unity. In this is the guaranty of our future victories and of the complete liberation of humanity.

Proletarians of all lands, unite.

PETROGRAD SOVIET OF WORKERS' AND SOLDIERS' DEPUTIES.

(*Izvestia*, No. 15, for March 15/28, 1917.)

EXCHANGE OF LETTERS BETWEEN THE WAR MINISTER, A. I. GUCHKOV, AND THE COMMANDER-IN-CHIEF, M. V. ALEKSEEV

Secret, to be delivered personally.

March 9, 1917 (old style).

My Dear Mikhail Vassilevitch:

We must both understand the present state of affairs, reckoning only with stern reality, putting aside all illusions. Only by establishing such unity of viewpoint we may, perhaps, succeed in taking some practicable measures for saving the Army and the state. We must proceed only on the basis of actual contemporary conditions in all operative plans which are prepared by us in coöperation with the Allied armies.

I ask you to believe that the present state of affairs is as follows:

1. The Provisional Government does not have at its disposal any real force, and its orders are carried out only to the extent permitted by the Soviet of Workers' and Soldiers' Deputies, which possesses the most important elements of real power, such as the troops, railroads, posts and telegraph communication. One may say directly that the Provisional Government exists only so long as the Soviet permits this. Especially in the military sphere it is possible now to give out only such orders as do not definitely conflict with the orders of the above mentioned Soviet.

2. The demoralization of the reserve units of the interior districts has set in and is making progress. Therefore the recruits included in these units for a long time (I suppose, not less than three or four months) cannot be used for reinforcing the Army. The reserve units do not possess sufficient moral and military training for this purpose. Therefore there can be no question of sending into the Army any considerable number of reinforcements during the next months.

3. Equally unpromising is the problem of filling up the horse requirements of the Army. The requisitions of horses in the districts, both those which have begun and those which were planned, had to be stopped and postponed until conditions of supply and transportation improve, so as not to exasperate the population and so as not to interfere with the sowing of the fields in good time, especially because a mobilization of horses, in view of the present condition of transportation and the lack of

fodder, would only lead to the useless perishing of the horses at the mobilization points.

4. The circumstances which are set forth in Points 2 and 3 make any new artillery and other formations impossible within the designated periods of time.

The details of the present situation will be reported to you by the Colonels Satterup and Prince Tumanov, who are despatched by me and who are fully informed both about the present conditions of reinforcing the Army and about the details of the state of affairs in Petrograd, because both these Staff officers from the first days of the Revolution were in the State Duma in close contact both with the members of the Provisional Government and with the members of the Soviet of Workers' and Soldiers' Deputies.

I ask you to accept my assurances of deep esteem and complete devotion.

A. GUCHKOV.
Acting Supreme Commander-in-Chief
Stavka

Secret, Copy
March 12, 1917 (old style).

My dear Alexander Ivanovitch:

I have received your letter of March 9, No. 33. In my turn I must inform you that the material condition of the armies in the field has become worse because, despite my judgment, which was expressed from Sevastopol, a broad change of organization began in January. All the infantry regiments are being organized on a three-battalion basis and sixty new infantry divisions are being formed out of those which already exist. As a result of the stoppage of the inflow of reinforcements and of horses a large part of the divisions, both old and new, face the most important spring period without being brought up to full strength and with disorganized baggage-trains. It is obvious that all new formations of infantry units without artillery lead to a continual decline in the number of cannon for every thousand soldiers, whereas this proportion on the side of our enemy is growing. We shall scarcely succeed in bringing up the number of machine-guns to eight per regiment, and this without proper equipment. Now it seems that we shall not receive even the prescribed number of rifles. Consequently part of the troops, especially on the Rumanian Front, will remain unarmed, to say nothing of the fact that there will be absolutely no rifles in reserve, in case of unavoidable losses in battle. Perhaps we will return to the hopelessly difficult situation of 1915.

The moral condition of the Army is still uncertain, as a result of all that has happened and that has not yet been digested by the minds of the officers and soldiers, and of the penetration into the ranks of propa-

ganda for ideas which violate the military order that has been established for generations. God grant that the Army may come out of the severe crisis more or less successfully. But we must reckon with the possibility of at least a temporary lowering of the fighting capacity of the Army. In the general course of events this will be the most dangerous moment for Russia. The well-informed enemy, of course, will appraise this circumstance and will attempt to exploit our period of weakness in order to deal a decisive blow. We do not know whom the general opinion of the Army will then hold responsible for the defeat.

As regards the "operative plans" which have been prepared by me, in coöperation with the Allied Armies, it is already late to discuss this at the present moment, because decisions were adopted at the conference in Chantilly on November 15 and 16, 1916, and at the conference in Petrograd in February, 1917. At these conferences we assumed definite *obligations,* and now it is a question of how to postpone or entirely to avoid these obligations with the least loss of dignity in the eyes of the Allies.

These obligations are as follows: the Russian Armies undertake to attack the enemy decisively not more than three weeks after the beginning of the offensive of the Allies. It has already been necessary to state that we cannot begin active operations earlier than the first days of May, because of organization work and the breakdown of transportation and reserves.

The facts communicated in your letter indicate that we cannot fulfill even this changed obligation. It would be unthinkable to begin any sort of operation on a large scale without reinforcements. We must say to the Allies that they cannot count on us before July, explaining this by some plausible pretexts.

I will do this, but I cannot assume responsibility for those consequences which our declining to fulfill the obligations which we have assumed will bring. We are so dependent on the Allies materially and financially that a refusal of the Allies to help us will place us in a still more difficult position than we are in now.

I think the Provisional Government must take care for the conclusion of an appropriate agreement.

So the force of circumstances brings us to the conclusion that during the next four months our armies must remain passive and not undertake operations of a decisive, broad character.

But in war one must reckon not only with one's own desires, but also with the will of the enemy. If the enemy attacks us we must fight a stubborn and prolonged battle, in order not to permit a defeat which would have fatal consequences both for the Army itself and for Russia.

This circumstance must be taken into account by the Government, whatever may be "the real conditions of the contemporary situation."

Defensive battles are accompanied by great human casualties, by

material losses and by the using up of ammunition. Without reinforcements, without a fresh supply of cannon, bullets and shells it will be impossible to carry on a battle which will be imposed on us by the enemy, apart from our own desire.

Some measures are immediately necessary. If the reserve units are demoralized, the best elements in them must be picked out and sent into the Army for the organization of special battalions, attached to the regiments. Although the general mood of the Army is still uncertain, proximity to the enemy and the larger number of officers create a more favorable atmosphere for the moral and military preparation of the reinforcements than exists in the reserve regiments of the interior districts.

Then energetic measures must be employed to bring back to service those numerous people who have left the reserve regiments and gone back to their homes without permission or who have turned to "peaceful" occupations in the towns. It is especially necessary to seek out the confused recruits of the last draft, because these represent the best fighting material, which can still be saved from demoralization. Out of these recruits reliable units can be prepared, part of which can be transferred to the fronts. In a word, the Army must be guarantied with at least some hundreds of thousands of new recruits, otherwise we will destroy our cadres.

The Army experiences an especially acute shortage of provisions. In days of moral crisis the question of provisioning becomes especially important. The well fed soldier sees in the fact that he is well fed proof that his superiors are taking care of him and is more inclined to listen to the voice of commonsense, calling him to order and obedience, to the preservation of the moral strength of his company and regiment. At the present time we are not emerging from the food crisis and live from day to day.

I ask you to accept my assurances of complete esteem and devotion.

MIKH. ALEKSEEV.

Signature confirmed by Lieut.-Col. Tikhobrazov, of the General Staff. (Delo Voenno-Uchenogo Arkhiva, No. 450.)

EXCERPTS FROM LETTER OF THE COMMANDER OF THE FIFTH ARMY, GENERAL DRAGOMIROV, TO THE COMMANDER OF THE NORTHERN FRONT, GENERAL RUZSKY

Commander of the Fifth Army.

March 29, 1917 (old style).

No. 2606

Secret

To the Commander of the Armies of the Northern Front, N. V. Ruzsky. My dear Nikolai Vladimirovitch:

The general mood in the Army becomes more strained every day. Some

pacification, which was noticed in the first days after the convocation of a general assembly of deputies from all units and departments of the Army, has been replaced by the manifestation of an extremely dangerous spirit.

Arrests of officers and commanders do not cease.* Recently, besides the former accusations of adherence to the old regime or unjust attitude toward the soldiers, commanders are accused of not observing order in sending troops into the front lines, of sending people to certain death in order to take prisoners. There were cases of refusal to go into the front line on the ground that last year the regiment was in the trenches on Easter night and therefore it is unjust to place it in the trenches before Easter, and other instances of the same kind. As an illustration of the demands which are presented by the troops and of the incredible difficulty with which the troops can be pacified I append the report of the commander of the 182nd Infantry Division, General Popov, from which it is evident that the soldiers begin to interfere even in questions of the distribution of the troops between the fighting lines and the reserve and respond very sullenly to the explanations and persuasions of their commanders.

Three days in succession regiments which had been in reserve came to me, expressing their readiness to carry on war to the end, declared themselves ready to go anywhere and to lay down their lives for the motherland at my first demand. But, along with this, they respond very unwillingly to any order to go into the trenches, and there are no volunteers for any fighting enterprise, even for the simplest scouting expedition, and there is no possibility to compel anyone to go out of the trenches. Fighting spirit declined. Not only has the soldier no desire to attack; even simple stubbornness in defense has declined to a degree that threatens the issue of the War.

All the thoughts of the soldiers are turned toward the rear. Everyone thinks only of whether it will soon be his turn to go into the reserve, and all dreams are fixed on being in Dvinsk. During the last days the soldiers live with the idea that they have fought enough and that it is time to withdraw them to the cities of the rear and to put in their place the troops of the Petrograd and of other large garrisons.

The demand for elected commanders is more and more definitely put forward by unknown agitators among the soldiers and proclamations about beating officers have already appeared. The former cases of arrest of generals and officers by soldiers, which all ended with the removal of the undesired commanders, while no punishments were inflicted upon the soldiers, have almost brought us to a state of affairs when the soldiers may remove anyone by the mere threat of violence against the person of the commander. The commanders are physically deprived of any

* Two days ago the commander of the 144th Infantry Kashira Regiment, Colonel Stefansky, and the regimental adjutant were arrested; now they have been released.

possibility of finding any support in the law and apparently the time will not soon come when the military courts will again occupy the position which they have completely lost.

Of course we all anticipated what is taking place. In the face of the enemy it was impermissible to bring into the Army such discord as was brought by all the orders of the Soviet of Workers' and Soldiers' Deputies and by that privileged position in which the Petrograd garrison was placed. Moreover, politics, widely occupying the attention of all ranks in the Army, involuntarily turned all attention away from the front to what is going on in Petrograd and compelled the whole mass of soldiers to desire one thing: the stopping of the war and return to their homes.

All the commanders clearly recognize how fatal is such a mood and bend all their energies to maintain fighting preparedness, to instill into the soldiers their determination to bring the War to a worthy end, but all their efforts up to this time have not led to real beneficial results. Morale has constantly fallen to such a degree that the simple replacement of one unit by another on the front already constitutes a risky operation, because no one is certain that the new unit at the last moment will not refuse to go into the trenches, as happened on March 28 with the Ryazhsk Regiment (which, after persuasion, did go into the trenches).

STATEMENT OF THE PROVISIONAL GOVERNMENT ABOUT THE ENDS OF THE WAR, OF APRIL 9, 1917

CITIZENS

The Provisional Government, having considered the military situation of the Russian state, decided to speak the whole truth to the people directly and openly, in the name of its duty to the country.

The regime which has now been overthrown left the cause of the defense of the country in a difficult, disorganized situation. By its criminal inactivity and its unwise measures it brought disorder into our finances, into the food supply and transportation system, into the supply of the Army. It undermined our economic life.

The Provisional Government, with the vigorous, active coöperation of the people, is making every effort to cure this grave inheritance from the old regime. But time does not wait. The blood of many sons has been flowing unceasingly during these two and a half long years of war.

But the country still remains under the attack of a powerful enemy, who has seized whole provinces of our territory and now, in the days of the birth of Russian freedom, threatens us with new, decisive attacks. Defense at any cost of our own, native land and liberation of the country from the enemy who has invaded its frontiers: this is the first insistent duty of our soldiers, who are defending the liberty of the people.

Leaving to the will of the people, in close union with our Allies, to

solve finally all the problems connected with the World War and its ending, the Provisional Government considers that it now has the right and the duty to state that the objective of free Russia is not domination over other peoples, not depriving them of their national possessions, not violent seizure of other peoples' territories, but the establishment of complete peace on the basis of the selfdetermination of nationalities.

The Russian people does not attempt to strengthen its external power at the expense of other peoples and does not set as its goal the enslavement and humiliation of anyone. In the name of the high principles of justice it has struck off the chains which fettered the Russian people. But the Russian people will not permit that its motherland should come out of the World War humiliated and undermined in its vital resources.

These principles will be made the basis of the foreign policy of the Provisional Government, which steadily carries out the will of the people and guards the rights of our motherland, fully observing the obligations which have been undertaken in regard to our Allies.

The Provisional Government of free Russia has not the right to hide the truth from the people. The state is in danger. All forces must be mobilized to save it. Let the reply of the country to the truth that has been said be not fruitless despair, not depression of spirit, but unanimous enthusiasm for the creation of a united popular will. This will give new forces for the struggle and will bring us to salvation.

In the hour of severe trial let the whole country find within itself the strength to fortify the liberty which it has conquered and to devote itself to unceasing work for the good of free Russia.

The Provisional Government, which has given a solemn vow to serve the people, firmly believes that, if it receives unanimous support, it will be able to fulfill its duty to the country to the end.

PREMIER PRINCE LVOV.

March 27/April 9, 1917

LENIN'S APRIL THESES, OF APRIL 20, 1917

1. In our attitude toward the War, which on Russia's side, also under the new Government of Lvov and Co. remains a predatory imperialistic war as a result of the capitalist character of this Government, not the least concessions to "revolutionary defensivism" are permissible.

The classconscious proletariat can give its consent to revolutionary war, which would really justify revolutionary defensivism, only on these conditions: (a) The passing of power into the hands of the proletariat and of those poorest groups of the peasantry who side with it; (b) Renunciation of all annexations in deeds, and not in words; (c) Complete breach with all the interests of capital.

In view of the unquestionable sincerity of the masses of the advocates of revolutionary defensivism, who recognize the War only as a matter of

necessity and not for the sake of conquests, in view of the fact that they are deceived by the bourgeoisie, we must especially fully, insistently, patiently explain to them their mistake, explain the inseparable connection of capital with imperialistic war, prove that without the overthrow of capital it is impossible to end the War with a truly democratic and not an annexationist peace.

Organization of the most widespread propaganda for this viewpoint in the Army in the field.

Fraternization.

2. The peculiarity of the present period in Russia is the transition from the first stage of the Revolution, which gave power to the bourgeoisie as a result of the insufficient classconsciousness and organization of the proletariat, to its second stage, which must give power into the hands of the proletariat and the poorest classes of the peasantry.

This transition is characterized, on the one hand, by the maximum of legal toleration (Russia *now* is the freest of all the belligerent countries in the world), on the other hand, by the absence of violence against the masses and, finally, by the ignorantly trustful attitude of the masses toward the Government of the capitalists, the worst enemies of peace and socialism.

This peculiarity demands from us the ability to adjust ourselves to the *special* conditions of Party work in the midst of unprecedentedly numerous masses of the proletariat, who are just awakening to political life.

3. No support to the Provisional Government, explanation of the complete falsity of all its promises, especially regarding the renunciation of annexations. Exposure, not the impermissible, illusion-breeding "demand" that this Government, a Government of capitalists, should *cease* to be imperialistic.

4. Recognition of the fact that in the majority of Soviets of Workers' Deputies our Party is in the minority, and so far in a weak minority, against the block of all the petty-bourgeois opportunist N. S. S. R.* elements, which succumb to the influence of the bourgeoisie and carry out its influence on the proletariat, including the OK † (Chkheidze, Tseretelli and others), Steklov, etc.

Explanation to the masses that the Soviet of Workers' Deputies is the sole possible form of revolutionary government, and that, therefore, our problem, so long as this Government submits to the influence of the bourgeoisie, can only be patient, systematic, insistent explanation of mistakes and tactics, adapted especially to the practical needs of the masses.

While we are in the minority we carry on the work of criticism and explanation of mistakes, at the same time advocating the necessity that

---

* N. S. was an abbreviation for People's Socialists; S. R. for Socialist Revolutionaries.—AUTHOR.

† The OK was a Menshevik organization.—AUTHOR.

all state power should pass into the hands of Soviets of Workers' Deputies, so that the masses by experience should free themselves from mistakes.

5. Not a parliamentary republic,—the return to this from the Soviet of Workers' Deputies would be a step backward,—but a republic of Soviets of Workers', Farmhands' and Peasants' Deputies in the whole country, from below to above.

Elimination of the police, army and bureaucracy (*i.e.*, replacement of the regular army by a general arming of the people).

Pay to all officials, who are to be elected and removed at any time, not more than the pay of a good worker.

6. In the agrarian programme the emphasis is to be placed on the Soviets of Farmhands' Deputies.

Confiscation of all land belonging to landlords.

Nationalization of all land in the country, management of the land by local Soviets of Farmhands' and Peasants' Deputies. Selection of Soviets of deputies from the poorest peasants. Creation out of every big estate (between 100 and 300 desyatinas in size *)of a model farm under the control of farmhands' deputies and at public expense.

7. Immediate fusion of all the banks of the country into one general national bank and the introduction of control of the Soviet of Workers' Deputies over this bank.

8. Not the "introduction" of socialism as our *immediate* task, but the transition only to control of the Soviet of Workers' Deputies over public production and distribution of products.

9. Party problems:

    (*a*)   Immediate convocation of a Party Congress.

    (*b*)   Change of the Party programme, mainly as follows:

        1. About imperialism and the imperialistic War.

        2. About the attitude to the state and *our* demand for a "state-commune" (*i.e.*, a state modelled on the Paris Commune).

        3. Correction of the out-of-date minimum programme.

    (*c*)   Change of the name of the Party.†

10. Revival of the International.

Initiative for the creation of a revolutionary International, an International against the social-chauvinists and against "the Centre." ‡

(Published in *Pravda*, of April 7 (old style), 1917, under signature: N. Lenin.)

---

* A desyatina is 2.7 acres.—AUTHOR.

† Instead of "Social-Democracy," the leaders of which all over the world betrayed socialism, passing over to the bourgeoisie ("defensists" and wavering "Kautskyans"), we must call ourselves the Communist Party.

‡ "The Centre" is the name of the group in the international Social Democracy which wavers between the chauvinists ("defensists") and the internationalists: Centrists are Kautsky and Co. in Germany, Longuet and Co. in France. Chkheidze and Co., in Russia, Turati and Co. in Italy, MacDonald and Co. in England, etc.

NOTE OF FOREIGN MINISTER P. N. MILYUKOV TO THE GOVERNMENTS OF
THE ALLIED POWERS OF MAY 1, 1917, COMMUNICATED THROUGH
THE RUSSIAN AMBASSADORS ABROAD

On March 27th of this year the Provisional Government published an appeal to citizens, which contained an exposition of the view of the Government of free Russia regarding the aims of the present War. The Minister for Foreign Affairs authorizes me to communicate the above mentioned document to you and to make the following comments in this connection. Our enemies recently attempted to bring discord into international relations, spreading fictitious reports that Russia is ready to conclude a separate peace with the Central European monarchs. The text of the appended document is the best refutation of such inventions. You see from it that the general views set forth by the Provisional Government fully correspond with those high ideals which were constantly expressed, up to the present time, by many prominent statesmen of the Allied countries and which found especially clear expression on the part of our new Ally, the great Trans-Atlantic Republic, in the declaration of its President. The Government of the old regime, of course, could not adopt and share these ideas of the liberating character of the War, of the creation of firm bases for the peaceful co-existence of peoples, of the selfdetermination of oppressed nationalities, etc. But liberated Russia at the present time can speak in a language which is understandable for the leading democracies of contemporary humanity, and it hastens to join its voice to the voices of its Allies. Of course the statements of the Provisional Government, which are permeated with this new spirit of freed democracy, cannot give the least reason to think that the revolution which has taken place has brought after it a weakening of the rôle of Russia in the general Allied struggle. Quite on the contrary, the popular aspiration to carry on the World War to a decisive victory has only become intensified, as a result of everyone's consciousness of the general responsibility. This aspiration became more real, being concentrated on a problem that is close to all and immediate: to drive back the enemy who has penetrated into the territories of our motherland. It may be taken for granted, as was stated in the appended document, that the Provisional Government, defending the rights of our motherland, will fully observe the obligations which were undertaken in regard to our Allies. Continuing to cherish complete confidence in the victorious ending of the present War, in full agreement with the Allies, the Provisional Government is quite confident that the problems raised by this War will be solved in a spirit of creating a firm basis for prolonged peace and that the leading democracies, inspired by the same aspirations, will find means to obtain those guaranties and sanctions which are necessary for the avoidance of new sanguinary clashes in the future.

Declaration of the Provisional Government in Connection with the Note to the Allied Powers (issued on May 4)

In view of the doubts which have arisen as regards the interpretation of the Note of the Minister for Foreign Affairs, which accompanied the communication to the Allied Governments of the declaration of the Provisional Government about the aims of the War, made on March 27 (old style), the Provisional Government considers it necessary to issue the following explanation:

The Note of the Minister for Foreign Affairs was the object of careful and prolonged consideration by the Provisional Government, and its text was accepted unanimously. Of course this Note, when it speaks of decisive victory over the enemies, has in view the achievement of those ends which were set forth in the Declaration of March 27 and were expressed in the following words:

"The Provisional Government considers it its right and duty to state that the objective of free Russia is not domination over other peoples, not depriving them of their national possessions, not violent seizure of other peoples' territories, but the establishment of complete peace on the basis of the selfdetermination of nationalities. The Russian people does not attempt to strengthen its external power at the expense of other peoples and does not set as its goal the enslavement and humiliation of anyone. In the name of the high principles of justice it has struck off the chains which fettered the Russian people. But the Russian people will not permit that its motherland should come out of the Great War humiliated and undermined in its vital resources."

The Provisional Government meant, in the sanctions and guaranties of lasting peace which were mentioned in the Note, limitation of armaments, establishment of an international tribunal, etc.

This explanation will be communicated by the Minister for Foreign Affairs to the Ambassadors of the Allied powers.

Appeal of the Central Committee of the Party of People's Freedom (Cadets) about the Note of May 1st

Citizens.

When the great Russian Revolution swept from the face of the earth the old monarchical order, the Provisional Government, created by the will of the people, recognized before the whole country that it was its duty to do what the Monarchy could not do. It decided, in close union with our Allies, to bring the war against German militarism to a victorious end. The statements of the Government then were supported by the unanimous voice of the people and the Army. Freed Russia then was united, and its unity created an invincible bulwark against the efforts and wiles of the enemy. But it is impossible to conceal the fact that great danger now threatens our unity. The agitation which has recently

been carried on for the immediate cessation of the War begins to yield its fruits. Led astray by this agitation, some circles of the population and even some troop units begin to protest against the foreign policy of the Government, which, as it were, bears an aggressive character, and to demand the retirement of the Minister for Foreign Affairs, P. N. Milyukov, who is regarded as responsible for this policy.

The Central Committee of the Party of People's Freedom at the present moment, responsible and difficult for the motherland, considers it a duty with all its power of conviction to warn the country against the fatal confusion into which some people want to lead it.

Neither the Provisional Government as a whole nor P. N. Milyukov as an individual carries on or can carry on an acquisitive policy, based on the desire for domination over other peoples. In agreement with the free peoples of the West they set as the goal of the War a stable peace, based on the selfdetermination of nations. This is clearly expressed both in the appeal which the Government addressed to the population and in the statement which accompanied the communication of this appeal to the peoples which are allied with us. This is also confirmed by the actions of the Provisional Government. How is it possible to accuse of imperialism, of desire to seize the possessions of other peoples, that Government which recognized the complete freedom and independence of Poland?

But those who now carry on agitation against the Government are not satisfied with its statements and actions. They desire the immediate conclusion of peace. Mistakenly thinking that it is possible to achieve this by changing our relations with the Allies, they desire that Russia should demand the changing of these treaties. Where this road will lead is clear to everyone. It will lead to the violation of confidence and unity between us and our Allies just at that moment when we need their help more than ever. Russia will not escape the sufferings of war by violating its obligations. It will only encounter new and very great dangers. The dreams that the Russian Revolution would evoke a revolution in Germany have not been realized. The German Social Democracy has not broken off with the German Monarchy. Before us, as formerly, stands the greedy Monarchy of the Hohenzollerns, basing all its reckonings on our disagreement with the Allies and on our internal disunion. It occupies our land and the land of the peoples who are our Allies. And there are people who call us to make peace quickly with Wilhelm and to sacrifice our friendship with the leading democracies of the world for the sake of this reconciliation. This road does not lead to peace. It leads to breach with the free peoples and to union with Prussian militarism.

Citizens. Is this really possible? Can free Russia betray the noble peoples of the West, who supported us at the most difficult times? Can it betray the devastated and tormented countries, Belgium, Serbia, Poland? Tsarism was unable to unite and organize Russia to resist the

enemy. Its adherents dreamed of a separate peace and were ready at any moment to stretch out their hands to Wilhelm. Is it possible that a free people, standing up in all its height on the ruins of Tsarism, would follow its example and seek a cowardly peace at any price? Such a blot cannot fall on Russian liberty.

The Central Committee of the Party of People's Freedom summons all who love Russia to firm, decisive support of the Provisional Government.

Citizens, don't believe those who say that the Provisional Government or the Minister for Foreign Affairs carry on an acquisitive policy. The policy which they carry on guards the freedom, dignity and safety of the Russian people. Don't follow those who demand from the Government the retirement of any one of its members, who threaten to disobey it. Such demands lead to anarchy and to the destruction of the new order. They play into the hands of lurking reaction, which awaits disagreement among the liberated people in order to raise its head. To sow dissension amid the population and the Army now, to excite distrust of the Provisional Government and its individual members is to prepare the destruction of the freedom of the Russian people. Russia now lives through the most decisive hour of its history. Everyone bears a great responsibility for the fate of the motherland. All who stand for Russia and its freedom must rally around the Provisional Government and support it. In its strength and firmness is the assurance of the strength and firmness of the new free order of state life.

CENTRAL COMMITTEE OF THE PARTY OF PEOPLE'S FREEDOM,
April 21, 1917 (O. S.).

(Reprinted by S. Piontkovsky in "Documents on the History of the October Revolution," pp. 86–89.)

DECLARATION OF PROVISIONAL GOVERNMENT OF MAY 19, 1917

Reorganized and strengthened by new representatives of the revolutionary democracy, the Provisional Government states that it is fully determined to carry out the ideas of liberty, equality and brotherhood, in the name of which the great Russian Revolution was made. The Provisional Government is especially united by the following basic principles in its future activity:

1. In foreign policy the Provisional Government, rejecting, in agreement with the whole people, any thought of separate peace, openly sets as its goal the speediest achievement of a general peace, which does not have as its objectives domination over other peoples or taking away from them of their national possessions or violent seizure of foreign territories,—a peace without annexations and contributions, on the basis of selfdetermination of the peoples.

Firmly convinced that with the fall of the Tsarist regime in Russia

and with the establishment of democratic principles in internal and foreign policy a new factor of aspiration for stable peace and brotherhood of peoples was created for the Allied democracies, the Provisional Government will undertake preparatory steps toward an agreement with the Allies on the basis of the declaration of the Provisional Government of March 27 (O. S.).

2. Convinced that the defeat of Russia and its Allies would not only be a source of the greatest sufferings of the peoples, but would postpone or make impossible the conclusion of general peace on the above mentioned basis, the Provisional Government firmly believes that the revolutionary Army of Russia will not permit the enemy to crush our Allies in the West and to turn with all its arms against us.

The most important problems of the Provisional Government are the strengthening of democratic principles in the Army, the organization and strengthening of its fighting power both for defensive and for offensive activities.

3. The Provisional Government will undeviatingly and decisively combat the economic breakdown of the country by means of further planned carrying out of state and public control of production, transportation, the exchange and distribution of products. In necessary cases it will also undertake the organization of production.

4. Measures for the general protection of labor will be energetically pushed forward further.

5. Leaving to the Constituent Assembly the solution of the problem of transferring the land to the possession of the toilers and carrying out preparatory work in this connection, the Provisional Government will take all measures which are necessary to assure the greatest production of bread for the country which needs it and to regulate the use of the land in the interests of the national economy and the working population.

6. Aiming at a logical reorganization of the financial system on democratic principles, the Provisional Government directs special attention to increasing the direct taxation of the propertied classes (taxes on inheritance, property, war super-profits).

7. The work of introducing and strengthening democratic organs of local administration will be carried on as vigorously and rapidly as possible.

8. The Provisional Government will also bend all its energies to convening the Constituent Assembly in Petrograd as soon as possible.

Setting as its goal the practical realization of the programme which has been outlined, the Provisional Government states categorically that it can work fruitfully only if it enjoys the complete and unreserved confidence of the revolutionary people and if it is able to exercise in fact those full powers which are so necessary for the strengthening of the conquests of the Revolution and for their further development.

Addressing an earnest and insistent appeal to all citizens, the Pro-

visional Government states that to save the motherland it will take the most energetic measures against any counterrevolutionary attempts and also against anarchical, illegal and violent actions, which disorganize the country and create soil for counterrevolution. The Provisional Government believes that on this road it will meet the support of all who love the freedom of Russia.

> PREMIER AND MINISTER FOR INTERNAL AFFAIRS,
>   PRINCE LVOV,
> MINISTER FOR WAR AND MARINE, KERENSKY,
> MINISTER FOR JUSTICE, PEREVERZEV,
> MINISTER FOR FOREIGN AFFAIRS, TERESCHENKO,
> MINISTER FOR COMMUNICATIONS, NEKRASOV,
> MINISTER FOR TRADE AND INDUSTRY, KONOVALOV,
> MINISTER FOR EDUCATION, MANUILOV,
> MINISTER FOR FINANCE, SHINGAREV,
> MINISTER FOR AGRICULTURE, CHERNOV,
> MINISTER FOR POST AND TELEGRAPH, TSERETELLI,
> MINISTER FOR LABOR, SKOBELEV,
> MINISTER FOR FOOD, PESHEKHONOV,
> OBER-PROCURATOR OF THE SYNOD, LVOV,
> STATE CONTROLLER, GODNEV.

(Reprinted in S. Piontkovsky's "Documents on the History of the October Revolution," pp. 103, 104.)

RESOLUTION ON MEASURES REQUIRED TO COMBAT INDUSTRIAL DIS-
ORGANIZATION, ADOPTED AT THE CONFERENCE OF FACTORY
COMMITTEES ON JUNE 16

1. The complete disorganization of all economic life in Russia has reached such a stage that an unprecedented catastrophe, bringing about the stoppage of a number of the most important industries, undermining agriculture, interrupting railroad communication, preventing the transportation of bread for millions of industrial workers in the cities,—such a catastrophe has become unavoidable. More than that, the breakdown has already begun and has affected a number of branches of economic life. A successful struggle with the breakdown is possible only if the people exert their efforts to the utmost and if a number of immediate revolutionary measures are adopted, both in the country and at the centre of state authority.

2. The catastrophe cannot be warded off either by the bureaucratic method, i.e., by the creation of institutions with a predominance of capitalists and officials, or by preserving the profits of the capitalists and their domination in production or by the rule of finance capital. Experience with a number of partial manifestations of the crisis in separate branches of industry showed this definitely and clearly.

3. The salvation of the country from catastrophe demands that the workingclass and peasant population of the country should be assured not by words but by deeds that the local and central governmental institutions will not hesitate to take over for the people a large part of the profits, income and property of the biggest magnates of banking and finance, trade and industry.

4. The road to salvation of the country from catastrophe lies only in the establishment of real workers' control over the production and distribution of products. Such control demands first of all that workers' organizations (trade-unions, Soviets of Workers' Deputies, factory committees) should be given not less than two thirds of all the votes in the central institutions which are concerned with this matter. There should be compulsory participation of those employers who have not withdrawn from production and of the technical personnel. Such control demands, secondly, that factory committees and trade-unions should receive the right to participate in the control of every undertaking. All commercial and bank books should be open for their inspection, and all information must be communicated to them.

5. On the same basis workers' control must also be extended to all financial and banking operations, and the entire financial side of the business must be made clear.

6. Workers' control, already recognized by the capitalists in a number of conflicts, must be immediately developed into complete regulation of the production and distribution of products by the workers by means of a number of measures which are carefully thought out, but carried into execution without any postponement.

7. In view of the complete breakdown of the whole financial and monetary system, in view of the impossibility of restoring it so long as the War continues, the exchange of agricultural machinery, clothing, shoes and other products for bread and other agricultural goods must be organized on a local and then a national scale, for the sake of supplying the city and village population with the necessities of life in the best possible manner. The city and country coöperatives must participate in this.

8. The introduction of general labor service, which alone can guaranty the most economical use of labor is possible and necessary only if the above mentioned measures are carried out. This measure in its turn demands the institution of a workers' militia. Only such a workers' militia can and must carry out labor service, not bureaucratically, not in the interest of the capitalists, but actually, in the interest of saving the people from catastrophe.

9. One of the most important conditions for eliminating the economic breakdown is the quickest possible cessation of the present imperialistic War. But already now a gradual transfer of labor power from the production of military munitions to the production of these objects which are necessary for the restoration of economic life must be carried out.

---

10. The systematic and successful carrying out of all the above mentioned measures is possible only if all state power is handed over to Soviets of Workers', Soldiers' and Peasants' Deputies.

("The Revolution of 1917," Vol. III, pp. 255–257.)

RESOLUTION OF THE BOLSHEVIKI ABOUT THE GOVERNMENT, INTRODUCED AT THE FIRST CONGRESS OF SOVIETS ON JUNE 21, 1917

The First Provisional Government, created by the Revolution, consisting of representatives of the imperialistic, landlord and capitalist classes, very quickly revealed its complete inability to satisfy the interests of the masses, to save the country from breakdown, to take steps toward the conclusion of a democratic peace.

The Second Coalition Government placed a cordon of "Socialist" Ministers between the people and the counterrevolutionary bourgeoisie. These Ministers were a most convenient weapon in the hands of the exploiting classes, so that the solution of all the basic problems of internal and foreign policy could be postponed, since a revolutionary statement of these problems would really affect the interests of Russian and of Allied imperialistic capital. The "Socialist" Ministers covered up the imperialistic bourgeois policy by means of promises which did not bind them to anything. Exploiting this covering up, the bourgeoisie clearly began to struggle against the Revolution and, in the name of the counterrevolutionists of June 3, openly proclaimed the slogan of an "immediate offensive." Such an offensive would mean not only transition to an active imperialistic policy, but also a decisive turn toward counterrevolution in all internal policy.

So a critical transitional period of the Russian Revolution developed. The increasing breakdown, caused by the anarchical management of the capitalists, who continue to heap up unprecedented profits on war orders, the national policy of the Coalition Government, which leads to needless conflicts with the nations which were oppressed by Tsarism (Finland and Ukraina), its policy of creating conflicts with local authorities because of anti-democratic pretensions to nominate or to confirm them, the policy of threatening the International elements in the Army—all this hastened and aggravated the present crisis of the whole Russian Revolution.

So, affirming the complete failure of the policy of compromise with the capitalists, the Congress recognizes as the sole way out of the crisis the passing of all state power into the hands of the All-Russian Soviet of Workers,' Soldiers' and Peasants' Deputies.

RESOLUTION ABOUT THE GOVERNMENT, PROPOSED BY THE SOCIALIST REVOLUTIONARIES AND MENSHEVIKI AND ACCEPTED BY THE CONGRESS OF SOVIETS ON JUNE 21

After hearing the report of the Executive Committee of the Petrograd Soviet of Workers' and Soldiers' Deputies the Congress recognizes:

1. That under the conditions which were created by the first Ministerial crisis the handing over of all power only to the bourgeois elements would have inflicted a blow upon the revolutionary cause;

2. That the passing of all power to the Soviets of Workers' and Soldiers' Deputies in the present period of the Russian Revolution would have considerably weakened its forces, would have prematurely pushed away from it elements which are still able to serve it and would have threatened the Revolution with disaster;—

Therefore, the All-Russian Soviet Congress approves the action of the Petrograd Soviet in finding a remedy for the crisis of April 20–21 (Old Style) in creating a Coalition Government on the basis of a decisive and logical democratic platform in the field of foreign and internal policy.

After hearing the explanations of the Comrades Ministers about the general policy of the Provisional Revolutionary Government the All-Russian Congress expresses its full confidence in them and recognizes that the direction of this policy corresponded with the interests of the Revolution.

The Congress urges the Provisional Government to carry out more vigorously and logically the democratic platform which it has accepted and especially:

(a) To struggle insistently for the speediest achievement of a general peace without annexations and contributions on the basis of selfdetermination of the peoples;

(b) To carry out the further democratization of the Army and to strengthen its fighting capacity.

(c) To adopt the most energetic measures for combating breakdown in the fields of finance, economic life and food supply, with the direct participation of the working masses.

(d) To carry out a systematic and decisive struggle with counter-revolutionary attempts.

(e) In the labor and land questions to put into effect most quickly measures which correspond with the demands of the organized working masses and which are dictated by the vital interests of the national economic life, which is undermined by the War.

(f) To contribute to the organization of the strength of revolutionary democracy by means of a speedy and radical reorganization of the system of local government on democratic principles and a speedy introduction of rural and town selfgovernment wherever they do not exist.

(g) The Congress especially demands the convocation at the earliest possible moment of the All-Russian Constituent Assembly.

Moreover, with a view to the more successful and vigorous execution of the above mentioned programme, to the complete union of the democratic forces and to the expression of the will of the democracy in all fields of state life, the Congress considers it necessary to create an authorized, united representative body of the whole organized revolutionary democracy of Russia. Representatives of the All-Russian Congress of Soviets of

Workers' and Soldiers' Deputies and of the All-Russian Congress of Peasants' Deputies must enter this body.

Before this All-Russian representative body the Socialist Ministers are responsible for the entire foreign and internal policy of the Provisional Government.

This responsibility gives assurance that, so long as the Socialist Ministers remain in the Provisional Government, this Government will act in agreement with the democracy and therefore must enjoy the active support of all the democratic forces of the country and full governmental authority.

The Congress summons the whole revolutionary democracy of Russia to rally its forces still more closely around the Soviets of Workers', Soldiers' and Peasants' Deputies, and energetically to support the Provisional Government in all its activity for strengthening and extending the conquests of the Revolution.

(Both these resolutions are reprinted in "The Revolution of 1917," Volume III, pp. 266–268.)

STATEMENT OF THE GROUP OF BOLSHEVIKI AND UNITED SOCIAL DEMOCRATS TO THE CONGRESS OF SOVIETS ON THE OCCASION OF THE BEGINNING OF THE OFFENSIVE, READ BY POZERN AT THE SESSION OF THE CONGRESS ON JULY 2

On the first day of the All-Russian Congress of Soviets of Workers' and Soldiers' Deputies we presented a statement, in which we pointed out that a policy directed toward the kindling of imperialist war, toward new stirring up of chauvinist passions, a policy of immediate offensive, is beneficial only to counterrevolution, that this policy has been dictated to the Russian Provisional Government by Anglo-French, American and Russian imperialists, that a policy of launching an offensive places in danger all the conquests of the Revolution.

The demonstration of June 18 (Old Style) in St. Petersburg showed very clearly that the vanguard of the Russian Revolution—the Petrograd proletariat and the Petrograd revolutionary garrison—demonstrated its solidarity with the above mentioned viewpoint of our Party.

To-day Kerensky's order for an offensive, dated June 16 (Old Style) is published.

We state that the entire responsibility for this policy falls on the Provisional Government and on the Parties, the Mensheviki and the Socialist Revolutionaries, which support it. We confirm the declaration which we made on the first day of the Congress. Along with the enormous majority of the Petrograd workers and soldiers we express our deep conviction that the end of the War can be brought about not by an offensive on the front, but only by the revolutionary efforts of the workers of all countries.

("Revolution of 1917," Vol. III, p. 289.)

DECLARATION OF THE PROVISIONAL GOVERNMENT TO THE UKRAINIAN RADA OF JULY 15, 1917

After hearing the communication of the Ministers Kerensky, Tereschenko and Tseretelli on the Ukrainian problem the Provisional Government adopted the following decision:

To nominate as the supreme authority for the administration of the local affairs of Ukraina a special organization—the General Secretariat, the composition of which will be decided by the Government in agreement with the Central Ukrainian Rada, the latter being filled up on a just basis by the representatives of other nationalities which live in Ukraina, through their democratic organizations.

Measures which affect the life and administration of the country will be carried out through this organization.

Considering that the Constituent Assembly must solve the problem of the national political organization of Ukraina and must decide the means of solving the agrarian problem in Ukraina, within the limits of general legislation providing that the land shall pass into the hands of those who work, the Provisional Government reacts sympathetically to the working out by the Ukrainian Central Rada, filled out as specified above, of a project for the national political organization of Ukraina which the Rada finds in harmony with the interests of the country, and also of a project for the solution of the agrarian problem in Ukraina, both these projects to be submitted to the Constituent Assembly.

The Provisional Government considers it necessary in time of war to preserve the fighting unity of the Army. It finds impermissible measures which may violate the unity of the Army organization and Command, as, for example, a change at the present moment of the mobilization plan by means of an immense transition to the system of territorial recruiting of military units or the granting of rights of command to any public organizations.

At the same time the Government considers it possible to continue to promote the closer national union of Ukrainians in the ranks of the Army itself or the recruiting of separate units exclusively from Ukrainians, inasmuch as such a measure, in the opinion of the War Minister, will seem technically possible and will not injure the fighting efficiency of the Army.

At the present time the Provisional Government, with a view to the more systematic and successful achievement of this objective, considers it possible to enlist the coöperation in this matter of the Ukrainian soldiers themselves. So, in agreement with the Central Rada, special Ukrainian delegates may be appointed and attached to the offices of the War Minister, of the General Staff and of the Commander-in-chief.

As regards the local Ukrainian committees, these carry out their

functions according to the general rules and their activity must be coördinated with the activity of other military public organizations.

("Revolution of 1917," Volume III, pp. 304, 305.)

RESOLUTION ADOPTED AT JOINT SESSION OF THE ALL-RUSSIAN
EXECUTIVE COMMITTEE AND OF THE EXECUTIVE COMMITTEE
OF THE ALL-RUSSIAN COUNCIL OF PEASANTS' DEPUTIES
ON JULY 16 IN CONNECTION WITH THE UPRISING
IN PETROGRAD WHICH BEGAN ON JULY 16

COMRADES WORKERS AND PEASANTS

Yesterday some members of the Provisional Government, members of the Cadet Party, resigned. In view of the crisis which was created a joint session of the Executive Committees of the All-Russian Soviets of Workers' and Peasants' Deputies was convoked. This joint session, as an authorized representative body of all revolutionary Russia, should adopt a decision about means of overcoming the crisis.

But the work of this meeting was interrupted, despite the repeated warning of the Soviet of Workers' and Peasants' Deputies.

Some military units came out on the streets with arms in their hands, attempting to master the city, seizing automobiles, arbitrarily arresting individual persons, acting with threats and violence. Coming to the Tauride Palace, with arms in their hands, they demanded that the Executive Committee should take all power into its own hands. Proposing that governmental authority should belong to the Soviets, they were the first to attack this governmental authority. The All-Russian Executive bodies of the Soviets of Workers' and Peasants' Deputies indignantly repudiate any attempt to bring pressure on their free will. It is unworthy by means of armed demonstrations to attempt to impose the will of certain parts of the garrison of one city upon the whole of Russia.

Those who ventured to call out armed men for this purpose are responsible for the blood which has flowed on the streets of Petrograd.

These actions are equivalent to treason to our revolutionary Army, which is defending the conquests of the Revolution on the front. Anyone who in the rear attacks the freedom of the authorized organizations of the democracy and thereby brings dissension into its ranks is plunging a knife into the back of the revolutionary Army, which is fighting against the troops of Wilhelm.

The All-Russian organizations of the Soviets of Workers' and Peasants' Deputies protest against these evil signs of undiscipline, which undermine any form of government by the people, not excepting the future government of the Constituent Assembly. The All-Russian Executive Committees of the Soviets of Workers', Soldiers' and Peasants' Deputies demand once for all a stoppage of such outbreaks, which disgrace

revolutionary Petrograd. The Executive Committees of the All-Russian Soviets of Workers', Soldiers' and Peasants' Deputies summon all who defend the Revolution and its conquests to await the decision of the authorized representative body of the democracy in the matter of the crisis of governmental authority. All who prize the cause of freedom must submit to this decision, in which the voice of all revolutionary Russia will be pronounced.

> THE EXECUTIVE COMMITTEES OF THE ALL-RUSSIAN SOVIET OF WORKERS' AND SOLDIERS' DEPUTIES AND OF THE SOVIET OF PEASANTS' DEPUTIES.

("The Revolution of 1917," Vol. III, pp. 315, 316.)

STATEMENT OF THE REPRESENTATIVES OF FIFTY-FOUR FACTORIES AT THE SESSION OF THE ALL-RUSSIAN SOVIET EXECUTIVE COMMITTEE ON JULY 17, 1917

The first representative says: "Fifty-four factories are represented here. It isn't necessary to talk about what has happened. It is strange when one has to read the appeal of the Central Committee,—the workers and soldiers are called counterrevolutionaries. Our demand is the general demand of the workers: all power to the Soviets of Workers' and Soldiers' Deputies. This demand has been presented to you. This fact has occurred. And you must reckon with it."

Statement of the second representative: "I am also the representative of fifty-four factories. You see what is written on the placards. The same question was discussed at all the factories. What were the decisions which the workers adopted? You know these resolutions. Hunger threatens us in the factories. We demand the withdrawal of the ten capitalist Ministers. We trust the Soviet, but not those whom the Soviet trusts. Our comrades, the Socialist Ministers, entered into an agreement with the capitalists, but these capitalists are our mortal enemies. We demand that the land should be seized immediately, that control over industry should be established immediately, we demand struggle against the threatening hunger."

The third representative says: "It is a matter not of words, but of actions. We are taking action and the Soviet unfortunately doesn't listen to what is taking place. We have been sent with the demand that the Soviets should immediately assume power. The land must be transferred immediately, without any constituent assembly. We have been fed with words long enough. I would like to ask the authors of the appeal: Who attacked the authority of the Soviets? And who imposed Revolution upon Russia? We need the immediate passing of power into the hands of the Soviets."

The fourth representative of the workers: "What the Cabinet Ministers decided theoretically the masses decided only by their feeling. The

mass sees that the present situation of the country is difficult. Before you is not a riot, but a fully organized demonstration. We demand that all the land should pass into the hands of the people. We demand that all orders, directed against the revolutionary army, should be cancelled. We demand the adoption of all measures for combating the sabotage and lockouts of the industrialists and capitalists. Control over industry must be established. There can be no peace in the country so long as the policy of compromise with the bourgeoisie will continue. We have nourished this snake in our bosoms long enough now. Now, when the Cadets refused to work with you, we ask: With whom will you make an agreement? We demand that all power should pass into the hands of the All-Russian Soviet of Workers', Soldiers' and Peasants' Deputies. This is the sole way out."

The representative of the Peterhof Soviet of Workers' and Soldiers' Deputies states: "Peterhof has 20,000 inhabitants, and I speak in their name. The present moment seems to us very dangerous. The ground is shaking. The Revolution develops. The masses do not desire the power of bourgeois Ministers. The masses go beyond the limits of organization. So the Third Revolutionary Regiment, without the consent of the Soviet, appeared to-day in Petrograd fully armed. You know yourselves what may happen here. Perhaps the Revolution will perish, if it doesn't now accept the demands of the democracy. The will of the democracy is quite clear: the transfer of power into the hands of the Soviets. Our Soviet in full agreement passed a quite definite resolution on this question."

(*Cf.* journal *Sovremennik*, No. 1, p. 7.)

Declaration of the Government of "Salvation of the Revolution," Organized after the July Uprising, Dated July 21, 1917

Citizens. A threatening hour has come. The troops of the German Emperor have broken through the front of the Russian people's revolutionary army. This terrible event was made easier for the German troops by the criminal lightmindedness and blind fanaticism of some, by the treachery of others. Both threatened the very foundation of new free Russia with decay and dissolution. In this menacing hour, when the hidden forces of counterrevolution may come out, exploiting the general confusion, the reorganized Provisional Government clearly recognizes the heavy responsibility which falls on its shoulders. But the Government, filled with firm faith in the powers of the great Russian people, believes in the speedy recovery of the political life of the country after the infectious disease which has undermined the national organism has come to the surface and been settled in an acute crisis. The Provisional Government believes that this is a crisis of recovery, not of death. Strong in this faith, the Provisional Government is ready to act, and will act with all the energy and decision which the extraordinary circumstances of the time demand. The Provisional Government regards as its primary task the

straining of all its resources for the struggle with the foreign enemy and for the protection of the new state order against any anarchist and counter-revolutionary attacks. Not hesitating to adopt the most decisive measures, the Government, through its foreign policy, at the same time confirms over and over again that not one drop of a Russian soldier's blood shall flow for the sake of ends which are alien to the sense of right of the Russian democracy, which has openly proclaimed its peace slogans to the whole world.

With these ends in view the Provisional Government, carrying out the principles of foreign policy which were announced in the Government's declaration of May 6, intends to propose to the Allies to meet in an Allied conference during August in order to define the general direction of the foreign policy of the Allies and the coördination of their activities, observing the principles which were proclaimed by the Russian Revolution. In the conference Russia's interests will be represented by spokesmen for the Russian democracy, along with persons of diplomatic training.

Continuing the work of state upbuilding in other fields on the principles which were announced in the declaration of May 6, the Provisional Government considers it necessary to execute a number of measures which put this decision into practise. The Provisional Government will make every effort to hold the election for the Constituent Assembly on the appointed date, September 17 (Old Style) and to complete in good time the preparatory measures which are to assure the correctness and freedom of the election. A primary problem of the Government in the sphere of internal policy is the speediest introduction of town and rural selfgovernment on the basis of general, equal, secret, direct balloting, together with its universal application.

Moreover, attaching special significance to the creation of local organs of administration which enjoy the confidence of the entire population, the Provisional Government invites local representatives to organize collegial organs of regional administration, which will unite a number of provinces.

In an effort to carry out logically the principles of civil responsibility the Provisional Government in the nearest future will issue a decree abolishing castes and finally eliminating titles and orders, with the exception of those which are granted for distinguished military services. The Economic Council and the Main Economic Committee, which have been instituted by the Provisional Government, will immediately proceed to work with a view to carrying on decisive struggle against economic breakdown and carrying out further measures for the defense of labor. Within the competence of these organizations are such matters as the organization of national economic life and labor, general measures for the regulation of economic life, control of industry and also a coördinated planned execution of such measures. In labor policy legal measures providing for freedom of trade-union association, labor exchanges and arbitration chambers will be worked out and carried into execution in the nearest future. A projected

law for the general protection of labor and for the introduction of all forms of social insurance, which are to be extended to all categories of hired labor, is being worked out.

As formerly, the measures of the Provisional Government in the agrarian question are defined by the conviction that, in harmony with the basic needs of our economic life and also as a result of the repeatedly expressed desires of the peasantry, proclaimed by all the democratic parties of the country, the future land reform must be based on the idea of transferring the land to the toilers. This is the basis of the projected land reform, which will be submitted for the consideration of the Constituent Assembly. The successive measures of the Provisional Government will be:

(1) Complete liquidation of the land arrangement policy, which is destructive and which disorganizes the village; (2) Measures which assure the complete freedom of the Constituent Assembly in disposing of the country's land reserves; (3) Regulation of land relations in the interests of state defense and of food supply of the country by means of extending and strengthening the network of land committees which are organized by the state (their functions in deciding current problems of agricultural policy are to be precisely defined by law and they are not to prejudge the basic question of the right of property in land, which falls only under the competence of the Constituent Assembly); (4) Removal, by means of such legal regulation of land relations, of that serious danger to the state and the future agrarian reform which is represented by land seizures and the organization of arbitrary local solutions for land shortage, which contradict the principle of a general state land reform. Making this declaration of its impending tasks, the Provincial Government supposes that it has the right to count on the enthusiastic support of all the vital forces of the country in its difficult and responsible work. It demands from all sacrificial readiness to give all their strength, property, life itself for the great cause of saving the country, which aspires to unite all its peoples on the basis of complete freedom and equality.

(Cited in S. A. Piontkovsky, "Documents on the History of the October Revolution," pp. 140–142.)

CIRCULAR DESPATCHED BY THE MINISTER FOR INTERNAL AFFAIRS, TSERETELLI, TO THE PROVINCIAL COMMISSARS ON AUGUST 4, 1917

The programme of the Provisional Government of July 8 (Old Style) and my telegrams of instructions of July 17 (Old Style) pointed out that the sole way out of the critical situation of the country lies in decisive struggle against any kind of anarchy and counterrevolution, combined with united action of all the living forces of the people. As a supplement to my former instructions I inform you as follows. The Commissar, supported in his activity by the united democratic organizations, is first of all the representative of the authority of the Central Government and is

bound to be guided by the instructions of the Provisional Government and to carry out its policy, without deviating from it in deference to local or party influences. I warn you that I shall consider any delay or inactivity in exercising power on the part of the Commissar (fatal in this period of great trials) as a sufficient and inevitable reason for dismissing the representative of the Government who has not proved fit for his appointment. For attempts to carry out any actions which are inconsistent with the policy of the Provisional Government and, still more, for encouragement or toleration of seizures and arbitrary actions of any groups or of counterrevolutionary movements I shall prosecute those Commissars who are guilty. There is no place for waverings or for disorganized activities. Only a strong united authority can save the country from dissolution. Immediately convey the above instructions for the guidance of all county commissars. Their activity is subject to your inspection and guidance.

("Revolution of 1917," Vol. III, p. 347.)

RESOLUTION ON THE PRESENT MOMENT AND THE WAR, ADOPTED BY THE SIXTH CONGRESS OF THE BOLSHEVIKI, HELD IN PETROGRAD FROM AUGUST 8 UNTIL AUGUST 16, 1917

1. The War has recently assumed the proportions of an all-embracing world clash. On the scene has appeared a new giant of imperialism and pretender to world hegemony—America. Under the pressure of America and the Allies China enters the War. The struggle of the imperialist powers is carried over into all countries. Along with the extension of the scope of the War, it is protracted by the struggle of the world bourgeoisie against the ripening proletarian revolution by means of preserving the regime of military dictatorship and breaking up the forces of the international proletariat.

2. The most dangerous event for the imperialists of all countries is the Russian Revolution, as the first outbreak of the masses which threatens, in the course of its development, to be transformed into a direct movement of the masses against war and imperialism and to draw into this struggle the proletarian masses of other countries.

3. From the very beginning of the Revolution the imperialists of the Allied countries opened an offensive against it (intriguing with the overthrown Nicholas, abuse of the Soviets, arrests of Russian Internationalists, etc.). This offensive developed into a direct storm against the Revolution, which found expression in the open alliance between the Allied bankers and the counterrevolutionary forces in Russia, the financing of the latter by British capital, the direct interference of the "Allied" authorities in the internal affairs of Russia, finally, in the demand that the Russian Army, despite its absolute unpreparedness for such a step, should undertake an offensive.

4. The victory of the advocates of the policy of offensive in Russia led to a new upsurge of chauvinism in all countries, to a strengthening of the imperialist dictatorship and to the creation of conditions which make difficult the work of international Socialists.

5. The upper classes of the small bourgeoisie and the peasantry and also part of the workers, who have not yet given up petty-bourgeois illusions, represented politically by the Socialist Revolutionary and Menshevik parties, favored the offensive and thereby fell into the power of the imperialist big bourgeoisie.

On the basis of general military problems a close union was created between them and the social-imperialists of the West, and this was inevitably transformed into a union of active support to the imperialism of the Entente countries.

6. The Russian petty-bourgeois democracy, the Socialist Revolutionary and Menshevik Parties, were drawn into the channel of general imperialist policy. In this respect there was a quite similar development in the policy of the social-patriots of all countries, who finally, also in Russia, became transformed into direct agents of imperialism. So the Mensheviki and the Socialist Revolutionaries aided counterrevolutionary finance capital to weaken the significance of Russia as a centre of international revolution.

7. The further continuation of the War, on one hand, hastens the process of destruction of productive forces. On the other hand, it leads to an extraordinary concentration of production and to centralization of it in the hands of the militarist state. At the same time the continuation of the War, which to an unprecedented degree has reduced the middle classes to the status of proletarians and has turned the proletariat into serfs of the imperialist state, which has brought about an absolute impoverishment of the workers and has turned against them police repressions, etc., unavoidably leads to a growth of the elements of proletarian revolution.

8. The campaign for peace by means of "pressure" on the Allied Governments and agreement with the social-imperialists, undertaken by the Soviets, who refused to break with imperialism in fact, could not but suffer complete failure. This failure confirmed the rightness of the standpoint of the revolutionary social-democracy that only the revolutionary struggle of the masses in all countries against imperialism, only the international proletarian revolution can lead to a democratic peace.

9. The liquidation of imperialist rule sets before the working class of that country which first realizes the dictatorship of the proletarians and semi-proletarians the problem of giving all kinds of support (including armed support) to the fighting proletariat of other countries. Such a problem especially lies before Russia if, as is very probable, the new inevitable upswing of the Russian Revolution places the workers and poorest peasants

in power before there is a revolution in the capitalist countries of the West.

10. Therefore the sole means by which the international proletariat can bring about a democratic liquidation of the war is to conquer power. For Russia the sole means is the conquest of power by the proletariat and the poorest peasants. Only these classes will be able to break with the capitalists of all countries and to contribute in fact to the growth of the international proletarian revolution, which must liquidate not only the War, but also capitalist slavery.

(Cited by S. A. Piontkovsky, in "Documents on the History of the October Revolution," pp. 143, 144.)

Kornilov's Appeal of September 9, 1917

Russian People.

Our great Motherland is perishing.

The final hour is near.

Compelled to come out openly, I, General Kornilov, declare that the Provisional Government under the pressure of the Bolshevik majority of the Soviets, acts in full agreement with the plans of the German General Staff, simultaneously with the impending descent of hostile forces on the Riga coast, destroys the Army and upsets the country from within. The painful consciousness of the inevitable destruction of the country commands me at this threatening moment to summon all Russian people to save the perishing motherland. Let all in whose breasts beat Russian hearts, all who believe in God and His churches pray to the Lord God for the greatest miracle: the salvation of our native land. I, General Kornilov, the son of a Cossack peasant, declare to all that personally I want nothing except the preservation of Great Russia, and I vow to bring the people, through victory over the enemy, to the Constituent Assembly, at which the people will itself decide its own fate and choose its own form of government. I cannot betray Russia into the hands of its historic enemy, the German tribe, and make the Russian people slaves of the Germans.

KORNILOV.

(Cited by S. A. Piontkovsky, "Documents on the History of the October Revolution," p. 162.)

Appeal of the Central Committee and the Petrograd Committee of the Bolshevik Party in Connection with the Kornilov Movement, of September 12, 1917

To all the Toilers, to all the Workers and Soldiers of Petrograd:

Counterrevolution is moving on Petrograd. The traitor to the Revolution and enemy of the people, Kornilov, is leading against Petrograd the troops which he has deceived. All the bourgeoisie, headed by the Cadet Party, which has been unceasingly slandering the workers and soldiers,

now greets the traitor and is ready to applaud with all its heart when Kornilov will make the streets of Petrograd red with the blood of the workers and revolutionary soldiers, when he will crush the proletarian, peasants' and soldiers' revolution with the hands of the ignorant people whom he has deceived. In order to make it easier for Kornilov to shoot down the proletariat the bourgeoisie put out the false idea that a revolt of the workers had triumphed in Petrograd. Now you see that not the workers, but the bourgeoisie and the Generals, headed by Kornilov, raised the rebellion. The victory of Kornilov means the destruction of liberty, the loss of land, the triumph and sole mastery of the landlord over the peasant, of the capitalist over the worker, of the general over the soldier.

The Provisional Government fell to pieces at the first movement of Kornilov's counterrevolution. This Government, in which part of the democracy repeatedly expressed its confidence, to which it entrusted all power,—this Government was not able to fulfill its first and immediate task: to strike down at the roots the counterrevolution of the generals and the bourgeoisie. The efforts to reach an agreement with the bourgeoisie weakened the democracy, stirred up the appetite of the bourgeoisie, gave it the audacity to decide on open uprising against the Revolution, against the people.

The salvation of the people, the salvation of the Revolution is in the revolutionary energy of the masses of workers and soldiers themselves. We can rely only on their forces, on their sense of discipline and organization. We entrust the leadership of the decisive struggle for the salvation of the whole Revolution, its conquests and its future to a Government which will unconditionally, devotedly, wholeheartedly undertake to carry out the demands of the masses of workers, soldiers and peasants. Only this Government will save the Revolution, will guard it against the onset of counterrevolution, will save it, despite the waverings, the shakiness, the lack of character of the wavering part of the democracy.

People of Petrograd! We summon you to the most decisive struggle with counterrevolution! Behind Petrograd stands all revolutionary Russia!

Soldiers! In the name of the Revolution—forward against General Kornilov!

Workers! In firm ranks guard the city of Revolution against the attack of the bourgeois counterrevolution!

Soldiers and workers! In brotherly union, cemented by the blood of the February days, show the Kornilovs that it is not the Kornilovs who will crush the Revolution, but the Revolution that will break and sweep from the earth the attempts of the bourgeois counterrevolution.

For the sake of the interests of the Revolution, for the sake of the power of the proletariat and the peasantry in liberated Russia and in the whole world,—as a united family, with firm ranks, hand in hand, all as one man, meet the enemy of the people, the betrayer of the Revolution, the assassin of liberty!

You could overthrow Tsarism,—show that you will not endure the rule of the upholder of the landlords and the bourgeoisie—Kornilov.

CENTRAL COMMITTEE OF THE RSDRP (BOLSHEVIKI),
PETROGRAD COMMITTEE OF THE RSDRP (BOLSHEVIKI),
MILITARY ORGANIZATION OF THE CENTRAL COMMITTEE OF THE RSDRP,
CENTRAL COUNCIL OF FACTORY COMMITTEES,
BOLSHEVIK FRACTION OF THE PETROGRAD AND CENTRAL SOVIETS OF WORKERS' AND SOLDIERS' DEPUTIES.

(*Cf.* "The Revolution of 1917," Vol. IV, pp. 345, 346.)

RESOLUTION OF THE PETROGRAD SOVIET OF OCTOBER 8, 1917, ABOUT THE RESULTS OF THE DEMOCRATIC CONFERENCE

The Petrograd Soviet states that after the experience of the Kornilov Affair, which revealed that all propertied Russia occupies a counterrevolutionary position, any attempt at coalition means nothing but a complete capitulation of the democracy to the Kornilovites. This capitulation finds expression in the make-up of the newly formed Cabinet, in which a decisive place is assigned to merchants and industrialists,—uncompromising enemies of the democracy constituted by the workers, soldiers and peasants. The so-called democratic Ministers, responsible to no one and to nothing, are unable either to change or to moderate the anti-democratic character of the new Government, which will go into the history of the Revolution as the Government of civil war. The Petrograd Soviet states: to this Government of bourgeois domination and counterrevolutionary violence we, the workers and garrison of Petrograd, will show no support. We express our firm confidence that the news of the organization of the new Government will meet one reply on the part of the whole revolutionary democracy: Resign. And, basing itself on this unanimous voice of the democracy, the All-Russian Congress of Soviets will create a genuinely revolutionary Government. At the same time the Petrograd Soviet summons the proletarian and soldiers' organization to intensified work in rallying their ranks around their Soviets, abstaining from any separate demonstrations.

(Cited by S. A. Piontkovsky, "Documents on the History of the October Revolution," p. 179.)

RESOLUTION OF THE CENTRAL COMMITTEE OF THE BOLSHEVIK PARTY IN FAVOR OF ARMED UPRISING, ADOPTED AT ITS SESSION ON OCTOBER 23, 1917

The Central Committee recognizes that both the international position of the Russian Revolution (the mutiny in the Navy in Germany as an extreme manifestation of the growth throughout Europe of the worldwide socialist revolution, together with the danger of a peace among the imperialists for the purpose of strangling the Revolution in Russia) and the

military situation (the unquestionable decision of the Russian bourgeoisie and Kerensky and Co. to surrender Peter [Petrograd] to the Germans) and the acquiring of a majority in the Soviets by the proletarian party,— all this, combined with the peasant uprising and with the turn of popular confidence toward our party (the election in Moscow), finally, the clear preparation of a second Kornilov movement (the withdrawal of troops from Peter, the bringing up of Cossacks to Peter, the surrounding of Minsk by Cossacks, etc.),—all this places armed uprising on the order of the day.

So, recognizing that armed uprising is inevitable, and that the situation is quite ripe for it, the Central Committee proposes to all Party organizations to be guided by this and to solve all practical problems (the Congress of Soviets of the Northern Region, the withdrawal of troops from Peter, the demonstrations of the Moscow and Minsk comrades) from this standpoint.

(*Cf. Proletarskaya Revolutsia,* No. 10, for 1922.)

ARTICLES OF SERVICE OF THE WORKERS' RED GUARD IN PETROGRAD, ADOPTED AT A CITY CONFERENCE OF THE RED GUARD ON NOVEMBER 4, 1917

1. The Workers' Red Guard is an organization of the armed forces of the proletariat for struggle with counterrevolution and defense of the conquests of the Revolution.

2. The Workers' Red Guard consists of workers who are recommended by Socialist Parties, factory committees and trade-unions.

3. Every member of the Workers' Red Guard is bound to submit to the discipline of the organization, to carry out all the points of the articles of service, to fulfill all obligations which are imposed on him by the organization and also to attend regularly the drills and meetings of the Workers' Guard.

Note—Persons who do not attend drills or meetings without sufficient cause for three successive times are expelled from the Workers' Guard.

4. Strict observance of discipline and unconditional subordination to elected authorities are based not on the force of blind obedience, but on a consciousness of the extraordinary importance and responsibility of the tasks of the Workers' Guard and also on a completely free and independent democratic organization.

5. One of the most important obligations of members of the Workers' Red Guard is the maintenance in good order and readiness for action of the arms which are given out by the organization.

6. The use of arms without the permission of the organization, and especially for impermissible purposes, is the greatest crime and is punished by expulsion from the Workers' Guard and by the declaration of a boycott against the offender.

7. Members of the Workers' Guard are liable to be brought before a comradely court if they violate the articles of service and do not submit to the discipline of the organization.

8. In order to maintain revolutionary order the Workers' Guard in troubled times takes over the protection of streets, of state and public institutions and of private buildings, wards off pogroms and suppresses the provocative activity of dark forces.

9. The maintenance of revolutionary order is carried out by the Command of the Workers' Guard according to the plan and under the general direction of the Soviet of Workers' and Soldiers' Deputies.

10. Military operations of the Workers' Guard and preparations for them are carried out according to the plan and under the general guidance of the Central Command of the Workers' Red Guard.

11. Numbered tickets, given out by the Central Command, serve as certificates of membership in the Workers' Red Guard.

ADMINISTRATION

12. The Workers' Red Guard is at the disposition of the Petrograd Soviet of Workers' and Soldiers' Deputies and is directly subordinated to the Central Command of the Workers' Red Guard.

13. The Central Command of the Workers' Guard consists of representatives of each of the city districts and of one representative of each of the following institutions: (1) the Petrograd Executive Committee, (2) the Military Department of the Petrograd Executive Committee, (3) the Inter-district Conference, (4) the Central Council of Factory Committees, (5) the Central Council of Trade-Unions.

14. The functions of the Central Command are: general guidance and inspection of the activity of the District Commands, supply of the districts with arms and necessary resources.

15. For the supervision of current work the Central Command appoints a bureau, consisting of five of its own representatives and one representative each of the Petrograd Executive Committee and of its Military Department.

16. An instructors' department is attached to the bureau of the Central Command. It takes charge of the training of the Workers' Guard in the districts and prepares commanders and specialists.

17. In the districts the Workers' Guard is under the control of the District Soviets of Workers' and Soldiers' Deputies and is subordinated to commanding staffs, one third of whose members are nominated by the District Soviets while two thirds are elected at a general meeting or a district conference of the Workers' Red Guard of the given district.

Note—The District Soviet has the right to dismiss for cause the chief of the Workers' Red Guard.

18. The District commanding staffs are to supervise the activity of the

Red Guard in the District and also to carry on direct practical work in the organization and guidance of the everyday activity of the Workers' Red Guard.

19. The Workers' Red Guard is organized in factories, where it is subordinated to elected factory commanders. Workers in small enterprises are united in groups of the regional commanding staff.

Note—If a factory guard (factory workers' militia) is selected from the personnel of the Workers' Red Guard, this body is under the command of a special Commissar of the Workers' Militia. In such cases the members of the Workers' Guard should bear this service in turn.

20. The Workers' Red Guard is divided into rifle units (tens, squads, companies, etc.) and into separate technical detachments (sapping, cycling, telegraph, machine-gun, artillery, etc.).

21. The basic fighting unit is the ten, which consists of thirteen men; four tens constitute a squad (53 men); three squads, a company (160 men); three companies, a battalion to the number of 480 men, amounting to 500 or 600 with the addition of special units.

22. All the battalions of a district make up the district detachment. If the battalions are very numerous the district detachment may be divided into regiments. In big factories detachments may be organized which enter into the district detachment with special names, as the Putilov Detachment.

23. The entire commanding staff (the commanders of the tens, squads, companies, etc.) is elective. It is desirable that comrades with special preparations should be chosen. If this qualification is lacking the commanders must take training under the direction of the bureau of the Central Command. Comrades who do not pass the special examination at the Instructors' Department of the Central Command are not confirmed in commanding posts.

(*Cf.* V. Malakhovsky, "History of the Red Guard," pp. 45–47.)

MANIFESTO OF THE MILITARY REVOLUTIONARY COMMITTEE BREAKING OFF RELATIONS WITH THE STAFF OF THE PETROGRAD MILITARY DISTRICT, OF NOVEMBER 4, 1917

To the Garrison of the City of Petrograd and its Environs. October 22 (Old Style), 1917.

At a meeting on October 21 (Old Style) the revolutionary garrison of Petrograd rallied around the Military Revolutionary Committee of the Petrograd Soviet of Workers' and Soldiers' Deputies as its leading organization.

Notwithstanding this the Staff of the Petrograd Military District on the evening of October 21 did not recognize the Military Revolutionary Committee and refused to work in coöperation with the representatives of the Soldiers' Section of the Soviet.

By this action the Staff breaks with the revolutionary garrison and with the Petrograd Soviet of Workers' and Soldiers' Deputies.

Breaking off with the organized garrison of the capital the Staff becomes a direct tool of counterrevolutionary forces.

The Military Revolutionary Committee repudiates all responsibility for the actions of the Staff of the Petrograd Military District.

Soldiers of Petrograd!

1. The defense of revolutionary order against counterrevolutionary attacks rests with you under the guidance of the Military Revolutionary Committee.

2. No orders to the garrison are valid, unless they are signed by the Military Revolutionary Committee.

3. All orders regarding to-day—the Day of the Petrograd Soviet of Workers' and Soldiers' Deputies—remain in full force.

4. It is the duty of every soldier of the garrison to maintain watchfulness, restraint and unwavering discipline.

5. The Revolution is in danger. Long live the revolutionary garrison!

THE MILITARY-REVOLUTIONARY COMMITTEE OF THE SOVIET OF WORKERS' AND SOLDIERS' DEPUTIES.

(*Cf.* "The Revolution of 1917," Vol. V, pp. 151, 152.)

ORDERS ISSUED BY COLONEL POLKOVNIKOV, COMMANDER OF THE PETROGRAD MILITARY DISTRICT, ON NOVEMBER 6, 1917, ON THE EVE OF THE BOLSHEVIK REVOLUTION

ORDER TO THE PETROGRAD MILITARY DISTRICT

1. I order all units to remain in the barracks where they are stationed until orders are received from the Staff of the District. I forbid any independent demonstrations. All who demonstrate with arms on the streets contrary to this order will be tried for armed rebellion.

2. In the event of any selfwilled armed outbreaks or in case separate units or groups of soldiers appear on the streets contrary to the orders issued by the Staff of the District, I order the officers to remain in the barracks. All officers who come out, despite the orders of their superiors, will be tried for armed rebellion.

3. I categorically forbid the troops to carry out any "orders," emanating from various organizations.

COMMANDER OF THE DISTRICT, COLONEL OF THE GENERAL STAFF POLKOVNIKOV.

DECLARATION

In order to avert the possibility of arbitrary seizures of automobiles I suggest that the owners of automobiles immediately send them to Palace

Square and place them at the disposal of the Staff of the Petrograd Military District.

Those who are guilty of not carrying out this order will be punished with all the strictness of the law.

COMMANDER OF THE PETROGRAD MILITARY DISTRICT, COLONEL OF THE GENERAL STAFF POLKOVNIKOV.

(*Cf.* "The Revolution of 1917," Vol. V, p. 264.)

MANIFESTO OF THE MILITARY REVOLUTIONARY COMMITTEE, PUBLISHED ON NOVEMBER 6

TO THE POPULATION OF PETROGRAD

Citizens!

Counterrevolution has raised its criminal head. The Kornilovites mobilize their forces, in order to smash the All-Russian Congress of Soviets and to prevent the meeting of the Constituent Assembly. At the same time the pogrom makers may attempt to cause brawling and bloodshed on the streets of Petrograd.

The Petrograd Soviet of Workers' and Soldiers' Deputies takes on itself the defense of revolutionary order against counterrevolutionary and pogrom attacks.

The Petrograd garrison will permit no acts of violence and disorder. The population is urged to detain hooligans and Black Hundred agitators and to bring them to the commissars of the Soviet in the nearest military unit. At the first attempt of dark elements to cause confusion, robbery, bloodshed or shooting on the streets of Petrograd those who are guilty will be wiped off the face of the earth.

Citizens! We call on you to maintain full calm and selfpossession. The cause of order and of revolution is in firm hands.

MILITARY REVOLUTIONARY COMMITTEE.

FROM THE MILITARY REVOLUTIONARY COMMITTEE, ATTACHED TO THE PETROGRAD SOVIET

Two revolutionary newspapers, *Rabochii Put* and *Soldat*, have been closed by the conspirators of the Staff. The Soviet of Workers' and Soldiers' Deputies cannot endure the suppression of freedom of speech. An honest press must be assured to the people, which is resisting the attacks of the pogrom-makers.

The Military Revolutionary Committee decides:

1. To open the printing shops of the revolutionary newspapers.

2. To propose to the editors and printers to continue the publication of the newspapers.

3. The honorable duty of guarding the revolutionary printing shops

against counterrevolutionary attempts is entrusted to the gallant soldiers of the Lithuanian Regiment and of the 6th Reserve Sappers' Battalion. (*Cf.* "The Revolution of 1917," Vol. V, pp. 265, 266.)

PROTESTS OF THE MENSHEVIK AND SOCIALIST REVOLUTIONARY DELEGATES
TO THE SECOND CONGRESS OF SOVIETS AGAINST THE BOLSHEVIK
REVOLUTION, READ AT THE SESSION OF THE CONGRESS
ON NOVEMBER 7, 1917

RESOLUTION OF THE MENSHEVIKI

Taking into consideration

1. That a military conspiracy was carried out and achieved by the Bolshevik Party in the name of the Soviet behind the backs of all the other parties and fractions, represented in the Soviets;

2. That the seizure of power by the Petrograd Soviet on the eve of the Congress of Soviets amounts to disorganization and break-up of the whole Soviet organization and undermined the significance of the Congress as the authorized representative of the revolutionary democracy;

3. That this conspiracy throws the country into civil strife, thwarts the Constituent Assembly, creates a threat of military catastrophe and leads to the triumph of counterrevolution;

4. That the sole possible peaceful way out of the situation is to negotiate with the Provisional Government about the organization of a Government, based on all groups of the democracy;

5. That the Russian Social Democratic Labor Party (united) considers it an obligation to the working class not only to repudiate, for itself, any responsibility for the activities of the Bolsheviki, who hide behind the Soviet banner, but also to warn the workers and soldiers against a policy of adventures that is fatal to the country and the Revolution,—

The fraction of the Russian Social Democratic Labor Party (united) leaves the present Congress, inviting all other fractions, which, like itself, refuse to bear responsibility for the activities of the Bolsheviki, to meet immediately to consider the situation.

DECLARATION OF THE CENTRAL COMMITTEE AND OF THE FRACTION OF
SOCIALIST REVOLUTIONARIES AT THE SECOND
CONGRESS OF SOVIETS

The Socialist Revolutionary Fraction of the Second All-Russian Congress of Soviets of Workers' and Soldiers' Deputies, in agreement with the Central Committee of the Socialist Revolutionary Party, declares:

1. The seizure of power, carried out by the Bolshevik Party and by the Petrograd Soviet of Workers' and Soldiers' Deputies on the eve of the Constituent Assembly and a day before the All-Russian Soviet Congress, is a crime against the motherland and the Revolution, signalizes the be-

ginning of civil war and the break-up of the Constituent Assembly and threatens to destroy the Revolution.

2. In anticipation of the outburst of popular indignation, which is inevitable as a result of the unavoidable breakdown of the Bolshevik promises, which are obviously unattainable at the present time, the Socialist Revolutionary fraction summons all the revolutionary forces of the country to organize and to stand on guard for the Revolution, in order, in the event of an impending catastrophe, to be able to take the fate of the country into their own hands and, without permitting counter-revolution to triumph, to bring about the speediest conclusion of a general democratic peace, the convocation of the Constituent Assembly at the appointed time and the socialization of the land;

3. Affirming the seizure of power by the Bolshevik Party and by the Petrograd Soviet, which is guided by them, the Socialist Revolutionary fraction imposes on them all the responsibility for the consequences of their insane and criminal step. Asserting, in view of this, the impossibility of common work with the Bolsheviki and, moreover, considering the Congress, because of the insufficient representation of the Front and of many Soviets, illegitimate, the Fraction of Socialist Revolutionaries leaves the Congress.

(*Cf.* S. Piontkovsky, "Documents on the History of the October Revolution," pp. 226, 227.)

APPEAL OF THE SECOND CONGRESS OF SOVIETS TO THE WORKERS, SOLDIERS AND PEASANTS IN CONNECTION WITH THE VICTORY OF THE BOLSHEVIK REVOLUTION, OF NOVEMBER 8, 1917

Workers, Soldiers and Peasants.

The Second All-Russian Congress of Soviets of Workers' and Soldiers' Deputies has opened. The enormous majority of the Soviets are represented in it. A number of delegates from the Peasant Soviets are present at the Congress. The powers of the compromising Central Executive Committee have expired. The Congress takes power into its hands, relying on the will of the enormous majority of the workers, soldiers and peasants, supported by the victorious uprising of the workers and the garrison which has taken place in Petrograd.

The Provisional Government is overthrown. The majority of the members of the Provisional Government are already arrested.

The Soviet power proposes an immediate democratic peace to all peoples and an immediate armistice on all fronts. It guaranties the transfer without compensation of landlords', Crown and monastery land to the disposition of peasant committees, defends the rights of the soldier, carrying out complete democratization of the army, establishes workers' control over production, insures the convocation of the Constituent Assembly at the appointed time, takes care for the provision of

bread in the towns and articles of primary necessity in the villages, assures to all the nations inhabiting Russia complete right to selfdetermination.

The Congress decrees: all power throughout the country passes into the hands of Soviets of Workers', Soldiers' and Peasants' Deputies, which must also guaranty genuine revolutionary order.

The Congress summons the soldiers in the trenches to watchfulness and firmness. The Congress of Soviets is convinced that the revolutionary army will be able to defend the Revolution against any attacks of imperialism until the new Government obtains the conclusion of a democratic peace, which it will propose directly to all peoples. The new Government will take all measures in order to insure the revolutionary army all necessary supplies, by means of a decisive policy of requisitioning and of imposing burdens on the propertied classes, and will also improve the position of the soldiers' families.

The Kornilovites—Kerensky, Kaledin and others—attempt to lead troops against Petrograd. Some detachments, which Kerensky moved by means of trickery, have passed over to the side of the insurgent people.

Soldiers, show active resistance to the Kornilovite Kerensky. Be on guard.

Railroad workers, stop all trains, despatched by Kerensky to Petrograd.

Soldiers, workers, employees,—in your hands is the fate of the Revolution and the fate of the democratic peace.

Long live the Revolution.

ALL-RUSSIAN CONGRESS OF SOVIETS OF WORKERS' AND SOLDIERS'
   DEPUTIES. DELEGATES FROM PEASANT SOVIETS.
(Published in *Pravda*, of November 9 [October 27.]

DECREE ON PEACE, ACCEPTED UNANIMOUSLY AT THE SESSION OF THE
   ALL-RUSSIAN CONGRESS OF SOVIETS ON NOVEMBER 8, 1917

The Workers' and Peasants' Government, created by the Revolution of October 24–25 (November 6–7) and supported by the Soviets of Workers', Soldiers' and Peasants' Deputies, proposes to all combatant peoples and to their governments to begin immediate negotiations for an honest democratic peace.

The Government regards as an honest or democratic peace, which is yearned for by the overwhelming majority of the workers and the toiling classes of all the fighting countries, who are exhausted, tormented and tortured by the War, which the Russian workers and peasants demanded most definitely and insistently after the overthrow of the Tsarist monarchy,—an immediate peace without annexations (*i.e.*, without the seizure of foreign land, without the forcible taking over of foreign nationalities) and without contributions.

Such a peace the Government of Russia proposes to all the fighting peoples to conclude immediately, expressing its readiness to take without the least delay immediately all the decisive steps, up to the final confirmation of all the conditions of such a peace by the authorized assemblies of peoples' representatives of all countries and all nations.

As annexation or seizure of alien lands the Government understands, in conformity with the conception of justice, of democracy in general and of the toiling classes in particular, any addition to a large or strong state of a small or weak nationality, without the precisely, clearly and voluntarily expressed agreement and desire of this nationality, irrespective of when this forcible annexation took place, and also irrespective of how advanced or how backward is the nation which is violently annexed or violently held within the frontiers of another state. Irrespective, finally, of whether this nation lives in Europe or in far-away transoceanic countries.

If any nation is kept within the frontiers of another state by violence, if it is not granted the right, despite its expressed desire,—regardless of whether this desire is expressed in the press, in people's meetings, in the decisions of parties or in riots and uprisings against national oppression, —to vote freely, with the troops of the annexationist or stronger nation withdrawn, to decide without the least compulsion the question of the form of its state existence, then the holding of such a nation is annexation, *i.e.*, seizure and violence.

To continue this War in order to decide how to divide between strong and rich nations the weak nationalities which they have seized, the Government considers the greatest crime against humanity; and it solemnly avows its decision immediately to sign conditions of peace which will stop this War on the terms which have been outlined, equally just for all nationalities, without exception.

Along with this the Government states that it does not regard the above mentioned conditions of peace as ultimative, *i.e.*, it is willing to consider any other conditions of peace, insisting only that these be presented as quickly as possible by one of the fighting countries, and on the fullest clarity, on the absolute exclusion of any ambiguity and secrecy in proposing conditions of peace.

The Government abolishes secret diplomacy, announcing its firm intention to carry on all negotiations quite openly before the whole people, proceeding immediately to the full publication of the secret treaties, ratified or concluded by the Government of landlords and capitalists between February and October 25, 1917. All the contents of these secret treaties, inasmuch as they are directed, as usually happened, toward the obtaining of advantages and privileges for Russian landlords and capitalists, toward the maintenance or the increase of Great Russian annexations, the Government declares unconditionally and immediately annulled.

Turning with its proposal to the Governments and peoples of all countries to begin immediately open negotiations for the conclusion of peace,

the Government expresses its readiness to carry on these negotiations by means of written communications, by telegraph, by means of negotiations between representatives of different countries or at a conference of such representatives. To facilitate such negotiations the Government will nominate its plenipotentiary representative in neutral countries.

The Government proposes to all Governments and peoples of all combatant countries immediately to conclude an armistice, considering it desirable that this armistice should be concluded for a period of not less than three months, in the course of which time it would be quite possible both to complete negotiations for peace with the participation of representatives of all nationalities or nations which have been drawn into the War or have been forced to participate in it and to convoke authoritative assemblies of peoples' representatives of all countries for the final confirmation of the peace conditions.

Turning with these proposals of peace to the Governments and the peoples of all the combatant countries, the Provisional Workers' and Peasants' Government of Russia also appeals especially to the class-conscious workers of the three leading nations of humanity and the largest states which are participating in the War, England, France and Germany. The workers of these countries rendered the greatest services to the cause of progress and socialism, and the great examples of the Chartist Movement in England, a number of revolutions of world significance, carried out by the French proletariat, finally the heroic struggle against the Exceptional Law in Germany and the long, stubborn, disciplined work of creating mass proletarian organizations in Germany (which was a model for the workers of the whole world),—all these examples of proletarian heroism and historic creation serve us as a guaranty that the workers of the above mentioned countries understand the problems which now fall on them, of liberating humanity from the horrors of war and its consequences, that these workers by their decisive and devotedly energetic activity will help us to bring successfully to its end the cause of peace and, along with this, the cause of freeing the toiling and exploited masses of the population from slavery and exploitation of every kind.

PRESIDENT OF THE SOVIET OF PEOPLES' COMMISSARS,

VLADIMIR ULIANOV-LENIN.

(Collection of Legislative Acts, No. 1, Article 2.)

DECREE ON LAND
ADOPTED AT THE CONGRESS OF SOVIETS ON NOVEMBER 8

1. The landlords' right of property in land is abolished immediately without any payment.

2. Landlords' estates, together with all Crown, monastery and Church lands, with all their livestock and machinery, buildings and everything

that belongs to them, pass into the administration of the township Land Committees and of the county Soviets of Peasant Deputies until the meeting of the Constituent Assembly.

3. Any damaging of the confiscated property, which henceforward belongs to the whole people, is declared a grave offense, to be punished by the revolutionary court. The county Soviets of Peasant Deputies are to take all the necessary measures for the maintenance of the strictest order in the confiscation of the landlords' estates, for defining which parts are subject to confiscation, for making up a precise list of all confiscated property and for the strictest revolutionary guarding of all the landed property which is now passing over to the people, with all the buildings, machines, cattle, stores of food, etc.

The following peasant resolution, made up on the basis of 242 local peasant resolutions by the editors of the *Izvestia of the All-Russian Soviet of Peasant Deputies* and published in number 88 of this *Izvestia* (Petrograd, No. 88, August 19, 1917), must everywhere serve as guidance in the realization of the great reorganization of the land system.

The land problem, in its full scope, can be solved only by the popularly elected Constituent Assembly.

The most equitable solution, of the land problem must be as follows:

1. The right of private property in land is forever abolished; land can be neither sold, nor bought, nor leased, nor pledged, nor alienated in any other way. All land, state, Crown, monastery, Church, which is owned by private persons, by public organizations, by peasants, etc., is taken away without compensation, becomes the property of the whole people and is transferred to the use of all those who work on it.

For those who suffer from this revolution in property only the right of public support during the period which is necessary for adaptation to the new conditions is recognized.

2. All the mineral resources of the earth, ore, oil, coal, salt, etc., and also forests and waters which are of general state significance pass into the exclusive possession of the state. All little streams, lakes, woods, etc., are transferred to the use of the peasant communities and are managed by the local institutions of selfgovernment.

3. Land sectors with a high degree of cultivation, gardens, plantations, model fields, orange-groves, etc., are not to be divided, but are to be transformed into model holdings and are to be handed over for the exclusive use of the state or of the local communities, depending upon the size and importance of the sectors.

Garden land in city and village, together with house gardens, remains for the use of its present owners. The size of such holdings and the amount of the tax for their use are defined by legislation.

4. State and private farms for breeding horses, blooded stock, poultry, etc., are confiscated, turned into public property and are transferred to

the exclusive use either of the state or of the community, depending on the size and importance of the farms.

5. Problems of purchase are to be considered by the Constituent Assembly. All the property, both livestock and material, of the confiscated land is transferred to the exclusive use of the state or of the community, depending upon its amount and its importance, without compensation.

The confiscation of property does not affect peasants with little land.

6. The right to use the land belongs to all citizens of the Russian state (without distinction of sex) who desire to farm it with their own labor, with the help of their families or in coöperative groups, and only so long as they are able to farm it themselves. Hired labor is not permitted.

In the event that any member of a village community is accidentally incapacitated the community, for a period of two years, until his working capacity is restored, is bound to come to his help by farming his land by common labor.

Farmers who have forever lost the ability to till their land, as a result of old age or illness, lose the right to farm the land, but receive in exchange a pension from the state.

7. The use of land must be on an equalized basis. The land must be distributed among those who work on it, according to local conditions, in accordance with a working or consuming norm.

The forms of using the land must be completely free. The land may be tilled individually, or by small or large communities, or by coöperative groups, as each village and settlement may decide.

All land, after it has been alienated, passes into a general people's land reserve. Local and central bodies of administration, beginning with democratically organized classless village and town communities and ending with central regional institutions, supervise the distribution of the land among those who work on it.

The land reserve is subject to periodic redivision, depending upon the growth of the population and the improved productivity and quality of the farming.

When the boundaries of allotments are changed the first nucleus of the allotment must remain untouched.

The land of members who pass out of the village community goes back into the land reserve. The nearest relatives of the persons who have withdrawn from the society and persons whom the latter have designated possess a preferential right to receive allotments.

The value of fertilizer and of basic improvements on the land, inasmuch as they have not been used up, must be paid for when an allotment is given back into the land reserve.

If in some places the available land reserve is insufficient to satisfy the entire local population the surplus population should be transferred elsewhere.

The state must assume responsibility for the organization of this transfer, including the expenses of moving, of supply with machinery, etc.

The transfer is carried out in the following order: first, landless peasants who desire to move, the porochni members of the community, deserters, etc., finally, by lot or by agreement.

Everything contained in this order, as an expression of the absolute will of the enormous majority of the classconscious peasants of all Russia, is declared a temporary law, which, until the convocation of the Constituent Assembly, is to be put into practise immediately when possible, in some of its parts with that necessary gradualness which must be defined by the county Soviets of Peasants' Deputies. The lands of ordinary peasants and rank-and-file Cossacks are not confiscated.

PRESIDENT OF THE COUNCIL OF PEOPLE'S COMMISSARS,

VLADIMIR ULIANOV-LENIN.

October 26, 1917 (old style).

(Cf. Izvestia for October 28, 1917 [Old Style].)

KERENSKY'S ORDER TO THE TROOPS OF THE PETROGRAD DISTRICT OF NOVEMBER 9, 1917

I declare that I, the Premier of the Provisional Government and the commander-in-chief of all the armed forces of the Russian Republic, arrived to-day at the head of troops from the front, devoted to the motherland.

I order all the units of the Petrograd Military District, which, from lack of understanding, have adhered to a band of traitors to the motherland and the Revolution, to return to the fulfilment of their duty without delaying one hour.

This order is to be read in all companies, commands and squadrons.

PREMIER OF THE PROVISIONAL GOVERNMENT AND

COMMANDER-IN-CHIEF, A. KERENSKY

Gatchina, October 27, 1917 (old style).

(Cf. S. Piontkovsky, "Documents on the History of the October Revolution," p. 227.)

APPEAL OF GENERAL P. N. KRASNOV TO THE COSSACKS, OF NOVEMBER 9, 1917

By the will of the Commander-in-chief I am appointed commander of the troops which are concentrated before Petrograd.

Citizen soldiers, valiant Cossacks of the Don, the Kuban, the Trans-Baikal, the Ussuri, the Amur and the Yenisei, all you who have remained true to your soldiers' oath, you who have sworn to keep the Cossack vow strong and inviolate,—to you I turn with an appeal to go and save Petrograd from anarchy, violence and hunger, and Russia from

the indelible mark of shame which has been thrown on it by a dark handful of ignorant men, led by the will and the money of Emperor Wilhelm.

The Provisional Government, to which you pledged allegiance in the great days of March, is not overthrown, but has been violently driven from its headquarters and holds its sessions with the great army from the front.

Faithful to its duty, the Council of the Union of the Cossack Troops has united all the Cossacks. Strong in the Cossack spirit, supported by the whole Russian people, it has vowed to serve the motherland as our ancestors served it in the terrible Time of Troubles in 1612, when the Don Cossacks saved Moscow, which was threatened by Swedes, Poles and Lithuanians and was torn up with internal strife.

The Front Congress of Cossacks in Kiev, which seized power, together with the Ukrainians and the troops which are faithful to their duty, is in full subordination to the Provisional Government.

All the Congresses of Peasants' Deputies have refused to have anything to do with a handful of traitors and betrayers.

The fighting Front looks on the enemies and traitors with inexpressible horror and contempt. Their robberies, murders and acts of violence, their truly German excesses against those who were defeated but did not surrender have alienated all Russia from them.

Citizen soldiers and valiant Cossacks of the Petrograd Garrison! Immediately send your delegates to me, so that I may know who is a traitor to freedom and the motherland and who is not, and so as not to shed accidentally innocent blood.

COMMANDER OF THE TROOPS OF THE RUSSIAN REPUBLIC, CONCENTRATED BEFORE PETROGRAD, MAJOR-GENERAL KRASNOV.

For the Chief of Staff Lieut.-Colonel Popov.

(*Cf. Rabochaya Gazeta* for October 28, 1917 [Old Style].)

APPEAL OF THE COMMITTEE FOR THE SALVATION OF THE MOTHERLAND, OF NOVEMBER 9, 1917

To the citizens of the Russian Republic.

On October 25 (Old Style) the Bolsheviki of Petrograd, notwithstanding the will of the revolutionary people, criminally arrested some members of the Provisional Government, dispersed the Provisional Council of the Russian Republic and declared an illegal regime.

Violence against the Government of revolutionary Russia, carried out at a time of greatest danger from the external enemy, is an unheard of crime against the motherland.

The revolt of the Bolsheviki inflicts a mortal blow upon the cause of defense and puts off the peace which everyone desires.

The civil war which the Bolsheviki have begun threatens to throw

the country into indescribable horrors of anarchy and counterrevolution and to break up the Constituent Assembly, which must strengthen the republican order and gain the land for the people once for all.

Preserving the continuity of the single state authority, the All-Russian Committee for the Salvation of the Motherland and the Revolution takes the initiative in re-creating the Provisional Government, which, supported by the forces of democracy, will bring the country to the Constituent Assembly and will save it from counterrevolution and anarchy.

The All-Russian Committee for the Salvation of the Motherland and the Revolution appeals to you, citizens:

Don't recognize the authority of the usurpers!

Don't fulfill their commands!

Rise for the defense of the Motherland and the Revolution!

Support the All-Russian Committee for the Salvation of the Motherland and the Revolution.

All-Russian Committee for the Salvation of the Motherland and the Revolution, with representatives of the Petrograd City Duma, the Provisional Council of the Russian Republic, the Central Executive Committee of the All-Russian Council of Peasants' Deputies, the Central Executive Committee of the Soviets of Workers' and Soldiers' Deputies, the Front Groups, Representatives of the Second Congress of Soviets of Workers' and Soldiers' Deputies, the delegations of the Socialist Revolutionaries and Social Democrats (Mensheviki), of the People's Socialists, the Group "Unity" and others.

(*Cf.* S. Piontkovsky, "Documents on the History of the October Revolution," pp. 242, 243.)

UNIVERSAL OF THE UKRAINIAN CENTRAL RADA, PROCLAIMING UKRAINA AN AUTONOMOUS REPUBLIC, OF NOVEMBER 20, 1917

Ukrainian People, and all the peoples of Ukraina. The Russian Republic is living through a hard and grievous time. Sanguinary civil war is going on in the North in the capitals.* There is no central authority. Anarchy, chaos and breakdown are increasing in the entire state.

Our country is also in danger. Without a strong, united, popular government Ukraina will also be cast into the pit of sanguinary civil strife and complete decline.

Ukrainian people, you along with the brotherly peoples of Ukraina, placed us here to watch out for the rights which were gained in struggle, to maintain order and to create a better future in our land. And we, the Ukrainian Central Rada, carrying out your will, in the name of the establishment of order in our country, in the name of the salvation of all Russia, declare:

From now on Ukraina will be the Ukrainian People's Republic.

* Petrograd and Moscow are often referred to as "the capitals."

Not separating from the Russian Republic, preserving union with it, we stand firmly on our land so that we can help all Russia with our forces, so that the whole Russian Republic may become a federation of free and equal peoples.

Until the Ukrainian Constituent Assembly meets, all authority to maintain order, to promulgate laws and to govern in our land belongs to us, the Ukrainian Central Rada, and to our Government—the General Secretariat of Ukraina.

Recognizing our power and authority in our native land we stand on guard for right and Revolution not only here but for all Russia.

And therefore we declare:

To the territory of the Ukrainian People's Republic belong the lands which are inhabited in the main by Ukrainians: the provinces of Kiev, Podolia, Volhynia, Chernigov, Poltava, Kharkov, Ekaterinoslav, Kherson and Tauride (without the Crimea). The final establishment of the frontiers of the Ukrainian People's Republic, both as regards the annexation of those parts of Kursk, Voronezh and Kholm Provinces which are inhabited mainly by Ukrainians and as regards other provinces with a mixed population, must follow in agreement with the organized will of the peoples.

To all citizens of these territories we declare:

Henceforward on the territory of the Ukrainian People's Republic rights of property in landlords' estates and in other agricultural land which is not farmed by the labor of its owners, in monastery, Crown and Church land are abolished. Recognizing that these lands belong to the whole working people and must be transferred to it without purchase, the Ukrainian Central Rada instructs the General Secretariat for Agriculture immediately to work out a law about the method of administering these lands through land committees, elected by the people, until the convocation of the Ukrainian Constituent Assembly.

The labor of the workers in the Ukrainian People's Republic must be regulated immediately. We now declare: the eight-hour working day is established on the territory of the People's Ukrainian Republic as from the present day.

The difficult and threatening hour which all Russia is experiencing, and, with Russia, our Ukraina, demands the regulation of production, the equal distribution of food products and better organization of labor. Therefore we instruct the General Secretariat for Labor, together with representatives of the workers, from the present day to establish state control over production in Ukraina, respecting the interests both of Ukraina and of all Russia.

For the fourth year blood is flowing on the fronts and the forces of all the peoples of the world are being expended in vain. By the will and in the name of the Ukrainian People's Republic we, the Ukrainian Central Rada, stand firmly for a speedy conclusion of peace. For this

purpose we are undertaking decisive measures in order, through the central government, to compel allies and enemies to begin immediate peace negotiations.

We shall also take care that at the peace congress the rights of the Ukrainian people inside and outside of Russia should not be violated in the conclusion of peace. But until the conclusion of peace every citizen of the Republic of Ukraina, together with the citizens of all the peoples of the Russian Republic, must stand firmly at his post, at the front or in the rear.

Recently the bright achievements of the Revolution were darkened by the reëstablishment of the death penalty. We declare:

Henceforward the death penalty is abolished on the territory of the Ukrainian Republic.

Complete amnesty is granted to all who have been arrested and imprisoned for political actions, committed up to the present day. This applies equally to those who have been condemned, to those who have not been condemned and to those who have not been brought to trial. A law will be promulgated immediately in this connection.

The courts in Ukraina must be just and must correspond with the spirit of the people. For this purpose we instruct the General Secretariat for Justice to take all measures in order to simplify judicial procedure and bring it into harmony with the people's conceptions of justice.

We instruct the General Secretariat for Internal Affairs to take all measures to strengthen and extend the rights of the local organs of self-government, which represent the supreme administrative power in the provinces, and to establish contact and coöperation between these organs of selfgovernment and the organizations of revolutionary democracy. This will be the best basis of a free democratic life.

All the liberties which were gained by the All-Russian Revolution will be preserved in the Ukrainian People's Republic: freedom of speech, press, faith, assembly, unions and strikes, immunity of personalty and dwelling, the right and possibility to use local languages in relations with all institutions.

The Ukrainian people, which for long years fought for its national freedom and has now received it, will firmly guard the freedom of national development of all the nationalities which live in Ukraina. There fore we declare that for the Great Russians, Jews, Poles and other peoples in Ukraina we recognize the right of national-personal autonomy, in order to guaranty them the right and freedom of selfgovernment in matters of their national life.

We commission our General Secretariat for international affairs to submit to us in the nearest future a law of national-personal autonomy.

The food question is the root of state strength in this difficult and responsible hour.

The Ukrainian People's Republic must strain all its energy and

save itself, the Front and those parts of the Russian Republic which need our help.

Citizens. In the name of the People's Ukrainian Republic and of Federative Russia, we, the Ukrainian Central Rada, summon all to a decisive struggle with disorder and destruction and to vigorous great up-building of new state forms, which will give the great and weakened Republic of Russia health, strength and new power. The working out of these forms must be completed at the Ukrainian and All-Russian Constittuent Assemblies.

We set as the day of election for the Ukrainian Constituent Assembly December 27, 1917, and as the day of the convocation of the Constituent Assembly January 9, 1918.

A law will be immediately published about the method of convening the Ukrainian Constituent Assembly.

Kiev, November 7, 1917 (Old Style).

(*Cf.* S. Piontkovsky, "The Civil War in Russia: Documents," pp. 334–336.)

DECREE ABOUT WORKERS' CONTROL, OF NOVEMBER 27, 1917

1. In the interest of planned regulation of national economic life workers' control over production, the purchase and sale of products and raw materials, the storage of these and over the financial side of the undertaking is introduced in all industrial, commercial, banking, agricultural, transport, coöperative, producers' coöperative and other enterprises which employ hired labor or give out work at home.

2. Workers' control is carried out by all the workers of a given enterprise through their elected bodies, such as factory committees, councils of elders, etc. Representatives of the employees and of the technical personnel are included in the personnel of these bodies.

3. A Council of Workers' Control is established in every large city, province or industrial region. This Council, being an organ of the Soviet of Workers', Soldiers' and Peasants' Deputies, is composed of representatives of trade-unions, factory and other workers' committees and workers' coöperatives.

4. Before the convocation of a congress of Councils of Workers' Control an All-Russian Council of Workers' Control is established in Petrograd. It is made up of the following number of representatives from the following organizations: 5 from the All-Russian Central Executive Committee of the Soviet of Workers' and Soldiers' Deputies; 5 from the All-Russian Central Executive Committee of the Peasants' Deputies; 5 from the All-Russian Council of Trade-Unions; 2 from the All-Russian Centre of Workers' Coöperation; 5 from the All-Russian Bureau of Factory Committees; 5 from the All-Russian Union of Engineers and Technicians; 2 from the All-Russian Union of Agronomes; 1 from every All-Russian

union of workers which has less than 100,000 members; 2 from each union with more than 100,000 workers; 2 from the Petrograd Council of Trade-Unions.

5. Commissions of specialists-examiners (technicians, bookkeepers, etc.) are attached to the higher organizations of Workers' Control. These commissions are sent to investigate the financial and technical aspects of undertakings both at the initiative of these higher organizations and at the request of the lower organizations of Workers' Control.

6. The organizations of Workers' Control possess the right to inspect production, to establish norms of output of the enterprise and to take measures to establish the costs of production.

7. The organizations of Workers' Control possess the right to control the entire business correspondence of the enterprise. The owners are legally responsible for the concealment of correspondence. Commercial secrecy is abolished. The owners are bound to submit to the organizations of Workers' Control all books and accounts, both for the current year and for past business years.

8. Decisions of the organizations of Workers' Control are obligatory for the owners of enterprises and may be cancelled only by the decision of the higher organizations of Workers' Control.

9. The owner or the directors of an enterprise are granted a period of three days in which to lodge a protest with the higher organizations of Workers' Control against any decisions of the lower organizations of Workers' Control.

10. In all enterprise the owners and the representatives of the workers and employees, elected to carry out Workers' Control, are declared responsible to the state for the strictest order, discipline and preservation of property. Those who are guilty of concealing material, products and orders and of making incorrect accounts and of similar abuses are liable to criminal responsibility.

11. Regional (according to Point 3) Councils of Workers' Control solve all disputed questions and conflicts between the lower organizations of control and also decide on the complaints of the owners of undertakings and issue, in conformity with the peculiarities of production and with local conditions, instructions within the limits of the decisions and instructions of the All-Russian Council of Workers' Control and supervise the activities of the lower organizations of control.

12. The All-Russian Council of Workers' Control works out the general plans of Workers' Control, issues instructions and compulsory decisions, regulates the relations between the regional Councils of Workers' Control and serves as the highest court of appeal for all matters connected with Workers' Control.

13. The All-Russian Council of Workers' Control coördinates the activity of the organizations of Workers' Control with all other institutions which are concerned with the organization of national economic life.

A statement about the relations between the All-Russian Council of Workers' Control and other institutions which organize and regulate the national economy will be issued separately.

14. All laws and circulars, restricting the activity of factory and other committees and councils of the workers and employees, are repealed. In the name of the Government of the Russian Republic,

PRESIDENT OF THE COUNCIL OF PEOPLE'S COMMISSARS,

VL. ULIANOV (LENIN),

PEOPLE'S COMMISSAR FOR LABOR, ALEXANDER SHLYAPNIKOV,

ADMINISTRATOR OF THE COUNCIL OF PEOPLE'S COMMISSARS,

VLAD. BONCH-BRUEVITCH,

SECRETARY OF THE COUNCIL, N. GORBUNOV.

(*Cf. Pravda* for November 30, 1917.)

DECREE OF THE COUNCIL OF PEOPLE'S COMMISSARS ABOUT THE LIMITS OF COMPENSATION FOR PEOPLE'S COMMISSARS AND FOR HIGHER EMPLOYEES AND OFFICIALS, DATED DECEMBER 1, 1917

Recognizing the necessity of taking the most energetic measures for the purpose of lowering the salaries of the higher employees and officials in all state, public and private institutions and undertakings, without exception, the Council of People's Commissars decides: (1) To establish the maximum salary for People's Commissars as 500 rubles a month for those who are without families, with an addition of 100 rubles a month for every member of the family who is unable to work; apartments must be limited to a basis of not more than one room for every member of the family; (2) To address to all local Soviets of Workers', Soldiers' and Peasants' Deputies the request to prepare and carry out revolutionary measures for the special taxation of higher employees; (3) To commission the Ministry for Finance to prepare a general legal project for such a reduction; (4) To commission the Ministry for Finance and all individual Commissars to examine immediately the budget accounts of the Ministries and to cut down all unduly high salaries and pensions.

SECRETARY OF THE COUNCIL OF PEOPLE'S COMMISSARS,

N. GORBUNOV.

(Published in *Pravda* for December 4, 1917.)

APPEAL TO THE WORKING MOSLEMS OF RUSSIA AND THE EAST, OF DECEMBER 3, 1917

To All the Working Moslems of Russia and the East.

Comrades! Brothers!

Great events are taking place in Russia. The end of the sanguinary war, which began for the sake of dividing up other people's countries, is approaching. The rule of the robbers, who have enslaved the peoples of

the world, is falling. Under the blows of the Russian Revolution the old edifice of servitude and slavery is shaking. The world of arbitrariness and oppression is living through its last days. A new world is being born, a world of workers and of freed people. At the head of this revolution stands the Workers' and Peasants' Government of Russia, the Council of People's Commissars.

All Russia is covered with a network of revolutionary Soviets of Workers' Soldiers' and Peasants' Deputies. Authority in the country is in the hands of the people. The working people of Russia burn with the sole desire to get a just peace and to help the oppressed peoples of the world conquer freedom for themselves.

Russia is not alone in this sacred cause. The great watchword of liberation, proclaimed by the Russian Revolution, is caught up by all the workers of the West and the East. The peoples of Europe, exhausted by the War, are already stretching out their hands to us and creating peace. The workers and soldiers of the West are already gathering under the banner of socialism, storming the ramparts of imperialism. And far-away India, the country which the "educated" robbers of Europe oppressed for centuries, has already raised the banner of uprising, organizing its Soviets of Deputies, casting from its shoulders the hateful yoke of slavery, calling the peoples of the East to struggle and liberation.

The reign of capitalist pillage and violence is crumbling. The ground is burning beneath the feet of the bandits of imperialism.

In the face of these great events we appeal to you, working and penniless Moslems of Russia and the East. Moslems of Russia, Tartars of the Volga and the Crimea, Kirghiz and Sarts of Siberia and Turkestan, Turks and Tartars of the Trans-Caucasus, Chechentsi and Gortsi of the Caucasus, all those whose mosques and prayer-houses were destroyed, whose beliefs and customs were trampled on by the Tsars and oppressors of Russia!

From now on your faiths and customs, your national and cultural institutions are declared free and untouchable. Arrange your national life freely and without obstacles. You have the right to do this. Know that your rights, as the rights of all the peoples of Russia, are guarded by all the power of the Revolution and of its organizations, the Soviets of Workers', Soldiers' and Peasants' Deputies.

Support this Revolution and its authorized Government!

Moslems of the East, Persians and Turks, Arabs and Hindus, all those whose heads and property, whose freedom and motherland have been objects of trade among the greedy robbers of Europe for centuries, all those whose countries the robbers who began the War want to divide up.

We say that the secret treaties of the overthrown Tsar, confirmed by the overthrown Kerensky, about the seizure of Constantinople are now torn up and destroyed. The Russian Republic and its Government, the

Council of People's Commissars, is against the seizure of other people's lands. Constantinople must remain in the hands of the Moslems.

We say that the treaty about the division of Persia is torn up and destroyed. As soon as military activities are stopped the troops will be withdrawn from Persia and the Persians will be freely granted the right to determine their own fate.

We say that the treaty about the division of Turkey and about the "taking away" of Armenia from it is torn up and destroyed. As soon as military activities cease the Armenians will be assured the right freely to determine their own political fate.

Enslavement awaits you not from Russia and its revolutionary Government, but from the robbers of European imperialism, from those who carry on the present War for the sake of despoiling your countries, from those who have turned your native countries into their robbed and oppressed "colonies."

Throw off these robbers and enslavers of your countries. Now, when war and economic breakdown shake the foundations of the old world, when the whole world burns with indignation against imperialist annexationists, when every spark of indignation is transformed into a powerful flame of revolution, when even the Indian Mohammedans, crushed and tortured by foreign yoke, rise up against their oppressors, now it is impossible to be silent. Don't lose time, but cast out those who have seized your lands. Don't let them rob your native hearths any longer. You yourselves must be the masters of your countries. You yourselves must arrange your lives as you choose. You have the right to do this, because your fate is in your own hands.

Comrades. Brothers.

Firmly and decisively we go toward an honest democratic peace.

On our banners we bring liberation to the oppressed peoples of the world.

Moslems of Russia. Moslems of the East.

On this road of renewing peace we expect from you sympathy and support.

PEOPLE'S COMMISSAR FOR NATIONAL AFFAIRS,

DZHUGASHVILI-STALIN,

PRESIDENT OF THE COUNCIL OF PEOPLE'S COMMISSARS,

V. ULIANOV (LENIN).

(*Cf. Izvestia* for December 5.)

ULTIMATUM OF THE COUNCIL OF PEOPLE'S COMMISSARS TO THE UKRAINIAN RADA, OF DECEMBER 17, 1917

Taking account of the interests of the unity and fraternal union of the workers and of the exploited masses in the struggle for socialism, taking account of the recognition of these principles by numerous decisions of the organizations of revolutionary democracy, the Soviets, and

especially of the Second All-Russian Congress of Soviets, the Socialist Government of Russia, the Council of People's Commissars, once again confirms for all nations which were oppressed by Tsarism and by the Great Russian bourgeoisie the right of selfdetermination, including the right of separation from Russia.

Therefore we, the Council of People's Commissars, recognize the People's Ukrainian Republic and its right to secede from Russia altogether or to conclude a treaty with the Russian Republic about mutual relations on a federative or similar basis.

All that concerns the national rights and national independence of the Ukrainian people is recognized by us, the Council of People's Commissars, immediately, without limitations and conditions.

We did not take one step against the Finnish bourgeois Republic, which still remains bourgeois, in the sense of limiting the national rights and national independence of the Finnish people, and we shall take no steps limiting the national independence of any nation which has entered or will desire to enter the Russian Republic.

We accuse the Rada of carrying on a two-faced bourgeois policy, concealing itself behind nationalist phrases. This policy finds expression in the nonrecognition by the Rada of the Soviets and the Soviet regime in Ukraina (among other things, the Rada refuses to convene a territorial congress of Soviets immediately, as the Ukrainian Soviets demand). This double-faced policy, which prevented us from recognizing the Rada as the authorized representative of the working and exploited masses of the Ukrainian Republic, recently led the Rada to actions which destroy any possibility of agreement.

Among such actions were, first, the disorganization of the front.

The Rada shifts and recalls Ukrainian units from the front, thus destroying the unity of the front before the demarcation which can only be achieved by an organized agreement of the Governments of the two Republics.

Second, the Rada has begun to disarm the Soviet troops in Ukraina.

Third, the Rada is supporting the Cadet-Kaledin conspiracy and uprising against the Soviet regime. Appealing to the notoriously false alleged autonomous rights of the "Don and Kuban," covering up with this Kaledin's counterrevolutionary outbreak, which is against the interests and demands of the enormous majority of the working Cossacks, the Rada permits troops to pass through its territory to Kaledin, *refusing to let through troops against Kaledin.*

Going on this road of unprecedented treason to the Revolution, on the road of supporting the worst enemies of the national independence of the peoples of Russia and of the Soviet regime, the enemies of the working and exploited masses, the Cadets and Kaledinists, the Rada would have compelled us, without any hesitation, to declare war on it, even if it were the formally recognized and indisputable organ of supreme state power of the independent bourgeois Republic of Ukraina.

At the present time, in view of all the above mentioned circumstances, the Council of People's Commissars, in the presence of the Ukrainian and Russian Republics, put to the Rada the following questions:

1. Does the Rada bind itself to abstain from attempts to disorganize the general front?

2. Does the Rada assume the obligation in the future not to permit any military units, bound for the Don, the Urals or for other places, to pass through its territory without the consent of the Supreme Commander-in-chief?

3. Does the Rada pledge itself to support the revolutionary troops in their struggle with the counterrevolutionary Cadet-Kaledinist uprising?

4. Does the Rada promise to stop all its attempts to disarm the Soviet regiments and the workers' Red Guard in Ukraina and to give back immediately arms to those from whom they were taken away?

In the event that a satisfactory reply to these questions is not received within forty-eight hours, the Council of People's Commissars will consider the Rada in a state of open war against the Soviet regime in Russia and in Ukraina.

COUNCIL OF PEOPLE'S COMMISSARS.

(*Cf. Izvestia* for December 19, 1917.)

DECREE ON THE ASSIGNMENT OF 2,000,000 RUBLES FOR THE NEEDS OF THE REVOLUTIONARY INTERNATIONALIST MOVEMENT, OF DECEMBER 24, 1917

Taking into consideration that the Soviet regime stands on the platform of the principles of international solidarity of the proletariat and of the brotherhood of the workers of all countries, that struggle against war and imperialism can lead to complete victory only on an international scale, the Council of People's Commissars considers it necessary to come to the aid of the Left, Internationalist wing of the workingclass movement of all countries with all possible resources, including money, quite irrespective of whether these countries are at war or in alliance with Russia, or whether they occupy a neutral position.

For this purpose the Council of People's Commissars decides to place at the disposal of the foreign representatives of the Commissariat for Foreign Affairs two million rubles for the needs of the revolutionary Internationalist movement.

PRESIDENT OF THE COUNCIL OF PEOPLE'S COMMISSARS,

V. ULIANOV (LENIN),

PEOPLE'S COMMISSAR FOR FOREIGN AFFAIRS,

L. TROTZKY,

ADMINISTRATOR OF THE COUNCIL OF PEOPLE'S COMMISSARS,

VLAD. BONCH-BRUEVITCH,

SECRETARY OF THE COUNCIL, N. GORBUNOV.

(*Cf. Investia* for December 26, 1917.)

Decree on the Nationalization of the Banks of December 27, 1917

In the interest of a correct organization of national economic life, in the interest of a decisive elimination of bank speculation and of general liberation of the workers, peasants and the entire toiling population from exploitation by bank capital, and for the purpose of organizing a single people's bank of the Russian Republic, which will really serve the interests of the people and of the poorest classes, the Central Executive Committee decrees:

1. Banking is declared a state monopoly.

2. All now existing private stock-company banks and bank offices are united with the State Bank.

3. The assets and liabilities of the liquidated undertakings are transferred to the State Bank.

4. The method of fusing the private banks with the State Bank will be defined in a special decree.

5. The temporary administration of the affairs of the private banks is handed over to the council of the State Bank.

6. The interests of the small depositors will be fully guarantied.

(*Cf. Izvestia* for December 28, 1917.)

Decree on the Election of Officers and on the Organization of Authority in the Army, of December 29, 1917

1. The Army, serving the will of the working people, is subordinated to the supreme representative of this will—the Soviet of People's Commissars.

2. Full power in every military unit belongs to the corresponding soldiers' committees and councils.

3. Those branches of the life and activity of the troops which are already in charge of the committees are now subject to their direct guidance. The control of the committees or councils is established over those branches of activity which they cannot directly assume.

4. Officers and persons in responsible posts are to be elected. Commanders, up to commanders of regiments, are to be elected by the general balloting of their detachments, squads, companies, commands, squadrons, batteries, divisions and regiments. Commanders above the rank of a regimental commander, up to and including the Commander-in-chief, are to be elected by the appropriate congresses or conferences held by the corresponding committees.

Note. Under the term conference is understood a meeting of the committee with the delegates of committees which are one degree lower.

5. The next highest committee confirms the elected commanders, above the rank of regimental commander.

Note. In the event of a refusal, for cause, by the higher committee to confirm the elected commander, the candidate, if he is chosen a second time by the corresponding lower committee, must be confirmed.

6. Commanders of the Armies are elected by Army Congresses. Commanders of the Fronts are elected by Front Congresses.

7. The committees of the special units appoint only persons with appropriate special knowledge to technical posts which demand special education, special knowledge or long practical preparation, for example: doctors, engineers, technicians, telegraphists, radio-telegraphists, aviators, automobile-drivers, etc.

8. Chiefs of Staffs are elected by Congresses from among persons with special training.

9. All other officers of the Staffs are nominated by the Chiefs of Staffs and confirmed by the appropriate congresses.

Note. All persons with specialized education are separately registered.

10. Officers above the mobilization age for soldiers who are not elected to any commanding posts and thereby acquire the status of rank-and-file soldiers are permitted to resign.

11. All other posts, not involving the command of troops, with the exception of offices in the supply department, are filled by nomination by the appropriate elected commander.

12. Detailed instructions about the elections of officers will be issued separately.

PRESIDENT OF THE COUNCIL OF PEOPLE'S COMMISSARS,

V. ULIANOV (LENIN),

PEOPLE'S COMMISSAR FOR MILITARY AND NAVAL AFFAIRS,

N. KRILENKO,

PEOPLE'S COMMISSAR FOR MILITARY AFFAIRS,

PODVOISKY,

ASSISTANTS OF THE PEOPLE'S COMMISSAR FOR MILITARY AFFAIRS,

KEDROV, SKYLANSKY, LEGRAN, MEKHONOSHIN.

(*Cf. Izvestia,* for December 30, 1917.)

GREETINGS TO THE WORKERS' AND PEASANTS' RADA, OF
DECEMBER 29, 1917

Greeting the organization in Kharkov of a truly popular Soviet regime in Ukraina, seeing in this Workers' and Peasants' Rada the true Government of the People's Ukrainian Republic, the Council of People's Commissars promises the new Government of the brotherly Republic complete and all possible support in the struggle for peace and also in the transfer of all land, factories and banks to the working people of Ukraina.

Long live the power of the Workers', Peasants' and Soldiers' Soviets!

Long live the brotherhood of the workers, soldiers and peasants of Ukraina and of Russia!

COUNCIL OF PEOPLE'S COMMISSARS.

(*Cf. Pravda* for December 30, 1917.)

DECREE ON THE STOPPAGE OF PAYMENT OF INTEREST AND DIVIDENDS, OF JANUARY 5, 1918

1. Until the promulgation of general legislation about the further nationalization of production and also about the method and extent of payment of interest on bonds and of dividends on shares and stocks of private undertakings, any payment of coupons is temporarily suspended.

2. All dealings in stocks and bonds are forbidden.

3. Persons guilty of violating the present decree are liable to prosecution and to confiscation of all their property.

PRESIDENT OF THE COUNCIL OF PEOPLE'S COMMISSARS,

V. ULIANOV (LENIN),

PEOPLE'S COMMISSARS:

V. MENZHINSKY, V. TRUTOVSKY, A. SHLICHTER, V. ALGASOV,

ADMINISTRATOR OF THE COUNCIL OF PEOPLE'S COMMISSARS,

VLAD. BONCH-BRUEVITCH,

SECRETARY OF THE COUNCIL, N. GORBUNOV.

("Collection of Laws" (*Sobranie Uzakonenii*), No. 13, Art. 185.)

DECLARATION OF THE RIGHTS OF THE WORKING AND EXPLOITED PEOPLE, ADOPTED BY THE ALL-RUSSIAN SOVIET EXECUTIVE COMMITTEE ON JANUARY 16, 1918, AND PROPOSED AT THE SESSION OF THE CONSTITUENT ASSEMBLY BY THE BOLSHEVIK DELEGATION

The Central Executive Committee puts forward the following basic propositions:

The Constituent Assembly resolves:

I

1. Russia is declared a Republic of Soviets of Workers', Soldiers' and Peasants' Deputies. All power in the centre and in the localities belongs to these Soviets.

2. The Soviet Russian Republic is established on the basis of a free union of free peoples, as a federation of Soviet national republics.

II

Setting as its fundamental task the destruction of any exploitation of man by man, the complete abolition of the division of society into classes, the merciless suppression of the exploiters, the establishment of a socialist organization of society and the victory of socialism in all countries, the Constituent Assembly further resolves:

1. In order to realize the socialization of the land, private property in land is abolished and the entire land reserve is declared the general

property of the people and is handed over to the workers without any purchase, on the principle of equalized use of the land.

All forests, minerals and waters of general state significance, all livestock and machinery, all estates and agricultural enterprises are declared national property.

2. The Soviet law on workers' control and on the Supreme Economic Council is confirmed for the purpose of assuring the power of the workers over the exploiters, as a first step toward the complete passing of the factories, mines, railroads and other means of production and transportation into the possession of the Soviet Workers' and Peasants' Republic.

3. The passing of all the banks into the possession of the workers' and peasants' state is confirmed as one of the conditions of the liberation of the working masses from the yoke of capital.

4. General liability to labor service is introduced for the purpose of destroying the parasite classes of society and for the organization of economic life.

5. The arming of the workers, the organization of a socialist Red Army of workers and peasants and the complete disarmament of the propertied classes are decreed in order to assure all power for the workers and in order to remove any possibility of the restoration of the power of the exploiters.

III

1. Expressing an unbending determination to tear humanity out of the claws of finance capital and imperialism, which has flooded the earth with blood in the present, most criminal of all wars, the Constituent Assembly fully adheres to the Soviet Government's policy of tearing up the secret treaties, organizing the broadest fraternization with the workers and peasants of the armies which are now fighting against each other and achieving, at any cost, by revolutionary measures, a democratic peace between peoples, without annexations and contributions, on the basis of free selfdetermination of the nations.

2. With the same objectives in view the Constituent Assembly insists on a complete breach with the barbarous policy of bourgeois civilization, building up the welfare of the exploiters in a few chosen nations on the enslavement of hundreds of millions of the working population in Asia, in the colonies in general and in little countries.

The Constituent Assembly greets the policy of the Council of People's Commissars, which has proclaimed the complete independence of Finland, has begun to withdraw troops from Persia and has declared freedom of selfdetermination for Armenia.

The Constituent Assembly regards the Soviet law about the annulment (destruction) of the loans, concluded by the Governments of the Tsar, the landlords and the bourgeoisie, as the first blow against inter-

national banking and finance capital and expresses confidence that the Soviet regime will firmly go forward on this road, until the complete victory of the international workingclass uprising against the yoke of capital has been achieved.

IV

Being elected on the basis of Party lists which were made up before the October Revolution, when the people could not rise up with all its masses against the exploiters, did not know all the strength of the resistance of the latter in defending their class privileges, when the people had still not started practically to create a socialist society, the Constituent Assembly would consider it fundamentally incorrect, even from the formal standpoint, to oppose itself to the Soviet regime.

In substance the Constituent Assembly assumes that now, at a time of decisive struggle of the people against its exploiters, there can be no place for the exploiters in any executive bodies. Power must belong entirely and exclusively to the working masses and to their authorized form of representation—Soviets of Workers', Soldiers' and Peasants' Deputies.

Supporting the Soviet regime and the decrees of the Council of People's Commissars, the Constituent Assembly recognizes that its own functions are confined to a general working out of the fundamental principles of the socialist reorganization of society.

Moreover, attempting to create a really free and voluntary, and consequently all the more complete and firm union of the working classes of all the nations of Russia, the Constituent Assembly limits itself to the establishment of the fundamental bases of the federation of Soviet Republics in Russia, leaving it to the workers and peasants of every nation to take an independent decision at their own authorized Soviet Congress as to whether and on what basis they desire to participate in the federal government and in the other federal Soviet institutions.

The above cited basic propositions must be immediately published and read by the official representatives of the Soviet regime, who open the Constituent Assembly, from the tribune of the Constituent Assembly and must be taken as a basis for the activity of the Constituent Assembly.

(Cf. Izvestia for January 17, 1918.)

Decree on the Dissolution of the Constituent Assembly, of January 19, 1918

The Russian Revolution, from its very beginning, put forward Soviets of Workers', Soldiers' and Peasants' Deputies as mass organizations of all the working and exploited classes, which alone could guide the struggle of these classes for their complete political and economic liberation.

In the course of the whole first period of the Russian Revolution the Soviets multiplied, grew and became stronger, outliving from their own

experience the illusions of compromise with the bourgeoisie and the deceptiveness of the forms of bourgeois-democratic parliamentarism, coming practically to the conclusion that the oppressed classes cannot be liberated without a breach with these forms and with all compromise. Such a breach was the October Revolution, the transfer of all power into the hands of the Soviets.

The Constituent Assembly, elected according to lists which were made up before the October Revolution, reflected the old relation of political forces, when the compromisers and the Cadets were in power.

At that time the people, voting for the candidates of the Socialist Revolutionary Party, could not choose between the Right Socialist Revolutionaries, the supporters of the bourgeoisie, and the Left Socialist Revolutionaries, upholders of socialism. So the Constituent Assembly, which had to be the crown of a bourgeois-parliamentary republic, could not but become an obstacle on the road of the October Revolution and the Soviet regime.

The October Revolution, which gave power to the Soviets and through the Soviets to the working and exploited classes, evoked the desperate resistance of the exploiters and in suppressing this resistance fully revealed itself as the beginning of a socialist revolution.

The working classes had to convince themselves by experience that the old bourgeois parliamentarism had outlived itself, that it was completely inconsistent with the problems of realizing socialism, that not general national, but only class institutions (such as the Soviets) are able to conquer the resistance of the propertied classes and to lay the foundation of a socialist party.

Any renunciation of the full power of the Soviets, of the Soviet Republic which has been conquered by the people, in favor of bourgeois parliamentarism and the Constituent Assembly would now be a step backward and a breakdown of the whole October workers' and peasants' revolution.

The Constituent Assembly, which opened on January 5 (Old Style), as a result of circumstances which are well known to everyone, gave a majority to the Party of Right Socialist Revolutionaries, the Party of Kerensky, Avksentiev and Chernov. It was natural that this Party refused to consider the quite definite, clear, uncompromising proposal of the highest organ of the Soviet regime, the Central Executive Committee of the Soviets, to recognize the programme of the Soviet regime, to recognize the "Declaration of the Rights of the Working and Exploited People," to recognize the October Revolution and the Soviet regime. Thereby the Constituent Assembly broke off any connection between itself and the Soviet Republic of Russia. The withdrawal from such a Constituent Assembly of the groups of the Bolsheviki and the Left Socialist Revolutionaries, who now, as is known, make up the vast majority in the Soviets and enjoy the confidence of the workers and of the majority of the peasants, was inevitable.

And outside the Constituent Assembly the parties of the majority in the Constituent Assembly, the Right Socialist Revolutionaries and the Mensheviki, carry on an open struggle against the Soviet regime, calling for its overthrow in their organizations, thereby objectively supporting the resistance of the exploiters to the transfer of the land and the factories into the hands of the toilers.

It is clear that the remaining part of the Constituent Assembly, as a result of this, can only play the rôle of a screen for the bourgeois counter-revolution, which aims at the overthrow of the power of the Soviets.

Therefore the Central Executive Committee decides:

The Constituent Assembly is dissolved.

(*Cf. Izvestia*, for January 20, 1918.)

MESSAGE OF THE PATRIARCH TIKHON, DENOUNCING THE BOLSHEVIKI, OF FEBRUARY 1, 1918

Humble Tikhon, by God's Grace Patriarch of Moscow and of all Russia, to the beloved in the Lord hierarchs, clergy and all faithful members of the Russian Orthodox Church:

The Lord will deliver us from this present evil world. (Galatians 1:4.)

The Holy Orthodox Church of Christ is at present passing through difficult times in the Russian land. The open and secret enemies of the Truth of Christ have begun to persecute that Truth and are striving to destroy the work of Christ by sowing everywhere, in place of Christian love, the seeds of malice, hatred and fratricidal warfare.

The commandments of Christ regarding love of one's neighbors are forgotten or trampled on; reports reach us daily about the astounding and bestial murders of quite innocent people, and even of the sick on their sickbeds, who are perhaps guilty only of having fulfilled their duty to the Fatherland, and of having spent all their strength in the service of the national welfare. This happens not only under cover of the nocturnal darkness, but openly, in daylight, with hitherto unheard-of audacity and merciless cruelty, without any kind of trial and despite all right and lawfulness and in our days it happens in almost all the towns and villages of our country, both in our capital and in outlying regions (Petrograd, Moscow, Irkutsk, Sevastopol and others).

All this fills our heart with a deep and bitter sorrow and obliges us to turn to such outcasts of the human race with stern words of accusation and warning, in accordance with the command of the Holy Apostle:

"Them that sin, reprove in the sight of all that the rest also may be in fear" (I Timothy 5:20).

Recall yourselves, ye senseless, and cease your bloody deeds. For what you are doing is not only a cruel deed; it is in truth a Satanic act, for which you shall suffer the fire of hell in the life to come, beyond the grave, and the terrible curses of posterity in this present, earthly life.

By the authority given us by God we forbid you to present yourselves for the sacraments of Christ, and anathematize you, if you still bear the name of Christians, even if, merely on account of your baptism, you still belong to the Orthodox Faith.

I adjure all of you who are faithful children of the Orthodox Church of Christ not to commune with such outcasts of the human race in any manner whatsoever: "Cast out the wicked from among you" (I Corinthians 5:13).

The most cruel persecution has likewise arisen against the Holy Church of Christ: the blessed sacraments, sanctifying the birth of man into the world, or blessing the marital union of the Christian family, have been pronounced superfluous; the holy churches are subjected either to destruction through gunfire directed against them (e.g., the holy cathedrals of the Moscow Kremlin) or to plunder and sacrilegious injury (e.g., the chapel of the Saviour in Petrograd). The sacred monasteries, revered by the people (as the Alexander Nevsky and Pochaevsky monasteries), are seized by the atheistic masters of the darkness of this world, and are declared to be in some manner national property. Schools, supported out of the resources of the Orthodox Church to train the ministers of churches and the teachers of the faith, are declared superfluous and are turned either into training institutes of infidelity or even into nurseries of immorality.

Property of monasteries and of Orthodox churches is alienated from them under the guise of being national property, but without any right and without even any desire to act in accordance with the lawful will of the nation. Finally, the Government, which is pledged to uphold right and truth in Russia, and to guaranty liberty and order everywhere, manifests only the most unbridled caprice and the crassest violence in dealing with the Holy Orthodox Church.

Where are the limits of such mockery of the Church of Christ? How may the attacks of its raging enemies upon it be stopped?

We appeal to all of you, believing you faithful children of the Church: rise up in defense of our injured and oppressed holy Mother.

The enemies of the Church seize power over her and her property by means of deadly weapons; but you rise to oppose them with the strength of your faith, with your own nationwide outcry, which would stop those senseless people and would show them that they have no right to call themselves champions of the people's welfare, initiators of a new life in accordance with the national ideal: for they are directly against the conscience of the people.

And if it should become necessary to suffer in the cause of Christ, we invite you, beloved children of the Church, to suffer along with us in accordance with the words of the Holy Apostle: "Who shall separate us from the love of God? Shall tribulation, or anguish, or persecution, or famine, or nakedness, or peril, or the sword?" (Romans 8:35.)

And you, brethren hierarchs and clergy, do not lose even an hour in your spiritual task, and with fiery zeal call upon your members to defend the offended rights of the Orthodox Church; convene religious gatherings; appeal not because of necessity, but take your place in the ranks of spiritual warriors of your own free choice, and oppose to outward violence the force of your genuine spirituality. We then positively affirm that the enemies of the Church of Christ will be shamed and will be dispersed by the power of the Cross of Christ, for the promise of the divine Cross-bearer is immutable: "I will build My Church and the gates of hell shall not prevail against it." (Matthew 16:18.)

TIKHON, PATRIARCH OF MOSCOW AND OF ALL RUSSIA

January 19, 1918

(*Cf.* A. Vedensky, "Church and State, 1918–1922," pp. 114–116.)

DECREE OF THE COUNCIL OF PEOPLE'S COMMISSARS ON THE SEPARATION OF CHURCH FROM STATE AND SCHOOL FROM CHURCH, OF FEBRUARY 5, 1918

1. The Church is separated from the state.

2. Within the boundaries of the Republic it is forbidden to publish any local laws or decisions which would obstruct or limit freedom of conscience or would establish any adventages or privileges based on the religious faith to which the citizens belong.

3. Every citizen may profess any religion or none. All disabilities connected with the profession of any faith or the nonprofession of any are abolished.

Note. Any indication of belonging or not belonging to some religious faith is removed from all official acts.

4. Acts of state and other public official functions are not accompanied by any religious rites or ceremonies.

5. Free practise of religious rites is guarantied in so far as this does not violate public order and is not accompanied by attacks on the rights of citizens of the Soviet Republic.

Local government bodies possess the right to put into effect all measures which are necessary to assure public order and safety in such cases.

6. No one may decline to carry out his civil obligations on account of his religious views. Exceptions to this rule, on the principle of replacing one civil duty by another, are permitted in each individual case by virtue of a decision of the People's Court.

7. Religious oaths are abolished. In necessary cases only a solemn promise is given.

8. Civil acts are under the exclusive control of the civil government: the departments of registration of marriages and births.

9. The school is separated from the church.

Religious teaching is not permitted in any state, public or private institution of learning where general educational subjects are taught.

Citizens may teach and study religion privately.

10. All church and religious societies are subject to the general rules about private societies and unions and do not receive any privileges or subsidies either from the state or from its local autonomous institutions of selfgovernment.

11. Compulsory collections or taxes for church or religious societies and measures of force or punishment applied by these societies against their members are not permitted.

12. No church or religious societies possess the right to own property. They do not possess the rights of a juridical person.

13. All the possessions of the church and religious societies existing in Russia are declared the property of the people.

Buildings and objects which are especially designed for purposes of service are handed over by special decisions of the central and local governmental authorities for the free use of the appropriate religious societies.

PRESIDENT OF THE COUNCIL OF PEOPLE'S COMMISSARS,

V. ULIANOV (LENIN),

PEOPLE'S COMMISSARS:

PODVOISKY, ALGASOV, TRUTOVSKY, SHLICHTER, PROSHIAN, MENZHINSKY, SHLYAPNIKOV, AND PETROVSKY,

ADMINISTRATOR OF THE COUNCIL OF PEOPLE'S COMMISSARS,

VLAD. BONCH-BRUEVITCH.

(*Cf. Gazeta Rab. i Krest Pravit.*, No. 15, for January 23, 1918 [O.S.].)

DECREE OF THE COUNCIL OF PEOPLE'S COMMISSARS, ANNULLING RUSSIA'S STATE DEBTS, OF FEBRUARY 10, 1918

1. All state loans, concluded by the representatives of the Russian landlords and the Russian bourgeoisie, enumerated in a list which is published separately, are annulled (repudiated) as from December, 1917. The December coupons of the above mentioned loans are not to be paid.

2. All the guaranties which the above mentioned governments gave in connection with the loans of different undertakings and institutions are similarly annulled.

3. All foreign loans are annulled unconditionally and without any exceptions.

4. Short-term obligations and notes of the State Treasury retain validity. Interest is not paid on them and the obligations themselves may circulate on an equal basis with currency.

5. Poorer citizens who own bonds of the annulled internal loans to a

value of not more than 10,000 rubles (according to the nominal value) receive in exchange personal certificates of the new loan of the Russian Socialist Federative Soviet Republic of a value which does not exceed 10,000 rubles. The conditions of the loan will be set forth separately.

6. Deposits in state savings-banks and interest on them are untouched. All the bonds of the annulled loans which belong to savings-banks are replaced by indebtedness of the Russian Socialist Federative Soviet Republic.

7. Coöperatives, organs of local selfgovernment and other socially useful or democratic institutions which own bonds of the annulled loans are compensated on the basis of rules which are worked out by the Supreme Economic Council in conjunction with representatives of the aforesaid institutions, if it is proved that these bonds were acquired before the publication of the present decree.

Note. It is left to the local organizations of the Supreme Economic Council to decide which local institutions fall under the definition of "socially useful or democratic."

8. General direction of the liquidation of state loans is entrusted to the Supreme Economic Council.

9. The whole business of the liquidation of the loans is entrusted to the State Bank, which is instructed to proceed immediately to the registration of all the bonds of state loans which are in the hands of different owners, and also of other interest-paying securities, both those which are and those which are not liable to annulment.

10. The Soviets of Workers', Soldiers' and Peasants' Deputies, in agreement with local economic councils, organize commissions to decide which citizens may be regarded as poor.

These commissions have the right to annul completely savings which were not acquired by labor, even if these savings do not exceed 5,000 rubles.

PRESIDENT OF THE ALL-RUSSIAN SOVIET CENTRAL EXECUTIVE COMMITTEE, Y. SVERDLOV,

SECRETARY AVANESOV.

(Published in No. 20 of *Gazeta Rabochego i Krestyanskogo Pravitelstva*, of January 28, 1918, [Old Style].)

SECRET RESOLUTION ON WAR AND PEACE, ADOPTED BY THE EIGHTH CONGRESS OF THE COMMUNIST PARTY, IN MARCH, 1918

The Congress recognizes that it is necessary to ratify the most oppressive and humiliating peace treaty, concluded with Germany, because of the incapacity of our Army, because of the extremely unhealthy condition of the demoralized Front units, because of the necessity of exploiting any, even the slightest possibility of a breathing-space before the assault of imperialism on the Soviet Socialist Republic.

Numerous military attacks of imperialist states (both from the West

and from the East) on Soviet Russia are historically inevitable in the present period, when the era of socialist revolution is beginning. The historical inevitability of such attacks, in view of the present extreme aggravation of all relations between states, classes and nationalities, may at any moment and even within a few days lead to new imperialistic aggressive wars against the socialist movement in general and against the Russian Socialist Republic in particular.

Therefore the Congress states that it regards as the first and basic problem of our Party, and of the whole vanguard of the classconscious proletariat, the adoption of the most energetic, pitilessly decisive and Draconian measures for raising the selfdiscipline and the discipline of the Russian workers and peasants, for explaining the inevitability of Russia's historical approach to liberating, fatherland, socialist war, for the creation everywhere of mass organizations, most strictly bound and strengthened by iron unity of will, organizations capable of united and selfsacrificing activities, both in everyday and in especially critical moments of the life of the people,—finally, for the all-around, systematic, general training of the adult population, without distinction of sex, in military science and operations.

The Congress sees the most hopeful guaranty of the strengthening of the socialist revolution, which has conquered in Russia, only in its transformation into an international workers' revolution.

The Congress is convinced that, from the standpoint of the international revolution, the step taken by the Soviet regime, in view of the existing relation of forces on the world arena, was necessary and inevitable.

Convinced that the workers' revolution is steadily growing in all the belligerent countries, the Congress states that the socialist proletariat of Russia, with all its forces and all the resources at its disposal, will support the brotherly revolutionary movement of the proletariat of all countries.

(Published in *Kommunar,* for January 1, 1919.)

THESES ON WAR AND PEACE, PROPOSED TO THE SEVENTH CONGRESS OF
THE RUSSIAN COMMUNIST PARTY BY A GROUP OF OPPONENTS OF
THE PEACE, OF MARCH 6–8, 1918

1. The imperialist war is everywhere already causing the disintegration of capitalist production relations, is making social antagonisms extremely sharp, disintegrating bourgeois groupings, placing whole countries (Austria) outside the number of capitalist organisms which are capable of living. All this, taken together, represents a basis for the ripening socialist revolution, the first signs of which in the West were the strikes and partial uprisings in Austria and Germany.

2. The war of imperialist coalitions may be regarded now from two standpoints: either the coalitions have come to secret temporary agreement with each other at Russia's expense or they are still ready to con-

tinue the War. In either case we must experience attempts of international capital, which is attacking us from all sides, to divide up Russia; in the second case Germany, just because it can only prolong the War by exploiting Russian grain and raw material, will inevitably try to crush the Soviet regime at any cost.

3. So both the element of class struggle and the element of imperialist exploitation under present conditions make impossible the peaceful coexistence of Soviet Russia with the imperialist coalition of the Central Powers.

4. This state of affairs was extremely clearly reflected in the peace conditions which were put forward by Germany and which really mean that the Soviet regime is undermined not only in its external, but in its internal policy.

5. These conditions cut off the centres of revolution from the producing regions which feed industry, divide the centres of the workers' movement, destroying a number of its largest centres (Latvia, Ukraina), undermine the economic policy of socialism (question of the annulment of loans, the socialization of production, etc.), bring to nothing the international significance of the Russian Revolution (renunciation of international propaganda), turn the Soviet Republic into a tool of imperialist policy (Persia, Afghanistan), last of all, attempt to disarm it (demand that old and new units be demobilized). All this does not give the possibility of a breathing-space, but places the struggle of the proletariat in worse conditions than ever.

6. Without giving any real postponement, the signing of the peace saps the revolutionary will of the proletariat to struggle and holds back the development of the international revolution. Therefore the sole correct tactics could be the tactics of revolutionary war against imperialism.

7. In view of the complete disintegration of the old army, the remnants of which are worse than useless, revolutionary war in its first stage can only be a war of flying partisan detachments, which will pull into the struggle both the city proletariat and the poorest peasantry and will transform military activities on our side into a civil war of the working classes against international capital. Such a war, whatever defeats it might bring in the beginning, would inevitably disintegrate the forces of imperialism.

8. Moreover, when the proletariat is breaking up as a productive class, as a result of unemployment and general economic breakdown, the mobilization of a proletarian army would save the proletariat from dissolution and would make, out of the unemployed, soldiers of the proletarian revolution.

9. Therefore the basis objective of the Party is a clear tactical line, based on war with imperialism, and most intensive work for the organization of the defense of socialism in the course of this war. The fighting capacity of a socialist army is created just in this process of direct struggle.

10. The policy of the leading institutions of our Party was a policy of waverings and compromises,—a policy which objectively obstructed the preparation of revolutionary resistance and, by its constant waverings, demoralized even those leading detachments which went into battle with enthusiasm.

11. The social basis of such a policy was the transformation of our Party from one that is purely proletarian into one that is "a general people's party," a process which was bound to take place, in view of its huge growth. The masses of soldiers, desiring peace at any price and on any conditions, not even reckoning with the socialist character of the Government of the proletariat, made its influence felt, and the Party, instead of raising the peasant masses to its own level, sank back to the level of the latter and was transformed from a vanguard of the revolution into an "average" organization.

12. And incidentally even the peasantry, in the event of a further struggle with international imperialism, will inevitably be drawn into this struggle, because it is threatened by the great danger of losing the land.

13. Under such conditions the objectives of the Party and of the Soviet Government are:

a. The annulment of the Peace Treaty.

b. Intensified propaganda and agitation against international capital, explaining the significance of this new civil war.

c. The creation of an efficient Red Army; the arming of the proletariat and the peasant population and proper instruction of the latter in military technique.

d. Decisive social measures, which will crush the bourgeoisie economically, will unite the proletariat and will increase the enthusiasm of the masses.

e. Merciless struggle with counterrevolution and compromise.

f. The most intensive international revolutionary propaganda and the recruiting for the Red Army of volunteers of all nationalities and states.

(*Cf.* "The All-Union Communist Party in the Resolutions of Its Congresses and Conferences [1898–1926]," pp. 203, 204.)

DECREE ON COMPULSORY MILITARY TRAINING, ADOPTED BY THE ALL-RUSSIAN SOVIET CENTRAL EXECUTIVE COMMITTEE, OF APRIL 22, 1918

One of the basic aims of socialism is to liberate humanity from the burden of militarism and from the barbarism of sanguinary clashes between peoples. The objective of socialism is general disarmament, perpetual peace and brotherly coöperation of all the peoples which inhabit the earth.

This aim will be realized when in all the powerful capitalist countries authority will pass into the hands of the working class, which will tear the means of production out of the hands of the exploiters, will hand them over for the general use of all workers and will establish the Communist system as the unshakable basis of the solidarity of all humanity.

At the present time state power belongs to the working class only in Russia. In all other countries the imperialistic bourgeoisie is in power. Its policy is directed toward the suppression of the Communist revolution and the enslavement of all weak peoples. The Russian Soviet Republic, surrounded by enemies on all sides, must create its own powerful army, which will defend the completion of the Communist reorganization of the country's public order.

The Workers' and Peasants' Government of the Republic sets as its direct aim the establishment of general liability to labor and military service for all citizens. This work encounters the stubborn resistance of the bourgeoisie, which does not wish to renounce its economic privileges and attempts to win back state authority for itself by means of conspiracies, uprisings and treacherous deals with foreign imperialists.

To arm the bourgeoisie would mean the bringing of continual strife into the Army and would thereby paralyze its strength in the struggle against foreign enemies. The parasitic and exploiting elements of society, which do not wish to assume equal obligations and rights with others, cannot be permitted to bear arms. The Workers' and Peasants' Government will seek out means to impose on the bourgeoisie in some form part of the burden of the defense of the Republic, which has been hurled into the greatest suffering and distress by the crimes of the propertied classes. But military training and the arming of the people in the coming transitional epoch will be extended only to the workers and to peasants who do not exploit hired labor.

Citizens between the ages of eighteen and forty who have passed through the course of military training will be registered as liable to military service. At the first call of the Workers' and Peasants' Government they will be obliged to take up arms and to fill up the ranks of the Red Army, which consists of the most devoted and selfsacrificing fighters for the freedom and independence of the Russian Soviet Republic and for the international socialist revolution.

1. Citizens of the Russian Soviet Federative Republic are subject to compulsory training in the following stages: (1) school training, the lowest stage of which is defined by the People's Commissariat for Education; (2) preparatory, between the ages of sixteen and eighteen; (3) mobilization, between the ages of eighteen and forty.

Women citizens, if they consent, are trained on the same general basis.

Note. Persons whose religious convictions do not permit the bearing

of arms are subject to training only in duties which are not connected with the bearing of arms.

2. The training of the preparatory and mobilization classes is entrusted to the People's Commissariat for War; the training of the school classes is committed to the People's Commissariat for Education, with the closest participation of the Commissariat for War.

3. Workers employed in factories, workshops, farms and villages and peasants who do not exploit the labor of others are summoned for training.

4. Military commissariats (district, provincial, county and township) must carry out the local organization of compulsory military training.

5. Persons in training receive no compensation for the time which is devoted to their compulsory exercises; the training must be organized in such a way that, so far as possible, those who are being trained are not kept away from their regular normal work during the period of training.

6. Training must proceed uninterruptedly for eight weeks, at a rate of not less than twelve hours a week. The terms of training of special branches of service and the method of repeated mobilizations will be defined in a special ruling.

7. Persons who have earlier undergone training in the ranks of the regular army may be exempted from training after they have passed an appropriate test, for which they are to receive corresponding certificates, given to them as to persons who have completed the course of compulsory training.

8. Training must be carried out by preparatory instructors according to a programme which has been confirmed by the People's Commissariat for War.

Persons who evade compulsory training and who do not faithfully carry out their obligations under general training are held to legal responsibility.

PRESIDENT OF THE ALL-RUSSIAN SOVIET CENTRAL EXECUTIVE COMMITTEE, Y. SVERDLOV,
SECRETARY, V. AVANESOV.

(*Cf.* S. Piontkovsky, "Civil War in Russia [1918–1921]: Documents," pp. 98–100.)

DECREE OF THE COUNCIL OF PEOPLE'S COMMISSARS ON THE
NATIONALIZATION OF FOREIGN TRADE, OF APRIL 22, 1918

I. All foreign trade is nationalized. Business dealings for the purchase and sale of any products (of the mining and manufacturing industries, agriculture, etc.) with foreign states and individual trade institutions

abroad are made in the name of the Russian Republic by organizations which have been granted special powers to do so. Outside the agency of these organizations any commercial dealings for import or export with foreign countries are forbidden.

Note. Rules about the importation and exportation of postal parcels and passengers' baggage will be issued separately.

II. The People's Commissariat for Trade and Industry is the institution which has charge of the nationalized foreign trade.

III. A Council of Foreign Trade, connected with the People's Commissariat for Trade and Industry, is established for the organization of export and import. This Council includes representatives of the following departments, institutions and organizations:

(a) Departments—War, Navy, Agriculture, Food, Ways of Communication, Foreign Affairs and Finance.

(b) Representatives of central organizations of regulation and management of individual branches of production, such as the Tea Centre, the Main Sugar Trust, the Textile Centre, etc., and representatives of all the departments of the Supreme Economic Council.

(c) Central organizations of the coöperatives.

(d) Central representatives of commercial, industrial and agricultural organizations.

(e) Central organizations of trade-unions and of employees in trade and industry.

(f) Central organizations of commercial bodies which import and export the most important products.

Note. The People's Commissariat for Trade and Industry has the right to bring into the membership of the Council of Foreign Trade representatives of organizations which are not mentioned here.

IV. The Council of Foreign Trade carries out the plan of goods exchange with foreign countries. This plan is worked out and approved by the People's Commissariat for Trade and Industry. Among the problems of the Council of Foreign Trade are: (1) taking account of the supply and demand of exported and imported goods; (2) organization of the preparation and purchase through the appropriate Centres of separate branches of industry (the Main Sugar Trust, the Main Oil Trust, etc.) and, if such Centres are lacking, through coöperatives, through the Commissariat's own agencies and trade firms; (3) the organization of purchasing abroad through the state purchasing commissions and agents, coöperative organizations and trade firms; (4) the fixing of prices for exported and imported goods.

V. 1. The Council of Foreign Trade is divided into departments according to branches of production and according to the most important categories of exports and imports. The presidents of these departments are the representatives of the People's Commissariat for Trade and Industry.

2. The president of the general assembly of the members of the Council of Foreign Trade and of its presidium, elected by the general assembly, is the representative of the People's Commissariat for Trade and Industry.

Note. The internal organization of the Council of Foreign Trade, the number of departments, their problems, rights and functions, will be worked out separately.

3. All the decisions of the departments are submitted by the presidium of the Council for the approval of the People's Commissariat for Trade and Industry.

PRESIDENT OF THE COUNCIL OF PEOPLE'S COMMISSARS, V. ULIANOV (LENIN),

PEOPLE'S COMMISSARS: STALIN, GUKOVSKY, CHICHERIN, BRONSKY,

ADMINISTRATOR OF THE COUNCIL OF PEOPLE'S COMMISSARS, VLAD. BONCH-BRUEVITCH.

(*Cf.* S. Piontkovsky, "Civil War in Russia [1918–1921]: Documents," pp. 57–58.)

DECREE OF THE ALL-RUSSIAN SOVIET CENTRAL EXECUTIVE COMMITTEE, OF MAY 1, 1918

I

Inheritance both by law and by testament is abolished. After the death of the owner the property which belongs to him (both movable and immovable) becomes the state property of the Russian Socialist Federative Republic.

Note. The cessation and the transfer of rights of utilizing agricultural sectors are defined by rules which are set forth in a special law about the nationalization of the land.

II

Until a decree is published on general social insurance needy (*i.e.,* those who do not possess a minimum living income) relatives who are incapable of working, full brothers and half brothers and sisters and wives and husbands of the deceased receive maintenance from the property which is left behind.

Note 1. No distinction is made between relationship in wedlock and out of wedlock.

Note 2. Relatives by adoption are placed in the same position as regards inheritance as relatives by blood.

III

If the remaining property is insufficient for the maintenance of the wife or husband and the other remaining relatives, the neediest of them are provided for first.

IV

The amount of maintenance to be paid to the wife or husband and to the other relatives out of the property of the deceased is defined by the institution which administers matters of social welfare in the provincial Soviets and, in Moscow and in Petrograd, in the city Soviets of Workers' and Peasants' Deputies, in agreement with the persons who have the right to receive maintenance. In the event of a dispute between them the decision of the local court is to settle the matter. Cases of this kind are under the jurisdiction of Soviets of Workers' and Peasants' Deputies and of local courts, depending on the last place of residence of the deceased.

V

All the property of the deceased, apart from what is enumerated in Article IX of the present decree, passes under the administration of the local Soviet, which transfers it to the management of institutions which administer locally the corresponding property of the Russian Republic, depending on the last place of residence of the deceased or on the place where the remaining property is located.

VI

The local Soviet publishes for general knowledge the news of the death of the owner of property and invites persons who possess the right to maintenance out of the proceeds of this property to appear within a year's time after the date of its publication.

VII

Persons who make no statement of their claims within the period of one year which is mentioned in the preceding article are deprived of the right to receive maintenance from the property of the deceased.

VIII

Expenses in connection with the management of the property are a first charge on the property of the deceased. The relatives and the wife or husband of the deceased receive maintenance from his property before the claims of his creditors are satisfied. The creditors of the deceased, if their claims are recognized as valid, are provided for out of the property which remains after the above mentioned deductions. In the event that there is not enough property to cover all the demands of the creditors the general principles of competition are applied.

IX

If the property of the deceased does not exceed ten thousand rubles, and consists partially of a garden, household furniture and means of a production of a working household in city or village it passes into the direct management and disposition of the wife or husband and relatives mentioned in Article II of the present decree. The method of management and disposition of the property is arranged by agreement between the mentioned wife or husband and relatives and, in the event of a dispute between them, by the local court.

X

The present decree has retrospective force in relation to all inheritances which were bequeathed before it was issued, if the heirs have not acquired or entered into possession of these inheritances.

XI

All disputes about inheritance, cases about the confirmation of wills and the ratification of the rights of inheritance, etc., which are now before the courts are regarded as terminated, and the inherited property involved is immediately transferred to the ownership of local Soviets or of the institutions which are mentioned in Article V of the present decree.

Note. A special ruling will be issued in connection with the cases of inheritance of the types of property which are enumerated in Article IX of the present decree, if these cases arose before the promulgation of the present decree.

XII

The People's Commissariat for Justice, in agreement with the People's Commissariats for Social Welfare and for Labor, are to issue detailed instructions as to how the present decree is to be put into operation.

The present decree comes into force from the day of its signature and is put into effect by telegraph.

PRESIDENT OF THE ALL-RUSSIAN SOVIET CENTRAL EXECUTIVE COMMITTEE, SVERDLOV.

SECRETARY, AVANESOV.

(*Cf. Izvestia* for May 1, 1918.)

DECREE OF THE ALL-RUSSIAN SOVIET CENTRAL EXECUTIVE COMMITTEE
GIVING THE FOOD COMMISSARIAT EXTRAORDINARY POWERS IN COM-
BATING THE VILLAGE BOURGEOISIE, WHICH IS CONCEALING AND SPEC-
ULATING WITH GRAIN RESERVES, OF MAY 9, 1918

The ruinous breakdown in the country's food supply, the disastrous
inheritance of four years of war, continues to spread and to become more
aggravated. While the consuming provinces are starving, there are now,
as formerly, large reserves of grain which has not even been milled, from
the harvests of 1916 and 1917, in the producing provinces. This grain
is in the hands of the kulaks and the rich, in the hands of the village
bourgeoisie. Well fed and provided for, having accumulated immense
sums of money during the years of war, the village bourgeoisie remains
stubbornly deaf and indifferent to the cries of the starving workers and
poor peasants, does not bring grain to the collection points. It counts on
forcing the Government to make new and further increases in grain
prices and at the same time sells grain in its own places at fabulous prices
to grain speculators and bagmen.

There must be an end of this stubbornness of the greedy village
kulaks and rich. Experience with the food problem in preceding years
has shown that the breakdown of fixed prices for grain and the abolition
of the grain monopoly, while it would make it possible for a handful of
our capitalists to feast, would place grain absolutely out of reach for
millions of the workers and would condemn them to an unavoidable
death from hunger. To the violence of the owners of the grain against
the starving poor the answer must be: violence against the bourgeoisie.
Not one pood of grain must remain in the hands of its holders, except
for the amount required for the sowing of their fields and the feeding of
their families until the new harvest.

And this must be carried out immediately, especially after the occupation of Ukraina by the Germans, when we are forced to satisfy ourselves with grain resources which scarcely suffice for seeding and cut
down the food supply.

Having considered the situation which has arisen and taking account
of the fact that only with the strictest account and even distribution
of all bread resources will Russia get out of the food crisis the All-
Russian Soviet Executive Committee decided:

1. Affirming the unalterable character of the grain monopoly and
of the fixed prices and also the necessity for a merciless struggle with
the grain speculators and bagmen, to force every owner of grain to
declare for delivery within a week after the announcement of this decision
in every township all the surplus above the amount required for the
seeding of the fields and for personal use, according to the established
scales, until the new harvest. The order of these declarations is determined

by the Food Commissariat through the local food organizations.

2. To call on all the working and unpropertied peasants to unite immediately for a merciless war against the kulaks.

3. To declare all who possess surplus grain and do not take it to the delivery points and also those who dissipate the grain reserves in making home-brewed liquor enemies of the people. To hand them over to a revolutionary court, with the provision that those who are found guilty should be condemned to imprisonment for not less than ten years, and should be driven forever from their village community, all their property being confiscated. The makers of liquor should also be condemned to forced labor.

4. In the event that someone is discovered with surplus grain which was not declared for delivery, according to Paragraph 1, the grain is taken away from him without compensation and the value of the undeclared surplus, reckoned in fixed prices, is paid half to the person who points out the hidden surplus and half to the village community, after the grain has actually been brought to the delivery points. Reports of hidden surplus stocks are to be made to the local food organizations.

Then, taking into consideration the facts that the struggle with the food crisis demands the application of quick and decisive measures, that the most effective carrying out of these measures, in turn, demands the centralization of all orders relating to food in a single institution and that this institution is the Food Commissariat, the All-Russian Soviet Central Executive Committee decides to give the Food Commissariat the following powers, to make possible a more successful struggle against the food crisis:

1. To promulgate compulsory decisions on food which go beyond the usual limits of the competence of the Food Commissariat.

2. To repeal the decisions of local food organizations and other bodies and institutions which contradict the plans and the information of the Food Commissariat.

3. To demand from institutions and organizations of all departments the unconditional and immediate execution of the orders of the Food Commissariat on the food question.

4. To apply armed force in the event that resistance is shown to the taking away of grain or other food products.

5. To dissolve or reorganize the local food organizations if they oppose the orders of the Food Commissariat.

6. To dismiss, replace, bring to revolutionary trial, arrest all holders of posts, employees of all departments and public organizations if they interfere with the orders of the Food Commissariat in a disorganizing way.

7. To transmit these powers (with the exception of the right to arrest, Point 6) to other persons and local institutions, with the approval of the Council of People's Commissars.

8. All those measures of the Food Commissariat which, by their nature, are connected with the departments of railroad transportation and of the Supreme Economic Council are put into effect in contact with the corresponding departments.

9. The decisions and orders of the Food Commissariat, issued in virtue of the present full powers, are examined by the Collegium of the Food Commissariat, which has the right, without stopping the execution of the orders, to lodge complaints about them with the Council of People's Commissars.

The present decree comes into force from the day of its signature and is put into effect by telegraph.

PRESIDENT OF THE ALL-RUSSIAN SOVIET CENTRAL EXECUTIVE COMMITTEE, Y. SVERDLOV,

PRESIDENT OF THE COUNCIL OF PEOPLE'S COMMISSARS, V. ULIANOV (LENIN),

SECRETARY OF THE ALL-RUSSIAN SOVIET CENTRAL EXECUTIVE COMMITTEE, AVANESOV.

(*Cf. Izvestia* for May 14, 1918.)

Library of Congress Cataloging-in-Publication Data

Chamberlin, William Henry, 1897–1969.
  The Russian revolution, 1917–1921.

  Reprint. Originally published: New York : Macmillan, 1954.
  Bibliography: p.
  Contents: v. 1. From the overthrow of the Tzar to the assumption of power by the Bol-
sheviks—v. 2. From the civil war to the consolidation of power.
  1. Soviet Union—History—Revolution, 1917–1921.
I. Title.
DK265.C43 1987   947.084′1   87-3719
ISBN 0-691-00816-7 (pbk. : set)
ISBN 0-691-05492-4 (v. 1 : alk. paper)
ISBN 0-691-00814-0 (pbk. : v. 1)
ISBN 0-691-05493-2 (v. 2 : alk. paper)
ISBN 0-691-00815-9 (pbk. : v. 2)

D1551692